Race, Class, and Gender in the United States

An Integrated Study

Second Edition

Paula S. Rothenberg

William Paterson College of New Jersey

ST. MARTIN'S PRESS   NEW YORK

Acquisitions Editor: Louise H. Waller
Project Management: Omega Publishing Services, Inc.
Cover Art: Sheree Goodman

HT
1521
.R 335
1992

For information, write:
St. Martin's Press, Inc.
175 Fifth Avenue
New York, NY 10010
ISBN: 0-312-05667-2 (paper)
      0-312-08578-8 (cloth)

Acknowledgments

It is a violation of the law to reproduce these selections by any means whatsoever without the written permission of the copyright holder.

"The Problem: Discrimination," from *Affirmative Action in the 1980s*, U.S. Commission on Civil Rights, 65, January, 1981, pp. 9–15.

"Domination and Subordination," from *Toward a New Psychology of Women* by Jean Baker Miller. Copyright © 1976, 1986 by Jean Miller. Reprinted by permission of Beacon Press.

"Racial Formations," from *Racial Formations in the United States* by Michael Omi and Harold Winant. Reprinted by permission of Routledge, Kegan and Paul.

"The Ethics of Living Jim Crow," from *Uncle Tom's Children* by Richard Wright. Copyright © 1936 by Richard Wright. Copyright renewed 1964 by Ellen Wright. Reprinted by permission of HarperCollins Publishers.

"Social Effects of Some Contemporary Myths about Women," by Ruth Hubbard. Reprinted from "Women's Nature," edited by Lowe and Hubbard, Pergamon Press, 1983, pp.1–8.

"Gender Issues in the College Classroom," by Edward B. Fiske. Copyright © 1990 by the New York Times Company. Reprinted by permission of the New York Times Company.

"Oppression," from *The Politics of Reality* by Marilyn Frye, The Crossing Press, 1983. Copyright © Marilyn Frye, 1983.

"Something about the Subject Makes it Hard to Name," by Jenny Yamato, from *Changing Our Power: An Introduction to Woman's Studies*, edited by Jo Whitehorse Cochron et al, Kendall/Hunt, 1987.

"'Bias Incident' at Staten Island's Miller Field," by Howard Blum. Copyright © 1983 by the New York Times Company. Reprinted by permission.

"Black vs. White in Howard Beach," by Richard Stengel, Joseph N. Boyce, and Mary Cronin. Copyright © 1986. Time Warner, Inc. Reprinted by permission.

"Death on a Mean Street," by Frank Tippett and Priscilla Painton. Copyright © 1989. The Time Inc. Magazine Company. Reprinted by permission.

"The Two Racisms," by Michael Eric Dyson, *The Nation* Magazine. The Nation Co., Inc. © 1989.

"Going 'Wilding' in the City," by David Gelman and Peter McKillop. From *Newsweek* 5/8/89 © 1989, Newsweek, Inc. Reprinted by permission.

"Boys Will Be Boys?" by Letty Cottin Pogrebin. From *Ms.* Magazine, September, 1989, p. 24. Permission granted by *Ms.* Magazine.

"A War on Women, Waged in the Dark," by Bob Herbert. From *New York Daily News*. Reprinted with permission.

"Female Midshipman Quits after Handcuff Incident." Reprinted by permission of Associated Press.

"Nude Pictures Are Ruled Sexual Harassment," by Tamar Lewin. Copyright © 1991 by The New York Times Company. Reprinted by permission.

(*Acknowledgments and copyrights are continued at the back of the book on pages 451–452, which constitute an extension of the copyright page.*)

Preface

Like its predecessor, this new version of Racism and Sexism: An Integrated Study undertakes a study of racism and sexism within the context of class. I have tried to build on the strengths of the original text and to go beyond its weaknesses. As I travelled around the country since the publication of Racism and Sexism, I have listened carefully to the many faculty and students who talked to me about the book, heartened that so many have found the book important to them. I have paid close attention to the concerns they wished to see receive greater attention—most significantly, that issues of class and heterosexism are more fully integrated into the text.

While devoting more space to issues of class proved to be a straightforward undertaking, adequately integrating issues of heterosexism and homophobia raised some serious structural and theoretical concerns. While some might treat those issues separately from gender issues and sexism, my analysis subsumes them under that broad category. While heterosexism and homophobia have taken on a life of their own in contemporary society, I believe that heterosexism, which plays an essential role in the subordination of all women, is best treated as part of the social construction of gender. Although "heterosexism" does not appear in the title, a concern with heterosexism and homophobia is reflected throughout the book.

The most basic challenge continues to be the need to explore each form or aspect of oppression while doing justice to the enormously complex ways in which they overlap and intersect. While we must at times focus on gender in the abstract, we must never forget that any woman or man always has a particular race or ethnic background, class identification, age, sexual orientation or preference, religion, etc., and the combination of these identities will inform and modify each of them separately and in combination with each other. Race, class, and sexuality are each modified, qualified, and informed by the other characteristics or identities that comprise the individual, and no one of them can exist in isolation.

Further, talking about racism and sexism within the context of class may require that we generalize about the experience of different groups of people, even while we realize that each individual is unique. To highlight similarities in the experiences of some individuals, I often talk about "people of color" or "women of color" even though these terms are not without difficulties. When I refer to "women" in this book instead of "white women" or "women of color," it is usually because I wish to focus on the particular experiences or legal status of women irrespective of race. In doing so, I use language in much the same way that one might discuss "the anatomy of the cat." There is no such thing as "the cat" anymore than there is "a woman" or "people of color." Yet for the purposes of discussion and analysis, we often make artificial distinctions that allow us to focus on particular aspects of experience that may not be separate in reality. One assumption reflected in this book is that language both mirrors reality and helps to structure it. Thus it is often difficult to use language in ways adequate to our topics without falling victim to the implicit racism and sexism that has rendered various individuals and groups invisible in the past.

iii

While we clearly need a theory or model for describing and analyzing experience that does justice to this complexity, our task is made harder by the narrow intellectual training so many of us have received. In the U.S. this training tends to be eurocentric, elitist, and male in orientation and perspective and often leaves out the rich intellectual traditions of the diverse cultures of the world and peoples of our own society, beginning with Native Americans. It has offered us a fairly narrow intellectual perspective and set of theoretical categories and treated them as if they were coextensive with human thought. This approach to conceptualizing reality overemphasizes oppositional thinking, individualism, and linear models. These are a few of the intellectual structures that limit our progress and make it difficult to deal with theoretical perspectives that emphasize complex interrelated elements.

Oppositional thinking and teaching encourage us to divide the world and its people into hard and fast categories: "black and white," "rational and emotional," "strong and weak," and then to divide these qualities among people or things instead of adopting a model for thought that posits continuums and complexities and embraces contradictions. Where models drawn from Native American cultures and many Eastern traditions posit opposites existing in harmony with each other and often see growth as the result of reconciliation among contradictory elements, education in a western tradition leaves little room for these possibilities.

This way of thinking is an important part of the social construction of gender, race, and class as difference in the sense that defines what is different as utterly other and insists that we either destroy difference entirely (as in the melting pot approach to ethnicity) or be divided forever by differences which are unbridgeable. Such an approach tends to regard those who are not white, male, heterosexual, and middle class as the ones who are in fact different; so that the very notion of difference comes to include hierarchy and to carry with it a rationale for the unequal distribution of power, privilege, and opportunity that characterizes society.

The other part of the dominant intellectual tradition in this country portrays reality as constructed out of simple and discrete (isolated) units or individuals and does not see relations and relationships as building blocks of reality (even though this contradicts the experience of so many ethnic and racial groups in this country). This approach views relations among discrete individuals or units as linear, and encourages simplistic thinking about social problems. Because of it, we are often inclined to look for the cause of events, feelings, and realities as if were possible to specify a single cause and then move on to the next effect in a simple linear progression. We must learn to spin theories that look more like cobwebs than railroad tracks and to construct models that look more like kaleidoscopes than pyramids. This is no easy task in a book that seeks to adequately reflect the incredible complexity of the ways race, gender, and class intersect and interact with each other and with other aspects of experience.

My experience teaching about race, gender, and class has convinced me that introducing these topics simultaneously creates serious difficulties. For this reason, I focus on racism and sexism in the first two sections of this book and examine each phenomenon separately and in relation to each other without looking at the way issues of class affect them; even though issues of class (and sexuality) occur throughout. Part III introduces the concept of class explicitly and presents data that reflect some of the ways class differences, along with difference in race and gender, intersect and mutually determine the economic reality of people's lives.

Those who prefer to introduce the "isms" in a different order, or all at once, will find this book adapts well to alternative orders of presentation. For example, while Suzanne Pharr's discussion of the relationship between heterosexism and homophobia and sexism and class privilege appears in the final Part of this book, some may choose to use it early in the course, perhaps even integrating it into Part I. I think this flexibility is one of the strong points of a collection which is genuinely interdisciplinary and firmly committed to an inclusive perspective.

This book remains in many respects incomplete. Some will be disappointed because a particular topic is omitted or does not receive the coverage they might wish. In some cases this is the result of a deficiency in my own perception or my failure to find an appropriate selection. In other cases, the omission results from a difference in analysis, as for example, in the case of anti-semitism. Although I deplore anti-semitism and other forms of religious prejudice and persecution, I do not believe that one can equate anti-semitism *in the United States* with racism; there are good reasons for keeping the distinction clear. This text does not undertake to examine every form of prejudice or victimization nor does it celebrate all people or every aspect of U.S. history deserving of celebration. Our topic, broad as it is, is too narrow to include all this. Clearly issues of age and ableism are extremely important today but, because of the structure and focus of this text, neither receives comprehensive treatment here. This book presents a core of readings designed to shed light on the nature of racism and sexism within class society and to highlight some of the ways members of so-called minority groups have drawn strength and pride from their heritage and culture. If I have succeeded, it should be possible to build upon this core, moving toward an ever more complex and inclusive account of the forces that shape our reality and the steps we must take to transform it in the interest of justice. I leave it to those who use this book to add to this account and I will be grateful to readers who offer concrete suggestions for enriching future editions.

ACKNOWLEDGMENTS

Many people contributed to this book. First, I owe a profound debt to the old 12th Street study group, with whom I first studied Black history and first came to understand the centrality of the issues of race, and to the group's members, who provided me with a lasting example of what it means to commit one's life to the struggle for justice to all people.

I owe an equally profound debt to my friends and colleagues in The New Jersey Project: Integrating the Scholarship on Gender and The New Jersey Multicultural Studies Project, and to friends, colleagues, and students at William Paterson College involved in the race and gender projects we have carried out for some years. I learned a great deal from all of them. I am especially grateful to J. Samuel Jordan and Leslie Agard-Jones with whom I have taught, learned, laughed, and cried. Les was available throughout every phase of the preparation of the first edition, and my debt to him is incalculable. I also wish to thank Della Capers of the African Afro-American Studies Department for her constant and professional attention to the details that make a book like this possible and for her friendship and encouragement.

Martina Nowak and Judy Baker Fronefield assisted me in many ways during different phases of this book's preparation. I am indebted to them for their diligence and enthusiasm.

I am also indebted to Norma Stoltz Chinchilla of California State University Long Beach, Alma M. Garcia of Santa Clara University, Patricia Samuel of St. Cloud State University, Margaret Stroebel of the University of Illinois at Chicago Circle, Margaret Anderson of the University of Delaware, and Pamela Hawkins of the California State University, Fresno, each of whom commented in great detail on the manuscript of the first version of this book and to the following reviewers: Regina Morantz-Sanchez, UCLA; Carl Allsup, University of Wisconsin-Plattesville; Estevan T. Flores, University of Colorado, Boulder; and Leona Fisher, Georgetown University, each of whom commented in detail on the manuscript for the new version of this book.

I am also grateful to the following questionnaire reviewers: Julie Andrzejewski, St. Cloud University; Jeanne Ballentine, Wright State University; Ellen Barry, Bowling Green State University; Jane Bradley, Virginia Polytechnic and State University; Noel Casenave, Temple University; Robert Claus, University of North Iowa; Kathleen Daly, Yale University; Norman Daniels, Tufts University; Christopher Dobb, Southern Connecticut State University; Carol Docan, California State University at Northridge; Laura Fishman, University of Vermont; Estevan Flores, University of Colorado; Bobbie Groth, Shimer College; David Iacoho-Harris, University of Texas at El Paso; M. Njeri Jackson, Southern University; Carolyn Jacobs, Smith College; Sue Ellen Jacobs, University of Washington; Alphine Jefferson, Southern Methodist University; Peter Kellog, University of Wisconsin-Green Bay; Patricia Klein, Western Michigan University; Seena Kohl, Webster University; Dorothy Kurz, University of Pennsylvania; Ann Parsons, University of Utah; Bronwyn Patulski, Syracuse University; Joan Strouse, Portland State University; Arlene Thorn, West Virginia State University; Karen Tolly, St. Lawrence University; Jacqueline Wilkotz, Towson University; and A. J. Williams-Meyers, SUNY New Paltz. The reviewers' thoughtful comments and suggestions have greatly strengthened the book's final form.

Many other people contributed to the book in a variety of ways. Some helped me track down articles or information, others discussed issues, and others were simply part of a broad learning experience that provided the context for the book. My thanks to Laura Aitken, Barbara Corrado Pope, Linda Day, Janet Falk, Ann Ferguson, Charley Flint, Carol Gruber, Joan Griscom, Linda Hamalian, Diane Harriford, Lee Hummel, Jean Levitan, Aubyn Lewis, Clara Lomas, Gregory Mantsios, Vernon McClean, Virginia Ramy Mollenkott, Mihri Reyes-Napoliello, Gladys Nussenbaum, Phyllis Palmer, Donna Perry, Susan Radner, William Rosa, Bob Rosen, Steve Shalom, Carole Sheffield, Vicki Spellman, Peter Stein, Karen Thompson, Isabel Tirado, Phyllis Vine, Bill Willis, Arlene Hirschfelder and Dennis White of the Association of American Indian Affairs, Susan Smith and Claudia Wayne of the National Committee on Pay Equity, and Marion Saviola of the Center for Independence of the Disabled, New York City.

Special thanks to the faculty and students, too numerous to name, at the many colleges and universities where I have lectured during the past several years. Their generous sharing of bibliographies, articles, insights, and questions has enriched this book immeasurably. I am particularly grateful to my friends at Frostburg State College in Maryland, Wooster College in Ohio, Clemson University in South Carolina, Sangamon State College in Illinois, Montgomery County College in Maryland, Rochester Institute of Technology in New York, Kenyon College in Ohio, and the State University of New York at Cortland, Binghamton, and Albany for their hospitality and lively conversation.

The book, in both its versions, has benefited greatly from the professional contributions of many people at St. Martin's Press. In particular, I would like to thank Andrea R. Guidoboni, Patricia Mansfield-Phelan, Beverly Hinton, Michael Weber, Louise Waller, Randi Israelow, and Huntley McNair Funston for their work on this book.

Finally, I want to thank Greg, Alexi, Andrea, and Daisy for their help and support and, above all, for just being there.

—Paula S. Rothenberg

Contents

PART III: THE ECONOMICS OF RACE, GENDER, AND CLASS IN THE UNITED STATES   91

PART IV: MANY VOICES, MANY LIVES   142

PART V: HOW IT HAPPENED: RACE AND GENDER ISSUES IN U.S. LAW

PART VI: CREATING AND MAINTAINING HIERARCHY: STEREOTYPES, IDEOLOGY, LANGUAGE, AND SOCIAL CONTROL   320

PART VII: REVISIONING THE FUTURE

Introduction

This book begins with the assumption that it is impossible to make sense out of either our past or our present without using race, class, and gender as central categories of description and analysis. Because issues of race, class, and gender are not merely topic areas like "pollution" or "health care," they cannot be treated in two-week course modules which adopt a smorgasbord approach to studying social problems. Rather, race, class, and gender are basic and central categories which must be studied in depth if we wish to understand our lives and our social, political, and economic institutions.

There was a time when theorists debated about the conceptual or structural primacy of these categories, arguing that one or the other was the most basic and most important category. Now the challenge is to find a model or a theory broad enough, flexible enough, and complex enough to capture and reflect the way these elements function together; to determine how we see ourselves and each other; and to circumscribe the opportunities and privileges to which each of us has access. This book grows out of the belief that an integrated study of racism and sexism, within the context of class, can provide us with the most comprehensive, accurate, and useful analysis of our society.

Our enterprise is not entirely without potential hazards. Racism and sexism are both comprehensive systems of oppression that deny individuals their personhood

1

and undermine the promise of democracy. They are not, however, identical in all respects, nor are they reducible to each other. There are important historical and contemporary differences between these forms of oppression, and we seek to recognize these differences and learn from them as well as from their similarities. The same may be said of class. Although introducing the notion of class can often help us understand puzzling differences in the experiences of individuals of the same race or gender, overemphasizing it can obscure the full impact of racism and sexism on people's lives at this moment in history. This book proceeds by integrating race, class, and gender in order to enhance our total understanding, but we must be ever mindful of the need to recognize and learn from difference.

Beginning

Beginning our study together presents some immediate differences from other academic enterprises. Whereas most students in an introductory literature or sociology class do not begin the semester with deeply felt and firmly entrenched attitudes toward the subject they are about to study, almost every student in a course on racism, sexism, and class privilege enters the room with strong feelings. These feelings can either provide the basis for a profoundly passionate and personal study of race, gender, and class that transforms its participants, or they can function as enormous obstacles that prevent our study from ever beginning in earnest. How we begin has critical implications for the success or failure of our enterprise.

It is important that we start by acknowledging the existence of these strong feelings and trying to come to terms with them. Why do we feel so strongly about issues of race, gender, and class? Why is it often difficult to examine critically our thoughts on the nature of women and men, sexuality, the family, racial difference, and equality of opportunity? Can we find a way to share these strong feelings and participate in an honest and open exploration of our attitudes while remaining respectful of and sensitive to the feelings of others? Are we willing to examine our beliefs and evaluate their accuracy? A good way to begin might be for each of us to try to remember when and how we first became aware of gender and race differences in the world and to share our memories with each other. When undertaken seriously and thoughtfully, this process reveals that much of what we believe was learned early in a thoroughly pre-critical context. Once we acknowledge the shaky basis for our attitudes toward race and gender, it may be easier for us to bracket those attitudes temporarily and begin our study of race, gender, and class in a changing society.

Structure of the Book

This book begins with definitions. What is "racism?" What is "sexism?" How shall we define these concepts? How shall we recognize instances of each? We are immediately confronted with another difference between this course and traditional courses. In the latter, teachers write definitions on the board, and students copy them down. The definitions are memorized, the problems or issues that define the subject matter are agreed upon, and the remainder of the course is spent examining different ways of solving the problems. In courses about race, class, and gender, definitions provoke all kinds of intense responses and inspire little agreement. Instead of copying them down and memorizing them, students argue, protest, and challenge. Instead of spending the semester solving mutually recognized problems, we spend it trying to agree on what the problems are.

Parts I and II of this book are designed to initiate this process. They allow us to examine fairly formal definitions of racism and sexism in relation to concrete manifestations of them in daily life. These two parts are not intended to end our discussion of the nature of race and gender difference in the United States but to begin it in a concrete and focused way, moving back and forth between theory and practice, using each to test the adequacy of the other.

After these preliminary attempts at definition, we are introduced to the notion of class and begin to examine the concrete impact of race, class, and gender on people's lives. Part III provides statistics and analyses, which allow us to formulate an understanding of the complex nature of the relations between and among these variables, and the differences in opportunity, expectations, and treatment their intersection produces. Part IV presents real-life experiences, which allow us to examine the impact of racism, sexism, and class privilege on people's daily lives. Many of these essays are highly personal, but each points beyond the individual's experience to social policy or practice or culturally conditioned attitudes. These articles should be used to further our discussion of the nature of racism and sexism and of the adequacy of the definitions examined in Part I.

When people first begin to recognize the enormous toll that racism and sexism take on human lives, they are often overwhelmed. How can they reconcile their belief that the United States provides liberty and justice and equal opportunity for all, with the reality presented in these pages? How did it happen? It is at this point that we turn to history.

Part V highlights important aspects of the history of subordinated groups in the United States by focusing on historical documents that focus on race and gender issues in U.S. law since the beginning of the Republic. Read in the context of the earlier material describing race, gender, and class differences in contemporary society, history becomes a way of using the past to make sense of the present. Focusing on the *legal* status of women and people of color allows us to telescope hundreds of years of history into manageable size, while still providing us with the historical information we need to make sense of contemporary society.

Our survey of racism and sexism in North America, past and present, has shown us that these phenomena function in a variety of ways. For some, the experiences that Richard Wright describes in "The Ethics of Living Jim Crow" are still all too real, but for most of us they describe a crude, blatant racism that seems incompatible with contemporary practice. How then are racism, sexism, and class privilege perpetuated in contemporary society? Why do these divisions and the accompany-

ing differences in opportunity and achievement continue? How are they reproduced? Why do we have so much difficulty recognizing the reality that lies behind a
rhetoric of equality of opportunity and justice for all? Part VI offers some suggestions.

An early essay on sex-role conditioning draws an important distinction between
discrimination, which frustrates choices already made, and the force of a largely
unconscious gender-role ideology, which frustrates the ability to choose.* Our
discussion of stereotypes, language, and social control is concerned with analyzing
how the way we conceive of others and, equally important, the way we have come to
conceive of ourselves help perpetuate racism, sexism, and class privilege. Our
discussion then moves beyond the specificity of stereotypes to analyze how our
modes of conceptualizing reality itself are conditioned by forces that are not always
obvious. Racism, sexism, and classism are not merely narrow but identifiable
attitudes, policies, and practices that affect individuals' lives. Rather, they operate
on a basic level to structure what we come to think of as "reality." In this way, they
cause us to limit our possibilities and personhood by internalizing beliefs that distort
our perspective and make it more difficult to blame the socioeconomic system that
benefits.

Finally, Part VII offers suggestions for moving beyond racism and sexism. These
suggestions are not definitive answers. They are offered to stimulate discussion about
the kinds of changes we might wish to explore in order to transform society. They
offer the reader a variety of ideas about the causes and cures for the pervasive social
and economic inequality and injustice this volume documents. They are meant to
initiate a process of reflection and debate about these social ills and about the kinds
of changes that can help address them. These solutions are neither comprehensive
nor definitive simply because we are light-years away from *global* change. Meaningful social change will occur first at the local level as individuals, working together,
begin to identify ways in which the institutions of which they are part perpetuate
domination and subordination so that they can then seek to alter those institutions.
Part VII is meant to provide a framework in which this process of identification and
alteration can occur.

*Sandra L. Bem and Daryl Bem: "Homogenizing the American Woman," from *Beliefs, Attitudes, and
Human Affairs* by D.J. Bem, Brooks/Cole Publishing Company, Monterey, California, 1970, pp. 89–99.

PART I

Defining "Racism" and "Sexism"

Refusing to hire a qualified person for a job because of their race or gender or refusing to rent someone an apartment or sell him or her a house because of their race or gender are fairly straightforward examples of discrimination. Most people would agree that such behavior is unfair or unjust. But once we move beyond these clear-cut cases of discrimination, it becomes more difficult to reach a consensus. Is the male supermarket manager or gas-station attendant just being friendly or is he acting in a sexist manner when he calls female customers "Sweetheart"? Is the underrepresentation of people of color in medical schools in the United States de facto proof of racism in the society, or does it result from a lack of qualified applicants? How do we arrive at the criteria which determines which applicants are "qualified"? Is it possible that the very criteria we employ for jobs and academic opportunities may themselves reflect subtle and pervasive racism and sexism? Can individuals and institutions be racist and sexist in the way they function normally, quite apart from their explicit intentions? These are the kinds of questions that will be raised in Part I as we attempt to arrive at some agreement about what constitutes racism and sexism.

Many people find the very words *racism* and *sexism* inflammatory and for this reason prefer to talk about *discrimination*. The members of the United States Commission on Civil Rights, authors of the first selection in this part, do just that.

5

They define the problem in terms of discrimination and present us with a survey of race and gender discrimination, past and present. They begin by citing examples of discrimination by individuals, move on to examine organizational and structural discrimination, and conclude with a discussion of the ways in which such treatment forms an interlocking and self-perpetuating *process of discrimination.*

Fundamental to the process of discrimination is the construction of *difference.* While the people, places, and things that make up our physical environment differ in a multitude of ways, only some of these differences are emphasized, treated as significant, and then employed by our society to justify and perpetuate inequality. Selection 2 examines the way in which relations of domination and subordination operate in order to insure the power and privileges of the dominant group. A key element here is the way difference becomes defined as defective or inferior and then is used to justify the hierarchical organization of society and the unequal distribution of wealth and opportunity.

While some people find it is tempting to think that racial and gender difference are given in nature, and that hierarchical social policies merely reflect natural difference, there is little evidence to support this point of view. In fact, an examination of the race and gender distinctions and stereotypes throughout our history indicates that what counts as race differences, and what defines "male" and "female," have changed repeatedly over the past several hundred years and continue to change today. Selection 3 argues that race is really more a political categorization than a biological or scientific category. The authors point to the relatively arbitrary way in which the category is constructed and employed, and suggest that changes in the meaning and use of racial distinctions can be correlated with economic and political changes in U.S. society. A similar point with respect to gender is made in Selection 6, which examines some of the myths and their claims to scientific corroboration that have been used to maintain the subordination of women.

Those who wish to emphasize the complex and powerful nature of relations of subordination and domination, as well as the interlocking and self-perpetuating nature of discrimination as a process, often claim that the term *discrimination* is itself too narrow and limited to do so effectively. They argue that words like *racism, sexism,* and *oppression* are more appropriate because they capture the comprehensive, systematic nature of the phenomena we are studying. They use these terms to point to a complex and pervasive system of beliefs, policies, practices, and attitudes that interrelate with incredible intricacy, subtlety, and force. The definitions provided in Part I are offered to give the reader an idea of the different ways thinkers have tried to describe the complexity of racism and sexism. None of these definitions is offered as *the* definition. In fact, defining racism and sexism within the context of class privilege is the project of this entire book, not merely the project of this single part. Nevertheless, this larger project requires some preliminary attempt to arrive at a set of working definitions. The examples provided in Selection 3 are a good place to begin. They ask us to move beyond a narrow understanding of discrimination and to think in more complex terms. They offer very different ways of expanding our thinking about the society we live in and how we think of ourselves and others.

Because they ask us to assume a critical perspective toward our experience, they are likely to strike some readers as provocative.

There is, for example, a great temptation to define *racism* as any policy, practice, belief or attitude that attributes characteristics or status to individuals based upon their race, and *sexism* as any one which does so according to sex. The appeal of this definition lies in its universal nature. It appeals to our sense of what it means to define a word according to the dictionary. But this approach to definitions fails to do the job of refining meanings adequately so that we can use language to clarify and analyze rather than to blur and oversimplify. In this book we will distinguish between *prejudice*, a general feeling of dislike for people based upon some characteristic they have (which may include race, sex, ethnicity, hair color, style of dress, etc.), and *racism* and *sexism* which are commonly said to require not merely *prejudice* but *prejudice plus power*. If we adopt this starting point we arrive at the following defining characteristics of both racism and sexism:

1. *Racism involves the subordination of people of color by white people.* While individual persons of color may well discriminate against a white person or another person of color because of their race, this does not qualify as *racism* according to our definition because that person of color cannot depend upon all the institutions of society to enforce or extend his or her personal dislike. Nor can he or she call upon the force of history to reflect and reinforce that prejudice. For example, the teacher at the front of the room may in fact be a person of color who, in any particular case, might conceivably be prejudiced against students of some race and act on that prejudice; but the distinguishing characteristic of racism is absent from this example. Outside the classroom, that teacher cannot call upon the various institutions of the society nor the force of history to recognize and support his or her power and prejudice. Quite the contrary. Outside the classroom, he or she will be the victim or object of institutionalized and comprehensive prejudice, which is what we mean by *racism*. History provides us with a long record of white people holding and using power and privilege over people of color to subordinate them, not the reverse.

2. *Sexism involves the subordination of women by men.* The reasoning here is similar. While some women may dislike men intensely and treat them unfairly, and while some women may be equally guilty of prejudice toward other women, the balance of power throughout most, if not all, of recorded history has allowed men to subordinate women in order to maintain their own privilege. Thus, an individual woman who treats men or other women unfairly simply because of their gender may be *prejudiced* and may be criticized as unjust, but she cannot be guilty of sexism. Of course, it is possible to imagine what it would mean for women to be guilty of sexism (or for people of color to be guilty of racism). If a reversal of power should come about so that women and people of color somehow gain fairly comprehensive control of the institutions and ideas of society and use them to subordinate

men and whites, respectively, we will alter our usage accordingly.

3. *Racism and sexism can be either conscious or unconscious, intentional or unintentional.* In Selection 4, Richard Wright describes growing up in the South during the early part of this century and provides us with dramatic examples of the kind of blatant, conscious, intentional racism that most of us take as stereotypical. But as other articles in this part of the book make clear, it is possible to reflect and perpetuate the racism and sexism of our society without having any intention or even any awareness of doing so.

One of these articles, Selection 7 by Marilyn Frye, explicitly introduces the concept of *oppression* to describe the pervasive nature of sexism and racism and illustrates how it is possible to participate unintentionally in the continued subordination of women of all colors and men of color. Frye uses the metaphor of a birdcage to illustrate how sexism imprisons its victims through the interlocking operation of a series of impediments to motion. Taken alone, none of the barriers seems very powerful or threatening; taken together, they construct a cage that appears light and airy, masking the fact that its occupants are trapped as firmly as if they were in a sealed vault. Although Frye focuses on sexism, it is relatively easy to apply the same metaphor and analysis to explicate racism.

Frye follows her discussion of the birdcage metaphor with some examples of seemingly innocent but oppressive practices that will undoubtably disturb some readers. She takes as her paradigm, or model, the "male door-opening ritual" and argues that its meaning and implications go far beyond the conscious intentions of the man who opens the door. As you think about her example, remember that Frye is analyzing the implications of a social ritual, not looking at any individual's motives for following that ritual. The point is that sexism and racism can be and are perpetuated by people who are just trying to be nice.

The final selection in Part 1 provides a kind of synthesis of many of the points that have already been made about racism. In her article, Jenny Yamato provides a good overview of the forms that racism can take and its connection to other systems of oppression. She concludes with some positive suggestions for all of us who want to come to terms with racism and, by implication, with sexism as well.

The Problem:
Discrimination

United States Commission on Civil Rights

Making choices is an essential part of everyday life for individuals and organizations. These choices are shaped in part by social structures that set standards and influence conduct in such areas as education, employment, housing, and government. When these choices limit the opportunities available to people because of their race, sex, or national origin, the problem of discrimination arises.

Historically, discrimination against minorities and women was not only accepted but it was also governmentally required. The doctrine of white supremacy used to support the institution of slavery was so much a part of American custom and policy that the Supreme Court in 1857 approvingly concluded that both the North and the South regarded slaves "as beings of an inferior order, and altogether unfit to associate with the white race, either in social or political relations; and so far inferior, that they had no rights which the white man was bound to respect."[1] White supremacy survived the passage of the Civil War amendments to the Constitution and continued to dominate legal and social institutions in the North as well as the South to disadvantage not only blacks,[2] but other racial and ethnic groups as well—American Indians, Alaskan Natives, Asian and Pacific Islanders and Hispanics.[3]

While minorities were suffering from white supremacy, women were suffering from male supremacy. Mr. Justice Brennan has summed up the legal disabilities imposed on women this way:

> [T]hroughout much of the 19th century the position of women in our society was, in many respects, comparable to that of blacks under the pre-Civil War slave codes. Neither slaves nor women could hold office, serve on juries, or bring suit in their own names, and married women traditionally were denied the legal capacity to hold or convey property or to serve as legal guardians of their own children.[4]

In 1873 a member of the Supreme Court proclaimed, "Man is, or should be, woman's protector and defender. The natural and proper timidity and delicacy

9

which belongs to the female sex evidently unfits it for many of the occupations of civil life."[5] Such romantic paternalism has alternated with fixed notions of male superiority to deny women in law and in practice the most fundamental of rights, including the right to vote, which was not granted until 1920;[6] the Equal Rights Amendment has yet to be ratified.[7]

White and male supremacy are no longer popularly accepted American values.[8] The blatant racial and sexual discrimination that originated in our conveniently forgotten past, however, continues to manifest itself today in a complex interaction of attitudes and actions of individuals, organizations, and the network of social structures that make up our society.

Individual Discrimination

The most common understanding of discrimination rests at the level of prejudiced individual attitudes and behavior. Although open and intentional prejudice persists, individual discriminatory conduct is often hidden and sometimes unintentional.[9] Some of the following are examples of deliberately discriminatory actions by consciously prejudiced individuals. Some are examples of unintentionally discriminatory actions taken by persons who may not believe themselves to be prejudiced but whose decisions continue to be guided by deeply ingrained discriminatory customs.

- Personnel officers whose stereotyped beliefs about women and minorities justify hiring them for low level and low paying jobs exclusively, regardless of their potential experience or qualifications for higher level jobs.[10]
- Administrators, historically white males, who rely on "word-of-mouth" recruiting among their friends and colleagues, so that only their friends and protégés of the same race and sex learn of potential job openings.[11]
- Employers who hire women for their sexual attractiveness or potential sexual availability rather than their competence, and employers who engage in sexual harassment of their female employees.[12]
- Teachers who interpret linguistic and cultural differences as indications of low potential or lack of academic interest on the part of minority students.[13]
- Guidance counselors and teachers whose low expectations lead them to steer female and minority students away from "hard" subjects, such as mathematics and science, toward subjects that do not prepare them for higher paying jobs.[14]
- Real estate agents who show fewer homes to minority buyers and steer them to minority or mixed neighborhoods because they believe white residents would oppose the presence of black neighbors.[15]
- Families who assume that property values inevitably decrease when minorities move in and therefore move out of their neighborhoods if minorities do move in.[16]
- Parole boards that assume minority offenders to be more dangerous or more

unreliable than white offenders and consequently more frequently deny parole to minorities than to whites convicted of equally serious crimes.[17]

These contemporary examples of discrimination may not be motivated by conscious prejudice. The personnel manager is likely to deny believing that minorities and women can only perform satisfactorily in low level jobs and at the same time allege that other executives and decisionmakers would not consider them for higher level positions. In some cases, the minority or female applicants may not be aware that they have been discriminated against—the personnel manager may inform them that they are deficient in experience while rejecting their applications because of prejudice; the white male administrator who recruits by word-of-mouth from his friends or white male work force excludes minorities and women who never learn of the available positions. The discriminatory results these activities cause may not even be desired. The guidance counselor may honestly believe there are no other realistic alternatives for minority and female students.

Whether conscious or not, open or hidden, desired or undesired, these acts build on and support prejudicial stereotypes, deny their victims opportunities provided to others, and perpetuate discrimination, regardless of intent.

Organizational Discrimination

Discrimination, though practiced by individuals, is often reinforced by the well-established rules, policies, and practices of organizations. These actions are often regarded simply as part of the organization's way of doing business and are carried out by individuals as just part of their day's work.

Discrimination at the organizational level takes forms that are similar to those on the individual level. For example:

- Height and weight requirements that are unnecessarily geared to the physical proportions of white males and, therefore, exclude females and some minorities from certain jobs.[18]
- Seniority rules, when applied to jobs historically held only by white males, make more recently hired minorities and females more subject to layoff—the "last hired, first fired" employee—and less eligible for advancement.[19]
- Nepotistic membership policies of some referral unions that exclude those who are not relatives of members who, because of past employment practices, are usually white.[20]
- Restrictive employment leave policies, coupled with prohibitions on part-time work or denials of fringe benefits to part-time workers, that make it difficult for the heads of single parent families, most of whom are women, to get and keep jobs and meet the needs of their families.[21]
- The use of standardized academic tests or criteria, geared to the cultural and

educational norms of the middle-class or white males, that are not relevant indicators of successful job performance. [22]
- Preferences shown by many law and medical schools in the admission of children of wealthy and influential alumni, nearly all of whom are white. [23]
- Credit policies of banks and lending institutions that prevent the granting of mortgage monies and loans in minority neighborhoods, or prevent the granting of credit to married women and others who have previously been denied the opportunity to build good credit histories in their own names. [24]

Superficially "color blind" or "gender neutral," these organizational practices have an adverse effect on minorities and women. As with individual actions, these organizational actions favor white males, even when taken with no conscious intent to affect minorities and women adversely, by protecting and promoting the status quo arising from the racism and sexism of the past. If, for example, the jobs now protected by "last hired, first fired" provisions had always been integrated, seniority would not operate to disadvantage minorities and women. If educational systems from kindergarten through college had not historically favored white males, many more minorities and women would hold advanced degrees and thereby be included among those involved in deciding what academic tests should test for. If minorities had lived in the same neighborhoods as whites, there would be no minority neighborhoods to which mortgage money could be denied on the basis of their being minority neighborhoods.

In addition, these barriers to minorities and women too often do not fulfill legitimate needs of the organization, or these needs can be met through other means that adequately maintain the organization without discriminating. Instead of excluding all women on the assumption that they are too weak or should be protected from strenuous work, the organization can implement a reasonable test that measures the strength actually needed to perform the job or, where possible, develop ways of doing the work that require less physical effort. Admissions to academic and professional schools can be decided not only on the basis of grades, standardized test scores, and the prestige of the high school or college from which the applicant graduated, but also on the basis of community service, work experience, and letters of recommendation. Lending institutions can look at the individual and his or her financial ability rather than the neighborhood or marital status of the prospective borrower.

Some practices that disadvantage minorities and women are readily accepted aspects of everyday behavior. Consider the "old boy" network in business and education built on years of friendship and social contact among white males, or the exchanges of information and corporate strategies by business acquaintances in racially or sexually exclusive country clubs and locker rooms paid for by the employer. [25] These actions, all of which have a discriminatory impact on minorities and women, are not necessarily acts of conscious prejudice. Because such actions are so often considered part of the "normal" way of doing things, people have difficulty recognizing that they are discriminating and therefore resist abandoning these practices despite the clearly discriminatory results. Consequently, many decision-makers have difficulty considering, much less accepting, nondiscriminatory alternatives that may work just as well or better to advance legitimate organizational interests but without systematically disadvantaging minorities and women.

This is not to suggest that all such discriminatory organizational actions are spurious or arbitrary. Many may serve the actual needs of the organization. Physical size or strength at times may be a legitimate job requirement; sick leave and insurance policies must be reasonably restricted; educational qualifications are needed for many jobs; lending institutions cannot lend to people who cannot reasonably demonstrate an ability to repay loans. Unless carefully examined and then modified or eliminated, however, these apparently neutral rules, policies, and practices will continue to perpetuate age-old discriminatory patterns into the structure of today's society.

Whatever the motivation behind such organizational acts, a process is occurring, the common denominator of which is unequal results on a very large scale.[26] When unequal outcomes are repeated over time and in numerous societal and geographical areas, it is a clear signal that a discriminatory process is at work.

Such discrimination is not a static, one-time phenomenon that has a clearly limited effect. Discrimination can feed on discrimination in self-perpetuating cycles.[27]

- The employer who recruits job applicants by word-of-mouth within a predominantly white male work force reduces the chances of receiving applications from minorities and females for open positions. Since they do not apply, they are not hired. Since they are not hired, they are not present when new jobs become available. Since they are not aware of new jobs, they cannot recruit other minority or female applicants. Because there are no minority or female employees to recruit others, the employer is left to recruit on his own from among his predominantly white and male work force.[28]
- The teacher who expects poor academic performance from minority and female students may not become greatly concerned when their grades are low. The acceptance of their low grades removes incentives to improve. Without incentives to improve, their grades remain low. Their low grades reduce their expectations, and the teacher has no basis for expecting more of them.[29]
- The realtor who assumes that white home owners do not want minority neighbors "steers" minorities to minority neighborhoods. Those steered to minority neighborhoods tend to live in minority neighborhoods. White neighborhoods then remain white, and realtors tend to assume that whites do not want minority neighbors.[30]
- Elected officials appoint voting registrars who impose linguistic, geographic, and other barriers to minority voter registration. Lack of minority registration leads to low voting rates. Lower minority voting rates lead to the election of fewer minorities. Fewer elected minorities leads to the appointment of voting registrars who maintain the same barriers.[31]

Structural Discrimination

Such self-sustaining discriminatory processes occur not only within the fields of employment, education, housing, and government but also between these structural areas. There is a classic cycle of structural discrimination that reproduces itself. Discrimination in education denies the credentials to get good jobs. Discrimination in employment denies the economic resources to buy good housing. Discrimination in housing confines minorities to school districts providing inferior education, closing the cycle in a classic form. [32]

With regard to white women, the cycle is not as tightly closed. To the extent they are raised in families headed by white males, and are married to or live with white males, white women will enjoy the advantages in housing and other areas that such relationships to white men can confer. White women lacking the sponsorship of white men, however, will be unable to avoid gender-based discrimination in housing, education, and employment. White women can thus be the victims of discrimination produced by social structures that is comparable in form to that experienced by minorities.

This perspective is not intended to imply that either the dynamics of discrimination or its nature and degree are identical for women and minorities. But when a woman of any background seeks to compete with men of any group, she finds herself the victim of a discriminatory process. Regarding the similarities and differences between the discrimination experienced by women and minorities, one author has aptly stated:

> [W]hen two groups exist in a situation of inequality, it may be self-defeating to become embroiled in a quarrel over which is more unequal or the victim of greater oppression. The more salient question is how a condition of inequality for both is maintained and perpetuated—through what means is it reinforced? [33]

The following are additional examples of the interaction between social structures that affect minorities and women:

- The absence of minorities and women from executive, writing, directing, news reporting, and acting positions in television contributes to unfavorable stereotyping on the screen, which in turn reinforces existing stereotypes among the public and creates psychological roadblocks to progress in employment, education, and housing. [34]
- Living in inner-city high crime areas in disproportionate numbers, minorities, particularly minority youth, are more likely to be arrested and are more likely to go to jail than whites accused of similar offenses, and their arrest and conviction records are then often used as bars to employment. [35]
- Because of past discrimination against minorities and women, female and minority-headed businesses are often small and relatively new. Further disadvantaged by contemporary credit and lending practices, they are more likely

than white male-owned businesses to remain small and be less able to employ full-time specialists in applying for government contracts. Because they cannot monitor the availability of government contracts, they do not receive such contracts. Because they cannot demonstrate success with government contracts, contracting officers tend to favor other firms that have more experience with government contracts.[36]

Discriminatory actions by individuals and organizations are not only pervasive, occurring in every sector of society, but also cumulative with effects limited neither to the time nor the particular structural area in which they occur. This process of discrimination, therefore, extends across generations, across organizations, and across social structures in self-reinforcing cycles, passing the disadvantages incurred by one generation in one area to future generations in many related areas.[37]

These interrelated components of the discriminatory process share one basic result: the persistent gaps seen in the status of women and minorities relative to that of white males. These unequal results themselves have real consequences. The employer who wishes to hire more minorities and women may be bewildered by charges of racism and sexism when confronted by what appears to be a genuine shortage of qualified minority and female applicants. The guidance counselor who sees one promising minority student after another drop out of school or give up in despair may be resentful of allegations of racism when there is little he or she alone can do for the student. The banker who denies a loan to a female single parent may wish to do differently, but believes that prudent fiscal judgment requires taking into account her lack of financial history and inability to prove that she is a good credit risk. These and other decisionmakers see the results of a discriminatory process repeated over and over again, and those results provide a basis for rationalizing their own actions, which then feed into that same process.

When seen outside the context of the interlocking and intertwined effects of discrimination, complaints that many women and minorities are absent from the ranks of qualified job applicants, academically inferior and unmotivated, poor credit risks, and so forth, may appear to be justified. Decisionmakers like those described above are reacting to real social problems stemming from the process of discrimination. But many too easily fall prey to stereotyping and consequently disregard those minorities and women who have the necessary skills or qualifications. And they erroneously "blame the victims" of discrimination,[38] instead of examining the past and present context in which their own actions are taken and the multiple consequences of these actions on the lives of minorities and women.

The Process of Discrimination

Although discrimination is maintained through individual actions, neither individual prejudices nor random chance can fully explain the persistent national patterns of inequality and underrepresentation. Nor can these patterns be blamed on the persons who are at the bottom of our economic, political, and social order. Overt racism and sexism as embodied in popular notions of white and male supremacy have been widely repudiated, but our history of discrimination based on race, sex, and national origin has not been readily put aside. Past discrimination continues to have present effects. The task today is to identify those effects and the forms and dynamics of the discrimination that produced them.

Discrimination against minorities and women must now be viewed as an inter-locking process involving the attitudes and actions of individuals and the organizations and social structures that guide individual behavior. That process, started by past events, now routinely bestows privileges, favors, and advantages on white males and imposes disadvantages and penalties on minorities and women. This process is also self-perpetuating. Many normal, seemingly neutral, operations of our society create stereotyped expectations that justify unequal results; unequal results in one area foster inequalities in opportunity and accomplishment in others; the lack of opportunity and accomplishment confirm the original prejudices or engender new ones that fuel the normal operations generating unequal results.

As we have shown, the process of discrimination involves many aspects of our society. No single factor sufficiently explains it, and no single means will suffice to eliminate it. Such elements of our society as our history of *de jure* discrimination, deeply ingrained prejudices,[39] inequities based on economic and social class,[40] and the structure and function of all our economic, social, and political institutions[41] must be continually examined in order to understand their part in shaping today's decisions that will either maintain or counter the current process of discrimination.

It may be difficult to identify precisely all aspects of the discriminatory process and assign those parts their appropriate importance. But understanding discrimination starts with an awareness that such a process exists and that to avoid perpetuating it, we must carefully assess the context and consequences of our everyday actions . . . .

NOTES

1. Dred Scott v. Sanford, 60 U.S. (19 How.) 393, 408 (1857).

2. For a concise summary of this history, see U.S., Commission on Civil Rights, *Twenty Years After Brown*, pp. 4–29 (1975); *Freedom to the Free: 1863, Century of Emancipation* (1963).

3. The discriminatory conditions experienced by these minority groups have been documented in the following publications by the U.S. Commission on Civil Rights: *The Navajo Nation: An American Colony* (1975); *The Southwest Indian Report* (1973); *The Forgotten Minority: Asian Americans in New York City* (State Advisory Committee Report 1977); *Success of Asian Americans: Fact or Fiction?* (1980); *Stranger in One's Land* (1970); *Toward Quality Education for Mexican Americans* (1974); *Puerto Ricans in the Continental United States: An Uncertain Future* (1976).

4. Frontiero v. Richardson, 411 U.S. 677, 684–86 (1973), citing L. Kanowitz, *Women and the Law: The Unfinished Revolution*, pp. 5–6 (1970), and G. Myrdal, *An American*

Dilemma 1073 (20th Anniversary Ed., 1962). Justice Brennan wrote the opinion of the Court, joined by Justices Douglas, White, and Marshall. Justice Stewart concurred in the judgment. Justice Powell, joined by Chief Justice Burger and Justice Blackmun, wrote a separate concurring opinion. Justice Rehnquist dissented. See also H. M. Hacker, "Women as a Minority Group," *Social Forces*, vol. 30 (1951), pp. 60–69; W. Chafe, *Women and Equality: Changing Patterns in American Culture* (New York: Oxford University Press, 1977).

5. Bradwell v. State, 83 U.S. (16 Wall) 130, 141 (1873) (Bradley, J., concurring), quoted in *Frontiero, supra* note 4.

6. U.S. Const. amend. XIX.

7. See U.S., Commission on Civil Rights, *Statement on the Equal Rights Amendment* (December 1978).

8. See note 4, Introduction.

9. See, e.g., R. K. Merton, "Discrimination and the American Creed," in R. K. Merton, *Sociological Ambivalence and Other Essays* (New York: The Free Press, 1976), pp. 189–216. In this essay on racism, published for the first time more than 30 years ago, Merton presented a typology which introduced the notion that discriminatory actions are not always directly related to individual attitudes of prejudice. Merton's typology consisted of the following: Type 1—the unprejudiced nondiscriminator; Type II—the unprejudiced discriminator; Type III—the prejudiced nondiscriminator; Type IV—the prejudiced discriminator. In the present context, Type II is crucial in its observation that discrimination is often practiced by persons who are not themselves prejudiced, but who respond to, or do not oppose, the actions of those who discriminate because of prejudiced attitudes (Type IV). See also D. C. Reitzes, "Prejudice and Discrimination: A Study in Contradictions," in *Racial and Ethnic Relations*, ed. H. M. Hughes (Boston: Allyn and Bacon, 1970), pp. 56–65.

10. See R. M. Kanter and B. A. Stein, "Making a Life at the Bottom," in *Life in Organizations, Workplaces as People Experience Them*, ed. Kanter and Stein (New York: Basic Books, 1976), pp. 176–90; also L. K. Howe, "Retail Sales Worker," ibid., pp. 248–51; also R. M. Kanter, *Men and Women of the Corporation* (New York: Basic Books, 1977).

11. See M. S. Granovetter, *Getting A Job: A Study of Contract and Careers* (Cambridge: Harvard University Press, 1974), pp. 6–11; also A. W. Blumrosen, *Black Employment and the Law* (New Brunswick, N.J.: Rutgers University Press, 1971), p. 232.

12. See U.S., Equal Employment Opprutnity Commission, "Guidelines on Discrimination Because of Sex," 29 C.F.R. §1604.4 (1979); L. Farley, *Sexual Shakedown: The Sexual Harassment of Women on the Job* (New York: McGraw-Hill, 1978), pp. 92–96, 176–79; C. A. Mackinnon, *Sexual Harassment of Working Women* (New Haven: Yale University Press, 1979), pp. 25–55.

13. See R. Rosenthal and L. F. Jacobson, "Teacher Expectations for the Disadvantaged," *Scientific American*, 1968 (b) 218, 219–23; also D. Bar Tal, "Interactions of Teachers and Pupils," in *New Approaches to Social Problems* ed. I. H. Frieze, D. Bar Tal, and J. S. Carrol (San Francisco: Jossey Bass, 1979), pp. 337–58; also U.S., Commission on Civil Rights, *Teachers and Students, Report V: Mexican American Education Study. Differences in Teacher Interaction With Mexican American and Anglo Students* (1973), pp. 22–23.

14. Ibid.

15. U.S., Department of Housing and Urban Development, "Measuring Racial Discrimination in American Housing Markets: The Housing Market Practices Survey" (1979); D. M. Pearce, "Gatekeepers and Home Seekers: Institutional Patterns in Racial Steering," in

Social Problems, vol. 26 (1979) pp. 325–42; "Benign Steering and Benign Quotas: The Validity of Race Conscious Government Policies to Promote Residential Integration," 93 *Harv. L. Rev.* 938, 944 (1980).

16. See M. N. Danielson, *The Politics of Exclusion* (New York: Columbia University Press, 1976), pp. 11–12; U.S., Commission on Civil Rights, *Equal Opportunity in Suburbia* (1974).

17. See L. L. Knowles and K. Prewitt, eds., *Institutional Racism in America* (Englewood Cliffs, N.J.: Prentice Hall, 1969) pp. 58–77, and E. D. Wright, *The Politics of Punishment* (New York: Harper and Row, 1973). Also, S. V. Brown, "Race and Parole Hearing Outcomes," in *Discrimination in Organizations*, ed. R. Alvarez and K. G. Lutterman (San Francisco: Jossey Bass, 1979), pp. 355–74.

18. Height and weight minimums that disproportionately exclude women without a showing of legitimate job requirement constitute unlawful sex discrimination. *See* Dothard v. Rawlinson, 433 U.S. 321 (1977); Bowe v. Colgate Palmolive Co., 416 F.2d 711 (7th Cir. 1969). Minimum height requirements used in screening applicants for employment have also been held to be unlawful where such a requirement excludes a significantly higher percentage of Hispanics than other national origin groups in the labor market and no job relatedness is shown. See Smith v. City of East Cleveland, 520 F.2d 492 (6th Cir. 1975).

19. U.S., Commission on Civil Rights, *Last Hired, First Fired* (1976); Tangren v. Wackenhut Servs., Inc., 480 F. Supp. 539 (D. Nev. 1979).

20. U.S., Commission on Civil Rights, *The Challenge Ahead, Equal Opportunity in Referral Unions* (1977), pp. 84–89.

21. A. Pifer, "Women Working: Toward a New Society," pp. 13–34, and D. Pearce, "Women, Work and Welfare: The Feminization of Poverty," pp. 103–24, both in K. A. Fernstein, ed., *Working Women and Families* (Beverly Hills: Sage Publications, 1979). Disproportionate numbers of single-parent families are minorities.

22. See Griggs v. Duke Power Company, 401 U.S. 424 (1971); U.S., Commission on Civil Rights, *Toward Equal Educational Opportunity: Affirmative Admissions Programs at Law and Medical Schools* (1978), pp. 10–12; I. Berg, *Education and Jobs: The Great Training Robbery* (Boston: Beacon Press, 1971), pp. 58–60.

23. See U.S., Commission on Civil Rights, *Toward Equal Educational Opportunity: Affirmative Admissions Programs at Law and Medical Schools* (1978), pp. 14–15.

24. See U.S., Commission on Civil Rights, *Mortgage Money: Who Gets It? A Case Study in Mortgage Lending Discrimination in Hartford, Conn.* (1974); J. Feagin and C. B. Feagin, *Discrimination American Style, Institutional Racism and Sexism* (Englewood Cliffs, N.J.: Prentice Hall, 1976), pp. 78–79

25. See *Club Membership Practices by Financial Institutions: Hearing Before the Comm. on Banking, Housing and Urban Affairs, United States Senate*, 96th Cong., 1st Sess. (1979). The Office of Federal Contract Compliance Programs of the Department of Labor has proposed a rule that would make the payment or reimbursement of membership fees in a private club that accepts or rejects persons on the basis of race, color, sex, religion, or national origin a prohibited discriminatory practice. 45 Fed. Reg. 4954 (1980) (to be codified in 41 C.F.R. §60–1.11).

26. See discussion of the courts' use of numerical evidence of unequal results in the text accompanying notes 4–21 in Part B of this statement.

27. See U.S., Commission on Civil Rights, *For All The People . . . By All the People* (1969), pp. 122–23.

28. See note 11.

29. See note 13.

30. See notes 15 and 16.

31. See Statement of Arthur S. Flemming, Chairman, U.S., Commission of Civil Rights, before the Subcommittee on Constitutional Rights of the Committee on the Judiciary of the U.S. Senate on S.407, S.903, and S.1279, Apr. 9, 1975, pp. 15–18, based on U.S., Commission on Civil Rights, *The Voting Rights Act: Ten Years After* (January 1975).

32. See, e.g., U.S., Commission on Civil Rights, *Equal Opportunity in Suburbia* (1974).

33. Chafe, *Women and Equality*, p. 78.

34. U.S., Commission on Civil Rights, *Window Dressing on the Set* (1977).

35. See note 17; Gregory v. Litton Systems, Inc., 472 F.2d 631 (9th Cir. 1972); Green v. Mo.-Pac. R.R., 523 F.2d 1290 (8th Cir. 1975).

36. See U.S., Commission on Civil Rights, *Minorities and Women as Government Contractors*, pp. 20, 27, 125 (1975).

37. See, e.g., A. Downs, *Racism in America and How to Combat It* (U.S., Commission on Civil Rights, 1970); "The Web of Urban Racism," in *Institutional Racism in America*, ed. Knowles and Prewitt (Englewood Cliffs, N.J.: Prentice Hall, 1969) pp. 134–76. Other factors in addition to race, sex, and national origin may contribute to these interlocking institutional patterns. In *Equal Opportunity in Suburbia* (1974), this Commission documented what it termed "the cycle of urban poverty" that confines minorities in central cities with declining tax bases, soaring educational and other public needs, and dwindling employment opportunities, surrounded by largely white, affluent suburbs. This cycle of poverty, however, started with and is fueled by discrimination against minorities. *See also* W. Taylor, *Hanging Together, Equality in an Urban Nation* (New York: Simon & Schuster, 1971).

38. The "self-fulfilling prophecy" is a well known phenomenon. "Blaming the victim" occurs when responses to discrimination are treated as though they were the causes rather than the results of discrimination. *See* Chafe, *Women and Equality* (New York: Oxford University Press, 1977) pp. 76–78; W. Ryan. *Blaming the Victim* (New York: Pantheon Books, 1971).

39. See, e.g., J. E. Simpson and J. M. Yinger, *Racial and Cultural Minorities* (New York: Harper and Row, 1965) pp. 49–79; J. M. Jones, *Prejudice and Racism* (Reading, Mass.: Addison Wesley, 1972) pp. 60–111; M. M. Tumin, "Who Is Against Desegregation?" in *Racial and Ethnic Relations*, ed. H. Hughes (Boston: Allyn and Bacon, 1970) pp. 76–85; D. M. Wellman, *Portraits of White Racism* (Cambridge: Cambridge University Press, 1977).

40. See, e.g., D. C. Cox, *Caste, Class and Race: A Study In Social Dynamics* (Garden City, N.Y.: Doubleday, 1948); W. J. Wilson, *Power, Racism and Privilege* (New York: Macmillan, 1973).

41. H. Hacker, "Women as a Minority Group," *Social Forces*, vol. 30 (1951) pp. 60–69; J. Feagin and C. B. Feagin, *Discrimination American Style*; Chafe, *Women and Equality*; J. Feagin, "Indirect Institutionalized Discrimination," *American Politics Quarterly*, vol. 5 (1977) pp. 177–200; M. A. Chesler, "Contemporary Sociological Theories of Racism," in *Towards the Elimination of Racism*, ed. P. Katz (New York: Pergamon Press, 1976); P. Van den Berghe, *Race and Racism: A Comparative Perspective* (New York: Wiley, 1967); S. Carmichael and C. Hamilton, *Black Power* (New York: Random House, 1967); Knowles and Prewitt, *Institutional Racism in America*; Downs, *Racism in America and How To Combat It* (1970).

2

Domination and Subordination

Jean Baker Miller

What do people do to people who are different from them and why? On the individual level, the child grows only via engagement with people very different from her/himself. Thus, the most significant difference is between the adult and the child. At the level of humanity in general, we have seen massive problems around a great variety of differences. But the most basic difference is the one between women and men.

On both levels it is appropriate to pose two questions. When does the engagement of difference stimulate the development and the enhancement of both parties to the engagement? And, conversely, when does such a confrontation with difference have negative effects: when does it lead to great difficulty, deterioration, and distortion and to some of the worst forms of degradation, terror, and violence—both for individuals and for groups—that human beings can experience? It is clear that "mankind" in general, especially in our Western tradition but in some others as well, does not have a very glorious record in this regard.

It is not always clear that in most instances of difference there is also a factor of inequality—inequality of many kinds of resources, but fundamentally of status and power. One useful way to examine the often confusing results of these confrontations with difference is to ask: What happens in situations of inequality? What forces are set in motion? While we will be using the terms "dominant" and "subordinate" in the discussion, it is useful to remember that flesh and blood women and men are involved. Speaking in abstractions sometimes permits us to accept what we might not admit to on a personal level.

Temporary Inequality

Two types of inequality are pertinent for present purposes. The first might be called temporary inequality. Here, the lesser party is *socially* defined as unequal. Major examples are the relationships between parents and children, teachers and students, and, possibly, therapists and clients. There are certain assumptions in these relationships which are often not made explicit, nor, in fact, are they carried through. But they are the social structuring of the relationship.

The "superior" party presumably has more of some ability or valuable quality, which she/he is supposed to impart to the "lesser" person. While these abilities vary with the particular relationship, they include emotional maturity, experience in the world, physical skills, a body of knowledge, or the techniques for acquiring certain kinds of knowledge. The superior person is supposed to engage with the lesser in such a way as to bring the lesser member up to full parity; that is, the child is to be helped to become the adult. Such is the overall task of this relationship. The lesser, the child, is to be given to, by the person who presumably has more to give. Although the lesser party often also gives much to the superior, these relationships are *based in service* to the lesser party. That is their *raison d'être*.

It is clear, then, that the paramount goal is to end the relationship; that is, to end the relationship of inequality. The period of disparity is meant to be temporary. People may continue their association as friends, colleagues, or even competitors, but not as "superior" and "lesser." At least this is the goal.

The reality is that we have trouble enough with this sort of relationship. Parents or professional institutions often tip toward serving the needs of the donor instead of those of the lesser party (for example, schools can come to serve teachers or administrators, rather than students). Or the lesser person learns how to be a good "lesser" rather than how to make the journey from lesser to full stature. Overall, we have not found very good ways to carry out the central task: to foster the movement from unequal to equal. In childrearing and education we do not have an adequate theory and practice. Nor do we have concepts that work well in such other unequal so-called "helping" relationships as healing, penology, and rehabilitation. Officially, we say we want to do these things, but we often fail.

We have a great deal of trouble deciding on how many rights "to allow" to the lesser party. We agonize about how much power the lesser party shall have. How much can the lesser person express or act on her or his perceptions when these definitely differ from those of the superior? Above all, there is great difficulty in maintaining the conception of the lesser person *as a person of as much intrinsic worth as the superior.*

A crucial point is that power is a major factor in all of these relationships. But power alone will not suffice. Power exists and it has to be taken into account, not denied. The superiors hold all the real power, but power will not accomplish *the task.* It will not bring the unequal party up to equality.

Our troubles with these relationships may stem from the fact that they exist within the context of a second type of inequality that tends to overwhelm the ways we learn to operate in the first kind. The second type molds the very ways we perceive and conceptualize what we are doing in the first, most basic kind of relationships.

The second type of inequality teaches us how to enforce inequality, but not how to make the journey from unequal to equal. Most importantly, its consequences are kept amazingly obscure—in fact they are usually denied. . . . However, the underlying notion is that this second type was determined, and still determines, the only ways we can think and feel in the first type.

Permanent Inequality

In these relationships, some people or groups of people are defined as unequal by means of what sociologists call ascription; that is, your birth defines you. Criteria may be race, sex, class, nationality, religion, or other characteristics ascribed at birth. Here, the terms of the relationships are very different from those of temporary inequality. There is, for example, no notion that superiors are present primarily to help inferiors, to impart to them their advantages and "desirable" characteristics. There is no assumption that the goal of the unequal relationship is to end the inequality; in fact, quite the reverse. A series of other governing tendencies are in force, and occur with great regularity. . . . While some of these elements may appear obvious, in fact there is a great deal of disagreement and confusion about psychological characteristics brought about by conditions as obvious as these.

Dominants.   Once a group is defined as inferior, the superiors tend to label it as defective or substandard in various ways. These labels accrete rapidly. Thus, blacks are described as less intelligent than whites, women are supposed to be ruled by emotion, and so on. In addition, the actions and words of the dominant group tend to be destructive of the subordinates. All historical evidence confirms this tendency. And, although they are much less obvious, there are destructive effects on the dominants as well. The latter are of a different order and are much more difficult to recognize.

Dominant groups usually define one or more acceptable roles for the subordinate. Acceptable roles typically involve providing services that no dominant group wants to perform for itself (for example, cleaning up the dominant's waste products). Functions that a dominant group prefers to perform, on the other hand, are carefully guarded and closed to subordinates. Out of the total range of human possibilities, the activities most highly valued in any particular culture will tend to be enclosed within the domain of the dominant group; less valued functions are relegated to the subordinates.

Subordinates are usually said to be unable to perform the preferred roles. Their incapacities are ascribed to innate defects or deficiencies of mind or body, therefore immutable and impossible of change or development. It becomes difficult for dominants even to imagine that subordinates are capable of performing the preferred activities. More importantly, subordinates themselves can come to find it difficult to believe in their own ability. The myth of their inability to fulfill wider or more valued roles is challenged only when a drastic event disrupts the usual arrangements. Such disruptions usually arise from outside the relationship itself. For instance, in the emergency situation of World War II, "incompetent" women suddenly "manned" the factories with great skill.

It follows that subordinates are described in terms of, and encouraged to develop, personal psychological characteristics that are pleasing to the dominant group. These characteristics form a certain familiar cluster: submissiveness, passivity, docility, dependency, lack of initiative, inability to act, to decide, to think, and the like. In general, this cluster includes qualities more characteristic of children than adults—immaturity, weakness, and helplessness. If subordinates adopt these characteristics they are considered well-adjusted.

However, when subordinates show the potential for, or even more dangerously have developed other characteristics—let us say intelligence, initiative, assertiveness—there is usually no room available within the dominant framework for acknowledgement of these characteristics. Such people will be defined as at least unusual, if not definitely abnormal. There will be no opportunities for the direct application of their abilities within the social arrangements. (How many women have pretended to be dumb!)

Dominant groups usually impede the development of subordinates and block their freedom of expression and action. They also tend to militate against stirrings of greater rationality or greater humanity in their own members. It was not too long ago that "nigger lover" was a common appellation, and even now men who "allow their women" more than the usual scope are subject to ridicule in many circles.

A dominant group, inevitably, has the greatest influence in determining a culture's overall outlook—its philosophy, morality, social theory, and even its science. The dominant group, thus, legitimizes the unequal relationship and incorporates it into society's guiding concepts. The social outlook, then, obscures the true nature of this relationship—that is, the very existence of inequality. The culture explains the events that take place in terms of other premises, premises that are inevitably false, such as racial or sexual inferiority. While in recent years we have learned about many such falsities on the larger social level, a full analysis of the psychological implications still remains to be developed. In the case of women, for example, despite overwhelming evidence to the contrary, the notion persists that women are meant to be passive, submissive, docile, secondary. From this premise, the outcome of therapy and encounters with psychology and other "sciences" are often determined.

Inevitably, the dominant group is the model for "normal human relationships." It then becomes "normal" to treat others destructively and to derogate them, to obscure the truth of what you are doing, by creating false explanations, and to oppose actions toward equality. In short, if one's identification is with the dominant group, it is "normal" to continue in this pattern. Even though most of us do not like to think of ourselves as either believing in, or engaging in, such dominations, it is, in fact, difficult for a member of a dominant group to do otherwise. But to keep on doing these things, one need only behave "normally."

It follows from this that dominant groups generally do not like to be told about or even quietly reminded of the existence of inequality. "Normally" they can avoid awareness because their explanation of the relationship becomes so well integrated *in other terms*; they can even believe that both they and the subordinate group share the same interests and, to some extent, a common experience. If pressed a bit, the familiar rationalizations are offered: the home is "women's natural place," and we know "what's best for them anyhow."

Dominants prefer to avoid conflict—open conflict that might call into question the whole situation. This is particularly and tragically so, when many members of the dominant group are not having an easy time of it themselves. Members of a dominant group, or at least some segments of it, such as white working-class men (who are themselves also subordinates), often feel unsure of their own narrow toehold on the material and psychological bounties they believe they desperately need. What dominant groups usually cannot act on, or even see, is that the situation of inequality in fact deprives them, particularly on the psychological level.

Clearly, inequality has created a state of conflict. Yet dominant groups will tend to suppress conflict. They will see any questioning of the "normal" situation as threatening; activities by subordinates in this direction will be perceived with alarm. Dominants are usually convinced that the way things are is right and good, not only for them but especially for the subordinates. All morality confirms this view, and all social structure sustains it.

It is perhaps unnecessary to add that the dominant group usually holds all of the open power and authority and determines the ways in which power may be acceptably used.

Subordinates.   What of the subordinates' part in this? Since dominants determine what is normal for a culture, it is much more difficult to understand subordinates. Initial expressions of dissatisfaction and early actions by subordinates always come as a surprise; they are usually rejected as atypical. After all, dominants *knew* that all women needed and wanted was a man around whom to organize their lives. Members of the dominant group do not understand why "they"—the first to speak out—are so upset and angry.

The characteristics that typify the subordinates are even more complex. A subordinate group has to concentrate on basic survival. Accordingly, direct, honest reaction to destructive treatment is avoided. Open, self-initiated action in its own self-interest must also be avoided. Such actions can, and still do, literally result in death for some subordinate groups. In our own society, a woman's direct action can result in a combination of economic hardship, social ostracism, and psychological isolation—and even the diagnosis of a personality disorder. Any one of these consequences is bad enough. . . .

It is not surprising then that a subordinate group resorts to disguised and indirect ways of acting and reacting. While these actions are designed to accommodate and please the dominant group, they often, in fact, contain hidden defiance and "put ons." Folk tales, black jokes, and women stories are often based on how the wily peasant or sharecropper outwitted the rich landowner, boss, or husband. The essence of the story rests on the fact that the overlord does not even know that he has been made a fool of.

One important result of this indirect mode of operation is that members of the dominant group are denied an essential part of life—the opportunity to acquire self-understanding through knowing their impact on others. They are thus deprived of "consensual validation," feedback, and a chance to correct their actions and expressions. Put simply, subordinates won't tell. For the same reasons, the dominant group is deprived also of valid knowledge about the subordinates. (It is particularly ironic that the societal "experts" in knowledge about subordinates are usually members of the dominant group.)

Subordinates, then, know much more about the dominants than vice versa. They have to. They become highly attuned to the dominants, able to predict their reactions of pleasure and displeasure. Here, I think, is where the long story of "feminine intuition" and "feminine wiles" begins. It seems clear that these "mysterious" gifts are in fact skills, developed through long practice, in reading many small signals, both verbal and nonverbal.

Another important result is that subordinates often know more about the dominants than they know about themselves. If a large part of your fate depends on accommodating to and pleasing the dominants, you concentrate on them. Indeed, there is little purpose in knowing yourself. Why should you when your knowledge of the dominants determines your life? This tendency is reinforced by many other restrictions. One can know oneself only through action and interaction. To the extent that their range of action or interaction is limited, subordinates will lack a realistic evaluation of their capacities and problems. Unfortunately, this difficulty in gaining self-knowledge is even further compounded.

Tragic confusion arises because subordinates absorb a large part of the untruths created by the dominants; there are a great many blacks who feel inferior to whites, and women who still believe they are less important than men. This internalization of dominant beliefs is more likely to occur if there are few alternative concepts at hand. On the other hand, it is also true that members of the subordinate group have certain experiences and perceptions that accurately reflect the truth about themselves and the injustice of their position. Their own more truthful concepts are bound to come into opposition with the mythology they have absorbed from the dominant group. An inner tension between the two sets of concepts and their derivatives is almost inevitable.

From a historical perspective, despite the obstacles, subordinate groups have tended to move toward greater freedom of expression and action, although this progress varies greatly from one circumstance to another. There were always some slaves who revolted; there were some women who sought greater development or self-determination. Most records of these actions are not preserved by the dominant culture, making it difficult for the subordinate group to find a supporting tradition and history.

Within each subordinate group, there are tendencies for some members to imitate the dominants. This imitation can take various forms. Some may try to treat their fellow subordinates as destructively as the dominants treat them. A few may develop enough of the qualities valued by the dominants to be partially accepted into their fellowship. Usually they are not wholly accepted, and even then only if they are willing to forsake their own identification with fellow subordinates. "Uncle

Toms" and certain professional women have often been in this position. (There are always a few women who have won the praise presumably embodied in the phrase "she thinks like a man.")

To the extent that subordinates move toward freer expression and action, they will expose the inequality and throw into question the basis for its existence. And they will make the inherent conflict an open conflict. They will then have to bear the burden and take the risks that go with being defined as "troublemakers." Since this role flies in the face of their conditioning, subordinates, especially women, do not come to it with ease.

What is immediately apparent from studying the characteristics of the two groups is that mutually enhancing interaction is not probable between unequals. Indeed, conflict is inevitable. The important questions, then, become: Who defines the conflict? Who sets the terms? When is conflict overt or covert? On what issues is the conflict fought? Can anyone win? Is conflict "bad," by definition? If not, what makes for productive or destructive conflict?

3

Racial Formations

Michael Omi and Harold Winant

In 1982–83, Susie Guillory Phipps unsuccessfully sued the Louisiana Bureau of Vital Records to change her racial classification from black to white. The descendant of an eighteenth-century white planter and a black slave, Phipps was designated "black" in her birth certificate in accordance with a 1970 state law which declared anyone with at least one-thirty-second "Negro blood" to be black. The legal battle raised intriguing questions about the concept of race, its meaning in contemporary society, and its use (and abuse) in public policy. Assistant Attorney General Ron Davis defended the law by pointing out that some type of racial classification was necessary to comply with federal record-keeping requirements and to facilitate programs for the prevention of genetic diseases. Phipps's attorney, Brian Begue, argued that the assignment of racial categories on birth certificates was unconstitutional and that the one-thirty-second designation was inaccurate. He called on a retired Tulane University professor who cited research indicating that most whites have one-twentieth "Negro" ancestry. In the end, Phipps lost. The court upheld a state law which quantified racial identity, and in so doing affirmed the legality of assigning individuals to specific racial groupings. [1]

The Phipps case illustrates the continuing dilemma of defining race and establishing its meaning in institutional life. Today, to assert that variations in human physiognomy are racially based is to enter a constant and intense debate. *Scientific* interpretations of race have not been alone in sparking heated controversy; *religious* perspectives have done so as well.[2] Most centrally, of course, race has been a matter of *political* contention. This has been particularly true in the United States, where the concept of race has varied enormously over time without ever leaving the center stage of US history.

What Is Race?

Race consciousness, and its articulation in theories of race, is largely a modern phenomenon. When European explorers in the New World "discovered" people who looked different than themselves, these "natives" challenged then existing conceptions of the origins of the human species, and raised disturbing questions as to whether *all* could be considered in the same "family of man."[3] Religious debates flared over the attempt to reconcile the Bible with the existence of "racially distinct" people. Arguments took place over creation itself, as theories of polygenesis questioned whether God had made only one species of humanity ("monogenesis"). Europeans wondered if the natives of the New World were indeed human beings with redeemable souls. At stake were not only the prospects for conversion, but the types of treatment to be accorded them. The expropriation of property, the denial of political rights, the introduction of slavery and other forms of coercive labor, as well as outright extermination, all presupposed a worldview which distinguished Europeans—children of God, human beings, etc.—from "others." Such a worldview was needed to explain why some should be "free" and others enslaved, why some had rights to land and property while others did not. Race, and the interpretation of racial differences, was a central factor in that worldview.

In the colonial epoch science was no less a field of controversy than religion in attempts to comprehend the concept of race and its meaning. Spurred on by the classificatory scheme of living organisms devised by Linnaeus in *Systema Naturae*, many scholars in the eighteenth and nineteenth centuries dedicated themselves to the identification and ranking of variations in humankind. Race was thought of as a *biological* concept, yet its precise definition was the subject of debates which, as we have noted, continue to rage today. Despite efforts ranging from Dr. Samuel Morton's studies of cranial capacity[4] to contemporary attempts to base racial classification on shared gene pools,[5] the concept of race has defied biological definition. . . .

Attempts to discern the *scientific meaning* of race continue to the present day. Although most physical anthropologists and biologists have abandoned the quest for a scientific basis to determine racial categories, controversies have recently flared in the area of genetics and educational psychology. For instance, an essay by Arthur Jensen which argued that hereditary factors shape intelligence not only revived the "nature or nurture" controversy, but raised highly volatile questions about racial equality itself.[6] Clearly the attempt to establish a *biological* basis of race has not been swept into the dustbin of history, but is being resurrected in various scientific arenas. All such attempts seek to remove the concept of race from fundamental social, political, or economic determination. They suggest instead that the truth of race lies in the terrain of innate characteristics, of which skin color and other physical attributes provide only the most obvious, and in some respects most superficial, indicators.

Race as a Social Concept

The social sciences have come to reject biologistic notions of race in favor of an approach which regards race as a *social* concept. Beginning in the eighteenth century, this trend has been slow and uneven, but its direction clear. In the nineteenth century Max Weber discounted biological explanations for racial conflict and instead highlighted the social and political factors which engendered such conflict.[7] The work of pioneering cultural anthropologist Franz Boas was crucial in refuting the scientific racism of the early twentieth century by rejecting the connection between race and culture, and the assumption of a continuum of "higher" and "lower" cultural groups. Within the contemporary social science literature, race is assumed to be a variable which is shaped by broader societal forces.

Race is indeed a pre-eminently *sociohistorical* concept. Racial categories and the meaning of race are given concrete expression by the specific social relations and historical context in which they are embedded. Racial meanings have varied tremendously over time and between different societies.

In the United States, the black/white color line has historically been rigidly defined and enforced. White is seen as a "pure" category. Any racial intermixture makes one "nonwhite." In the movie *Raintree County*, Elizabeth Taylor describes the worst of fates to befall whites as "havin' a little Negra blood in ya'—just one little teeny drop and a person's all Negra."[8] This thinking flows from what Marvin Harris has characterized as the principle of *hypo-descent*:

> By what ingenious computation is the genetic tracery of a million years of evolution unraveled and each man [sic] assigned his proper social box? In the United States, the mechanism employed is the rule of hypo-descent. This descent rule requires Americans to believe that anyone who is known to have had a Negro ancestor is a Negro. We admit nothing in between. . . . "Hypo-descent" means affiliation with the subordinate rather than the superordinate group in order to avoid the ambiguity of intermediate identity. . . . The rule of hypo-descent is, therefore, an invention, which we in the United States have made in order to keep biological facts from intruding into our collective racist fantasies.[9]

The Susie Guillory Phipps case merely represents the contemporary expression of this racial logic.

By contrast, a striking feature of race relations in the lowland areas of Latin America since the abolition of slavery has been the relative absence of sharply defined racial groupings. No such rigid descent rule characterizes racial identity in many Latin American societies. Brazil, for example, has historically had less rigid conceptions of race, and thus a variety of "intermediate" racial categories exist. Indeed, as Harris notes, "One of the most striking consequences of the Brazilian system of racial identification is that parents and children and even brothers and sisters are frequently accepted as representatives of quite opposite racial types."[10] Such a possibility is incomprehensible within the logic of racial categories in the US.

To suggest another example: the notion of "passing" takes on new meaning if we compare various American cultures' means of assigning racial identity. In the United States, individuals who are actually "black" by the logic of hypo-descent have attempted to skirt the discriminatory barriers imposed by law and custom by attempting to "pass" for white.[11] Ironically, these same individuals would not be able to pass for "black" in many Latin American societies.

Consideration of the term "black" illustrates the diversity of racial meanings which can be found among different societies and historically within a given society. In contemporary British politics the term "black" is used to refer to all nonwhites. Interestingly this designation has not arisen through the racist discourse of groups such as the National Front. Rather, in political and cultural movements, Asian as well as Afro-Caribbean youth are adopting the term as an expression of self-identity.[12] The wide-ranging meanings of "black" illustrate the manner in which racial categories are shaped politically.[13]

The meaning of race is defined and contested throughout society, in both collective action and personal practice. In the process, racial categories themselves are formed, transformed, destroyed and re-formed. We use the term *racial formation* to refer to the process by which social, economic and political forces determine the content and importance of racial categories, and by which they are in turn shaped by racial meanings. Crucial to this formulation is the treatment of race as a *central axis* of social relations which cannot be subsumed under or reduced to some broader category or conception.

Racial Ideology and Racial Identity

The seemingly obvious, "natural" and "common sense" qualities which the existing racial order exhibits themselves testify to the effectiveness of the racial formation process in constructing racial meanings and racial identities.

One of the first things we notice about people when we meet them (along with their sex) is their race. We utilize race to provide clues about *who* a person is. This fact is made painfully obvious when we encounter someone whom we cannot conveniently racially categorize—someone who is, for example, racially "mixed" or of an ethnic/racial group with which we are not familiar. Such an encounter becomes a source of discomfort and momentarily a crisis of racial meaning. Without a racial identity, one is in danger of having no identity.

Our compass for navigating race relations depends on preconceived notions of what each specific racial group looks like. Comments such as, "Funny, you don't look black," betray an underlying image of what black should be. We also become disoriented when people do not act "black," "Latino," or indeed "white." The content of such stereotypes reveals a series of unsubstantiated beliefs about who these groups are and what "they" are like.[14]

In US society, then, a kind of "racial etiquette" exists, a set of interpretative codes and racial meanings which operate in the interactions of daily life. Rules shaped by our perception of race in a comprehensively racial society determine the "presentation of self,"[15] distinctions of status, and appropriate modes of conduct. "Etiquette" is not mere universal adherence to the dominant group's rules, but a more dynamic combination of these rules with the values and beliefs of subordinated groupings. This racial "subjection" is quintessentially ideological. Everybody learns some combination, some version, of the rules of racial classification, and of their own racial identity, often without obvious teaching or conscious inculcation. Race becomes "common sense"—a way of comprehending, explaining and acting in the world.

Racial beliefs operate as an "amateur biology," a way of explaining the variations in "human nature."[16] Differences in skin color and other obvious physical characteristics supposedly provide visible clues to differences lurking underneath. Temperament, sexuality, intelligence, athletic ability, aesthetic preferences and so on are presumed to be fixed and discernible from the palpable mark of race. Such diverse questions as our confidence and trust in others (for example, clerks or salespeople, media figures, neighbors), our sexual preferences and romantic images, our tastes in music, films, dance, or sports, and our very ways of talking, walking, eating and dreaming are ineluctably shaped by notions of race. Skin color "differences" are thought to explain perceived differences in intellectual, physical and artistic temperaments, and to justify distinct treatment of racially identified individuals and groups.

The continuing persistence of racial ideology suggests that these racial myths and stereotypes cannot be exposed as such in the popular imagination. They are, we think, too essential, too integral, to the maintenance of the US social order. Of course, particular meanings, stereotypes and myths can change, but the presence of a *system* of racial meanings and stereotypes, of racial ideology, seems to be a permanent feature of US culture.

Film and television, for example, have been notorious in disseminating images of racial minorities which establish for audiences what people from these groups look like, how they behave, and "who they are."[17] The power of the media lies not only in their ability to reflect the dominant racial ideology, but in their capacity to shape that ideology in the first place. D. W. Griffith's epic *Birth of a Nation*, a sympathetic treatment of the rise of the Ku Klux Klan during Reconstruction, helped to generate, consolidate and "nationalize" images of blacks which had been more disparate (more regionally specific, for example) prior to the film's appearance.[18] In US television, the necessity to define characters in the briefest and most condensed manner has led to the perpetuation of racial caricatures, as racial stereotypes serve as shorthand for scriptwriters, directors and actors, in commercials, etc. Television's tendency to address the "lowest common denominator" in order to render programs "familiar" to an enormous and diverse audience leads it regularly to assign and reassign racial characteristics to particular groups, both minority and majority.

These and innumerable other examples show that we tend to view race as something fixed and immutable—something rooted in "nature." Thus we mask the historical construction of racial categories, the shifting meaning of race, and the crucial role of politics and ideology in shaping race relations. Races do not emerge full-blown. They are the results of diverse historical practices and are continually subject to challenge over their definition and meaning.

Racialization: The Historical Development of Race

In the United States, the racial category of "black" evolved with the consolidation of racial slavery. By the end of the seventeenth century, Africans whose specific identity was Ibo, Yoruba, Fulani, etc., were rendered "black" by an ideology of exploitation based on racial logic—the establishment and maintenance of a "color line." This of course did not occur overnight. A period of indentured servitude which was not rooted in racial logic preceded the consolidation of racial slavery. With slavery, however, a racially based understanding of society was set in motion which resulted in the shaping of a specific *racial* identity not only for the slaves but for the European settlers as well. Winthrop Jordan has observed: "From the initially common term *Christian*, at mid-century there was a marked shift toward the terms *English* and *free*. After about 1680, taking the colonies as a whole, a new term of self-identification appeared—*white*."[19]

We employ the term *racialization* to signify the extension of racial meaning to a previously racially unclassified relationship, social practice or group. Racialization is an ideological process, an historically specific one. Racial ideology is constructed from pre-existing conceptual (or, if one prefers, "discursive") elements and emerges from the struggles of competing political projects and ideas seeking to articulate similar elements differently. An account of racialization processes that avoids the pitfalls of US ethnic history[20] remains to be written.

Particularly during the nineteenth century, the category of "white" was subject to challenges brought about by the influx of diverse groups who were not of the same Anglo-Saxon stock as the founding immigrants. In the nineteenth century, political and ideological struggles emerged over the classification of Southern Europeans, the Irish and Jews, among other "non-white" categories.[21] Nativism was only effectively curbed by the institutionalization of a racial order that drew the color line *around*, rather than *within*, Europe.

By stopping short of racializing immigrants from Europe after the Civil War, and by subsequently allowing their assimilation, the American racial order was reconsolidated in the wake of the tremendous challenge placed before it by the abolition of racial slavery.[22] With the end of Reconstruction in 1877, an effective program for limiting the emergent class struggles of the later nineteenth century was forged: the definition of the working class *in racial terms*—as "white." This was not accomplished by any legislative decree or capitalist maneuvering to divide the working class, but rather by white workers themselves. Many of them were recent immigrants, who organized on racial lines as much as on traditionally defined class lines.[23] The Irish on the West Coast, for example, engaged in vicious anti-Chinese race-baiting and committed many pogrom-type assaults on Chinese in the course of consolidating the trade union movement in California.

Thus the very political organization of the working class was in important ways a racial project. The legacy of racial conflicts and arrangements shaped the definition of interests and in turn led to the consolidation of institutional patterns (e.g., segregated unions, dual labor markets, exclusionary legislation) which perpetuated the color line *within* the working class. Selig Perlman, whose study of the development of the labor movement is fairly sympathetic to this process, notes that:

> The political issue after 1877 was racial, not financial, and the weapon was not merely the ballot, but also "direct action"—violence. The anti-Chinese agitation in California, culminating as it did in the Exclusion Law passed by Congress in 1882, was doubtless the most important single factor in the history of American labor, for without it the entire country might have been overrun by Mongolian [sic] labor and *the labor movement might have become a conflict of races instead of one of classes*.[24]

More recent economic transformations in the US have also altered interpretations of racial identities and meanings. The automation of southern agriculture and the augmented labor demand of the postwar boom transformed blacks from a largely rural, impoverished labor force to a largely urban, working-class group by 1970.[25] When boom became bust and liberal welfare statism moved rightwards, the majority of blacks came to be seen, increasingly, as part of the "underclass," as state "dependents." Thus the particularly deleterious effects on blacks of global and national economic shifts (generally rising unemployment rates, changes in the employment structure away from reliance on labor intensive work, etc.) were explained once again in the late 1970s and 1980s (as they had been in the 1940s and mid-1960s) as the result of defective black cultural norms, of familial disorganization, etc.[26] In this way new racial attributions, new racial myths, are affixed to "blacks."[27] Similar changes in racial identity are presently affecting Asians and Latinos, as such economic forces as increasing Third World impoverishment and indebtedness fuel immigration and high interest rates, Japanese competition spurs resentments, and US jobs seem to fly away to Korea and Singapore.[28]. . .

Once we understand that race overflows the boundaries of skin color, super-exploitation, social stratification, discrimination and prejudice, cultural domination and cultural resistance, state policy (or of any other particular social relationship we list), once we recognize the racial dimension present to some degree in *every* identity, institution and social practice in the United States—once we have done this, it becomes possible to speak of *racial formation*. This recognition is hard-won; there is a continuous temptation to think of race as an *essence*, as something fixed, concrete and objective, as (for example) one of the categories just enumerated. And there is also an opposite temptation: to see it as a mere illusion, which an ideal social order would eliminate.

In our view it is crucial to break with these habits of thought. The effort must be made to understand race as *an unstable and "decentered" complex of social meanings constantly being transformed by political struggle.* . . .

NOTES

1. *San Francisco Chronicle*, 14 September 1982, 19 May 1983. Ironically, the 1970 Louisiana law was enacted to supersede an old Jim Crow statute which relied on the idea of "common report" in determining an infant's race. Following Phipps's unsuccessful attempt to change her classification and have the law declared unconstitutional, a legislative effort arose which culminated in the repeal of the law. See *San Francisco Chronicle*, 23 June 1983.

2. The Mormon church, for example, has been heavily criticized for its doctrine of black inferiority.

3. Thomas F. Gossett notes:

Race theory . . . had up until fairly modern times no firm hold on European thought. On the other hand, race theory and race prejudice were by no means unknown at the time when the English colonists came to North America. Undoubtedly, the age of exploration led many to speculate on race differences at a period when neither Europeans nor Englishmen were prepared to make allowances for vast cultural diversities. Even though race theories had not then secured wide acceptance or even sophisticate formulation, the first contacts of the Spanish with the Indians in the Americas can now be recognized as the beginning of a struggle between conceptions of the nature of primitive peoples which has not yet been wholly settled. (Thomas F. Gossett, *Race: The History of an Idea in America* (New York: Schocken Books, 1965), p. 16).

Winthrop Jordan provides a detailed account of early European colonialists' attitudes about color and race in *White Over Black: American Attitudes Toward the Negro, 1550–1812* (New York: Norton, 1977 [1968]), pp. 3–43.

4. Pro-slavery physician Samuel George Morton (1799–1851) compiled a collection of 800 crania from all parts of the world which formed the sample for his studies of race.

Assuming that the larger the size of the cranium translated into greater intelligence, Morton established a relationship between race and skull capacity. Gossett reports that:

> In 1849, one of his studies included the following results: The English skulls in his collection proved to be the largest, with an average cranial capacity of 96 cubic inches. The Americans and Germans were rather poor seconds, both with cranial capacities of 90 cubic inches. At the bottom of the list were the Negroes with 83 cubic inches, the Chinese with 82, and the Indians with 79. (Ibid., p. 74).

On Morton's methods, see Stephen J. Gould, "The Finagle Factor," *Human Nature* (July 1978).

5. Definitions of race founded upon a common pool of genes have not held up when confronted by scientific research which suggests that the differences *within* a given human population are greater than those *between* populations. See L. L. Cavalli-Sforza, "The Genetics of Human Populations," *Scientific American* (September 1974), pp. 81–9.

6. Arthur Jensen, "How Much Can We Boost IQ and Scholastic Achievement?", *Harvard Educational Review*, vol. 39 (1969), pp. 1–123.

7. Ernst Moritz Manasse, "Max Weber on Race," *Social Research*, vol. 14 (1947), pp. 191–221.

8. Quoted in Edward D.C. Campbell, Jr, *The Celluloid South: Hollywood and the Southern Myth* (Knoxville: University of Tennessee Press, 1981), pp. 168–70.

9. Marvin Harris, *Patterns of Race in the Americas* (New York: Norton, 1964), p. 56.

10. Ibid., p. 57.

11. After James Meredith had been admitted as the first black student at the University of Mississippi, Harry S. Murphy announced that he, and not Meredith, was the first black student to attend "Ole Miss." Murphy described himself as black but was able to pass for white and spent nine months at the institution without attracting any notice (ibid., p. 56).

12. A. Sivanandan, "From Resistance to Rebellion: Asian and Afro-Caribbean Struggles in Britain," *Race and Class*, vol. 23, nos. 2–3 (Autumn-Winter 1981).

13. Consider the contradictions in racial status which abound in the country with the most rigidly defined racial categories—South Africa. There a race classification agency is employed to adjudicate claims for upgrading of official racial identity. This is particularly necessary for the "coloured" category. The apartheid system considers Chinese as "Asians" while the Japanese are accorded the status of "honorary whites." This logic nearly detaches race from any grounding in skin color and other physical attributes and nakedly exposes race as a juridicial category subject to economic, social and political influences. (We are indebted to Steve Talbot for clarification of some of these points.)

14. Gordon W. Allport, *The Nature of Prejudice* (Garden City, New York: Doubleday, 1958), pp. 184–200.

15. We wish to use this phrase loosely, without committing ourselves to a particular position on such social psychological approaches as symbolic interactionism, which are outside the scope of this study. An interesting study on this subject is S.M. Lyman and W.A. Douglass, "Ethnicity: Strategies of Individual and Collective Impression Management," *Social Research*, vol. 40, no. 2 (1973).

16. Michael Billig, "Patterns of Racism: Interviews with National Front Members," *Race and Class*, vol. 20, no. 2 (Autumn 1978), pp. 161–79.

17. "Miss San Antonio USA Lisa Fernandez and other Hispanics auditioning for a role

in a television soap opera did not fit the Hollywood image of real Mexicans and had to darken their faces before filming." Model Aurora Garza said that their faces were bronzed with powder because they looked too white. "'I'm a real Mexican [Garza said] and very dark anyway. I'm even darker right now because I have a tan. But they kept wanting me to make my face darker and darker'" (*San Francisco Chronicle*, 21 September 1984). A similar dilemma faces Asian American actors who feel that Asian character lead roles inevitably go to white actors who make themselves up to be Asian. Scores of Charlie Chan films, for example, have been made with white leads (the last one was the 1981 *Charlie Chan and the Curse of the Dragon Queen*). Roland Winters, who played in six Chan features, was asked by playwright Frank Chin to explain the logic of casting a white man in the role of Charlie Chan: "'The only thing I can think of is, if you want to cast a homosexual in a show, and you get a homosexual, it'll be awful. It won't be funny . . . and maybe there's something there . . .'" (Frank Chin, "Confessions of the Chinatown Cowboy," *Bulletin of Concerned Asian Scholars*, vol. 4, no. 3 (Fall 1972)).

18. Melanie Martindale-Sikes, "Nationalizing 'Nigger' Imagery Through 'Birth of a Nation'," paper prepared for the 73rd Annual Meeting of the American Sociological Association, 4–8 September 1978 in San Francisco.

19. Winthrop D. Jordan, op. cit., p. 95; emphasis added.

20. Historical focus has been placed either on particular racially defined groups or on immigration and the "incorporation" of ethnic groups. In the former case the characteristic ethnicity theory pitfalls and apologetics such as functionalism and cultural pluralism may be avoided, but only by sacrificing much of the focus on race. In the latter case, race is considered a manifestation of ethnicity. See Chapter 1 above.

21. The degree of antipathy for these groups should not be minimized. A northern commentator observed in the 1850s: "An Irish Catholic seldom attempts to rise to a higher condition than that in which he is placed, while the Negro often makes the attempt with success." Quoted in Gossett, op. cit., p. 288.

22. This analysis, as will perhaps be obvious, is essentially DuBoisian. Its main source will be found in the monumental (and still largely unappreciated) *Black Reconstruction in the United States, 1860–1880* (New York: Atheneum, 1977 [1935]).

23. Alexander Saxton argues that:

North Americans of European background have experienced three great racial confrontations: with the Indian, with the African, and with the Oriental. Central to each transaction has been a totally one-sided preponderance of power, exerted for the exploitation of nonwhites by the dominant white society. In each case (but especially in the two that began with systems of enforced labor), white workingmen have played a crucial, yet ambivalent, role. They have been both exploited and exploiters. On the one hand, thrown into competition with nonwhites as enslaved or "cheap" labor, they suffered economically; on the other hand, being white, they benefited by that very exploitation which was compelling the nonwhites to work for low wages or for nothing. Ideologically they were drawn in opposite directions. *Racial identification cut at right angles to class consciousness.* (Alexander Saxton, *The Indispensable Enemy: Labor and the Anti-Chinese Movement in California* (Berkeley and Los Angeles: University of California Press, 1971), p. 1, emphasis added.)

24. Selig Perlman, *The History of Trade Unionism in the United States* (New York: Augustus Kelley, 1950), p. 52; emphasis added.

25. Whether southern blacks were "peasants" or rural workers is unimportant in this context. Some time during the 1960s blacks attained a higher degree of urbanization than whites. Before World War II most blacks had been rural dwellers and nearly 80 percent lived in the South.

26. See George Gilder, *Wealth and Poverty* (New York: Basic Books, 1981); Charles Murray, *Losing Ground* (New York: Basic Books, 1984) See Chapter 7 below.

27. A brilliant study of the racialization process in Britain, focused on the rise of "mugging" as a popular fear in the 1970s, is Stuart Hall *et al.*, *Policing the Crisis* (London: Macmillan, 1978).

28. The case of Vincent Chin, a Chinese American man beaten to death in 1982 by a laid-off Detroit auto worker and his stepson who mistook him for Japanese and blamed him for the loss of their jobs, has been widely publicized in Asian American communities. On immigration conflicts and pressures, see Michael Omi, "New Wave Dread: Immigration and Intra-Third World Conflict," *Socialist Review*, no. 60 (November–December 1981).

4

The Ethics of Living Jim Crow:

An Autobiographical Sketch

Richard Wright

I

My first lesson in how to live as a Negro came when I was quite small. We were living in Arkansas. Our house stood behind the railroad tracks. Its skimpy yard was paved with black cinders. Nothing green ever grew in that yard. The only touch of green we could see was far away, beyond the tracks, over where the white folks lived. But cinders were good enough for me and I never missed the green growing things. And anyhow cinders were fine weapons. You could always have a nice hot war with huge black cinders. All you had to do was crouch behind the brick pillars of a house with your hands full of gritty ammunition. And the first woolly black head you saw pop out from behind another row of pillars was your target. You tried your very best to knock it off. It was great fun.

I never fully realized the appalling disadvantages of a cinder environment till one day the gang to which I belonged found itself engaged in a war with the white boys who lived beyond the tracks. As usual we laid down our cinder barrage, thinking that this would wipe the white boys out. But they replied with a steady bombardment of broken bottles. We doubled our cinder barrage, but they hid behind trees, hedges, and the sloping embankments of their lawns. Having no such fortifications, we retreated to the brick pillars of our homes. During the retreat a broken milk bottle caught me behind the ear, opening a deep gash which bled profusely. The sight of blood pouring over my face completely demoralized our ranks. My fellow-combatants left me standing paralyzed in the center of the yard, and scurried for their homes. A kind neighbor saw me and rushed me to a doctor, who took three stitches in my neck.

I sat brooding on my front steps, nursing my wound and waiting for my mother to come from work. I felt that a grave injustice had been done me. It was all right to throw cinders. The greatest harm a cinder could do was leave a bruise. But broken bottles were dangerous; they left you cut, bleeding, and helpless.

When night fell, my mother came from the white folks' kitchen. I raced down the street to meet her. I could just feel in my bones that she would understand. I knew she would tell me exactly what to do next time. I grabbed her hand and babbled out the whole story. She examined my wound, then slapped me.

"How come yuh didn't hide?" she asked me. "How come yuh awways fightin'?"

I was outraged, and bawled. Between sobs I told her that I didn't have any trees or hedges to hide behind. There wasn't a thing I could have used as a trench. And you couldn't throw very far when you were hiding behind the brick pillars of a house. She grabbed a barrel stave, dragged me home, stripped me naked, and beat me till I had a fever of one hundred and two. She would smack my rump with the stave, and, while the skin was still smarting, impart to me gems of Jim Crow wisdom. I was never to throw cinders any more. I was never to fight any more wars. I was never, never, under any conditions, to fight *white* folks again. And they were absolutely right in clouting me with the broken milk bottle. Didn't I know she was working hard every day in the hot kitchens of the white folks to make money to take care of me? When was I ever going to learn to be a good boy? She couldn't be bothered with my fights. She finished by telling me that I ought to be thankful to God as long as I lived that they didn't kill me.

All that night I was delirious and could not sleep. Each time I closed my eyes I saw monstrous white faces suspended from the ceiling, leering at me.

From that time on, the charm of my cinder yard was gone. The green trees, the trimmed hedges, the cropped lawns grew very meaningful, became a symbol. Even today when I think of white folks, the hard, sharp outlines of white houses surrounded by trees, lawns, and hedges are present somewhere in the background of my mind. Through the years they grew into an overreaching symbol of fear.

It was a long time before I came in close contact with white folks again. We moved from Arkansas to Mississippi. Here we had the good fortune not to live behind the railroad tracks, or close to white neighborhoods. We lived in the very heart of the local Black Belt. There were black churches and black preachers; there were black schools and black teachers; black groceries and black clerks. In fact, everything was so solidly black that for a long time I did not even think of white folks, save in remote and vague terms. But this could not last forever. As one grows older one eats more. One's clothing costs more. When I finished grammar school I had to go to work. My mother could no longer feed and clothe me on her cooking job.

There is but one place where a black boy who knows no trade can get a job, and that's where the houses and faces are white, where the trees, lawns, and hedges are green. My first job was with an optical company in Jackson, Mississippi. The morning I applied I stood straight and neat before the boss, answering all his questions with sharp yessirs and nosirs. I was very careful to pronounce my *sirs* distinctly, in order that he might know that I was polite, that I knew where I was, and that I knew he was a *white* man. I wanted that job badly.

He looked me over as though he were examining a prize poodle. He questioned me closely about my schooling, being particularly insistent about how much mathematics I had had. He seemed very pleased when I told him I had had two years of algebra.

"Boy, how would you like to try to learn something around here?" he asked me.

"I'd like it fine, sir," I said, happy. I had visions of "working my way up." Even Negroes have those visions.

"All right," he said. "Come on."

I followed him to the small factory.

"Pease," he said to a white man of about thirty-five, "this is Richard. He's going to work for us."

Pease looked at me and nodded.

I was then taken to a white boy of about seventeen.

"Morrie, this is Richard, who's going to work for us."

"Whut yuh sayin' there, boy!" Morrie boomed at me.

"Fine!" I answered.

The boss instructed these two to help me, teach me, give me jobs to do, and let me learn what I could in my spare time.

My wages were five dollars a week.

I worked hard, trying to please. For the first month I got along O.K. Both Pease and Morrie seemed to like me. But one thing was missing. And I kept thinking about it. I was not learning anything and nobody was volunteering to help me. Thinking they had forgotten that I was to learn something about the mechanics of grinding lenses, I asked Morrie one day to tell me about the work. He grew red.

"Whut yuh tryin' t' do, nigger, get smart?" he asked.

"Naw; I ain' tryin' t' git smart," I said.

"Well, don't, if yuh know whut's good for yuh!"

I was puzzled. Maybe he just doesn't want to help me, I thought. I went to Pease.

"Say, are yuh crazy, you black bastard?" Pease asked me, his gray eyes growing hard.

I spoke out, reminding him that the boss had said I was to be given a chance to learn something.

"Nigger, you think you're *white*, don't you?"

"Naw, sir!"

"Well, you're acting mighty like it!"

"But, Mr. Pease, the boss said. . . ."

Pease shook his fist in my face.

"This is a *white* man's work around here, and you better watch yourself!"

From then on they changed toward me. They said good-morning no more. When I was just a bit slow in performing some duty, I was called a lazy black son-of-a-bitch.

Once I thought of reporting all this to the boss. But the mere idea of what would happen to me if Pease and Morrie should learn that I had "snitched" stopped me. And after all the boss was a white man, too. What was the use?

The climax came at noon one summer day. Pease called me to his work-bench. To get to him I had to go between two narrow benches and stand with my back against a wall.

"Yes, sir," I said.

"Richard, I want to ask you something," Pease began pleasantly, not looking up from his work.

"Yes, sir," I said again.

Morrie came over, blocking the narrow passage between the benches. He folded his arms, staring at me solemnly.

I looked from one to the other, sensing that something was coming.

"Yes, sir," I said for the third time.

Pease looked up and spoke very slowly.

"Richard, *Mr.* Morrie here tells me you called me *Pease*."

I stiffened. A void seemed to open up in me. I knew this was the show-down.

He meant that I had failed to call him Mr. Pease. I looked at Morrie. He was gripping a steel bar in his hands. I opened my mouth to speak, to protest, to assure Pease that I had never called him simply *Pease*, and that I had never had any intentions of doing so, when Morrie grabbed me by the collar, ramming my head against the wall.

"Now, be careful, nigger!" snarled Morrie, baring his teeth. "*I* heard yuh call 'im *Pease*! 'N' if yuh say yuh didn't, yuh're callin' me a *lie*, see?" He waved the steel bar threateningly.

If I had said: No, sir Mr. Pease, I never called you *Pease*, I would have been automatically calling Morrie a liar. And if I had said: Yes, sir, Mr. Pease, I called you *Pease*, I would have been pleading guilty to having uttered the worst insult that a Negro can utter to a southern white man. I stood hesitating, trying to frame a neutral reply.

"Richard, I asked you a question!" said Pease. Anger was creeping into his voice.

"I don't remember calling you *Pease*, Mr. Pease," I said cautiously. "And if I did, I sure didn't mean. . . ."

"You black son-of-a-bitch! You called me *Pease*, then!" he spat, slapping me till I bent sideways over a bench. Morrie was on top of me, demanding:

"Didn't yuh call 'im *Pease?* If yuh say yuh didn't, I'll rip yo' gut string loose with this bar, yuh black granny dodger! Yuh can't call a white man a lie 'n' git erway with it, you black son-of-a-bitch!"

I wilted. I begged them not to bother me. I knew what they wanted. They wanted me to leave.

"I'll leave," I promised. "I'll leave right *now.*"

They gave me a minute to get out of the factory. I was warned not to show up again, or tell the boss.

I went.

When I told the folks at home what had happened, they called me a fool. They told me that I must never again attempt to exceed my boundaries. When you are working for white folks, they said, you got to "stay in your place" if you want to keep working.

II

My Jim Crow education continued on my next job, which was portering in a clothing store. One morning, while polishing brass out front, the boss and his twenty-year-old son got out of their car and half dragged and half kicked a Negro woman into the store. A policeman standing at the corner looked on, twirling his night-stick. I watched out of the corner of my eye, never slackening the strokes of my chamois upon the brass. After a few minutes, I heard shrill screams coming from the rear of the store. Later the woman stumbled out, bleeding, crying, and holding her stomach. When she reached the end of the block, the policeman grabbed her and accused her of being drunk. Silently, I watched him throw her into a patrol wagon.

When I went to the rear of the store, the boss and his son were washing their hands at the sink. They were chuckling. The floor was bloody and strewn with wisps of hair and clothing. No doubt I must have appeared pretty shocked, for the boss slapped me reassuringly on the back.

"Boy, that's what we do to niggers when they don't want to pay their bills," he said, laughing.

His son looked at me and grinned.

"Here, hava cigarette," he said.

Not knowing what to do, I took it. He lit his and held the match for me. This was a gesture of kindness, indicating that even if they had beaten the poor old woman, they would not beat me if I knew enough to keep my mouth shut.

"Yes, sir," I said, and asked no questions.

After they had gone, I sat on the edge of a packing box and stared at the bloody floor till the cigarette went out.

That day at noon, while eating in a hamburger joint, I told my fellow Negro porters what had happened. No one seemed surprised. One fellow, after swallowing a huge bite, turned to me and asked:

"Huh! Is tha' all they did t' her?"

"Yeah. Wasn't tha' enough?" I asked.

"Shucks! Man, she's a lucky bitch!" he said, burying his lips deep into a juicy hamburger. "Hell, it's a wonder they didn't lay her when they got through."

III

I was learning fast, but not quite fast enough. One day, while I was delivering packages in the suburbs, my bicycle tire was punctured. I walked along the hot, dusty road, sweating and leading my bicycle by the handle-bars.

A car slowed at my side.

"What's the matter, boy?" a white man called.

I told him my bicycle was broken and I was walking back to town.

"That's too bad," he said, "Hop on the running board."

He stopped the car. I clutched hard at my bicycle with one hand and clung to the side of the car with the other.

"All set?"

"Yes, sir," I answered. The car started.

It was full of young white men. They were drinking. I watched the flask pass from mouth to mouth.

"Wanna drink, boy?" one asked.

I laughed as the wind whipped my face. Instinctively obeying the freshly planted precepts of my mother, I said:

"Oh, no!"

The words were hardly out of my mouth before I felt something hard and cold smash me between the eyes. It was an empty whisky bottle. I saw stars, and fell backwards from the speeding car into the dust of the road, my feet becoming entangled in the steel spokes of my bicycle. The white men piled out and stood over me.

"Nigger, ain' yuh learned no better sense'n tha' yet?" asked the man who hit me. "Ain't yuh learned t' say *sir* t' a white man yet?"

Dazed, I pulled to my feet. My elbows and legs were bleeding. Fists doubled, the white man advanced, kicking my bicycle out of the way.

"Aw, leave the bastard alone. He's got enough," said one.

They stood looking at me. I rubbed my shins, trying to stop the flow of blood. No doubt they felt a sort of contemptuous pity, for one asked:

"Yuh wanna ride t' town now, nigger? Yuh reckon yuh know enough t' ride now?"

"I wanna walk," I said, simply.

Maybe it sounded funny. They laughed.

"Well, walk, yuh black son-of-a-bitch!"

When they left they comforted me with:

"Nigger, yuh sho better be damn glad it wuz us yuh talked t' tha' way. Yuh're a lucky bastard, 'cause if yuh'd said tha' t' somebody else, yuh might've been a dead nigger now."

IV

Negroes who have lived South know the dread of being caught alone upon the streets in white neighborhoods after the sun has set. In such a simple situation as this the plight of the Negro in America is graphically symbolized. While white strangers may be in these neighborhoods trying to get home, they can pass unmolested. But the color of a Negro's skin makes him easily recognizable, makes him suspect, converts him into a defenseless target.

Late one Saturday night I made some deliveries in a white neighborhood. I was pedaling my bicycle back to the store as fast as I could, when a police car, swerving toward me, jammed me into the curbing.

"Get down and put up your hands!" the policemen ordered.

I did. They climbed out of the car, guns drawn, faces set, and advanced slowly.

"Keep still!" they ordered.

I reached my hands higher. They searched my pockets and packages. They seemed dissatisfied when they could find nothing incriminating. Finally, one of them said:

"Boy, tell your boss not to send you out in white neighborhoods after sundown."

As usual, I said:

"Yes, sir."

V

My next job was a hall-boy in a hotel. Here my Jim Crow education broadened and deepened. When the bell-boys were busy, I was often called to assist them. As many of the rooms in the hotel were occupied by prostitutes, I was constantly called to carry them liquor and cigarettes. These women were nude most of the time. They did not bother about clothing, even for bell-boys. When you went into their rooms, you were supposed to take their nakedness for granted, as though it startled you no more than a blue vase or a red rug. Your presence awoke in them no sense of shame, for you were not regarded as human. If they were alone, you could steal sidelong glimpses at them. But if they were receiving men, not a flicker of your eyelids could show. I remember one incident vividly. A new woman, a huge, snowy-skinned blonde, took a room on my floor. I was sent to wait upon her. She was in bed with a thick-set man; both were nude and uncovered. She said she wanted some liquor and slid out of bed and waddled across the floor to get her money from a dresser drawer. I watched her.

"Nigger, what in hell you looking at?" the white man asked me, raising himself upon his elbows.

"Nothing," I answered, looking miles deep into the blank wall of the room.

"Keep your eyes where they belong, if you want to be healthy!" he said.

"Yes, sir."

VI

One of the bell-boys I knew in this hotel was keeping steady company with one of the Negro maids. Out of a clear sky the police descended upon his home and arrested him, accusing him of bastardy. The poor boy swore he had had no intimate relations with the girl. Nevertheless, they forced him to marry her. When the child arrived, it was found to be much lighter in complexion than either of the two supposedly legal parents. The white men around the hotel made a great joke of it. They spread the rumor that some white cow must have scared the poor girl while she was carrying the baby. If you were in their presence when this explanation was offered, you were supposed to laugh.

VII

One of the bell-boys was caught in bed with a white prostitute. He was castrated and run out of town. Immediately after this all the bell-boys and hall-boys were called together and warned. We were given to understand that the boy who had been castrated was a "mighty, mighty lucky bastard." We were impressed with the fact that next time the management of the hotel would not be responsible for the lives of "trouble-makin' niggers." We were silent.

VIII

One night, just as I was about to go home, I met one of the Negro maids. She lived in my direction, and we fell in to walk part of the way home together. As we passed the white night-watchman, he slapped the maid on her buttock. I turned around, amazed. The watchman looked at me with a long, hard, fixed-under stare. Suddenly he pulled his gun and asked:

"Nigger, don't yuh like it?"

I hesitated.

"I asked yuh don't yuh like it?" he asked again, stepping forward.

"Yes, sir," I mumbled.

"Talk like it, then!"

"Oh, yes sir!" I said with as much heartiness as I could muster.

Outside, I walked ahead of the girl, ashamed to face her. She caught up with me and said:

"Don't be a fool! Yuh couldn't help it!"

This watchman boasted of having killed two Negroes in self-defense.

Yet, in spite of all this, the life of the hotel ran with an amazing smoothness. It would have been impossible for a stranger to detect anything. The maids, the hall-boys, and the bell-boys were all smiles. They had to be.

IX

I had learned my Jim Crow lessons so thoroughly that I kept the hotel job till I left Jackson for Memphis. It so happened that while in Memphis I applied for a job at a branch of the optical company. I was hired. And for some reason, as long as I worked there, they never brought my past against me.

Here my Jim Crow education assumed quite a different form. It was no longer brutally cruel, but subtly cruel. Here I learned to lie, to steal, to dissemble. I learned to play that dual role which every Negro must play if he wants to eat and live.

For example, it was almost impossible to get a book to read. It was assumed that after a Negro had imbibed what scanty schooling the state furnished he had no further need for books. I was always borrowing books from men on the job. One day I mustered enough courage to ask one of the men to let me get books from the library in his name. Surprisingly, he consented. I cannot help but think that he consented because he was a Roman Catholic and felt a vague sympathy for Negroes, being himself an object of hatred. Armed with a library card, I obtained books in the following manner: I would write a note to the librarian, saying: "Please let this nigger boy have the following books." I would then sign it with the white man's name.

When I went to the library, I would stand at the desk, hat in hand, looking as unbookish as possible. When I received the books desired I would take them home. If the books listed in the note happened to be out, I would sneak into the lobby and forge a new one. I never took any chances guessing with the white librarian about what the fictitious white man would want to read. No doubt if any of the white patrons had suspected that some of the volumes they enjoyed had been in the home of a Negro, they would not have tolerated it for an instant.

The factory force of the optical company in Memphis was much larger than that in Jackson, and more urbanized. At least they liked to talk, and would engage the Negro help in conversation whenever possible. By this means I found that many subjects were taboo from the white man's point of view. Among the topics they did not like to discuss with Negroes were the following: American white women; the Ku Klux Klan; France, and how Negro soldiers fared while there; French women; Jack Johnson; the entire northern part of the United States; the Civil War; Abraham Lincoln; U. S. Grant; General Sherman; Catholics; the Pope; Jews; the Republican Party; slavery; social equality; Communism; Socialism; the 13th and 14th Amendments to the Constitution; or any topic calling for positive knowledge or manly self-assertion on the part of the Negro. The most accepted topics were sex and religion.

There were many times when I had to exercise a great deal of ingenuity to keep out of trouble. It is a southern custom that all men must take off their hats when they enter an elevator. And especially did this apply to us blacks with rigid force. One day I stepped into an elevator with my arms full of packages. I was forced to ride with my hat on. Two white men stared at me coldly. Then one of them very kindly lifted my hat and placed it upon my armful of packages. Now the most accepted response for a Negro to make under such circumstances is to look at the white man out of the corner of his eye and grin. To have said: "Thank you!" would have made the white man *think* that you *thought* you were receiving from him a personal service. For such an act I have seen Negroes take a blow in the mouth. Finding the first alternative distasteful, and the second dangerous, I hit upon an acceptable course of action which fell safely between these two poles. I immediately—no sooner than my hat was lifted—pretended that my packages were about to spill, and appeared deeply distressed with keeping them in my arms. In this fashion I evaded having to acknowledge his service, and, in spite of adverse circumstances, salvaged a slender shred of personal pride.

How do Negroes feel about the way they have to live? How do they discuss it when alone amongst themselves? I think this question can be answered in a single sentence. A friend of mine who ran an elevator once told me:

"Lawd, man! Ef it wuzn't fer them polices 'n' them ol' lynch-mobs, there wouldn't be nothin' but uproar down here!"

5

Social Effects of Some Contemporary Myths about Women

Ruth Hubbard

Social Myths and Social Control

The dominant belief system of a society is often completely intertwined and hidden in the ordinary truths and realities that the people who live in that society accept without question. This tends to obscure the fact that these beliefs are actively generated and furthered by members of the dominant group because they are consistent with that group's interests. Further, these beliefs are intended to stabilize the social conditions that are required to perpetuate the hegemony of the dominant group. This is how we must regard present day scientific ideas about women's nature. They are part of the dominant belief system, but are myths that do not offer an accurate description of women's lives or explain the differences in the social and economic status of women and men.

Oppressive ideas and explanations that derive women's roles from women's "nature" are grounded in the material conditions in which the scientists who generate them live. These scientists are predominantly university-educated, economically privileged white men, who either belong to the hegemonic group or identify with its interests. (The few women and Third World men who have recently gained access to the scientific elite generally have the same economic and educational backgrounds as the traditional, white male members and often identify with the same interests.) It is therefore not an accident that scientists' perceptions of reality, as well as their descriptions of it, often serve to perpetuate and bolster the privileges of that disproportionately small group of people who have economic and social power in society.

One way that scientific explanations have served the ends of those in power has been by "proving" that the economic, social, and political roles of members of the different classes, races, and/or other socially significant groupings within the society are consistent with their biological natures and derive naturally from them. This is the way the ideology of woman's nature functions. It provides justifications for setting limits on women's roles, activities, and aspirations that are consistent with the social needs and goals perceived by those who have power to rule the society and to generate its ruling ideas. The roles women (and men) occupy in society are thus said to originate in mother nature, rather than in the society in which we live. Internalized by women, this ideology helps to make us, too, accept our allocated roles as natural.

Although the grounding of social roles in biological differences takes a scientific form in our society, it is important to see clearly that the basis for the theories is political, not simply a matter of science gone astray. Other theories have appeared in other cultures and play similar functions there. For example, Beatrice Medicine discusses views held by the Lakota Sioux and points out the several, and sometimes contradictory ways, that notions of woman's nature are used to socialize American Indian girls to accept traditional and contemporary Native American norms, as well as Anglo ones—norms that often are oppressive, though they occasionally also acknowledge women's strengths.

Because the ideology of woman's nature plays a critical role in keeping women "in our place," in this scientific age it is important to examine scientific theories that are used to support it. Therefore I shall describe some of the ways that scientific assumptions about women's biology have led us to accept discriminatory social arrangements as appropriate and natural. Indeed, the very notion that there exists a prototypical woman who can be described in ways that reflect and have meaning for the lives of the many different women living in very different geographical, economic, political, and social needs to be challenged. For example, Marian Lowe shows that naturalistic explanations of women's status in society can be quite insidious because they can affect and literally *shape* our biology by determining the material conditions in which we live—what and how much we eat and do, how stressful our lives are, and so on. For example, women are on average weaker than men at least partly because boys are encouraged to be more active than girls from earliest childhood, and girls are admonished to act like ladies. Thus, to some extent—though we do not know how much—the biological sex differences that are not specifically involved with reproduction reflect the different ways that girls and boys and women and men live.

Women's Lives: Myth and Reality

It is important to be aware that the *ideology* of woman's nature can differ drastically from, and indeed be antithetical to, the *realities* of women's lives. In fact, the ideology often serves as a smokescreen that obscures the ways women live by making people (including women) look away from the realities or ask misleading questions about them.

What are some of the realities? One is that women, with few exceptions, work and have always worked, though the term work has over the centuries been increasingly defined to mean what men do. Women's work is often trivialized, ignored, and undervalued, both in economic and political terms. For example, it is not called work when women "only" care for their households and children. Indeed, much of the work women do does not appear in the GNP and hence has no reality and value in standard descriptions of the economy. It is a fact that women work considerably more than men if *all* the work women do is counted—on average, about 56–65 hours per week as against men's 40–48—since in addition to working for pay, most women do most or all housework, as well as most volunteer work in schools, hospitals, and other parts of the community. Women earn 57 cents for every dollar men earn, not because we do not work as much or are less effective, but because women usually are paid less than men in work places and because much of women's work is unpaid. If women stopped doing all the work for which we are not paid, this society would grind to a halt, since much of the paid work men do depends heavily on women's unacknowledged and unpaid household labor.

The ideology that labels women as the natural reproducers of the species, and men as producers of goods, has not been used to exempt women from also producing goods and services, but to shunt us out of higher paying jobs, professional work, and other kinds of paid work that require continuity and give some power over one's own and, at times, other people's lives. Most women who work for pay do so in job categories such as secretary or nurse, which involve a great deal of concealed responsibility, but are underpaid. This is one reason why affirmative action *within* job categories cannot remedy women's economic disadvantage. Women will continue to be underpaid as long as access to better paying job categories is limited by social pressures, career counseling, training and hiring practices, trade union policies, and various other subtle and not so subtle societal mechanisms (such as discouraging the interest of girls in mathematics and scientific subjects). An entire range of discriminatory practices is justified by the claim that they follow from the limits that biology places on women's capacity to work. Though exceptions are made during wars and other emergencies, these are forgotten as soon as life resumes its normal course. Then women are expected to return to their subordinate roles, not because the quality of their work during the emergencies has been inferior, but because these roles are seen as natural.

A number of women employees in the chemical and automotive industries actually have been forced to choose whether to work at relatively well-paying jobs or be able ever to have children. In one instance, five women were required to submit to sterilization *by hysterectomy* in order to avoid being transferred from work in the lead pigment department at the American Cyanamid plant in Willow Island, West Virginia to janitorial work at considerably lower wages and benefits. Even though none of these women was pregnant or planning a pregnancy in the near future (indeed, the husband of one had had a vasectomy), they were considered pregnant or "potentially pregnant" unless they could prove that they were sterile. This goes on despite the fact that exposure to lead can damage sperm as well as eggs and can affect the health of workers (male and female) as well as a "potential fetus." But it is important to notice that this vicious choice has been forced only on women who have recently entered what had previously been relatively well-paid male jobs. Women whose work routinely involves exposure to chemical or radiation hazards in traditionally female jobs such as nurses, X-ray technologists, cleaning women in surgical operating rooms, beauticians, secretaries, workers in the ceramic industry, and domestic workers are not warned about the presence of chemical or physical hazards to their health or to that of a fetus, should they be pregnant. In other words, protection of women's reproductive integrity is being used as a pretext to exclude women from better paid job categories from which they had previously been excluded by discriminatory employment practices, but women (or, indeed, men) are not protected against health endangering work in general.[1]

The ideology of woman's nature that is invoked at these times would have us believe that a woman's capacity to become pregnant leaves her at all times physically disabled by comparison with men. The scientific underpinnings for these ideas were elaborated in the nineteenth century by the white, university-educated, mainly upper class men who made up the bulk of the new professions of obstetrics and gynecology, biology, psychology, sociology and anthropology. But these professionals used their theories of women's innate frailty only to disqualify the girls and women of their own race and class who would be in competition with them for education and professional status and might also deprive them of the kinds of personal attention and services they were accustomed to receive from their mothers, wives, and sisters. They did not invoke women's weakness to mitigate the exploitation of poor women working long hours in homes and factories that belonged to members of the upper classes, nor against the ways Black slave women were forced to work for no wages in the plantations and homes of their white masters and mistresses. Dorothy Burnham eloquently tells us about slave women's lives.

Nineteenth century biologists and physicians claimed that women's brains were smaller than men's, and that women's ovaries and uteruses required much energy and rest in order to function properly. They "proved" that therefore young girls must be kept away from schools and colleges once they had begun to menstruate and warned that without this kind of care women's uteruses and ovaries would shrivel, and the human race would die out. Yet again, this analysis was not carried over to poor women, who were not only required to work hard, but often were said to reproduce *too* much. Indeed, the fact that they could work so hard while bearing children was taken as a sign that these women were more animal-like and less highly evolved than upper class women.

Science and Social Myths

During the last decade, many feminist scholars have reminded us of this history. They have analyzed the self-serving theories and documented the absurdity of the claims as well as their class and race biases and their glaringly political intent. But this kind of scientific mythmaking is not past history. Just as medical men and biologists in the nineteenth century fought women's political organizing for equality by claiming that our reproductive organs made us unfit for anything but childbearing and childrearing, and Freud declared women to be intrinsically less stable and intellectually less inventive and productive than men, so beginning in the 1970s, there has been a renaissance in sex differences research that has claimed to prove scientifically that women are *innately* better than men at home care and mothering while men are *innately* better fitted than women for the competitive life of the market place.

Questionable experimental results obtained with animals (primarily that proto-typic human, the white laboratory rat) are treated as though they can be applied equally well to people. On this basis, some scientists are now claiming that the secretion of different amounts of so-called male hormones (androgens) by male and female fetuses produces life-long differences in women's and men's brains. They claim not only that these (unproved) differences in fetal hormone levels exist, but imply (without evidence) that they predispose women and men *as groups* to exhibit innate differences in our abilities to localize objects in space, in our verbal and mathematical aptitudes, in aggressiveness and competitiveness, nurturing ability, and so on.[2] Other scientists, sociobiologists, claim that some of the sex differences in social behavior that exist in our society (for example, aggressiveness, competitiveness, and dominance among men; coyness, nurturance, and submissiveness among women) are human universals that have existed in all times and cultures. Because these traits are ever-present, they deduce that they must be adaptive (that is, promote human survival), and that they have evolved through Darwinian natural selection and are now part of our genetic inheritance.

In recent years, sociobiologists have tried to prove that women have a greater biological investment in our children than men, and that women's disproportionate contributions to child- and homecare are biologically programmed to help us insure that our "investments" mature—in other words, that our children live long enough to have children themselves. The rationale is that an organism's biological fitness, in the Darwinian sense, depends on producing the greatest possible number of offspring, who themselves survive long enough to reproduce. This is what deter-

mines the frequency of occurrence of an individual's genes in successive generations. Following this logic a step further, sociobiologists argue that women and men
must adopt basically different strategies to maximize the spreading of genes over
future generations. The calculus goes as follows: because women cannot produce as
many eggs as men can sperm and, in addition, must "invest" at least the nine
months of pregnancy (whereas it takes a man only the few minutes of heterosexual
intercourse to send a sperm on its way to personhood), each egg and child represents
a much larger fraction of the reproductive fitness a woman can achieve in her
lifetime than a sperm or a child does in a man's life. From this biological asymme-
try, follow female fidelity, male promiscuity, and the unequal division and valuing of
labor by sex in this society. As sociobiologist, David Barash, presents it, "mother
nature is sexist," so don't blame her human sons. [3]

In devising these explanations, sociobiologists ignore the fact that human societies do not operate with a few superstuds; nor do stronger or more powerful men
usually have more children than weaker ones. Though men, in theory, could have
many more children than women can, in most societies equal numbers of men and
women engage in *producing* children, but not in caring for them. But these kinds of
theories are useful to people who have a stake in maintaining present inequalities.
They have a superficial ring of plausibility and thus offer naturalistic justifications
for discriminatory practices.

It is important to recognize that though sociobiologists have argued that we must
come to understand these intrinsic biological realities so that we may bring our
social arrangements into conformity with them, scientists generally have not been
reluctant to tamper with nature. Scientists are proud of the technical and chemical
innovations that have transformed the natural environment. And they pride themselves on the medical innovations through which healthy women's normal biology
is routinely altered by means of the pill or by surgical operations that change breast
or thigh size. At present, physicians routinely intervene in the normal course of
pregnancy and birth, so that in the United States one out of five births is a major
surgical event—a Caesarean section. Truly, physicians and scientists are not noted
for their reluctance to interfere with nature!

Though many people would like to see less interference with normal biological
functions than now occurs in this overmedicated and highly technological society,
the fact is that human living necessarily involves an interplay between biological and
social forces. We have no way of knowing what people's "real" biology is, because
the concept has no meaning. There is no such thing as human biology in the pure.
In other words, what we think of as women's biology is a political construct, not a
scientific one.

However, within this constraint, it is important to recognize that we have much
less solid and reliable information about how our bodies function than we could
have if women asked the questions that are of importance and interest to us. For
example, we do not know the normal range of women's experiences of menstrua-
tion, pregnancy, childbirth, lactation, and menopause. If women want to learn
about our biology, we will have to share our knowledge and experiences of how our

bodies function *within the context of our lives*. We must also become alert and sensitive to the ways that many of the standard descriptions of women's biology *legitimize* women's economic and social exploitation and reinforce the status quo. To summarize:

- People's biology develops in reciprocal and dialectical relationships with the ways in which we live. Therefore human biology cannot be analyzed or understood in social isolation.
- Reconstructions of women's "intrinsic" biological nature are scientifically meaningless and usually are politically and ideologically motivated.
- Scientists and physicians have asked scientific questions from a male-supremist perspective, with the conscious or unconscious intention of proving that a woman's place in society derives naturally from her biological being.
- It is important to dispel naturalistic explanations that provide biological justifications for the economic and social limitations with which women must struggle.
- We do not know much about how our bodies function within the context of our lives because the right questions have not yet been asked, nor in the right ways. It is therefore worthwhile for women to generate meaningful and important questions that can yield practical information about how to live more healthfully and productively.

NOTES

1. This is discussed by Jeanne M. Stellman and Mary Sue Henifin in their article, "No Fertile Women Need Apply: Employment Discrimination and Reproductive Hazards in the Workplace," in, Ruth Hubbard, Mary Sue Henifin, and Barbara Fried, eds., *Biological Woman—The Convenient Myth* (Cambridge, Mass.: Schenkman, 1982), pp. 117–145.

2. Several recent publications have been concerned with hormones and the brain. Up to date summaries to research can be found in Robert W. Goy and Bruce S. McEwen, *Sexual Differentiation of the Brain* (Cambridge, Mass.: M.I.T. Press, 1980) and in a series of review articles published in *Science* 211 (1981): 1263–1324. Articles intended for general readers have appeared in *Quest* (October, 1980), *Discover* (April, 1981), *Newsweek* (May 18, 1981), *Playboy* (January–July, 1982), and other magazines. Feminist criticisms of sex differences research, including research on hormones and the brain, can be found in Ruth Hubbard and Marian Lowe, eds., *Genes and Gender II: Pitfalls in Research on Sex and Gender* (New York: Gordian Press, 1979); Brighton Women and Science Group, eds., *Alice Through the Microscope* (London: Virago, 1980); Ruth Hubbard, Mary Sue Henifin, and Barbara Fried, eds., *Biological Woman—The Convenient Myth* (Cambridge, Mass.: Schenkman, 1982).

3. The investment calculus of sex differences in social and economic roles is presented in many recent publications on sociobiology. Examples are Edward O. Wilson, *Sociobiology: The New Synthesis* (Cambridge, Mass.: Harvard University Press, 1975), chapters 15 and 16; David Barash, *The Whispering Within* (New York: Harper & Row, 1979); Donald Symons, *The Evolution of Human Sexuality* (New York: Oxford University Press, 1979). Criticisms are included in Arthur L. Caplan, ed., *The Sociobiology Debate* (New York: Harper & Row, 1978) and in Ashley Montagu, ed., *Sociobiology Examined* (New York: Oxford University Press, 1980).

6

Gender Issues in the College Classroom

Edward B. Fiske

Do men get more for their money than women do when they slap down $50,000 to $100,000 for a college education? Based on her analysis of thousands of hours of college teaching, Catherine G. Krupnick says the answer is a resounding yes.

Detailed observations of thousands of hours of videotapes of college classrooms show that faculty members consistently take male students and their contributions more seriously than females and their ideas. Moreover, they permit males to dominate discussions far out of proportion to their numbers.

"College catalogues should carry warnings: The value you receive will depend on your sex," she suggested.

Ms. Krupnick's conclusions are bad news for Wheaton College. Until two years ago, it was an all-female institution selling itself as a place where women could flex their intellectual and leadership muscles before moving out into male-dominated work places.

Now Wheaton has bowed to economic necessity, become coeducational and taken up the challenge of providing what Alice F. Emerson, president of the college, calls "gender-balanced" education. To do so, they have turned to Ms. Krupnick, a researcher at the Harvard Graduate School of Education, for help.

Ms. Krupnick's findings are among the latest in a steady stream of research over the last two decades showing that while they may be sitting side by side, male and female undergraduates have substantially different educational experiences.

In a survey of the literature on the subject for the Association of American Colleges, Roberta Hall argued that women face a "chilly climate" in most college classrooms. Professors are more likely to remember men's names, call on them in class and listen attentively to their answers. By contrast, they feel freer to interrupt women and ask them "lower order" questions.

For example, an English professor might ask a woman for the year when Wordsworth wrote the first version of "the Prelude," but turn to a male student to ask, "What are the thematic differences between the 1805 and 1850 versions?"

A study released last month by the Harvard Assessment Seminars reported that men and women often approach their studies with sharply different values. The satisfaction men get from college years tends to correlate well with the grades they achieve, and they look for faculty advisers who will give them "concrete and directive suggestions." Women, by contrast, tend to put the heart before the course. Their overall academic satisfaction, the study found, is shaped "far more by personal relationships and by informal encounters and meetings with faculty and advisers."

When she was first hired by Wheaton as a consultant, Ms. Krupnick expected to find no problems. "Half of the faculty members were women, and women still predominated in every class," she recalled. "I assumed that they would still be holding their own. But I was wrong."

Detailed analysis of videotapes of Wheaton classes showed that in a class where they made up one-tenth of the students, male students would do a quarter of the speaking. They also tended to be more impulsive. "You ask what's the meaning of life, and four hands will shoot up, most of them male," she said.

Ms. Krupnick said that female students, by contrast, tended to want time to think about a question before offering an answer and that when they did respond, they were more likely than men to "enlarge on the ideas of a previous speaker rather than to challenge his or her initial assumption."

Women at Wheaton tend to do better than their male classmates on written papers, but according to Ms. Krupnick, the cost of not becoming proficient in holding an audience can be high. "In a vast number of careers," she said, "it's the ability to use language in public settings, like meetings, that leads to advancement, not the quality of work done in private."

Ms. Krupnick suggested that the goal for Wheaton—or any college, for that matter—should be to promote all strengths in all students. "Teachers should encourage women to initiate comments, resist interruptions and be willing to assume the risks of a public role," she said. "Likewise, men need listening skills. They must also be shown that when they give instant answers to complicated questions, mostly for the sake of social posturing, they are not getting a very good education."

Wheaton faculty members have been working with Ms. Krupnick on techniques for reaching such goals.

"The most important thing is to be aware of the space in the room and think about who is speaking," said Richard Pearce, a professor of English. "Then you can consciously, even physically, turn away from over-participators."

Another technique is to pause for five or ten seconds after asking a question and not accept the first hand that goes up. "Americans are nudgy about silence," said Ms. Krupnick. "You have to learn to say: 'Not yet.'"

Either that, she says, or issue warning labels.

7

Oppression

Marilyn Frye

It is a fundamental claim of feminism that women are oppressed. The word "oppression" is a strong word. It repels and attracts. It is dangerous and dangerously fashionable and endangered. It is much misused, and sometimes not innocently.

The statement that women are oppressed is frequently met with the claim that men are oppressed too. We hear that oppressing is oppressive to those who oppress as well as to those they oppress. Some men cite as evidence of their oppression their much-advertised inability to cry. It is tough, we are told, to be masculine. When the stresses and frustrations of being a man are cited as evidence that oppressors are oppressed by their oppressing, the word "oppression" is being stretched to meaninglessness; it is treated as though its scope includes any and all human experience of limitation or suffering, no matter the cause, degree or consequence. Once such usage has been put over on us, then if ever we deny that any person or group is oppressed, we seem to imply that we think they never suffer and have no feelings. We are accused of insensitivity, even of bigotry. For women, such accusation is particularly intimidating, since sensitivity is one of the few virtues that has been assigned to us. If we are found insensitive, we may fear we have no redeeming traits at all and perhaps are not real women. Thus are we silenced before we begin: the name of our situation drained of meaning and our guilt mechanisms tripped.

But this is nonsense. Human beings can be miserable without being oppressed, and it is perfectly consistent to deny that a person or group is oppressed without denying that they have feelings or that they suffer.

We need to think clearly about oppression, and there is much that mitigates against this. I do not want to undertake to prove that women are oppressed (or that men are not), but I want to make clear what is being said when we say it. We need this word, this concept, and we need it to be sharp and sure.

The root of the word "oppression" is the element "press." *The press of the crowd; pressed into military service; to press a pair of pants; printing press; press the button.* Presses are used to mold things or flatten them or reduce them in bulk, sometimes to reduce them by squeezing out the gasses or liquids in them. Something pressed is something caught between or among forces and barriers which are so related to each other that jointly they restrain, restrict or prevent the thing's motion or mobility. Mold. Immobilize. Reduce.

The mundane experience of the oppressed provides another clue. One of the most characteristic and ubiquitous features of the world as experienced by oppressed people is the double bind—situations in which options are reduced to a very few and all of them expose one to penalty, censure or deprivation. For example, it is often a requirement upon oppressed people that we smile and be cheerful. If we comply, we signal our docility and our acquiescence in our situation. We need not, then, be taken note of. We acquiesce in being made invisible, in our occupying no space. We participate in our own erasure. On the other hand, anything but the sunniest countenance exposes us to being perceived as mean, bitter, angry or dangerous. This means, at the least, that we may be found "difficult" or unpleasant to work with, which is enough to cost one one's livelihood; at worst, being seen as mean, bitter, angry or dangerous has been known to result in rape, arrest, beating and murder. One can only choose to risk one's preferred form and rate of annihilation.

Another example: It is common in the United States that women, especially younger women, are in a bind where neither sexual activity nor sexual inactivity is all right. If she is heterosexually active, a woman is open to censure and punishment for being loose, unprincipled or a whore. The "punishment" comes in the form of criticism, snide and embarrassing remarks, being treated as an easy lay by men, scorn from her more restrained female friends. She may have to lie and hide her behavior from her parents. She must juggle the risks of unwanted pregnancy and dangerous contraceptives. On the other hand, if she refrains from heterosexual activity, she is fairly constantly harassed by men who try to persuade her into it and pressure her to "relax" and "let her hair down"; she is threatened with labels like "frigid," "uptight," "man-hater," "bitch" and "cocktease." The same parents who would be disapproving of her sexual activity may be worried by her inactivity because it suggests she is not or will not be popular, or is not sexually normal. She may be charged with lesbianism. If a woman is raped, then if she has been heterosexually active she is subject to the presumption that she liked it (since her activity is presumed to show that she likes sex), and if she has not been heterosexually active, she is subject to the presumption that she liked it (since she is supposedly "repressed and frustrated"). Both heterosexual activity and heterosexual nonactivity are likely to be taken as proof that you wanted to be raped, and hence, of course, weren't *really* raped at all. You can't win. You are caught in a bind, caught between systematically related pressures.

Women are caught like this, too, by networks of forces and barriers that expose one to penalty, loss or contempt whether one works outside the home or not, is on welfare or not, bears children or not, raises children or not, marries or not, stays married or not, is heterosexual, lesbian, both or neither. Economic necessity; confinement to racial and/or sexual job ghettos; sexual harassment; sex discrimination; pressures of competing expectations and judgments about *women, wives* and *mothers* (in the society at large, in racial and ethnic subcultures and in one's own mind); dependence (full or partial) on husbands, parents or the state; commitment to political ideas; loyalties to racial or ethnic or other "minority" groups; the demands of self-respect and responsibilities to others. Each of these factors exists in complex tension with every other, penalizing or prohibiting all of the apparently available options. And nipping at one's heels, always, is the endless pack of little things. If one dresses one way, one is subject to the assumption that one is advertising one's sexual availability; if one dresses another way, one appears to "not care about oneself" or to be "unfeminine." If one uses "strong language," one invites categorization as a whore or slut; if one does not, one invites categorization as a "lady"—one too delicately constituted to cope with robust speech or the realities to which it presumably refers.

The experience of oppressed people is that the living of one's life is confined and shaped by forces and barriers which are not accidental or occasional and hence avoidable, but are systematically related to each other in such a way as to catch one between and among them and restrict or penalize motion in any direction. It is the experience of being caged in: all avenues, in every direction, are blocked or booby-trapped.

Cages. Consider a birdcage. If you look very closely at just one wire in the cage, you cannot see the other wires. If your conception of what is before you is determined by this myopic focus, you could look at that one wire, up and down the length of it, and be unable to see why a bird would not just fly around the wire any time it wanted to go somewhere. Furthermore, even if, one day at a time, you myopically inspected each wire, you still could not see why a bird would have trouble going past the wires to get anywhere. There is no physical property of any one wire, *nothing* that the closest scrutiny could discover, that will reveal how a bird could be inhibited or harmed by it except in the most accidental way. It is only when you step back, stop looking at the wires one by one, microscopically, and take a macroscopic view of the whole cage, that you can see why the bird does not go anywhere; and then you will see it in a moment. It will require no great subtlety of mental powers. It is perfectly *obvious* that the bird is surrounded by a network of systematically related barriers, no one of which would be the least hindrance to its flight, but which, by their relations to each other, are as confining as the solid walls of a dungeon.

It is now possible to grasp one of the reasons why oppression can be hard to see and recognize: one can study the elements of an oppressive structure with great care and some good will without seeing the structure as a whole, and hence without seeing or being able to understand that one is looking at a cage and that there are people there who are caged, whose motion and mobility are restricted, whose lives are shaped and reduced.

The arresting of vision at a microscopic level yields such common confusion as that about the male door-opening ritual. This ritual, which is remarkably widespread across classes and races, puzzles many people, some of whom do and some of whom do not find it offensive. Look at the scene of the two people approaching a door. The male steps slightly ahead and opens the door. The male holds the door open while the female glides through. Then the male goes through. The door closes after them. "Now how," one innocently asks, "can those crazy womenslibbers say that is oppressive? The guy *removed* a barrier to the lady's smooth and unruffled progress." But each repetition of this ritual has a place in a pattern, in fact in several patterns. One has to shift the level of one's perception in order to see the whole picture.

The door-opening pretends to be a helpful service, but the helpfulness is false. This can be seen by noting that it will be done whether or not it makes any practical sense. Infirm men and men burdened with packages will open doors for able-bodied women who are free of physical burdens. Men will impose themselves awkwardly and jostle everyone in order to get to the door first. The act is not determined by convenience or grace. Furthermore, these very numerous acts of unneeded or even noisome "help" occur in counterpoint to a pattern of men not being helpful in many practical ways in which women might welcome help. What *women* experience is a world in which gallant princes charming commonly make a fuss about being helpful and providing small services when help and services are of little or no use, but in which there are rarely ingenious and adroit princes at hand when substantial assistance is really wanted either in mundane affairs or in situations of threat, assault or terror. There is no help with the (his) laundry; no help typing a report at 4:00 A.M.; no help in mediating disputes among relatives or children. There is nothing but advice that women should stay indoors after dark, be chaperoned by a man, or when it comes down to it, "lie back and enjoy it."

The gallant gestures have no practical meaning. Their meaning is symbolic. The door-opening and similar services provided are services which really are needed by people who are for one reason or another incapacitated—unwell, burdened with parcels, etc. So the message is that women are incapable. The detachment of the acts from the concrete realities of what women need and do not need is a vehicle for the message that women's actual needs and interests are unimportant or irrelevant. Finally, these gestures imitate the behavior of servants toward masters and thus mock women, who are in most respects the servants and caretakers of men. The message of the false helpfulness of male gallantry is female dependence, the invisibility or insignificance of women, and contempt for women.

One cannot see the meanings of these rituals if one's focus is riveted upon the individual event in all its particularity, including the particularity of the individual man's present conscious intentions and motives and the individual woman's conscious perception of the event in the moment. It seems sometimes that people take a deliberately myopic view and fill their eyes with things seen microscopically in order not to see macroscopically. At any rate, whether it is deliberate or not, people can and do fail to see the oppression of women because they fail to see macroscopically and hence fail to see the various elements of the situation as systematically related in larger schemes.

As the cageness of the birdcage is a macroscopic phenomenon, the oppressiveness of the situations in which women live our various and different lives is a macroscopic phenomenon. Neither can be *seen* from a microscopic perspective. But when you look macroscopically you can see it—a network of forces and barriers which are systematically related and which conspire to the immobilization, reduction and molding of women and the lives we live.

8

Something about the Subject Makes It Hard to Name

Jenny Yamato

Racism—simple enough in structure, yet difficult to eliminate. Racism—pervasive in the U.S. culture to the point that it deeply affects all the local town folk and spills over, negatively influencing the fortunes of folk around the world. Racism is pervasive to the point that we take many of its manifestations for granted, believing "that's life." Many believe that racism can be dealt with effectively in one hellifying workshop, or one hour-long heated discussion. Many actually believe this monster, racism, that has had at least a few hundred years to take root, grow, invade our space and develop subtle variations . . . this mind-funk that distorts thought and action, can be merely wished away. I've run into folks who really think that we can beat this devil, kick this habit, be healed of this disease in a snap. In a sincere blink of a well-intentioned eye, presto—poof—racism disappears. "I've dealt with my racism . . . (envision a laying on of hands) . . . Hallelujah! Now I can go to the beach." Well, fine. Go to the beach. In fact, why don't we all go to the beach and continue to work on the sucker over there? Cuz you can't even shave a little piece off this thing called racism in a day, or a weekend, or a workshop.

When I speak of *oppression*, I'm talking about the systematic, institutionalized mistreatment of one group of people by another for whatever reason. The oppressors are purported to have an innate ability to access economic resource, information, respect, etc., while the oppressed are believed to have a corresponding negative innate ability. The flip side of oppression is *internalized oppression*. Members of the target group are emotionally, physically, and spiritually battered to the point that they begin to actually believe that their oppression is deserved, is their lot in life, is natural and right, and that it doesn't even exist. The oppression begins to feel comfortable, familiar enough that when mean ol' Massa lay down de whip, we got's to pick up and whack ourselves and each other. Like a virus, it's hard to beat racism, because by the time you come up with a cure, it's mutated to a "new cure-resistant" form. One shot just won't get it. Racism must be attacked from many angles.

The forms of racism that I pick up on these days are 1) aware/blatant racism, 2) aware/covert racism, 3) unaware/unintentional racism, and 4) unaware/self-righteous racism. I can't say that I prefer any one form of racism over the others, because they all look like an itch needing a scratch. I've heard it said (and understandably so) that the aware/blatant form of racism is preferable if one must suffer it. Outright racists will, without apology or confusion, tell us that because of our color we don't appeal to them. If we so choose, we can attempt to get the hell out of their way before we get the sweat knocked out of us. Growing up, aware/covert racism is what I heard many of my elders bemoaning "up north," after having escaped the overt racism "down south." Apartments were suddenly no longer vacant or rents were outrageously high, when black, brown, red, or yellow persons went to inquire about them. Job vacancies were suddenly filled, or we were fired for very vague reasons. It still happens, though the perpetrators really take care to cover their tracks these days. They don't want to get gummed to death or slobbered on by the toothless laws that supposedly protect us from such inequities.

Unaware/unintentional racism drives usually tranquil white liberals wild when they get called on it, and confirms the suspicions of many people of color who feel that white folks are just plain crazy. It has led white people to believe that it's just fine to ask if they can touch my hair (while reaching). They then exclaim over how soft it is, how it does not scratch their hand. It has led whites to assume that bending over backwards and speaking to me in high-pitched (terrified), condescending tones would make up for all the racist wrongs that distort our lives. This type of racism has led whites right to my doorstep, talking 'bout, "We're sorry/we love you and want to make things right," which is fine, and further, "We're gonna give you the opportunity to fix it while we sleep. Just tell us what you need. 'Bye!!"—which *ain't* fine. With the best of intentions, the best of educations, and the greatest generosity of heart, whites, operating on the misinformation fed to them from day one, will behave in ways that are racist, will perpetuate racism by being "nice" the way we're taught to be nice. You can just "nice" somebody to death with naïveté and lack of awareness of privilege. Then there's guilt and the desire to end racism and how the two get all tangled up to the point that people, morbidly fascinated with their guilt, are immobilized. Rather than deal with ending racism, they sit and ponder their guilt and hope nobody notices how awful they are. Meanwhile, racism picks up momentum and keeps on keepin' on.

Now, the newest form of racism that I'm hip to is unaware/self-righteous racism. The "good white" racist attempts to shame Blacks into being blacker, scorns Japanese-Americans who don't speak Japanese, and knows more about the Chicano/a community than the folks who make up the community. They assign themselves as the "good whites," as opposed to the "bad whites," and are often so busy telling people of color what the issues in the Black, Asian, Indian, Latino/a communities should be that they don't have time to deal with their errant sisters and brothers in the white community. Which means that people of color are still left to deal with what the "good whites" don't want to . . . racism.

Internalized racism is what really gets in my way as a Black woman. It influences the way I see or don't see myself, limits what I expect of myself or others like me. It results in my acceptance of mistreatment, leads me to believe that being treated with less than absolute respect, at least this once, is to be expected because I am Black, because I am not white. "Because I am (*you fill in the color*)," you think, "Life is going to be hard." The fact is life may be hard, but the color of your skin is not the cause of the hardship. The color of your skin may be used as an excuse to mistreat you, but there is no reason or logic involved in the mistreatment. If it seems that your color is the reason; if it seems that your ethnic heritage is the cause of the woe, it's because you've been deliberately beaten down by agents of a greedy system until you swallowed the garbage. That is the internalization of racism.

Racism is the systematic, institutionalized mistreatment of one group of people by another based on racial heritage. Like every other oppression, racism can be internalized. People of color come to believe misinformation about their particular ethnic group and thus believe that their mistreatment is justified. With that basic vocabulary, let's take a look at how the whole thing works together. Meet "the Ism Family," racism, classism, ageism, adultism, elitism, sexism, heterosexism, physicalism, etc. All these ism's are systematic, that is, not only are these parasites feeding off our lives, they are also dependent on one another for foundation. Racism is supported and reinforced by classism, which is given a foothold and a boost by adultism, which also feeds sexism, which is validated by heterosexism, and so it goes on. You cannot have the "ism" functioning without first effectively installing its flip-side, the internalized version of the ism. Like twins, as one particular form of the ism grows in potency, there is a corresponding increasing in its internalized form within the population. Before oppression becomes a specific ism like racism, usually all hell breaks loose. War. People fight attempts to enslave them, or to subvert their will, or to take what they consider theirs, whether that is territory or dignity. It's true that the various elements of racism, while repugnant, would not be able to do very much damage, but for one generally overlooked key piece: power/privilege.

While in one sense we all have power we have to look at the fact that, in our society, people are stratified into various classes and some of these classes have more privilege than others. The owning class has enough power and privilege to not have to give a good whinney what the rest of the folks have on their minds. The power and privilege of the owning class provides the ability to pay off enough of the working class and offer that paid-off group, the middle class, just enough privilege to make it agreeable to do various and sundry oppressive things to other working-class and outright disenfranchised folk, keeping the lid on explosive inequities, at least for a minute. If you're at the bottom of this heap, and you believe the line that says you're there because that's all you're worth, it is at least some small solace to believe that there are others more worthless than you, because of their gender, race, sexual preference . . . whatever. The specific form of power that runs the show here is the power to intimidate. The power to take away the most lives the quickest, and back it up with legal and "divine" sanction, is the very bottom line. It makes the difference between who's holding the racism end of the stick and who's getting beat with it (or beating others as vulnerable as they are) on the internalized racism end of the stick.

What I am saying is, while people of color are welcome to tear up their own neighborhoods and each other, everybody knows that you cannot do that to white folks without hell to pay. People of color can be prejudiced against one another and whites, but do not have an ice-cube's chance in hell of passing laws that will get whites sent to relocation camps "for their own protection and the security of the nation." People who have not thought about or refuse to acknowledge this imbalance of power/privilege often want to talk about the racism of people of color. But then that is one of the ways racism is able to continue to function. You look for someone to blame and you blame the victim, who will nine times out of ten accept the blame out of habit.

So, what can we do? Acknowledge racism for a start, even though and especially when we've struggled to be kind and fair, or struggled to rise above it all. It is hard to acknowledge the fact that racism circumscribes and pervades our lives. Racism must be dealt with on two levels, personal and societal, emotional and institutional. It is possible—and most effective—to do both at the same time. We must reclaim whatever delight we have lost in our own ethnic heritage or heritages. This so-called melting pot has only succeeded in turning us into fast food-gobbling "generics" (as in generic "white folks" who were once Irish, Polish, Russian, English, etc. and "black folks," who were once Ashanti, Bambara, Baule, Yoruba, etc). Find or create safe places to actually *feel* what we've been forced to repress each time we were a victim of, witness to or perpetrator of racism, so that we do not continue, like puppets, to act out the past in the present and future. Challenge oppression. Take a stand against it. When you are aware of something oppressive going down, stop the show. At least call it. We become so numbed to racism that we don't even think twice about it, unless it is immediately life-threatening.

Whites who want to be allies to people of color: You can educate yourselves via research and observation rather than rigidly, arrogantly relying solely on interrogating people of color. Do not expect that people of color should teach you how to behave non-oppressively. Do not give into the pull to be lazy. Think, hard. Do not blame people of color for your frustration about racism, but do appreciate the fact that people of color will often help you get in touch with that frustration. Assume that your effort to be a good friend is appreciated, but don't expect or accept gratitude from people of color. Work on racism for your sake, not "their" sake. Assume that you are needed and capable of being a good ally. Know that you'll make mistakes and commit yourself to correcting them and continuing on as an ally, no matter what. Don't give up.

People of color, working through internalized racism: Remember always that you and others like you are completely worthy of respect, completely capable of achieving whatever you take a notion to do. Remember that the term "people of color" refers to a variety of ethnic and cultural backgrounds. These various groups have been oppressed in a variety of ways. Educate yourself about the ways different peoples have been oppressed and how they've resisted that oppression. Expect and insist that whites are capable of being good allies against racism. Don't give up. Resist the pull to give out the "people of color seal of approval" to aspiring white allies. A moment of appreciation is fine, but more than that tends to be less than helpful. Celebrate yourself. Celebrate yourself. Celebrate the inevitable end of racism.

Suggestions for Further Reading

Andreas, Carol: *Sex and Caste in America*, Prentice-Hall, Englewood Cliffs, NJ, 1971.

Banton, M., and J. Harwood: *The Race Concept*, Praeger, New York, 1975.

De Beauvoir, Simone: *The Second Sex*, Alfred A. Knopf, New York, 1952.

Gould, Stephen J.: *The Mismeasure of Man*, W.W. Norton & Co., New York, 1984.

Kitano, Harry H.L.: *Race Relations*, Third Edition, Prentice-Hall, Englewood Cliffs, NJ, 1985.

Levin, Jack, and William Levin: *The Functions of Discrimination and Prejudice*, Second Edition, Harper & Row, New York, 1982.

Lipman-Blumen, Jean: *Gender Roles and Power*, Prentice-Hall, Englewood Cliffs, NJ, 1984.

Lowe, M., and R. Hubbard (eds.): *Women's Nature: Rationalizations of Inequality*, Pergamon Press, New York, 1983.

Memmi, Albert: *Dominated Man*, Boston, Beacon Press, 1969.

Montagu, M.F. Ashley: *Man's Most Dangerous Myth*, Harper & Row, New York, 1952.

Knowles, Louis L., and Kenneth Prewitt (eds.): *Institutional Racism in America*, Prentice-Hall, Englewood Cliffs, NJ, 1969.

Omi, Michael, and Harold Winnat: *Racial Formations in the United States*, Routledge and Kegan Paul, New York, 1986.

Smith, Dorothy E.: *The Everyday World As Problematic: A Feminist Sociology*, Northeastern Press, Boston, 1987.

United States Commission on Civil Rights: *Racism in America and How to Combat It*, Washington, DC, 1970.

Wellman, David T.: *Portraits of White Racism*, Cambridge University Press, Cambridge, 1977.

PART II

Bias Incidents and Harassment: Some Examples

While Richard Wright's chilling account of growing up as a Negro in the South during the early part of this century, which appears in Part I, leaves no doubt in people's minds that he has been the victim of crude, brutal, conscious, and intentional racism, no such consensus exists about many of the "bias incidents" or incidents of harassment reported in the press. In Part II we examine a number of such cases. Drawn from newspapers and magazines, these accounts present a picture of the concrete ways in which racism, sexism, homophobia, and class inequities are often played out in contemporary U.S. society. Although we examine only a sampling of such incidents, we can use them to begin to make some general observations about the dynamics involved in bias incidents and to think about the way such incidents are perceived and interpreted.

"Bias incidents" are different from other acts of violence insofar as the race, ethnicity, sex, or sexual preference, real or imagined, of the victims are key elements in the attack. Racist and other stereotyping plays a major role in the perceptions and actions of the attackers, as do deeply held beliefs about social roles and values. For example, in "'Bias Incident' at Staten Island's Miller Field: A Tale of Two Neighborhoods," the stereotypes of African-Americans and Hispanics held by the white teenagers are so powerful they prevent those involved from accurately perceiving the age and status of the sixth graders they attack. Frequently, those carrying out the assault believe themselves to be in some way under attack even as they beat, maim, or kill the nonviolent targets of their violence. For example, in the first three incidents described in this section, the white youths who carry out the attacks actually believe that their neighborhoods and way of life are under attack. For them, the presence of people of a different race in their neighborhood in itself constitutes an act of violence that must be answered. Although the targets of the attack were in one case sixth graders on a school picnic and in another buyers in search of a used car, the attackers saw an invasion of their community that had to be repelled at any cost.

Reaction to such attacks, both by those directly and indirectly involved and those who simply hear about them through the press, often reflect the contradictory beliefs and pervasive stereotyping that produces the incident in the first place. For example, in Selection 8, the administration at Annapolis, the U.S. Naval Academy, dismisses the incident in which a female midshipman was handcuffed to a urinal by two male midshipmen as "a good-natured exchange that got out of hand." Often, only those who already acknowledge the pervasive sexism and racism of the society will readily acknowledge that these isms played a role in any particular alleged bias incident. Others may feel angered, victimized, or even betrayed by the charge that a bias incident has occured.

Accounts of rapes and assaults committed against women, like the cashier from Queens or the Central Park jogger, often imply that the women are responsible for their attack because they were in the wrong part of town, or were out too late, or were in a place women should not go, or were wearing the wrong kinds of clothes. In a society where white, male prerogatives legislate acceptable and unacceptable forms of behavior for everyone else, it is easy for so-called minorities to violate unwritten laws and become objects of extraordinary violence which is then regarded by some as largely deserved. Implicit in both racism and sexism is a picture of the world in which large areas of physical space are simply "off-limits" to women of all colors and men of color. Transgressing these invisible boundaries leaves members of so-called minority groups open to violent assault (and worse) and is usually taken as proof that the violence was provoked and even deserved.

This attitude has its roots in our history, as several selections from Part V make clear. For example, the reader might wish to look ahead to "An Act for the Better Ordering and Governing of Negroes and Slaves, South Carolina, 1712," which makes it a crime for virtually all "negroes and slaves" to be off the master's plantation and gives virtually all white men both the right and responsibility to apprehend, punish, and even kill any negro who enters white territory. Judging by the violence that often greets people of color who find themselves in "white neighborhoods," things haven't changed very much over the past two or three hundred years.

Another element at play in this sense of territory is both the stereotype of the non-white male as a sexual predator, and the definition of manhood as carrying with it responsibility of males to protect "their" women from possible attack by an outsider. That many men and women often hold simultaneously the contradictory beliefs that women, in contrast to men, are "pure" and spiritual creatures, and that they are inherently sexual and seductive or provocative, only complicates matters further. These beliefs, combined with a failure to permit and encourage women to assume responsibility for their own sexuality, add to a mentality which consistently blames the victim.

While violence against lesbians and homosexuals is often excused or explained similarly by the need to protect society in general and children in particular from the imagined overtures of gay people, the territorial imperative is lacking or, perhaps more correctly, is generalized. Where the mythology suggests that women of all colors and men of color who conform to appropriate social roles (as defined by patriarchy and white supremacy) will not be subject to assault, heterosexism and homophobia make it clear that lesbians and gays have no place in society. Their sexual being, in itself, is perceived as constituting an assault on the greater good and is not to be tolerated. As Suzanne Pharr points out in her essay in Part VII, and as the last selection in this part makes clear, homophobia and the violence that often accompanies it are a threat to us all, since anyone, at any time, can be taken to be homosexual or lesbian and targeted for attack.

"'Bias Incident' at Staten Island's Miller Field: A Tale of Two Neighborhoods" is particularly useful because it includes most if not all of the characteristics of the classic bias incident which we have been discussing. Reports from many of those involved in the attack on a group of multiracial, sixth graders on a school picnic, indicate the attackers are unable to distinguish between the stereotypes they hold of African-Americans and Hispanics and the actual children who were at Miller Field. Insisting the children were "really big dudes—huge," the attackers deny that they were in fact only sixth graders. When pressed to acknowledge this distortion, one of the Staten Island teenagers assures us that if there were little kids they were "day-care center kids." Unable to see the people who are in front of their nose, these teenagers can't see past the stereotypes they have internalized in a racist society.

The parents of these teens seem equally to be victims of such racist stereotyping. Take for example the fear expressed by the mother of one of the boys that if the family's name is in the paper, relatives of the kids from Brooklyn will come after her and rob her. The picture of the world she carries in her head is one in which African-Americans and Hispanics are criminals who spend their time mugging people and committing robberies. There is no room in this picture for minority group teachers, nurses, bus drivers, doctors, fire fighters, or ministers. Although her own son is the perpetrator of a vicious assault on sixth grade school children, she both feels and believes that she and her son are under attack.

Not only does racism undermine the ability of people to perceive events and other people accurately, the intensity and passion with which such deeply held prejudices are maintained often leads people to hold and assert contradictory beliefs and values, and renders them unable to recognize the contradictory nature of their stand. In this case, for example, seventeen-year-old Charles Trainer says, "sure black people got a right to come to the field. It's public property," and thus acknowledges a reality that most people would find indisputable. He continues on to say, "But they should know they don't belong here. The teachers who took them here are to blame." He and others see no contradiction between asserting a right and simulta-neously denying people the right to exercise it; in this case by pelting them and their school bus with rocks and bottles. It is no surprise to find these same youths and other members of their community expressing surprise and denial over the sugges-tion that this was a racial incident, or over the charge that they are racists.

It is axiomatic that in the United States the lives of African-Americans, and by extension, the lives of other people of color, are not valued as highly as those of white people. Beginning with the U.S. Constitution's determination that African-Ameri-cans counted for three-fifths of a man (see page 264), and further institutionalized by the differentials in punishment proscribed and actually prescribed by our laws and our courts depending upon the color and class position of the accused and their victim, this inequality has a long and tragic history. It continues to be played out in the attitudes of young whites who believe passionately in white supremacy at the same time that they recite the pledge of allegiance and parrot back the democratic values they have been taught in high school social studies courses. Because they have learned the litany of democracy by heart, they are confident that they are not racists, even as they attack African-Americans with baseball bats while screaming "Niggers Go Home."

The class tensions that underly these expressions of racism cannot be overstated. As several of the pieces in this section point out, racial violence frequently occurs in "down and out white ethnic neighborhoods" pitting "the powerless against the powerless." In a society which provides mediocre education at best to the great majority of its youth, and has little to offer in the way of meaningful employment to so many, racism effectively blinds the victims of class inequities to the true origins of their plight. It serves effectively to pit "the powerless against the powerless," leaving those who benefit from class stratification to enjoy the fruits of their privilege.

Taken together the articles in this section raise important and difficult questions about the ways in which issues of race, gender, and class intersect to create the context in which hate violence is acted out. In all such cases the same mentality that causes the attackers to blame the victims of their attack for the incident is what makes the attack possible in the first place. In a society where women of all colors, men of color, working class and poor people, and gay and lesbian people are defined as "different" or "other," and treated both implicitly and explicitly as less valuable than white, middle class, heterosexual males, acts of hate violence are inevitable.

"Bias Incident" at Staten Island's Miller Field:
A Tale of Two Neighborhoods

Howard Blum

The selection that follows is a newspaper account of an incident that occurred in New York City in August 1983.

Gregory Cotton had adjusted the tan leather cap on his head to a jaunty angle and was returning to the punchball game when he found his path blocked by two husky teen-agers.

"This field is for white people only," Gregory, a sixth grader, remembers one of the youths calling to him. The other motioned with a can of beer as if to underline the threat.

Some of Gregory's classmates saw the confrontation by the water fountain and walked across Staten Island's Miller Field to intervene.

There were more threats. A punch was thrown. And then another. And suddenly the Public School 139 graduation picnic had turned into what the New York City police would later call "a confirmed bias incident."

All this happened on June 17, but weeks later it still affects the lives of those involved, young and old. The children from Flatbush certainly remember it. So do the teen-agers from Staten Island. One of them was sentenced on July 19 to perform 70 hours of community service for his actions that afternoon on Miller Field.

"Our reports show there was a racial incident that afternoon," said Lieut. James I. Radney of the Federal park police, which patrols the field, part of the Federal Gateway National Recreation Area.

It was only one racial incident in a city where, according to the Police Department, there were 71 "confirmed bias incidents" in the first six months of this year.

But what happened that afternoon remains a jumble of frightening images to the 12-year-olds from the Brooklyn school: a group of perhaps 15 white teen-agers throwing rocks and shouting racial epithets as they chased them across the field; cries of "Go back to where you belong"; a teacher swinging a bat frantically as he tried to

67

defend his pupils, and rocks and bottles flying through the air, hitting children, crashing through school bus windows.

The sixth grade of P.S. 139 left the picnic on Staten Island under a police escort. The pupils made the trip back to Brooklyn in different buses from those in which they had arrived; the original school buses, their windows shattered, were littered with shards of glass. Six of the pupils—one Hispanic youth and five blacks—were treated in the emergency room of Staten Island Hospital for minor cuts and bruises.

Their class picnic had become a racial incident. And it had become the story of two divergent communities and a generation coming of age on the issue of race.

"A Neighborhood to Protect"

The bungalows at New Dorp Beach on Staten Island were built after World War II as summer getaway homes. As the completion of the Verrazano-Narrows Bridge made Staten Island more accessible to the rest of the city and the economy made second homes less accessible to many, these bungalows, with some insulation, gradually became year-round residences.

It was not long before developers moved in to plow dusty roads through the woods and erect rows of adjoining red-brick town houses and clapboard houses with neat front lawns. A community, just a stone's throw from the Atlantic Ocean, evolved.

Many of the second generation of New Dorp Beach residents—the teenage children of Civil Service and other middle-class workers—hang out on summer nights at the General Store on Topping Street, across from a strip of dunes leading to a rocky beach. Seated on a low fence near the store is a row of teen-agers, boys and girls, in an orderly line like birds perched on a wire.

Two antiquated gas pumps stand in front and the inside is crowded with a haphazard assortment of food and soda. A video game across from the front door is surrounded by youngsters; the machine fills the store with a steady background of shrill, high-pitched noises. About a block away is Miller Field.

"We got a neighborhood to protect," explains Ralph Fellini, 31, the owner of the General Store and the only one in the crowd outside willing to answer questions. "That's really what the whole thing on Miller Field was about."

"Hey, you guys know what went down at the field that day," he says to a group of uncommunicative youths. "You got nothing to be ashamed of. Tell the man."

"Well, if Ralphie says it's all right," decides a youth who had moments before denied even knowing the location of Miller Field.

"This is our neighborhood," says Darren Scaffidi, 15. "You let in one colored, you gotta let in a thousand."

"They don't have to come to Staten Island," says Petey Smith, 14. "Couldn't they go to Prospect Park in Brooklyn or some place like that?"

"I mean what would happen if we went up to Harlem?" asks Mike Cumminsky, 17.

"Look," says Charles Trainer, 17, "sure black people got a right to come to the field. It's public property. But they should know they don't belong here. The teachers who took them here are to blame."

The specifics of the incident have also taken on a reality unique to the logic of the neighborhood: A half-dozen voices insist that it could not have been a sixth-grade class that was attacked.

"They were really big dudes—huge," John Coe argues.

"Oh, maybe there were some little kids," Kevin McCarthy Jr., 15, finally agrees. "But they were day-care center kids. They should know better than to bus day-care center kids out here."

Mr. Fellini, a parent himself, sums it up: "These are good kids. They're not troublemakers. They're like I was when I was growing up in this neighborhood. They're just trying to make sure New Dorp Beach stays the kind of place where they'll want to raise their kids someday."

"The Racial Mix of the Real World"

P.S. 139 on Cortelyou Road in the Flatbush section of Brooklyn is on the fringe of a neighborhood of grand Victorian homes that seem out of place in Brooklyn. Tiled fireplaces, paneled rooms, wainscoting, parquet floors—all are common amenities surviving from a more comfortable era. Even the street names—Buckingham, Marlborough, Rugby—suggest the sort of gracious and static vision of Britannia that fuels romantic imaginations.

Yet Flatbush is a neighborhood hectic with modern-day problems and transition. Signs on the streets announce that private security police patrol the neighborhood. It is not an unrealistic precaution: in the 70th Precinct, which includes P.S. 139, the police report there were 3,534 burglaries in 1982.

And although the people whose children were attacked on Staten Island talk as though it could not happen here, there were also, police records show, four "confirmed bias incidents" in the precinct during that year. The incidents involved anti-Semitic actions and resulted in the arrests of youths aged 10 to 17.

From a population that was heavily Jewish and white in 1970, the 1980 census found Flatbush 30 percent white, 50 percent black, 13 percent Hispanic and 7 percent Asian.

P.S. 139 also reflects the changing character of the neighborhood. According to Lawrence Levy, the school's principal, 70 percent of the school's 1,500 pupils are black, Hispanic or Asian.

It was this racial cross-section of students that the principal addressed at a special assembly two days after the events in Staten Island.

"I simply told the children," Mr. Levy recalled, "that there are some people in this world who are determined to hate other people because of their race or religion. This is not the way things are at P.S. 139, but we can't ignore that such hatred exists elsewhere."

"Part of the strength of P.S. 139 is that it reflects the racial mix of the real world," said Jackie Lieberman, whose sixth-grade child had been at the picnic. "And it would be wrong for our children simply to forget what happened that day. They should remember so that they can someday do something about the hatred which exists in this very imperfect but very real world."

So one day, a group of sixth graders gathered in a shady corner planted with day lilies across the from the school's playground to discuss how they felt about what happened at Miller Field.

"They think we're still going to be slaves," says Bruce Johnston, 11. "I was scared, but I'd rather be scared than a racist."

"I was angry," says Charlene Ohayon, 11. "This is a free a country, and we got a right to play anywhere."

"They could come here if they want," says Stephen Delabstide, 12. "Maybe they should. Those kids from Staten Island in their punk rock T-shirts should see that all kinds of kids can get along out here."

"Yeah," says Tricia Moretti, 11. "They grow up in that neighborhood hating people who are strange to them. It's their parents who teach them that. Their parents taught them to hate people who are different, and now it's too late. Their parents are to blame."

"We Don't Want All This Destroyed"

Rose Lanza's 16-year-old son, Nicholas, was arrested and charged with six counts of second-degree assault, reckless endangerment, criminal mischief and resisting arrest for his purported role in the incident on Miller Field. On July 19, after plea bargaining, Nicholas was sentenced to perform 70 hours of community service.

The boy's lawyer, Dennis M. Karsch, contends that his client is not guilty. "Nicholas Lanza did nothing wrong," says Mr. Karsch. "He was just walking up the street when he was arrested. He didn't call any names or throw any rocks. He didn't do anything."

"What really bothers me," Mr. Karsch continues as he sits in his Staten Island office, "is the way some people have thrown racism into this. There's no proof. Some people are just trying to fire things up by calling this a racial issue. I think it was just a group of kids who had an argument that led to a fight with another group of kids."

Mrs. Lanza, a school crossing guard, breaks into tears when she discusses her son. In the living room of her brick town house, there are plastic seat covers on the blue couch and a wedding picture of her and her husband on a wooden coffee table.

"I'm a widow," she manages to say through her tears, "and I have to raise Nick all by myself. Now look what they done to him. They kept him in jail overnight. Jail in Brooklyn. They made him drink coffee. I never let my son drink coffee. He's just a boy. A good boy. How could they do that to him?"

"And now what's going to happen to us? If our name is in the paper, they'll come back here and rob us. Those kids from Brooklyn have relatives. Uncles. Brothers. What if those people from Brooklyn come after us? I was robbed last winter. I couldn't live through another robbery. Why did they have to pick on my son?"

Esther Scaffidi's son Kevin, 15, was also arrested by the park police after the incident at Miller Field. Kevin was arrested in front of the General Store while he was trying to prevent the park police from arresting a friend who he said was innocent.

The authorities agreed that Kevin had not been at Miller Field that afternoon, and he was released after his mother paid a $25 fine and he promised to buy a new pair of sunglasses for a park police officer who had his broken in the scuffle.

Mrs. Scaffidi is disabled. She sits in the living room of her bungalow in New Dorp Beach while her son and Ralph Fellini listen.

"I don't know the Lanza boy," she says, "but I'm sure he's a good kid like all the other kids in the neighborhood. It isn't that we're prejudiced. People out here just work hard. We don't want all this destroyed. It's wrong for black people to yell prejudice. We're not racists."

2

Black vs. White in Howard Beach

Richard Stengel, Joseph N. Boyce, and Mary Cronin

The people of Howard Beach, Queens, have always been proud that their neighborhood is set apart, insulated from the rest of New York City. A close-knit community of modest row houses and trim gardens, it is bordered by Jamaica Bay to the south, Spring Creek Park to the west, Kennedy Airport to the east and a highway to the north. Along Cross Bay Boulevard, the community's main artery, clam bars and pizza parlors contend for local business, while above the street sea gulls lazily flap their wings. Most of Howard Beach's inhabitants are Italians, and its older section feels more like a slightly run-down seaside resort than a corner of the nation's largest city. To ensure safety and enforce quiet, householders pay $220 a year to maintain a private security force.

But the sleepy insularity of Howard Beach ended last week. Overnight a brutal attack against three young black men at a local pizza parlor turned the neighborhood into a national synonym for flagrant racial violence. The death of one of the young blacks and the apparently unprovoked beating of all three at the hands of a gang of white teenagers caused New York City's Mayor Ed Koch to describe what happened as the "most horrendous incident" of violence in his nine years as mayor. Local civil rights leaders saw the attack not as an isolated outbreak but as the latest example of a pervasive prejudice that lurks just below the surface of New York life. It was, said Roscoe Brown Jr., president of Bronx Community College, an example of the "institutional racism that permeates this city, in business and in government." When some 2,000 black and white civil rights advocates marched in Howard Beach on Saturday, they were jeered at with obscenities by a large crowd of young whites from the community.

On Friday evening, Dec. 19, Howard Beach was humming with holiday festivities. Residents cruised slowly in their cars to gape at the Vigliarolo family's front lawn, an electrified montage of Santa's workshop. Around the corner, more cars were parked in front of Steven Schorr's house, where 30 of his friends were helping him celebrate his 18th birthday. Among them were Jon Lester, 17, Jason Ladone, 16, and Scott Kern, 17. Shortly before midnight, according to police, several guests, including Lester, left the party to drive a young woman home. Along Cross Bay Boulevard their headlights caught three blacks walking toward the New Park pizza parlor. "Niggers!" yelled the whites.

Earlier that evening the three black men, Michael Griffith, 23, Cedric Sandiford, 36, and Timothy Grimes, 18, along with Griffith's cousin Curtis Sylvester, 20, had left the Griffith home in Brooklyn. They later told police they had gone to Far Rockaway in Queens to pick up Griffith's paycheck from a construction site. On their way back to Brooklyn, their 1976 Buick broke down on Cross Bay Boulevard. Sylvester stayed with the car, and the other three went off to look for help. They stopped about three miles away at the pizza parlor, a ramshackle fixture in Howard Beach, ordered some slices of pizza and sat down.

When the three left the restaurant at 12:40 A.M., they were accosted by eleven white teenagers—led, say police, by Lester, who brandished a baseball bat, Kern, who had a tree limb, and Ladone. The whites first taunted the blacks and then began beating them. Grimes was hit once before he managed to escape. Griffith and Sandiford tried to get away, but the teenagers caught up with them along a fence that bordered the Shore Parkway and continued their assault. Sandiford feigned unconsciousness. Griffith, severely beaten, dove through a 3-ft. hole in the fence and staggered onto the parkway. He was struck and killed by an automobile driven by Dominick Blum, 24, of Brooklyn, a court officer and the son of a policeman.

Two days later Lester, Ladone and Kern were arrested and charged with second-degree murder, manslaughter and assault. Lester, a slight, baby-faced junior at John Adams High School, who immigrated to the U.S. with his family from England four years ago, had one previous arrest, for possession of a loaded .32-cal. handgun. The family of the murdered man, Michael Griffith, had also immigrated to New York, having come from Trinidad 18 years ago. According to a medical examiner's report, the dead man had a bullet in his chest, the result of a dispute. Griffith never pressed charges.

Timothy Mitchell, pastor of the Ebenezer Baptist Church in Queens, declared that Howard Beach is representative "of the deep-seated enclave mentality of the Borough of Queens." Noting that Mafia Boss John Gotti lives in Howard Beach, Mitchell suggested that Gotti's presence, as well as that of other Mob leaders, contributes greatly to a "macho Mafia mentality" on the part of local young people.

In the neighborhood, many residents seemed unrepentant. Youngsters from Howard Beach, claimed Joe Funaro, a longtime resident, are "abused by blacks" in other parts of the city. "They know when they go out there, they don't feel safe." At the local John Adams High School, where whites and nonwhites are almost equally represented, Lester has become a folk hero to some of the white students. But to the friends and relatives of Michael Griffith who jammed a funeral service for him in Bedford-Stuyvesant last Friday, Lester is a symbol of society gone awry. "We wonder why these events are happening," said the Rev. Robert Seay in his eulogy. "The great [civil rights] movement was to have ended all this. But society admits and encourages violence and bigotry. When teenagers commit a crime like this, the blame is not only on them, but on their parents and on society."

3

Death on a Mean Street

Frank Tippett and Priscilla Painton

Around his neighborhood in mostly black East New York, Yusuf Hawkins was known as an easygoing kid, good at games, dutiful in class, eager to get on with high school. No one would have thought him a world shaker. Yet last week, when his funeral was held, it was clear that the 16-year-old Brooklyn boy, gunned down on the night of Aug. 23, had not merely shaken up New York City but had become a national reminder that there are streets in white America where a black man dares not tread.

It was Hawkins' misfortune to have set foot on such a street in the Bensonhurst section of Brooklyn that fateful night. He and some friends had entered the largely Italian, working-class neighborhood to inspect a used car advertised for sale there. They were suddenly surrounded by ten or so white youths. Inflamed by the fact that a former girlfriend of their ringleader was associating with blacks and Hispanics, the whites were looking for trouble. They carried baseball bats and at least one gun. It was fired four times. Hawkins died shortly afterward.

When scores of blacks marched into Bensonhurst to protest the slaying, numerous residents screamed at the protesters, "Niggers, go home!" and mockingly held aloft watermelons. Mayor Edward Koch, running for his fourth term in office, added to his reputation for insensitivity to black concerns by complaining (even before criticizing the racist hecklers) that protest marches would increase tensions. For Manhattan Borough President David Dinkins, a black running for Koch's job, the death became an occasion to blame the mayor for creating the hostile atmosphere in which it occurred. Swiftly, Hawkins' death transformed the election campaign and provoked the most sulfurous racial exchanges since 1986, when a young black named Michael Griffith was killed in the Howard Beach section of Queens after a mob of white youths chased him into the path of a moving car.

It is no coincidence that both racial episodes took place in down-at-the-heels, ethnic white neighborhoods like Howard Beach and Bensonhurst. According to a study done at Temple University's Institute for Public Policy Studies, racial violence occurs most frequently in poor or lower-middle-class white urban neighborhoods, especially those in which housing values are in decline and manufacturing jobs have been lost.

Other cities, particularly in the Northeast and the Rust Belt, have similar districts that are tinderboxes for violence: Chicago's Marquette Park, Baltimore's Hampden section and Philadelphia's Fishtown and Feltonville, where a young Hispanic was killed by a white mob in July. Such confrontations "pit the powerless against each other," observes J. Anthony Lukas, a Pulitzer prizewinning author who often writes about racial conflict. "These swaggering kings of the walk in Bensonhurst are as ill equipped to make their way in the late 1980s as the blacks from Bed-Stuy, and they know it at some level of their being."

Last week a grand jury indicted Keith Mondello, 18, and Pasquale Raucci, 19, for second-degree murder and lesser offenses related to Hawkins' death. The youth suspected of pulling the trigger, Joseph Fama, 18, surrendered the day after the funeral to police in Oneonta, N.Y.

Hawkins' funeral drew New York Governor Mario Cuomo, Mayor Koch and three candidates running against him. While some mourners objected to their presence, the Rev. Curtis Wells, who led the service, addressed them directly, "Mr. Mayor, Mr. Governor, let freedom ring in Howard Beach. Let freedom ring, yes, from Bensonhurst." To some, the ceremony had an all too familiar ring. Said Jean Griffith, mother of Michael Griffith: "It seems like I'm burying my son again."

4

The Two Racisms

Michael Eric Dyson

The racially motivated murder of Yusuf Hawkins, a 16-year-old New Yorker, symbolizes the continuing and bitter crisis in American race relations. More poignant, his death is a dangerous point along the tortuous trajectory of New York's racial problem.

Young Hawkins was murdered on August 23, in Bensonhurst, Brooklyn, a predominantly Italian blue-collar neighborhood. He and three friends went there to meet the owner of an automobile that one of them hoped to purchase. En route they walked past the apartment of 18-year-old Gina Feliciano, who shortly before had severed a relationship with 18-year-old Keith Mondello and was now reputedly dating blacks and Latinos. Mondello was allegedly seeking revenge on Feliciano's date for her birthday party.

At least ten and perhaps as many as thirty youths, including Mondello, gathered in front of Feliciano's apartment, apparently unaware that she had canceled her party because of threats of trouble. As Hawkins and his friends approached, four shots were fired; Hawkins, hit twice in the chest, died shortly afterward. To lend absurdity to the tragedy, Hawkins was not Feliciano's new suitor.

In a year already marked by new rioting in Miami over a black man murdered by police and by steadily increasing racial violence on college campuses, Hawkins's senseless death is a forceful reminder of America's unresolved racist history, and the circumstances of the murder are rife with the iconography of New York's racial antipathy: baseball bats wielded by several of the white youths; the mostly black marches of protest in the aftermath, and the controversial police tactics in one of them. Those who deemed Spike Lee's portrayal of the deep divide between Italians and African-Americans in his film *Do the Right Thing* to be overdrawn, art intimidating life as it were, have now been tragically rebutted.

The ready temptation is to view the troubling escalation of racial violence in tightly turfed, blue-collar communities like Bensonhurst as isolated from other varieties of racism. Admittedly several factors intensify racism's violent expression in white working-class communities. For one, there is the machismo-laden bonding process fostered through loosely associated groups of young men. These gangs commit random acts of racial violence in retaliation against a perceived invasion of their turf by blacks or other minorities. Also, a generation removed from the immediate social, historical and political background of the civil rights movement,

75

these white youths find white supremacist groups like the Klan, the boot boys and the skinheads appealing. Their racist message, coupled with the older generation's resentment of the limited racial progress that *has* been made, renders the white youths devoid of a sense of why strategies like affirmative action were developed. Furthermore, the dislocation of many blue-collar whites within the economy, with its shift from manufacturing to service employment, means that there is intense intraclass as well as racial conflict, especially in competition for low-skilled, high-wage jobs.

However, while racism is perhaps most violently expressed in blue-collar communities, both its logic and life are sustained across class lines. Racism is embedded and expressed in the classroom by racist teachers and professors; in the white-collar workplace by career ceilings on black managers; in the judicial system in recent Supreme Court attacks on the spirit of affirmative action; in housing by the ongoing real estate practice of "steering"; in local government (New York City Mayor Edward Koch's racial insensitivity stands out); and for most of this decade by national policies under Reaganism. What occurred in Bensonhurst, and in Howard Beach before it, is the conspicuous harvest of the seeds of bigotry sowed in a thousand insidiously subtle gestures of racial antagonism, insensitivity and resentment. Our task, in formulating strategies of resistance, is to understand the relationship between the two racisms. In so doing, we help reveal how racism's violent, working-class expression is linked to, and nourished by, its less visible but just as vicious middle- and upper-class counterparts. Otherwise, Yusuf Hawkins's tragic death will have been in vain.

5

Going "Wilding" in the City

David Gelman and Peter McKillop

On a warm April night two weeks ago a band of young black and Hispanic teenagers chased down a young Wall Street investment banker out jogging by herself, rather daringly for that late hour, in Central Park. They hit the slightly built woman with fists and rocks, stabbed her head five times and then repeatedly raped and sodomized her. When she was found hours later she had suffered multiple skull fractures and lost most of her blood. Last week she remained in a coma, with indications of serious brain damage.

By early accounts, the seven youths charged with the attack were hardly case-book sociopaths. They were variously vouched for by friends, teachers and relatives as industrious, churchgoing, "shy." Individually there seemed nothing especially intimidating about them. Yet together they stood accused of an assault so wantonly vicious that, as an investigator for the Manhattan district attorney's office remarked, "even New York" was unprepared for its brutality.

Indeed, besides their shock at the savagery of the attack, New Yorkers were scarcely ready for yet another explosion of the white-black tensions that have wracked the city in recent years. Many, white and nonwhite alike, hastened to say the incident had more to do with class than race—a lashing out of resentful ghetto residents against privileged Yuppies. In that view, they were supported by at least one black psychiatrist, James Comer of the Yale Child Study Center, for whom the episode seemed "as much an issue of the haves and have-nots as it is race." But to Comer and others, there appeared also to be forces at work—part adolescent restlessness, part "herd" mentality—having little to do with either race or class.

Originally, police say, about 35 youths, some as young as 13, had gone into the park "wilding"—a variety of bash-as-bash-can gang rampage that has disrupted some of the city's public places recently. After a couple of desultory attempts on a male jogger and a homeless man, the group dwindled to a hard core of about eight to 13. Ultimately, seven are believed to have participated in the rape of the woman jogger. Such expeditions usually begin spontaneously. Teenagers hanging around a housing project often have no agenda but to stir up a little excitement. "They may have said, 'Let's go wilding'," notes Franklin Zimring, director of the Earl Warren Legal Institute at the University of California, "but nobody said. 'Let's go raping'." Zimring, who conducted a 1984 study of youth homicide in New York, thinks the group may have been swayed by what he calls "government by dare—you do it because you don't want to back out."

Behavioral experts agree that in the dynamics of a group, there is often at least one leader able to control the rest by playing on their need to prove themselves. The instigator of a gang rape gains a double sense of mastery, not only over the victim but over his cohorts, who feel obliged to equal his audacity. There is an undeniably subtle power in the group: it has the ability to validate and thereby embolden behavior. That may be especially true of teenagers, who are particularly susceptible to pressure from peers. But the essential element is the anonymity group membership confers, and thus the relative freedom from accountability. "Basically, it's a loss of the individual's personality," says Robert Panzarella, a professor of police science at New York's John Jay College of Criminal Justice. "Things he would never think of doing by himself he does in the group." There is also a kind of division of labor, with the chilling result that "while the action of each individual can seem relatively minor, the action of the whole may be horrific."

Frenzied attack: Something like that process was evident in the Central Park rape. As the defendants themselves told it later, it was one of the group, a 15-year-old, who first spotted the woman and said, "Go get her." Another, 14, helped knock her down, then punched and kicked her. Others, in turn, hit her with a rock, a brick and a length of lead pipe, pinioned her legs and arms, ripped off her shirt and sweat pants, and committed the actual rape and sodomy. "No one really knows these kids or what was in their minds," cautions Yale's Comer. But by their own description there appears to have been an accelerating frenzy that is often seen in gang rapes. Momentum builds as the assailants try to outdo one another, in this case a momentum that carried them over the edge into horror.

Although newspapers reported when the youths were arraigned that they appeared to show no "remorse," some observers doubt that they have yet grasped the enormity of their collective act. On the other hand, Dorothy Lewis, a criminal psychiatrist known for her work with serial killer Ted Bundy, warns that initial newspaper reports stressing the apparent wholesomeness of some of the group should be viewed with a measure of skepticism. Lewis believes further investigation will show that the teenagers who committed the rape were damaged in some way. In similar cases, she says, people who commit such acts have either been victims of abuse themselves or have witnessed terrible scenes of domestic violence. These early experiences make the youths "unable to control their impulses," and, in essence, she thinks that is what could have happened that night in Central Park. "I see something," says Lewis, "that started out as a roaming gang, but degenerated into a heinous, aberrant crime."

⑥

Boys Will Be Boys?

Letty Cottin Pogrebin

I'm writing this column in mid-June. Two months after the rape of the Central Park jogger, her medical progress is still making headlines. The young men accused of the "wilding" attack remain the subject of talk shows and feature stories analyzing their behavior, their families, the brutality of the crime. All over the country people are comparing other acts of violence to this one, pawing at the facts like a dog with a bone, seeking some marrow of meaning that might explain the unexplainable.

Unlike the attention paid to other nationally publicized victims—such as Bonnie Garland (beaten to death with a hammer by her rejected boyfriend), Karen Straw (raped by her husband at knife point in front of her children), Jennifer Levin (choked by Robert Chambers), or Hedda Nussbaum (maimed and dehumanized by Joel Steinberg)—the outcry in the jogger's case seems to be saying, "Things have gone too far; *something* must be done."

That reaction reminds me of the 1964 murder of Kitty Genovese, when 38 people witnessed a protracted, bloody attack and not one tried to help or even to call the police from behind the safety of their window blinds. As that crime symbolized issues of collective passivity and disengagement, the Central Park rape seems to have crystallized society's fears of violence, moving us beyond horrified fascination to palpable anger and a demand for action.

By the time you read this September issue, nearly five months will have passed since the rape. Will we still be obsessed and angry? Will the rhetoric of outrage have been translated into anything concrete? Will people in power be ready to change the way violence is understood and treated in our society? I doubt it. Because despite the brouhaha, I don't see any willingness to address the real root of the problem.

Most people deal with unthinkable behavior by seeking causes and finding fault. They submit savagery to the yoke of reason. If they can blame something or someone, they can think about the "contributing factors" rather than the knife at the throat, the kicking and punching, the penis as tool of suffocation or rubbed-raw penetration, the screams and the terror. They don't have to relate this ugliness to their world if they can deplore the "animals" among us and blame the madness on drugs, racial tensions, poverty, family background, TV violence, or educational deprivation. Better still, if they can imagine that a woman "deserved" the assault— said the wrong thing, wore the wrong clothes, went to the wrong neighborhood— then the attack can be made to "make sense."

But in the Central Park case, these formulas don't work. It was rape but the jogger wasn't "provocative." It was a white woman but other "wilding" victims were black and Hispanic and nothing suggests that race was pertinent. It was ghetto kids versus a Wall Street achiever but the woman wasn't parading her status, and the kids didn't seem to be stereotypical "hard cases": addicts, homeless, or on welfare. So how do you figure it? The neighbors shrug. The psychologists speculate. The pundits are stumped.

That the answer might have more to do with gender than race or class has occurred to a few commentators who recognize that what happened, first and foremost, was an act of violence by males against a female—an occurrence as commonplace and all-American as apple pie. But until we go deeper in our search for causation the jogger will symbolize nothing but another horror story and our calls for action will fade into the wind. Before we can *do* anything, we've got to trace the crime to its roots: patriarchy, misogyny, and childhood sex-role socialization.

Isn't it time to examine why so many sweet, affectionate little boys grow up to be men who feel the need to hurt women? Can't we figure out once and for all what happens to make males so much more violent than females and find a way to neutralize this behavior for the good of both sexes? Isn't it clear by now that the bifurcations of masculinity and femininity lead boys to compensate for being raised primarily by women in a culture where femininity is despised as weak? How can we expect young men to come of age in a society where masculinity is equated with dominance and male supremacy when it is clear that for most young men, dominance is out of reach, concentrated in the hands of older white males? Shouldn't we be exploring the connection between this culturally programmed craving for dominance and the fact that hundreds of thousands of men turn to violence against women to prove their masculine power?

Escalating male aggression has become a form of terrorism in women's lives. For that reason, if no other, these questions, long on feminists' minds, belong up front in public discourse. To guarantee women the basic rights of life, liberty, and the pursuit of happiness, all of us need to rethink the way we raise boys into men, and the meaning of masculinity in America.

7

A War on Women, Waged in the Dark

Bob Herbert

It happened about 6 o'clock on a cold morning in January 1989. The young woman was a cashier who worked at a firm in Manhattan. She was on her way to the Grand Ave. subway station in Elmhurst, Queens.

There were not a lot of people out at that hour of the morning. The woman could hear her own footsteps as she neared the station. Occasionally, a car would pass.

One of them stopped.

According to police, it was a dark brown car with tinted windows. In what seemed like an instant, two teenagers, one 17 and the other 14, jumped out and grabbed the woman.

They tried to force her into the car, but the woman fought back furiously. Her shoes flew off. Still she fought. She began screaming for help.

As she wrestled with the two boys, one of them pulled her coat from her and angrily threw it into the street. Finally, with the woman still screaming desperately for help, they got her into the car and slammed the door.

Two other boys were waiting inside.

An off-duty transit cop had spotted the attack and had run to help the woman. But the car pulled off just as he got there. He picked up the shoes and the coat that were lying on the sidewalk and in the street, and then he called 911.

For the next hour and a half, the woman was at the mercy of the four boys in the car. They tormented her. They beat her, they pulled her clothes off, they raped and sodomized her.

They also stole her jewelry.

When they were finished with the woman, they opened the door of the car and threw her into the street outside Marcy Homes, a public housing project in Brooklyn.

A maintenance worker found her and called police.

"She was normal when they grabbed her," said a source very close to the case. "Now she'll never be the same."

The attack happened three months before the rape and near-fatal beating of the jogger in Central Park, but it didn't get much press coverage. It didn't cause a sensation.

Maybe the perps didn't beat her badly enough. Maybe it was because she was just a cashier from Queens. Maybe it was because she was Hispanic.

Anyway, the boys who attacked this woman were something less than geniuses. On Jan. 13, Otis Mitchell Lee, 17, and Wayne Strawder 16, were in a car that crashed in Jamaica, Queens. The cops hauled them in and it wasn't long before investigators linked them to the rape.

The boys weren't any good at stonewalling, either. Soon after Lee and Strawder were busted, two of their buddies were also arrested—Rodney Bacchus, 17, and David Clarke, 14.

The indictment was lengthy, containing charges of kidnaping, rape, sodomy, sex abuse, assault, grand larceny and robbery.

But nothing too terrible happens to youthful sex offenders. After pleading guilty to various counts, Bacchus was sentenced to 3 1/3 to 10 years in prison, and Strawder and Clarke were each sentenced to 2 to 6 years. If they behave themselves, they can get off with the minimum, which means they could all be back on the street before they're old enough to drink legally.

Lee pleaded innocent. He's on trial right now in Queens and there are some real ironies here. For one thing, his lawyer is worried that the publicity from the jogger trial will hurt Lee. At the lawyer's request, the judge is asking prospective jurors if they have been prejudiced by media coverage of the Central Park attack.

A lawyer who was in the courthouse on an unrelated matter laughed and said, "They sure haven't been prejudiced by coverage of *this* case, because it's not getting any coverage."

Another irony is the absence of a vocal black clique in the courtroom rooting for the defendant, who is black. There is a small group of observers at the jogger trial who are convinced that Antron McCray, Raymond Santana and Yusef Salaam are being persecuted because they are black or Hispanic.

Lee has not enjoyed such unsolicited support. Also missing is the widespread sense of outrage at the plight of the victim, who was only 19 when the attack occurred.

No one cares very much what ultimately happened to her. If she called a press conference today, no one would come. If the jogger called a press conference, look out—you could get trampled in the rush.

There are other cases that have gotten similar short shrift from the media. There was, for example, the woman in Brooklyn who was attacked by three youths, raped and sodomized at knifepoint, and then thrown half-naked off a rooftop. She landed at the bottom of an airshaft, injured for life.

This happened two weeks after the attack on the jogger. By comparison, it got very little coverage and there are very few people now who bother to ask how she's doing.

Just last month, a woman was attacked by five youths who surrounded her on a subway platform in Brooklyn. They raped, sodomized and robbed her, and then fled.

No one's been caught, and there's been no public outcry over the attack.

If the cashier attacked in Queens had been a Wall Street yuppie raped on her way to work, we would have had headlines from here to the hereafter. If the woman gang-raped in the subway in Brooklyn had been dragged instead from a limo on the upper East Side, we would still be squeezing into press conferences about it. . . .

Female Midshipman Quits after Handcuff Incident

The Star-Ledger

A female midshipman resigned from the Naval Academy after two male midshipmen handcuffed her to a urinal and taunted her as others snapped pictures, a newspaper reported yesterday.

The culprits were punished with demerits and loss of leave time because the elite academy's administration decided the incident was a good-natured exchange that got out of hand and didn't merit stronger punishment, the Capital said.

The incident involving Gwen Marie Dreyer was not an isolated one, according to Dreyer's father Gregory, a 1967 academy graduate, and another academy graduate who is conducting a poll of women in the military.

Gwen Dreyer resigned last month, dissatisfied with the investigation of the Dec. 8 incident at the once all-male academy, the Annapolis newspaper said. She plans to study engineering at California State Polytechnic Institute in San Luis Obispo.

Gregory Dreyer said his daughter was intimidated by classmates who warned her not to testify at a formal disciplinary hearing. "She was told her life would be made miserable," he said.

Midshipmen 2d Class John Hindinger and Tom Rosson were punished with demerits and loss of leave time, the Capital said, citing records. Six other midshipmen later received written warnings for lesser roles in the incident.

The academy ruled that the assault wasn't premeditated and therefore couldn't be considered hazing, which can lead to dismissal.

"Don't get me wrong, I was bowled over when I heard about this," said academy Superintendent Virgil L. Hill Jr. "It has never happened before to my knowledge.

"But this escalated from a snowball-throwing incident minutes earlier. So what started out as good-natured exchange got out of hand. They overstepped a boundary."

Dreyer, who was pulled from her dormitory room and dragged to the bathroom by male midshipmen, was eventually freed by her roommates. They shoved their way into the fracas and pleaded for the keys to the handcuffs.

The Encinitas, Calif., woman declined to comment on the incident when asked by the paper. But in her letter of resignation she said resentment expressed toward women at the academy crushes their spirits, according to the newspaper.

"What disgusts me most about the academy is to see people who once had tremendous drive and determination feel crushed and therefore satisfied with just getting by," Dreyer's letter said.

"I understand that steps are now being taken to correct some very serious human relations problems," she wrote. "However, after what I've been through and have seen, not only because of what has happened to me personally, I have decided to leave."

About 3,000 midshipmen attend the historic academy; about 10 percent are women.

"There still are large cliques of men who want to make it a men's school again," said Lt. Barbette Lowndes, a 1980 academy graduate polling women in the military.

"They ignore you, keep you isolated, just let you know that you're not wanted. It's more mental abuse," she said.

"We've heard similar horror stories since we started looking into all this," Gregory Dreyer said.

He said academy officials would not solve the problem if they "keep sweeping things under the rug."

"Something needs to be done to change the attitudes of the macho guys who just don't want women at that school," he said.

9

Nude Pictures Are Ruled Sexual Harassment

Tamar Lewin

A female shipyard welder who accused her employer of sexual harassment has won a groundbreaking ruling that posting pictures of nude and partly nude women is a form of sexual harassment.

While rulings in other cases have found that pornographic pictures may contribute to an atmosphere of sexual harassment, the new decision is thought to be the first finding that such pictures are, in and of themselves, harassment.

The judge, Howell Melton, of Federal District Court in Jacksonville, Fla., found on Friday that Jacksonville Shipyards Inc. and two of its employees were directly liable for the harassment. He rejected what he called the company's "ostrich defense" that it was unaware of many of the complaints made by the plaintiff, Lois Robinson.

Judge Melton said the shipyard, where Ms. Robinson has worked since 1977, maintained a boys' club atmosphere with an unrelenting "visual assault on the sensibilities of female workers," including pinup calendars and close-ups of women's genitals posted on the walls. He said the sexualized atmosphere of the workplace had worked to keep women out of the shipyard.

New Policy Is Ordered

"A pre-existing atmosphere that deters women from entering or continuing in a profession or job is no less destructive to and offensive to workplace equality than a sign declaring "men only," the opinion said.

Judge Melton ordered the shipyard to institute a comprehensive sexual harassment policy written by the NOW Legal Defense and Education Fund, the New York-based women's advocacy group that brought the case.

Eric Holshouser, a lawyer for the shipyard, said the company had no comment on the decision, or any possible appeal. But at the trial, the company said it had not known of all of Ms. Robinson's complaints and presented expert witnesses to testify that the pictures would not create substantial harm or offense to the average woman.

In addition, the company said that since 1980 it had a policy prohibiting abuse of dignity through sexist slurs. But the court found that the policy was ineffective and that many employees were unaware of it.

The courts have previously ruled that sexual harassment in the workplace is a form of illegal sex discrimination, forbidden by Title VII of the Civil Rights Act of 1964.

Women's rights lawyers hailed the Florida case as an important advance for women in construction jobs that have customarily been held by men.

Judith Vladeck, a New York lawyer who specializes in sex discrimination cases, said, "If women in the construction trades are getting any recognition from the courts, that's a big deal, because they have been so horribly abused and harassed for so long, with the courts believing that because they do hard labor, they do not get protection."

The decision, which found both verbal and visual sexual harassment, describes 30 pornographic pictures displayed at the shipyard, including a picture of a woman's pubic area with a spatula pressed on it. The pictures, many of which came from calendars provided by tool supply companies, also included a nude woman bending over with her buttocks and genitals exposed. Another showed a frontal view of a nude female torso with the words "U.S.D.A. Choice" written on it. The verbal harassment included explicit sexual remarks.

When Ms. Robinson told co-workers that she considered their behavior to be sexual harassment, the decision said, they took that as a new subject of ridicule, denying that they were engaging in harassment because they had not actually propositioned her for sexual favors. Two women who worked with Ms. Robinson testified that they too were subjected to frequent sexual harassment, including remarks, pinches and sexual teasing.

Ms. Robinson repeatedly complained to her supervisors about the pictures, according to the testimony. At one meeting where she made a formal complaint, the opinion said, a supervisor told her that the company had no policy against the pictures, and that the men had "constitutional rights" to post the pictures, so he would not order their removal. According to the opinion, the shipyard had no system to record complaints about sexual harassment, and supervisors had no instructions to document such complaints.

Judge Melton ordered the shipyard to pay the legal fees of Ms. Robinson but did not order back pay for the time she was absent because of the strain of harassment, saying that her estimates of days missed were too vague. Other damages are not available in Title VII cases.

The Jacksonville case is the first sexual harassment case in which expert testimony on sexual stereotyping was used, lawyers in the case said. Based on the testimony, Judge Melton found that the women at the shipyard were affected by "sex role spillover," where the evaluation of women by their coworkers and supervisors takes place in terms of the sexuality of the women and their sexual worth rather than their merit as craft workers.

"Judge Melton understands how damaging and illegal it is for women workers to be given the message that they are welcome at work only so long as they accept the stereotypical role of sex object," said Alison Wetherfield of the NOW Legal Defense and Education Fund. "The decision recognizes the impossible position many harassed women are in, in a very sensitive and unusual way."

Few Jobs for Women

Women are still extremely rare in skilled shipyard jobs. According to the decision, 6 women and 846 men were employed as skilled craft workers at the shipyard in 1986, and the company has never employed a women in a supervisory job like foreman, coordinator, leaderman or quarterman.

In 1987, a year after Ms. Robinson filed her lawsuit, the shipyard adopted a new sexual harassment policy prohibiting employees from making any kind of sexual conduct a condition of employment or creating an "intimidating, hostile or offensive working environment"

The policy was posted on bulletin boards, but employees were given no special training. The court found that the policy had little or no effect on what it found to be a sexually hostile work environment. It also said that the company had failed to adequately communicate the policy to employees.

10

Aqui No Se Habla Español

Shirley Perez West

Saying they were there to celebrate diversity, about 40 people rallied Friday outside the Howdy Pardner tavern on Highway 99. The crowd included two of three women who have filed a discrimination lawsuit against the tavern.

The women's civil lawsuit against the tavern and the Eugene Police Department alleges that the three were kicked out of the tavern for speaking Spanish.

The rally, organized by members of the University of Oregon's Chicano/Latino student union, began shortly after noon with songs by members of the Eugene Peace Choir. It continued for about two hours as the crowd marched in a circle in front of the empty tavern, which did not open until 4 p.m.

Occasionally, protesters waved signs saying "Practice Spanish at the Howdy Pardner," and "Stop Fearing Our Differences," among others. Some signs were printed in French and Russian.

The atmosphere became tense when owner Welton Wilson arrived.

Wilson, flanked by three friends, stood briefly outside the entrance to his tavern as reporters and a few protesters encircled him.

The question of whether the civil rights of Magadelena Portillo, Susan Loren and Mireya Hill were violated is at the center of the lawsuit filed Sept. 19 in Lane County Circuit Court.

According to the lawsuit, the three Eugene women claim that on Oct. 26, 1989, bartender Debrah Ann Goding told them and a fourth, non-Spanish-speaking woman that they would all have to leave the tavern if they continued to speak Spanish.

Goding said it was the owner's policy that only English be spoken at the tavern, the lawsuit claims.

The women then called Eugene police, who "aided and abetted the tavern's discriminatory conduct," by failing to enforce a city ordinance that makes it illegal to refuse accommodations on the basis of race or national origin, the lawsuit claims.

Hill, who attended Friday's rally, said she called police expecting that they would tell Goding she could not discriminate against Hill and her companions.

"(The police officer) told us it would be better if we just left," Hill said.

According to the police report filed by Officer Tony Veach, Goding denied asking the women to leave because they were speaking Spanish. Goding told Veach she did not ask Hill to leave until Hill walked out of the tavern with a drink in her hand, violating Oregon Liquor Control Commission regulations.

Hill and the others walked out of the tavern to talk with police, the report says.

"I think they're being used as pawns," Wilson said of the protesters marching outside his tavern. "There's no one here who was evicted for speaking Spanish. She was evicted because she took a drink outside."

Wilson acknowledged that Hill went outside the tavern to greet police, but he said he did not know why she felt it necessary to call them.

"Up to that point she hadn't been asked to leave," he said.

Wilson said he was bewildered by the protesters' belief that his tavern discriminated against the three women. "Nothing's been proven. How can they say this for sure?" he said.

Outside the tavern, various speakers talked of the incident as an example of a pervasive problem.

"One important point is to begin changing the way we view racial incidents," said a woman who called herself TK. "Instead of us vs. them, we have to view racism as a human rights issue, not just one that affects people of color."

Eric Ward, co-director of the UO Black Student Union, told the crowd that Eugene is not the nice liberal town it thinks it is.

"We're out here today, not because of one particular owner, but because of a system that allows . . . racism," Ward said.

11

S.I. Man Stabbed Dead on Beach:

Anti-Gay Bias Is Called a Motive

James C. McKinley, Jr.

A Vietnam War veteran suffering from emotional problems was hunted down and stabbed to death on a remote beach on Staten Island Monday night by two men because they thought he was a homosexual, the police said yesterday.

A Staten Island man was arrested in the killing yesterday and the police said they were searching for a second suspect.

A police spokesman, Inspector Richard Mayronne, said detectives concluded after talking with a suspect that James Zappalorti, 44 years old, was killed because his attackers "thought he was homosexual."

"It's a bias incident," Inspector Mayronne said. Although the Staten Island house where Mr. Zappalorti lived with his parents was ransacked, the police said robbery was not the motive. The police said they did not know if Mr. Zappalorti was gay.

Face Down on Beach

Investigators said Mr. Zappalorti's attackers knew him and purposely hunted him down Monday on the Arthur Kill beach where he had a small, snug house built of scrap lumber. "They knew he was there," a police official said, "They went looking for him."

Mr. Zappalorti, was found by his brother, Michael, at 2:15 P.M. Tuesday, lying face down on the beach at the end of Androvette Street, across the street from the family house and stained-glass workshop, Inspector Mayronne said.

Mr. Zappalorti's mother said yesterday that her son, who lived at home, was left "shell-shocked" by his experience in Vietnam. A neighbor described him as "intelligent, but socially maladjusted."

"His life was his beach house," said Owen Reiter, who lives across the street from the Zappalortis. "He was like Gilligan from 'Gilligan's Island'—very innocent. He wouldn't hurt a fly."

When he wasn't helping neighbors with odd jobs or working in the family's stained-glass business, he could usually be found sitting in the beach house, watching the waters of the Arthur Kill, Mr. Reiter said.

The police said he he had been killed a few minutes before 9 P.M. Monday on the beach. He had been stabbed many times in the chest, and his throat had been slashed. His trousers and boots were lying nearby, along with a blood-stained knife, the inspector said.

Twelve hours later, detectives arrested Michael Taylor, of 83 Androvette Street, as he came out of a bar, the Surf Club, at 124 Ocean Avenue in South Beach, and charged him with second-degree murder, Inspector Mayronne said. The police said they were searching for a friend of Mr. Taylor, Phillip Sarlo, 26, of 138 Joseph Avenue.

After questioning Mr. Taylor yesterday, the police announced that they had evidence the two men sought out and attacked Mr. Zappalorti because they believed he was homosexual. Police officials would not elaborate on what Mr. Taylor said.

Inspector Mayronne said that, right after the killing, the two men used Mr. Zappalorti's keys to get into his house, which they ransacked. Mr. Zappalorti's elderly invalid mother, Mary, surprised them in the living room, and they told her that her son had met them in a bar and given them the keys, she said last night. Then, after asking to use the phone and being told to use the kitchen one, they left. Only after they were gone did she realize some things were missing, she said. They took a crystal rosary that belonged to the victim, Inspector Mayronne said.

'86 Arrests

Mr. Zappalorti's father, Michael, was at church at the time.

In April 1986, Mr. Sarlo and Mr. Taylor were arrested and accused of kidnapping a man, putting him into the trunk of a car and threatening to blow the car up or slide it into the Arthur Kill, a police official said.

Mr. Sarlo was charged with attempted murder, forcible theft, kidnapping and possession of a knife but pleaded guilty to a reduced charge of robbery. He was paroled in March 1989. Mr. Taylor, charged as a juvenile offender, also pleaded guilty and served 18 months in state prison. It was unclear last night whether the kidnapping was motivated by anti-homosexual hatred.

Mr. Reiter, the neighbor, said Mr. Zappalorti was a kind man who helped his older brother, Michael, in the stained-glass shop, called Michael and Sons, which had been founded by their great-grandfather. He said the beach house was decorated with "old furniture, a crucifix and an American flag," and described a man who was harmless and pleasant, and very attached to the isolated neighborhood at the southwestern end of Staten Island, where tall weeds edge the streets and dead-end roads taper off into forest.

"My kids played in the woods with him, and we never had any fears about Jimmy," he said.

Mrs. Zappalorti said in a telephone interview last night that she had heard a noise in the house and thought it was her son. When someone passed by her bedroom door, she said, she called out, "Jimmy."

"I think I shocked the man more than he shocked me," she said of the intruder. "He thought the house was empty."

"The man said, 'Your son gave me the key to meet him here,'" she said. "I thought that unusual and walked him to the door. When I put the light on I saw another man." After they left, she said she noticed some things were missing.

"But I did see them, and I identified them from mug shots," she said. "So thank God for that."

Mrs. Zappalorti said her son attended Tottenville High School but left before graduating to enlist in the Navy in 1962, and was discharged on April 5, 1965, with a disability.

"He had a nervous breakdown," she said, adding that he had been on shipboard and saw combat but she could not recall where.

Mr. Zappalorti's entire world revolved around the street where he lived, Mr. Reiter said. Without asking for payment, he swept the street, trimmed hedges, mowed lawns and put away garbage cans.

While other Arthur Kill beaches are covered with landfill, the local bit of waterfront "is cleaner than Jones Beach," he said. "Jimmy would rake the sand. He collected broken bits of bottles and made windows in the hut. He built a walkway of discarded bricks. He was a harmless person."

Suggestions for Further Reading

Watch daily papers and weekly and monthly national magazines for accounts of bias incidents.

PART III

The Economics of Race, Gender, and Class in the United States

In an ideal world, every child born would have the same opportunity to realize his or her potential. In the real world, this is not yet the case. Although many factors play a role in defining and limiting opportunity, three factors are of primary importance: *race, gender,* and *class.* For purposes of clarity, this book begins by looking at issues of race and gender and treating them almost as if they were separable from issues of class, but as several selections in Part II make abundantly clear, it's impossible to talk very long about either gender or race without factoring in class and looking at the way differences in class impact on race and gender difference. In Part III we focus on the issue of class directly and examine the ways in which class privilege intersects with race and gender to affect how others treat us and how we come to think of ourselves.

Most Americans dislike talking about class and have been taught to be suspicious of those who do. It is fashionable to deny the existence of rich and poor and to proclaim us all as "middle class." However, [class divisions are real, and recent economic data show that [the gap between rich and poor in this country is growing larger. Being born to the upper class, the middle class, or the lowest class in the United States has repercussions that affect every aspect of a person's life. Furthermore, our class position affects our relation to others of our gender and race, as well as our relations with people of a different gender and/or race. For example, while all women earn less than all men, white women in general earn more and experience less unemployment than do women of color, who must confront the double burden of racism and sexism. And while two individuals may both earn the identical salary, a salary which qualifies both for middle-class status, differences in race and/or gender will mean very different life choices and chances for them in spite of their "shared" class position. Privilege is not something that one either has or does not have; each of us can be privileged in certain respects but not in others. In this sense, race, gender, and class differences create enormously complex sets of relationships between and among individuals. The same individual may experience feelings of superiority and may exercise privilege over some, while finding themselves subordinate and demeaned in relation to others. A young white, working-class male can often call upon either or both white skin privilege and male privilege to dominate some, but may feel anything but privileged in relation to those who can use their class privilege to dominate him. A middle-class white woman may simultaneously be the victim of sexism and the recipient of race and class privilege.

In addition to denying or underestimating the existence and importance of class divisions in the United States, many people are quick to argue that though racism and sexism existed in the past, they have now been replaced by "reverse discrimination," a kind of preferential treatment afforded white women and people of color to the detriment of white males. This erroneous belief is created and reinforced by advertising, the media, and even by statements of misinformation from people in high places. Magazine covers and television stories about female African-American, and Asian astronauts, female jockeys, and Latin and African-American politicians and business executives would have us believe that women and people of color have been fully integrated into society. But is this the case? Do these highly touted "firsts" indicate profound and fundamental changes in the distribution of wealth and opportunity in society, or do they merely serve to distract our attention from the reality of most people's lives?

In Part III, we attempt to answer these critical questions about the impact of race, gender and class by turning our attention from magazine covers and sports stars' salaries to statistics that reveal the economic realities that most ordinary people face in their daily lives. Most of the statistics cited here are drawn from United States government publications. It is important to understand that a gap exists between the time these statistics were collected and the time they were published. For the most part, however, it is reasonable to regard figures gathered within the past ten years as current.

Another concern that arises is the accuracy of statistics. For example, according to figures for 1983 published by the United States Census Bureau, the population of the United States breaks down into the following percentages: non-Hispanic whites made up 78.7 percent of the population; African-Americans, 12.0 percent; Hispanics, 6.7 percent; and others, 2.6 percent. In reporting these statistics, The Council on Interracial Books for Children, an important source of data analyzed in terms of race and gender, offered the following qualifications on its accuracy:

It is also important to note that the Census acknowledges serious undercounts of the Black and Hispanic populations, so that the actual statistics for U.S. minorities is likely to be almost 25% of all U.S. residents, counting undocumented workers and people who are not located by the Census. For example, according to the *New York Times*, 5/11/84, the census undercount of working age Black men is more than 10% compared to less than 1% for working age White men.

Although no statistic should be treated as literally true, statistics are enormously useful for gaining a general picture of conditions in a society. In addition, they allow us to make reasonably accurate judgments about the relative position of various groups in the work force and economy over a period of years.

Another problem that we should remember is that statistics are not always available in the form we might wish. For example, although it is now possible to obtain data that compare the situation of women and men with regard to a whole series of concerns, it is not always possible to get data that break down "male" and "female" into such other categories as African-Americans, Hispanics, and Asians. Obtaining statistics on each specific group included under the catchall heading "Hispanics" is often difficult, and getting any statistics at all for other groups—for example, American Indians and Alaskan natives—can be impossible.

Finally, what statistics shall we examine? If we want to learn something about the economic realities of daily life, where should we look? Should we look at the Dow-Jones average and the gross national product, or should we look at take-home pay, infant mortality, and the cost-of-living index? The Dow-Jones average tells us something about the level of activity in the stock market and gives us an idea of how investors view the overall health of the economy, while the GNP tells us something about productivity levels in the society. However, it is difficult to make direct inferences from such figures to the actual economic well-being of individuals. To draw conclusions about the latter, it is obviously more relevant to look, for example, at statistics on mean earnings of full- and part-time workers that are broken down by race and gender or at poverty figures for families broken down along similar lines as well as age and marital status. If our concern is with determining whether race and gender discrimination continue to play an important role in determining people's opportunities and realities, then it will be necessary to make comparisons between past and present statistics in these and related areas.

The first selection in Part III suggests that U.S. society is characterized by a dramatically unequal distribution of wealth and opportunity—all the more shocking because of the persistent refusal of so many Americans to acknowledge that we are a class society. In his article, Greg Mantsios describes the nature of the gap between wealth and poverty and looks at the ways class position shapes virtually every aspect of our lives. He is particularly critical of the myth that education functions as a great equalizer in U.S. society, providing all those who work hard and persevere with an opportunity to achieve success. In fact, statistics indicate that the class position of one's family is probably the single greatest determinant of future success, quite apart from intelligence and determination. Mantsios goes on to examine the forces that succeed in making class invisible to so many, and concludes by arguing that differences in class in our society are the results of institutional structures and policies which are designed to see to it that the rich get richer and the rest of us fall further behind.

In 1990, The Business-Higher Education Forum published a major study of minority life in American entitled *Three Realities*. In it, this group of corporate and education leaders from around the country paint a disturbing picture of the opportunities and realities that define the lives of minority group members in the United States. While deploring the abysmal conditions that define the lives of the poorest third of this group, the Forum suggests that focusing exclusively on its plight prevents us from acknowledging the strides toward a better life made by the most successful members of minority communities. It analyzes their economic and social success as well as the failure of other African-Americans to achieve even a part of the American dream by using the ethnicity paradigm, or model, which discounts the impact of racism and slavery and assumes that hard work and ability will always be rewarded.

As the next article makes clear, even African-Americans who qualify for middle-class standing based upon family earnings, face very different realities than many whites with similar status. For example, though many white middle-class families count on two incomes to get by, most middle-class minority group families owe their middle-class status to the presence of two full time salaries in the family and, unlike their white counterparts, would not qualify as middle class without both incomes. Further, African-Americans and other so-called minority group families are more likely to be called upon to support a large extended family with their middle-class earnings than are whites and, because of the effects of racism and long-term discrimination, are less likely to have the financial assets of whites whose families have been middle class for several generations.

Selection 5 presents an overview of the way that differences in race and sex affect occupation and earnings in the U.S. today. It shows significant occupational segregation by both race and sex, and broad disparities in earnings between all women and men. As the charts make clear, Hispanic/Latina, African-American, and Native American women who bear the double burden of race and sex earn the lowest wages of all. (For an interesting perspective on Asian women's earnings relative to the wages of other women the reader may wish to look ahead to Deborah Woo's article, "The Gap between Striving and Achieving: The Case of Asian American Women" in Part IV.) At the same time that it documents a persistent wage gap based on race and sex over many years, this selection examines the various explanations commonly offered for this discrepancy, and concludes that racism and sexism, not ability or qualifications, have determined what jobs women and men do and how much worth is attached to their work.

But statistics alone cannot tell the whole story. That is why it is important to place statistics within the context of personal narratives like the one offered by Teresa Funiciello in "The Poverty Industry." In describing her own personal interaction with the poverty industry, Funiciello raises serious questions about the real impact of government and social agency policies designed to deal with poverty in the United States.

"Being Poor Isn't Enough" goes a step further and argues that there are serious flaws in the way our government calculates who qualifies as "poor," thus denying even limited assistance to large numbers of U.S. citizens living in poverty, if not actually living below the poverty line. The actual distribution of wealth in the society is described in the final section which reports that the gap between the very wealthy and all other Americans has been increasing, while the tax burden continues to fall disproportionally on middle class and poor Americans. The wealthy are actually paying less taxes now than they did a decade ago. Since this is largely due to the tax policies of the last two Presidents and their administrations, policies routinely reported in the media, it is interesting to speculate about why the majority of people in the country continue to vote into office administrations whose tax policies result in the rich getting richer. To this end, it might be useful to look at the way in which racism and sexism are used to divide poor, working class, and middle class people from each other in ways that obscure the privileges of a tiny fraction of people who profit from them.

Rewards and Opportunities:
*The Politics and Economics of Class in the U. S.**

Gregory Mantsios

"[Class is] for European democracies or something else—it isn't for the United States of America. We are not going to be divided by class."
GEORGE BUSH, 1988[1]

Strange words from a man presiding over a nation with more than 32 million people living in poverty and one of the largest income gaps between rich and poor in the industrialized world.** Politicians long before and long after George Bush have made and will continue to make statements proclaiming our egalitarian values and denying the existence of class in America. But they are not alone: most Americans dislike talking about class. We minimize the extent of inequality, pretend that class differences do not really matter, and erase the word "class" from our vocabulary and from our mind. In one survey, designed to solicit respondents' class identification, 35% of all those questioned told interviewers they had never thought about their class identification before that very moment.[2]

"We are all middle-class" or so it would seem. Our national consciousness, as shaped in large part by the media and our political leadership, provides us with a picture of ourselves as a nation of prosperity and opportunity with an ever expanding middle class life style. As a result, our class differences are muted and our collective character is homogenized.

Yet class divisions are real and arguably the most significant factor in determining both our very being in the world and the nature of the society we live in.

* The author wishes to thank Bill Clark for his assistance in preparing this selection.

** The income gap in the United States, measured as a percentage of total income held by the wealthiest 20% of the population vs. the poorest 20% is approximately 11 to 1. The ratio in Great Britain is 7 to 1; in Japan, it is 4 to 1. (see "U.N. National Accounts Statistics", Statistical Papers, Series M no. 79. N.Y. U.N. 1985 pp 1–11.)

The Extent of Poverty in the U. S.

The official poverty line in 1990 was $12,675 for an urban family of four and $9,736 for a family of three. For years, critics have argued that the measurements used by the government woefully underestimate the extent of poverty in America.[3] Yet even by the government's conservative estimate, nearly one in eight Americans currently lives in poverty.

As deplorable as this is, the overall poverty rate for the nation effectively masks both the level of depravation and the extent of the problem within geographic areas and within specific populations. Three short years prior to George Bush's speech, the Physicians Task Force on Hunger in America declared that "Hunger is a problem of epidemic proportion across the nation." Upon completing their national field investigation of hunger and malnutrition, the team of twenty-two prominent physicians estimated that there were up to 20 million citizens hungry at least some period of time each month.

Touring rural Mississippi the Task Force filed this report from one of the many such homes they visited:

Inside the remnants of a house, alongside a dirt road in Greenwood, lived a family of thirteen people. Graciously welcomed by the mother and father, the doctors entered another world—a dwelling with no heat, no electricity, no windows, home for two parents, their children, and several nieces and nephews. Clothes were piled in the corner, the substitute location for closets which were missing; the two beds in the three-room house had no sheets, the torn mattresses covered by the bodies of three children who lay side by side. In the kitchen a small gas stove was the only appliance.

No food was in the house. The babies had no milk; two were crying as several of the older children tried to console them. "These people are starving," the local guide told the doctors. Twice a week she collected food from churches to bring to the family. . . . Only the flies which crawled on the face of the smallest child seemed to be well fed. The parents were not; they had not eaten for two days. The children had eaten some dried beans the previous evening.

from *Hunger in America: The Growing Epidemic*, the Physicians Task Force[4]

Nearly a quarter of the population of the state of Mississippi lives below the federal poverty level. Over a third of the population of Mississippi is so poor it qualifies for food stamps, although only 15% actually receive them.[5]

The face of poverty in Greenwood, Mississippi, is not much different than that in other parts of the deep south and beyond. Appalling conditions of poverty are facts of life in the foothills of Appalachia, the reservations of Native America, the barrios of the Southwest, the abandoned towns of the industrial belt, and the ghettoes of the nation's urban centers. There are more than 2 million poor people in New York City alone, a figure than exceeds the entire population of some nations.

Today, the poor include the very young and the elderly, the rural poor and the urban homeless: increasingly, the poor also include men and women who work full time. When we examine the incidence of poverty within particular segments of the population, the figures can be both shameful and sobering:

- more than one out of every five children in the U.S. (all races) lives below the poverty line[6]
- 39% of Hispanic children and 45% of Black children in the U.S. live below the poverty line[7]
- one in every four rural children is poor[8]
- if you are Black and 65 years of age or older, your chances of being poor are one in three[9]
- roughly 60% of all poor work at least part-time or in seasonal work[10]
- 2 million Americans worked full time throughout the year and were still poor[11]

Poverty statistics have either remained relatively constant over the years or have shown a marked increase in the incidence of poverty. The number of full-time workers below the poverty line, for example, increased by more than 50% from 1978 to 1986.[12]

The Level of Wealth

Business Week recently reported that the average salary for the CEO of the nation's top 1,000 companies was $841,000.[13] As high as this figure is, however, it fails to capture the level of compensation at the top of the corporate world. Short-term and long-term bonuses, stock options and stock awards can add significantly to annual compensation. Take the following examples:

- annual compensation in 1989, including short-term bonuses, for the Chief Executive Officer of UAL, came to $18.3 million; for the head of Reeboks, compensation came to $14.6 million (in what was not a particularly hot year in the sneaker business).[14]
- annual compensation, including short-term and long-term bonuses and stock awards, for the head of Time Warner Inc. totaled $78.2 million; for the CEO of LIN Broadcasting, it came to a whooping $186 million.[15]

The distribution of income in the United States is outlined in Table 1.

TABLE 1
Income Inequality in the U.S.[16]

Income group (families)	Percent of income received
Lowest fifth	4.6
Second fifth	10.8
Middle fifth	16.8
Fourth fifth	24.0
Highest fifth	43.7
(Highest 5 percent)	(17.0)

By 1990, according to economist Robert Reich, the top fifth of the population took home more money than the other four-fifths put together.[17]

Wealth, rather than income, is a more accurate indicator of economic inequality. Accumulated wealth by individuals and families runs into the billions, with the U.S. now boasting at least 58 billionaires, many of them multi-billionaires. The distribution of wealth is far more skewed than the distribution of income. In 1986, the Joint Economic Committee of the U.S. Congress released a special report entitled "The Concentration of Wealth in the United States." Table 2 summarizes some of the findings.

TABLE 2
Distribution of Wealth in the U.S.[18]

Families	Percent of wealth owned
The richest 10%	71.7
(The top 1/2%)	(35.1)
Everyone else, or 90% of all families	28.2

It should be noted that because of the way the statistics were collected by the Congressional Committee, the figure for 90% of all other families includes half of the families who fall into the wealthiest quintile of the population. The "super rich," that is, the top one-half of one percent of the population, includes approximately 420,000 households with the average value of the wealth for each one of these households amounting to $8.9 million.[19]

Most people never see the opulence of the wealth, except in the fantasy world of television and the movies. Society pages in local newspapers, however, often provide a glimpse into the real life-style of the wealthy. A recent article in the New York Times, described the lifestyle of John and Patricia Kluge.

Mr. Kluge, chairman of the Metromedia Company, has an estimated worth of $5.2 billion. . . . The Kluges (pronounced Kloog-ee) have an apartment in Manhattan, an estate in the Virginia hunt country, and a horse farm in Scotland. . . .

They are known in Washington and New York social circles for opulent parties. Mr. Kluge had the ballroom of the Waldorf done up like the interior of a Viennese belle epoque palace for Mrs. Kluge's 49th birthday.

Her birthday parties for him have been more intimate, friends say. Typically these involve, only one or two other couples (once it was Frank and Barbara Sinatra) who take over L'Orangerie, a private dining room at Le Cirque that seats 100. The room was turned into an English garden for Mr. Kluge's 70th birthday, with dirt covering the carpet, flowering plants and trees. Hidden among the trees were nine violinists. The wine was a Chateau Lafite from 1914, the year of his birth. The birthday cake was in the shape of a $1 billion bill.[20]

The Plight of the Middle Class

The percentage of households with earnings at a middle-income level has been falling steadily.[21] The latest census figures show that the percentage of families with an annual income between $15,000 and $50,000 (approximately 50% and 200% of the median income) has fallen by nearly 10 percentage points since 1970.[22] While some of the households have moved upward and others have moved downward, what is clear is that the United States is experiencing a significant polarization in the distribution of income. The gap between rich and poor is wider and the share of income earned by middle-income Americans has fallen to the lowest level since the census bureau began keeping statistics in 1946. More and more individuals and families are finding themselves at one or the other end of the economic spectrum as the middle class steadily declines.

Furthermore, being in the middle class is no longer what it used to be. Once, middle class status carried the promise that one's standard of living would steadily improve over time. Yet 60% of Americans will have experienced virtually no income gain between 1980 and 1990. (Compare this to the income gains experienced by the wealthiest fifth of the population—up by 33%, and the wealthiest one percent of the population—up by 87%.)[23] One study showed that only one in five (males) will surpass the status, income, and prestige of their fathers.[24]

Nor does a middle class income any longer guarantee the comforts it once did. Home ownership, for example, has increasingly become out of reach for a growing number of citizens. During the last decade home ownership rates dropped from 44%

to 36% among people in the 25–29 year old age group and from 61% to 53% among those in their thirties.[25]

The Rewards of Money

The distribution of income and wealth in the U.S. is grossly unequal and becomes increasingly more so with time. The rewards of money, however, go well beyond those of consumption patterns and life style. It is not simply that the wealthy live such opulent life styles, it is that class position determines one's life chances. Life chances include such far-reaching factors as life expectancy, level of education, occupational status, exposure to industrial hazards, incidence of crime victimization, rate of incarceration, etc. In short, class position can play a critically important role in determining how long you live, whether you have a healthy life, if you fail in school, or if you succeed at work.

The link between economic status and health is perhaps the most revealing and most disheartening. Health professionals and social scientists have shown that income is closely correlated to such factors as infant mortality, cancer, chronic disease, and death due to surgical and medical complications and "misadventures."[26]

The infant mortality rate is an example that invites international as well as racial and economic comparisons. At 10.6 infant deaths per 1,000 live births, the U.S. places nineteenth in the world—behind such countries as Spain, Singapore, and Hong Kong; a statistic that is in and of itself shameful for the wealthiest nation in the world. When infant mortality only among Blacks in the U.S. is considered, the rate rises to 18.2 and places the U.S. 28th in rank—behind Bulgaria and equal to Costa Rica. The infant mortality rate in poverty stricken areas, such as Hale County, Alabama, is three times the national rate and nearly twice that of the nation of Malaysia (whose GNP per capita is one tenth that of the U.S.).[27]

TABLE 3
Infant mortality rate per 1,000 births[28]

Total (national, all racial and ethnic groups)	10.6
Among Blacks only	18.2
In Hale County, Alabama	31.0

Analyses of the relationship between health and income are not always easy to come by. A recent study conducted in New York City, however, provided some important information. The study examined the difference in health status and delivery of health services among residents from different neighborhoods. The data provided allows for comparing incidents of health problems in neighborhoods where

40% or more of the population lives below the poverty line with those in other neighborhoods where less than 10% of the population lives below the poverty line. The study found that the incidence of health problems, in many categories, was several times as great in poorer neighborhoods. For example, death associated with vascular complications (from the heart or brain) occurred nearly twice as often in poor areas than in non-poor. Similarly, chances of being afflicted with bronchitis is 5 times as great in poor areas than in non-poor areas.[29] The study concluded, "The findings clearly indicate that certain segments of the population—poor, minority, and other disadvantaged groups—are especially vulnerable and bear a disproportionate share of preventable, and therefore unnecessary deaths and diseases."[30]*

The reasons for such a high correlation are many and varied: inadequate nutrition, exposure to occupational and environmental hazards, access to health-care facilities, quality of health services provided, ability to pay and therefore receive medical services, etc. Inadequate nutrition, for example, is associated with low birth weights and growth failure among low-income children and with chronic disease among the elderly poor. It has also been shown that the uninsured and those covered by Medicaid are far less likely to be given common hospital procedures than are patients with private medical coverage.

The relationship between income and health is similar to that of income and rate of incarceration. One in four young Black men, age 20 to 29, are either in jail or court supervised (i.e., on parole or probation). This figure surpasses the number of Black men enrolled in higher education. The figure also compares negatively to that for white men where 1 in 16 are incarcerated in the same age group.[31]

While it is often assumed that differences in rates of arrest and incarceration reflect differences in the incidents of crime, a recent study conducted in Pinellas County, Florida, found that most women prosecuted for using illegal drugs while pregnant have been poor members of racial minorities, even though drug use in pregnancy is equally prevalent in white middle class women. Researchers found that about 15% of both the white and the Black women used drugs, but that the Black women were 10 times as likely as whites to be reported to the authorities and poor women were more likely to be reported than middle class women. Sixty percent of the 133 women reported had incomes of less than $12,000 a year. Only 8% had incomes of more than $25,000 a year.

Differences in Opportunity

The opportunity for social and economic success are the hallmarks of the American Dream. The dream is rooted to two factors: education and jobs.

Our nation prides itself on its ability to provide unprecedented educational

---

* It should be noted that the study was conducted in a major metropolitan area where hospitals and health-care facilities are in close proximity to the population, rich and poor. One might expect the discrepancies to be even greater in poor, rural areas where access to health care and medical attention is more problematic.

opportunities to its citizens. As well it should. It sends more of its young people to college than any other nation in the world. There are nearly 13 million Americans currently enrolled in colleges and universities around the country, a result of the tremendous expansion of higher education since World War II. The establishment of financial assistance for veterans and for the needy, and the growth of affordable public colleges all have had an important and positive effect on college enrollment. Most importantly from the point of view of a national consciousness, the swelling of college enrollments has affirmed our egalitarian values and convinced us that our educational system is just and democratic.

Our pride, however, is a false pride. For while we have made great strides in opening the doors of academe, the system of education in the United States leaves much to be desired and is anything but egalitarian.

More than a quarter of our adult population has not graduated from high school, nearly three quarters do not hold a college degree.[32] This is a record that does not bode well for the most industrialized and technologically advanced nation in the world. Perhaps more importantly, the level of educational achievement is largely class determined.

At least equal in importance to the amount of education received, is the quality of education. The quality of primary and secondary schools is largely dependent on geography and proximity to schools with adequate resources. Educational funding, and the tax base for it, are determined by residency and who can afford to live where. Schools in poorer districts are just not as likely to provide a high-quality education.

Student achievement in the classroom and on standardized tests is also class determined. Studies from the late 1970s showed a direct relation between SAT scores and family income. Grouping SAT scores into twelve categories from highest to lowest, researchers found that the mean family income decreased consistently from one group to the next as test scores declined. The study was done by examining the test results and family income of over 600,000 students![33] In other words, the higher the family income, the higher the test scores and vice versa.

Furthermore, for that segment of the population that does enter and complete a college education (approximately 18% of the population, including Associate degrees), the system is highly stratified. Precious few from poor and working class families have gained access to the elite colleges. For the most part, these have remained the bastion of the wealthy, leaving the less prestigious two year colleges almost exclusively the domain of the poor and the disadvantaged. The result is that colleges today are performing the same sorting function previously performed by high schools, where students are divided into vocational and academic tracks. The rate of participation in vocational programs at the college level is closely related to socioeconomic class, so that students from poorer backgrounds who do enroll in college are still being channeled into educational programs and institutions that are vocational in nature and that lead to less desirable occupations and futures.[34*]

---

* This does not deny the intrinsic value of vocational education, but points to the fact that poor and working class students are found in the sector of education that yields the smallest socioeconomic return.

The "junior" colleges, whose growth once promised to serve as a stepping stone for the disadvantaged and the underprepared to gain access to four year liberal arts colleges have been transformed into "community" colleges which provide vocational programs and terminal degrees in fields that narrow occupational options. The effect is to limit opportunity and to provide what some critics have referred to as a "cooling out function"—the managing of ambitions of the poor and working class who might otherwise take the American dream seriously.[35]

Some might argue that intelligence and drive are more significant than education in determining a young person's future. For example, a study by the Carnegie Foundation found that even when IQ test scores were the same, a young person's ability to obtain a job that will pay in the top 10% of the income structure is 27 times as great if he or she comes from a wealthy background.[36]

Culture, the Media, and Ideology

If the U.S. is so highly stratified and if economic class makes such a difference, why is it then, that we retain such illusions about an egalitarian society? In part, it is because for many of us it is simply more comfortable to deny the class nature of our society and the rigid boundaries such a society suggests: we would rather consider our economic predicament, whatever our class standing, to be temporary and anticipate a brighter future in what we prefer to believe is a fluid and open opportunity structure. In part, it is also because we are constantly bombarded with cultural messages from the media and other sources that tell us that class in America, if it exists at all, does not really matter.

Both in entertainment and in relating the news of the day, the media convey important, albeit contradictory messages: classes do not exist, the poor and the working class are morally inferior, America is a land of great social and economic mobility, class is irrelevant.

TV sitcoms and feature films have traditionally ignored class issues. There have been relatively few serious portrayals of the poor or the working class in the history of film and television. Television, in particular, presents a view of America where everyone is a professional and middle class: daddy, it seems, always goes to the office, not to the factory.[37] There are notable exceptions and these are of particular interest in that they usually present story lines that distort class realities even further.

Story lines about class do one of three things. First, they present and reinforce negative class stereotypes. The poor are presented as hapless or dangerous and the working class as dumb, reactionary, and bigoted. Those not members of the professional middle class are to be laughed at, despised, or feared.[38] Second, they portray instances of upward mobility and class fluidity. These include rags-to-riches stories, Pygmalion tales, and comic instances of downward mobility. Third, they stress that the people who think firm class lines exist come to discover that they are mistaken: everybody is really the same.[39] These are often rich girl/poor boy romances or their opposite.

Story lines about class make for good comedy, good romance, and in the last example, even good lessons in human relations. They also perform, however, a great disservice: "treating class differences totally inconsequential strengthens the national delusion that class power and position are insignificant".[40]

A Structural Perspective

Vast differences in wealth have serious consequences and are neither justifiable nor a result of individual and personal deficiencies. People are poor because they have no money and no power to acquire money. The wealthy are rich because they have both.

The distribution of income and wealth occurs because a society is structured and policies are implemented in such a way to either produce or alleviate inequalities. A society can choose to minimize the gaps in wealth and power between its most privileged and its most disenfranchised. Government can serve as the equalizer by providing mechanisms to redistribute wealth from the top to the bottom. The promise of government as the great equalizer has clearly failed in the U.S. and rather than redoubling the efforts to redistribute wealth, traditional redistributive mechanisms, such as the progressive income tax, have declined in use in recent years. The tax rate for the wealthiest segment of the population, for example, steadily declined in spite of, or perhaps because of, the increasing concentration of wealth and power at the top. In 1944 the top tax rate was 94%, after World War II it was reduced to 91%, in 1964 to 72%, in 1981 to 50%, in 1990 to 28% (for those with an annual income over $155,000).*

Nor is it the case that conditions of wealth simply coexist side-by-side with conditions of poverty. The point is not that there are rich and poor, but that some are rich precisely because others are poor, and that one's privilege is predicated on the other's disenfranchisement. If it were not for the element of exploitation, we might celebrate inequality as reflective of our nation's great diversity.

The great anti-poverty crusader, Michael Harrington, tells of the debate in Congress over Richard Nixon's Family Assistance Plan during the 1970s. If the government provided a minimum income to everyone, "Who," asked a southern legislator, "will iron my shirts and rake the yard?"[41]

The legislator bluntly stated the more complex truth: the privileged in our society require a class-structured social order in order to maintain and enhance their economic and political well-being. Industrial profits depend on cheap labor and on a pool of unemployed to keep workers in check. Real estate speculators and developers create and depend on slums for tax-evading investments. These are the injustices and irrationalities of our economic system.

What is worse is that inequalities perpetuate themselves. People with wealth are the ones who have the opportunity to accumulate more wealth.

---

* Ironically those with an annual income between $75,000 and $150,000 pay a higher rate of 33%.

The fortune of Warren Buffett is estimated to be approximately $4 billion dollars. He is one of 71 billionaires in the United States (their average holding is about $3 billion each).[42] Calculated below is the interest generated by Buffett's wealth at an 8% return.
Interest generated by $4 billion, at 8% return
$10 each second
$600 each minute
$36,000 each hour
$864,000 each day
$6,048,000 each week
$320,000,000 each year ($320 million)
In other words, Mr. Buffett makes more money in two days of non-work than most people earn in a lifetime of work.

It is this ability to generate additional resources that most distinguishes the nation's upper class from the rest of society. It is not simply bank interest that generates more money, but income producing property: buildings, factories, natural resources; those assets Karl Marx referred to as the means of production. Today, unlike the early days of capitalism, these are owned either directly or indirectly through stocks. Economists estimate that for the super rich, the rate of return on such investments is approximately 30%.[43] Economists have also designed a device, called Net Financial Assets (NFA), to measure the level and concentration of income-producing property. While Net Worth (NW), a figure that considers all assets and debts, provides a picture of what kind of life-style is being supported, the NFA figure specifically excludes in its calculation ownership of homes and motor vehicles. By doing so, the NFA figure provides a more reliable measure of an individual's life chances and ability to accumulate future resources. A home or a car are not ordinarily converted to purchase other resources, such as a prep school or college education for one's children. Neither are these assets likely to be used to buy medical care, support political candidates, pursue justice in the courts, pay lobbyists to protect special interests, or finance a business or make other investments. Net financial assets include only those financial assets normally available for and used to generate income and wealth.[44] Stock ownership, for example, is a financial asset and is highly concentrated at the top, with the wealthiest 10% of the population owning over 89% of the corporate stocks.[45] Since home ownership is the major source of wealth for those who own a house, removing home equity as well as car ownership from the calculations has a significant impact on how we view the question of equity.

- The median net household income in the U. S. is $21,744, net worth in the U.S. is $32,609, and the median Net Financial Assets is $2,599.
- While the top 20% of American households earn over 43% of all income, that same 20% holds 67% of Net Worth, and nearly 90% of Net Financial Assets.

- The median income of the top one percent of the population is 22 times greater than that of the remaining 99%. The median Net Financial Assets of the top one percent is 237 times greater than the median of the other 99% of the population.[46]

The ability to generate wealth on the part of this class of owners is truly staggering. It contrasts sharply with the ability of those who rely on selling their labor power. For those with income under $25,000, wage and salary income from labor comprised 90% of their total income.

There is also an entrepreneurial middle class in America that includes farmers, shopkeepers, and others. The small entrepreneurs, however, are becoming increasingly marginal in America and their income-producing property hardly exempts them from laboring.

The wealthy usually work too: their property income, however, is substantial enough to enable them to live without working if they chose to do so.

People with wealth and financial assets have disproportionate power in society. First, they have control of the workplace in enterprises they own. They determine what is produced and how it is produced. Second, they have enormous control over the media and other institutions that influence ideology and how we think about things, including class. Third, they have far greater influence over the nations' political institutions than their numbers warrant. They have the ability to influence not only decisions affecting their particular business ventures, but the general political climate of the nation.

Spheres of Power and Oppression

When we look at society and try to determine what it is that keeps most people down—what holds them back from realizing their potential as healthy, creative, productive individuals—we find institutionally oppressive forces that are largely beyond their individual control. Class domination is one of these forces. People do not choose to be poor or working class; instead they are limited and confined by the opportunities afforded or denied them by a social system. The class structure in the United States is a function of its economic system—capitalism, a system that is based on private rather than public ownership and control of commercial enterprises and on the class division between those who own and control and those who do not. Under capitalism, these enterprises are governed by the need to produce a profit for the owners, rather than to fulfill collective needs.

Racial and gender domination are other such forces that hold people down. Although there are significant differences in the way capitalism, racism and sexism affect our lives, there are also a multitude of parallels. And although race, class, and gender act independently of each other, they are at the same time very much interrelated.

On the one hand, issues of race and gender oppression cut across class lines.

Women experience the effects of sexism whether they are well-paid professionals or poorly paid clerks. As women, they face discrimination and male domination, as well as catcalls and stereotyping. Similarly, a Black man faces racial oppression whether he is an executive, an auto worker, or a tenant farmer. As a Black, he will be subjected to racial slurs and be denied opportunities because of his color. Regardless of their class standing, women and members of minority races are confronted with oppressive forces precisely because of their gender, color, or both.

On the other hand, class oppression permeates other spheres of power and oppression, so that the oppression experienced by women and minorities is also differentiated along class lines. Although women and minorities find themselves in subordinate positions vis-à-vis white men, the particular issues they confront may be quite different depending on their position in the class structure. Inequalities in the class structure distinguish social functions and individual power, and these distinctions carry over to race and gender categories.

Power is incremental and class privileges can accrue to individual women and to individual members of a racial minority. At the same time, class-oppressed men, whether they are white or Black, have privileges afforded them as men in a sexist society. Similarly, class-oppressed whites, whether they are men or women, have privileges afforded them as whites in a racist society. Spheres of power and oppression divide us deeply in our society, and the schisms between us are often difficult to bridge.

Whereas power is incremental, oppression is cumulative, and those who are poor, Black, and female have all the forces of classism, racism, and sexism bearing down on them. This cumulative oppression is what is meant by the double and triple jeopardy of women and minorities.

Furthermore, oppression in one sphere is related to the likelihood of oppression in another. If you are Black and female, for example, you are much more likely to be poor and working class than you would be as a white male. Census figures show that the incidence of poverty and near-poverty (calculated as 125% of the poverty line) varies greatly by race and gender.

TABLE 4
Chances of Being Poor in America[47]

	White male & female	White female head	Black male & female	Black female head
Poverty	1 in 9	1 in 4	1 in 3	1 in 2
Near Poverty	1 in 6	1 in 3	1 in 2	2 in 3

In other words, being female and being nonwhite are attributes in our society that increase the chances of poverty and of lower-class standing. Racism and sexism compound the effects of classism in society.

NOTES

1. Quoted in George Will, "A Case for Dukakis," in *The Washington Post*, November 13, 1988, p. A27.

2. Marian Irish and James Prothro, *The Politics of American Democracy*, Engelwood Cliffs, N. J., Prentice-Hall, 1965, p. 2, 38.

3. See, for example, Patricia Ruggles, "The Poverty Line—Too Low for the 90's," in the *New York Times*, April 26, 1990, p. A31.

4. Physicians Task Force on Hunger in America, *Hunger in America: The Growing Epidemic*, Wesleyan University Press, 1985, p. 27.

5. Ibid.

6. Bureau of Census, "Statistical Abstract of the U.S. 1990," Department of Commerce, Washington, D.C., 1990, p. 460.

7. Ibid.

8. Ibid.

9. Ibid.

10. *U. S. News and World Report*, January 1, 1988, pp. 18–24.

11. Ibid.

12. Ibid.

13. *Business Week*, October 19, 1990, p. 11.

14. Ibid, p. 12.

15. *Business Week*, May 6, 1991, p. 90.

16. U. S. Department of Commerce, "Statistical Abstract of the U.S. 1988," Washington, D.C., 1988, p. 428.

17. Robert Reich, "Secession of the Successful," *New York Times*, January 20, 1991, p. M42.

18. Joint Economic Committee of the U.S. Congress, "The Concentration of Wealth in the United States," Washington, D.C., 1986, p. 24.

19. Richard Roper, *Persistent Poverty: The American Dream Turned Nightmare*, Plenum Press, 1991, p. 60.

20. *New York Times*, April 29, 1990, p. 48.

21. Chris Tilly, "U-Turn on Equality," *Dollars and Sense*, May 1986, p. 84.

22. Census, ibid, p. 450.

23. "And the Rich Get Richer," *Dollars and Sense*, October 1990, p. 5.

24. Richard DeLone, *Small Futures*, Harcourt Brace Jovanovich, 1978, pp. 14–19.

25. Roper, ibid, p. 32.

26. Melvin Krasner, *Poverty and Health in New York City*, United Hospital Fund of New York, 1989. See also, U.S. Dept of Health and Human Services, *Health Status of Minorities and Low Income Groups*, 1985; and Dana Hughes, Kay Johnson, Sara Rosenbaum, Elizabeth Butler, Janet Simons, *The Health of America's Children*, The Children's Defense Fund, 1988.

27. Physicians Task Force, ibid; Hughes, et al, ibid; and "World Development Report 1990," World Bank, Oxford University Press, 1990, pp. 232–233.

28. Ibid.

29. Krasner, ibid, p. 134.

30. Ibid, p. 166.

31. *Washington Post*, February 27, 1990, p. A3, citing Marc Mauer, "Young Black Men and the Criminal Justice System: A Growing National Problem," The Sentencing Project January 1990.

32. The Chronicle of Higher Education, *The Almanac of Higher Education, 1989–1990*, The University of Chicago Press, 1989.

33. Richard DeLone, ibid, p. 102.

34. David Karen, "The Politics of Class, Race, and Gender," paper presented at Conference on "Class Bias in Higher Education," Queens College, Flushing N.Y., November 1990.

35. Steven Brint and Jerome Karabel, *Diverted Dream: Community Colleges and the Promise of Educational Opportunity in America, 1990 to 1985*, Oxford University Press, 1989.

36. Richard DeLone, ibid.

37. Barbara Ehrenreich, *Fear of Falling: The Inner Life of the Middle Class*, Pantheon, 1989, p. 140.

38. See Barbara Ehrenreich, ibid.

39. Benjamin DeMott, *The Imperial Middle: Why Americans Can't Think Straight About Class*, William Morrow, 1990.

40. DeMott, ibid.

41. Michael Harrington, *The New American Poverty*, Penguin, 1985, p. 3.

42. *Fortune Magazine*, September 10, 1990, p. 98; *Forbes*, October 21, 1991, pp. 145–160.

43. E. K. Hunt and Howard Sherman, *Economics*, Harper and Row, 1990, pp. 254–257.

44. Melvin Oliver and Thomas Shapiro, "Wealth of a Nation," *The American Journal of Economics and Sociology*, April 1990, p. 129.

45. The Joint Economic Committee, ibid.

46. Oliver, ibid, p. 129.

47. "Characteristics of the Population Below the Poverty Line: 1984," from Current Population Reports, Consumer Income Series P-60, No. 152, Washington, D.C., U.S. Department of Commerce, Bureau of the Census, June 1986, pp. 5–9.

Three Realities:
Minority Life in America

Business—Higher Education Forum

As measured by virtually all statistical measures of income, opportunity, education, access to health care, and personal security, it is clear that the *typical* minority American does not begin to enjoy anything close to parity with the life experiences of the average white American.

The general picture is deeply disturbing: the statistics chart a wide gulf between the races. For example, life expectancy figures for whites and blacks are heading in opposite directions. After narrowing for decades, the gap in life expectancy between blacks and whites has grown for the last three years in a row, according to the most recent data from the National Center for Health Statistics—increasing between 1984 and 1987 from 5.6 years to 6.2 years.

In 1986, poverty rates for all black individuals, from infancy through old age, were nearly three times the rate for whites (31 percent and 11 percent, respectively). Poverty rates for other minority groups are also extraordinarily high. American Indians living on reservations experience the highest rates of poverty in the United States, followed by Puerto Ricans. The median wealth (assets less liabilities) of black households is 9 percent of the white household median.

In any given month, Hispanic unemployment is about 50 percent higher than the rate for whites, and black unemployment is 2.5 times as high. In a 45-year work career, a white man, on average, can expect to work for 36 years, to be unemployed for 2, and to be "out of the labor force" for 7. Comparable figures for a black man are 29 years of work, 5 years of unemployment, and 11 years out of the labor force.

Less money, on average, is spent on public education for minority group members, who are frequently isolated in cities or in rural areas where the tax base cannot adequately support the public schools. The National Assessment of Educational Progress reveals that despite progress in recent years the average performance of young blacks and Hispanics in reading, mathematics, and science still lags far behind that of their white peers.

But useful though these statistics may be, they conceal as much as they reveal about the nation's 30 million black and 18 million Hispanic citizens. Just as understanding the average daily temperature in the continental United States does not prepare the visitor for August heat or January frost, so, too, understanding the average situation for members of minority groups does not illuminate the diversity of minority life in this country.

That diversity, as a recent exhaustive analysis by the National Research Council points out, reflects the confluence of two major developments in the status of all Americans. First, between 1940 and 1973, real earnings for all, including members of minority groups, appreciated steadily, after which they stagnated. Second, since 1973, inequality among all Americans increased as the least skilled were the most damaged by economic change. These two developments are reflected in minority communities as well, including, in the words of the National Research Council, pronounced differences in the "material well-being and opportunities among blacks."

As a result, three separate realities exist for minority Americans.

The first reality is that a significant number of minority group members—black and Hispanic—are succeeding in the American society, economy, and culture. They are repeating the successes of ethnic immigrants and doing it in much the same way: by insisting they be treated with the dignity to which every human being is entitled; by demanding the equal treatment that is every citizen's due; by diligence and education; by seizing each new opportunity; and by sacrificing today for the tomorrow of their children. More than a third of *all* blacks and Hispanics are included in this group. The proportion of the *working-age* minority population is even larger, probably exceeding 40 percent.

The second reality is more troublesome. It involves, overwhelmingly, working minority Americans who are at the margin of making it in American life. Despite their best efforts, limited educational opportunities, low levels of literacy, and the lack of marketable skills prevent them from keeping pace with the rising demands of the workplace. They are falling behind economically and receive little attention from policymakers. About a third of all blacks and Hispanics are included in this precarious position. For the working-age minority population, the figure appears to be slightly lower, between 25 and 30 percent.

The third reality—severe minority poverty—confounds America's fundamental concept of itself. The persistence of severe minority poverty in the United States remains a paradox in a just and compassionate society.

In any given year, three out of 10 minority Americans live below the poverty line. We estimate that roughly 25 percent of working-age minority Americans are poor.

What's more, of all those Americans living in poverty in one year, about three-quarters are still living in poverty the next year. Analysts refer to this group as the "persistently poor." The persistently poor include a group frequently referred to as the underclass, a group that is largely black and Hispanic, and most readily apparent in the nation's cities. But the underclass also exists in isolated rural areas where large numbers of people, majority *and* minority, live in poverty. The underclass is defined in various ways, but is generally said to include individuals who are chronically jobless, who are living in communities that have very high rates of poverty, or who do not embrace mainstream norms.

The underclass has endured for nearly two generations. Despite the piecemeal strategies developed since the 1960s, this human tragedy in the midst of plenty threatens to become permanent. A new pathology is overwhelming many communities. Hope for the future, dreams for one's children, and aspirations for a better life are being replaced by the anesthetic of drugs, dependency on public assistance, and the destructiveness of violence.

3

Middle Class Blacks Try to Grip a Ladder While Lending a Hand

Isabel Wilkerson

Joyce Ford, the daughter of laborers, fled the hand-to-mouth world of Washington's black housing projects and now has amenities of the middle class: a good job in the Government, an office across the street from the White House, a merit raise and an American Express card. But she still has the bone-deep worries of the poor.

Sitting at her desk the other day, she got yet another call from a frantic relative with bad news and high expectations. "Your brother's sick," the caller said. "He needs to see somebody. What are you going to do?"

What else could she do? She spent the better part of the day trying to figure out where her out-of-work brother should go for treatment, and how to pay for it.

Mrs. Ford, 44 years old, is among tens of thousands of black people who are the first in their families to break out of poverty and take a tenuous place in the American middle class. Many are scaling the economic ladder with one hand on the middle rung and the other still outstretched to the relatives who need them.

The Peril of Falling Back

To the outside world, Mrs. Ford and those like her are examples of how far this nation has come since the civil rights movement opened up legions of professional jobs previously closed to black people. To their families, they are the American dream come true, showpieces to brag about.

But even in the best of times, these newly arrived blacks have a loose grasp on prosperity. And as a faltering economy tumbles toward recession, they may slip out of the middle class altogether, many economists and sociologists fear, creating an even deeper well of need among impoverished blacks to whom they now lend support.

Two main things tend to distinguish black middle-class people from middle-class whites. One is the likelihood that many more of their relatives will come to them for

113

help. The other is that they tend to lack the resources of people who started life in the middle class.

There is no clear-cut definition of "middle class," a concept that can embrace not just how much money people make but the way they make it: usually not with their hands. Most economists and sociologists agree that the middle class includes mainly professionals, skilled service and clerical workers and entrepreneurs, each one earning $25,000 to about $50,000 a year, or more if the person lives in an expensive city or has a lot of children.

Under those criteria, about 40 percent of blacks fall into the category of middle class or above while 30 percent are blue-collar working class and 30 percent are the unskilled poor.

But unlike the white middle and upper classes, which include nearly 70 percent of all white households and have been a fixture for three or four generations, the vast majority of the black middle class is starting from scratch.

Census Bureau figures for 1989 show that in median annual income, the households of black college graduates trailed those of white college graduates by more than a third: $37,958 for blacks as against $48,862 for whites.

And while all couples earn more if both husband and wife work, a second income for black families is usually what allows them to be middle class.

When both spouses work, the median income of black couples is $37,787, according to 1989 census figures. But when one spouse did not bring home a paycheck, the black couple's median income dropped to $18,727—out of the middle class. White couples, by contrast, tend to keep their middle-class status even when one spouse does not work. Last year, white couples earned a median figure of $45,803 with two paychecks and $29,689 with one.

Perhaps equally important, economists say, black people often enter the middle class with a slight fraction of the financial assets of middle-class whites whose parents and grandparents were middle class. So blacks lack the reserve of money and property needed to buy a house, to finance a college education, to weather a personal catastrophe or a national recession.

"Middle-class blacks are much more vulnerable than whites because they tend to be new to their positions and don't have the seniority of accumulated wealth," said William Julius Wilson, a professor of sociology at the University of Chicago.

Reminders of Desperation

Unlike most middle-class whites, they live with daily, personal reminders of the poverty and desperation they are trying to put behind them, as the loved ones back home who have not fared so well turn to them for help with the rent, use of a car, a place to stay.

"We're all tied together because upward mobility is recent for us," said Dr. Andrew Billingsly, chairman of the Department of Family and Community Development at the University of Maryland and a leading researcher on the black middle class.

The topic can be painful. Many middle-class black people were reluctant to talk to a reporter about their experiences out of a sense of duty and protectiveness toward their loved ones. Some did not want to take credit or appear to be holding themselves above the people they once played stickball with.

And in a society that in many ways judges people not only by where they are but by where they came from, many feared that their backgrounds and family responsibilities would subject them to unwanted scrutiny at work, or even be held against them.

In dozens of interviews, middle-class black people said they were proud to be the ones able to help their families, but were frustrated by their inability to get ahead.

"You can never accomplish anything," said Mrs. Ford, the Government worker in Washington. "As soon as you get anything, there's something there to take it away. I often wonder what will happen if something happens to me. Who'll be there for me?"

Some Dependents Aren't Declared

Donald Sheppard, an assistant professor of social work at Texas Southern University in Houston, has a wife and five children, but they are just the dependents the Internal Revenue Service gives him credit for.

When a brother needs a loan, when a sister needs a job, when a nephew needs a car, when a cousin needs a credit card or a friend needs a place to stay, they come to him.

"I know that when I get paid on the first of the month, I'm going to get a call," Mr. Sheppard, 40, said. "It's expected that I have it and that I'm going to give it. I feel I'm working for the whole extended family. It's not a question of *if* they're going to need it. I know they're going to need it."

His relatives have looked to him for help since he was in grade school. "When the television would get those horizontal lines, they would always call on me," Mr. Sheppard recalled. "I didn't know what to do any more than they did. But I'd turn some screw and it would work. Even as a child, people expected me to do everything."

By the time he was 11, he was catching the bus to go pay the family's utility bills. His father, a wool presser at a Houston dry cleaners with not a day of high school, could not dare ask for the time off; his mother, a maid, had suffered a stroke and was too sick. So she kept him out of school to pay the bills. He remembers being stopped by a truant officer and telling him, "Sir, my mama's sick. I'm going to go to school as soon as I pay the bills."

Mr. Sheppard became the only one of eight children to get a college degree and carry a briefcase to work. A sister once told him, "You're almost like a god in our family."

He and his wife, Jina, both social workers, earned their master's degrees at the University of Chicago in the mid-1980's by packing their five children in their 1971 station wagon and all their belongings in a U-Haul truck, driving north and feeding seven mouths on what was left of their scholarship money.

Sometimes He Gets Burned

They returned to Houston to an extended family of relatives and friends who needed them. Mr. Sheppard has gone into the refrigerator to get chicken broilers and T-bone steaks for them; he has had to choose between helping a relative out with the rent or fixing the boiler at his house. The family always wins.

Lately, he has been trying to provide services rather than money. He recently got one of his nephews a maintenance job at the university. "I have to do it for me," Mr. Sheppard said. "If I get them a job, they won't have to be asking me for something."

Last August, a childhood friend of Mr. Sheppard's who was down on his luck and recently evicted asked if he could move his family in with Mr. Sheppard and his family. The answer was yes, and Mr. Sheppard's children slept on the floor to make room. They stayed for five weeks.

"Every day, I had to buy milk and bread and cereal," Mr. Sheppard said. "I had 12 people in the house, and I was the provider."

Some of his investments have begun to pay off. For instance, he saw promise in the young son of one of his sisters, who was raising the boy as a single parent. Mr. Sheppard signed the boy up for Little League Baseball, coached him and counseled him as a surrogate father. The boy is now a senior in high school, at the top of his class and a drum major in the band.

Mr. Sheppard is still paying for the help he has given. His credit cards are up to their limit and the car needs fixing. Even on his and his wife's combined income of $60,000 a year, they have only a $5,000 cushion for their retirement and have not been able to save for their children's college education.

"In my family's eyesight, we've made it," Mr. Sheppard said. "But we're living paycheck to paycheck. To lavish and wallow in the status of the middle class, we can't do it. And I can't give like I used to. But it doesn't seem to register. People still come up to me and say, 'I know it's rough on you, but it's rougher on me, so can you give me this?'"

His goal is to build up reserves so he can provide for relatives without depleting his own money. But he is a long way from that. "When I think about it, it really kind of frightens me," he said. "Sometimes I find myself frustrated and depressed. I'm called on by my children, my wife, family members, students, colleagues, friends, needing, asking, wanting. The cycle never ends."

An Easier Road for Immigrants?

The role of family pathfinder is not new. Immigrants who flocked here from Europe early in this century typically relied on the first child who got an education and a foothold to serve as ambassador and teacher for the rest of the family.

But there are key differences for today's black people. For one, while many unskilled immigrants were able to get relatively good-paying factory jobs or make connections with local political machines to vault their children into the middle class, discrimination prohibited the parents and grandparents of most of today's black middle class from nearly all but menial positions in industry or politics. That meant black families had far less than white families to pass on.

Soon after civil rights measures created a more even playing field, the economy changed: once-dependable, relatively lucrative factory jobs started to vanish just as they began opening up to blacks.

Sociologists, however, point to the effects of lingering racial discrimination as the main difference. Dr. Joe R. Feagin, a professor of sociology at the University of Florida who is completing a book on racial discrimination and the black middle class, contrasts his experiences as an Irish-American with those of black Americans.

"My great-great-grandparents saw signs that said, 'No Irish or dogs allowed,'" Dr. Feagin said. "But once we lost the brogue and the look of the Irish, we could pass. People couldn't single us out for discrimination anymore. That has not been the case for blacks, no matter what their status."

Indeed, the civil rights gains of the last 20 years have done little to even out the huge gaps in white and black wealth. Census figures from 1984, the most recent available for this category, showed that for black households, the median net worth, or total value of what they own (cars, houses, stocks, equity in a business, for example) minus what they owe, such as an outstanding mortgage or education loan, was $3,397. For white households, it was $39,135.

More disturbing, perhaps, nearly a third of blacks have zero or negative net worth, meaning they owe more than they own. Only 8 percent of whites are in that category.

Giving Help, Giving Space

When Marjorie Ellis, 38, is not punching blueprint data into a computer as a drafting clerk at the Southern Bell Telephone Company, she runs a boarding-house—for her own family. Her two-bedroom ranch house just south of Atlanta bustles with the banter and footsteps of her sister, her sister's children, her elderly aunt and her mother.

They are all in transition. Her sister has a job as a civilian worker in the military and is trying to get on her feet, one of the nephews is in college, the aunt is recovering from hip surgery and her mother is struggling on a pension. They all turned to Miss Ellis when they needed help and now share space in the house, chipping in whenever they can.

Their fortune is tied to her fortune. "If there's a middle class, I'm in the poor section," said Miss Ellis, who earns about $30,000 a year.

In the months since her relatives moved in, she has depleted her savings and fallen behind on her house payments.

She doesn't have the $2,500 she needs to get the engine fixed for her 1984 Thunderbird. The car sits cold and idle in her driveway as she leaves to catch the 5:30 bus each dark morning to get to work by 7.

"I'm behind and it's hard to catch up," Miss Ellis said. "I pay one bill one week, the others when I can. I might be late a month. That doesn't mess your credit up too bad. Sometimes I sit and pray and cry. Then I figure it'll be all right somehow. I'm not going to let any of my relatives go wanting if I can help them."

A Wreck Is Disastrous

A few years ago, when her nephew needed a car to get to school, for instance, she bought a car, for which he agreed to make the payments if she covered the down payment and insurance. He never got the money. Worse, the car was in an accident and she ended up owing $1,300 on it. She is still paying for the car, which neither of them can use.

Miss Ellis's father was a cement finisher who died when she was in grade school; her mother was a maid. She and her sister were the first to graduate from high school and work behind a desk.

She remembers her minister's words when she got her house: "You're coming up in the world. You're coming up slow, but you're coming up in the world."

Between the economy and her family responsibilities, she doesn't feel that way anymore. She sleeps on the speckled beige sofa in the den, beneath pictures of the assorted relatives who rely on her. There is also a dog-eared picture of her grandmother, posing not with any of the 25 children she bore but with one of the white children she tended to for a living.

Under the strain, Miss Ellis has developed a bleeding ulcer, diabetes and chronic depression for which she takes regular medication. Her nightmares are not of ghosts and gremlins but of becoming homeless.

Her mother has begun to catch on. She has seen the somber-looking letters from the Department of Housing and Urban Development, which backed her mortgage. But Miss Ellis doesn't want to let on to her situation. Her relatives look up to her. She wouldn't want to let them down.

"What are you studying about?" her mother will ask in rural Georgiaspeak when she sees her daughter thinking of the weight on her shoulders.

"Nothing," Miss Ellis will answer, and smile not very convincingly. "I'm fine."

Saying "No" to Relatives

Glen Giles of Atlanta doesn't go out for lunch or take his family on trips to Florida anymore. And for the first time in his life, he must sometimes say no when relatives need money. It is not easy for a man who, after he got his degree, sent $25 every week to the next sibling in line to go to college.

But he is an insurance account agent with an office to run and a commission to earn at a time when people are not buying houses or cars, two of the biggest things people insure.

Since the first of the year, his business has been off 50 percent as the housing market in Atlanta has slowed. Last summer he had to lay off his entire office staff: a secretary and two other agents.

Now the shiny new desks sit empty in his gray-carpeted office, and he answers the phone, takes orders and messages himself.

So when relatives need help with the electric bill or the rent, he can't help them as he used to. One brother-in-law spent several nights in jail on a traffic violation because no one in the family could bail him out.

"I don't have it to give," said Mr. Giles, 43. "It takes everything we make to pay the bills. I have to dip into my own money to pay the office bills. Some bills go lacking as long as they can. We're borrowed out."

He is the third of 10 children born to textile workers in South Carolina, and even though his siblings are all college graduates and all working, they have limited resources just as he does. So he has no place to turn. "It's just me and whatever financial institution that will help me," Mr. Giles said.

Decades Behind in Prosperity

Jared Samples presumably went from working poor to middle class overnight when he won a seat on the Atlanta City Council last year. One of the first things he did when he got his first paycheck was to move out of the Perry Homes housing project where he grew up. The next thing he wants to do is get his mother out.

He is saving for the house he wants to buy for her, but he is finding that the $25,000 he makes as a full-time public servant doesn't go very far, especially when he still tries to give money to his nephew in college or a sister to pay her car insurance when he can.

He drives a 1975 Dodge. "My family knows I'm still poor," he said. "I might be able to loan somebody a little money, but I need my money back. We're four generations out of slavery and one generation out of the projects."

He knows he is starting from a deficit. "I'm working for my nephews and nieces," he said. "My life is pretty much set. I can work every day but I can't get but so far."

Waiting for the Century?

Many economists say it will take much of the next century to close the gap between the security levels of the black and white middle class. "Blacks can try to do better than in the past and save up, but the best they can do is to try to provide an education for their children so that by the second or third generation, perhaps there will be parity," said William D. Bradford, a professor of finance at the University of

Maryland who has written extensively on race and wealth. "I don't see anything in the next 20 years. We're looking at 40 to 60 years."

And many public policy analysts say that such an outcome will require continuing Government intervention. "Blacks are dependent on the Government opening doors and keeping those doors open," said Dr. Walter Allen, a professor of sociology at the University of California at Los Angeles.

Much is at stake for the entire country, sociologists say. "If the black middle class is not stable and secure, they will fall into the lower classes and not be able to pay their bills, their fair share of taxes, and will use a larger share of public services," Dr. Billingsly of the University of Maryland said.

Black people say they are doing what they can to help themselves. Betty Brown Chappell, a social worker and a doctoral candidate at the University of Chicago, remembers her tough freshman year at the University of Michigan, when she arrived on campus with not even enough money for books and food. She remembers how her father, a factory worker, sent what he had—a $10 bill. She gave $5 of it to one sister in college, who then sent $2.50 to another sister in college.

Mrs. Chappell wanted things to be different for the next generation. So when her niece, Alea, was born 18 years ago, she bought $150 in savings bonds for her. Last September, Alea enrolled at the University of Michigan. The savings bonds had doubled in value. She used the money to buy her books.

4

The Poverty Industry

Theresa Funiciello

Firefighters returning from a false alarm in Queens, New York, one beautiful October day in 1989 were gazing into the sky when they passed an apartment complex. Ten stories up, a body was dangling from the window. Hector Faberlle and his coworkers yelled up front to get the rig turned around. Just as it arrived back at the building, a little girl, naked, hit the ground. Faberlle ran to resuscitate her as two other firefighters dashed into the building.

According to Faberlle, "We tried to stabilize her. Just as she was breathing on her own, I heard people screaming. I looked up and saw another small child spinning down." Witnesses said a woman had seemed to dangle him before she let go of him. Hussein, age three, fell on his seven-year-old sister. "After that we couldn't get a pulse from her and blood was spilling from her mouth."

Ameenah Abdus-Salaam, a 32-year-old black middle-class Muslim housewife, was trying to send all five of her children back to Allah, through their apartment window. Her daughter Zainab was pronounced dead at the hospital. Hussein survived and a year later is still in rehabilitation. Just as Ms. Abdus-Salaam was about to toss out her one-year-old, firefighters burst in. As they were overtaking her, she urged the children to go quickly, as if they would go on their own. All were naked. According to one news report, she said, "We came into this world with nothing and that's how we're going to leave." Three children and their mother, who intended to jump when she completed the task, were rescued.

Ms. Abdus-Salaam was charged with murder, attempted murder, first- and second-degree assault, reckless endangerment, and endangering the welfare of a child. Neighbors said the mother was loving and the children were always polite and clean, as if that rendered the occurrence more mysterious. And then Ameenah Abdus-Salaam and her children vanished from our collective memory.

When I was young I could not possibly have understood or forgiven (as if it were mine to forgive) the acts of Ameenah Abdus-Salaam on October 5, 1989. Some of that youth I spent as a Muslim—drapes for clothes, virtually nonstop prayers, my two feet of hair cordoned with a bolt of white cloth bound so tightly I could never forget it was there. I took this religion as seriously as those that preceded it, starting with Catholicism (I went to *that* church every day until I was 18). My religion was as solid as a rock mountain pervious only to centuries of dripping water. (Latent feminism finally crept up on me.)

In Islam, everything is ritualized, from sex to eating. That's how I know what Ameenah Abdus-Salaam was doing calmly while she held Hussein out of the window before letting go. She was praying.

In form and function, as in other patriarchal religions, Muslim women are buried alive in contradictions. They are equal; no, superior; no, inferior—to men, to snakes, to witches. Make no mistake: an Islamic woman without a man, especially a woman with children, isn't remotely like a fish without a bicycle.

This woman had five children, aged one to eight years, and was recently separated from her husband. She had trouble making her last month's rent. She surely feared a descent into poverty and probably homelessness. (As of this writing she is not granting interviews.) Ahead lay the streets. Welfare. Welfare hotels. Drugs, prostitution, guns, knives, gambling, drunkenness, and all manner of spiritual death. But for a woman with the option of deliverance, it wasn't inevitable.

Some years after shedding my Muslim garb, I had a baby and ended up homeless and on welfare myself. Not long after, I organized a welfare rights center, where we (the mothers trapped in this system) tried, among other things, to sort out the differences between "us" and "them" (mothers not on welfare). One subject was the stereotype of child abuse. It was something each of us understood at some terribly private gut level, but never articulated outside our circle; even then, we were cautious.

My own revelation came when my daughter was about a year old. At one point, she was sick and cried almost nonstop for a week. I was experiencing severe sleep deprivation coupled with the trauma of being unable to comfort her. For one horrible moment, I felt like hurling her against the wall. Fortunately, my mother came by unexpectedly and held the baby for a couple of hours, giving me time to gather composure. My daughter's fever broke and we both survived. But ever since, I have understood child abuse. And any parent who claims not to understand it in that context, ain't hardly trying.

I had been very close to where Ameenah Abdus-Salaam was. On another level, our circumstances were very different. A homeless mother of five (I had only one) has virtually no chance of being taken in by friends or family for more than a night or two. A homeless mother of four or more has only a 16 percent chance of keeping her children together. If she stays in an abandoned building with them and gets caught, they'll be taken away for "neglect." Still, there are commonalities shared by women of all races and religions, from rural to urban poverty. The merciless anxiety, the humiliation of being shuttled back and forth like herded animals, the stress of keeping kids in school, are constant. Only the details vary.

In New York City, if she were able to keep them together, at some point they would approach an Emergency Assistance Unit (EAU), which is obligated to shelter them in some way. This would mean waiting for hours, sometimes even days, on plastic chairs or the bare floor. If the family didn't eat pork, they'd eat nothing, since baloney sandwiches are about all they'd get for several meals. Some nights they might be moved (often after midnight) to a roach, lice, and rat infested welfare hotel for a few hours. In the morning the family would be shuttled back to wait again.

If they were lucky, after some days they would finally be placed in a welfare hotel or "transitional" shelter. These often provide less space per family member than that required for jail cells. Because the family was large, they wouldn't even get apartment referrals from city workers until after they'd been in this hell for months. (One rural homeless mother told me her family was placed in a motel with bars instead of windows and not one store or school within walking distance. She was at the mercy of a barely functional shuttle system for the homeless.)

At first, many mothers try to continue taking children to their previous schools. In New York City, this usually means traveling with them (other babies in tow) to another borough in the morning and returning for them in the afternoon. When one child is too sick to travel, none go to school. After a while, the mother might try to place the children in a school closer to the shelter. Legal, yes. Easy, no. If the mother does accomplish this, other kids in the new school will soon realize her children are "untouchables." School life will become anathema to her kids. They'll begin to adopt the coping mechanisms of other homeless kids who *will* associate with them.

Night brings scant respite. Police sirens. Gunshots from outside or down the hall. Families fighting. Too many people and too few beds, often with neither sheets nor blankets, much less pillows. The mattresses have long since burst like pastry puffs. Bedbugs pinch.

Those of us who are lucky have a little stove in the room. I'll never forget the first time I used one in a welfare hotel. I had just added eggs to the frying pan when swarms of roaches scrambled out of the lit burner in every direction—including into the frying pan. It was days before I could bring myself to try it again. All the things most people take for granted become little horrors.

If the Abdus-Salaam family emerged from the "temporary" shelter intact and were placed in an apartment, the world would think their problems solved. But now they would be a welfare family. Overnight she would switch from homeless victim to society's victimizer. Her living conditions would not improve nor her stress diminish, but she would join the larger class of poor women—despised abusers of the system—welfare mothers. To have come this far would have been a heroic feat, but what would be said of her is that she's a drain on national resources, has too many children she shouldn't have had if she couldn't afford to, and she doesn't "work."

On welfare, the chances of having enough money to live in a remotely decent neighborhood and pay for basic human needs are laughable—even in New York, where welfare benefits are "high." On the day when the Abdus-Salaam family almost came to total halt, the *maximum* monthly grant in New York City for a mother and five children was $814.20—or *less than three fifths of the federal poverty threshold for the same size family.* The *average* New York grant for six was $655 per month. (In January 1990 there was a slight, almost negligible increase in aggregate benefits.) Assuming the family received the maximum, the rent allotment would have been $349. Assuming the absurd—that they could find habitable housing for that price in New York or most any other U.S. city—they would be left with $465.20, or about $2.50 per person, per day, for most of their food. (Food stamps would provide less than two weeks of nutritionally adequate food for the month.) That same $2.50 must cover some of their medical expenses, and *all* their utilities, toothpaste, toilet paper, furniture, soap, baby bottles, diapers, laundry, transportation, kitchen utensils, and clothing. If Ms. Abdus-Salaam lived in South Dakota, she'd have had just about $1.88 for all those things. If she were a single mother living in California aged 25 or less, she'd have a 98 percent chance of landing on welfare. In New York, if she took one subway ride in search of an elusive job, she'd use up over 90 percent of her daily ration. If she's menstruating and needs to buy a box of sanitary napkins, she'd have to dip into her children's share. Like millions of women, she has at her disposal only one commodity guaranteed to produce sufficient income to keep her family together: her body. For some women that's unthinkable; for example, to a devout Muslim, even survival does not justify such a damning act. Yet to kill herself—only herself—would be to act irresponsibly to her children. Had *Mr.* Abdus-Salaam died instead of leaving the family, everything would have been different.

Ameenah would have been the recipient of sympathy and support. As a widow with minor children, she would become a Social Security recipient instead of a welfare mother. (The maximum family benefit for survivor families on Social Security in 1989—$1,898.90 per month—could be enough to continue living modestly where she was. While this sum is hardly lavish, the family would remain above poverty.) No social policy experts would go nuts because she didn't have a "job." In fact, she would be thought a good mother for taking care of her children full-time, "at least while they're small." If and when she did get a paying job, she could earn thousands of dollars without a reduction in her Social Security check. (On welfare, a job would be taxed at 100 percent. Outside of minimal work-related expenses, for the most part her welfare check would be reduced one dollar for every dollar she was paid.) The message: the needs and rights of women and children are determined by the nature of their prior relationship to a man; the only difference between "survivor" families and "welfare" families is the imprimatur of the father. How did such a cruel policy come to be?

Whose Welfare?

The Social Security Act of 1935 was the legislative blast-off point. From the start it had the aim of protecting men—and only incidentally their families—from the vagaries of the marketplace. It insured most citizens, but *not* mothers separated from living husbands. The elderly—men, by more than two to one because of their labor-force participation rates back then—were designated beneficiaries of old age insurance. It was also this bill that created unemployment insurance, intended primarily to cover males temporarily disjointed from the waged labor market. Widows (the *good* single mothers/wives) and their children were to receive survivors' benefits. (Early on, if the father divorced his wife two minutes before he died, she was not eligible for "his" Social Security benefits.) Children with living but absent fathers were almost left out, but Frances Perkins and others fought to cover them through what came to be called Aid to Dependent Children (ADC). ADC kids were presumed to live with their mothers, as in fact almost all did. But *no sum of money was designated for the women*; Perkins lost that one. It wasn't until the 1950s that the caretaker parent (mother) was added to the beneficiary unit, and ADC was changed to AFDC, or Aid to *Families* with Dependent Children.

AFDC is the program most frequently thought of today as "welfare"; 94 percent of its recipients are single mothers and their children. Conservatives, especially during the Reagan era, argued recipients opted out of the job market in favor of plentiful dollars on the dole, offered by Lyndon Johnson's Great Society legacy. In fact, for most of the post 1960s, the purchasing power of cash assistance to poor families plummeted, though aggregate social spending soared. The Great Society was a culprit—but for different reasons than those given by Reaganites. *It emphasized a service strategy to the near exclusion of income security*—with the long-term effect of eroding the income security of millions of people, thousands of whom became homeless. The conceptual framework that supported this disaster held into the 1990s, long after the nation had surrendered in the War on Poverty.

War (Games) on Poverty

The foundation for the Great Society was laid in the Kennedy administration. Income maintenance had been ruled out; it was thought to breed a degenerative social disease—dependency. (There was no rigorous examination of this notion, although income maintenance was really the same as Social Security payments to survivor families, and "dependency" didn't destroy *them*.)

President Johnson declared War on Poverty not only because he felt the political necessity to carry on where Kennedy left off, but because big spending programs aimed at reducing the effects of poverty had been his turf as far back as the New Deal. He liked programs that doled out contracts across the country. Although income maintenance strategy was discussed during (and after) his administration, he too rejected it. But he did appoint an investigatory Commission on Income Maintenance Programs, which continued into the Nixon administration. Barbara Jordan, then a Texas state senator, was one of the few commission members not from the business community; still, even dominated by such stalwart capitalists as IBM's Thomas Watson and the Rand Corporation's Henry Rowen, the commission ultimately endorsed the "creation of a universal income supplement program . . . to all members of the population in need."

Why did Johnson reject income redistribution? The decline in the industrial base had limited certain jobs, and Democratic reform movements had put a stranglehold on party machines accustomed to wielding power through the jobs *they* controlled. Johnson's War on Poverty must have seemed an excellent chance to rebuild the party machine. So services emerged with regularity, each new "need" defined by the helping industry and by elected officials shagging dollars or votes. (When it works to their advantage, Republicans have shown they can also use service money to control allegiances. But generally, Republican conservatives, while railing about "big government," hand out their patronage through the military. Government spending is rarely about social remedies or defense; it's a contemporary form of patronage.)

The Great Society programs were the perfect vehicle for distributing patronage on a grand scale: Community Action, Vista, Model Cities. The service (plus economic development) strategy was to achieve a marriage of otherwise feuding factions: mayors, poor people (who at first had cause for optimism), civil rights leaders, liberals, and the press. Were it not for the Vietnam war, Johnson had every reason to believe reelection in the bag. His programs were shoring up a deteriorating political machine while providing the rhetorical posture for an end to poverty.

Among the War on Poverty designers was Kennedy administration holdover Richard Boone, who repeatedly urged citizen participation in the Office of Economic Opportunity (OEO) programs, believing institutional change possible only with the "maximum feasible participation" of community (poor) people. Community Action Agencies (CAAs) were hatched to do the job.

But with the exception of a few highly publicized locations, input by poor people was nonexistent. In *Betrayal of the Poor*, Stephen Rose wrote that no poor people or neighborhood representatives were involved in any of the 20 cities, although—*after* programs were designed and money budgeted—some members of groups to be served appeared on the agencies' boards of directors. In *The Great Society's Poor Law*, Sar Levitan concurred, noting that "affluent citizens who happened to live in a 'target area' could represent the poor. The law could therefore be observed without having a single low-income person on the CAA board."

CAAs genuinely committed to citizen participation were either swiftly defunded or never got out of the planning stages. Participation of poor people never took place; only the appearance of it occurred.

The mirage of participation had value, though. The impact of the civil rights, women's, and welfare rights movements was felt strongly through the 1970s, so that it was politically uncouth for advantaged parties to act in the absence of input from the disadvantaged. By manipulating the input, the social welfare establishment could appear to address poverty with the imprimatur of poor people (most commonly, women on welfare). The resulting aura of equality made it easier to get and maintain government and private foundation grants. The pretense of poor people's participation thus legitimized the social welfare institutions. The Great Society *did* offer a guaranteed income—to the social welfare establishment. By the 1980s, genuflecting to "participation" was dispensed with altogether.

Meanwhile, various other legislative events also displaced income needs in favor of "service." The 1962 and 1967 Amendments to Social Security Law set the stage. First, the federal government moved to increase the states' revenue share for family services from 50 to 75 percent. Second, states were allowed to contract these services out to *nongovernmental agencies* (previously, local welfare departments were the sole service providers using federal dollars).

Those states that previously and systematically had denied welfare benefits to millions of needy families (especially black families) were now eager to qualify for the windfall revenue sharing. But first they had to find people categorically eligible for welfare. Furthermore, in order to capture services dollars from the feds, states would actually have to pay the families welfare benefits (which were also federally subsidized, but not so liberally). Not to worry. Cash assistance levels were set *by* the states, so it was (1) possible to find families eligible for welfare (to get the federal funding for services) and (2) *set AFDC levels so low that families would stay poor*.

The welfare rolls climbed so fast the phenomenon was characterized as an "explosion." This legislated windfall to states (combined with the War on Poverty strategy of delivering megabucks to state and local governments for "services" to the poor) set off a spending spree—that was peaking just when purchasing power of cash assistance began to decline.

The decrease was coupled with an increase in rhetoric about "dependency" and the necessity for women to "work." Never mind that the jobs didn't (and still don't) exist that would pay enough to lift them out of poverty. Never mind that single parenting under any circumstances *is* "work," and even harder work in poverty.

The Birth of an Industry

What became the professionalization of being human took off, bloating under government contracts. For every poverty problem, a self-perpetuating profession proposed to ameliorate the situation without altering the poverty. In *The Politics of a Guaranteed Income*, published in 1973, Daniel Patrick Moynihan noted the "astonishing consistency" with which middle-class professionals "improved" the condition of lower-class groups by devising schemes that would first improve their *own* condition. It doesn't take a genius to figure out that paying the administrators of a homeless shelter two or three thousand dollars a month for each family instead of providing a permanent apartment is ludicrous. Yet the most massive growth in AFDC spending in the 1980s has been for just that purpose. Furthermore, to keep the "service" engine stoked, every manner of failure has been ascribed to the families themselves. Laziness. Cheating. Dependency. The families lack resources to defend themselves, though the "helping" institutions always have government and/or foundation funds to lobby (ostensibly on the families' behalf) for *more* funding.

What has happened over the last quarter century *has* been an income redistribution scheme, the most disturbing one this country has ever seen: a redistribution from poor women and children to middle-class professionals—with men at the top calling the shots.

This has been done not only with government tax dollars but also with private charitable (and tax deductible) dollars. The United Way. The American Red Cross. The Children's Aid Society. The independent federations of Protestant, Jewish, and Catholic charities. Hands Across America. . . . Each year, the New York *Times* begs its readers daily, from Thanksgiving to February, for its "Neediest Cases Fund." For nearly a century the *Times* has reported that all the money goes to the poor through eight social service agencies who distribute it, with no funds spent on "administration or fundraising." This is a wild exaggeration from the venerable newspaper; most of the money pays workers' salaries in the agencies, and has for years. Not to mention that the male directors of several of these already obese agencies are paid salaries in excess of $100,000 annually. Not bad for social work.

The "Workfare" Myth

In the great welfare reform debates of the late 1980s, social welfare professionals fell all over each other running after more funding (for themselves) through the jobs, training, and child care provisions of the so-called welfare reform bill, ironically presided over by Moynihan. Forgotten were the words of the President's Commission on Income Maintenance two decades earlier: "Services cannot be a substitute for adequate incomes; they cannot pay rent or buy food for a poor family." (The few surviving organizations of poor women put guaranteed income at the top of their lists, but they are rarely listened to. After all, they have no money.)

What stalled the "reform" debates for months was the issue of how much money would be allocated for those running the "reform" programs, and a turf war over whether the programs would be run by welfare departments or contracted out to private charities. (Everybody knew getting the women to "work" didn't mean getting them out of poverty.) Welfare rolls dipped slightly and briefly, but are now on the rise again nationwide. And the number and percent of single-parent female families living in profound poverty continues to climb. The relentless theme, from both the right and the left, still is to get those "nonworking" mothers to work.

In fact, the key to the tragedy of U.S. welfare policies is the notion of work—specifically, the unpaid and uncounted labor of women outside the waged labor market. About the only time the word labor is applied to women outside the wage system is in reference to the birthing process.

If any woman reading this were penniless today and went to apply for welfare to feed her children, she would not receive her first welfare check for about a month. Not because the welfare is prohibited from giving her money sooner, but because they are allowed to take 30 days to determine the obvious: that she is poor. The 30-day deadline might come and go with no relief. Or destructive policies plus bureaucratic bungling might prevent a check from ever coming. If she did make it onto the rolls, she might—like at least one million needy U.S. citizens every year—be cut off despite being still legally entitled to welfare. This process has been given the name "churning" by the welfare department, as needy people are routinely cut off and sometimes put back on months later.

One ghastly result of such U.S. social policy is that far more children die from poverty than slip away at the hands of mothers like Ameenah Abdus-Salaam. Twelve times as many poor children die in fires than do nonpoor children. Eight times as many die of disease, according to a study done by the state of Maine—where, by the way, 98 percent of the population is white. Thirty times as many low birth weight babies die as do normal weight babies. In 1987, one in two homeless mothers in New York reported *losing* weight during pregnancy. Even at the bottom, luck plays a role: whose kid is hit by a stray bullet, whose kitchen stove explodes because it was used nonstop as the only source of heat in a frozen apartment, whose infant dies of pneumonia. Poverty is the number one killer of children in the U.S.A. Murder by malfeasance.

Children are poor because their mothers are poor.

Ameenah Abdus-Salaam's tragic acts may not be so mysterious, after all. The miracle is that more women, facing similar anguish, don't do the same.

On September 19, 1990, I attended a court hearing. Ameenah Abdus-Salaam's male attorney had pleaded her "not responsible by reason of mental disease or defect." Two court-appointed psychiatrists agreed, and recommended she be released—no longer a danger to herself or anyone else. District Attorney John Santucci's office refused to accept the recommendation until another psychiatrist, of the D.A.'s choosing, can evaluate her. The case could drag on indefinitely. The male judge has consistently refused to set bail. Ameenah herself was not "produced" for the proceedings. All four walls of the courtroom are of elaborately carved wood. Above the judge's throne, in raised gold letters, gleam the words *In God We Trust*. However misguided it may seem to outsiders, that was the one thing Ameenah Abdus-Salaam intended to do.

5

The Wage Gap:
Myths and Facts

National Committee on Pay Equity

1. The United States Labor Force Is Occupationally Segregated by Race and Sex.

- In 1990, women constituted 45.4 percent of all workers in the civilian labor force (over 53 million women).[1]
- People of Color constituted 14.1 percent of all workers.[2]
- Labor force participation is almost equal among white women, Black women and women of Hispanic origin. In 1990, 57.8 percent (6.8 million) of Black women, 57.5 percent (47.9 million) of white women and 53.2 percent (3.6 million) of Hispanic women were in the paid labor force.[3]
- In 1990, women were:
  - 99.1 percent of all secretaries
  - 94.5 percent of all registered nurses
  - 97.0 percent of all child care workers
  - 89.0 percent of all telephone operators
  - 73.7 percent of all teachers (excluding colleges and universities)
  - 87.2 percent of all data entry keyers

  Women were only:
  - 9.5 percent of all dentists
  - 8.0 percent of all engineers
  - 20.8 percent of all lawyers and judges
  - 13.8 percent of all police and detectives
  - 8.5 percent of all precision, production, craft and repair workers
  - 19.3 percent of all physicians[4]

The U.S. Labor force is segregated by sex and race:

Occupations with the Highest Concentration by Race/Ethnicity/Sex

Black women:	Private household workers, cooks, housekeepers, welfare aides
Black men:	Stevedores, garbage collectors, longshore equipment operators, baggage porters
Hispanic women:	Graders and agricultural workers, housekeepers, electrical assemblers, sewing machine operators
Hispanic men:	Farm workers, farm supervisors, elevator operators, concrete finishers
Asian women:	Marine life workers, electrical assemblers, dressmakers, launderers
Asian men:	Physicians, engineers, professors, technicians, baggage porters, cooks, launderers, longshore equipment operators
Native American women:	Welfare aides, child care workers, teacher's aides, forestry (except logging)
Native American men:	Marine life workers, hunters, forestry (except logging), fishers
White women:	Dental hygienists, secretaries, dental assistants, occupational therapists[5]

2. Economic Status.

- In (March) 1988, 59% of all women were either the sole supporter of their families or their husbands earned $15,000 or less per year.[6] (Source: *20 Facts*)
- Over 11.1 million women work full time in jobs which pay wages below the poverty line (in 1989 for a family of three the poverty line was $9,890 per year). They work in jobs such as day care, food counter, and many service jobs. Many more women than men are part of the working poor (125 percent of the poverty level) and work in jobs such as clerical, blue collar, and sales jobs.[7a]
- In 1987, married couple families with 2 children present had a median income of $36,807 while female headed households with 2 children present had a median income of only $11,257.[7b]

Women of color are in the lowest paid jobs.

Occupations and Average Salaries of Occupations with a High Percentage of Women of Color[8]

Occupation	Annual Salary	Percentage of Women of Color*
Child care worker	$7,119	26.4
Sewing machine operator	7,568	29.6
Maids and housemen	7,945	35.5
Nursing aides	8,778	29.6
Health aides	9,489	19.5
Food preparation workers	7,132	18.9

*Women of color represented 7.59 percent of the United States workforce in the 1979 Census data.

The majority of women, just as the majority of men, work out of economic necessity to support their families. Women do not work for "pin money."

3. The Wage Gap Is One of the Major Causes of Economic Inequality in the United States Today.

- In 1989, all men, working year-round full-time, were paid a median salary of $27,430 per year.
- All women, working year-round full-time, were paid a median salary of $18,780 per year.
- Therefore, women were paid 68.5 cents compared to each dollar paid to men.

The breakdown by race shows the double burden that women of color face because of race and sex discrimination.

Year-Round Full-Time Earnings for 1989[9]

Race/Sex	Earnings	Earnings as a Percentage of White Men's
White men	$28,541	100
Black men	20,426	71.5
Hispanic men	18,358	64.3
White women	18,922	66.2
Black women	17,389	60.9
Hispanic women	15,662	54.8

- In 1980 according to the United States Census Bureau, workers were paid the following average annual salaries based on race and sex:

Race/Sex	1980 Earnings	Earnings as a Percentage of White Men's
White men	$20,335	100
Asian men	20,148	99.1
Native American men	16,019	78.8
Hispanic men	14,935	73.4
Black men	14,372	70.7
Asian women	12,432	60.0
White women	11,213	55.1
Black women	10,429	51.3
Native American women	10,052	49.4
Hispanic women	9,725	47.8

4. The Wage Gap Has Fluctuated, But Has Not Disappeared in the Last Several Decades.

Comparison of Median Earnings of Year-Round Full-Time Workers, by Sex, Selected Years

Year	Median Earnings WOMEN	MEN	Women's Earnings as a Percent of Men's	Year	Median Earnings WOMEN	MEN	Women's Earnings as a Percent of Men's
1989	$18,780	$27,430	68.5	1972	$5,903	$10,202	57.9
1988	17,606	26,656	66.0	1971	5,593	9,399	59.5
1987	16,909	26,008	65.0	1970	5,323	8,966	59.4
1986	16,232	25,256	64.3	1969	4,977	8,227	60.5
1985	15,624	24,195	64.5	1966	3,973	6,848	58.0
1984	14,780	23,218	63.7	1965	3,823	6,375	60.0
1983	13,915	21,881	63.6	1964	3,690	6,195	59.6
1982	13,014	21,077	61.7	1963	3,561	5,978	59.6
1981	12,001	20,260	59.2	1962	3,446	5,974	59.5
1980	11,197	18,612	60.2	1961	3,351	5,644	59.4
1979	10,151	17,014	59.7	1960	3,293	5,317	60.8
1978	9,350	15,730	59.4	1959	3,193	5,209	61.3
1977	8,618	14,626	58.9	1958	3,102	4,927	63.0
1976	8,099	13,455	60.2	1957	3,008	4,713	63.8
1975	7,504	12,758	58.8	1956	2,827	4,466	63.3
1974	6,772	11,835	57.2	1955	2,719	4,252	63.9
1973	6,335	11,186	56.6	1946	1,710	2,588	66.1

5. The Cause of the Wage Gap Is Discrimination.

Differences in education, labor force experience, and commitment (years in the labor force) do not account for the entire wage gap.

- The National Academy of Sciences found in 1981 that usually less than a quarter (25 percent), and never more than half (50 percent), of the wage gap is due to differences in education, labor force experience, and commitment.
- According to the 1986 NAS study, entitled *Women's Work, Men's Work,* "each additional percentage point female in an occupation was associated with $42 less in median annual earnings."
- According to the 1987 NCPE study, in New York State, for every 5 to 6 percent increase in Black and Hispanic representation in a job there is a one salary grade decrease. (A one salary grade decrease amounts to a 5 percent salary decrease.)
- In 1985, both women and men had a median educational level of 12.8 years.
- In 1985, the United States Bureau of the Census reported that differences in education, labor force experience, and commitment account for only 14.6% of the wage gap between women and men.

White Vs. Minority Wage Inequity By Education for Entry Level Jobs

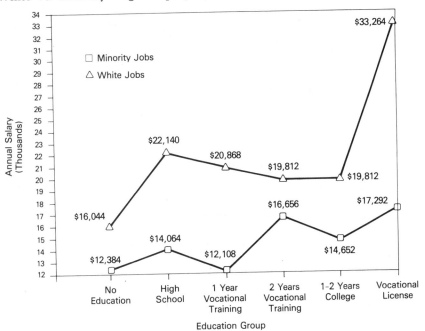

6. Employers Are Always Comparing Different Jobs in Order to Set Wages.

- Two-thirds (⅔) of employees are paid according to a formal job evaluation system

7. The Cost of Implementing Pay Equity.

- Achieving pay equity usually costs about 2 to 5 percent of an employer's pay roll budget.

For example, in the State of Minnesota, after conducting a job evaluation study, it was determined that there was a 20 percent gap between comparable male-dominated and female-dominated jobs. It cost the state 3.7 percent of the payroll budget to eliminate this inequity. The adjustments are being phased-in over a 4-year period.

8. Pay Equity Is Not a "Looney Tunes" Idea; It Is Being Addressed All Over the Country.

- All but 5 states (Alaska, Arkansas, Delaware, Georgia, and Idaho) have addressed the issue of pay equity
- 22 states and Washington, D.C. have conducted or are conducting job evaluation studies to determine if their wage setting systems are discriminatory
- 20 states have begun to make pay equity adjustments
- 4 states (New York, New Jersey, Florida, and Wisconsin) and Washington, D.C. have addressed race in addition to sex discrimination[10]

9. Everyone in Society Benefits from Pay Equity.

A. Men's wages will not be lowered. Employers cannot remedy discrimination by penalizing another group. Men who are working in predominantly female jobs will also be paid more if pay equity adjustments are made.
   Everyone benefits from women being paid fairly. Whether it is your mother, sister, wife or daughter, wage discrimination hurts the entire family
   Men of color will benefit in additional ways to those listed for all men
   - elimination of race from the wage setting system.
   - more likely to be in undervalued women's occupations.
B. Employers benefit because the employees' productivity will increase if there is a sense of fairness in how wages are set.

C. Society benefits because if wage discrimination is eliminated, the need for government subsidies for food stamps, health care, etc., will not be necessary. In addition when workers whose wages were lowered by discrimination are paid fairly, their pensions will be greater upon retirement.

Where We Get the Statistics

The U.S. Census Bureau collects wage data every 10 years. This data provides in-depth data for Blacks, whites, Hispanics, Asian Pacific Islanders and Native Americans.

The most recent salary data is from 1979. The United States Census Bureau also provides annual salary data for Blacks, whites, and Hispanics. They gather this information in March of the following year and release it in August. Therefore, the annual salary data for 1986 will not have been released until August of 1987.

The Bureau of Labor Statistics (BLS) provides quarterly reports each year on weekly salaries for Blacks, whites and Hispanics. They also provide an annual average of weekly wages.

The Women's Bureau releases "20 Facts on Working Women" on an annual basis.

The BLS and the Women's Bureau are part of the United States Department of Labor.

NOTES

1. *Employment and Earnings*, Bureau of Labor Statistics, Jan., 1991.
2. U.S. Census Bureau, represents Black, Asian, Native American, and some but not all persons of Hispanic origin.
3. Employment and Earnings, Black and white women; Women of Hispanic Origin in the Labor Force, Women's Bureau, Aug., 1989, Hispanic women.
4. *Employment and Earnings.*
5. *Pay Equity: An Issue of Race, Ethnicity and Sex,* by the NCPE, February, 1987.
6. *20 Facts.*
7a. U.S. Census Bureau, Current Population Series P-60 #168.
7b. Working Mothers and Their Children, Women's Bureau, Aug., 1989.
8. *Pay Equity: An Issue of Race, Ethnicity and Sex.*
9. U.S. Census Bureau, Current Population Series P-60 #154, most recent annual data available.
10. Pay Equity Activity in the Public Sector 1979–1989, by the NCPE, October, 1989.

6

Being Poor Isn't Enough

Tim Wise

Consider a hypothetical case: Cheryl R., a single mother of two, earns $5.25 an hour as a full-time maid in a downtown hotel, roughly $10,920 a year. She pays $450 a month to rent a two-bedroom apartment, which is cheap by Washington-area standards. So is her county-subsidized child care, at $30 a week. Still, rent, child care, and taxes absorb about 80% of Cheryl's income, leaving about $40 a week for food, clothing, transportation, medical care, and other necessities for her family.

Nevertheless, the federal government says Cheryl isn't poor. To the feds, Cheryl could earn no more than $10,560 for her family to be considered poor. This limits her access to some federal anti-poverty programs.

Why is the poverty line so out of touch with reality? "The answer," explains Patricia Ruggles, who works for Congress' Joint Economic Committee and is the author of a new book on poverty measures, "is that it is based on estimates of family needs calculated in 1963, using consumption data from a 1955 survey. The basic definition has never been updated for changes in family needs."

Ruggles estimates that today's line would have to be 50% higher than it is now just to match the standard of living provided by the 1967 poverty line (the year for which the government first set an official line). Under her recommended new poverty line, nearly one in four Americans would be considered poor, almost double the official rate.

Defining Poverty

But calculating poverty rates is not the most important function of the poverty line. The government uses the line to determine eligibility cutoffs and benefit levels for several federal poverty programs. Food stamps, for example, are available to those earning less than 130% of the poverty line. Similarly, pregnant women and children under six can receive Medicaid if their family earns less than 133% of the poverty threshold. Head Start and the national school breakfast and lunch programs are also tied to the poverty line. (State governments determine eligibility levels for Aid to Families with Dependent Children, the principal welfare program. Both eligibility and benefit levels fall well below the federal poverty standard. The median state AFDC benefit level is only 44% of the poverty line.)

Given its extensive application, the poverty line is a remarkably arbitrary and outdated measure. Using work by researcher Mollie Orshansky, the Social Security Administration set the first official poverty standard in the 1960s. Orshansky extrapolated the poverty line from the Department of Agriculture's 1955 Food Consumption Survey and "economy" food budget (the cost of a minimally adequate diet). The survey indicated that a typical family spent about a third of its budget on food, so Orshansky simply multiplied the cost of the economy food plan by three to get poverty thresholds for each family type and size.

In 1969, the Bureau of the Budget slightly revised Orshansky's scale and declared it the official poverty measure. Using this poverty line, the government has produced poverty statistics for every year since 1967. It updates the threshold each year using the Consumer Price Index (CPI). Except for minor technical adjustments in 1981, however, the initial formula remains unchanged. Ironically, Orshansky herself advocated regular revisions to it to account for changing consumption patterns.

According to Ruggles, revisions are long overdue. In the first place, poverty is a changeable term, based in part on social norms. Ruggles cites Adam Smith, who 200 years ago defined necessities as commodities "the custom of the country renders it indecent for creditable people, even of the lowest order, to be without."

Certainly, the custom of this country has changed since 1955. Thirty-five years ago, few people would have considered a telephone, refrigerator, or even indoor plumbing necessities. Moreover, changing work and family patterns have made child care a necessity for many.

Not only has the expanding list of necessities made Orshansky's three-to-one calculation irrelevant, but the original formula also rests on a conceptual fallacy. It assumes that poor families can limit other expenses just as they trim their food budgets. But expenses for some necessities are not so easily reduced. Skyrocketing housing costs provide the case in point.

The Poverty Line

Family Size	Official Measure[1]	Corrected Measure[2]
1	$6,280	$9,922
2	$8,420	$13,304
3	$10,560	$16,685
4	$12,700	$20,066
5	$14,840	$23,447
6	$16,980	$26,828
7	$19,120	$30,210
8	$21,260	$33,591

[1]1990 U.S. Department of Health and Human Services poverty guidelines.
[2]Patricia Ruggles' estimate of the poverty line for 1990 using updated consumption data.
Sources: Federal Register, February 16, 1990; Patricia Ruggles, *Drawing the Line,* 1990.

1987 Poverty Rates, Official and Real

	Official Rate[1]	Corrected Rate[2]
All persons	13.5	24.1
Children 18 or under	20.6	32.6
Elders 65 or over	12.2	29.7
Persons in female-headed families	33.6	49.8

[1]Census Bureau, *Current Population Survey.*
[2]Ruggles' estimate using updated poverty line.
Source: Patricia Ruggles, *Drawing the Line,* 1990.

In 1952–53, the average household spent 32% of its budget on food and 34% on housing, so food did, in fact, take about a third of the total. In a 1982–84 survey, food costs were down to 18%; housing had risen to 42%.

But that is an average. Because poor families spend virtually all their incomes on necessities, they are more sensitive to price hikes for those items. In 1985, half of low-income renters spent at least 65% of their incomes on housing. Two necessities, housing and food, took over 85% of a typical poor family's budget.

Just as Orshansky's original formula fails to adequately account for rising housing prices, so does the annual cost-of-living adjustment using the CPI. Though the government periodically adjusts the relative weights of the items in its CPI market basket (which includes housing costs) to reflect changing consumption patterns, it looks at prices for the average consumer. Because poor families use a higher percentage of their income for housing, the market basket for the typical low-income family over the last 20 years would yield a much higher inflation rate.

Drawing the Line

In her work for Congress's Joint Economic Committee and in her new book, Ruggles advocates thoroughly revamping the poverty line to make it a more accurate measure. She points out that the government already collects the data needed to calculate the cost of a minimum basket of goods for different family sizes and types, regions of the country, and income levels. "All I'm advocating is doing with the poverty line what we already do for the CPI," she says.

For now, Ruggles has recalculated the poverty line herself, updating Orshansky's food-based standard to better reflect the amount the poor spend on food. Her updated poverty threshold for a family of three in 1987 is $14,308, compared to the official $9,056. (The 1990 poverty line, adjusted for inflation, is $10,560. See table.)

That's not overgenerous, yet the effect on poverty rates is astounding, particularly for children, the elderly, and female-headed families. Overall, the 1987 poverty rate leaps from 13.5% to 24.1% using Ruggles' measure. For children 18 years old and younger, the rate jumps from 20.6% to 32.6%. Nearly half of female-headed families would be considered in poverty, compared to the official rate of one-third.

The vault in the poverty rate for elders is even more dramatic. The current poverty line says 12.2% of people 65 years old and over are poor, but with the updated threshold almost 30% would be considered in poverty. Raising the threshold highlights the tenuous situation of elders, many of whom live one nursing-home payment away from the official measure.

Ruggles' updating also paints a different picture of the progress the nation has made in eliminating poverty. Officially, poverty rates peaked in the 1982 recession and have been easing since then. Yet Ruggles' line shows poverty rates rising throughout the 1980s, even while the economy expanded. Similarly disturbing, the current 24% poverty rate is actually two points higher than Orshansky's estimate for 1960, suggesting poverty actually worsened during a period many associate with gains.

This year, the Joint Economic Committee held a hearing on revising the poverty line, and Rep. Stephen Solarz (D-N.Y.) has called for a commission to study the issue. But little action is expected soon. One potential obstacle is the budget deficit. Some $100 billion in federal and state programs are tied in some way to the poverty line. Raising the threshold could make millions more people eligible for food stamps, Medicaid, and other entitlement programs.

To avoid this dilemma, Ruggles suggests separating the poverty definition from the program guidelines. For example, the poverty line could be redefined while keeping the food-stamp income cutoff constant. After a new poverty measure is in place, she argues, the government can take up the issue of appropriate eligibility and benefit levels.

In the short run, of course, such a strategy misses the point, which is to define poverty in order to ensure that poverty programs provide a minimum standard of living to those on the margins of the U.S. economy. Still, Ruggles' research highlights the inadequacy of the current poverty measure. Only when the government recognizes that Cheryl and her two children are in poverty is there a chance that legislators will recognize their obligation to help lift them out of it.

7

And the Rich Got Richer . . .

According to a new report, the gap between the very wealthy and other Americans has become so great that by the end of 1990 the top 1% of the population (2.5 million Americans) will have almost as much income after taxes as the bottom 40%

(100 million Americans), and the share of income earned by middle-income Americans will have fallen to the lowest level since World War II.

The report, "Drifting Apart: New Findings on Growing Income Disparities Between the Rich, the Poor, and the Middle Class," by the Center on Budget and Policy Priorities is based on data prepared by the Congressional Budget Office (CBO). The CBO figures are based on actual data for 1980 through 1988 and projections for 1989 and 1990.

The Center attributes much of the growing income gap during the 1980s to a striking increase in capital gains received by the wealthiest Americans and a shift in the federal tax burdens. A capital gain is income from the sale of personal asset that has gone up in value. Between 1980 and 1990, capital gains for households in the top 1% of the population more than doubled from $83,000 to $175,000, after adjusting for inflation. Those in the bottom 90% of the population will receive an average increase in capital gain of just $12.

The shift in federal tax burdens has also placed more demands on the poor and fewer on the wealthy. For example, the percentage of income that the poorest one-fifth of households will pay in major federal taxes will be 16% higher in 1990 than it was in 1980. For middle-income Americans the projected rise is 1%. But for the wealthiest 1% of households, the percentage of income going to federal taxes will actually fall between 1980 and 1990.

By the end of 1990, the Center estimates that the richest 1% of Americans will have made income gains of 87%, while the poorest 20% will have lost 5% of their income. Sixty percent of Americans will have made virtually no income gain from 1980 through 1990.

Suggestions for Further Reading

Amott, Theresa L. and Julie Atthaei: *Race, Gender and Work: a Multicultural History of Women in the U.S.*, South End Press, Boston, 1991.

Blumberg, Paul: *Inequality in an Age of Decline*, Oxford University Press, Oxford, 1980.

DeMott, Benjamin, *The Imperial Middle*, William Morrow and Company, Inc., New York, 1990.

Domhoff, G. William: *Who Rules America Now?* Simon and Schuster, New York, 1983.

Hacker, Andrew: *US. A Statistical Portrait of the American People*, Viking Press, New York, 1983.

Horwitz, Lucy and Lou Ferleger: *Statistics for Social Change*, South End Press, Boston, 1980.

Jaynes, Gerald David and Robin M. Williams, Jr. (eds): *A Common Destiny: Blacks and American Society*, National Academy Press, Washington, D.C., 1989.

Newman, Katherine S.: *Falling from Grace: The Experience of Downward Mobility in the American Middle Class*, Vintage Books, New York, 1989.

Phillips, Kevin: *The Politics of the Rich and the Poor*, Random House, New York, 1990.

Rix, Sara E. for the Women's Research and Education Institute: *The American Woman, 1990–91 Status Report,* W. W. Norton and Co., New York, 1990.

Sennet, Richard and Jonathan Cobb: *The Hidden Injuries of Class,* Vintage Books, New York, 1973.

In addition to these books, the following organizations are good sources for obtaining current statistics analyzed in terms of race, class, and gender:

The Association for American Indian Affairs, 432 Park Avenue South, New York, NY 10016.

The Council on Interracial Books for Children, 1841 Broadway, New York, NY 10023.

Institute for Women's Policy Research, 1400 20th Street, NW, Suite 104, Washington, DC.

The National Urban League, Inc., 500 East 62nd Street, New York, NY 10021.

The National Committee on Pay Equity, 1201 Sixteenth Street, NW, Room 422, Washington, DC 20036.

Southern Regional Council, Inc., 60 Walton, NW, Atlanta, GA 30303.

PART IV

Many Voices,
Many Lives

Statistics can tell us a great deal about living conditions in a given society, but they paint only part of the picture. They can tell us that more and more women and children are living in poverty, but they cannot make that poverty real to us. They can tell us that a woman is raped in the United States at least as often as every two minutes, but they cannot help us share her pain, anger, or terror.[1] They can tell us that one-third of the adult population in this country cannot read well enough to get through the front page of a daily newspaper, but they cannot translate those numbers into lived experience.[2] For that, we must turn to stories about people's lives.

Who will tell these stories? For many years, it was difficult to find books about the experiences of women and minorities. Even books about breast-feeding and childbirth were authored almost exclusively by male "experts," who described and defined a reality that they had never known. White sociologists and anthropologists set themselves up as experts on Black, Hispanic, and American Indian experiences and offered elaborate, critical accounts of the family structure and life-style of each. Novels chronicling the growth to manhood of young white males from the upper or upper-middle class were routinely assigned in high-school and college English courses and examined for "universal themes," while novels about women's lives or the experiences of minorities or working people were relegated to "special-interest" courses and treated as marginal. In short, by definition, great literature has been that which was by well-to-do white males and about their experiences; accounts of the lives of other groups, if available at all, were rarely written by members of these groups.

During the recent past, more accounts of the lives of ordinary people have become available, thus bridging some of the gaps in the limited experience each of us brings to our study of race, class, and gender. The selections in Part IV are offered as a way of putting flesh and blood around the bare-bones facts provided in Part III. Some of the selections are excerpts from novels; others are nonfiction pieces drawn from magazines and books. All of them are offered as a vehicle for shedding our own particular identity, at least for a few minutes, and finding out what it is like to live as someone who is of a different gender or is from another race or class or who lives a different lifestyle. They can begin to suggest to us something of the terrible price that is paid in the destruction of human lives by the racism, sexism, homophobia, and class differences that define our world, at the same time that they reflect and celebrate the richness of different cultures and lifestyles.

While race, class, and gender are the primary factors that define opportunity and limit possibility for people in the United States at this time, other factors can also have a significant impact on life choices: among them are age, sexual orientation or preference, disability, and whether one lives in a rural or an urban area. Some of these factors are touched upon or highlighted in the selections included in Part IV. In some contexts, these factors play a major role in shaping the way others treat us, in how much we are paid, in what kinds of educational opportunities are available to us, and in where and how we live. In other contexts, these variables may well be irrelevant. Reading about them adds another dimension to our understanding of the complex set of additional factors that interact with issues of race, class, and gender.

But even as we acknowledge how much there is to learn from looking at the lives and experiences of many different people, there is also a danger in this project—the danger of overgeneralizing. It is easy to take the particular experience of one member of a group and attribute it to all members of that group. Many students who are members of a racial or ethnic minority have had the uncomfortable experience of being asked to speak for all African-Americans or all Asians or all Latinas at some point in their college experience. Failing to see members of minority groups as individuals is typical of a society where stereotyping flourishes. On the other hand, for the purposes of studying race, class, and gender, it is often necessary to look beyond individual differences and generalize about "Native Americans" or "Chicanas" or "men" in order to highlight aspects of their experience which are more typical of that group's experience than of others. As we have already seen, it would be naive to think that the individual exists in a vacuum, untouched by the racism, sexism, and class bias of society. Unless we understand something about the ways different *groups* experience life in the United States, we will never adequately understand the particular experiences of individual people.

The articles in this part have been selected because they give us some sense of the diversity of life in the United States at the same time that they reflect some of the consequences of the racial, gender, and class inequalities documented in Part II. For the most part, these stories, articles, poems, and essays need no introduction. They speak for themselves.

NOTES

1. The statistic on rape is drawn from the FBI's Uniform Crime Report for 1985.

2. The statistic on literacy is drawn from an article Jonathan Kozol wrote for the *New York Times* Book Review Section, March 3, 1985. There he writes: "Among adults, 16 percent of whites, 44 percent of blacks and 56 percent of Hispanic people are either total, functional or marginal nonreaders."

Racial and Ethnic Minorities:

An Overview

Beth B. Hess, Elizabeth W. Markson, and Peter J. Stein

Racial Minorities

Native Americans

Estimates of the size of the Native American population prior to the invasion of Europeans in North America vary; a conservative estimate is 5 million when Columbus discovered America. It was not long after the arrival of Europeans that Native American tribes were reduced to a racial and ethnic group "inferior" to the "more civilized" white newcomers. Because Europeans viewed their own cultures as superior, the physical characteristics of Native Americans were taken as evidence of biological inferiority. All Native Americans were categorized as "Indians" and their widely varying cultures destroyed. Disease was a major factor in reducing the Native American population; frequently, entire communities became ill, halting everyday life and enabling conquest by white settlers. Remarkably, Native Americans had previously been almost free of infectious diseases such as smallpox and measles, and they lacked any biological defenses against epidemics (Thornton, 1987) brought by Europeans.

Because Native Americans were not considered to be entitled to equal status with whites, treaties with the "Indians" were ignored. During the 1800s, whole tribes were resettled forcibly into reservations distant from centers of population and business. The complex interaction of relocation, war, and forced culture change combined with disease to reduce the Native American population to its low point of roughly 250,000 people in 1900 (Thornton, 1987). By the early 1980s, about 53 million acres, or 2.4 percent, of U.S. land was managed in trust by the Bureau of Indian Affairs. These reservations became notorious for their lack of economic opportunities. Moreover, most tribes own only a small part of their reservations.

Native Americans remain the poorest and the most disadvantaged of all racial or ethnic groups in the United States. Contrary to popular belief, only slightly more than half of all Native Americans live on reservations. Many live in metropolitan areas such as Los Angeles, Chicago, Seattle, and Minneapolis–St. Paul. Others are farmers and migrant laborers in the Southwest and north central regions, and many live in New York State and New England. The earnings of metropolitan Native Americans are higher than those of nonmetropolitan Native Americans. Better jobs and higher levels of education of metropolitan Native Americans account for these differences (Snipp and Sandefur, 1988). . . .

Self-determination and economic self-sufficiency cannot be achieved easily when the most basic needs, such as adequate education, housing, and health care, have not yet been met. Death rates from a range of diseases are greater than among the U.S. population as a whole. Mortality from alcohol-related causes among Native Americans remains about 22 times higher than the national average, and the suicide rate is twice the national average. Housing is substandard, and nearly half the hospitals built by the Indian Health Service were built before 1940 and are both understaffed and in need of repairs.

Far from being on the verge of extinction, however, the Native American population is growing faster than the U.S. population as a whole. According to Government statistics, there are around 1.5 million Native Americans, most heavily concentrated in California, Oklahoma, Arizona, New Mexico, and North Carolina. It is difficult, however, to know the precise size of the current Native American population, as the Federal government uses a variety of criteria to count "Indians." Although the birthrate among Native Americans accounts for a small proportion of the increase in their numbers, it seems likely that many people who identified themselves as belonging to some other race or ethnicity in earlier censuses now identify themselves as Native Americans, reflecting a new militancy.

Demonstrations and lawsuits have called attention to the treaties broken by the U.S. government and the unmet needs of Native Americans. Several lawsuits have resulted in a return of native lands and/or reparation payments in the millions. But despite the rising tide of political activity illustrated by the American Indian Movement (AIM), it has been difficult for Native Americans to create a unified political front. The variety among tribes is great, and there is no typical Native American, no one Indian culture, language, religion, or physical type.

African-Americans in America

AFRICAN-AMERICANS AND STRATIFICATION HIERARCHIES.   In 1989, 30 million African-Americans accounted for almost 13 percent of the total population of the United States. To what extent have African-Americans moved into and up the stratification system?

Although all legal barriers to voting have been removed, African-Americans are less likely to vote than whites, partly because of difficulties encountered in register-ing and voting in the South but primarily as a result of lower income and less education, which, in turn, are associated with lower voter turnout in general. Also, feelings of powerlessness and alienation reduce the motivation to vote ("What good would it do?"). Although African-Americans constitute about 12 percent of the country's voting-age population, it will not be until 1998 that they achieve parity in voting in congressional elections (National Urban League, 1989).

The number of African-American state legislators rose from about 168 in 1970 to over 400 today. Other elected officials increased, and an African-American political elite has begun to emerge. But the rate of increase of elected African-American officials has declined and is about only one-third of what it was from 1970 to 1976. At the moment, elected African-American officials represent considerably fewer than the almost 13 percent that would reflect their percentage in the American population. . . .

In the arenas of employment, occupation, income, and wealth, African-Ameri-cans remain disadvantaged compared to whites. . . . The average income for white families was 78 percent higher than for African-American families in 1987 dollars. Economic disparity between the two racial groups has increased since 1978 (Urban League, 1989). Indeed, analysis of trend data show that the income gap between African-Americans and white men has not lowered since 1948 (Farley and Allen, 1987). About one African-American in three lives below the poverty line today compared to about one in ten whites (U. S. Bureau of the Census, Series P-20, No. 442). At the current rate of progress of African-Americans, parity with whites will not be achieved in individual poverty rates until the year 2148 for individuals and 2158 for families (National Urban League, 1989). The rate of unemployment for young African-American men is three times that of young white men—a disparity in-creasing since 1948. Among young central-city African-American men, unemploy-ment rates (excluding "discouraged workers") are as high as 50 percent (Farley and Allen, 1987). Although African-American women fare somewhat better, their higher income in comparison to white females is primarily due to lower earnings of women regardless of race or ethnicity. In 1980, more than a century after the abolition of slavery, there were still more African-American women employed as domestics than there were African-American women professionals (Farley and Allen, 1987). . . .

High unemployment, poverty, and economic tension have taken their toll among African-Americans. An African-American male teenager is six times as likely as a white male teenager to be a victim of homicide (National Urban League, 1989). African-Americans suffer from higher rates of almost all cancers and are 33 percent more likely to develop diabetes. Higher rates of heart disease and stroke among African-American women account for nearly half of the black-white differ-ence in their life expectancy: cancer, homicide, and strokes account for 50 percent of the six-year difference between African-American and white men (Farley and Allen, 1987). Nearly 40 percent of all African-American mothers receive no prenatal care in the first trimester of pregnancy. One in eight African-American infants is born at a low birth weight, and the infant mortality rate is twice that of white infants. The infant mortality rate for whites ranks with Britain and West Germany; for African-Americans it ranks with Cuba. African-American children are more likely to drop out of elementary or high school and less likely to attend college.

Much has been written about the increasing numbers of African-American families that have moved into the middle class (Wilson, 1980, 1981), but they still work harder for equal rewards. At the same level of education and occupation, African-American wages are lower than those of whites.

Given the political, income, and occupational data just presented, it is evident that sources of personal and social prestige are systematically denied to African-Americans. In one area of most rapid gains, education, advancement may be more apparent than real. . . .

African-Americans have made occupational gains since 1960, but they have not been as significant as those of whites, particularly white males. In football, for example, although 57 percent of total members of the NFL were African-American by 1987, only 6.5 percent of the administrative posts were held by African-Americans. Even African-Americans in positions that pay well and sound prestigious have complained that they have been placed in high-visibility dead-end jobs.

The evidence supports the caste model of stratification in the United States today, although debates over the relative importance of class and race continue. Some analysts (Wilson, 1978, 1986) claim that race itself is less important than the overwhelming effects of poverty. Others cite continuing racism as a major factor in perpetuating the cycle of poverty. That African-Americans have fared poorly in our economic system seems evident. Although African-Americans have achieved higher levels of education and have greater opportunities for political activity, they remain outside the mainstream stratification system. And their disadvantages have been built into the social structure. For generations, despite their familiarity with American customs and language, African-Americans were systematically denied the right to vote, to be on juries, and even to be promoted in the military long after newer immigrant groups had achieved these goals (Lieberson, 1981).

Comparative studies of African-American and white ethnic immigrants indicate that the greater success of whites in achieving middle-class status has been aided by "a set of bootstraps that must be government issued . . . a system of protection that takes the civil rights of groups to acquire property and to pursue a wide range of economic opportunities" (Smith, 1987, p. 168). African-Americans have not been issued similar bootstraps enabling collective entry into the middle class. . . .

Asians in the United States

Like European-Americans, Asian-Americans come from different cultures and religious backgrounds and speak different languages. Yet, a tendency to classify all Asians together has dominated both immigration policy and popular attitudes. . . .

The Asian-American population increased by 142 percent between 1970 and 1980. Despite the growing importance of Asians, the decennial census is the only source of detailed information currently available. Unlike Latinos, on whom data are collected by the federal government each year, Asians are still too small a category to be captured in sample surveys. It will not be until the results of the 1990 Census are available that we will have more recent counts. Those people described by the Bureau of the Census as Asian are diverse, representing different languages, religions, cultural traditions, time of immigration, and poverty level. . . . The only other source of national data on Asians comes from the Immigration and Naturalization Service, which collects annual information on immigrants. Immigration data indicate that the three largest groups of Asian immigrants during the past few years have been Chinese, Filipino, and Korean. These three groups make up more than 20 percent of the total number of legal immigrants coming to the United States.

CHINESE.   In the mid-nineteenth century, young Chinese males were imported to work on the transcontinental railroad. Unable to bring a wife with them or to send for a woman to marry, those who remained in the United States formed an almost exclusively male community, concentrated in a few occupations (Siu, 1987). Chinese men were victims of extreme prejudice, discrimination, and open violence until the outbreak of World War II, when suddenly they became the "good" Asians compared to the "evil" Japanese. Restrictive immigration laws ended in the 1960s, and . . . 63.3 percent of Chinese-Americans in 1980 were foreign born.

The majority of Chinese live in seven states, with California having the highest concentration (40 percent), followed by New York, Hawaii, Illinois, Texas, Massachusetts, and New Jersey. As older immigrant groups have left the garment industry, an increasing number of immigrant Chinese entrepreneurs in New York have opened small manufacturing plants that do not require large initial capital investments; they have also recruited workers through kin and friendship networks (Waldinger, 1987).

As barriers to discrimination were lifted, Chinese-Americans entered colleges and universities in growing numbers. . . . A high proportion of both American- and foreign-born Chinese in the labor force held jobs as managers, professionals, or executives in 1980, and this percentage is growing. Although residential discrimination still exists in some areas, it has been less difficult for Chinese than for African-Americans to assimilate culturally or to amalgamate.

JAPANESE.   According to one social scientist (Kitano, 1976), Japanese immigrants "came to the wrong country and the wrong state (California) at the wrong time (immediately after the Chinese) with the wrong race and skin color, with the wrong religion, and from the wrong country" (p. 31). After the outbreak of World War II, the Japanese in North America were forcibly moved from their homes and "relocated." Inasmuch as hostility toward Japan was high in the United States during World War II, Japanese-Americans provided visible targets for its expression. Their appearance, language, and culture were interpreted as indications of disloyalty to the United States. More than 100,000 West Coast Japanese-Americans were placed in detention camps, with guard towers and barbed-wire fences. Their property was confiscated, sold, or stolen. Among the long-term effects of relocation were a reduction in the relative power of men over women in the family, a weakening of control over offspring, and reinforcement of a sense of ethnic identity.

Has the pattern of Japanese-American assimilation been similar to that of other minority . . . groups, or are they still excluded from the majority society, as their relocation during World War II dramatically illustrated? In the history of U. S. race relations, few nonwhite minorities have established as secure an economic position as whites. The Japanese-Americans in California are a notable exception and have been upwardly mobile in part because of their economic ethnic hegemony. *Ethnic hegemony* refers to the power exerted by one ethnic group over another. Japanese-Americans achieved economic control over produce agriculture, thereby dominating an important economic area that permitted them to interact from a position of power with the majority culture (Jiobu, 1988).

Greater mobility, in turn, has been associated with a shift from jobs in the ethnic community to employment in the corporate economy, and to greater assimilation. For example, third-generation Japanese-Americans have a higher percentage of non-Japanese friends than do first- or second-generation Japanese-Americans. They are also more likely to have non-Japanese spouses, to live in a non-Japanese neighborhood, and to profess non-Japanese religious beliefs (Montero, 1981). Moreover, the Japanese are the only Asian-American group to have a higher proportion of childless couples than do whites (Robey, 1985). In short, as occupational and financial mobility has occurred, greater cultural, structural, and marital assimilation has taken place.

Can the Japanese-American community remain intact or will it be amalgamated into the majority society? The answer will depend on whether Japanese-Americans develop a broader identity as Asian-Americans. But the most highly educated and most successful Japanese-Americans have become the most cut off from their ethnic background; for example, 40 percent have non-Japanese spouses. The irony of this trend toward amalgamation is that the Japanese may lose their roots in the tradition that gave rise to their upward mobility.

THE INDOCHINESE.   Indochina is a region in southeast Asia that includes Vietnam, Cambodia, Thailand, and Laos. In 1960, a total of only 59 immigrants were admitted to the United States from Vietnam, Laos, and Cambodia combined; all but 3 of these came from Vietnam. However, in the decade following the end of the Vietnam War, about 842,000 Indochinese immigrants, primarily refugees, arrived in the United States. In 1987 alone, more than 50,000 Indochinese immigrated to the United States (*Statistical Abstract*, 1989). Indochinese now represent more than one Asian-American in five.

Within the Indochinese population, there are marked cultural and linguistic variations. Only about one-sixth came as part of the largely elite first wave of South Vietnamese who brought with them money and skills. In contrast, recent arrivals have been both more numerous and more diverse: Vietnamese "boat people," lowland Laotians, almost all of the Hmong or Laotian hill tribes, and Cambodians. Many of these people came from rural backgrounds, had little education or transferable occupational skills, no knowledge of English, and had spent long periods in refugee camps overseas prior to coming to the United States. Moreover, their arrival coincided with inflation, recession, and growing fears of displacement among the native-born population (Rumbaut, 1986). Despite government policies that attempted to settle these new refugees throughout the United States, about 40 percent of Indochinese immigrants live in California, and 8 percent in Texas. Vietnamese also cluster in Washington, Pennsylvania, New York, Louisiana, and the District of Columbia. Laotians can be found in places as diverse as Minnesota, Rhode Island, and Oregon, with a large concentration of Hmong in agricultural central California.

OTHER ASIANS.   In 1980, there were about 1.7 million people of other Asian ethnicities in the United States. Filipinos accounted for 45 percent, followed by Asian Indians and Koreans. Koreans showed the most remarkable growth, increasing from 69,999 in 1970 to 357,000 by 1980. The welcome given to the arrival of Asian-Americans, like that of most new immigrants who are not of northern European origin, has been mixed. However, Asians, whether from Korea, India, or elsewhere, may be the achievers of the future. An incredible 52 percent of adult Asian Indians and more than one-third of Filipinos are college graduates. (It is important to note that most Asian Indians admitted to this country already had a good educational background upon arrival.)

Ethnic Minorities

The great variety of nationalities is a defining characteristic of American society. To illustrate general themes in the immigrant experiences and to introduce you to the fastest growing ethnic minorities in the United States, our discussion will focus on two recent entrants: Latinos and Middle-Easterners.

Latinos

Latino is a category made up of many separate cultural and racial subgroups bound together by a common language, Spanish (although even language patterns vary by country of origin). In 1989, about 21 million Spanish-speaking people were officially recorded as residing in the United States, and several million others are believed to have entered without official documents. Because of their generally younger ages and high birthrates, it is likely that Spanish-speaking Americans will soon outnumber African-Americans as the single largest minority group in the United States.

In 1989, the four major ethnic subdivisions within the Spanish-speaking population were Mexican-Americans; Puerto Ricans; Cubans; and people from Central and South American countries, particularly the Dominican Republic, Colombia, and El Salvador. . . . The remainder were from other Spanish-speaking nations. . . . Differences within the Spanish-speaking minority are striking, especially in terms of education and income. Each ethnic group has its own immigration history, cultural patterns, and its own internal diversity.

There is a stratification system within the Latino population, based not only on indicators of socioeconomic status but also on skin color. Race and ethnicity combine to determine the relative status of Spanish-speaking Americans, both within the stratification system of the wider society and within the hierarchy of the Latino subculture. These divisions reduce the likelihood of the development of shared interests necessary to build a unified Latino power base.

MEXICAN-AMERICANS. When the United States conquered Mexico in 1848 the Southwest had already been settled by Mexicans. A gradual pattern of economic and social subordination of the Mexicans, as well as Native Americans, developed as white Americans ("Anglos") migrated into the Southwest.

Like many other ethnic groups that have not been accepted by the majority group, Mexican-Americans tend . . . to live in particular geographic areas, such as southern California, south Texas, and New Mexico. . . . Although the stereotype of the Mexican farm laborer persists, relatively few Mexican-Americans today work on farms, in contrast to the employment pattern of their parents. This change reflects the increasing industrialization of agriculture rather than gains in job status or income. The occupational mobility of Mexican-Americans has been horizontal rather than vertical. That is, the present generation has moved from farm labor into other unskilled jobs, such as work in canning factories. Relatively few have moved into semiskilled or higher-status occupations. Many undocumented workers from Mexico have been employed in low-wage service and manufacturing jobs to keep labor costs low and to prevent unionization.

On various measures of social mobility, Mexican-Americans rank below the average for the population as a whole. In general they have less education than do non-Latinos or African-Americans. The traditional Mexican family is an extended one, with the kinship group being both the main focus of obligation and the source of emotional and social support. Birthrates are relatively high, especially among first-generation and poorly educated women (Bean and Swicegood, 1985). Within the family, gender roles are well defined. Both mothers and daughters are expected to be protected and submissive and to dedicate themselves to caring for the males of the family. For the Mexican male, *machismo*, or the demonstration of physical and sexual prowess, is basic to self-respect.

These traditional patterns protect Mexican-Americans against the effects of prejudice and discrimination, but they also reinforce isolation from the majority culture. An upwardly mobile Mexican-American must often choose between remaining locked into a semi-isolated ethnic world or becoming alienated from family, friends, and ethnic roots (Arce, 198).

PUERTO RICANS. Technically U.S. citizens since the United States took the island after the Spanish-American War in 1898, Puerto Ricans began to arrive on the mainland in large numbers in the 1950s because of the collapse of the sugar industry on their island. One-third of the world's Puerto Ricans now reside in the mainland United States. Of the 2.3 million mainland Puerto Ricans, 80 percent live in six states: New York, New Jersey, Connecticut, Illinois, Pennsylvania, and Massachusetts. Although almost two-fifths of the Puerto Ricans in the continental United States have incomes below the poverty level, their expectations of success are higher than the expectations of those who have remained in Puerto Rico.

Although Puerto Ricans are often grouped with Mexican-Americans, the two populations are very different in history, culture, and racial composition. Puerto Rico's culture is a blend of African and Spanish influences, with a heavy dose of American patterns. In Mexico, both Spanish and Native American elements combine.

The Puerto Rican experience on the mainland has included a continuing struggle for stability and achievement in education, politics, the arts, and community control. Puerto Ricans have been elected to the U.S. Congress, to state legislatures, and to city councils. Growing numbers of Puerto Ricans have moved from the inner city to middle-income, homeowner suburbs, and young Puerto Ricans are entering the fields of law, business, medicine, and teaching. . . . Others continue to have difficulty on standardized English and math tests, to drop out of school, and to face unemployment. About 43 percent of Puerto Rican families are likely to be headed by a woman with no husband present.

CUBANS. Cuban immigration to the United States began in large numbers when Fidel Castro came to power in the mid-1950s. Between 1954 and 1978, more than 325,000 Cubans were admitted as permanent residents in the United States, especially in the Miami, Florida, area. In early 1980, an additional 115,000 refugees entered the country in a sudden, somewhat chaotic exodus from Cuba. Although it is too early to determine how these new Cuban immigrants will fare in the United States, many earlier immigrants have achieved success operating businesses within Cuban communities . . . and a Cuban-American woman from Florida was elected to Congress.

Of all Spanish-speaking subgroups in the U.S. the Cubans are older and better educated; are more likely to live in metropolitan areas, though not the central city; and have the highest median income. Much of their success, however, can be attributed to the educational and occupational characteristics with which they entered America. Theirs was an upper- and middle-class emigration in contrast to that of the Cuban newcomers of 1980, who were, on the average, younger, less educated, and less skilled. Recent Cuban immigrants have also been received with greater hostility and fear, and they are experiencing barriers to mobility within established Cuban communities as well as outside.

Middle Easterners

In recent years, a new group of immigrants from the Middle East has begun to emerge as a visible urban minority. The number of immigrants from Middle Eastern countries has averaged more than 18,000 annually since 1970. Yet, little is known about them. . . . They have come from a number of different countries such as

Egypt, Syria, Lebanon, Iran, and Jordan, and they speak a number of languages. Their religious affiliations include Muslim, Coptic Christian, and Melkite Catholic, and they bring with them diverse cultural norms. Many would not describe themselves as "Arabs." They do not speak Arabic or identify with Arabic history and culture. The one common denominator of these different ethnic groups is their Middle Eastern origin. The socioeconomic position of the various ethnic groups also varies: the Lebanese, the Syrians, and the Iranians are primarily middle class, whereas other groups are mostly working class. . . .

In the Detroit area, which now has the largest concentration of Arabic-speaking people outside the Middle East—more than 200,000 Lebanese, Palestinians, Yemenis, and Iraqi-Chaldeans—there has been conflict between Middle Easterners and other ethnic groups. From the limited information available, however, there seems to be little racial tension, juvenile delinquency, or crime within Near Eastern immigrant communities. Tensions are caused by drinking, dating, and language, as younger people become acculturated to the norms of the dominant society and reject traditional values and behavior. As with most other immigrant groups, length of residence in the United States is an important factor both in acculturation and in socioeconomic status.

REFERENCES

Thorton, Russell. *American Indian Holocaust and Survival: A Population History Since 1492.* Norman: University of Oklahoma Press, 1987.

Snipp, C. Matthew, and Gary D. Sandefur. "Earnings of American Indians and Alaskan Natives: The Effects of Residence and Migration." *Social Forces* 66(4) (1988):994–1008.

National Urban League. *Stalling Out: The Relative Progress of African-Americans.* New York: National Urban League. 1989.

Farley, Reynolds and Walter R. Allen, *The Color Line and the Quality of Life in America.* New York: Russell Sage Foundation, 1987.

U. S. Bureau of the Census. "The Black Population in the United States: March 1988." *Current Population Reports*, Series P-20, No. 442. Washington, D.C.: U.S. Government Printing Office, 1989.

Wilson, William Jullus. "Cycles of Deprivation and the Underclass Debate." *Social Service Review* 59 (1986):541–559.

Lieberson, Stanley. *A Piece of the Pie: Black and White Immigrants Since 1880.* Berkeley and Los Angeles: University of California Press, 1981.

Smith, J. Owens. *The Politics of Racial Inequality: A Systematic Comparative Macro-Analysis from the Colonial Period to 1970.* Westport, CT: Greenwood Press, 1987.

Siu, Paul C. P. *The Chinese Laundryman: A Study of Social Isolation.* New York: New York University Press, 1987.

Waldinger, Roger. *Through the Eye of the Needle: Immigrants and Enterprise in the New York Garment Trade.* New York: New York University Press, 1987.

Kitano, Harry. *Japanese Americans.* Englewood Cliffs, NJ: Prentice-Hall, 1976.

Jiobu, Robert M. "Ethnic Hegemony and the Japanese of California." *American Sociological Review* 53 (June 1988):353–367.

Montero, Darrel, "The Japanese Americans: Changing Patterns of Assimilation over Three Generations." *American Sociological Review* 46 (1981):829–839.

Roby, Bryant. "America's Asians." *American Demographics* 7 (1985):22–25.

U.S. Bureau of the Census, *Statistical Abstract of the United States 1989*. Washington, D.C.: U.S. Department of Commerce, 1989.

Rumbaut, G, Ruben. "Southeast Asian Refugees in the United States: A Portrait of a Decade of Migration and Resettlement, 1975–1985." Paper presented at the 81st annual meeting of the American Sociological Association, New York, August 1986.

Bean, Frank D., and Gary Swicegood. *Mexican-American Fertility Patterns*. Austin: University of Texas Press, 1985.

2

Sun Chief:
Autobiography of a Hopi Indian

Leo W. Simmons, Editor

I grew up believing that Whites are wicked, deceitful people. It seemed that most of them were soldiers, government agents, or missionaries, and that quite a few were Two-Hearts. The old people said that the Whites were tough, possessed dangerous weapons, and were better protected than we were from evil spirits and poison arrows. They were known to be big liars too. They sent Negro soldiers against us with cannons, tricked our war chiefs to surrender without fighting, and then broke their promises. Like Navahos, they were proud and domineering—and needed to be reminded daily to tell the truth. I was taught to mistrust them and to give warning whenever I saw one coming.

Our chief had to show respect to them and pretend to obey their orders, but we knew that he did it halfheartedly and that he put his trust in our Hopi gods. Our ancestors had predicted the coming of these Whites and said that they would cause us much trouble. But it was understood that we had to put up with them until our gods saw fit to recall our Great White Brother from the East to deliver us. Most people in Oraibi argued that we should have nothing to do with them, accept none of their gifts, and make no use of their building materials, medicine, food, tools, or clothing—but we did want their guns. Those who would have nothing to do with

Whites were called "Hostiles" and those who would cooperate a little were called "Friendlies." These two groups were quarreling over the subject from my earliest memories and sometimes their arguments spoiled the ceremonies and offended the Six-Point-Cloud-People, our ancestral spirits, who held back the rain and sent droughts and disease. Finally the old chief, with my grandfather and a few others, became friendly with the Whites and accepted gifts, but warned that we would never give up our ceremonies or forsake our gods. But it seemed that fear of Whites, especially of what the United States Government could do, was one of the strongest powers that controlled us, and one of our greatest worries.

A few years before my birth the United States Government had built a boarding school at the Keams Canyon Agency. At first our chief, Lolulomai, had not wanted to send Oraibi children, but chiefs from other villages came and persuaded him to accept clothes, tools, and other supplies, and to let them go. Most of the people disliked this and refused to cooperate. Troops came to Oraibi several times to take the children by force and carry them off in wagons. The people said that it was a terrible sight to see Negro soldiers come and tear children from their parents. Some boys later escaped from Keams Canyon and returned home on foot, a distance of forty miles.

Some years later a day school was opened at the foot of the mesa in New Oraibi, where there were a trading post, a post office, and a few government buildings. Some parents were permitted to send their children to this school. When my sister started, the teacher cut her hair, burned all her clothes, and gave her a new outfit and a new name, Nellie. She did not like school, stopped going after a few weeks, and tried to keep out of sight of the Whites who might force her to return. About a year later she was sent to the New Oraibi spring to fetch water in a ceremonial gourd for the Ooqol society and was captured by the school principal who permitted her to take the water up to the village, but compelled her to return to school after the ceremony was over. The teachers had then forgotten her old name, Nellie, and called her Gladys. Although my brother was two years older than I, he had managed to keep out of school until about a year after I started, but he had to be careful not to be seen by Whites. When finally he did enter the day school at New Oraibi, they cut his hair, burned his clothes, and named him Ira. . . .

3

A Farewell to Manzanar

Jeanne Wakatsuki Houston and
James D. Houston

At seven I was too young to be insulted. The camp worked on me in a much different way. I wasn't aware of this at the time, of course. No one was, except maybe Mama, and there was little she could have done to change what happened.

It began in the mess hall. Before Manzanar, mealtime had always been the center of our family scene. In camp, and afterward, I would often recall with deep yearning the old round wooden table in our dining room in Ocean Park, the biggest piece of furniture we owned, large enough to seat twelve or thirteen of us at once. A tall row of elegant, lathe-turned spindles separated this table from the kitchen, allowing talk to pass from one room to the other. Dinners were always noisy, and they were always abundant with great pots of boiled rice, platters of home-grown vegetables, fish Papa caught.

He would sit at the head of this table, with Mama next to him serving and the rest of us arranged around the edges according to age, down to where Kiyo and I sat, so far away from our parents, it seemed at the time, we had our own enclosed nook inside this world. The grownups would be talking down at their end, while we two played our secret games, making eyes at each other when Papa gave the order to begin to eat, racing with chopsticks to scrape the last grain from our rice bowls, eyeing Papa to see if he had noticed who won.

Now, in the mess halls, after a few weeks had passed, we stopped eating as a family. Mama tried to hold us together for a while, but it was hopeless. Granny was too feeble to walk across the block three times a day, especially during heavy weather, so May brought food to her in the barracks. My older brothers and sisters, meanwhile, began eating with their friends, or eating somewhere blocks away, in the hope of finding better food. The word would get around that the cook over in Block 22, say, really knew his stuff, and they would eat a few meals over there, to test the rumor. Camp authorities frowned on mess hall hopping and tried to stop it, but the good cooks liked it. They liked to see long lines outside their kitchens and would work overtime to attract a crowd.

Younger boys, like Ray, would make a game of seeing how many mess halls they could hit in one meal period—be the first in line at Block 16, gobble down your food, run to 17 by the middle of the dinner hour, gulp another helping, and hurry to 18 to make the end of that chow line and stuff in the third meal of the evening. They didn't *need* to do that. No matter how bad the food might be, you could always eat till you were full.

Kiyo and I were too young to run around, but often we would eat in gangs with other kids, while the grownups sat at another table. I confess I enjoyed this part of it at the time. We all did. A couple of years after the camps opened, sociologists studying the life noticed what had happened to the families. They made some recommendations, and edicts went out that families *must* start eating together again. Most people resented this; they griped and grumbled. They were in the habit of eating with their friends. And until the mess hall system itself could be changed, not much could really be done. It was too late.

My own family, after three years of mess hall living, collapsed as an integrated unit. Whatever dignity or feeling of filial strength we may have known before December 1941 was lost, and we did not recover it until many years after the war, not until after Papa died and we began to come together, trying to fill the vacuum his passing left in all our lives.

The closing of the camps, in the fall of 1945, only aggravated what had begun inside. Papa had no money then and could not get work. Half of our family had already moved to the east coast, where jobs had opened up for them. The rest of us were relocated into a former defense workers' housing project in Long Beach. In that small apartment there never was enough room for all of us to sit down for a meal. We ate in shifts, and I yearned all the more for our huge round table in Ocean Park.

Soon after we were released I wrote a paper for a seventh-grade journalism class, describing how we used to hunt grunion before the war. The whole family would go down to Ocean Park Beach after dark, when the grunion were running, and build a big fire on the sand. I would watch Papa and my older brothers splash through the moonlit surf to scoop out the fish, then we'd rush back to the house where Mama would fry them up and set the sizzling pan on the table, with soy sauce and horseradish, for a midnight meal. I ended the paper with this sentence: "The reason I want to remember this is because I know we'll never be able to do it again."

You might say it would have happened sooner or later anyway, this sliding apart of such a large family, in postwar California. People get married; their interests shift. But there is no escaping the fact that our internment accelerated the process, made it happen so suddenly it was almost tangible.

Not only did we stop eating at home, there was no longer a home to eat in. The cubicles we had were too small for anything you might call "living." Mama couldn't cook meals there. It was impossible to find any privacy there. We slept there and spent most of our waking hours elsewhere.

Mama had gone to work again soon after we arrived. The call went out for people with any kind of skill to offer their services. Thousands were responding, with great surges of community spirit, sometimes with outright patriotism, wanting "to do their part." Woody signed on as a carpenter. One of my brothers-in-law was a roofing foreman. Another ran a reservoir crew. Mama had worked as a dietician in Washington after she was married. In camp this was high-priority training. In addition to the daily multitude, those amateur cooks were faced with allergy cases, diabetics, nursing mothers, infants who required special feedings. For Mama it was also a way to make a little money. Nineteen dollars a month. This was top wage for an internee. Unskilled labor started at eight. All volunteer of course. You didn't have to get out of bed in the morning if you didn't want to. Mama wanted the work. She had a monthly fee to pay the warehouse in Los Angeles where she had stored what remained of our furniture and silver just before we evacuated. She worried about this constantly.

She worried about Papa too. Letters from him trickled in, once or twice a month, with half the words blacked out, calling her "Sweetheart" for the first time in fifteen years. She was always distracted, staring at things I could never see. I would try to get her attention, grab her around the legs. At night, in bed, she would hug me close. But during the day she never seemed to notice me.

Adrift, I began to look elsewhere for attention and thus took the first steps out of my child's realm toward a world of grownups other than my parents. Though I was only seven, my images of certain people from this period are very precise, because I had begun to *see* adults for the first time. On Terminal Island I first *saw* Orientals, those demon-children who had terrorized me. At Manzanar, past the fear of slanted eyes and high cheekbones, I watched with fresh amazement the variety of faces and bodies and costumes all around me. This may have resulted, in part, from the life Manzanar had forced upon us all. Once the weather warmed up, it was an out-of-doors life, where you only went "home" at night, when you finally had to: 10,000 people on an endless promenade inside the square mile of barbed wire that was the wall around our city.

One of our neighbors was a tall, broad woman, taller than anyone in camp, as far as I recall. She walked erectly and wore an Aunt Jemima scarf around her head. She was married to a Japanese man, and they had adopted a little Japanese girl I sometimes played with. But this woman, I realized much later, was half-black, with light mulatto skin, passing as a Japanese in order to remain with her husband. She wore scarfs everywhere to cover her give-away hair.

In the barracks facing ours there lived an elegant woman who astounded me each time I saw her. She and her husband both came from Japan, and her long aristocratic face was always a ghastly white. In traditional fashion she powdered it with rice flour every morning. By old-country standards this made her more beautiful. For a long time I thought she was diseased.

Two more white faces stand out in my memory, a pair of nurses I saw from time to time in the clinic. They wore white shoes, white hose, and white dresses. Above their bleached faces their foreheads had been shaved halfway over their scalp's curve to make a sharp widow's peak where starched black hair began to arch upward, reminding me of a cobra's hood. Their lips were gone. Their brows were plucked. They were always together, a pair of reptilian kabuki creatures at loose in the camp hospital.

You might say they were the negatives for two other women I soon began to see almost every day and, in fact, saw more of for a while than I did my mother. Their robes were black, their heads were hooded in white. Sister Mary Suzanne was about forty then, a frail, gentle woman from Japan who could speak no English. Sister Mary Bernadette was a feisty, robust little Canadian Japanese who spoke both languages fluently.

They were Maryknoll nuns, members of that missionary order whose special task is to go into a country, with knowledge of its language, and convert its people to the Catholic faith. Before the war they had run an orphanage in Los Angeles for children of Japanese ancestry. Evacuated to Manzanar and given the job of caring for some fifty orphans interned there, they set up what came to be known as "Children's Village," and they had one barracks turned into a chapel. They were joined by Father Steinback, one of the few Caucasians to live among us inside the compound and eat in our mess halls. He was greatly admired for this, and many internees converted to Catholicism before the camp was closed.

I was almost one of them. Papa stepped in just before my baptism day. If he had been there during those early months I probably would never have started spending time with the Maryknolls. He was always suspicious of organized religions. I think he had already tried to scare me away from Catholics. That was one of his prime methods of instruction: fear. On my way home from school each day in Ocean Park I would break into a run as I passed the local Catholic church. The nuns I glimpsed were robed and ghostly figures I wanted no part of.

Culturally we were like those Jews who observe certain traditions but never visit a synagogue. We kept a little Buddhist shrine in the house, and we celebrated a few Japanese holidays that were religiously connected—the way Christmas is. But we never said prayers. I had never been inside a Buddhist church. And as for Christianity, I had not heard the word God until we reached Terminal Island. I first heard about Jesus when the one friend I made there—another Japanese girl—took me to a Baptist Sunday School on the island, where a Caucasian teacher bewildered me with pictures of lambs and donkeys and golden-domed pavilions.

For some reason these did not appeal to me nearly as much as the stories of the saints and martyrs I heard a few months later when I began to study catechism with the Maryknolls. Soon I was over there every afternoon and most of Sunday. With no regular school to attend and no home to spend time in, it's no mystery that I should have been drawn to these two kind and generous women. They had organized a recreation program. They passed out candy. But what kept me coming back, once I started, were the tales of the unfortunate women like Saint Agatha, whose breasts were cut off when she refused to renounce her faith.

I had to walk nearly a mile to reach their chapel, and walk a mile back. That summer it was miserably hot, over one hundred degrees most days. Yet I made the trip gladly. A big homely girl about twenty years old who wore boys' shoes and an Eisenhower jacket taught catechism to the younger kids. She loved to sit us down and fix us with the eye of a mother superior and tell us about Saint Agatha, or Saint Juliana, who was boiled alive, or Saint Marcella, who was whipped to death by the Goths.

I was fascinated with the miseries of women who had suffered and borne such afflictions. On my way home, I would hike past row upon row of black barracks, watching mountains waver through that desert heat, with the sun trying to dry up my very blood, and imagine in some childish way that I was among them, that I too was up there on the screen of history, in a white lace catechism dress, sweating and grimy, yet selflessly carrying my load.

I fulfilled this little fantasy one blistering afternoon when the heat finally got me. Sunstroke. While crossing one of the wide sandy firebreaks that separated some of the blocks, I passed out.

This put me in bed for a week. After I recovered, several months went by before I resumed my catechism. For one thing, Papa discouraged me. It was just before this happened that he had returned from Fort Lincoln. He was back among us, making decisions, giving commands. For a while it seemed we would almost be a family again. But it didn't turn out that way. He was not the same man. Something terrible had happened to him in North Dakota.

He arrived at Manzanar on a Greyhound bus. We all went down to the main gate to meet him, everyone but Woody's wife, Chizu, who was in the camp hospital. The previous day she'd given birth to Papa's first grandson. She named him George, in honor of Papa's return. Two of my sisters were pregnant at the time, and they were there at the gate in hot-weather smocks, along with Woody, who had left the hospital long enough to welcome Papa back, and Granny and Mama and the rest of the family, a dozen of us standing in the glare, excited, yet very reverent as the bus pulled in.

The door whished open, and the first thing we saw was a cane—I will never forget it—poking from the shaded interior into sunlight, a straight, polished maple limb spotted with dark lidded eyes where small knotholes had been stained and polished.

Then Papa stepped out, wearing a fedora hat and a wilted white shirt. This was September 1942. He had been gone nine months. He had aged ten years. He looked over sixty, gaunt, wilted as his shirt, underweight, leaning on that cane and favoring his right leg. He stood there surveying his clan, and nobody moved, not even Mama, waiting to see what he would do or say, waiting for some cue from him as to how we should deal with this.

I was the only one who approached him. I had not thought of him much at all after he was taken away. He was simply gone. Now I was so happy to see him that I ran up and threw my arms around his waist and buried my face in his belt. I thought I should be laughing and welcoming him home. But I started to cry. By this time everyone was crying. No one else had moved yet to touch him. It was as if the youngest, the least experienced, had been appointed to display what the others, held back by awe or fear, or some old-country notion of respect for the patriarch, could not. I hugged him tighter, wanting to be happy that my father had come back. Yet I hurt so inside I could only welcome him with convulsive tears.

4

The Circuit

Francisco Jiménez

It was that time of year again. Ito, the strawberry sharecropper, did not smile. It was natural. The peak of the strawberry season was over and the last few days the workers, most of them braceros, were not picking as many boxes as they had during the months of June and July.

As the last days of August disappeared, so did the number of braceros. Sunday, only one—the best picker—came to work. I liked him. Sometimes we talked during our half-hour lunch break. That is how I found out he was from Jalisco, the same state in Mexico my family was from. That Sunday was the last time I saw him.

When the sun had tired and sunk behind the mountains, Ito signaled us that it was time to go home. "Ya esora," he yelled in his broken Spanish. Those were the words I waited for twelve hours a day, every day, seven days a week, week after week. And the thought of not hearing them again saddened me.

As we drove home Papá did not say a word. With both hands on the wheel, he stared at the dirt road. My older brother, Roberto, was also silent. He leaned his head back and closed his eyes. Once in a while he cleared from his throat the dust that blew in from outside.

Yes, it was that time of year. When I opened the front door to the shack, I stopped. Everything we owned was neatly packed in cardboard boxes. Suddenly I felt even more the weight of hours, days, weeks, and months of work. I sat down on a box. The thought of having to move to Fresno and knowing what was in store for me there brought tears to my eyes.

That night I could not sleep. I lay in bed thinking about how much I hated this move.

A little before five o'clock in the morning, Papá woke everyone up. A few minutes later, the yelling and screaming of my little brothers and sisters, for whom the move was a great adventure, broke the silence of dawn. Shortly, the barking of the dogs accompanied them.

While we packed the breakfast dishes, Papá went outside to start the "Carcanchita." That was the name Papá gave his old '38 black Plymouth. He bought it in a used-car lot in Santa Rosa in the winter of 1949. Papá was very proud of his little jalopy. He had a right to be proud of it. He spent a lot of time looking at other cars before buying this one. When he finally chose the "Carcanchita," he checked it thoroughly before driving it out of the car lot. He examined every inch of the car. He listened to the motor, tilting his head from side to side like a parrot, trying to detect any noises that spelled car trouble. After being satisfied with the looks and sounds of the car, Papá then insisted on knowing who the original owner was. He never did find out from the car salesman, but he bought the car anyway. Papá figured the original owner must have been an important man because behind the rear seat of the car he found a blue necktie.

Papá parked the car out in front and left the motor running. "Listo," he yelled. Without saying a word, Roberto and I began to carry the boxes out to the car. Roberto carried the two big boxes and I carried the two smaller ones. Papá then threw the mattress on top of the car roof and tied it with ropes to the front and rear bumpers.

Everything was packed except Mamá's pot. It was an old large galvanized pot she had picked up at an army surplus store in Santa Maria the year I was born. The pot had many dents and nicks, and the more dents and nicks it acquired the more Mamá liked it. "Mi olla," she used to say proudly.

I held the front door open as Mamá carefully carried out her pot by both handles, making sure not to spill the cooked beans. When she got to the car, Papá reached out to help her with it. Roberto opened the rear car door and Papá gently placed it on the floor behind the front seat. All of us then climbed in. Papá sighed, wiped the sweat off his forehead with his sleeve, and said wearily: "Es todo."

As we drove away, I felt a lump in my throat. I turned around and looked at our little shack for the last time.

At sunset we drove into a labor camp near Fresno. Since Papá did not speak English, Mamá asked the camp foreman if he needed any more workers. "We don't need no more," said the foreman, scratching his head. "Check with Sullivan down the road. Can't miss him. He lives in a big white house with a fence around it."

When we got there, Mamá walked up to the house. She went through a white gate, past a row of rose bushes, up the stairs to the front door. She rang the doorbell. The porch light went on and a tall husky man came out. They exchanged a few words. After the man went in, Mamá clasped her hands and hurried back to the car. "We have work! Mr. Sullivan said we can stay there the whole season," she said, gasping and pointing to an old garage near the stables.

The garage was worn out by the years. It had no windows. The walls, eaten by termites, strained to support the roof full of holes. The dirt floor, populated by earth worms, looked like a gray road map.

That night, by the light of a kerosene lamp, we unpacked and cleaned our new home. Roberto swept away the loose dirt, leaving the hard ground. Papá plugged the holes in the walls with old newspapers and tin can tops. Mamá fed my little brothers and sisters. Papá and Roberto then brought in the mattress and placed it on the far corner of the garage. "Mamá, you and the little ones sleep on the mattress. Roberto, Panchito, and I will sleep outside under the trees," Papá said.

Early next morning Mr. Sullivan showed us where his crop was, and after breakfast, Papá, Roberto, and I headed for the vineyard to pick.

Around nine o'clock the temperature had risen to almost one hundred degrees. I was completely soaked in sweat and my mouth felt as if I had been chewing on a handkerchief. I walked over to the end of the row, picked up the jug of water we had brought, and began drinking. "Don't drink too much; you'll get sick," Roberto shouted. No sooner had he said that than I felt sick to my stomach. I dropped to my knees and let the jug roll off my hands. I remained motionless with my eyes glued on the hot sandy ground. All I could hear was the drone of insects. Slowly I began to recover. I poured water over my face and neck and watched the dirty water run down my arms to the ground.

I still felt a little dizzy when we took a break to eat lunch. It was past two o'clock and we sat underneath a large walnut tree that was on the side of the road. While we ate, Papá jotted down the number of boxes we had picked. Roberto drew designs on the ground with a stick. Suddenly I noticed Papá's face turn pale as he looked down the road. "Here comes the school bus," he whispered loudly in alarm. Instinctively, Roberto and I ran and hid in the vineyards. We did not want to get in trouble for not going to school. The neatly dressed boys about my age got off. They carried books under their arms. After they crossed the street, the bus drove away. Roberto and I came out from hiding and joined Papá. "Tienen que tener cuidado," he warned us.

After lunch we went back to work. The sun kept beating down. The buzzing insects, the wet sweat, and the hot dry dust made the afternoon seem to last forever. Finally the mountains around the valley reached out and swallowed the sun. Within an hour it was too dark to continue picking. The vines blanketed the grapes, making it difficult to see the bunches. "Vámonos," said Papá, signaling to us that it was time to quit work. Papá then took out a pencil and began to figure out how much we had earned our first day. He wrote down numbers, crossed some out, wrote down some more. "Quince," he murmured.

When we arrived home, we took a cold shower underneath a water-hose. We then sat down to eat dinner around some wooden crates that served as a table. Mamá had cooked a special meal for us. We had rice and tortillas with "carne con chile," my favorite dish.

The next morning I could hardly move. My body ached all over. I felt little control over my arms and legs. This feeling went on every morning for days until my muscles finally got used to the work.

It was Monday, the first week of November. The grape season was over and I could now go to school. I woke up early that morning and lay in bed, looking at the stars and savoring the thought of not going to work and of starting sixth grade for the first time that year. Since I could not sleep, I decided to get up and join Papá and Roberto at breakfast. I sat at the table across from Roberto, but I kept my head down. I did not want to look up and face him. I knew he was sad. He was not going to school today. He was not going tomorrow, or next week, or next month. He would not go until the cotton season was over, and that was sometime in February. I rubbed my hands together and watched the dry, acid stained skin fall to the floor in little rolls.

When Papá and Roberto left for work, I felt relief. I walked to the top of a small grade next to the shack and watched the "Carcanchita" disappear in the distance in a cloud of dust.

Two hours later, around eight o'clock, I stood by the side of the road waiting for school bus number twenty. When it arrived I climbed in. Everyone was busy either talking or yelling. I sat in an empty seat in the back.

When the bus stopped in front of the school, I felt very nervous. I looked out the bus window and saw boys and girls carrying books under their arms. I put my hands in my pant pockets and walked to the principal's office. When I entered I heard a woman's voice say: "May I help you?" I was startled. I had not heard English for months. For a few seconds I remained speechless. I looked at the lady who waited for an answer. My first instinct was to answer her in Spanish, but I held back. Finally, after struggling for English words, I managed to tell her that I wanted to enroll in the sixth grade. After answering many questions, I was led to the classroom.

Mr. Lema, the sixth grade teacher, greeted me and assigned me a desk. He then introduced me to the class. I was so nervous and scared at that moment when everyone's eyes were on me that I wished I were with Papá and Roberto picking cotton. After taking roll, Mr. Lema gave the class the assignment for the first hour. "The first thing we have to do this morning is finish reading the story we began yesterday," he said enthusiastically. He walked up to me, handed me an English book, and asked me to read. "We are on page 125," he said politely. When I heard this, I felt my blood rush to my head; I felt dizzy. "Would you like to read?" he asked hesitantly. I opened the book to page 125. My mouth was dry. My eyes began to water. I could not begin. "You can read later," Mr. Lema said understandingly.

For the rest of the reading period I kept getting angrier and angrier with myself. I should have read, I thought to myself.

During recess I went into the restroom and opened my English book to page 125. I began to read in a low voice, pretending I was in class. There were many words I did not know. I closed the book and headed back to the classroom.

Mr. Lema was sitting at his desk correcting papers. When I entered he looked up at me and smiled. I felt better. I walked up to him and asked if he could help me with the new words. "Gladly," he said.

The rest of the month I spent my lunch hours working on English with Mr. Lema, my best friend at school.

One Friday during lunch hour Mr. Lema asked me to take a walk with him to the music room. "Do you like music?" he asked me as we entered the building.

"Yes, I like corridos," I answered. He then picked up a trumpet, blew on it and handed it to me. The sound gave me goose bumps. I knew that sound. I had heard it in many corridos. "How would you like to learn how to play it?" he asked. He must have read my face because before I could answer, he added: "I'll teach you how to play it during our lunch hours."

That day I could hardly wait to tell Papá and Mamá the great news. As I got off the bus, my little brothers and sisters ran up to meet me. They were yelling and screaming. I thought they were happy to see me, but when I opened the door to our shack, I saw that everything we owned was neatly packed in cardboard boxes.

5

The Puerto Rican Community in the South Bronx:

Contradictory Views from Within and Without

Clara E. Rodriguez

The South Bronx in New York City has always been home to me. As a young girl growing up in the southern-most part of the South Bronx, I was surrounded by a stable family and a sense of community. I was part of a sizable and dynamic Puerto Rican community. However, the South Bronx was viewed, even when I was a child, as a place where only "the poorest of the poor" lived (*New York Times*, November 2, 1950).

My earliest recollection of my neighborhood is of an energetic and alive community with a great deal of social interaction. I recall being wheeled with my sister in a huge baby carriage in front of what the *New York Times* would subsequently call those "solid, grimy five-story tenements." My parents would stop to converse with neighbors, chatting about people and life in the neighborhood. We were part of a network of people who knew each other well and who helped each other.

My South Bronx had a richness of life, a dynamism and stability of relations that few other places have. However, as I matured, I came to understand that the world beyond my community's boundaries had a different view of us. That world saw us as "different" and poor. It was a world that was often instinctively hostile or afraid of us. Yet, I never felt poor, deprived, or disadvantaged. I also never understood what inspired hostility, particularly hostility toward those I held dear. I never accepted it as right.

At an early age I came to puzzle over this contradiction, that is, why the view from within was so different from the view from without; why hostility, fear, or disrespect should exist without cause. This developed in me a basic curiosity about

166

the view of those affected and the factors that affected them, or, in other words, about the interaction of micro- and macroprocesses.

The world within which I grew up was not all roses and *pasteles* (a festive Puerto Rican dish). My childhood was as full of traumas, joys, and disappointments as the next person's. There were the usual struggles to survive that all people who have little money or who have strong differences of culture, color, and language experience. Life was hard, but life was manageable. As I was growing up, I witnessed my community and others like it destroyed by forces over which the Puerto Rican community has little control, the forces of urban decay: drugs, urban renewal, and housing abandonment.

The extent of the housing decline and urban devastation is made dramatic by the following data. Between 1970 and 1980, the Bronx and Brooklyn, the two New York City boroughs with the largest Puerto Rican populations, accounted for more than 80 percent of housing units either abandoned or destroyed in the *entire country*. During this time, the South Bronx, which has the largest Puerto Rican community in the United States, lost 27,763 units of housing, or 10.5 percent of all its housing stock. Additional buildings that had roofs but were abandoned and not inhabited were not included in this count. Moreover, a high proportion of Puerto Ricans still residing there live in units with three or more maintenance deficiencies and live in areas with boarded-up buildings on their blocks.

What were some of the reasons behind this dramatic urban decay? Foremost were the redlining policies of insurance companies and banks, which made very little money available for local residential development, and the policies of the federal government, which emphasized highway construction and suburban residential development while ignoring local residential development. Other reasons included the failure of local government policy, arson for profit, rent control (which did not allow a large enough profit for the maintenance of buildings), drug trafficking and other crimes, poorly planned housing projects, and the gutting of neighborhoods for the construction of the Cross Bronx Expressway. Because the loss of housing was not evenly distributed across the South Bronx, certain neighborhoods were hit hard and swept with devastation, leaving local landscapes with one or two buildings as lone survivors in an unabated process of destruction. The dynamism and stability of the communities of the South Bronx had been severely damaged by external forces.

Not all Puerto Ricans fled; some fought to maintain their neighborhoods, fought drug dealers, and organized to get support from the city and federal governments. Currently, the decline has slowed and signs of revitalization have appeared. The South Bronx has bottomed out, but the history lived there will remain a bitter chapter for all concerned. . . .

6

"Nopalitos":
The Making of Fiction

Helena Maria Viramontes

Fiction is my jugular. For me it is a great consolation to know that whatever miserable things happen in my lifetime, goodness will inevitably result because I will write about it. There is strength in this when none is left in the soul.

I was born and raised in the U.S., East L.A., Califas, to be more exact, on First Street not too far from Whittier Blvd., close enough to enable me to see the smoke from the Chicano Moratorium riots. I come from a family of eleven, six sisters and three brothers, but the family always extended its couch or floor to whomever stopped at our house with nowhere else to go. As a result, a variety of people came to live with us. Former boyfriends of my sisters who were thrown or pushed out of their own homes, friends who stayed the night but never left, relatives who crossed the border and stayed until enough was saved. Through all this I remember two things well: first, the late night kitchen meetings where everyone talked and laughed in low voices, played cards, talked of loneliness, plans for the future, of loves lost or won. I heard men cry, drunken stories, women laughing. It was fascinating to listen in the dark, peek into the moments of their lives. For me, it seemed like a dream to wake up at midnight and hear the voices and listen to the soft music, see the light under the door. This was adulthood and I yearned to one day be the one on the other side of that door.

Little did I realize that this is the stuff good fiction is made of: the stories, the fascination of the subject matter, capturing the moments and fleeing with them like a thief or lover. I began my apprenticeship without even knowing it.

The other thing I remember is my mother. Her relentless energy. She must have been tired a good part of her life and yet she had to keep going and going and going. I also remember her total kindness, the way a sad story made her cry, the way she always found room somehow in an already-crowded household for those with the sad stories. The nights she would stay up, a small black and white T.V. blaring, waiting for the girls to come home. The mornings she would get up, KWKW Spanish radio low, making the big stack of tortillas for the morning breakfast.

These two things, love of stories and love of my mother, or all that seemed female in our household, influenced me to such an extent that it became an unconscious part of me, so unconscious that I didn't realize it until just moments ago. In fact, the first story that I wrote, titled "Requiem for the Poor," opened with my mother awaking to make breakfast. To think: she was the first image in my mind, my heart, my hand. Naturally.

If my mother was the fiber that held a family together, it was my father who kept snapping it with his oppressive cruelty. With virtually no education, stressed with the responsibility of supporting such a large family, he worked as a hod carrier—a carrier of cement in construction. He drank, and was mean. Impatient, screaming a lot of the time, temper tantrums, we were often trembling in his presence. If my mother showed all that is good in being female, my father showed all that is bad in being male. I'm only now understanding the depth of this conclusion, and am making a serious effort to erase this black and white. See the good and bad in both sexes. That's the power of imagination, peeking beyond the fence of your personal reality and seeing the possibilities thereafter.

A basic problem for any writer is time. I lament the lack of time. As I pass my shelves of books, I think, these are books I will never read; or as my notebooks pile up, spilling over with plots, characters, great and moving sentences, I think, these are the words that will never find a story. Ideally, it would be bliss to manipulate the economic conditions of our lives and thus free our minds, our hands, to write. But there is no denying that this is a privilege limited to a certain sex, race, and class. The only bad thing about privilege, Virginia Woolf wrote (I'm paraphrasing from Tillie Olsen) was that not every one could have it.

How does one solve the problem of time? Fortunately, we mujeres are an inventive people. My mother, for example, faced the challenge of feeding eleven people every evening. Time and time again, I saw her cut four pork chops, add this and that and this, pour water, and miraculously feed all of us with a tasty guiso. Or the nopales she grew, cleaned, diced, scrambled with eggs, or meat, or chile, or really mixed with anything her budget could afford, and we had such a variety of tasty dishes!

I have never been able to match her nopales, but I have inherited her capacity for invention. I myself invent time by first conjuring up the voices and spirits of the women living under brutal repressive regimes. In the light of their reality, my struggles for a few hours of silence seem like such a petty problem. I am humbled, and no sooner do I think of their courage than I find my space on the kitchen table, my time long after midnight and before the start of the children's hectic morning. Because I want to do justice to their voices. To tell these women, in my own gentle way, that I will fight for them, that they provide me with my own source of humanity. That I love them, their children. Once seen in this perspective, the lack of sleep is more of an inconvenience than a sacrifice.

What little time we do invent we guard like our children. Interruption is a fact in our lives and is as common as pennies. Solely because we are women. A man who aspires to write is sanctioned by society. It is an acceptable and noble endeavor. As for us, writing is seen as a hobby we do after all our responsibilities are fulfilled. Nay, to write while the baby is crying is a crime punishable by guilt. Guilt is our Achilles' heel. Thus the work of the mujer suffers immensely, for the leisure of returning to her material, to rework it, polish it, is almost impossible. Because phones will ring, children will cry, or mothers will ask for favors. My mother, it seemed for a time, believed me to be half-baked for wanting desperately to write. It was inconceivable to her that I spent mornings scratching a sharpened pencil against paper. She would stand and look over my shoulder, try to read a paragraph or two, and seeing that I was simply wasting my time staring into space, she'd ask me to go get some tortillas, or could you vacuum the living room, maybe water the plants outside? After turning her away with a harsh no, guilt would engulf me like a blob, and although I hated myself for doing it, there I was, once again, holding a garden hose, watering her roses.

We must come to understand that stifling a woman's imagination is too costly a price to pay for servitude. The world would be void of any depth or true comprehension if we were not allowed to exercise our imaginations. We must challenge those beliefs which oppress us within our family, our culture, in addition to those in the dominant culture.

Family ties are fierce. Especially for mujeres. We are raised to care for. We are raised to stick together, for the family unit is our only source of safety. Outside our home there lies a dominant culture that is foreign to us, isolates us, and labels us illegal alien. But what may be seen as a nurturing, close unit, may also become suffocating, manipulative, and sadly victimizing. As we slowly examine our own existence in and out of these cultures, we are breaking stereotypes, reinventing traditions for our own daughters and sons.

What a courageous task! In the past, we have been labeled as the weaker sex, and it is logical to assume that we are of weaker minds as well. As women, we have learned to listen, rather than speak, causing us, historically, to join with others who maintain we have nothing to say. Only now we are discovering that we do. And those who do not seem interested in knowing our voices are just plain foolish. To limit their knowledge of people, places, cultures, and sexes is to live in a narrow, colorless world. It is not only a tragedy, but just plain silly, for only foolish people would not be interested in embracing such knowledge.

We can not, nor will we divorce ourselves from our families. But we need a change in their attitudes. If I am to succeed as a writer, I need my family to respect my time, my words, myself. This goes for my parents, brothers, sisters, my children, my husband. Respectability is a long and sometimes nasty struggle. But you'd be surprised at the progress one can make. Eventually, my mother proved to be very flexible. When I signed my first honorarium over to her, she discreetly placed it in her pocket. Later, as I spread my notebooks over the dining room table, she carried in a steaming cup of coffee, sweetened just the way I like it.

Now for some nopalitos.

My tio Rogelio was one of those who stayed for years. I became his consentida, he my best friend, until other interests developed in my life. He eventually moved and the distance between his house and mine became so far it took years to get together again. Recently, he visited me and was astonished to find that I spoke only in English. Straightforward, as has always been his manner, he asked me: "Why don't you speak Spanish anymore?"

Good question. What happened? I did as a child, I know only from others' recollection, but what happened? Somewhere along the educational system I lost it, and with it I lost a part of me. Yes, I can communicate all right now, but to feel that it is my own, to feel comfortable enough to write in it, that's what I am missing. As a result, I will not be a whole person until I reacquire this part of me. For you see, a good part of my upbringing was in Spanish. Spanish images, words, moods that I feel I must explore before they are buried for good.

Of course English is my language too. I'm entitled to it, though it is the one I have learned artificially. But having Spanish stolen from me is lingual censorship. A repression that reveals to me the power of the language itself.

Consequently, I do not feel comfortable in either language. In fact, I majored in English and acquired a degree to erase what Lorna Dee Cervantes calls "my excuse me tongue." However, my English is often awkward, and clumsy, and it is this awkwardness that I struggle so hard with. But isn't that what writing is all about? The struggle with the word for the perfect meaning? Sometimes my mistakes turn out to be my best writing. Sometimes I think in Spanish and translate. Sometimes I go through the dictionary and acquaint myself with words I wouldn't otherwise use in conversation. Sometimes I am thrilled by the language and play with its implications. And sometimes I hate it, not feeling comfortable.

And yet, I am amazed when people say one of my greatest strengths is my language. Funny, no? I was also recently informed that my book, *The Moths and Other Stories*, will be included as required reading in the English Department's qualifying exam for the Ph.D. program at University of Texas, Austin.

I still say that if my works were translated into Spanish, they would somehow feel better. More, more, what's the word? At home.

In my case, Faulkner was right; I became a short story writer because I was a failed poet. But when I began to write, I honestly went into it rather blindly. I never once thought of a potential audience. Perhaps just starting out, I didn't have the confidence to think that people would actually be interested in reading it. I wrote what was natural, personal to me. I showed my work to Chicanas mostly, and since they related to it, they became supportive and thrilled at what I was doing. And the more they were thrilled and supportive, the more I wrote.

By that time, I had discovered the Latin American writers: Borges, García Márquez, Rulfo, Yañez, to name a few. Their exploration with form and voice was a thrilling experiment in modern fiction, I felt, and was eager to try my hand at it. It was a rebellion against accepted rules that, in essence, reflected their politics as well. Like Faulkner, they sought to see what they could get away with, and, as a result, gave birth to such a rich texture of literature that it is a sheer celebration to read.

This is where I got my angst for form, technique. But my worldview was obviously a different one because I was a Chicana. Once I discovered the Black women writers—Walker, Morrison, Brooks, Shange, again to name a few— womanism as subject matter seemed sanctioned, illuminating, innovative, honest, the best in recent fiction that I've seen in a long time.

Subject matter and form. They met, became lovers, often quarrelled, but nonetheless, Helena Maria Viramontes was born.

As Chicanas, we must continue to have the courage to examine our lives. Some- times, when I see all that goes on around me, I begin to question the importance of fiction and its value against the face of a starving child. Yet, we continue to write. Perhaps it is because we have such a strong belief in the power of the written word. It is a link which bonds us. Their starvation becomes mine, their death becomes mine. Our destiny is not embedded in cement. We can determine its destination. Some use the soapbox, others, weapons. I choose to write.

I am genuinely happy to be a part of a growing, nurturing group of writers, radical women of color who are not afraid to explore culture, politics, humanity, womanism, not afraid to sabotage the stereotypes with whatever words are necessary to get the job done.

7

Suicide Note

Janice Mirikitani

. . . An Asian American college student was reported to have jumped to her death from her dormitory window. Her body was found two days later under a deep cover of snow. Her suicide note contained an apology to her parents for having received less than a perfect four point grade average . . .

> How many notes written . . .
> ink smeared like birdprints in snow.

>   not good enough   not pretty enough   not smart enough
> dear mother and father.
> I apologize
> for disappointing you.
> I've worked very hard,

        not good enough
harder, perhaps to please you.
If only I were a son, shoulders broad
as the sunset threading through pine,
I would see the light in my mother's
eyes, or the golden pride reflected
in my father's dream
of my wide, male hands worthy of work
and comfort.
I would swagger through life
muscled and bold and assured,
drawing praises to me
like currents in the bed of wind, virile
with confidence.
        not good enough   not strong enough   not good enough

I apologize.
Tasks do not come easily.
Each failure, a glacier.
Each disapproval, a bootprint.
Each disappointment,
ice above my river.
So I have worked hard.
            not good enough
My sacrifice I will drop
bone by bone, perched
on the ledge of my womanhood,
fragile as wings.
            not strong enough
It is snowing steadily
surely not good weather
for flying—this sparrow
sillied and dizzied by the wind
on the edge.
            not smart enough
I make this ledge my altar
to offer penance.
This air will not hold me,
the snow burdens my crippled wings,
my tears drop like bitter cloth
softly into the gutter below.
        not good enough   not strong enough   not smart enough

        Choices thin as shaved

ice. Notes shredded
drift like snow

on my broken body,
covers me like whispers
of sorries
sorries.
Perhaps when they find me
they will bury
my bird bones beneath
a sturdy pine
and scatter my feathers like
unspoken song
over this white and cold and silent
breast of earth.

The Gap between Striving and Achieving:
The Case of Asian American Women

Deborah Woo

Much academic research on Asian Americans tends to underscore their success, a success which is attributed almost always to a cultural emphasis on education, hard work, and thrift. Less familiar is the story of potential not fully realized. For example, despite the appearance of being successful and highly educated, Asian American women do not necessarily gain the kind of recognition or rewards they deserve.

The story of unfulfilled dreams remains unwritten for many Asian Americans. It is specifically this story about the gap between striving and achieving that I am concerned with here. Conventional wisdom obscures the discrepancy by looking primarily at whether society is adequately rewarding individuals. By comparing how minorities as disadvantaged groups are doing relative to each other, the tendency is to view Asian Americans as a "model minority." This practice programs us to ignore structural barriers and inequities and to insist that any problems are simply due to different cultural values or failure of individual effort.

Myths about the Asian American community derive from many sources. All ethnic groups develop their own cultural myths. Sometimes, however, they create myths out of historical necessity, as a matter of subterfuge and survival. Chinese Americans, for example, were motivated to create new myths because institutional opportunities were closed off to them. Succeeding in America meant they had to invent fake aspects of an "Oriental culture," which became the beginning of the Chinatown tourist industry.

What has been referred to as the "model minority myth," however, essentially originated from without. The idea that Asian Americans have been a successful group has been a popular news media theme for the last twenty years. It has become a basis for cutbacks in governmental support for all ethnic minorities—for Asian Americans because they apparently are already successful as a group; for other ethnic minorities because they are presumably not working as hard as Asian Americans or they would not need assistance. Critics of this view argue that the portrayal of Asian Americans as socially and economically successful ignores fundamental inequities. That is, the question "Why have Asians been successful vis-à-vis other minorities?" has been asked at the expense of another equally important question: "What has kept Asians from *fully* reaping the fruits of their education and hard work?"

The achievements of Asian Americans are part reality, part myth. Part of the reality is that a highly visible group of Asian Americans are college-educated, occupationally well-situated, and earning relatively high incomes. The myth, however, is that hard work reaps commensurate rewards. This essay documents the gap between the level of education and subsequent occupational or income gains.

The Roots and Contours of the "Model Minority" Concept

Since World War II, social researchers and news media personnel have been quick to assert that Asian Americans excel over other ethnic groups in terms of earnings, education, and occupation. Asian Americans are said to save more, study more, work more, and so achieve more. The reason given: a cultural emphasis on education and hard work. Implicit in this view is a social judgment and moral injunction: if Asian Americans can make it on their own, why can't other minorities?

While the story of Asian American women workers is only beginning to be pieced together, the success theme is already being sung. The image prevails that despite cultural and racial oppression, they are somehow rapidly assimilating into the mainstream. As workers, they participate in the labor force at rates higher than all others, including Anglo women. Those Asian American women who pursue higher education surpass other women, and even men, in this respect. Moreover, they have acquired a reputation for not only being conscientious and industrious but docile, compliant, and uncomplaining as well.

In the last few decades American women in general have been demanding "equal pay for equal work," the legitimation of housework as work that needs to be recompensed, and greater representation in the professional fields. These demands, however, have not usually come from Asian American women. From the perspective of those in power, this reluctance to complain is another feature of the "model minority." But for those who seek to uncover employment abuses, the unwillingness to talk about problems on the job is itself a problem. The garment industry, for example, is a major area of exploitation, yet it is also one that is difficult to investigate and control. In a 1983 report on the Concentrated Employment Program of the California Department of Industrial Relations, it was noted:

> The major problem for investigators in San Francisco is that the Chinese community is very close-knit, and employers and employees cooperate in refusing to speak to investigators. In two years of enforcing the Garment Registration Act, the CEP has never received a complaint from an Asian employee. The few complaints received have been from Anglo or Latin workers.[1]

While many have argued vociferously either for or against the model minority concept, Asian Americans in general have been ambivalent in this regard. Asian Americans experience pride in achievement born of hard work and self-sacrifice, but at the same time, they resist the implication that all is well. Data provided here indicate that Asian Americans have not been successful in terms of benefitting fully, (i.e., monetarily), from their education. It is a myth that Asian Americans have proven the American Dream. How does this myth develop?

The working consumer: income and cost of living.   One striking feature about Asian Americans is that they are geographically concentrated in areas where both income and cost of living are very high. In 1970, 80 percent of the total Asian American population resided in five states—California, Hawaii, Illinois, New York, and Washington. Furthermore, 59 percent of Chinese, Filipino, and Japanese Americans were concentrated in only 5 of the 243 Standard Metropolitan Statistical Areas (SMSA) in the United States—Chicago, Honolulu, Los Angeles/Long Beach, New York, and San Francisco/Oakland.[2] The 1980 census shows that immigration during the intervening decade has not only produced dramatic increases, especially in the Filipino and Chinese populations, but has also continued the overwhelming tendency for these groups to concentrate in the same geographical areas, especially those in California.[3] Interestingly enough, the very existence of large Asian communities in the West has stimulated among more recent refugee populations what is now officially referred to as "secondary migration," that is, the movement of refugees away from their sponsoring communities (usually places where there was no sizable Asian population prior to their own arrival) to those areas where there are well-established Asian communities.[4]

This residential pattern means that while Asian Americans may earn more by living in high-income areas, they also pay more as consumers. The additional earning power gained from living in San Francisco or Los Angeles, say, is absorbed by the high cost of living in such cities. National income averages which compare the income of Asian American women with that of the more broadly dispersed Anglo women systematically distort the picture. Indeed, if we compare women within the same area, Asian American women are frequently less well-off than Anglo American females, and the difference between women pales when compared with Anglo males, whose mean income is much higher than that of any group of women.[5]

When we consider the large immigrant Asian population and the language barriers that restrict women to menial or entry-level jobs, we are talking about a group that not only earns minimum wage or less, but one whose purchasing power is substantially undermined by living in metropolitan areas of states where the cost of living is unusually high.

Another striking pattern about Asian American female employment is the high rate of labor force participation. Asian American women are more likely than Anglo American women to work full time and year round. The model minority interpretation tends to assume that mere high labor force participation is a sign of successful employment. One important factor motivating minority women to enter the work force, however, is the need to supplement family resources. For Anglo American women some of the necessity for working is partly offset by the fact that they often share in the higher incomes of Anglo males, who tend not only to earn more than all other groups but, as noted earlier, also tend to receive higher returns on their education. Moreover, once regional variation is adjusted for, Filipino and Chinese Americans had a median annual income equivalent to black males in four mainland SMSAs—Chicago, Los Angeles/Long Beach, New York, San Francisco/Oakland.[6] Census statistics point to the relatively lower earning capacity of Asian males compared to Anglo males, suggesting that Asian American women enter the work force to help compensate for this inequality. Thus, the mere fact of high employment must be read cautiously and analyzed within a larger context.

The different faces of immigration. Over the last decade immigration has expanded the Chinese population by 85.3 percent, making it the largest Asian group in the country at 806,027, and has swelled the Filipino population by 125.8 percent, making it the second largest at 774,640. Hence at present the majority of Chinese American and Filipino American women are foreign-born. In addition the Asian American "success story" is misleading in part because of a select group of these immigrants: foreign-educated professionals.

Since 1965 U.S. immigration laws have given priority to seven categories of individuals. Two of the seven allow admittance of people with special occupational skills or services needed in the United States. Four categories facilitate family reunification, and the last applies only to refugees. While occupation is estimated to account for no more than 20 percent of all visas, professionals are not precluded from entering under other preference categories. Yet this select group is frequently offered as evidence of the upward mobility possible in America when Asian Americans who are born and raised in the United States are far less likely to reach the doctoral level in their education. Over two-thirds of Asians with doctorates in the United States are trained and educated abroad.[7]

Also overlooked in some analyses is a great deal of downward mobility among the foreign-born. For example, while foreign-educated health professionals are given preferential status for entry into this country, restrictive licensing requirements deny them the opportunity to practice or utilize their special skills. They are told that their educational credentials, experience, and certifications are inadequate. Consequently, for many the only alternatives are menial labor or unemployment.[8] Other highly educated immigrants become owner/managers of Asian businesses, which also suggests downward mobility and an inability to find jobs in their field of expertise.

"Professional" obscures more than it reveals.   Another major reason for the perception of "model minority" is that the census categories implying success, "professional-managerial" or "executive, administrative, managerial," frequently camouflage important inconsistencies with this image of success. As managers, Asian Americans, usually male, are concentrated in certain occupations. They tend to be self-employed in small-scale wholesale and retail trade and manufacturing. They are rarely buyers, sales managers, administrators, or salaried managers in large-scale retail trade, communications, or public utilities. Among foreign-born Asian women, executive-managerial status is limited primarily to auditors and accountants.[9]

In general, Asian American women with a college education are concentrated in narrow and select, usually less prestigious, rungs of the "professional-managerial" class. In 1970, 27 percent of native-born Japanese women were either elementary or secondary school teachers. Registered nurses made up the next largest group. Foreign-born Filipino women found this to be their single most important area of employment, with 19 percent being nurses. They were least represented in the more prestigious professions—physicians, judges, dentists, law professors, and lawyers.[10] In 1980 foreign-born Asian women with four or more years of college were most likely to find jobs in administrative support or clerical occupations.

Self-help through "taking care of one's own."   Much of what is considered ideal or model behavior in American society is based on Anglo-Saxon, Protestant values. Chief among them is an ethic of individual self-help, of doing without outside assistance or governmental support. On the other hand, Asian Americans have historically relied to a large extent on family or community resources. Their tightly-knit communities tend to be fairly closed to the outside world, even when under economic hardship. Many below the poverty level do not receive any form of public assistance.[11] Even if we include social security benefits as a form of supplementary income, the proportion of Asian Americans who use them is again very low, much lower than that for Anglo Americans.[12] Asian American families, in fact, are more likely than Anglo American families to bear economic hardships on their own.

While Asian Americans appear to have been self-sufficient as communities, we need to ask, at what personal cost? Moreover, have they as a group reaped rewards commensurate with their efforts? The following section presents data which document that while Asian American women may be motivated to achieve through education, monetary returns for them are less than for other groups.

The Nature of Inequality

The decision to use white males as the predominant reference group within the United States is a politically charged issue. When women raise and push the issue of "comparable worth," of "equal pay for equal work," they argue that women frequently do work equivalent to men's, but are paid far less for it.

The same argument can be made for Asian American women, and the evidence of inequality is staggering. For example, after adjustments are made for occupational prestige, age, education, weeks worked, hours worked each week, and state of residence in 1975, Chinese American women could be expected to earn only 70 percent of the majority male income. Even among the college-educated, Chinese American women fared least well, making only 42 percent of what majority males earned. As we noted earlier, the mean income of all women, Anglo and Asian, was far below that of Anglo males in 1970 and 1980. This was true for both native-born and foreign-born Asians. In 1970 Anglo women earned only 54 percent of what their male counterparts did. Native-born Asian American women, depending on the particular ethnic group, earned anywhere from 49 to 57 percent of what Anglo males earned. In 1980, this inequity persisted.

Another way of thinking about comparable worth is not to focus only on what individuals do on the job, but on what they bring to the job as well. Because formal education is one measure of merit in American society and because it is most frequently perceived as the means to upward mobility, we would expect greater education to have greater payoffs.

Asian American women tend to be extraordinarily successful in terms of attaining higher education. Filipino American women have the highest college completion rate of all women and graduate at a rate 50 percent greater than that of majority males. Chinese American and Japanese American women follow closely behind, exceeding both the majority male and female rate of college completion.[13] Higher levels of education, however, bring lower returns for Asian American women than they do for other groups.

While education enhances earnings capability, the return on education for Asian American women is not as great as that for other women, and is well below parity with white males. Data on Asian American women in the five SMSAs where they are concentrated bear this out.[14] In 1980 all these women fell far behind Anglo males in what they earned in relation to their college education. Between 8 and 16 percent of native-born women earned $21,200 compared to 50 percent of Anglo males. Similar patterns were found among college-educated foreign-born women.

The fact that Asian American women do not reap the income benefits one might expect given their high levels of educational achievement raises questions about the reasons for such inequality. To what extent is this discrepancy based on outright discrimination? On self-imposed limitations related to cultural modesty? The absence of certain social or interpersonal skills required for upper managerial positions? Or institutional factors beyond their control? It is beyond the scope of this paper to address such concerns. However, the fact of inequality is itself noteworthy and poorly appreciated.

In general, Asian American women usually are overrepresented in clerical or administrative support jobs. While there is a somewhat greater tendency for foreign-born college-educated Asian women to find clerical-related jobs, both native- and foreign-born women have learned that clerical work is the area where they are most easily employed. In fact, in 1970 a third of native-born Chinese women were doing clerical work. A decade later Filipino women were concentrated there. In addition Asian American women tend to be overrepresented as cashiers, file clerks, office machine operators, and typists. They are less likely to get jobs as secretaries or receptionists. The former occupations not only carry less prestige but generally have "little or no decision-making authority, low mobility and low public contact."[15]

In short, education may improve one's chances for success, but it cannot promise the American Dream. For Asian American women education seems to serve less as an opportunity for upward mobility than as protection against jobs as service or assembly workers, or as machine operatives—all areas where foreign-born Asian women are far more likely to find themselves.

Conclusion

In this essay I have attempted to direct our attention on the gap between achievement and reward, specifically the failure to reward monetarily those who have demonstrated competence. Asian American women, like Asian American men, have been touted as "model minorities," praised for their outstanding achievements. The concept of model minority, however, obscures the fact that one's accomplishments are not adequately recognized in terms of commensurate income or choice of occupation. By focusing on the achievements of one minority in relation to another, our attention is diverted from larger institutional and historical factors which influence a group's success. Each ethnic group has a different history, and a simplistic method of modeling which assumes the experience of all immigrants is the same ignores the sociostructural context in which a certain kind of achievement occurred. For example, World War II enabled many Asian Americans who were technically trained and highly educated to move into lucrative war-related industries.[16] More recently, Korean immigrants during the 1960s were able to capitalize on the fast-growing demand for wigs in the United States. It was not simply cultural ingenuity or individual hard work which made them successful in this enterprise, but the fact that Korean immigrants were in the unique position of being able to import cheap hair products from their mother country.[17]

Just as there are structural opportunities, so there are structural barriers. However, the persistent emphasis in American society on individual effort deflects attention away from such barriers and creates self-doubt among those who have not "made it." The myth that Asian Americans have succeeded as a group, when in actuality there are serious discrepancies between effort and achievement, and between achievement and reward, adds still further to this self-doubt.

While others have also pointed out the myth of the model minority, I want to add that myths do have social functions. It would be a mistake to dismiss the model minority concept as merely a myth. Asian Americans are—however inappropriately—thrust into the role of being models for other minorities.

A closer look at the images associated with Asians as a model minority group suggests competing or contradictory themes. One image is that Asian Americans exemplify a competitive spirit enabling them to overcome structural barriers through perseverance and ingenuity. On the other hand, they are also seen as complacent, content with their social lot, and expecting little in the way of outside help. A third image is that Asian Americans are experts at assimilation, demonstrating that this society still functions as a melting pot. Their values are sometimes equated with white, middle-class, Protestant values of hard work, determination, and thrift. Opposing this image, however, is still another, namely that Asian Americans have succeeded because they possess cultural values unique to them as a group—their family-centeredness and long tradition of reverence for scholarly achievement, for example.

Perhaps, then, this is why so many readily accept the myth, whose tenacity is due to its being vague and broad enough to appeal to a variety of different groups. Yet to the extent that the myth is based on misconceptions, we are called upon to reexamine it more closely in an effort to narrow the gap between striving and achieving.[18]

NOTES

1. Ted Bell, "Quiet Loyalty Keeps Shops Running," *Sacramento Bee*, 11 February 1985.

2. Amado Y. Cabezas and Pauline L. Fong, "Employment Status of Asian-Pacific Women" (Background paper; San Francisco: ASIAN, Inc., 1976).

3. U.S. Bureau of the Census, *Race of the Population by States* (Washington, D.C., 1980). According to the census, 40 percent of all Chinese in America live in California, as well as 46 percent of all Filipinos, and 37 percent of all Japanese. New York ranks second for the number of Chinese residing there, and Hawaii is the second most populated state for Filipinos and Japanese.

4. Tricia Knoll, *Becoming Americans: Asian Sojourners, Immigrants, and Refugees in the Western United States* (Portland, Oreg.: Coast to Coast Books, 1982), 152.

5. U.S. Commission on Civil Rights, *Social Indicators of Equality for Minorities and Women* (Washington, D.C., 1978), 24, 50, 54, 58, 62.

6. David M. Moulton, "The Socioeconomic Status of Asian American Families in Five Major SMSAs" (Paper prepared for the Conference of Pacific and Asian American Families and HEW-related Issues, San Francisco, 1978). No comparative data were available on blacks for the fifth SMSA, Honolulu.

7. James E. Blackwell, *Mainstreaming Outsiders* (New York: General Hall, Inc., 1981), 306; and Commission on Civil Rights, *Social Indicators*, 9.

8. California Advisory Committee, "A Dream Unfulfilled: Korean and Filipino Health Professionals in California" (Report prepared for submission to U.S. Commission on Civil Rights, May 1975), iii.

9. See Amado Y. Cabezas, "A View of Poor Linkages between Education, Occupation and Earnings for Asian Americans" (Paper presented at the Third National Forum on Education and Work, San Francisco, 1977), 17; and Census of Population, PUS, 1980.

10. Census of the Population, PUS, 1970, 1980.

11. A 1977 report on California families showed that an average of 9.3 percent of Japanese, Chinese, and Filipino families were below the poverty level, but that only 5.4 percent of these families received public assistance. The corresponding figures for Anglos were 6.3 percent and 5.9 percent. From Harold T. Yee, "The General Level of Well-Being of Asian Americans" (Paper presented to U.S. government officials in partial response to Justice Department amicus).

12. Moulton, "Socioeconomic Status," 70–71.

13. Commission on Civil Rights, *Social Indicators*, 54.

14. The few exceptions occur in Honolulu with women who had more than a high school education and in Chicago with women who had a high school education or three years of college. Even these women fared poorly when compared to men, however.

15. Bob H. Suzuki, "Education and the Socialization of Asian Americans: A Revisionist Analysis of the 'Model Minority' Thesis," *Amerasia Journal* 4:2 (1977): 43. See also Fong and Cabezas, "Economic and Employment Status," 48–49; and Commission on Civil Rights, *Social Indicators*, 97–98.

16. U.S. Commission on Civil Rights, "Education Issues" in *Civil Rights Issues of Asian and Pacific Americans: Myths and Realities* (Washington, D.C., 1979), 370–376. This material was presented by Ling-chi Wang, University of California, Berkeley.

17. Illsoo Kim, *New Urban Immigrants: The Korean Community in New York* (Princeton, N.J.: Princeton University Press, 1981).

18. For further discussion of the model minority myth and interpretation of census data, see Deborah Woo, "The Socioeconomic Status of Asian American Women in the Labor Force: An Alternative View," *Sociological Perspectives* 28:3 (July 1985):307–338.

9

Black Hispanics:
The Ties That Bind

Vivian Brady

At the bottom of the Spring semester course selection sheet is an optional question: students are requested to supply the college with their ethnicity for federal reporting requirements. Six categories are provided: White non-Hispanic, Black non-Hispanic, Puerto Rican, Hispanic other, Asian/Pacific Islander and Native American/Alaskan. Students must choose only one category, the one that best describes them.

I have always found the restriction to only one choice incredibly frustrating. As someone who describes herself as Black-Puerto Rican, there never seems to be any category that acknowledges the strong African heritage of Hispanic people in the Caribbean and Latin America. We, as Hispanics, are isolated as if we were a separate race unto ourselves. Unlike English and French-speaking people of the Caribbean, the kinship ties of Puerto Ricans to the Black American community are often ignored or denied. Our common bond of African heritage, as people of color in this hemisphere and our implicit sisterhood and brotherhood are often left unrecognized, even on my course selection sheet.

My recognition of myself as a Black-Puerto Rican may be facilitated by the fact that my parents come from two different islands. My mother is from Puerto Rico and my father from St. Thomas VI, but I have met many Hispanics who do not have mixed parentage who see themselves as I do. My mother emigrated to this country from Puerto Rico when she was three years old. The economic situation in Puerto Rico during the War was harsh and her family came to find a better life, settling in *El Barrio*, East Harlem. She has always viewed herself as a Black woman, a brave and independent stance to take in the 1940s and 50s. To my mother, separating the communities was a dangerous thing. She believes that it strengthens us to find our commonalities and stand united because the price of separation can be great in the face of racist oppression.

The "West Side Story" of my mother's time was more the relationship between the newly arrived Puerto Ricans and American Blacks than the romanticized tensions between the Italians and the Puerto Ricans of that musical's fame. An imaginary line was drawn on Lenox Avenue creating two insular communities, one Black and one Puerto Rican, and even though their lives and experiences were startlingly similar there was ambivalence. This ambivalence still survives today and divides us. Both groups fell into the trap of believing what the racist dogma of the day heralded. Many Puerto Ricans accepted on face value that Black was synonymous with inferiority. They believed the stereotypes about Blacks being "bad" and shied away from building a relationship with them, not wanting to be tainted by their status. Black Americans also fell into the mire of white racism; Puerto Ricans were loud, heavy drinkers and the men were womanizing Latinos. It seems funny to list these ridiculous images, yet they live on. I know because I have lived on both sides of the issue, red faced and embarrassed at how glibly we apply these stereotypes to each other; the multitudes of accusatory general statements not based on direct knowledge. Underneath it all is a wealth of strength that can help us discard the pervasive racism that our country is shackled to, but it must be a combined effort.

Our shared experience is not just the oppression that we have had to survive in this country, although it is of crucial importance and should serve to bind us together politically in order to create change and support each other's self determination. We live together in some of the poorest communities, are racked by a drug epidemic, inadequate housing, and an educational system that leaves us unqualified and intellectually stifled. We ride the subways together every day, feeling much the same anger and despair, yet there is uncertainty between us. We are determined to see our cultural differences as insurmountable even though we have a shared heritage. The core of this uncertainty and divisiveness is ignorance.

My grandmother lives in Ceiba, a sleepy town near the Navy base in Puerto Rico where all the houses are painted in tropical pastels and one can hear the war games being executed along the coast. I see in her brown face my African heritage. Slaves were imported into Puerto Rico like the other neighboring islands for their cheap labor. They were exploited in the sugar cane fields under the hot sun. They brought with them their music, spirit and culture, enriching Puerto Rico. Black people in the Spanish-speaking Caribbean and in Latin America have left us with great legacies: The quilombo leader Ganga Zambi in Brazil, the African rhythms of the *merengue* and the spiritual influences in our religions. My grandmother would never call herself Black though; she is firstly and lastly Puerto Rican. Most Puerto Ricans describe their country like a rainbow, a mixture and blend of African, European and Indian. The manner in which they view their "blackness" is directly related to their environment and culture.

I have often heard Black Americans alienated by this concept; they see a woman as dark as my grandmother not identifying herself as Black and conclude that "Puerto Ricans don't know what they are" or that they seek to deny their blackness. Sadly enough this is true for some. I certainly don't wish to obscure the issues of race, color and class among Puerto Ricans. We are afflicted by these prejudices, much like Black Americans. It is Puerto Rican to recognize our mixed heritage. It is a mulatto country, not the stark Black and White of the United States.

When I learn about Afro-American history I treat it as my own, as part of my identity as a Black woman. I see the accomplishments and survival as a testimony to all people of color. I hope that Black Americans can find pride and strength in Puerto Rican and other Afro-Latin histories, but I know that it will take time for people to see this global Pan-Africanist view.

Things are not simple though, and viewing the situation perched on the edge of both communities I see that though we may socialize, form committees and lobby together, we must learn more about each other to see the merits of standing non-judgmentally side by side. A good place to begin is to examine our histories.

I recently asked some of my Black American friends, "What if Michael Griffith were Puerto Rican? Would you fight racist aggression in Howard Beach if the lynch mob were out to kill "dirty spics" with bats and pipes?" Most said their response would have been tempered by the fact that the victim was Hispanic and that they would not be as passionate. By the same token I would have liked to see a stronger voice made by the Hispanic community during the case. We do not yet see that the enemy and the issue are the same: we must both be energized to see the struggle.

I have been told that it is impossible for me to continue being both Puerto Rican and Black and that I will inevitably need to choose sides, perhaps as a way to show my allegiance to my chosen community. But I, like many other Hispanics, know that the blood I share with Afro-Americans links me to the survival and work necessary in both communities equally.

10

Blacks and Hispanics:
A Fragile Alliance

Jacqueline Conciatore and Roberto Rodriguez

On the stone steps of City Hall, a leader of Latino workers makes a decision. Standing above an assemblage of microphones and tape recorders, he angrily tells reporters that African Americans are making gains at the expense of his people. "Blacks had their turn in the fight for equality," he says. "Now it's our turn." The next day on the same steps, a Black labor leader hosts the same audience. "Latinos," he says, "are pimping off the civil rights struggle. They didn't sacrifice their lives 25 years ago—or get beat with their own picket signs. They can't benefit from our fight." Both leaders take to the airwaves. People listen as they accuse each other of being racially motivated and of taking each other's jobs. In a number of inner-city schools, fights between Black and Latino students break out. Gang wars, already a problem, escalate into racial battles. Newspapers begin to report a killing a day. The leaders of the Latino and African American employees associations call for a truce. It is a show of unity. Restore peace to this city, they say. But the wrong people are talking. Nobody's listening. In a racially mixed community, tension is palpable. The possibility of violence is a hair trigger away. . . Sound familiar?

Los Angeles? New York? Chicago? Houston? Philadelphia? Washington, DC? Miami? Oakland? Denver? Phoenix?

Some cities have already witnessed Black-Latino conflicts such as the one just described. Typically, tensions between the two groups arise from a perception that they must compete for scant educational and economic opportunities. "Any time communities of color have been locked out of the American dream," says Antonio Villaraigoza, past co-chair of the Los Angeles Black/Latino Agenda, "they have had to fight over the same limited resources—jobs, education."

As the above scenario illustrates, what leaders do and say are crucial to the state of Black-Latino relations. Many leaders recognize the potential revolutionary impact of a real alliance and are calling on Blacks and Hispanics to mobilize around a host of common concerns.

They stress that for people of color, alliance is not a luxury, not a utopian ideal, but a necessity. Creative and forceful initiatives are needed to confront the problems of the '90s, they say, to lift both communities out of the bottom of the barrel they share. If Blacks and Latinos do it together, the climb will be all the faster.

Demographic Changes: Impacting Race Relations

In a working class neighborhood in Washington, DC, a priest has a dilemma.

His 12:30 Spanish-language Mass is getting to be overcrowded. Standing shoulder to shoulder, patrons fill the pews, then take scattered positions at the back of the church.

The 9:30 Mass must become a Spanish service as well. But to accomplish this will take a doctorate in diplomacy, says Father Robert McCrary. People from the neighborhood—African Americans, Vietnamese, some whites—have been going to that Mass in English for years and years. When the transition happens, McCrary predicts, "the fur will fly."

The population changes that require solutions in McCrary's Mount Pleasant parish are also occurring in nearby Northern Virginia, in suburban Maryland, throughout the metropolitan area. With a wider lens, one can see the same demographic tides in Florida, Chicago and on the West Coast. The nation as a whole, in fact, has seen a 39 percent increase in Hispanic members—both immigrants and those born here—since 1980. This compares to a total population growth of 9.5 percent.

For a nation that likes to call itself a melting pot, shifts in the demographic makeup of its citizenry are nothing new. Never before, however, has the emergence of a population promised to so significantly alter the racial balance of the nation, as is happening with the current influx of Latinos (and Asian Americans as well).

The change forces Black Americans to alter their conception of race relations, to make room for new players. Says Dr. Manning Marable of the Center for Studies of Ethnicity and Race in America: "Black Americans are still accustomed to thinking of race relations in Black and white terms." But that conceptual framework, he says, has not been appropriate for 50 years at least.

Ben Benavidez, director of the Fresno-based Mexican American Political Association (MAPA), agrees: "Black people have to remember they're not the only minority. And they're not the only oppressed minority."

In Fresno and its San Joaquin Valley, there is some tension between Blacks and Mexican-Americans as they struggle for a share of power in the educational system. Local board members are apt to see "minority progress" as putting one or two Blacks in high administrative posts, Benavidez says. But Mexican-American children are the majority school-age population.

"We're not fighting to see who's the most oppressed," Benavidez says. But, he adds, "there are going to be some struggles, and the powers that be love that."

Economic Competition

In Miami's Black community, says Guillermo Grenier, director of the Center for Labor Research, everyone knows that you can't get a job if you can't speak Spanish.

"In the Black community, you have common knowledge that Blacks were displaced by Latins," he says.

Although Blacks in many urban areas say they are losing economic ground to immigrants and their offspring, nowhere is that plaint heard more clearly than in Miami. Since Cuban exiles laid stakes there 30 years ago, the city has erupted into periodic race-related violence.

The Black sense of displacement, along with Cuban-Black political differences and a police force that many say is racist, combine to create tensions that lead to riots, says Marvin Dunn, author of a book on the Miami riots of 1980.

But Dunn says objective evidence does not bear out the perception that Miami's Blacks have been displaced by Hispanics. In the last decade, the number of Blacks earning $35,000 or more has doubled. Black median family incomes have also improved, while they held steady for whites and dropped for Hispanics he says.

These upward trends, however, do not hold true for low-income Blacks, who comprise 30 percent of the city's Black population. This group has indeed lost access to housing, health care and early intervention programs such as Head Start, Dunn says. "In the competition for basic services, lower income Blacks have definitely lost out," he says. Dunn attributes this economic decline to an influx of "new poor," many of them Cubans who came in the Mariel exodus of 1980, when Fidel Castro packed American-bound boats with convicts and those diagnosed as mentally ill.

Grenier counters that the Cuban presence impacts more affluent Blacks in less measurable ways. "The managers and city mothers and fathers, when they look at, 'Should we include minorities in our doings?,' They say, 'Yes,' but they will include mostly Latinos." Middle-class Blacks are not being displaced in the upper levels of business and government, he says, because "they were never there to begin with."

The belief that the success of Hispanics means the failure of Blacks, and vice versa, is not unique to Miami. But a recent study by Paula McClain of Arizona State University and Albert Karnig of the University of Wyoming indicates that Blacks and Latinos have reason to celebrate each other's success. McClain and Karnig analyzed the distribution of power and resources in 49 U.S. cities with populations exceeding 25,000 and at least 10 percent Black and 10 percent Hispanic populations. They found that where Blacks are succeeding in some measure with respect to education, income, and employment, Hispanics are likely to be successful as well.

In the end, it is a waste of energy to focus on the deprivation of one's group relative to another, Marable says. "The whole approach is wrong. It's like battling for crumbs." The correct approach, he says, is to determine "how race and ethnicity are used to perpetuate the inferior status for people of color across the board."

Political Differences

When Miami officials did not give Nelson Mandela a celebratory welcome this past summer because the Cuban community objected to Mandela's stated affiliation with Fidel Castro, Black residents were outraged and chagrined.

While the incident was an illustration of how diverse the Latino community is (Cubans shunned Mandela, while Mexican Americans, Central Americans, South Americans and Latinos from the Caribbean welcomed him with open arms), it also illustrated how political differences work to separate Blacks and Latinos. In Miami, many Blacks feel Cuban Americans care only about Castro and have no appreciation of their experience of oppression in the United States, said Dunn.

That perception in some cases is well founded, said Max Castro, head of Greater Miami United, a multicultural coalition of activists. When Cuban Americans first arrived, the civil rights struggle was flowering. "It was like watching the person that threw the second punch and not seeing all the punches that were thrown before that," he said. Because Cubans were relatively well-treated here, "they kind of overestimate the benevolence of the system and may not be sufficiently critical of the way [it] treats other minorities—and even ourselves on some occasions," he said.

The two groups have a gap in their world views as well, Max Castro said. Cubans see the world in terms of "communist or noncommunist," he said. Blacks tend to see the world in terms of race. "Cubans see Nelson Mandela as someone allied with the African Nationalist party. . . . African Americans see Mandela as a liberator in the struggle for equality. Cubans attack Mandela for ideological reasons. African Americans see that as a racial attack."

Racism

Racism occupies a place in the Black-Hispanic dynamic as well. Blacks have been known to question the right of Hispanics to empowerment because some do not have legal status as citizens. Hispanics have been known to argue that many Blacks cannot beat the system because they are unwilling to work.

Says Ona Alston, a former Howard University student body president who works as project manager for the Committee in Solidarity with the People of El Salvador in

Washington, DC: "Even when African Americans and Latinos live in close proximity, which is generally not the case, there is a tremendous amount of ignorance and misunderstanding."

But, she says, proximity improves the chances for understanding. "Where there is proximity, African Americans and Latinos can see they have a lot more in common than, say, African Americans and European Americans do, or Latinos and European Americans do.

"But if there's one thing that America is good at . . . it's letting people know, when you come to these shores, whatever you are, you aren't Black. We are at the bottom of the totem pole—'These are the people to be dumped on.' And that's very real."

11

Legal Alien

Pat Mora

Bi-lingual, Bi-cultural,
able to slip from "How's life?"
to *"Me'stan volviendo loca,"*
able to sit in a paneled office
drafting memos in smooth English,
able to order in fluent Spanish
at a Mexican restaurant,
American but hyphenated,
viewed by Anglos as perhaps exotic,
perhaps inferior, definitely different,
viewed by Mexicans as alien,
(their eyes say, "You may speak
Spanish but you're not like me")
an American to Mexicans
a Mexican to Americans
a handy token
sliding back and forth
between the fringes of both worlds
by smiling
by masking the discomfort
of being pre-judged
Bi-laterally.

12

Her Rites of Passage

Lynda Marín

In the stairwell of the apartment building lobby, she had made a tent palace of sheets, bed pillows, and one of Mary's forbidden quilts. Through the palace door flap she marched the buggy, delivering into the great dining hall Corky the rabbit and Brown Doggy. A soft knocking from beyond the palace walls interrupted the feasting. She popped her head under a sheet to see. From the other side of the lobby glass door a large man bent to meet her eyes. He knocked again, pleadingly, as if he were carrying a heavy burden and would be relieved of it only when the big, latched door was opened. Her first impulse—to let him in—was halted instantly by Mary's repeated warning. "Don't ever open that door to anyone who doesn't live here. No matter what!" But now here were his eyes, so sorrowful, and his insistent knocking, so sure, so right. He was a man, after all, and important for that reason. Perhaps just this time.

She was surprised to find that he did not rush right past her but took an interest in her tent palace. He asked if he might have a peek inside. Shyly she lifted the flap, and in he crawled, raising the ceiling with his big head. "What about you?" he asked, cheery. A pause, then she followed. He took up almost all the space. He pointed to his lap and pulled her onto himself jerkily. When she shrank away, his arms tightened around her and his face scratched her cheek. "You be a good girl, and I'll show you something." He fumbled at his pants. His eyes looked cloudy and seemed not to be pointed at her anymore. She thought of screaming but could not. Even now she was not sure he meant to harm her. "Look at this," he commanded. He had taken his pants down to his knees and held a rubbery tube of skin in his hand. "Take a hold of it," he whispered. He grabbed her reluctant hand and rubbed her fisted fingers along the tube. It was warm and smelled like Mary's Chinese herbs only more sour, like stomach flu. She wrenched her nose away, and then, to her surprise, her body sprang free of the sheets and followed after. At the threshold of her own second-story apartment she stopped her legs. If she went in now, heart thumping and wild, Mary might guess, might find him still in her tent palace, his tube hanging from him like a dead bird. And too, she would see the quilt. Better to hide and wait.

The click of the lobby door below released her. She approached the tent warily, but she knew he was gone. In his place, a tidy, piled bowel movement on Mary's quilt. He had used Corky and Brown Doggy to wipe himself. She staggered to the other side of the lobby and wept. Later she was to explain that she'd made the mess herself, for which she received a memorable whipping. That was when she was six years old. . . .

13

is not so gd to be born a girl

Ntozake Shange

Is not so gd to be born a girl/ some times. that's why societies usedta throw us away/ or sell us/ or play with our vaginas/ cuz that's all girls were gd for/ at least women cd carry things & cook/ but to be born a girl is not good sometimes/ some places/ such abominable things cd happen to us. i wish it waz gd to be born a girl everywhere/ then i wd know for sure that no one wd be infibulated/ that's a word no one wants us to know/ "infibulation" is sewing our vaginas up with cat gut or weeds or nylon thread to insure our virginity/ virginity insurance = infibulation/ that can also make it impossible for us to live thru labor/ make it impossible for the baby to live thru labor/ infibulation lets us get infections that we cant mention cuz disease in the ovaries is a sign that we're dirty anyway/ so wash yrself cuz once infibulated we have to be cut open to have you know what/ the joy of the phallus/ that we may know nothing abt/ ever/ especially if something else not good that happens to little girls happens/ if we've been excised/ had our labia removed with glass or scissors/ if we've lost our clitoris because our pleasure is profane & the presence of our naturally evolved clitoris wd disrupt the very unnatural dynamic of polygamy/ so with no clitoris, no labia, & infibulation/ we're sewn-up, cut-up, pared down & sore if not dead/ & oozing puss, if not terrified that so much of our body waz wrong & did not belong on earth/ such thoughts lead to a silence/ that hangs behind veils & straight jackets/ it really is not so good to be born a girl when we have to be infibulated, excised, clitorectomized & still be afraid to walk the streets or stay home at night.

i'm so saddened that being born a girl makes it dangerous to attend midnight mass unescorted. some places if we're born girls & some one else who's very sick & weak & cruel/ attacks us & breaks our hymen/ we have to be killed/ sent away from our families/ forbidden to touch our children. these strange people who wound little girls are known as attackers, molesters, & rapists. they are known all over the world

& are proliferating at a rapid rate. to be born a girl who will always have to worry not only abt the molesters, the attackers & the rapists/ but also abt their peculiarities/ does he stab too/ or shoot/ does he carry an ax/ does he spit on you/ does he know if he doesn't drop sperm we cant prove we've been violated/ those subtlties make being a girl too complex/ for some of us & we go crazy/ or never go anyplace.

some of us have never had an open window or a walk alone/ but sometimes our homes are not safe for us either/ rapists & attackers & molesters are not strangers to everyone/ they are related to somebody/ & some of them like raping & molesting their family members better than a girl-child they don't know yet/ this is called incest & girl children are discouraged from revealing attacks from uncle or daddy/ cuz what wd mommy do/ after all daddy may have seen to it that abortions were outlawed in his state/ so that mommy might have too many children/ to care abt some "fun" daddy might have been having with the 2 year old/ she's a girl after all/ we have to get used to it/ but infibulation, excision, clitorectomies, rape, & incest/ are irrevocable life-deniers/ life-stranglers & disrespectful of natural elements/ i wish these things wdnt happen anywhere anymore/ then i cd say it waz gd to be born a girl everywhere/ even though gender is not destiny/right now being born a girl is to be born threatened/ i dont respond well to threats/ i want being born a girl to be a cause for celebration/ cause for protection & nourishment of our birth-right/ to live freely with passion, knowing no fear/ that our species waz somehow incorrect.

& we are now plagued with rapists & clitorectomies. we pay for being born girls/ but we owe no one anything/ not our labia, not our clitoris, not our lives. we are born girls & live to be women who live our own lives/ to live our lives/
to have/
our lives/
to live.

14

The Tyranny of Slenderness

Kim Chernin

A woman should never give the impression that she is so capable, so self-sufficient, that she doesn't need him at all. Men are enchanted by minor, even amusing frailties. This quality of vulnerability, of needing a man, is something that the mature woman should study very carefully. Because it's that quality that she loses most easily. Years of dealing with home and family, of making decisions, of coping, can turn the woman of forty-plus into a brusque, cold-eyed, and somewhat frightening figure.

GLORIA HEIDI

Is it a conspiracy, unknown even to those who participate in it?

A whole culture busily spinning out images and warnings intended to keep women from developing their bodies, their appetites, and their powers?

Maybe, when we see another calorie counter on the stand, or read of another miracle diet in a women's magazine, or pick up another container of low-calorie cottage cheese, we must begin to understand these trivial items symbolically and realize that what we are purchasing is the covert advice not to grow too large and too powerful for our culture.

Maybe, indeed, this whole question of the body's reduction is analogous to the binding of women's feet in prerevolutionary China?*

"My mother buys me a girdle when I am fifteen years old," says Louise Bernikow, "because she doesn't like the jiggle. . . . Tighter. I hold myself tighter, as my mother has taught me to do. . . . Is the impulse to cripple a girl peculiar to China between the eleventh and twentieth centuries? The lotus foot was the size of a doll's and the woman could not walk without support. Her foot was four inches long and two inches wide. A doll. A girl-child. Crippled, indolent, and bound."[1]

There is a relationship between the standards set for women's beauty and the desire to limit their development. In the name of a beautiful foot, the women of China were deprived of autonomy and made incapable of work. A part of the body was forced to remain in a childish condition. They did not walk, they hobbled. In the name of beauty they were crippled.

What happens to women today in the name of beauty?

I'd never wear a girdle, she said,
just medieval throwbacks
to whale baleen brassieres 'n
laced-up waist confiner corsets.
We burned em in the sixties,
girdles, she said walking
into Bloomingdales, grabbing
a pair of cigarette-legged
tight denim jeans off the rack.
Hoisting them up to her hips,
how do ya get em on, she said,
have surgery, take steam baths,
slimnastic classes'n Dr. Nazi's
diet clinic fatshots for a month?
These aren't jeans for going

---

*Alice Walker, in a conversation about women and their body, suggested this analogy to me.

to lunch in, she said trying
to do the snap, these
aren't even jeans
for eating an hour
before ya put em on, just
for standin up in without
your hands in the pockets,
there's not even room
in here for my underpants.
One hour later she returns
to the store for a new zipper,
front snap, and the side seams
re-stitched. These're jeans
for washing in cold water only
then wearin round the house
til they dry on yr shape,
put em in a clothes dryer,
she said, and you'll get
all pinch bruised
round the crotch'n
your stomach covered
with red streak marks
cross the front.

We burned em in the sixties,
girdles, she said.[2]

We must not imagine that it is only the fashion industry that is upset about the large size of our bodies. Fashion creates and it reflects. Creates, as we have seen, an image few women in this culture are able to realize for themselves. Creates longing—and we all know this longing to win the approval of our culture even at cost to our health, our identity as women, our experience of pleasure in our bodies. But fashion also reflects hidden cultural intentions, as it did in China with the binding of women's feet. As it does in our own day, with pants so tight they serve as an adequate replacement for the girdles that used to bind us. Fashion, for all its appearance of superficiality, is a mirror in which we can read the responses of conventional culture to what is occurring, at the deepest levels of cultural change, among its people.

For instance: if the problem of body and mind is as old in this culture as I have suggested, why is anorexia a new disease and bulmarexia a condition first named during the 1970s? Why for that matter is Christine Olman a model now and not twenty years ago when Marilyn Monroe inspired our admiration?

These questions may help us to understand that something has happened in our culture during the last twenty years that has made us particularly uneasy about the abundance of our flesh. Something, unnamed as yet, which fashion expresses as a shift from the voluptuous to the ascetic.

I wish to place before us a cluster of related facts that constitutes an important cultural synchronicity.

FACT: During the 1960s Marilyn Monroe stood for the ideal in feminine beauty. Now Christine Olman represents that ideal.

FACT: During the 1960s anorexia nervosa began to be a widespread social disease among women.

FACT: During the late 1960s and early 1970s bulmarexia began to be observed as a condition among women.

FACT: During the 1960s Weight Watchers opened their doors. In 1965 Diet Workshop appeared, in 1960s Over-Eaters Anonymous, in 1966 Why Weight, in 1968 Weight Losers Institute, in 1969 Lean Line.

FACT: During the 1960s the Feminist Movement began to emerge, asserting woman's right to authority, development, dignity, liberation and above all, power.

What am I driving at here? I am suggesting that the changing awareness among women of our position in this society has divided itself into two divergent movements, one of which is a movement toward feminine power, the other a retreat from it, supported by the fashion and diet industries, which share a fear of women's power.

In this light it is significant that one of the first feminist activities in our time was an organized protest against the Miss America Contest and the idea of feminine beauty promulgated by the dominant culture through this pageant, in which women strut and display their bodies, as men sit passively, judging them. It is interesting, further, that as a significant portion of the female population in the last two decades began to go to consciousness-raising groups and to question the role and subservience of women in this society, other women hastened to groups where the large size of their bodies was deplored. The same era gave birth to these two contradictory movements among women.

Yet we sense that there is an underlying similarity of motive in both movements. In both, women are driven to gather together and make confessions and find sisterly support for the new resolutions they are taking. In both, women have created new forms of social organization, apart from the established institutions of the dominant culture.

There is, however, also a fundamental divergence here. The groups that arise among feminists are dedicated to the enlargement of women. Confessions made in these groups reveal anger over rape and the shame women have been taught to feel about their bodies; there is interest in the longing to develop the self, concern for the boredom and limitations of motherhood, acknowledgement of the need for sisterly support in the resolution to return to work, go back to school, become more of oneself, grow larger. But in the other groups, confessions are voiced about indulgence in the pleasures of eating, and resolutions are made to control the amount of food consumed, and sisterly support is given for a renewed warfare against the appetite and the body.

Listen to the spontaneous metaphor that finds its way into the discussions of these two groups. In the feminist group it is *largeness* in a woman that is sought, the *power* and *abundance* of the feminine, the assertion of a woman's right to be taken seriously, to *acquire weight*, to *widen* her *frame* of reference, to be *expansive, enlarge* her views, *acquire gravity, fill out,* and *gain* a sense of self-esteem. It is always a question of *widening, enlarging, developing* and *growing*. But in the weight-watching groups the women are trying to *reduce* themselves; and the metaphoric consistency of this is significant: they are trying to make themselves *smaller,* to *narrow* themselves, to become *lightweight,* to lose *gravity,* to be-*little* themselves. Here, emphasis is placed upon *shrinking* and *diminution, confinement* and *contraction,* a *loss* of pounds, a *losing* of flesh, a *falling* of weight, a *lessening.*

These metaphoric consistencies reveal a struggle that goes beyond concern for the body. Thus, in the feminist groups the emphasis is significantly upon liberation—upon release of power, the unfettering of long-suppressed ability, the freeing of one's potential, a woman shaking off restraints and delivering herself from limitations. But in the appetite control groups the emphasis is upon restraint and prohibition, the keeping of watch over appetites and urges, the confining of impulses, the control of the hungers of the self.

When all other personal motives for losing weight are stripped away—the desire to be popular, to be loved, to be successful, to be acceptable, to be in control, to be admired, to admire one's self—what unites the women who seek to reduce their weight is the fact that they look for an answer to their life's problems in the control of their bodies and appetites. A woman who walks through the doors of a weight-watching organization and enters the women's reduction movement has allowed her culture to persuade her that significant relief from her personal and cultural dilemma is to be found in the reduction of her body. Thus, her decision, although she may not be aware of it, enters the domain of the body politic and becomes symbolically a political act.

It is essential to interpret anorexia nervosa, that other significant movement among women during the last decades so that it, too, can be understood as part of women's struggle for liberation during the last decades. Indeed, Hilde Bruch calls it a new disease because in the last fifteen or twenty years it has occurred at a "rapidly increasing rate." From 1960 on, she writes, "reports on larger patient groups have been published in countries as far apart as Russia and Australia, Sweden and Italy, England and the United States."[3]

The fact that these are highly developed industrial countries, and that anorexia occurs primarily among girls of the upper-middle class, should remind us that anorexia is a symbolic illness. Where hunger is imposed by external circumstances, the act of starvation remains literal, a tragic biological event that does not serve metaphoric or symbolic purposes. It is only in a country where one is able to choose hunger that elective starvation may come to express cultural conflict or even social protest.

"You go over to the high school today and it's like walking into a concentration camp," says the mother of an anorexic girl, in a telephone conversation with a friend, whose daughter has just lost fifty pounds in five months. "Betty Talbot has the same problem, I understand. . . . And of course you know about Kimmy Sanders, don't you? That absolutely gorgeous girl. What a tragedy."[4]

This conversation between mothers, about their anorexic daughters, would not have been heard during the 1950s, or only in rare and isolated cases. Today, however, we may expect to find this conversation in most affluent communities, where families raise daughters who are not able to express their angers and rebellions directly, yet who feel a distinct reluctance to become the conventional people their mothers are.

"Ugh, wretched curves," says the daughter of the mother whose telephone conversation we have just overheard. "I grab my breasts, pinching them until they hurt. If only I could eliminate them, cut them off if need be to become as flat-chested as a child again. It is better now than before I started dieting. To think that I needed a size B bra! Now I don't even need to wear one, but the womanly outline still remains, and I'm afraid that if I should gain again they'll blow up like zeppelins. I would probably start having periods again as well. I would probably look and function just like my mother."[5]

Anorexia nervosa speaks exactly the same protest being spoken by the women's liberation movement. Feminists, it is true, in an outspoken gesture of refusal to comply with the conventional expectations for a woman in this culture, take off their bras. The anorexic girl starves herself instead, so that she does not develop the breasts that would require the bra. The underlying emotional attitude of anorexia is clear: "I don't want to be an imitation," says the anorexic girl. "I don't want to be a victim of fate. . . . I want to make my own name, cut my own image, set my own trend. I want to surpass [my mother], not follow her lead."

This rebellious attitude toward the mother seems to be directed less against the personal mother, more against the limitations of woman's social destiny. Indeed, the mothers of anorexic girls "had often been career women, who felt they had sacrificed their aspirations for the good of the family. In spite of superior intelligence and education, practically all had given up their careers when they married." Their daughters feel impatience with their mothers, dreading that they will share their mothers' fate, which one anorexic girl characterizes in the following way: "to be a nothing, to be devoted to a husband, to be devoted to her children, but without a life of her own."[6] . . .

Anorexic girls continue to get good grades, they graduate with honors from their high schools, but they sit on the stage in all the terrible, mute eloquence of their rebellion. This is how an anorexic girl, looking at her high school graduating class, describes them: "Nan, so frail these days, looks as though she's ready to pass out"; Candy, who has been "released from the hospital on the condition that she gain ten pounds by the end of the month"; Kim, "wraithlike and miserable, her ghostly eyes staring vacantly toward the speaker's podium."[7]

In America . . . no woman can possibly remain unaware of the fact that significant numbers of her sisters are asserting their rights to autonomy, to power, to the development of their full emotional and creative capacities. This movement of women into their enlargement is likely to affect her in a number of ways. She may grow depressed with the life she is living and rebel against it. She may refuse to recognize that her life depresses her and fail to develop a meaningful analysis of her condition as a woman. Or she may feel the force of these contradictory tendencies and enact her entire response to them through her body.

Let us imagine then that a woman comes to awareness of her condition one day in 1969. She is, let us say, forty-five years old, she wears old, dreary clothes, and she is seriously depressed. She is a woman who has tried to diet and failed and who has exhausted her tolerance for weight-watching groups. For her the anorexic solution is simply not a possibility. And so she decides to join a women's consciousness-raising group. There, she tells the other women that her husband has just left her after twenty-five years. She tells how she is stuck in a job with a poverty wage in an insurance company, how she feels a thousand years old. She blames herself, she says, and the fatness in her body, for everything that has gone wrong with her life. But now, because she is encouraged to talk and because no one here believes her rounded belly is the cause of these complex failures, she speaks about a dream she had once as a young girl when she wished to become a writer. She tells how absurd this old dream seems now and how she is afraid. But because the women listen to her fears and encourage her to speak further, she goes home and she begins to dream that she might want to dream of becoming a writer.

Let us also imagine that another similar woman comes to a group intended to help women change their lives. But here, in fact, we do not have to provide the script, for the story of a middle-aged woman named Faye has been written for us by Gloria Heidi, in her unintentionally revealing book:

> She was about forty-five years old when she enrolled in my class—a gray, doughy woman in a dreary maroon, half-size dress—a woman who had obviously come to me as a last resort. "Look, my husband Harry has just walked out after twenty-five years. I'm stuck in a poverty-wage, nowhere job at the insurance company. I feel a thousand years old—and look sixty. But I'm determined to be a new me . . . and I want to start by losing this excess weight. After all, now that I've lost Harry"—her eyes filled with tears—"what else have I got to lose?"[8]

In this group, where the woman comes with a complex social and personal situation, her terrible despair is attributed to the fact that she is fat. She is therefore encouraged to lose weight; a chart is kept of the weight she loses. When the magical transformation finally takes place we are told that the horror of her personal and social position has miraculously altered. A moral is drawn. We are assured that we, too, if only we will lose weight, can be "filled with energy, go aggressively after a better job and with a new figure, a revitalized personality, and an exciting new social life, [like] formerly dowdy and half-sized Faye, [soon] be sitting on top of the world."

The hidden message in this story is profoundly disturbing. Implicitly, we are asked to believe that if every woman lost twenty-five or thirty pounds she would be able to overcome the misogyny in our land; her social problems would be solved, the business world would suddenly fling wide its gates and welcome her into its privileges. Isn't it incredible? We, as women, need only lose weight and all of us will find jobs equal in authority and status and salary to those of men? The need for the Equal Rights Amendment will vanish? Unemployment figures will dissolve and the very structure of our society will be transformed?

There is a profound untruth here and a subversion of the radical discontent women feel. In a class of this sort, women are directed to turn their dissatisfaction and depression toward their own bodies. They are encouraged to look at their large size as the cause of the failure they sustain in their lives. Consider what it means to persuade a woman who is depressed and sorrowful and disheartened by her entire life, that if only she succeeds in reducing herself, in becoming even less than she already is, she will be acceptable to this culture which cannot tolerate her if she is any larger or more developed than an adolescent girl. The radical protest she might utter, if she correctly understood the source of her despair and depression, has been directed toward herself and away from her culture and society. Now, she will not seek to change her culture so that it might accept her body; instead, she will spend the rest of her life in anguished failure at the effort to change her body so that it will be acceptable to her culture.*

We should not be misled by the fact that we feel more at home in our culture when we lose weight. It may indeed happen that a woman becomes more attractive to men, finds it easier to get a job, experiences less discrimination, receives fewer gibes from strangers, and endures far less humiliation in her own family. Culture rewards those who comply with its standards. But we have to wonder what cost the woman is paying when she sacrifices her body in this way for the approval of her culture. . . .

NOTES

1. Louise Bernikow, *Among Women*, New York, 1980.
2. Jana Harris, *Manhattan as a Second Language*, Harper & Row, forthcoming.
3. Bruch, *The Golden Cage*.
4. Liu, *Solitaire*.
5. Ibid.
6. Bruch, *The Golden Cage*.
7. Liu, *Solitaire*.
8. Heidi, *Winning the Age Game*.

*Adapted from a very similar utterance by Louise Wolfe, "The Politics of Body Size," Pacifica Tape Library.

15

Bloody and Bowed

Anna Quindlen

Some days it seems that all the troubles in the world are coming through the phone lines into this unprepossessing suite of offices just outside the city limits.

"National Domestic Violence Hotline," says one of the women answering the phones at 1-800-333-SAFE, her face mottled in the glow of the computer screen. "Are you safe?"

"Do you and your children have a place to spend the night?"

"Have you called the police?"

"How often has he hit you?"

The single largest cause of injury to women in the United States is abuse by the men they live with and, often, love. This comes as a surprise to many people, but not to the women who answer the hotline. They know that more than a quarter of the women treated at hospital emergency rooms have been abused, and that a third of the women murdered each year are killed by their husband or boyfriend.

Domestic Violence Awareness Month is drawing to a close. There have been TV feature reports, proclamations and magazine stories. Right in there with the silver patterns, Bride's magazine provides advice on how to spot an abuser before the wedding. Miss America has taken an interest in the subject.

It has become common to cast a bright light on our social problems: rape, incest, child abuse. This is a good thing, but it convinces us that things are better when they are not. Years ago women were afraid to say they were beaten because nobody talked about it; today it's talked about so frequently on TV shows and radio call-ins that they may be afraid to tell because they fear their friends would be incredulous. We assume rape victims go to the police. We assume children know adults are not to touch them that way. We assume it because the problem is out in the open.

The problem is out in the open, but the people are still behind closed doors.

Treatment is easier than prevention. If we really tried to unravel why so many men beat their wives, it would tell us something about ourselves, male and female alike, that we don't want to know, something humiliating and perhaps indelible. I told a woman in this field that I had heard many men were using their fists because they were threatened by the new liberated woman. "Yeah," she said, "and before that they were doing it because their dinner was cold."

So we make things better after, after the bruises and the broken bones. When Debi Cain, who runs a shelter in Pontiac, got started 13 years ago, there were no shelters for battered women in Michigan. Now there are 48. . . .

And many women do leave, finding a haven at a shelter, rebuilding a life. But it requires much more courage than a movie of the week would suggest. Many of them stay because they suspect they can't raise their children on one income in a two-income world. So they become adept at the use of foundation to conceal bruises. It is axiomatic that hardly anyone ever really runs into a door.

Debi Cain still marks the anniversary of the day when a nurse who came to the shelter after yet another fierce beating went home. Her husband called and told her that if she didn't, he would kill their kids. Then he put his gun on the hall table, and said, "When Mommy comes, go outside and play." He shot her in the head, on their front lawn on a summer day. The children watched.

There is a new generation of boys and girls out there who will believe that a relationship between a man and a woman is like a boxing match in which one contestant has no arms. Teaching them otherwise is the real answer, but the people who could take care of that are at the other end of the phones, knocking the receiver halfway across the room because if he told her once, he told her a million times not to tell, and anyway she drove him to it, and it's only because he goes a little crazy when he gets jealous, or when he's drunk, or when he's had a hard day at work. And the telephone—he knows it's her boyfriend, no matter what she says. It's her fault he has to hit her. He's sorry. It won't happen again. He knows he said that the last time. But this time he means it. Don't cry.

And the children listen and watch and learn.

16

He Defies You Still:
The Memoirs of a Sissy

Tommi Avicolli

You're just a faggot
No history faces you this morning
A faggot's dreams are scarlet
Bad blood bled from words that scarred[1]

Scene One

A homeroom in a Catholic high school in South Philadelphia. The boy sits quietly in the first aisle, third desk, reading a book. He does not look up, not even for a moment. He is hoping no one will remember he is sitting there. He wishes he were invisible. The teacher is not yet in the classroom so the other boys are talking and laughing loudly.

Suddenly, a voice from beside him:

"Hey, you're a faggot, ain't you?"

The boy does not answer. He goes on reading his book, or rather pretending he is reading his book. It is impossible to actually read the book now.

"Hey, I'm talking to you!"

The boy still does not look up. He is so scared his heart is thumping madly; it feels like it is leaping out of his chest and into his throat. But he can't look up.

"Faggot, I'm talking to you!"

To look up is to meet the eyes of the tormentor.

Suddenly, a sharpened pencil point is thrust into the boy's arm. He jolts, shaking off the pencil, aware that there is blood seeping from the wound.

"What did you do that for?" he asks timidly.

"Cause I hate faggots," the other boy says, laughing. Some other boys begin to laugh, too. A symphony of laughter. The boy feels as if he's going to cry. But he must not cry. Must not cry. So he holds back the tears and tries to read the book again. He must read the book. Read the book.

When the teacher arrives a few minutes later, the class quiets down. The boy does not tell the teacher what has happened. He spits on the wound to clean it, dabbing it with a tissue until the bleeding stops. For weeks he fears some dreadful infection from the lead in the pencil point.

Scene Two

The boy is walking home from school. A group of boys (two, maybe three, he is not certain) grab him from behind, drag him into an alley and beat him up. When he gets home, he races up to his room, refusing dinner ("I don't feel well," he tells his mother through the locked door) and spends the night alone in the dark wishing he would die. . . .

These are not fictitious accounts—I *was* that boy. Having been branded a sissy by neighborhood children because I preferred jump rope to baseball and dolls to playing soldiers, I was often taunted with "hey sissy" or "hey faggot" or "yoo hoo honey" (in a mocking voice) when I left the house.

To avoid harassment, I spent many summers alone in my room. I went out on rainy days when the street was empty.

I came to like being alone. I didn't need anyone, I told myself over and over again. I was an island. Contact with others meant pain. Alone, I was protected. I began writing poems, then short stories. There was no reason to go outside anymore. I had a world of my own.

> *In the schoolyard today*
> *they'll single you out*
> *Their laughter will leave your ears ringing*
> *like the church bells*
> *which once awed you. . . .*[2]

School was one of the more painful experiences of my youth. The neighborhood bullies could be avoided. The taunts of the children living in those endless repetitive row houses could be evaded by staying in my room. But school was something I had to face day after day for some two hundred mornings a year.

I had few friends in school. I was a pariah. Some kids would talk to me, but few wanted to be known as my close friend. Afraid of labels. If I was a sissy, then he had to be a sissy, too. I was condemned to loneliness.

Fortunately, a new boy moved into our neighborhood and befriended me; he wasn't afraid of the labels. He protected me when the other guys threatened to beat me up. He walked me home from school; he broke through the terrible loneliness. We were in third or fourth grade at the time.

We spent a summer or two together. Then his parents sent him to camp and I was once again confined to my room.

Scene Three

High school lunchroom. The boy sits at a table near the back of the room. Without warning, his lunch bag is grabbed and tossed to another table. Someone opens it and confiscates a package of Tastykakes; another boy takes the sandwich. The empty bag is tossed back to the boy who stares at it, dumbfounded. He should be used to this; it has happened before.

Someone screams, "faggot," laughing. There is always laughter. It does not annoy him anymore.

There is no teacher nearby. There is never a teacher around. And what would he say if there were? Could he report the crime? He would be jumped after school if he did. Besides, it would be his word against theirs. Teachers never noticed anything. They never heard the taunts. Never heard the word, "faggot." They were the great deaf mutes, pillars of indifference; a sissy's pain was not relevant to history and geography and god made me to love honor and obey him, amen.

Scene Four

High school Religion class. Someone has a copy of *Playboy*. Father N. is not in the room yet; he's late, as usual. Someone taps the boy roughly on the shoulder. He turns. A finger points to the centerfold model, pink fleshy body, thin and sleek. Almost painted. Not real. The other asks, mocking voice, "Hey, does she turn you on? Look at those tits!"

The boy smiles, nodding meekly; turns away.

The other jabs him harder on the shoulder, "Hey, whatsamatter, don't you like girls?"

Laughter. Thousands of mouths; unbearable din of laughter. In the Arena: thumbs down. Don't spare the queer.

"Wanna suck my dick? Huh? That turn you on, faggot!"

The laughter seems to go on forever. . . .

Behind you, the sound of their laughter
echoes a million times
in a soundless place
They watch how you walk/sit/stand/breathe. . . .[3]

What did being a sissy really mean? It was a way of walking (from the hips rather than the shoulders); it was a way of talking (often with a lisp or in a high-pitched voice); it was a way of relating to others (gently, not wanting to fight, or hurt anyone's feelings). It was being intelligent ("an egghead" they called it sometimes); getting good grades. It means not being interested in sports, not playing football in the street after school; not discussing teams and scores and playoffs. And it involved not showing fervent interest in girls, not talking about scoring with tits or *Playboy* centerfolds. Not concealing naked women in your history book; or porno books in your locker.

On the other hand, anyone could be a "faggot." It was a catch-all. If you did something that didn't conform to what was the acceptable behavior of the group, then you risked being called a faggot. If you didn't get along with the "in" crowd, you were a faggot. It was the most commonly used put-down. It kept guys in line. They became angry when somebody called them a faggot. More fights started over someone calling someone else a faggot than anything else. The word had power. It toppled the male ego, shattered his delicate facade, violated the image he projected. He was tough. Without feeling. Faggot cut through all this. It made him vulnerable. Feminine. And feminine was the worst thing he could possibly be. Girls were fine for fucking, but no boy in his right mind wanted to be like them. A boy was the opposite of girl. He was not feminine. He was not feeling. He was not weak.

Just look at the gym teacher who growled like a dog; or the priest with the black belt who threw kids against the wall in rage when they didn't know their Latin. They were men, they got respect.

But not the physics teacher who preached pacifism during lectures on the nature of atoms. Everybody knew what he was—and why he believed in the anti-war movement.

My parents only knew that the neighborhood kids called me names. They begged me to act more like the other boys. My brothers were ashamed of me. They never said it, but I knew. Just as I knew that my parents were embarrassed by my behavior.

At times, they tried to get me to act differently. Once my father lectured me on how to walk right. I'm still not clear on what that means. Not from the hips, I guess, don't "swish" like faggots do.

A nun in elementary school told my mother at Open House that there was "something wrong with me." I had draped my sweater over my shoulders like a girl, she said. I was a smart kid, but I should know better than to wear my sweater like a girl!

My mother stood there, mute. I wanted her to say something, to chastise the nun; to defend me. But how could she? This was a nun talking—representative of Jesus, protector of all that was good and decent.

An uncle once told me I should start "acting like a boy" instead of like a girl. Everybody seemed ashamed of me. And I guess I was ashamed of myself, too. It was hard not to be.

Scene Five

Priest: Do you like girls, Mark?
Mark: Uh-huh.
Priest: I mean *really* like them?
Mark: Yeah—they're okay.
Priest: There's a role they play in your salvation. Do you understand it, Mark?
Mark: Yeah.
Priest: You've got to like girls. Even if you should decide to enter the seminary, it's
   important to keep in mind God's plan for a man and a woman. . . .[4]

Catholicism of course condemned homosexuality. Effeminacy was tolerated as long as the effeminate person did not admit to being gay. Thus, priests could be effeminate because they weren't gay.

As a sissy, I could count on no support from the church. A male's sole purpose in life was to father children—souls for the church to save. The only hope a homosexual had of attaining salvation was by remaining totally celibate. Don't even think of touching another boy. To think of a sin was a sin. And to sin was to put a mark upon the soul. Sin—if it was a serious offense against god—led to hell. There was no way around it. If you sinned, you were doomed.

Realizing I was gay was not an easy task. Although I knew I was attracted to boys by the time I was about eleven, I didn't connect this attraction to homosexuality. I was not queer. Not I. I was merely appreciating a boy's good looks, his fine features, his proportions. It didn't seem to matter that I didn't appreciate a girl's looks in the same way. There was no twitching in my thighs when I gazed upon a beautiful girl. But I wasn't queer.

I resisted that label—queer—for the longest time. Even when everything pointed to it, I refused to see it. I was certainly not queer. Not I.

We sat through endless English classes, and History courses about the wars between men who were not allowed to love each other. No gay history was ever taught. No history faces you this morning. You're just a faggot. Homosexuals had never contributed to the human race. God destroyed the queers in Sodom and Gomorrah.

We learned about Michelangelo, Oscar Wilde, Gertrude Stein—but never that they were queer. They were not queer. Walt Whitman, the "father of American poetry," was not queer. No one was queer. I was alone, totally unique. One of a kind. Were there others like me somewhere? Another planet, perhaps?

In school, they never talked of the queers. They did not exist. The only hint we got of this other species was in religion class. And even then it was clouded in mystery—never spelled out. It was sin. Like masturbation. Like looking at *Playboy* and getting a hard-on. A sin.

Once a progressive priest in senior year religion class actually mentioned homosexuals—he said the word—but was into Erich Fromm, into homosexuals as pathetic and sick. Fixated at some early stage; penis, anal, whatever. Only heterosexuals passed on to the nirvana of sexual development.

No other images from the halls of the Catholic high school except those the other boys knew: swishy faggot sucking cock in an alley somewhere, grabbing asses in the bathroom. Never mentioning how much straight boys craved blowjobs, it was part of the secret.

It was all a secret. You were not supposed to talk about the queers. Whisper maybe. Laugh about them, yes. But don't be open, honest; don't try to understand. Don't cite their accomplishments. No history faces you this morning. You're just a faggot   faggot   no history   just a faggot

Epilogue

The boy marching down the Parkway. Hundreds of queers. Signs proclaiming gay pride. Speakers. Tables with literature from gay groups. A miracle, he is thinking. Tears are coming loose now. Someone hugs him.

> *You could not control*
> *the sissy in me*
> *nor could you exorcise him*
> *nor electrocute him*
> *You declared him illegal illegitimate*
> *insane and immature*
> *But he defies you still.*[5]

NOTES

1. From the poem "Faggot" by Tommi Avicolli, published in *GPU News*, Sept. 1979.

2. Ibid.

3. Ibid.

4. From the play *Judgment of the Roaches* by Tommi Avicolli, produced in Philadelphia at the Gay Community Center, the Painted Bride Arts Center and the University of Pennsylvania; aired over WXPN-FM, in four parts; and presented at the Lesbian/Gay Conference in Norfolk, VA, July, 1980.

5. From the poem "Sissy Poem," published in *Magic Doesn't Live Here Anymore* (Philadelphia: Spruce Street Press, 1976).

17

Silent Scream

Carole R. Simmons

My late Uncle Harold was an effervescent man. Just give him an audience and he'd bubble over with stories of growing up black in the South. A sudden increase in the day's temperature would remind him of having to work for endless hours under the hot Georgia sun in Mr. John's fields. A newscaster's mention of racial rebellion would prompt Uncle Harold to retell the story about his left eyebrow's three-inch scar, a souvenir from a 1966 trip to Jackson, Mississippi, where he was clubbed by a state patrolman who was unsatisfied with the volume of Uncle Harold's "sir."

He lived through a lot of unpleasant situations, my uncle, and each one made him stronger and wiser. But I never really believed him when he'd say, "Baby girl, as long as dey call you nigga to yo face, you ain't got nothin' to worry 'bout. When dey don't call you nothin', you bettuh look out." Now I understand completely what Uncle Harold meant because at the University of Georgia at Athens, where I'm a journalism graduate student, they ain't callin' me nothin'.

When I was in high school, there was no question that I'd go to college. And like most of my classmates, both black and white, I'd heard that those four years would be the best of my life. I daydreamed about debating the issues of the day. I looked forward to bundling up against winter winds to cheer the football team. I thought I might join a few clubs. I sure never thought that the color of my skin could prevent me from achieving those simple dreams. I was wrong.

Despite federally mandated desegregation, affirmative action, and a succession of intelligent black UG graduates, racism thrives at this predominantly white Southern institution of 25,000. It's as alive as the azalea bushes in the spring, as plentiful as beer on a football weekend, and as much a part of college as the overcrowded bookstore on the first day of class or the lack of student parking spaces.

But to expedite buying books, people discussed the problem and enlarged the bookstore. To make more parking spaces available to students, administrators admitted the problem and approved the construction of several lots.

Meanwhile, not many people want to hear about how I feel when I get on a campus bus and watch the seats around me fill up while the one next to me remains empty until some other minority student takes it or a white student is left with no other choice.

Few nonblacks here are willing to talk about how I lost my first roommate. I never actually met her. When I checked in, her belongings were already in the room. She'd written a chatty note introducing herself and informing me that she was eating dinner with her family and would meet me later. I unpacked my bags, set a few family photos on my desk, and went to dinner. When I returned a few hours later, a picture of my mother was facedown on my bed. My roommate's things were gone.

I remember starting a journal when I first arrived in 1981. I was so excited; everything was new and promising. But I stopped writing the journal at the end of my first term. The last entry reads, "I feel as if I've been invited to dinner and everybody's eating, but there's no seat at the table for me." Five years later I've returned to attend graduate school, and I could write that same line again.

I've often asked myself why I returned to UG. I knew it hadn't changed. I told myself that I returned to get my master's degree and that nothing would alter that goal. My resolve was unshakable until the first day of orientation, when I overheard one white professor tell another that he had two blacks in his class that quarter. He was anxious, he said, to see how they'd do. I was one of those students.

To an outsider it could very easily look as though black students don't attend UG. I know that for some, owning up to the fact that there are more than 1,000 black students on this campus would be inconvenient. It would mean giving up things like the annual Old South Ball, at which the women dress up in crinolines and hoop skirts, the men don Confederate uniforms, and everyone frolics on the lawn while little black boys serve mint juleps.

And the university would have to relinquish the acts of bias it appears to sanction. Black students are never featured in the pages of the student newspaper unless it's football or basketball season. Of the scores of lecturers, entertainers, and special events brought to campus, few programs reflect that there's any ethnic diversity here.

But by far the most troublesome act of omission is repeated in the classroom every day. During my enrollment the only time that a professor mentioned the name of any ethnic person, group, or publication was in an American history class. We spent a week on the Civil War; we barely covered slavery.

When I tell my friends at other schools about feeling isolated here, they say that at least I haven't experienced the overt racial acts many of them have recently lived through. When my friend Donna attended Carleton College in Minnesota, she was often told that the coursework was too tough for her and was repeatedly encouraged to leave. She now attends graduate school. While at Yale, my friend Terry attended an antiapartheid rally she helped organize, then returned to her car to find its tires slashed and a dead bird hanging from the antenna. Around the bird's neck was a note that read, SOUTH AFRICA HAS THE RIGHT IDEA.

I guess I've been lucky as I've rarely been the recipient of such open hostility. Still the frustration I experience on a daily basis, just dealing with an ongoing succession of insensitivities, makes me angry.

Educated people at UG believe that not making "special provisions" for minority students is a cause for celebration. But what they seem to have made is an institution that resists change and rationalizes insensitivity. In failing to understand that black students have their own culture that should be incorporated into the academic structure, UG appears to subscribe to "the notion that one ethnic stock is superior"—which, according to my dictionary, is the definition of racism.

As far back as I can remember, I'd always heard that education is the great equalizer of people. That philosophy was taught in my family, in my secondary schools, and in my church. And despite what I've experienced at UG, I believe education has that potential; I believe that college campuses should be among the most civil places on earth. Places where we learn to appreciate one another's differences. Places where we're not afraid to admit our transgressions and to work to change them. Places where the only name we call one another is friend.

18

Being Black Is Dangerous to Your Health

Denise Foley

At 16, Deirdre appears to have all the advantages of her white classmates—a good family, a good education, promising job prospects when she graduates from college. In fact, Deirdre has all the advantages but one, the most important one.

Because she is black, she is 1.3 times as likely to die of heart disease and cancer and three times as likely to die of conditions associated with pregnancy and childbirth as her white classmates.

At 55, Earl has never missed a day's work in his 35-year career as a loading-dock foreman. These days, he dreams of retiring with his wife to a little farm in North Carolina, where they'll live the simple life on his small pension and Social Security. But Earl may not live long enough to realize his dream.

Because he is black, he is almost twice as likely to die of stroke, 2.2 times as likely to die of diabetes mellitus, 3.2 times as likely to die of kidney disease and almost 6 times as likely to be murdered as his white co-workers. In fact, on the average, black men like Earl don't survive long enough to collect Social Security.

Today, after more than a century of social progress, a young black girl can grow up to be Miss America, a young black boy to be an astronaut, and the son of a struggling black sharecropper can become mayor of the fifth largest city in the nation. But when it comes to health, it's a different story. Disease appears to have its own kind of bigotry.

"Former National Urban League President Vernon Jordan put it very well," says Ed Pitt, co-author of the League's *Black Health Status Report*. "He said, 'Being black is dangerous to your health.'"

Indeed, statistically, being black seems to be a risk factor in almost every killer disease.

Black death rates are higher for all but two of the 15 leading causes of death in the United States. (Those two are suicide and chronic obstructive pulmonary diseases.) The most chilling are infant and maternal mortality rates. A black child is almost twice as likely to die before its first birthday than a white child—and is three times as likely to be left motherless. Though infant mortality rates have been steadily declining for both races, the gap between the two shows no sign of diminishing.

Heredity? That's the easy answer, but not the real one.

Blacks are not being felled in such large numbers by genetics, but by lifestyle risk factors such as poor diet and stress, alterable behaviors that can affect anyone. There is, of course, a complicating factor. For black people, these high-risk behaviors are, in large part, a legacy of economic deprivation and social oppression.

A Look at Hypertension

Hypertension is a good example. Among blacks, high blood pressure is a virtual epidemic. One out of every four blacks is hypertensive compared to one out of 10 people in the white population. The course the disease takes is particularly vicious. Hypertensive blacks have higher blood pressure than hypertensive whites, which in turn may contribute to the greater incidences of hypertension-related diseases such as coronary heart disease, stroke, and kidney disease, says Gerald Thomson, M.D., a leading expert on black hypertension. "Depending on age, the death rates from those diseases are several times higher for blacks. For young blacks—those under 50—they're four to five times higher," says Dr. Thomson, who is director of medicine at New York's Harlem Hospital and professor of medicine at Columbia University.

There is some speculation that a greater percentage of blacks have an inability to excrete excess sodium, but the hardest evidence points to lifestyle. Some studies indicate that blacks have tended to eat more salt than whites. But, even more important, they seem to eat less potassium. Potassium has been shown to regulate blood pressure in several significant ways, including helping the body excrete excess sodium.

In fact, when a Veterans Administration study measured sodium and potassium excretion in a racially mixed group of untreated mild and moderate hypertensives, both blacks and whites were excreting about the same amount of sodium. But the blacks excreted about two-thirds as much potassium as their white counterparts.

Researcher William Cushman, M.D., attributes the marked difference to potassium intake.

"Blacks are simply getting less potassium in their diet," says Dr. Cushman, chief of the hypertension clinic at the Veterans Administration Medical Center in Jackson, Mississippi. "Urinary excretion of electrolytes is almost always a reflection of dietary intake. Other studies done in Evans County, Georgia, and in the Bogalusa Heart Study reported similar findings. And though we don't know for sure why, we can conjecture: It's more expensive to eat a high-potassium diet. Fresh fruit, vegetables and lean meats are costly. It could possibly be something in cooking practices. It has been proved that when vegetables are cooked for a long time, as they are in Southern-style cooking, potassium leaches out. But what it may all come down to is economics."

The Poverty Risk Factor

In several studies, poverty has been pinpointed as a risk factor in hypertension for both blacks *and* whites. And poverty may have another kind of fall-out—by limiting access to health care.

Hypertensive blacks in Edgecombe County, a poor, rural community in North Carolina, reported less use of medical care than their white counterparts, with more difficulties getting into the health-care system and less satisfaction with the treatment they received. It is probably no coincidence that black hypertensives in the ongoing Edgecombe high-blood-pressure study were also "worse off," according to researchers, particularly younger black men, many of whom were unaware their blood pressures were high and, in fact, have the highest death rates from hypertension-related diseases.

There appears to be a strange mythology at work when it comes to black health, particularly when the focus is on heart disease. Blacks are widely thought to have some inherent protections against coronary heart disease, particularly myocardial infarctions (heart attacks) and angina pectoris. There is some evidence from a number of leading studies that blacks have a higher level of blood fibrinolytic activity—an ability to resist clotting—and a higher ratio of high-density lipoproteins to low-density lipoproteins, a factor that is believed to protect against the collection of cholesterol plaque in the arteries. But the bottom line is that heart disease is the leading cause of death among blacks and their mortality rates are actually higher than most white populations in the world.

Richard F. Gillum, M.D., of the University of Minnesota, is a researcher in the area of blacks and coronary heart disease. In an article in the *American Heart Journal*, he postulated that the "myth" of black immunity to heart disease is the result of a tragedy of errors: statistical mistakes, lack of accurate data, underdiagnoses and inadequate accessibility of blacks to modern diagnostic techniques and medical services. Not only do blacks have higher rates of death from heart disease, says Dr. Gillum, there are certain important differences in their disease experience. Though blacks and whites suffer from heart attacks and angina with about the same frequency, evidence shows that the conditions are more often fatal in blacks. Though many researchers are still pursuing the genetic angle, Dr. Gillum suggests that the statistics may reflect lack of adequate diagnosis and treatment rather than anything physiological.

That is not to say there aren't some correctable lifestyle factors involved in the development of disease in blacks. Studies show that more black men than white men smoke, a risk factor in both cardiovascular diseases and cancer. More black women than white women are obese, a cardiovascular risk factor that may also account for the extraordinarily high rate of type II diabetes—often called adult-onset diabetes—in middle-aged and older black women.

In fact, says James R. Gavin III, M.D., Ph.D., assistant professor of medicine at Washington University School of Medicine, in St. Louis, Missouri, 60 to 90 percent of all type II diabetics develop the disease because of obesity.

"That is very important," he says. "Here is the one factor over which we may exert a great deal of control. If these people lose weight, the improvement in glucose tolerance will very often greatly exceed the amount of weight loss. The loss of just a few pounds will result in a great improvement in carbohydrate tolerance. At normal weight, glucose tolerance actually may be normal."

There is some suspicion that the predisposition to obesity has a genetic connection, though the precise link is murky. The environmental factors are clearer: For many blacks, a good, healthful weight-loss diet simply isn't affordable.

"When we look at the eating habits of our urban patients, we see diets rich in simple carbohydrates and saturated fats," says Dr. Gavin. "Lean meats, vegetables and complex carbohydrates are generally precluded because of economics. . . ."

It is well known that nutritional deficiencies over time lead not only to specific ailments such as scurvy and beriberi, but also leave the body more vulnerable to infection and disease. Poor prenatal nutrition is widely recognized as a primary factor in the distressingly high infant-mortality rates among blacks.

Low birth weight and prematurity are leading causes of death among infants. According to the latest figures, 12.5 percent of all black infants weighed less than the standard weight of five pounds, eight ounces at birth and 17 percent were premature, a fact that in itself accounts for at least some of the low-birth-weight babies born to black mothers. Another figure too is significant—the month prenatal care begins. Although most black mothers begin care early—as do most white mothers—9 percent received either delayed or no care prior to the birth of their babies.

"And you've got to look at the population whose babies are dying," says Byllye Avery, executive director of the fledgling National Black Women's Health Project, headquartered in Atlanta. "They're of lower economic status and many of them are teenagers. Now, teenagers can have healthy babies. But if a teenager denies her pregnancy and doesn't get the proper food, she gets a little sickly baby. And that starts the chain."

Teenage mothers tend to be the children of teenage mothers. "If you look at a lot of teenage black mothers, they have mamas who are grandmas in their 30's—and great-grandmas in their 40's," says Ms. Avery. "So you aren't starting out with a healthy group of people. Instead, you've got a group of people predisposed toward high-risk pregnancy."

For that reason, groups like the National Urban League focus much of their attention on prenatal care and nutrition for the young, usually unwed mother, and fight tooth and nail to preserve federal nutrition programs that have been rapidly disappearing.

The Cancer Epidemic

Less attention has been paid to cancer, which has been insidiously gaining ground among blacks even as death rates for some cancers drop among whites. Just this year, Lucius C. Earles III, M.D., president of the black National Medical Association, called cancer an epidemic in the black community.

Cancer is perhaps the best example of how social and economic conditions dictate the individual experience blacks have with disease. While medical advances in diagnostic techniques have increased the amount of early detection—often the difference between life and death with cancer—blacks are not being diagnosed in the early, curable stages.

In fact, a national survey by the American Cancer Society showed that urban blacks tend to be less knowledgeable about cancer's warning signs, less likely to see a doctor and more likely to underestimate both the prevalence of cancer and chance for a cure.

Even after cancer is detected, the black experience is different. Survival rates are far lower than for whites, according to a study by the National Cancer Institute, which suggested that the wide variation in survival figures was due not to any genetic cause but because blacks, for economic or social reasons, were less likely to get the most up-to-date treatment or follow-up care.

Dietary deficiencies of vitamins A and C, two vitamins believed to protect against cancer, may also play a role in the gloomier cancer prognosis for blacks. In the case of esophageal cancer, which kills blacks at a rate four times higher than whites, smoking and drinking may be implicated, although the link is uncertain.

The Stress of Being Black

Stress may also play a role in the higher death rates from cancer and other diseases among blacks, although the connection, again, is not clear. Studies have shown that stress acts on the body directly by suppressing the disease-fighting capabilities of the immune system. Indirectly, it may increase life-threatening behaviors such as drinking and drug abuse which, in turn, can lead to nutritional deficiencies and diseases like cirrhosis of the liver. Stress may also be a factor in high blood pressure.

"I don't think it's a coincidence that most of the diseases that affect blacks more severely are the so-called stress diseases," says Byllye Avery.

Women seem particularly hard hit by stress. In a national survey, black women reported not only the lowest level of positive well-being, but more than half reported moderate to severe levels of distress, and a third showed a level of distress comparable to that reported by many mental patients.

Clearly, improving the black health picture is far from simple. Lifestyle changes—losing weight, reducing salt, eating three well-balanced meals a day, quitting smoking—require more than vigorous individual effort when poor health habits are dictated by economic or social conditions.

For most of us, good health is a priceless commodity. For many blacks, it's just expensive.

"The basic solution isn't personal," says Alvin F. Poussaint, M.D., professor of psychiatry at Harvard Medical School. "It's a full-employment economy, government support services such as health care, health education, prenatal nutrition programs, that insure good health from infancy on. It's not in the national interest to have families and children in such dire straits. It's too much of a risk for us not to insure that healthy children are born. To allow the birth of a defective infant that society has to take care of for 60 years—when it can be avoided—makes no sense. It's bad economics, bad medicine, and bad preventive medicine."

19

The Case of Sharon Kowalski and Karen Thompson:
Ableism, Heterosexism, and Sexism

Joan L. Griscom

In November, 1983, in Minnesota, Sharon Kowalski was in a head-on collision with a drunk driver. Her four-year old niece died soon after; her seven-year old nephew survived; and she suffered a severe brain-stem injury. As a result, she was paralyzed and lost the ability to speak. Kowalski was living in a committed partnership with Karen Thompson, although only their closest friends knew. Soon after the accident, serious conflict developed between Thompson and Kowalski's parents, which erupted in a series of law-suits that still continue. Thompson has been fighting in the courts of Minnesota to secure adequate rehabilitation for her as well as access to friends and family of her choice. In July, 1985, acting under Minnesota guardianship laws, her father placed Kowalski in a nursing home that lacked adequate rehabilitation facilities and prohibited Thompson and other friends from visiting her. If Thompson had not continued the struggle in the courts, Kowalski would probably still be locked away in this home. While in January, 1989, she was finally transferred to an appropriate rehabilitation center and reunited with lover and friends, she still is not free to make her own choices.

In this article I tell the story of Sharon Kowalski and Karen Thompson and show how prejudices deeply entrenched in our medical and legal systems intertwined to deny Kowalski the fullest quality of life. Among these modes of oppression are ableism, discrimination against disabled persons; heterosexism, the belief structured into our institutions that only heterosexual relationships are legitimate; and sexism, discrimination against women.

A History of the Events

By November of 1983, Sharon Kowalski and Karen Thompson had lived in partnership for almost four years. Karen was thirty-six years old, an assistant professor of physical education at St. Cloud State University in Minnesota. Devoutly religious, conservative in social outlook, three years earlier she had refused to join a class action sex discrimination suit at her university since it seemed irrelevant to her. Sharon was twenty-seven years old, an outstanding athlete who had graduated from St. Cloud in physical education and had just accepted a job coaching golf at St. Cloud for the next spring. She had grown up in the Iron Mine area of northern Minnesota, a conservative world where women are expected to marry young and have children. Defying such expectations, she became the first member of her family to attend college and earned her own tuition by working part-time in the mines. After she and Karen fell in love, they exchanged rings, bought a house together, and vowed a lifetime commitment to each other.

After the accident, it was unclear if Sharon would live. For weeks she lay in a coma, and Karen spent as many as eight or ten hours a day talking to her, reading the Bible, massaging and stretching her neck, shoulders, and hands. As medical staff explained, it is essential to massage and stretch brain-injured patients in a coma, for they tend to curl up tightly and permanently damage their muscles in the process. The next concern was the degree to which she would recover. Doctors were pessimistic. However, in January, 1984, Karen noticed that Sharon was moving her right index finger, and discovered that Sharon could indicate yes-and-no answers to questions by moving her finger. Later she began to tap her fingers, and then slowly learned to write letters and words.

The Kowalski parents became increasingly suspicious of the long hours Karen was spending with their daughter. Increasingly Karen feared they would take steps to prevent her from participating in medical decisions and to exclude her from Sharon's life. Initially the parents stayed at Karen's and Sharon's home, but one day, they moved out, without telling her; and in the evening, Donald Kowalski told her she was visiting too often, that only family could really love Sharon. After consulting a hospital psychologist, Karen wrote the parents a letter explaining their love, in hopes they would understand her need to be with Sharon and her importance to Sharon. They reacted with shock, denial, and rage. As the nightmare deepened, Karen consulted an attorney and learned she had no legal rights, unless she won guardianship. In March, 1984, she therefore filed for guardianship, and Donald Kowalski immediately counterfiled.

The results of the hearing at first appeared positive. In an out-of-court settlement, guardianship was awarded to Donald Kowalski, but Karen was granted equal access to medical and financial information and full visitation rights. She participated in both the physical and occupational therapy. Sharon continued to improve slowly, responding more often than before and more fully. Karen made her an alphabet board, and Sharon began to spell out answers to questions. Subsequently she began to communicate by using a typewriter, and in August she spoke a few words. However, conflicts continued. The day after the hearing, Donald Kowalski incorrectly told Karen she did not have visitation rights. Later, when it became necessary to move Sharon to another institution, he tried to cancel Karen's arrangements to work with Sharon and her therapists. When Karen and other friends took Sharon out on day passes, to church and other events, he objected, and subsequently testified in court that he did not want her out in public. In October, 1984, by court order, Sharon was moved further away to Duluth, and Kowalski filed a motion to gain full power as guardian and deny Karen visitation. Karen counterfiled to remove him as guardian.

The hearings on these motions took months to complete. During this period Sharon was moved several times, regressed in her skills, and became clinically depressed. By this time the Minnesota Civil Liberties Union had entered the case, arguing that Sharon's rights of free speech and free association, under the First Amendment, were being violated. The Handicap Services Program of Tri-County Action Programs, Inc., submitted lengthy testimony of Sharon's capacity to communicate, including a long conversation with her in which she stated that she was gay and Karen was her lover. At Sharon's request, the MCLU asked for the right to represent her and suggested she might eventually testify for herself. Ultimately the court refused both requests. They found that Sharon lacked sufficient understanding to make decisions for herself, and wrote that the elimination of the conflict between the Kowalski's and Karen was in her best interest. Accordingly, on July 23, 1985, the court awarded Donald Kowalski full guardianship, including the right to determine visitation. Within a day he denied visitation to Karen, other friends of Sharon, the MCLU, various disability rights groups, and others. In two days, he transferred her to a nursing home near his home with only minimal rehabilitation facilities. In August, 1985, Karen saw Sharon for what would be the last time for over three years.

As this summary indicates, the medical system had failed Sharon in at least three respects. First, they failed to supply her with necessary rehabilitation in the years when it was vital to her recovery. Following brain-stem injury, the initial months and years are crucial in rehabilitation; the longer the incapacity lasts, the more permanent the damage. As the legal battles protracted themselves, her chances of rehabilitation diminished. Stark in the medical record is the fact that this woman who was starting to stand and starting to feed herself was locked away for over three years with an implanted feeding tube, insufficiently stretched and exercised so that muscles that were starting to work curled back on themselves again. Second, she was deprived of the bombardment of emotional and physical stimulation needed to regenerate her cognitive faculties. For example, once she was in the nursing home, the regenerative outside excursions were forbidden. Third, although medical staff often recognized Sharon's unusual response to Karen, they failed to explain to her parents the importance of maintaining the connection. There was an urgent need for counseling to assist the parents, but except for one court-mandated session, there was none.

The failure of the medical system was consistently supported by the legal system.

Initially the court ruled that Sharon must be in a nursing home with a young adult rehabilitation ward. But once Donald Kowalski was awarded full guardianship, he was able to move her to a nursing home without such a ward. Another contradiction occurred in late 1985 when the Minnesota Office of Health Facility Complaints investigated Sharon's right to visitors of her choice, a right guaranteed under the Minnesota Patient Bill of Rights. They found that indeed her right was being violated. However, the state appeals court held that visitation rights under the Patient Bill of Rights were inapplicable to this case, since the healthcare facility was not restricting the right of visitation, the guardian was.

The deficiencies of guardianship law are a key problem throughout this case. First, a guardian can restrict a patient's rights and there is no legal recourse. As is often said, under present laws, a guardian can lock a person up and throw away the key. This is a national problem, affecting disabled people, elderly people, and others who are presumed incompetent for whatever reason. Second, guardians are inadequately supervised. Under Minnesota statutes, a guardian is required to have the ward tested annually for competency. Donald Kowalski never did so, and for over three years the courts did not require him to do so. As early as December, 1985, Karen filed a motion in district court to hold the guardian in contempt for failure to arrange competency testing and for failure to heed Sharon's "reliably expressed" wishes for visitation. The courts routinely rejected such motions until 1988.

Between 1985 and 1988 Karen and the Minnesota Civil Liberties Union pursued repeated appeals to various Minnesota courts, and all were denied. By now, since the legal system had failed her, Karen had begun to speak publicly and to seek help from the media, disability rights groups, gay and lesbian groups, and women's groups. She recognized that the legal precedents set in this case could be devastating for others, whether gay/lesbian couples, unmarried heterosexual people, or people living in communities of choice. The reserved, closeted, conservative professor slowly transformed into a passionate speaker in her quest to secure freedom and adequate rehabilitation for Sharon; and slowly she gained national attention. The alternative press, in particular, responded: national groups such as the National Organization for Women passed resolutions of support; the National Committee to Free Sharon Kowalski, a coalition of activists, formed with regional chapters. Finally the mainstream media, initially hostile, began publishing supportive articles; Karen appeared on national T.V. programs; and significant politicians, including Jesse Jackson, began to express concern and support. Meanwhile Sharon remained in the nursing home, cut off from many former friends, physically regressing and psychologically depressed.

In September, 1987, Karen filed a new request to have Sharon tested for competency. February, 1988, brought the first break in the case; the judge ruled the testing should be done, and finally, in July, ordered it. In January, 1989, Sharon was moved to the Miller-Dwan Medical Center in Duluth for a 60-day evaluation. Through his attorney, Donald Kowalski unsuccessfully argued against both the move and the testing. At Miller-Dwan, Sharon immediately expressed her wish to see Karen, as well as her awareness that her father would disapprove. On February 2, 1989, Karen visited her for the first time in three and a half years, an event which made banner headlines in the alternative press across the nation. She was, however, highly depressed, and there were numerous physical changes: for example, her feet had curled up so tightly that she was no longer able to stand. A more significant issue was her cognitive ability; her short-term memory loss remains considerable.

The competency evaluation nevertheless demonstrated that she could communicate on an adult level and that she had significant potential for rehabilitation. As a long-term goal Miller-Dwan recommended "her return to pre-morbid home environment" and added,

> We believe Sharon has shown areas of potential and ability to make rational choices in many areas of her life. She has consistently indicated a desire to return home and, by that, means to St. Cloud to live with Karen Thompson again.

Soon after the release of this report, Donald Kowalski resigned as guardian, for both financial and health reasons, and the parents stopped attending medical conferences. In June, 1989, Sharon was transferred to Travilla, a long-term rehabilitation center in Minneapolis for brain-injured young adults. Here she has continued to have extensive occupational, physical, and speech therapy. Karen again has been able to spend many hours with her, taking her out on passes. She had surgery on her legs, feet, toes, left shoulder and arm to reverse the results of three years of inadequate care. She uses both a speech synthesizer and a motorized wheel chair. However, major issues remain unsettled.

Karen subsequently filed for guardianship, and Sharon's court-appointed attorney and medical staff from Miller-Dwan and Travilla testified positively in favor of their relationship. The medical personnel testified unanimously that Sharon is capable of deciding for herself what kinds of relationships she wants and with whom, and that she responds more to Karen than to anyone else. Further, they testified that Sharon is capable of living outside an institution, that returning home to St. Cloud would be best for her, and that Karen is best qualified to care for her in a home environment. However, witnesses for the Kowalski's strenuously opposed the petition. According to one report, they stated they would not continue to see Sharon if Karen became her guardian. The judge appeared increasingly uncomfortable with the national publicity generated by the case. While in August, 1990, he allowed Sharon and Karen to fly out to San Francisco for the national convention of the National Organization for Women, where they each received a Woman of Courage award, in October he denied permission for Sharon to attend the first Disability Pride Day in Boston. He issued a gag order against Karen, which was overturned on appeal. Finally, in April, 1991, in a lengthy decision, he denied guardianship to Karen and awarded it to a supposedly "neutral third party," a former classmate of Sharon who lives near the Kowalski parents and testified against Karen in a 1984 hearing. He based his decision in part on the Kowalskis' opposition, in part on his belief that while Sharon is capable of expressing wishes for visitation, her expressed wish to live with Karen in St. Cloud is "not tantamount to a preference of who should be her guardian." Karen will appeal this decision.

Readers who wish more information about the details of this case may consult items listed at the end of this article.[1,3] Up-to-date information is regularly published in feminist, gay, and disability rights newspapers such as *off our backs*, *National NOW Times*, *Gay Community News*, *The Disability Rag*, and others.

The Three Modes of Oppression

Sharon Kowalski has been denied the fullest quality of life by three interacting systems of oppression: ableism, heterosexism, and sexism. These are not simply prejudices held by individuals; they also pervade social structures such as the medical and legal systems and thus become modes of oppression. Originally Karen believed that their difficulties were merely personal problems. She had believed all her life that the institutions of our society are basically fair and reasonable and support the rights of individuals. In the book[3] she co-authored with her St. Cloud colleague Julie Andrzejewski, she documented the development of her awareness that wide social and political forces were involved in their supposedly personal problems and that the oppression they have experienced is systemic.

Ableism has been rampant throughout this case. Sharon's inability to speak has often been construed as a lack of competence, and her particular kinds of communication have not been recognized. Quite early Karen noticed that some people did not speak to Sharon, some raised their voices as if she was deaf, and others spoke to her as if she was a child. A doctor spoke about Sharon in her presence as if she was not there. When Karen later asked her how she felt about this, Sharon typed out, "Shitty." Probably one reason Sharon has responded to Karen more than anyone else is that from the start Karen has talked directly to her, at length, has read to her, has played music for her, and has consulted her wishes at every point. Although the MCLU and the Handicap Services Program submitted extensive transcripts of conversations with Sharon, the courts did not accept these as evidence of competence, relying instead on the testimony of people who had much less interaction with her. In a major article in the St. Paul *Pioneer Press* (1987), the reporter described the Kowalskis' visiting the room "where their eerily silent daughter lies trapped in her twisted body." Eerily silent? This is the person who typed out "columbine" when asked what her favorite flower is, answered arithmetical questions correctly, and responded to numerous questions about her life, her feelings, and her wishes. She also communicates nonverbally in many ways: gestures, facial expressions, smiles, tears, and laughter.

Thanks to ableism, Sharon has often been stereotyped as helpless. The presumption of helplessness "traps" her far more severely than her "twisted body." Once a person is stereotyped as helpless, then there is no need to consult her wishes; her testimony is unnecessary; her written communications can be ignored. When Sharon was transferred to Miller-Dwan in 1989 for competency testing, Karen reported with joy that the staff was giving her full information and allowing her to make choices, even if her choice was to do nothing. Most seriously, if a person is seen as helpless, then there is no potential for rehabilitation. As Ellen Bilofsky[1] has written, Sharon was presumed "incompetent until proven competent." If the courts had not accepted Karen's 1987 motion for competency testing, Sharon could have remained in the nursing home indefinitely, presumed incompetent.

Finally, ableism can lead to keeping disabled people invisible and hidden, literally out of sight. This is clearly illustrated in Donald Kowalski's responses to his daughter. He argued strenuously against day passes and resented Karen's efforts to take her out. He testified that he would not take her to a shopping center or to church because he did not wish to put her "on display . . . in her condition." Although it was clear to medical staff that outside excursions provided Sharon with important pleasure and stimulation, both vital for rehabilitation, they often cooperated with the father in denying her the possibility. According to an article in the *Washington Post*, Kowalski once said, "What the hell difference does it make if she's gay or lesbian or straight or anything because she's laying there in diapers? . . .let the poor kid rest in peace." Invisible in the nursing home to which he had moved her, cut off from lover and friends, there was little chance for Sharon to demonstrate competence. The wonder is that after three and a half years of loss, loneliness, and lack of proper physical care, she was able to emerge from her depression and respond to her examiners. To retain her capacity for response, through such an experience, suggests a strong spirit.

The second mode of oppression infusing this case is homophobia, the fear and dislike of homosexuality, and heterosexism, the structuring of our institutions so that only heterosexual relationships are legitimated. Glaringly apparent throughout is the failure to recognize committed gay/lesbian partnerships. Donald Kowalski has consistently denied the possibility. When Karen first arrived at the hospital after the accident, the first on the scene, she was not allowed access to Sharon or even to any information because she was not "family." Seeing her anguish, a Roman Catholic priest interceded, brought information, and arranged for a doctor to speak with her. Although the two women considered themselves married, in law they were not, and therefore lacked any social or legal rights as a couple. If recognized as a couple, there would have been no question of denying visitation, and the long nightmare of the three-and-a-half year separation would have been impossible. While unmarried heterosexual partners might still have trouble securing guardianship, there would be little or no problem for a married partner.

Because of heterosexism, it was not important to honor Sharon's obvious emotional need for her partner and Karen's rehabilitative effect on her. Since it was clear that Sharon responded actively to Karen, she was often included in the therapeutic work. Yet, prior to 1989, medical staff often were unwilling to testify to this positive effect, even when they had privately noted it to Karen. Perhaps they feared condoning the same-sex relationship if they reported positively about it; perhaps they did not wish to be involved in the conflict. One neurologist, Dr. Keith Larson, did testify, although he stipulated that he spoke as a friend of the court, not as one of Karen's witnesses. His testimony is worth looking at in detail.

> The reason I'm here today is . . . to deliver an observation that I have agonized over, and thought a great deal about, and prayed a little bit . . . I cannot help but say that Sharon's friend, Karen, can get out of Sharon physical actions, attempts at vocalization, and longer periods of alertness and attention than can really any of our professional therapists.

Why was it necessary to "agonize" over this testimony? To pray about it? Why such a tremendous effort? Clearly, had one of the partners been male, Larson would have had no such difficulty. He simply would have reported the obvious fact: that the patient responded far more to her partner than to anyone else. Some medical staff did testify to Karen's positive effects: psychologists, nurses, occupational therapists. And since 1989 the testimony of medical personnel from Miller-Dwan and Travilla has been consistent, strong, and unanimous. However, in repeated decisions, including the most recent (1991), the courts have ignored this testimony.

Finally, heterosexism is evident in a consistent tendency to exaggerate the role of sex in same-sex relationships. In general our society believes that the lives of gay/lesbian people revolve around sex, although evidence from all social-psychological research is that homosexual people are no more sexually active than heterosexual people. Further, gay/lesbian sex is often perceived as sexual exploitation rather than an appropriate expression of mutual caring. The final denial of Karen's visitation rights was based on the charge that she might sexually abuse Sharon. A physician hired by the Kowalskis, Dr. William L. Wilson, levelled this charge as follows:

> It has come to my attention that Karen Thompson has been involved in bathing Sharon Kowalski behind a closed door for a prolonged period of time. It has also come to my attention that Ms. Thompson has alleged a sexual relationship with Sharon Kowalski that existed prior to the accident. Based on this knowledge and my best medical judgment concerning Sharon and her welfare, I feel that visits by Karen Thompson at this time would expose Sharon Kowalski to a high risk of sexual abuse.

Accordingly, as Sharon's physician, Wilson directed the nursing home staff not to permit Karen to visit. Even though under legal statute Karen could have continued her visits while the various decisions were under appeal, the nursing home was obliged to obey the doctor's order.

In this instance, ableism and heterosexism merge. Had Sharon and Karen been unmarried heterosexual partners, sexual abuse probably would have not been a significant argument. Had they been married, the issue would not exist. Ableism often denies disabled persons their sexuality. However, a person does not lose her sexuality simply because she becomes disabled. Furthermore, a person who loses the capacity to speak has a special need for touching. What are Sharon's sexual rights? Karen has written that when Sharon was starting to emerge from the coma, she once reached out and touched Karen's breast, and later placed Karen's hand on her breast. At the time Karen did not dare to ask medical advice, for fear of revealing their relationship, and she recognized that if they were a heterosexual couple, she would have been free to ask advice. Even to raise such questions could have exposed her to further charges of sexual abuse. Thus ableism and heterosexism combined to deny both Sharon and Karen the chance to explore such questions.

Heterosexism dictates that only heterosexual partnership can form the basis for a family. While same-sex partnerships are often called "anti-family" in our homophobic society, actually such relationships create family, in that they create stable emotional and economic units. *Family*, in this sense, may be defined as a kin-like unit of two or more persons who are related by blood, marriage, adoption, or primary commitment, and who usually share the same household. Sharon and Karen considered themselves married. Karen's long pilgrimage over almost nine years is testimony to an extraordinary depth of commitment; she would not permit her loved one to be locked away without rehabilitation. Sharon, similarly, has consistently said that she is gay, Karen is her lover, and she wishes to live again with her in St. Cloud. While marriage has historically occurred between two sexes, we cannot determine our definition from history. In United States history, for example, marriage between black and white persons was forbidden for centuries. In 1967, when the Supreme Court finally declared miscegenation laws unconstitutional, there were still such laws on the books in sixteen states.

Sexism is sufficiently interfused with heterosexism that it is difficult to separate them. Heterosexism often enforces a social role on women in which they are subordinated to men. For example, women in the social world of the area in Minnesota where Sharon grew up were expected to marry young and submit to the authority of their husbands, a model that is intrinsically sexist. From the perspective of this model, Sharon's partnership with Karen was illegitimate. Sexism is also apparent in the awarding of full guardianship to the father. In a sexist society, it is appropriate to assign a woman to her male parent; had Sharon been a man rather than a twenty-eight year old "girl," such a decision might have been less possible. In a sexist society, women are not encouraged to take responsibility for their sexuality, just as society denies sexual rights to the disabled and the elderly. Finally, our society devalues friendship, especially friendship between women. Soon after the accident, a doctor advised Karen to go away and forget Sharon. The gist of his remarks were that "Sharon's parents will always be her parents. They have to deal with this, but you don't. Maybe you should go back to leading your own life." Friendship between two women was unimportant. Ableism as well as sexism is apparent in this advice.

It is sometimes impossible to separate the modes of oppression even for the purpose of analysis. It is tempting to ask which mode was the most significant in denying Sharon her rights. However, this case makes clear that all the issues work simultaneously and dealing with any one of them in isolation from the others is mistaken. Like Audre Lorde[2], I argue that "there is no hierarchy of oppressions." Admittedly, any individual's perspective on the case is likely to reflect the issue most central to their life: e.g., the gay press emphasizes heterosexism, and the disability rights press emphasizes ableism. Unfortunately, however, each all too often slights or omits the other. While working in coalition on the case, some women were ill at ease with disability rights activists, and some disability rights groups were anxious about associating themselves with gay/lesbian issues. But the fact is that there are lesbians and gays in the disabled community, and disabled folks in the women's community. Karen experienced the inseparability of the issues on one occasion when she was invited to speak to a Presbyterian disability rights concerns group. They asked her to speak only about ableism, since they had already "done" gay concerns. She tried, but found it nearly impossible; she had to censor her material, ignore basic facts, and leave out crucial connections.

What the three modes of oppression have in common is that in each case one group of people take power over another. Disabled people, women, gays and lesbians are all to some degree denied their full personhood by the structures of our society. Their self-determination is limited; their choices can be denied. Their sexuality is controlled. On the basis of ableism, heterosexism, and sexism, Sharon Kowalski's opportunity for the fullest quality of life was permanently taken from her. She was denied proper medical care, legal counsel of her choice, and access to the people she wished to see. As the Minnesota Civil Liberties Union put it, "The convicted criminal loses only his or her liberty; Sharon Kowalski has lost the right to choose who she may see, who she may like, and who she may love." Even her right to be tested for competency was denied for years. Since that right was restored, she now has access to good medical treatment and the people she loves, but she is still denied the right to live where she chooses.

Conclusion

Many activists and coalition groups have become involved nationally in the struggle to provide rehabilitation for Sharon Kowalski and bring her home. These include disability rights activists, gays and lesbians, feminists and their male supporters, and civil rights workers. In addition there have been many hundreds, perhaps by now thousands, of people who are not involved in activist work but are drawn to this case by the dimension of human rights. After all, any of us could be hit by a drunk driver, become disabled, and in the process lose our legal and medical rights in comparable ways. The Kowalski/Thompson case stands as a warning that in our deeply divided society, freedom is still a privilege and rights are fragile.

People living in nontraditional families—whether gay/lesbian, unmarried heterosexuals, or communities of choice—need legal protection to secure their legal and medical rights. Karen Thompson has suggested the importance of making your relationships known to your family of birth, if possible, and informing them of your wishes in case of accident. Also, it is essential to execute a durable power of attorney, a document in which you stipulate a person to make medical and financial decisions for you in case you are incapacitated. Copies should be given to your physicians. While requirements vary from state to state and such powers of attorney are not always enforceable, they may serve to protect your rights. Information about how to execute them may be found in your public library, in consultation with a competent lawyer, or in Appendix B of the book *Why Can't Sharon Kowalski Come Home?*[3]

NOTES

1. Ellen Bilofsky. "The Fragile Rights of Sharon Kowalski." *Health/PAC Bulletin*, 1989, *19*, 4–16.

2. Audre Lorde. "There Is No Hierarchy of Oppressions." *Interracial Books for Children Bulletin*, 1983, *14*, 9. See also "Age, Race, Class, and Sex: Women Redefining Difference" in *Sister Outsider*. Trumansburg, New York: The Crossing Press, 1984.

3. Karen Thompson and Julie Andrzejewski. *Why Can't Sharon Kowalski Come Home?* San Francisco: Spinster/Aunt Lute, 1988.

20

Poem for the Young White Man Who Asked Me How I, an Intelligent, Well-read Person Could Believe in the War between Races

Lorna Dee Cervantes

In my land there are no distinctions.
The barbed wire politics of oppression
have been torn down long ago. The only reminder
of past battles, lost or won, is a slight
rutting in the fertile fields.

In my land
people write poems about love,
full of nothing but contented childlike syllables.
Everyone reads Russian short stories and weeps.
There are no boundaries.
There is no hunger, no
complicated famine or greed.

I am not a revolutionary.
I don't even like political poems.
Do you think I can believe in a war between races?
I can deny it. I can forget about it
when I'm safe,
living on my own continent of harmony
and home, but I am not
there.

I believe in revolution
because everywhere the crosses are burning,
sharp-shooting goose-steppers round every corner,
there are snipers in the schools . . .
(I know you don't believe this.
You think this is nothing
but faddish exaggeration. But they
are not shooting at you.)

I'm marked by the color of my skin.
The bullets are discrete and designed to kill slowly.
They are aiming at my children.
These are facts.
Let me show you my wounds: my stumbling mind, my
"excuse me" tongue, and this
nagging preoccupation
with the feeling of not being good enough.

These bullets bury deeper than logic.
Racism is not intellectual.
I can not reason these scars away.

Outside my door
there is a real enemy
who hates me.

I am a poet
who yearns to dance on rooftops,
to whisper delicate lines about joy
and the blessings of human understanding.
I try. I go to my land, my tower of words and
bolt the door, but the typewriter doesn't fade out
the sounds of blasting and muffled outrage.
My own days bring me slaps on the face.
Every day I am deluged with reminders

that this is not
my land

and this is my land.

I do not believe in the war between races

but in this country
there is war.

21

Listening

Sey Chassler

One morning, about 20 years ago, my wife and I were arguing about whether or not I ever listened to her. It was one of those arguments that grow into passion and pain and, often, for me at least, into a kind of hysteria. This one became one of those that do not go away with the years. Suddenly, she threw something at me, and said: "From now on you do the shopping, plan the meals, take care of the house, everything. I'm through!"

I was standing in the kitchen looking at the shelves of food, at the oven, at the sink, at the refrigerator, at the cleaning utensils. At my wife.

My reaction was orgasmic. Somewhere inside of me there was screaming, hurting, a volcanic gush of tears flooded my head and broke down over me. I shook and sobbed. I was terrified. No matter what, I knew I could not handle the burden. I could not do my job and be responsible for the entire household. How could I get through a day dealing with personnel, budgets, manuscripts, art departments, circulation statistics, phone calls, people, agents, management, writers, and *at the same time* plan dinner for tonight and tomorrow night and breakfast and a dinner party Thursday night and shopping for it all and making sure the house is in good shape and the woman who cleans for us is there and on time and the laundry done and the children taken to the doctor, and the children taken care of? How could *any* one person do all that and stay sane? No one could do that properly. No one. Natalie simply watched me for a while. Finally she said: "Okay. Don't worry. I'll keep on doing it." She put on her coat and went to her office.

Despite her simple statement that she would go on doing it, I stood awhile telling myself that *no one* could do all of that. No one. There was a *click* in my head—and it dawned on me that *she* was doing it.

How invisible my wife's life was to me. How invisible to men women are.

Shortly afterward, in 1963 or 1964, not long after *The Feminine Mystique* was published, Betty Friedan and I were invited to speak to the nation's largest organization of home economists. As executive editor of *Redbook* magazine, I was asked to talk about the magazine's view of women. Betty was talking about the thesis of her book—that all American women were trapped in their homebound positions and that women's magazines, among others, put out propaganda to keep them trapped.

I had read *The Feminine Mystique*, of course, and felt I was fully prepared to answer it and, thereby, to defend not only *Redbook* from Friedan's attack but to defend American women, as well.

In mid-speech I proclaimed that, despite what Friedan had written, women, in this day and in this country, were free to be whatever they wished to be, that they were not children to be told what they might and might not do, that they could work at whatever profession they chose or whatever job, that they were free to be wives if they wished, and truck drivers if they wished, and mothers if they wished or homemakers if they wished. The list was growing longer and the speech was getting more and more impassioned in its proclamation of freedoms. I paused and waited for the applause. I had, after all, just proclaimed freedom throughout the land! I looked out at the audience. The hall was silent.

My pause became a dark empty cavern, and I could feel myself groping for a way out, wondering what had gone awry. I felt naked, stripped bare before 800 women. I could not understand what I had said that was wrong. Looking for comfort, I thought of my wife, and—*click!* I suddenly realized that my wife was a woman who was free to choose a career and *had*—but who also had delayed that career until her children—*her* children!—were in school. She was not as free as I thought, nor was any married woman.

While my enthusiasm had diminished, I went on with my speech. But whatever it was that had clicked in my head first in the kitchen and then in Kansas City, stayed there. And for a long time afterward, there were things going on in my head that I couldn't quite get hold of.

Whatever they were, I found myself listening for clicks in my head while thinking about, talking to, or dealing with women. And since I worked with more than 60 women every day and came home to my wife every night, I had a good deal of listening to do.

At home one night after dinner, I sat down to read the paper, as usual, while my wife went into the kitchen to do the dishes. I could see her in the kitchen. She looked happy, or at least not unhappy, there in the pretty kitchen she had designed— and she was probably appreciating the change of pace after a hard day as chief of service in a mental hospital dealing with a staff of three or four dozen employees and a hundred or more patients, some of whom threatened her from time to time. Yes, she was using the time well, since she had no hobbies to break the tension. I was feeling comfortably and happily married, when—*click!*—the view changed, and I saw a hardworking woman doing something she'd rather not be doing just now.

When my wife finished and sat down near me, I kissed her with a special tenderness, I thought. She didn't. As a matter of fact, she turned the other cheek. Something was going on in both our heads.

The next night *I* decided to do the dishes and she read the paper. At the sink, I began to think about male arrogance. Why did I have the choice of doing or not doing the dishes, while my wife did not? By the same token, why had she had to wait until our children were in school to exercise her "free" choice of working at her career? Our jobs were equally pressured and difficult (hers more harrowing than mine) and yet, if I chose to sit and read after dinner, I could. She could not, unless I decided she could by *offering* to do the dishes. My definition of freedom was based on a white male conception: the notion that because I am free, because I can make choices, anyone can make choices. I was defining "anyone" in my terms, in masculine terms. I am anyone, unqualified. She is anyone, gender female. So you can take your tender kisses and shove them.

I felt I had caught the edge of an insight about the condition of women and while I wanted to, I found I couldn't discuss it with men; it made them uneasy and defensive. They'd fight off the conversation. They'd say things like "But that's the way it is supposed to be, Sey. Forget it!" After a while, I began to feel like one of those people who carry signs in the street announcing the end of the world. Pretty soon I got defensive, too—and my questions produced terrific dinner-table fights with other male guests. The women almost always remained silent, seeming to enjoy watching the men wrestle. The men were convinced that I was a nut. And several, including my father, accused me of "coming out for women," because in my job as editor of a women's magazine that would be "smart" and "profitable."

I certainly couldn't talk to any woman directly, because I was embarrassed. I didn't believe women would tell me the truth—and, more important, I was not going to let them know I was worried or thinking about the matter or afraid to find the answer.

If you are one of those men who feel trapped by women, who think they are fine for sex but interfere with living, all of the above may not be very clear to you. Maybe the following will set some clicks off for you.

The other day I was reading *The Intimate Male*, by Linda Levine, ACSW, and Lonnie Barbach, Ph.D. It is one of those books in which men reveal all their sexual secrets, fantasies, and so on. It is supposed to help us understand each other, I guess. All I ever get out of such books is the discovery that other guys and I share the same fantasies. Well, in this one, I read about a guy who likes his wife to walk around the house without any underwear under her skirt. Innocent enough, you guess? But what he *really* likes is to "lay on the floor while my wife does the dishes, and look up her dress"!

I told this story to a couple of men I know, and they thought it beat all hell how he got his wife to walk around without her pants on. They loved it. Hey, what a crazy guy!

But wait. Let's try it from the wife's point of view: here is this nice woman who has spent her day working somewhere, either out on a job of some kind or taking care of this romantic fellow's house. She is about as beat as he is by the end of the day and maybe she'll be ready for sex later, but not right now. Right now her hands are full of dirty dishes and wet garbage, so what can she be thinking of? *He* doesn't have to do anything but work his eyeballs.

Everyone to her or his own kink, of course. But it isn't kink that is going on here. What is going on here is a neat exercise in power. The man on the floor is proving to his wife and to himself that he is the boss. He can take his pleasure while she works. Of course, she can tell him to knock it off and keep her pants on, but that is going to make him very unhappy. Unhappy enough maybe to go out for a few beers until she comes to her senses. "This freaking wife of mine," he'll say to the guys in the bar, "every time I want it, she's doing the dishes or too tired or something."

So the chances are she doesn't tell him to knock it off, because the implied threat of walking out for a while gains the husband the privilege of turning his wife into a dancing girl while she's doing the dishes. In other words, here is a neat form of blackmail—"Do as I say, or you'll get my mad side and everyone will know I married a cold little bitch." This is known as dominance—and you should have heard a click in your head.

The episode on the kitchen floor is, admittedly, a bit unusual. That sort of thing doesn't go on with most people. Here's one that is more familiar. As reported in *The Wall Street Journal* in a story on sex discrimination in law firms, King & Spalding of Atlanta had a company picnic last summer. Initially proposed for the festivities was a "wet T-shirt" contest, but, in the end, the firm merely decided to hold a bathing-suit competition. It was open only to the company's women summer associates. A third-year law student from Harvard University won. While awarding her the prize, a partner of the firm said, "She has the body we'd like to see more of." King & Spalding is no small company. Among its clients are Coca-Cola Company, Cox Broadcasting Corporation, and General Motors.

The question here is: why would a Harvard law student parade around in a bathing suit for a bunch of rowdy male lawyers? It's easy to say she was looking for a job with a good firm. Since the bathing-suit competition incident, King & Spalding has promised it will not practice sex discrimination, and the student who won the contest has agreed to join the firm. But the question remains: why would she enter such a contest?

I refer you to the woman in the kitchen, above. Why did she take her pants off?

Dominance. Male dominance. Someone calls the shots, someone else does as she is told.

What would you say to your boss if he announced that he was thinking of having a wet jockstrap contest at the company picnic? Or if your best girl asked you to take your pants off, while you crawled under the car to have a look at the manifold? What would you say? If your wife asked you to stay home with the baby or to meet the plumber or to do the shopping or to clean the toilet bowl some day, what would you say?

Click?

My wife and I have been married 41 years. We think of ourselves as being happily married—and we are. But the dominance is there. It means that in my relationship with my wife, I am almost totally the boss. When we have a discussion (that's marital-ese for argument), more often than not it is I who declare when the end of it arrives. If we make a plan together and she does most of the work on the plan, it is given to me for *approval*. If I do most of the work on the plan, I submit it to her for her *information*. If she agrees to the plan, she'll say "Good, should we do it?" If *I* agree to the plan, I'll say, "Good, let's go." That doesn't mean that I make all the decisions, control all the funds, make all the choices, talk louder than she does. I don't have to. It simply means that I do not have to ask my wife for permission to do anything. Whether she does or says anything about it or not, everything my wife does is to a large extent qualified by what I think or will think. In effect, she must ask my permission. What's more, as husband, I seem—no matter how I try to avoid it—to assign all the jobs in our family. In effect, I win all the arguments—even the ones we don't have. That's emotional dominance—and it means that everything that occurs between us, everything we do together, is monitored by me.

Once during a lecture tour I was talking to undergraduates at the University of Indiana about the Women's Movement and how important it is. One of the women, a senior, asked a question and then she said: "I don't want to get married when I graduate. I want to be someone." *Click.*

That statement haunts me. I never had to say anything like that. I had always thought I would get married *and* be somebody. What's more, I took it for granted that my wife would be responsible for the family in addition to her job. I would love and care for my children, but I wouldn't have to deal with their phone calls at the office. They'd call my wife at the office. That's what mommies are for, aren't they? No one had to tell the children that. No one had to tell me that. No one had to tell my wife that. We all *knew* it. And everyone knew that men not only had freedom of choice but freedom to grant permission to women to make choices.

I had freedom, yes, but as my children were growing up, as I looked at my family, I began to struggle with a barely conscious knowledge that the happy group of people with whom I lived—my two sons, my daughter, my wife—were feeling uneasy when I was around. They shifted stiffly, muffled their voices, stifled their laughter when I arrived in their midst. They could feel the dominant grown male arrive. I didn't want that. It was simply there—where I was.

As the years went by and my consciousness grew, I began to recall for examination not only those uneasy days, but really angry ones. What was I angry about? I was angry that I was not always my wife's center of attention. I had been brought up thinking I would be. That made our early days very rough, indeed. I was angry when our first son was born. Those were the days when women had babies and men simply were proud, frightened, and prepared to pay the bills.

The birth of my first child was traumatic, as it was with each of the others. Beyond admiring the growing child in my wife's body, I played virtually no part in any of their births. As each child was about to be born, I got to drive my wife to the hospital. I was kept in the waiting room for expectant fathers. I could read and smoke and bite my nails. No one came to tell me anything. The movies had told me childbirth is painful, dangerous, life-threatening for a woman. I stood in the corner of the waiting room—all three times—fearful, out of touch with whatever dark things were happening in an operating room somewhere above me, sick with wanting to be near my wife.

In the evening before my second son was born, it was extremely hot, and the nurses sent me home to await his arrival. Nervous and feeling abandoned, I took a shower with an electric fan whirring in the bathroom. As I reached for the towel, I stuck my fingers into the metal blades of the fan. I screamed for my wife and cursed that she was not there. I raced around looking for bandages, found a handkerchief, wrapped it around my fingers, shoved a months-old condom on them to stem the flow of blood, dressed, ran to a doctor down the street, was stitched up, and finally rushed off to the hospital—to wait. And he was born. But I didn't get to see him right away.

It was always the same: when my first son was born, they didn't let me see him for a while. A nurse simply came and told me to be proud. "It's a boy!" she said. I had to ask if my wife was all right. I had to ask when I would see our baby. After a half hour or so, they took me up to a nursery window and pointed to a bundle in a tiny basket. They took me to see my wife and let me kiss her. They sent me away. They did the same with our second son. They did the same with my daughter. Only, they didn't say, "Be proud," they said, "You have a beautiful little girl this time!" I was proud. But they did not let me use my love, touch my world.

I was angry. I felt left out, put off, unable to feel entirely that I, too, had had a baby, had given (*given*) birth to a child—just as my wife had. I think sometimes that the anger of those days has carried into all of our lives. I, in some kind of crazy partnership with my past, my traditions, put it there—in the lives of my wife, and of our children.

Now, as I look back at the time of the births, when I was kept out, given no choice over urgent and vital matters affecting my life, I understand how it feels to be a woman and have no choices—how it feels not to be heard. I have finally discovered what it is to be like the undergraduate who wanted to be someone. She, too, I realize now was in a waiting room waiting to be proud—and knowing her pride would be controlled by others.

Last year, after a board meeting of one of the nation's best-known women's organizations, I was sitting with a group of women who are legislators, corporate executives, lawyers, broadcasters—big shots. One of them said: "We've been at it for about twenty years now, and we've made real progress—why then does the pain still linger?" Another answered simply: "Because the men still keep the lid on."

Click.

The Women's Movement has made some remarkable changes in our lives, but it hasn't changed the position of the male much at all. Men still make the moves. They are the ones who, in their own good time, move in. And in their own good time, move out. Someone makes the rules, someone else does as she is told.

About eight years ago, my wife suggested—finally—that I must be hard of hearing because I never seemed to hear what she said, even though I answered all questions and conducted real conversations with her. She made me promise to see an ear doctor. I did. He found nothing wrong. When I told him that this whole idea was my wife's, he sent me home. "Most of my male patients," he said, "are here on the advice of their wives." I laughed. But . . . *click*!

We don't have to listen. As men we simply are in charge. It comes with the territory. Popeye sings "I am what I am." God said the same thing to Moses in the wilderness. Male images. They're built into us. Images of dominance.

I got to be the editor of *Redbook* because I was the second in line. There was at least one woman on the staff who could have done the job as well or better than I, but the president of the company had, in his time, passed over many women—and this time there was no exception. While I knew about editing and writing and pictures, I didn't know beans about fiction or recipes and fashion and cosmetics and all of those things; still, having the responsibility and the authority, I had to act as if I did. I was forced, therefore, to listen very carefully to the women who worked with me and whose help I needed. And, listening, I learned to talk with them and talking with them I began to hear them.

Most of the editors in the company were women, most of the sales and business people were men. The men could never figure out how to talk to the women. They seemed to think that I had learned some secrets about women, and they'd stop me in the halls and say things like "How can I tell Anne such and such about this advertising account?" And I'd say, "Just tell her." And they'd say, "But can you say that to a woman? Will she understand?"

Click.

In the beginning, I found myself using my position as a male. I *talked* to the men; I gave orders to the women.

By the same token, the men and women dealt with me differently. In an argument, a man would feel comfortable telling me I was wrong and, if necessary, call me a damn fool. Two hours later we'd be working together without grudge. But most women would give silent assent and do as they were told. They obeyed. The stronger ones *would* call me stupid or whatever they needed to, but they (and I) would hurt for days. They had breached the rules. Some would come up to apologize, and we both would wind up with tears in our eyes. Dominance. When we learned to work with each other as equals, we learned to be angry as equals—and to respect each other, to love each other as equals.

And yet, while I began to feel some measure of equality with the women, I could not, for a very long time, figure out how to achieve the kind of camaraderie, the palship, the mutual attachment to team, the soldierly equality of action, that men feel for each other. I could never feel comfortable putting my arm around a woman as we walked down a corridor talking business or conspiring against some agent or corporate plan—as I would with a man. Out of sheer good feeling and admiration for a job well done and a fight well fought, there were days when I wanted to throw my arms around women I worked with—as I would with a man—but I never really felt fully free to.

While it was hard to achieve camaraderie, as we worked hand-in-hand, eye-to-eye, shoulder-to-shoulder, mind-to-mind warm, erotic, sexy—yet not sexy—feelings would begin to flow. While they were mutual, they were not feelings to be turned into acts of sex. They were feelings that came out of—and went into—the intensity of the work at hand.

What were they like, these erotic feelings? They were like the feelings of a locker room after a game played hard and won. They felt like sweat. They felt like heroism. They felt like bodies helping bodies. They felt like those urges that make it all right to smack a guy on the ass in congratulation and gratitude, to throw your arms around him and hug him for making the winning point. And they felt like the secret admiration of his body—because he was a hero—as he stood in the shower. How marvelous to feel that way about a woman—and not want to go to bed with her! Just to admire and love her for being with you—and for helping you to play the game. I recommend the feeling. And I think, perhaps, in prehistory when female and male hunted and gathered side-by-side in the frightening wilderness—sharing their fears, their losses, their gains and their triumphs equally—it must have been this way. In the time before the gods. In the time before I-am-what-I-am.

I was telling a woman friend about all of this. She asked: "Do you deal with your women colleagues and friends differently from the way you deal with your wife?"

Click.

I was sitting with a man friend, when, in relation to nothing in particular, he said: "Guys get to be heroes. Girls get to be cheerleaders. Guys get to be dashing womanizers, great studs. Women get to be sluts."

Click.

A lot of us men think of these things and we hurt when we do. And a lot of us—most of us—simply don't think of these things. Or we think of them as something that will go away—the complaints from women will go away, as they always seem to.

Still, as men, we recognize Freud's question: "Good God, what do women *want?*"

To be heard.

My 89-year-old mother, married 65 years to my 89-year-old father, says to him, "Someday you'll let me talk when I want to."

On the grimy wall of the 23rd Street station of the New York subway a woman's hand has written: "Women Lib gonna get your girl!"

In H. G. Wells's book, *The Passionate Friends*, Mary writes to Stephen: "Womankind isn't human, it's reduced human."

Margaret Mead, in a conversation, remarks that in American households, the man decides whether the toilet paper leads from the top of the roll or the bottom of the roll.

Will men ever appreciate fully what women are saying?

I don't think I will ever, fully. No matter what clicks in my head.

The world belongs to men. It is completely dominated by us—and by our images.

What men see when they look out and about are creatures very like themselves—in charge of everything. What women see when they look out and about is that the creatures in charge of everything are *unlike* themselves.

If you are a man, think of a world, your world, in which for everything you own or do or think you are accountable to women. Women are presidents, bankers, governors, door holders, traffic cops, airline pilots, bosses, supervisors, landlords. Shakespeare. The whole structure is completely dominated by women. Your doctor, your lawyer, your priest, minister, rabbi are women. The figure on the cross is a woman. God is a woman. Every authoritative voice and every authoritative image is the image and voice of women: Buddha, Mohammed, Moses, Matthew, Luke, Paul, the guy who does the voice-over on the commercial and Ben Franklin—all are women. So are Goliath and David. So are the Supreme Court, the tax collector, the head of the CIA, the mechanic who fixes your transmission, the editor of your daily newspaper. Jack the Giant Killer. Walter Mondale. St. Patrick. Ronald Reagan is a woman. Walter Cronkite is a woman. George Steinbrenner is a woman. Think of such a world. The Pope is a woman. JR is a woman. Casper Weinberger. Think of yourself in such a world. Think of your father in it. Think of *him* as a woman. Think about it.

Don't just brush it off, for Mary's sake—think about it.

Suggestions for Further Reading

Anzaldua, Gloria (ed.): *Making Faces, Making Soul: Creative and Critical Perspectives by Women of Color,* An aunt lute foundation book, San Francisco, 1990.
Bean, Joseph: *In the Life: A Black Gay Anthology,* Alyson Publishers, Boston, 1986.
Chinese Historical Society of Southern California: *Linking Our Lives: Chinese American Women of Los Angeles,* Chinese Historical Society of Southern California, Los Angeles, 1984.
Brown, R. M.: *RubyFruit Jungle,* Bantam, New York, 1977.
David, J. (ed): *The American Indian: The First Victim,* William Morrow and Co., New York, 1972.
Native Americans 500 Years After: photographs by Joseph C. Farner, text by Michael Dorris, Thomas Crowell & Co., New York, 1975.
Flores, Angel and Kate Flores: *The Defiant Muse: Hispanic Feminist Poems from the Middle Ages to the Present,* The Feminist Press, New York, 1986.
Gwaltney, J.: *Drylongso: A Self-Portrait of Black America,* Vintage Books, New York, 1981.
Haley, A.: *The Autobiography of Malcolm X,* Grove Press, New York, 1964.
Kingston, M. H.: *The Woman Warrior,* Vintage Books, New York, 1981.
Moody, A.: *Coming of Age in Mississippi,* Dell Publishing Co., New York, 1968.
Moore, Joan and Harry Pachon: *Hispanics in the U.S.,* Prentice-Hall, New York, 1985.
Naylor, G.: *The Women of Brewster Place,* Penguin Books, New York, 1983.
Reid, John: *The Best Little Boy in the World,* G. P. Putnam's Sons, New York, 1973.
Rivera, E.: *Family Installments: Memories of Growing Up Hispanic,* Penguin Books, New York, 1983.
Rubin, L. B.: *Worlds of Pain: Life in the Working Class Family,* Basic Books, New York, 1976.

Shulman, A. K.: *Memoirs of an Ex-Prom Queen*, Knopf, New York, 1972.

Silko, L. M.: *Ceremony*, New American Library, New York, 1972.

Smith, B. (ed.): *Home Girls: A Black Feminist Anthology*, Kitchen Table: Women of Color Press, New York, 1983.

Tan, Amy: *The Joy Luck Club*, Ivy Books, New York, 1990.

Thompson, Karen and Julie Andrzejewski: *Why Can't Sharon Kowalski Come Home?*, Spinsters/Aunt Lute, San Francisco, 1988.

Turkel, S.: *Working*, Avon Books, New York, 1972.

Warshaw, Robin: *I Never Called it Rape*, Harper and Row, New York, 1988.

Winged Words: American Indian Writers Speak: University of Nebraska Press, 1990.

Zahava, Irene (ed.): *Speaking for Ourselves: Short Stories by Jewish Lesbians*, Crossing Press, Freedom, California, 1990.

PART V

How It Happened: Race and Gender Issues in U.S. Law

It is clear that being born a woman, a person of color, or both, in addition to being poor, makes it far more likely that an individual will have less education, inferior health care, a lower standard of living, and a diminished set of aspirations compared with those who are born white, wealthy, and male. How does this happen? Is the lack of equality of opportunity and condition documented in the first four parts of this book accidental and aberrant? Or is it the inevitable result of a system designed to perpetuate the privileges of wealthy, white males? To answer these questions, we must turn to history.

But whose history shall we study? History can be written from many perspectives. The lives of "great men" will vary greatly depending upon whether their biographers are their mothers, their peers, their wives, their lovers, their children, or their servants. And there is no basis for singling out one point of view as more correct or appropriate than any other, for each tells us part of the history of the person. Furthermore, we might ask why history should be the history of "great men" exclusively. What about the lives of valets, dancers, carpenters, teachers, and mothers? Aren't their experiences essential to reconstructing the past? Can history omit the lives of the majority of people in a society and still claim to give us an accurate account of the past?

We can even question who decides what counts as history. In the past, the war diaries of generals were kept as prized historical documents, whereas diaries written by women giving an account of their daily lives were ignored or discounted. What makes one invaluable and the other irrelevant? Many historians have chosen to call one particular point of view *history* and have used it to evaluate the relevance and worth of all else—this point of view being that of white men of property. It is this point of view that has permeated our American history texts and classes. The greatest secret kept by many traditional history texts was that women and people of color and working people created the wealth and culture of this country.

History, we are told, involves collecting and studying facts. But what counts as a "fact," and who decides which facts are important? Whose interests are served or furthered by these decisions? For many years, one of the first "facts" that grade-school children learned was that Christopher Columbus discovered America. And yet this "history" is neither clear nor incontrovertible. It is a piece of the past examined from the point of view of white Europeans; it is to their interest to persuade others to believe it, since this "fact" undermines the claims of others. American Indians might well ask how Columbus could have discovered America in 1492 if they had already been living here for thousands of years. Teaching children that bit of fiction about Columbus served to render Native Americans invisible and thus tacitly excused or denied the genocide carried out by European settlers.

During the contemporary period, many new approaches to history have arisen to remedy the omissions and distortions of the past. Women's history, Black history, gay history, ethnic history, labor history, and others all propose to transform traditional history so that it more accurately reflects the reality of people's lives past and present.

Part V does not attempt to provide a comprehensive history of the American Republic since its beginning. Rather it is designed to trace the legal status of people of color and women since the first Europeans came to this land. After two preliminary readings which present an overview of legal issues as they apply to Native Americans and African-Americans in particular, this part of the book proceeds by reproducing legal documents that highlight developments in legal status. In a few cases, these legal documents are supplemented with materials that help paint a clearer picture of the issues involved or their implications.

Much is left out by adopting this framework for our study. Most significantly, the actual political and social movements that brought about the changes in the legal realm are omitted. For this reason, students are urged to supplement their study of the legal documents with the rich accounts of social history from the "Suggested Readings" listed at the end of Part V.

However, the legal documents themselves are fascinating. They make it possible for us to reduce hundreds of years of history to a manageable size. We can thus form a picture of the rights and status of many so-called minority groups in this country, a picture that contrasts sharply with the one usually offered in high-school social-studies classes. Most importantly, the documents can help us answer the question raised by material in the first four parts of this text: how did it happen that all women and all people of color came to have such limited access to power and opportunity?

The readings here show that, from the country's inception, the laws and institutions of the United States were designed to create and maintain the privileges of wealthy white males. The discrimination documented in the early parts of this book is no accident. It has a long and deliberate history. Understanding this history is essential if we are to create a more just and democratic society.

On July 4, 1776, the thirteen colonies set forth a declaration of independence from Great Britain. In that famous document, the founders of the Republic explained their reasons for separating from the homeland and expressed their hopes for the new republic. In lines that are rightly famous and often quoted, the signatories proclaimed that "all Men are created equal, that they are endowed by their Creator with certain unalienable Rights, that among these are Life, Liberty and the Pursuit of Happiness." They went on to assert that "to secure these Rights, Governments are instituted among Men, deriving their just Powers from the Consent of the Governed." When these words were written, however, a large portion of the population of the United States had no legal rights whatsoever. American Indians, women, indentured servants, poor white men who did not own property, and, of course, slaves could not vote, nor were they free to exercise their liberty or pursue their happiness in the same way that white men with property could. When the authors of the Declaration of Independence proclaimed that all men were created equal and endowed with unalienable rights, they meant "men" quite literally and white men specifically. Negro slaves, as it turned out, were worth "three fifths of all other Persons," a figure stipulated in Article I, Section 2, of the United States Constitution. This section of the Constitution, which is often referred to as the "three-fifths compromise," undertook to establish how slaves would be counted for the purposes of determining taxes as well as for calculating representation of the states in Congress.

Faced with the need for an enormous work force to cultivate the land, the European settlers first tried to enslave the American Indian population. Later, the settlers brought over large numbers of "indentured workers" from Europe. These workers were poor white men, women, and children, some serving prison sentences at home, who were expected to work in the colonies for a certain period of time and then receive their freedom. When neither of these populations proved suitable, the settlers began importing African Negroes to serve their purposes.

Records show that the first African Negroes were brought to this country as early as 1526. Initially, the Negroes appear to have had the same status as indentured servants, but the laws reflect a fairly rapid distinction between the two groups. Maryland law made this distinction as early as 1640; Massachusetts legally recognized slavery in 1641; Virginia passed a law making Negroes slaves for life in 1661; and so it went until the number of slaves grew to roughly 600,000 at the time of the signing of the Declaration of Independence.[1] Numerous legal documents, such as An Act for the Better Ordering and Governing of Negroes and Slaves passed in South Carolina in 1712 and excerpted in Selection 3, prescribed the existence of the slaves, as did the acts modeled on An Act Prohibiting the Teaching of Slaves to Read, a North Carolina statute reprinted here in Selection 5.

When the early European settlers came to this country, there were approximately 2.5 million Native Americans living on the land that was to become the United States. These Indian peoples were divided among numerous separate and autonomous tribes, each with its own highly developed culture and history. The white man quickly lumped these diverse peoples into a single and inferior category, "Indians," and set about destroying their culture and seizing their lands. The Indian Removal Act of 1830 was fairly typical of the kinds of laws that were passed to carry out the appropriation of Indian lands. Believing the Indians to be inherently inferior to whites, the United States government had no hesitation about legislating the removal of the Indians from valuable ancestral lands to ever more remote and barren reservations. The dissolution of the Indian tribal system was further advanced by the General Allotment Act (Dawes Act) of 1887, which divided tribal landholdings among individual Indians and thereby successfully undermined the tribal system and the culture of which it was a part. In addition, this act opened up lands within the reservation area for purchase by the United States government, which then made those lands available to white settlers for homesteading. Many supporters of the allotment policy, who were considered "friends" of the Indians, argued that the benefits of individual ownership would have a "civilizing effect" on them.[2] Instead, it ensured a life of unrelenting poverty for most because it was usually impossible for a family to derive subsistence from the use of a single plot of land and without the support of the tribal community.

While John Adams was involved in writing the Declaration of Independence, his wife, Abigail Adams, took him to task for failing to accord women the same rights and privileges as men. "I cannot say that you are very generous to the ladies; for whilst you are proclaiming peace and good will to men, emancipating all nations, you insist upon retaining an absolute power over wives."[3] Although law and custom consistently treated women as if they were physically and mentally inferior to men, the reality of women's lives was very different. Black female slaves were forced to perform the same inhuman fieldwork as Black male slaves and were expected to do so even in the final weeks of pregnancy. They were routinely beaten and abused without regard for the supposed biological fragility of the female sex. White women settlers gave birth to large numbers of children, ten and twelve being quite common and as many as twenty births not being unusual. And they did so in addition to working side by side with men to perform all those duties necessary to survival in a new and unfamiliar environment. When her husband died, a woman often assumed his responsibilities as well. It was not until well into the 1800s, primarily as a result of changes brought about by the Industrial Revolution, that significant class differences began to affect the lives and work of white women.

As women, both Black and white, became increasingly active in the antislavery movement during the 1800s, many noticed certain similarities between the legal status of women and the legal status of slaves. Participants at the first women's rights convention held at Seneca Falls, New York, in 1848 listed women's grievances and specified their demands. At this time, married women were regarded as property of their husbands and had no direct legal control over their own wages, their property, or even their children. The Declaration of Sentiments issued at Seneca Falls was modeled on the Declaration of Independence in the hope that men would extend the declaration's rights to women. Similar emotional attacks are still used today to ridicule and then dismiss contemporary feminist demands.

The abysmal legal status of women and people of color in the United States during the nineteenth century is graphically documented in a series of court decisions reproduced in this part. In *People* v. *Hall*, 1854, the California Supreme Court decided that a California statute barring Indians and Negroes from testifying in court cases involving whites also applied to Chinese Americans. The judges asserted that the Chinese are "a race of people whom nature has marked as inferior, and who are incapable of progress or intellectual development beyond a certain point." The extent of anti-Chinese feeling in parts of the United States can be further inferred from portions of the California Constitution adopted in 1876 and included in this part.

In a more famous case, *Dred Scott* v. *Sanford*, 1857, the United States Supreme Court was asked to decide whether Dred Scott, a Negro, was a citizen of the United States with the rights that that implied. Scott, a slave who had been taken from Missouri, a slave state, into the free state of Illinois for a period of time, argued that because he was free and had been born in the United States, he was therefore a citizen. The Court ruled that this was not the case and, using reasoning that strongly parallels *People* v. *Hall*, offered a survey of United States law and custom to show that Negroes were never considered a part of the people of the United States. In *Bradwell* v. *Illinois*, 1873, the Supreme Court ruled that women could not practice law and used the opportunity to carefully distinguish the rights and prerogatives of women from those of men. The Court maintained that "civil law, as well as nature herself, has always recognized a wide difference in the respective spheres and destinies of man and woman" and went on to argue that women belong in the "domestic sphere."

During the period in which these and other court cases were brought, the United States moved toward and ultimately fought a bloody civil war. Allegedly fought "to free the slaves," much more was at stake. The Civil War reflected a struggle to the death between the Southern aristocracy, whose wealth was based on land and whose power rested on a kind of feudal economic-political order, and the Northern capitalists, who came into being by virtue of the Industrial Revolution and who wished to restructure the nation's economic-political institutions to better serve the needs of the new industrial order. Chief among these needs was a large and mobile work force for the factories in the North. Hundreds of thousands of soldiers died in the bloody conflict, while other men purchased army deferments and used the war years to amass tremendous personal wealth. On the Confederate side, men who owned fifty or more slaves were exempted from serving in the army, while wealthy Northern men were able to purchase deferments from the Union for the sum of $300. Among those who purchased deferments and went on to become millionaires as a result of war profiteering were John D. Rockefeller, Andrew Carnegie, J. Pierpont Morgan, Philip Armour, James Mellon, and Jay Gould.[4]

In September 1862, President Abraham Lincoln signed the Emancipation Proclamation (Selection 10) as part of his efforts to bring the Civil War to an end by forcing the Southern states to concede. It did not free all slaves; it freed only those in states or parts of states in rebellion against the federal government. Only in September 1865, after the conclusion of the war, were all slaves freed by the Thirteenth Amendment (Selection 11). However, Southern whites did not yield their privileges easily. Immediately after the war, the Southern states began to pass laws known as "The Black Codes," which attempted to reestablish the relations of slavery. Some of these codes are described in this part in a selection written by W. E. B. Du Bois.

In the face of such efforts to deny the rights of citizenship to Black men, Congress passed the Fourteenth Amendment (Selection 11) in July 1868. This amendment, which continues to play a major role in contemporary legal battles over discrimination, includes a number of important provisions. It explicitly extended citizenship to all those born or naturalized in the United States and guarantees all citizens "due process" and "equal protection" of the law. In addition, it cancelled all debts incurred by the Confederacy in its unsuccessful rebellion while recognizing the validity of the debts incurred by the federal government. This meant that wealthy Southerners who had extended large sums of money or credit to the Confederacy would lose it, while wealthy Northern industrialists would be paid.

Southern resistance to extending the rights and privileges of citizenship to Black men persisted, and the Southern states used all their powers, including unbridled terror and violence, to subvert the intent of the Thirteenth and Fourteenth Amendments. The Fifteenth Amendment (Selection 11), which explicitly granted the vote to Black men, was passed in 1870 but it was received by the Southern states with as little enthusiasm as had greeted the Thirteenth and Fourteenth Amendments.

As the abolitionist movement grew and the Civil War became inevitable, many women's rights activists, also active in the struggle to free the slaves, argued that the push for women's rights should temporarily defer to the issue of slavery. In fact, after February 1861, no women's rights conventions were held until the end of the war. Although Black and white women had long worked together in both movements, the question of which struggle took precedence created serious splits among women's rights activists, including such strong Black allies as Frederick Douglass and Sojourner Truth. Some argued that the evils of slavery were so great that they took precedence over the legal discrimination experienced by middle-class white women. They resented attempts by Elizabeth Cady Stanton and others to equate the condition of white women with that of Negro slaves and argued, moreover, that the women's rights movement had never been concerned with the extraordinary suffering of Black women or the special needs of working women. The explicitly racist appeals made by some white women activists as they sought white men's support for women's suffrage did nothing to bridge this schism. While Black men received the vote in 1868, at least on paper, women would have to continue their fight until the passage of the Nineteenth Amendment (Selection 18) in 1920. As a result, many women and Blacks saw each other as adversaries or obstacles in their struggle for legal equality, deflecting their attention from the privileged white men who provoked the conflict and whose power was reinforced by it.

One special cause for bitterness was the Fourteenth Amendment's reference to *male* inhabitants and the right to vote. This was the first time that voting rights had explicitly been rendered gender-specific. The Fourteenth Amendment was tested in 1874 by *Minor* v. *Happersett* (Selection 14), in which the court was asked to rule directly on the question of whether women had the vote by virtue of their being citizens of the United States. The Court ruled unanimously that women did *not* have the vote, arguing that women, like criminals and mental defectives, could legitimately be denied the vote by the states.[5] In a somewhat similar case, *Elk* v. *Wilkens*, 1884 (Selection 16), John Elk, an American Indian who had left his tribe and lived among whites, argued that he was a citizen by virtue of the Fourteenth Amendment and should not be denied the right to vote by the state of Nebraska. The Supreme Court ruled that neither the Fourteenth nor Fifteenth Amendments applied to Elk. Native Americans became citizens of the United States three years later, under one of the provisions of the Dawes Act of 1887.

Unsuccessful in their attempts to reinstate some form of forced servitude by passage of "The Black Codes," Southern states began to legalize the separation of the races in all aspects of public and private life. In *Plessy* v. *Ferguson*, 1896, (Selection 17), the Supreme Court was asked to rule on whether segregation by race in public facilities violated the Thirteenth and Fourteenth Amendments. In a ruling that was to cruelly affect several generations of Black Americans, the Supreme Court ruled that restricting Negroes to the use of "separate but equal" public accommodations did not deny them equal protection of the law. This decision remained in effect for almost sixty years until *Brown* v. *Board of Education of Topeka*, 1954 (Selection 20). In the historic *Brown* decision, the Court ruled, in effect, that "separate" could not possibly be "equal." Nonetheless, abolishing segregation on paper was one thing; actually bringing about the integration of public facilities was another. The integration of public schools, housing, and employment in both the North and the South has been a long and often bloody struggle that continues to this day.

The racist attitudes toward Chinese Americans, reflected in the nineteenth-century California statutes and constitution as we have already seen, extended toward Japanese Americans as well. This racism erupted during the twentieth century after the bombing of Pearl Harbor by Japan on December 7, 1941. Anti-Japanese feelings ran so high that President Franklin Roosevelt issued an executive order allowing the military to designate "military areas" from which it could then exclude any persons it chose. On March 2, 1942, the entire West Coast was designated as such an area, and within a few months, everyone of Japanese ancestry (defined as those having as little as one-eighth Japanese blood) was evacuated. More than 110,000 people of Japanese descent, most of them American citizens, were forced to leave their homes and jobs and to spend the war years in so-called relocation camps behind barbed wire.[6] Although the United States was also at war with Germany, no such barbaric treatment was afforded German Americans. The military evacuation of Japanese Americans was challenged in *Korematsu* v. *United*

States, 1944. In its decision, excerpted in Selection 19, the Supreme Court upheld the forced evacuation.

The twentieth century has seen the growth of large and diverse movements for race and gender justice. These movements precipitated the creation of a number of commissions and government agencies, which were to research and enforce equal treatment for people of color and women; the passage of a number of statutes to this end; and a series of Supreme Court decisions in the area. For women, one of the most significant Court decisions of the recent past was *Roe* v. *Wade*, 1973 (Selection 21), which, for the first time, gave women the right to terminate pregnancy by abortion. Rather than affirming a woman's right to control her body, however, the *Roe* decision is based upon the right to privacy. The impact of *Roe* was significantly blunted by *Harris* v. *McRae*, 1980, in which the Court ruled that the right to privacy did not require public funding of medically necessary abortions for women who could not afford them. In practice, this meant that white middle-class women who chose abortion could exercise their right but that many poor white women and women of color could not. The single biggest defeat for the Women's Movement of this period was the failure to pass the much misunderstood Equal Rights Amendment, which is reproduced in Selection 22.

More recently, the Supreme Court was asked to rule on the constitutionality of homosexual intercourse when Michael Hardwick, a practicing homosexual, brought suit challenging the constitutionality of Georgia's sodomy law. In *Bowers* v. *Hardwick* (Selection 23), the Court upheld that law. In a broad decision that could have disturbing implications for many different kinds of private sexual conduct between consenting adults, the Supreme Court ruled that it is not unconstitutional to legislate against certain forms of sexual activity. The prohibition against sodomy as well as other legal issues that might impact directly on lesbian and gay people are surveyed in Selection 24, "Gay/Lesbian Rights: Report from the Legal Front."

NOTES

1. W. Z. Foster: *The Negro People in American History*, International Publishers, New York, 1954, p. 37.

2. United States Commission on Civil Rights: *Indian Tribes: A Continuing Quest for Survival*, a report of the United States Commission on Civil Rights, June 1981, p. 34.

3. Letter to John Adams, May 7, 1776.

4. H. Wasserman: *Harvey Wasserman's History of the United States*, Harper & Row, New York, 1975, p. 3.

5. E. Flexner: *Century of Struggle*, Harvard University Press, Cambridge, Massachusetts, 1976, p. 172.

6. R. E. Cushman & R. F. Cushman: *Cases in Constitutional Law*, Appleton-Century-Crofts, New York, 1958, p. 127.

Indian Tribes:
A Continuing Quest for Survival

U.S. Commission on Human Rights

Traditional civil rights, as the phrase is used here, includes those rights that are secured to individuals and are basic to the United States system of government. They include the right to vote and the right to equal treatment without discrimination on the basis of race, religion, or national origin, among others, in such areas as education, housing, employment, public accommodations, and the administration of justice.

In order to understand where American Indians stand today with respect to these rights, it is important to look at historical developments of the concept of Indian rights along with the civil rights movement in this country. The consideration given to these factors here will not be exhaustive, but rather a brief look at some of the events that are most necessary to a background understanding of this area.

A basic and essential factor concerning American Indians is that the development of civil rights issues for them is in reverse order from other minorities in this country. Politically, other minorities started with nothing and attempted to obtain a voice in the existing economic and political structure. Indians started with everything and have gradually lost much of what they had to an advancing alien civilization. Other minorities have had no separate governmental institutions. Their goal primarily has been and continues to be to make the existing system involve them and work for them. Indian tribes have always been separate political entities interested in maintaining their own institutions and beliefs. Their goal has been to prevent the dismantling of their own systems. So while other minorities have sought integration into the larger society, much of Indian society is motivated to retain its political and cultural separateness.

Although at the beginning of the colonization process Indian nations were more numerous and better adapted to survival on this continent than the European settlers, these advantages were quickly lost. The colonization period saw the rapid expansion of non-Indian communities in numbers and territory covered and a shift in the balance of strength from Indian to non-Indian communities and governments. The extent to which Indians intermingled with non-Indian society varied by time period, geographical location, and the ability of natives and newcomers to get along with one another. As a general matter, however, Indians were viewed and treated as members of political entities that were not part of the United States. The Constitution acknowledges this by its separate provision regarding trade with the Indian tribes.[1] Indian tribes today that have not been forcibly assimilated, extinguished, or legally terminated still consider themselves to be, and are viewed in American law, as separate political units.

The Racial Factor

An important element in the development of civil rights for American Indians today goes beyond their legal and political status to include the way they have been viewed racially. Since colonial times Indians have been viewed as an "inferior race"; sometimes this view is condescendingly positive—the romanticized noble savage—at other times this view is hostile—the vicious savage—at all times the view is racist. All things Indian are viewed as inherently inferior to their counterparts in the white European tradition. Strong racist statements have appeared in congressional debates, Presidential policy announcements, court decisions, and other authoritative public utterances. This racism has served to justify a view now repudiated, but which still lingers in the public mind, that Indians are not entitled to the same legal rights as others in this country. In some cases, racism has been coupled with apparently benevolent motives, to "civilize" the "savages," to teach them Christian principles. In other cases, the racism has been coupled with greed; Indians were "removed" to distant locations to prevent them from standing in the way of the development of the new Western civilization. At one extreme the concept of inferior status of Indians was used to justify genocide; at the other, apparently benevolent side, the attempt was to assimilate them into the dominant society. Whatever the rationale or motive, whether rooted in voluntary efforts or coercion, the common denominator has been the belief that Indian society is an inferior lifestyle.

> It sprang from a conviction that native people were a lower grade of humanity for whom the accepted cannons of respect need not apply; one did not debase oneself by ruining a native person. At times, this conviction was stated explicitly by men in public office, but whether expressed or not, it generated decision and action.[2]

Early assimilationists like Thomas Jefferson proceeded from this assumption with benevolent designs.

> Thus, even as they acknowledged a degree of political autonomy in the tribes, their conviction of the natives' cultural inferiority led them to interfere in their social, religious, and economic practices. Federal agents to the tribes not only negotiated treaties and tendered payments; they pressured husbands to take up the plow and wives to learn to spin. The more conscientious agents offered gratuitous lectures on the virtues of monogamy, industry, and temperance.

The same underlying assumption provided the basis for Andrew Jackson's attitude. "I have long viewed treaties with the Indians an absurdity not to be reconciled to the principles of our government," he said. As President he refused to enforce the decisions of the U. S. Supreme Court upholding Cherokee tribal autonomy, and he had a prominent role in the forced removal of the Cherokees from Georgia and the appropriation of their land by white settlers. Other eastern tribes met a similar fate under the Indian Removal Act of 1830.[3]

Another Federal Indian land policy, enacted at the end of the 19th century and followed until 1934, that shows the virulent effect of racist assumptions was the allotment of land parcels to individual Indians as a replacement for tribal ownership. Many proponents of the policy were considered "friends of the Indians," and they argued that the attributes of individual land ownership would have a great civilizing and assimilating effect on American Indians. This action, undertaken for the benefit of the Indians, was accomplished without consulting them. Had Congress heeded the views of the purported beneficiaries of this policy, allotment might not have been adopted. Representatives of 19 tribes met in Oklahoma and unanimously opposed the legislation, recognizing the destructive effect it would have upon Indian culture and the land base itself, which was reduced by 90 million acres in 45 years.

An important principle established by the allotment policy was that the Indian form of land ownership was not "civilized," and so it was the right of the Government to invalidate that form. It is curious that the principle of the right to own property in conglomerate form for the benefit of those with a shareholder's undivided interest in the whole was a basis of the American corporate system, then developing in strength. Yet a similar form of ownership when practiced by Indians was viewed as a hallmark of savagery. Whatever the explanation for this double standard, the allotment policy reinforced the notion that Indians were somehow inferior, that non-Indians in power knew what was best for them, and that these suppositions justified the assertion that non-Indians had the power and authority to interfere with the basic right to own property.

Religion is another area in which non-Indians have felt justified in interfering with Indian beliefs. The intent to civilize the natives of this continent included a determined effort to Christianize them. Despite the constitutional prohibition, Congress, beginning in 1819, regularly appropriated funds for Christian missionary efforts. Christian goals were visibly aligned with Federal Indian policy in 1869 when a Board of Indian Commissioners was established by Congress under President Grant's administration. Representative of the spectrum of Christian denominations, the independently wealthy members of the Board were charged by the Commissioner of Indian Affairs to work for the "humanization, civilization and Christianization of the Indians." Officials of the Federal Indian Service were supposed to cooperate with this Board.

The benevolent support of Christian missionary efforts stood in stark contrast to the Federal policy of suppressing tribal religions. Indian ceremonial behavior was misunderstood and suppressed by Indian agents. In 1892 the Commissioner of

Indian Affairs established a regulation making it a criminal offense to engage in such ceremonies as the sun dance. The spread of the Ghost Dance religion, which promised salvation from the white man, was so frightening to the Federal Government that troops were called in to prevent it, even though the practice posed no threat to white settlers.

The judiciary of the United States, though it has in many instances forthrightly interpreted the law to support Indian legal claims in the face of strong, sometimes violent opposition, has also lent support to the myth of Indian inferiority. For example, the United States Supreme Court in 1883, in recognizing the right of tribes to govern themselves, held that they had the exclusive authority to try Indians for criminal offenses committed against Indians. In describing its reasons for refusing to find jurisdiction in a non-Indian court in such cases, the Supreme Court said:

> It [the non-Indian court] tries them, not by their peers, nor by the customs of their people, nor the law of their land, but by *superiors* of a different race, according to the law of a social state of which they have an imperfect conception, and which is opposed to the traditions of their history, to the habits of their lives, to the strongest prejudices of their *savage nature*; one which measures the red man's revenge by the maxims of the white man's morality.[4] (emphasis added)

In recognizing the power of the United States Government to determine the right of Indians to occupy their lands, the Supreme Court expressed the good faith of the country in such matters with these words: "the United States will be governed by such considerations of justice as will control a Christian people in their treatment of an ignorant and dependent race."[5]

Another example of racist stereotyping to be found in the courts is this example from the Supreme Court of Washington State:

> The Indian was a child, and a dangerous child, of nature, to be both protected and restrained. . . . True, arrangements took the form of treaty and of terms like "cede," "relinquish," "reserve." But never were these agreements between equals . . . [but rather] that "between a superior and an inferior."[6]

This reasoning, based on racism, has supported the view that Indians are wards of the Government who need the protection and assistance of Federal agencies and it is the Government's obligation to recreate their governments, conforming them to a non-Indian model, to establish their priorities, and to make or approve their decisions for them.

Indian education policies have often been examples of the Federal Government having determined what is "best" for Indians. Having judged that assimilation could be promoted through the indoctrination process of white schools, the Federal Government began investing in Indian education. Following the model established by army officer Richard Pratt in 1879, boarding schools were established where Indian children were separated from the influences of tribal and home life. The boarding schools tried to teach Indians skills and trades that would be useful in white society, utilizing stern disciplinary measures to force assimilation. The tactics used are within memory of today's generation of tribal leaders who recall the policy of deterring communication in native languages. "I remember being punished many times for. . . singing one Navajo song, or a Navajo word slipping out of my tongue just in an unplanned way, but I was punished for it."

Federal education was made compulsory, and the policy was applied to tribes that had sophisticated school systems of their own as well as to tribes that really needed assistance to establish educational systems. The ability of the tribal school to educate was not relevant, given that the overriding goal was assimilation rather than education.

Racism in Indian affairs has not been sanctioned recently by political or religious leaders or other leaders in American society. In fact, public pronouncements over the last several decades have lamented past evils and poor treatment of Indians.[7] The virulent public expressions of other eras characterizing Indians as "children" or "savages" are not now acceptable modes of public expression. Public policy today is a commitment to Indian self-determination. Numerous actions of Congress and the executive branch give evidence of a more positive era for Indian policy.[8] Beneath the surface, however, the effects of centuries of racism still persist. The attitudes of the public, of State and local officials, and of Federal policymakers do not always live up to the positive pronouncements of official policy. Some decisions today are perceived as being made on the basis of precedents mired in the racism and greed of another era. Perhaps more important, the legacy of racism permeates behavior and that behavior creates classic civil rights violations. . . .

NOTES

1. U.S. Const. art. 1, §8.
2. D'Arcy McNickel, *Native American Tribalism* (New York: Oxford University Press, 1973), p. 56.
3. Act of May 28, 1830, ch. 148, 4 Stat. 411.
4. Ex Parte Crow Dog, 109 U.S. 556, 571 (1883).
5. Missouri, Kansas, and Texas Railway Co. v. Roberts, 152 U.S. 114, 117 (1894).
6. State v. Towessnute, 154 P. 805, 807 (Wash. Sup. Ct. 1916), quoting Choctaw Nation v. United States, 119 U.S. 1, 27 (1886).
7. See, e.g., President Nixon's July 8, 1970, Message to the Congress, Recommendations for Indian Policy, H. Doc. No. 91–363, 91st Cong., 2d sess. (hereafter cited as *Recommendations for Indian Policy*).
8. Ibid; Indian Self-Determination and Education Assistance Act, Pub. L. No. 93–638, 88 Stat. 2203 (1975); Indian Child Welfare Act of 1978, Pub. L. No. 95–608, 92 Stat. 3096; U.S., Department of the Interior, *Report on the Implementation of the Helsinki Final Act* (1979).

2

Race and the American Legal Process

A. Leon Higginbotham, Jr.

"Why of all of the multitudinous groups of people in this country [do] you have to single out Negroes and give them this separate treatment."
—*Oral argument before the United States Supreme Court by Thurgood Marshall, then Chief Counsel for the Plaintiffs in* Brown v. Board of Education.

At approximately 7:17 P.M., April 4, 1968, an assassin fired a shot mortally wounding Martin Luther King. Late that evening I received a call from the President, Lyndon Johnson, who had appointed me four years earlier to the United States District Court, asking me to come to the White House early the next morning to discuss with others who were being called the national significance of Dr. King's death. Though the President acted quickly in collecting his counselors for a meeting the next morning, another section of the nation would not wait the night to express its own response to this national tragedy. Ten blocks from the White House, buildings in the largely black ghettoes of Washington, D.C. were already in flames. As the painful night lingered on, news reports indicated that more and more people had taken to the streets, many striking out irrationally and in anger, in city after city, in response to the senseless death of the prophet of nonviolence.

President Johnson opened the meeting at the White House the next morning with the question, "What can we do now?"

There were many thoughtful responses. Some talked of strengthening civil rights legislation, others spoke of further improving manpower programs, still others argued for additional condemnations of racism. The idea for appointing yet another presidential commission was also introduced. Although the discussion was calm and dispassionate, a deep sense of shared pain was apparent. Most of us present had known Dr. King intimately and had worked with him in the attempt to obliterate racism from American life.

As I listened and reflected on the various suggestions made from such thoughtful and well-meaning people, I kept thinking of the question Thurgood Marshall had asked the Supreme Court thirteen years earlier: "Why," he had asked, "of all the multitudinous groups of people in this country, do you have to single out Negroes and give them this separate treatment." That morning, sitting in the White House, I knew there was an indisputable nexus between the dark shadow of repression under which, historically, most American blacks have lived and the rioting occurring within ten blocks of the White House. Why, I thought to myself, in the land of the free and the home of the brave, had even brave blacks so often failed to get free? Why had that very legal process that had been devised to protect the rights of individuals against the will of the government and the whim of the majority been often employed so malevolently against blacks? What were the options that ought to have been exercised years ago, even centuries ago, to narrow those disparities in meted-out justice that had periodically—and had now once more—kindled black hatred and white fear?

In the company of the great lawyers present at the President's meeting—Supreme Court Associate Justice Thurgood Marshall and Attorney General Ramsey Clark—as well as the other notable government and public officials—Cabinet officer Robert C. Weaver, Civil Rights leaders Roy Wilkins, Whitney Young, Clarence Mitchell, Reverend Leon Sullivan, and Vice President Humphrey—it was inevitable that I would ponder how the legal process had contributed to this malaise. For in 1968, in this nation's 192nd year, things could have been different. If the legal process had been racially just, the nation in the 1960s would not have been torn asunder as it was by the unrelenting demands by blacks for dignity and equal justice under the law pulling against the stubborn resistance of those who had been conditioned to believe in the status quo as the ultimate expression of "liberty and justice for all." The institutionalized injustice of racial apartness had first brought Martin Luther King to the forefront and now, ultimately, had brought him to his death.

Particularly during this Bicentennial era, it is appropriate to assess the interrelationship of race and the American legal process. This nation has just celebrated its 200th birthday in a most grandiose fashion. Conventions have been held in almost every town to reaffirm those "self-evident truths," and the oratory will continue to 1987, the 200th anniversary of the United States Constitution. As praise is heaped on the great leaders of yesterday, and as some laud 1776 as the Golden Era of liberty, it is often suggested that if only today's leaders had the integrity and character of Jefferson, Franklin, John Adams, Washington, and Madison, today's racial difficulties might be quickly resolved. Few have had the temerity to contradict this general but misdirected consensus, for it is bad bicentennial form to refer to the fact that many of America's founding fathers owned slaves and that most, either directly or indirectly, profited from the evil institution that enslaved black human beings only.

The bicentennial drum roll of revolutionary heroes and events, then, symbolizes one thing to white Americans but quite another to blacks. From a predominantly white perspective, the Declaration of Independence is viewed as former President Nixon described it: "the greatest achievement in the history of man. We are the beneficiaries of that achievement." But who, until recently, did the "we" describe?

Not black America. Frederick Douglass, a leading abolitionist who was born a slave, described Independence Day in 1852 from the perspective of blacks and slaves rather than whites and slaveholders:

> This Fourth of July is *yours*, not mine. You may rejoice, I must mourn. To drag a man in fetters to the grand illuminated temple of liberty, and call upon him to join you in joyous anthems, were inhuman mockery and sacrilegious irony. . . . I say it with a sad sense of the disparity between us. I am not included within the pale of this glorious anniversary. . . . The blessings in which you, this day, rejoice, are not enjoyed in common. The rich inheritance of justice, liberty, prosperity and independence, bequeathed by your fathers, is shared by you, not by me. The sunlight that brought light and healing to you, has brought stripes and death to me.

Likewise, from a predominantly white perspective, the pledges of the Preamble to the Constitution honestly set out the largest principles for which the new American legal process would strive.

> We the people . . . in order to form a more perfect union, establish justice, . . . promote the general welfare, and secure the blessings of liberty to ourselves and our posterity. . . .

From a black perspective, however, the Constitution's references to justice, welfare, and liberty were mocked by the treatment meted out daily to blacks from the seventeenth to nineteenth centuries through the courts, in legislative statutes, and in those provisions of the Constitution that sanctioned slavery for the majority of black Americans and allowed disparate treatment for those few blacks legally "free."

Further, whatever opening there might have been for one day peacefully redefining "We the people" to include, as it should have in the first place, black Americans, was abruptly closed with the 1857 U.S. Supreme Court decision *Dred Scott* v. *Sandford*. When asked if the phrase "We the people" included black people and whether blacks were embraced in the egalitarian language of the Declaration of Independence, Chief Justice Roger Taney, speaking for the majority, wrote:

> [A]t the time of the Declaration of Independence, and when the Constitution of the United States was framed and adopted . . . [blacks] had no rights which the white man was bound to respect.

In effect, Taney had not answered the question. Rather, he had gone back in time in an attempt to determine what the founding fathers had intended, and in so doing, had argued from the untenable position that the Constitution might never be any larger than the restrictive vision of eighteenth-century America.

Thus, for black Americans today—the children of all the hundreds of Kunta Kintes unjustly chained in bondage—the early failure of the nation's founders and their constitutional heirs to share the legacy of freedom with black Americans is at least one factor in America's perpetual racial tensions. Twenty years after the Civil

War, over one hundred years after the Declaration of Independence, two hundred fifty years after the first black man set foot in America, in *Huckleberry Finn*, Mark Twain, in a parody of white attitudes, suggested that as late as 1884 many white Americans still failed to perceive blacks as human beings. He writes:

> "Good gracious. Anybody hurt?"
> "No'm. Killed a nigger."
> "Well, it's lucky because sometimes people do get hurt." . . .

This book will treat from a legal standpoint this historically persistent failure of perception. What should have been on the minds of all in power during the seventeenth and eighteenth centuries was the question James Otis raised in his provocative paper of 1764:

> Does it follow that, tis right to enslave a man because he is black?

. . . I am aware that an analysis of cases, statutes, and legal edicts does not tell the whole story as to why and how this sordid legal tradition managed to establish itself. Nevertheless, there is merit in abolitionist William Goodell's statement: "No people were ever yet found who were better than their laws, though many have been known to be worse."

While I recognize that a view of slavery from the perspective of the law does not make a complete picture, I join in the conclusions of Winthrop D. Jordan when writing on the Colonial period and C. Vann Woodward when writing on the Reconstruction period. Jordan has advised us:

> while statutes usually speak falsely as to actual behavior, they afford probably the best single means of ascertaining what a society thinks behavior ought to be; they sweep up the felt necessities of the day and indirectly expound the social norm of the legislators.

And C. Vann Woodward has stated:

> I am convinced that law has a special importance in the history of segregation, more importance than some sociologists would allow, and that the emphasis on legal history is justified.

While I do not represent what I put forward here as a complete picture of the practices of the society, that canvas will never be painted unless someone first treats adequately the interrelationship of race and the American legal process.

Obviously, there were several factors that contributed to the inclination of the legal process to treat blacks so differently from all others. Many have written in great detail on some of these factors. For instance, in so many legal decisions, there was the powerful presence of the economics of slavery. The key question for many a righteous and learned community leader was whether it was cheaper to have blacks as slaves or to have blacks as "free" labor. Or, possibly, instead of black slaves would it have been cheaper to have had white indentured servants or white free labor.

The issue of safety and the natural fear of slave revolts was also intertwined in the chain of legal judgments. While never reluctant to protect and maximize their property rights in the slaves, many judges and legislators were reluctant to recognize that slaves had, in their own right, any basic human rights. Many feared that any judicial protection of the slave would trigger further challenges to the legitimacy of the dehumanized status of blacks and slaves. Since the plantations were often in isolated settings and there was an ever threatening possibility that the slaves might rise up and slay their oppressors, any judge whose decision criticized racial injustice might be accused of weakening the master-slave system. For instance, in a famous North Carolina decision *State* v. *Mann* involving the issue of whether or not it was a criminal offense to subject a slave woman to "a cruel and unreasonable battery," the court stated that a slave was to "labor upon a principle of natural duty," to disregard "his own personal happiness," and that the purpose of the legal system was to convince each slave that he had

> no will of his own [and that he must surrender] his will in implicit obedience to that of another. Such obedience is the consequence only of uncontrolled authority over the body. There is nothing else that can operate to produce the effect. The power of the master must be absolute to render the submission of the slave perfect.

The court emphasized that for the slave "there is no remedy," that "[w]e cannot allow the right of the master to be brought into discussion in the courts of justice. The slave, to remain a slave, must be made sensible that there is no appeal from his master; that his power is in no instance usurped; but is conferred by the laws of man at least, if not by the law of God." The court noted that this unlimited "dominion is essential to the value of slaves as property, and to the security of the master, and the public tranquility."

The control the court sought was the *total* submission of blacks. It had incorporated into its law-made morality the psychological conceptions Frederick Douglass subsequently described:

> Beat and cuff the slave, keep him hungry and spiritless, and he will follow the chain of his master like a dog, but feed and clothe him well, work him moderately and surround him with physical comfort, and dreams of freedom will intrude. . . . You may hurl a man so low beneath the level of his kind, that he loses all just ideas of his natural position, but elevate him a little, and the clear conception of rights rises to life and power, and leads him onward.

With only slightly less paranoia, white society feared that slaves and free blacks would form an alliance with either indentured servants or poor whites to topple the plantation aristocracy, which exploited both blacks and poor whites. As the percentage of blacks, slave or free, increased, the probability of successful rebellions and revolts became greater. Thus, in examining degrees of repression one can almost correlate a rise in the black population with an increased level of legal repression.

In terms of moral and religious issues, there was the underlying question of whether or not America had the right to treat differently and more malevolently people whose skins were darker. From this perspective it became necessary to determine whether blacks were part of the human family and whether, after they had adopted your "religion," they were then entitled to be treated as equals, or at least less harshly. In a nation "under God" the moral or religious rationale that justified or rejected the institution of slavery had to have been an important factor. But what tortuous moral or religious rationale had to have been devised for a religious people to have tolerated treating black human beings more like horses or dogs than white human beings?

Finally, there was always the issue of whether or not blacks were inherently inferior to whites. If blacks could be perceived as inferior, basically uneducable and inherently venal, it might be intellectually less self-condemnatory to relegate them because of their "lower status" to a subordinate role—either for "their own good" or, as one judge had the audacity to express it, for the good of the total society, whites and blacks alike.

Thus it was that even the man many Americans see as one of the major forces for liberty and equality, Thomas Jefferson, found blacks to be "inferior to whites in the endowments both of body and mind." After comparing the characteristics of the three major races in America, white, black, and red, Jefferson concluded that although the condition of slavery imposed great misery on blacks, the inferiority of the black race was caused by more than mere environmental factors:

> The improvement of the blacks in body and mind, in the first instance of their mixture with the whites, has been observed by everyone, and proves that their inferiority is not the effect merely of their condition of life. . . . This unfortunate difference of color, and perhaps of faculty, is a powerful obstacle to the emancipation of these people.

Yet even during the seventeenth and eighteenth centuries, there were voices that challenged the morality and legality of slavery. . . . As early as February, 1688 the Germantown Mennonites of Philadelphia had issued a proclamation against slavery, having found it inconsistent with Christian principles. . . . In 1772, four years prior to our Declaration of Independence and fifteen years prior to the Constitution, Lord Mansfield, Chief Justice of the King's Bench, said that "the state of slavery is of such a nature that it is incapable of being introduced on any reasons moral or political, . . . It is so odious that nothing can be suffered to support it, but positive law." And with that statement, Lord Mansfield freed the slave, Sommersett, demonstrating that there was no universal view on slavery among the civilized nations of the world.

As we survey . . . legislative and judicial doctrines, it will be difficult to isolate one and only one factor as the sole explanation for the legislated, adjudicated, and upheld racial deprivation that gained the official approval of the American legal establishment. As in most things, the causal factors were multifaceted. On some occasions the economic concerns seemed the dominating influence, while in other instances a moral or religious aspect appeared to be more significant. But however tightly woven into the history of their country is the legalization of black suppression, many Americans still find it too traumatic to study the true story of racism as it has existed under their "rule of law." For many, the primary conclusion of the National Commission on Civil Disorders is still too painful to hear:

> What white Americans have never fully understood—but what the Negro can never forget—is that white society is deeply implicated in the ghetto. White institutions created it, white institutions maintain it, and white society condones it.

Since the language of the law shields one's consciousness from direct involvement with the stark plight of its victims, the human tragedy of the slavery system does not surface from the mere reading of cases, statutes, and constitutional provisions. Rather it takes a skeptical reading of most of the early cases and statutes to avoid having one's surprise and anger dulled by the casualness with which the legal process dealt with human beings who happened to be slaves. Generally neither the courts nor the legislatures seemed to have been any more sensitive about commercial transactions involving slaves than they were about sales of corn, lumber, horses, or dogs. This casualness is reflected in a perfectly legal and acceptable advertisement of that era:

> One hundred and twenty Negroes for sale—The subscriber has just arrived from Petersburg, Virginia, with one hundred and twenty likely young Negroes of both sexes and every description, which he offers for sale on the most reasonable terms. The lot now on hand consists of plough-boys, several likely and well-qualified house servants of both sexes, several women and children, small girls suitable for nurses, and *several small boys without their mothers*. Planters and traders are earnestly requested to give the subscriber a call previously to making purchases elsewhere, as he is enabled to sell as cheap or cheaper than can be sold by any other person in the trade.
>
> —Hamburg, South Carolina, Benjamin Davis

The advertisement of Benjamin Davis was not unique; it was typical of thousands of advertisements posted in newspapers and bulletin boards throughout our land. In the *New Orleans Bee* an advertisement noted:

> Negroes for sale—a Negro woman, 24 years of age, and her two children, one eight and the other three years old. Said Negroes will be sold separately or together, as desired. The woman is a good seamstress. She will be sold low for cash, or exchange for groceries. For terms apply to Matthew Bliss and Company, 1 Front Levee.

How could a legal system encourage and sanction such cruelty—cruelty that permitted the sale, as Benjamin Davis bragged, of "several small boys without their mothers"? Was there any justice in a legal process that permitted a mother, twenty-four years of age, to be sold in exchange for groceries and separated from her children, only eight and three years old? Looking past the commercial façade, one sees the advertisement as stating that American laws encouraged the destruction of black families and the selling of human beings. The only criterion was the demand of the marketplace.

. . . For example, we cite several statutes that offered rewards to bounty hunters bringing in the scalp and ears of runaway slaves. These statutes, subtly cast in the language of lawyers, can make one oblivious to the fact that the lives of human beings were involved. From one perspective, it appears that these two legislatures were merely defining penalties and granting rewards—just as they would do upon the recovery of an individual's lost property or as a reward for the slaying of a bear or wild coyote. Yet the scalps and the ears referred to in the Georgia and South Carolina statutes were *not* those of wild animals. They were not those of murderers or traitors. They were the scalps and ears of human beings, persons who had committed no crime other than that of seeking that same freedom the colonists declared to be the birthright of all whites.

As I reflect on these statutes, I think of my experiences as a youngster forty years ago viewing the local cowboy and Indian movies. The bad guys—the Indians, naturally—would occasionally scalp some white adult. Always as my friends and I left the movies, we were angry because of the cruelty the Indians had inflicted on those innocent pioneers, who were merely traveling over Indian land. Thus, it was a matter of astonishment to learn as an adult that the legislatures of Georgia, South Carolina and many of the other colonies actually legalized acts as inhumane as those dreamt up by movie producers. Perhaps the movies were fictionalized accounts representing Hollywood screenwriters' vivid imagination. But the colonial statutes were not bits of fiction; they were the reality of the colonial legal process, a process that rewarded those who were willing to scalp and cut off the ears of blacks who dared to seek freedom.

While we recognize today how inhumane and how immoral this legal process was, it seems that Americans would rather distort their history than face the extraordinary brutality to which these advertisements attest and the inadequacy of a system of laws that promoted and sanctioned such brutality.

The legal process has never been devoid of values, preferences, or policy positions. By the very nature of its pronouncements, when the legal process establishes a right of one particular person, group, or institution, it simultaneously imposes a restraint on those whose preferences impinge on the right established. Ultimately, the legal process has always acted as an expression of social control. Professor Vilhelm Aubert has argued that "beneath the veneer of consensus on legal principles, a struggle of interest is going on, and the law is seen as a weapon in the hands of those who possess the power to use it for their own ends."

The mechanisms of control through judicial decisions and statutes span the sanctioning of slavery and the special limitations imposed on free blacks, to the prohibitions against interracial marriage and sexual activity, to the eliminating of the legal significance of blacks' "conversions to Christianity," to generally restricting any activities or aspirations of blacks that might threaten the groups in control. The law is usually perceived as a normative system, founded on a society's custom and convention.

Charles Warren, one of the most distinguished scholars on the history of the Supreme Court, observed:

> The Court is not an organism dissociated from the conditions and history of the times in which it exists. It does not formulate and deliver its opinions in a legal vacuum. Its Judges are not abstract and impersonal oracles, but are men whose views are necessarily, though by no conscious intent, affected by inheritance, education and environment and by the impact of history past and present. . . .

Oliver Wendell Holmes shared this perception:

> The life of the law has not been logic: it has been experience. The felt necessities of the time, the prevalent moral and political theories, intuitions of public policy, avowed or unconscious, even the prejudices which judges share with their fellowmen, have had a good deal more to do than the syllogism in determining the rules by which men should be governed.

3

An Act for the Better Ordering and Governing of Negroes and Slaves, South Carolina, 1712

Colonial America had a role for the Negro. But the presence of a servile population, presumably of inferior stock, made it necessary to adopt measures of control. As might be expected, the southern colonies had the most highly developed codes governing Negroes. In 1712 South Carolina passed "An Act for the better ordering and governing of Negroes and Slaves." This comprehensive measure served as a model for slave codes in the South during the colonial and national periods. Eight of its thirty-five sections are reproduced below.

Whereas, the plantations and estates of this province cannot be well and sufficiently managed and brought into use, without the labor and service of negroes and other slaves; and forasmuch as the said negroes and other slaves brought unto the people of this Province for that purpose, are of barbarous, wild, savage natures, and such as renders them wholly unqualified to be governed by the laws, customs, and practices of this Province; but that it is absolutely necessary, that such other constitutions, laws and orders, should in this Province be made and enacted, for the good regulating and ordering of them, as may restrain the disorders, rapines and inhumanity, to which they are naturally prone and inclined, and may also tend to the safety and security of the people of this Province and their estates; to which purpose,

I. *Be it therefore enacted*, by his Excellency, William, Lord Craven, Palatine, and the rest of the true and absolute Lords and Proprietors of this Province, by and with the advice and consent of the rest of the members of the General Assembly, now met at Charlestown, for the South-west part of this Province, and by the authority of the same, That all negroes, mulatoes, mustizoes or Indians, which at any time heretofore have been sold, or now are held or taken to be, or hereafter shall be bought and sold for slaves, are hereby declared slaves; and they, and their children, are hereby made and declared slaves, to all intents and purposes; excepting all such negroes, mulatoes, mustizoes or Indians, which heretofore have been, or hereafter shall be, for some particular merit, made and declared free, either by the Governor and council of this Province, pursuant to any Act or law of this Province, or by their respective owners or masters; and also, excepting all such negroes, mulatoes, mustizoes or Indians, as can prove they ought not to be sold for slaves. And in case any negro, mulatoe, mustizoe or Indian, doth lay claim to his or her freedom, upon all or any of the said accounts, the same shall be finally heard and determined by the Governor and council of this Province.

II. And for the better ordering and governing of negroes and all other slaves in this Province, *Be it enacted* by the authority aforesaid, That no master, mistress, overseer, or other person whatsoever, that hath the care and charge of any negro or slave, shall give their negroes and other slaves leave, on Sundays, hollidays, or any other time, to go out of their plantations, except such negro or other slave as usually wait upon them at home or abroad, or wearing a livery; and every other negro or slave that shall be taken hereafter out of his master's plantation, without a ticket, or leave in writing, from his master or mistress, or some other person by his or her appointment, or some white person in the company of such slave, to give an account of his business, shall be whipped; and every person who shall not (when in his power) apprehend every negro or other slave which he shall see out of his master's plantation, without leave as aforesaid, and after apprehended, shall neglect to punish him by moderate whipping, shall forfeit twenty shillings, the one half to the poor, to be paid to the church wardens of the Parish where such forfeiture shall become due, and the other half to him that will inform for the same, within one week after such neglect; and that no slave may make further or other use of any one ticket than was intended by him that granted the same, every ticket shall particularly mention the name of every slave employed in the particular business, and to what place they are sent, and what time they return; and if any person shall presume to give any negro or slave a ticket in the name of his master or mistress, without his or her consent, such person so doing shall forfeit the sum of twenty shillings; one half to the poor, to be disposed of as aforesaid, the other half to the person injured, that will complain against the person offending, within one week after the offence committed. And for the better security of all such persons that shall endeavor to take any runaway, or shall examine any slave for his ticket, passing to and from his master's plantation, it is hereby declared lawful for any white person to beat, maim or assult, and if such negro or slave cannot otherwise be taken, to kill him, who small refuse to shew his ticket, or, by running away or resistance, shall endeavor to avoid being apprehended or taken.

III. *And be it further enacted* by the authority aforesaid, That every master, mistress or overseer of a family in this Province, shall cause all his negro houses to be searched diligently and effectually, once every fourteen days, for fugitive and runaway slaves, guns, swords, clubs, and any other mischievous weapons, and finding any, to take them away, and cause them to be secured; as also, for clothes, goods, and any other things and commodities that are not given them by their master, mistress, commander or overseer, and honestly come by; and in whose custody they find any thing of that kind, and suspect or know to be stolen goods, the same they shall seize and take into their custody, and a full and ample description of the particulars thereof, in writing, within ten days after the discovery thereof, either to the provost marshall, or to the clerk of the parish for the time being, who is hereby required to receive the same, and to enter upon it the day of its receipt, and the particulars to file and keep to himself; and the clerk shall set upon the posts of the church door, and the provost marshall upon the usual public places, or places of notice, a short brief, that such lost goods are found; whereby, any person that hath lost his goods may the better come to the knowledge where they are; and the owner going to the marshall or clerk, and proving, by marks or otherwise, that the goods lost belong to him, and paying twelve pence for the entry and declaration of the same, if the marshall or clerk be convinced that any part of the goods certified by him to be found, appertains to the party inquiring, he is to direct the said party inquiring to the place and party where the goods be, who is hereby required to make restitution of what is in being to the true owner; and every master, mistress or overseer, as also the provost marshall or clerk, neglecting his duty in any the particulars aforesaid, for every neglect shall forfeit twenty shillings.

IV. And for the more effectual detecting and punishing such persons that trade with any slave for stolen goods, *Be it further enacted* by the authority aforesaid, That where any person shall be suspected to trade as aforesaid, any justice of the peace shall have power to take from him suspected, sufficient recognizance, not to trade with any slave contrary to the laws of this Province; and if it shall afterwards appear to any of the justices of the peace, that such person hath, or hath had, or shipped off, any goods, suspected to be unlawfully come by, it shall be lawful for such justice of the peace to oblige the person to appear at the next general sessions, who shall there be obliged to make reasonable proof, of whom he brought, or how he came by, the said goods, and unless he do it, his recognizance shall be forfeited. . . .

VII. And *whereas*, great numbers of slaves which do not dwell in Charlestown, on Sundays and holidays resort thither, to drink, quarrel, fight, curse and swear, and profane the Sabbath, and using and carrying of clubs and other mischievous weapons, resorting in great companies together, which may give them an opportunity of executing any wicked designs and purposes, to the damage and prejudice of the inhabitants of this Province; for the prevention whereof, *Be it enacted* by the authority aforesaid, That all and every the constables of Charlestown, separately on every Sunday, and the holidays at Christmas, Easter and Whitsonside, together with so many men as each constable shall think necessary to accompany him, which he is hereby empowered for that end to press, under the penalty of twenty shillings to the person that shall disobey him, shall, together with such persons, go through all or any the streets, and also, round about Charlestown, and as much further on the neck as they shall be informed or have reason to suspect any meeting or concourse of any such negroes or slaves to be at that time, and to enter into any house, at Charlestown, or elsewhere, to search for such slaves, and as many of them as they can apprehend, shall cause to be publicly whipped in Charlestown, and then to be delivered to the marshall, who for every slave so whipped and delivered to him by the constable, shall pay the constable five shillings, which five shillings shall be repaid the said marshall by the owner or head of that family to which the said negro or slave, doth belong, together with such other charges as shall become due to him for keeping runaway slaves; and the marshall shall in all respects keep and dispose of such slave as if the same was delivered to him as a runaway, under the same penalties and forfeiture as hereafter in that case is provided; and every constable of Charlestown which shall neglect or refuse to make search as aforesaid, for every such neglect shall forfeit the sum of twenty shillings. . . .

IX. *And be it further enacted* by the authority aforesaid, That upon complaint made to any justice of the peace, of any heinous or grievous crime, committed by any slave or slaves, as murder, burglary, robbery, burning of houses, or any lesser crimes, as killing or stealing any meat or other cattle, maiming one the other, stealing of fowls, provisions, or such like trespasses or injuries, the said justice shall issue out his warrant for apprehending the offender or offenders, and for all persons to come before him that can give evidence; and if upon examination, it probably appeareth, that the apprehended person is guilty, he shall commit him or them to prison, or immediately proceed to tryal of the said slave or slaves, according to the form hereafter specified, or take security for his or their forthcoming, as the case shall require, and also to certify to the justice next to him, the said cause, and to require him, by virtue of this Act, to associate himself to him, which said justice is hereby required to do, and they so associated, are to issue their summons to three sufficient freeholders, acquainting them with the matter, and appointing them a day, hour and place, when and where the same shall be heard and determined, at which day, hour and place, the said justices and freeholders shall cause the offenders and evidences to come before them, and if they, on hearing the matter, the said freeholders being by the said justices first sworn to judge uprightly and according to evidence, and diligently weighing and examining all evidences, proofs and testimonies (and in case of murder only, if on violent presumption and circumstances), they shall find such negro or other slave or slaves guilty thereof, they shall give sentence of death, if the crime by law deserve the same, and forthwith by their warrant cause immediate execution to be done, by the common or any other executioner, in such manner as they shall think fit, the kind of death to be inflicted to be left to their judgment and discretion; and if the crime committed shall not deserve death, they shall then condemn and adjudge the criminal or criminals to any other punishment, but not extending to limb or disabling him, without a particular law directing such punishment, and shall forthwith order execution to be done accordingly.

X. And in regard great mischiefs daily happen by petty larcenies committed by negroes and slaves of this Province, *Be it further enacted* by the authority aforesaid, That if any negro or other slave shall hereafter steal or destroy any goods, chattels, or provisions whatsoever, of any other person than his master or mistress, being under the value of twelve pence, every negro or other slave so offending, and being brought before some justice of the peace of this Province, upon complaint of the party injured, and shall be adjudged guilty by confession, proof, or probable circumstances, such negro or slave so offending, excepting children, whose punishment is left wholly to the discretion of the said justice, shall be adjudged by such justice to be publicly and severely whipped, not exceeding forty lashes; and if such negro or other slave punished as aforesaid, be afterwards, by two justices of the peace, found guilty of the like crimes, he or they, for such his or their second offence, shall either have one of his ears cut off, or be branded in the forehead with a hot iron, that the mark thereof may remain; and if after such punishment, such negro or slave for his third offence, shall have his nose slit; and if such negro or other slave, after the third time as aforesaid, be accused of petty larceny, or of any of the offences before mentioned, such negro or other slave shall be tried in such manner as those accused of murder, burglary, *etc.* are before by this Act provided for to be tried, and in case they shall be found guilty a fourth time, of any the offences before mentioned, then such negro or other slave shall be adjudged to suffer death, or other punishment, as the said justices shall think fitting; and any judgment given for the first offence, shall be a sufficient conviction for the first offence; and any after judgment after the first judgment, shall be a sufficient conviction to bring the offender within the penalty of the second offence, and so for inflicting the rest of the punishments; and in case the said justices and freeholders, and any or either of them, shall neglect or refuse to perform the duties by this Act required of them, they shall severally, for such their defaults, forfeit the sum of twenty-five pounds. . . .

XII. *And it is further enacted* by the authority aforesaid, That if any negroes or other slaves shall make mutiny or insurrection, or rise in rebellion against the authority and government of this Province, or shall make preparation of arms, powder, bullets or offensive weapons, in order to carry on such mutiny or insurrection, or shall hold any counsel or conspiracy for raising such mutiny, insurrection or rebellion, the offenders shall be tried by two justices of the peace and three freeholders, associated together as before expressed in case of murder, burglary, *etc.*, who are hereby empowered and required to try the said slaves so offending, and inflict death, or any other punishment, upon the offenders, and forthwith by their warrant cause execution to be done, by the common or any other executioner, in such manner as they shall think fitting; and if any person shall make away or conceal any negro or negroes, or other slave or slaves, suspected to be guilty of the beforementioned crimes, and not upon demand bring forth the suspected offender or offenders, such person shall forfeit for every negro or slave so concealed or made away, the sum of fifty pounds; *Provided, nevertheless,* that when and as often as any of the beforementioned crimes shall be committed by more than one negro, that shall deserve death, that then and in all such cases, if the Governor and council of this Province shall think fitting, and accordingly shall order, that only one or more of the said criminals should suffer death as exemplary, and the rest to be returned to the owners, that then, the owners of the negroes so offending, shall bear proportionably the loss of the said negro or negroes so put to death, as shall be allotted them by the said justices and freeholders; and if any person shall refuse his part so allotted him, that then, and in all such cases, the said justices and freeholders are hereby required to issue out their warrant of distress upon the goods and chattels of the person so refusing, and shall cause the same to be sold by public outcry, to satisfy the said money so allotted him to pay, and to return the overplus, if any be, to the owner; *Provided, nevertheless,* that the part allotted for any person to pay for his part or proportion of the negro or negroes so put to death, shall not exceed one sixth part of his negro or negroes so excused and pardoned; and in case that shall not be sufficient to satisfy for the negro or negroes that shall be put to death, that the remaining sum shall be paid out of the public treasury of this Province.*

*Thomas Cooper and David J. McCord, eds., *Statutes at Large of South Carolina* (10 vols., Columbia, 1836–1841), VII, 352–357.

The "Three-Fifths Compromise":
The U.S. Constitution, Article I, Section 2

One of the major debates in the Constitutional Convention hinged on the use of slaves in computing taxes and fixing representation. Southern delegates held that slaves should be computed in determining representation in the House, but that they should not be counted in determining a state's share of the direct tax burden. The northern delegates' point of view was exactly the opposite. A compromise was reached whereby three fifths of the slaves were to be counted in apportionment of representation and in direct taxes among the states. Thus the South was victorious in obtaining representation for her slaves, even though delegate Luther Martin might rail that the Constitution was an insult to the Deity "who views with equal eye the poor African slave and his American master." The "three-fifths compromise" appears in Article I, Section 2.

Representatives and direct Taxes shall be apportioned among the several States which may be included within this Union, according to their respective Numbers, which shall be determined by adding to the whole Number of free Persons, including those bound to Service for a Term of Years, and excluding Indians not taxed, three fifths of all other Persons.

5

An Act Prohibiting the Teaching of Slaves to Read*

To keep the slaves in hand it was deemed necessary to keep them innocent of the printed page. Otherwise they might read abolitionist newspapers that were smuggled in, become dissatisfied, forge passes, or simply know too much. Hence most states passed laws prohibiting anyone from teaching slaves to read or write. The North Carolina statute was typical.

An Act to Prevent All Persons from Teaching Slaves to Read or Write, the Use of Figures Excepted

Whereas the teaching of slaves to read and write, has a tendency to excite dissatisfaction in their minds, and to produce insurrection and rebellion, to the manifest injury of the citizens of this State:

Therefore,

Be it enacted by the General Assembly of the State of North Carolina, and it is hereby enacted by the authority of the same, That any free person, who shall hereafter teach, or attempt to teach, any slave within the State to read or write, the use of figures excepted, or shall give or sell to such slave or slaves any books or pamphlets, shall be liable to indictment in any court of record in this State having jurisdiction thereof, and upon conviction, shall, at the discretion of the court, if a white man or woman, be fined not less than one hundred dollars, nor more than two hundred dollars, or imprisoned; and if a free person of color, shall be fined, imprisoned, or whipped, at the discretion of the court, not exceeding thirty-nine lashes, nor less than twenty lashes.

II. *Be it further enacted,* That if any slave shall hereafter teach, or attempt to teach, any other slave to read or write, the use of figures excepted, he or she may be carried before any justice of the peace, and on conviction thereof, shall be sentenced to receive thirty-nine lashes on his or her bare back.

III. *Be it further enacted,* That the judges of the Superior Courts and the justices of the County Courts shall give this act in charge to the grand juries of their respective counties.

*Acts Passed by the General Assembly of the State of North Carolina at the Session of 1830–1831 (Raleigh, 1831), 11.

6

Declaration of Sentiments and Resolutions, Seneca Falls Convention, 1848

The Declaration of Sentiments, adopted in July 1848 at Seneca Falls, New York, at the first woman's-rights convention, is the most famous document in the history of feminism. Like its model, the Declaration of Independence, it contains a bill of particulars. Some people at the meeting thought the inclusion of disfranchisement in the list of grievances would discredit the entire movement, and when the resolutions accompanying the Declaration were put to a vote, the one calling for the suffrage was the only one that did not pass unanimously. But it did pass and thus inaugurated the woman-suffrage movement in the United States.

Declaration of Sentiments

When, in the course of human events, it becomes necessary for one portion of the family of man to assume among the people of the earth a position different from that which they have hitherto occupied, but one to which the laws of nature and of nature's God entitle them, a decent respect to the opinions of mankind requires that they should declare the causes that impel them to such a course.

We hold these truths to be self-evident: that all men and women are created equal; that they are endowed by their Creator with certain inalienable rights; that among these are life, liberty, and the pursuit of happiness; that to secure these rights governments are instituted, deriving their just powers from the consent of the governed. Whenever any form of government becomes destructive of these ends, it is the right of those who suffer from it to refuse allegiance to it, and to insist upon the institution of a new government, laying its foundation on such principles, and organizing its powers in such form, as to them shall seem most likely to effect their safety and happiness. Prudence, indeed, will dictate that governments long established should not be changed for light and transient causes; and accordingly all experience hath shown that mankind are more disposed to suffer, while evils are sufferable, than to right themselves by abolishing the forms to which they were accustomed. But when a long train of abuses and usurpations, pursuing invariably the same object, evinces a design to reduce them under absolute depotism, it is their duty to throw off such government, and to provide new guards for their future security. Such has been the patient sufferance of the women under this government, and such is now the necessity which constrains them to demand the equal station to which they are entitled.

The history of mankind is a history of repeated injuries and usurpations on the part of man toward woman, having in direct object the establishment of an absolute tyranny over her. To prove this, let facts be submitted to a candid world.

He has never permitted her to exercise her inalienable right to the elective franchise.

He has compelled her to submit to laws, in the formation of which she had no voice.

He has withheld from her rights which are given to the most ignorant and degraded men—both natives and foreigners.

Having deprived her of this first right of a citizen, the elective franchise, thereby leaving her without representation in the halls of legislation, he has oppressed her on all sides.

He has made her, if married, in the eye of the law, civilly dead.

He has taken from her all right in property, even to the wages she earns.

He has made her, morally, an irresponsible being, as she can commit many crimes with impunity, provided they be done in the presence of her husband. In the covenant of marriage, she is compelled to promise obedience to her husband, he becoming, to all intents and purposes, her master—the law giving him power to deprive her of her liberty, and to administer chastisement.

He has so framed the laws of divorce, as to what shall be the proper causes, and in case of separation, to whom the guardianship of the children shall be given, as to be wholly regardless of the happiness of women—the law, in all cases, going upon the false supposition of the supremacy of man, and giving all power into his hands.

After depriving her of all rights as a married woman, if single, and the owner of property, he has taxed her to support a government which recognizes her only when her property can be made profitable to it.

He has monopolized nearly all the profitable employments, and from those she is permitted to follow, she receives but a scanty remuneration. He closes against her all the avenues to wealth and distinction which he considers most honorable to himself. As a teacher of theology, medicine, or law, she is not known.

He has denied her the facilities for obtaining a thorough education, all colleges being closed against her.

He allows her in Church, as well as State, but a subordinate position, claiming Apostolic authority for her exclusion from the ministry, and, with some exceptions, from any public participation in the affairs of the Church.

He has created a false public sentiment by giving to the world a different code of morals for men and women, by which moral delinquencies which exclude women from society, are not only tolerated, but deemed of little account in man.

He has usurped the prerogative of Jehovah himself, claiming it as his right to assign for her a sphere of action, when that belongs to her conscience and to her God.

He has endeavored, in every way that he could, to destroy her confidence in her own powers, to lessen her self-respect, and to make her willing to lead a dependent and abject life.

Now, in view of this entire disfranchisement of one-half the people of this country, their social and religious degradation—in view of the unjust laws above mentioned, and because women do feel themselves aggrieved, oppressed, and fraudulently deprived of their most sacred rights, we insist that they have immediate admission to all the rights and privileges which belong to them as citizens of the United States.

In entering upon the great work before us, we anticipate no small amount of misconception, misrepresentation, and ridicule; but we shall use every instrumentality within our power to effect our object. We shall employ agents, circulate tracts, petition the State and National legislatures, and endeavor to enlist the pulpit and the press in our behalf. We hope this Convention will be followed by a series of Conventions embracing every part of the country.

Resolutions

Whereas, The great precept of nature is conceded to be, that "man shall pursue his own true and substantial happiness." Blackstone in his Commentaries remarks, that this law of Nature being coeval with mankind, and dictated by God himself, is of course superior in obligation to any other. It is binding over all the globe, in all countries and at all times; no human laws are of any validity if contrary to this, and such of them as are valid, derive all their force, and all their validity, and all their authority, mediately and immediately, from this original; therefore,

Resolved, That such laws as conflict, in any way, with the true and substantial happiness of woman, are contrary to the great precept of nature and of no validity, for this is "superior in obligation to any other."

Resolved, That all laws which prevent woman from occupying such a station in society as her conscience shall dictate, or which place her in a position inferior to that of man, are contrary to the great precept of nature, and therefore of no force or authority.

Resolved, That woman is man's equal—was intended to be so by the Creator, and the highest good of the race demands that she should be recognized as such.

Resolved, That the women of this country ought to be enlightened in regard to the laws under which they live, that they may no longer publish their degradation by declaring themselves satisfied with their present position, nor their ignorance, by asserting that they have all the rights they want.

Resolved, That inasmuch as man, while claiming for himself intellectual superiority, does accord to woman moral superiority, it is pre-eminently his duty to encourage her to speak and teach, as she has an opportunity, in all religious assemblies.

Resolved, That the same amount of virtue, delicacy, and refinement of behavior that is required of woman in the social state, should also be required of man, and the same transgressions should be visited with equal severity on both man and woman.

Resolved, That the objection of indelicacy and impropriety, which is so often brought against woman when she addresses a public audience, comes with a very ill-grace from those who encourage, by their attendance, her appearance on the stage, in the concert, or in feats of the circus.

Resolved, That woman has too long rested satisfied in the circumscribed limits which corrupt customs and a perverted application of the Scriptures have marked out for her, and that it is time she should move in the enlarged sphere which her great Creator has assigned her.

Resolved, That it is the duty of the women of this country to secure to themselves their sacred right to the elective franchise.

Resolved, That the equality of human rights results necessarily from the fact of the identity of the race in capabilities and responsibilities.

Resolved, therefore, That, being invested by the Creator with the same capabilities, and the same consciousness of responsibility for their exercise, it is demonstrably the right and duty of woman, equally with man, to promote every righteous cause by every righteous means; and especially in regard to the great subjects of morals and religion, it is self-evidently her right to participate with her brother in teaching them, both in private and in public, by writing and by speaking, by any instrumentalities proper to be used, and in any assemblies proper to be held; and this being a self-evident truth growing out of the divinely implanted principles of human nature, any custom or authority adverse to it, whether modern or wearing the hoary sanction of antiquity, is to be regarded as a self-evident falsehood, and at war with mankind.

[All the above resolutions had been drafted by Elizabeth Cady Stanton. At the last session of the convention Lucretia Mott offered the following, which, along with all the other resolutions except the ninth, was adopted unanimously.—*Ed.*]

Resolved, That the speedy success of our cause depends upon the zealous and untiring efforts of both men and women, for the overthrow of the monopoly of the pulpit, and for the securing to woman an equal participation with men in the various trades, professions, and commerce.

7

The Antisuffragists:
Selected Papers, 1852–1887

Editorial, New York Herald (1852)*

The farce at Syracuse has been played out. . . .

Who are these women? What do they want? What are the motives that impel them to this course of action? The *dramatis personae* of the farce enacted at Syracuse present a curious conglomeration of both sexes. Some of them are old maids, whose personal charms were never very attractive, and who have been sadly slighted by the masculine gender in general; some of them women who have been badly mated, whose own temper, or their husbands', has made life anything but agreeable to them, and they are therefore down upon the whole of the opposite sex; some, having so much of the virago in their disposition, that nature appears to have made a mistake in their gender—mannish women, like hens that crow; some of boundless vanity and egotism, who believe that they are superior in intellectual ability to "all the world and the rest of mankind," and delight to see their speeches and addresses in print; and man shall be consigned to his proper sphere—nursing the babies, washing the dishes, mending stockings, and sweeping the house. This is "the good time coming." Besides the classes we have enumerated, there is a class of wild enthusiasts and visionaries—very sincere, but very mad—having the same vein as the fanatical Abolitionists, and the majority, if not all of them, being, in point of fact, deeply imbued with the anti-slavery sentiment. Of the male sex who attend these Conventions for the purpose of taking part in them, the majority are henpecked husbands, and all of them ought to wear petticoats. . . .

How did woman first become subject to man as she now is all over the world? By her nature, her sex, just as the negro is and always will be, to the end of time, inferior to the white race, and, therefore, doomed to subjection; but happier than she would be in any other condition, just because it is the law of her nature. The women themselves would not have this law reversed. . . .

*"The Woman's Rights Convention—The Last Act of the Drama," editorial, New York *Herald*, September 12, 1852.

What do the leaders of the Woman's Rights Convention want? They want to vote, and to hustle with the rowdies at the polls. They want to be members of Congress, and in the heat of debate to subject themselves to coarse jests and indecent language. . . . They want to fill all other posts which men are ambitious to occupy—to be lawyers, doctors, captains of vessels, and generals in the field. How funny it would sound in the newspapers, that Lucy Stone, pleading a cause, took suddenly ill in the pains of parturition, and perhaps gave birth to a fine bouncing boy in court! Or that Rev. Antoinette Brown was arrested in the middle of her sermon in the pulpit from the same cause, and presented a "pledge" to her husband and the congregation; or, that Dr. Harriot K. Hunt, while attending a gentleman patient for a fit of the gout or *fistula in ano*, found it necessary to send for a doctor, there and then, and to be delivered of a man or woman child—perhaps twins. A similar event might happen on the floor of Congress, in a storm at sea, or in the raging tempest of battle, and then what is to become of the woman legislator?

New York State Legislative Report (1856)*

Mr. Foote, from the Judiciary Committee, made a report on Women's rights that set the whole House in roars of laughter:

"The Committee is composed of married and single gentlemen. The bachelors on the Committee, with becoming diffidence, having left the subject pretty much to the married gentlemen, they have considered it with the aid of the light they have before them and the experience married life has given them. Thus aided, they are enabled to state that the ladies always have the best place and choicest titbit at the table. They have the best seat in the cars, carriages, and sleighs; the warmest place in the winter, and the coolest place in the summer. They have their choice on which side of the bed they will lie, front or back. A lady's dress costs three times as much as that of a gentleman; and, at the present time, with the prevailing fashion, one lady occupies three times as much space in the world as a gentleman.

"It has thus appeared to the married gentlemen of your Committee, being a majority (the bachelors being silent for the reason mentioned, and also probably for the further reason that they are still suitors for the favors of the gentler sex), that, if there is any inequality or oppression in the case, the gentlemen are the sufferers. They, however, have presented no petitions for redress; having, doubtless, made up their minds to yield to an inevitable destiny. . . ."

---

*This Report on Woman's Rights, made to the New York State Legislature and concerning a petition for political equality for women, was printed in an Albany paper in March 1856.

Orestes A. Brownson, The Woman Question (1869 and 1873)*

The conclusive objection to the political enfranchisement of women is, that it would weaken and finally break up and destroy the Christian family. The social unit is the family, not the individual; and the greatest danger to American society is, that we are rapidly becoming a nation of isolated individuals, without family ties or affections. The family has already been much weakened, and is fast disappearing. We have broken away from the old homestead, have lost the restraining and purifying associations that gathered around it, and live away from home in hotels and boarding-houses. We are daily losing the faith, the virtues, the habits, and the manners without which the family cannot be sustained; and when the family goes, the nation goes too, or ceases to be worth preserving. . . .

Extend now to women suffrage and eligibility; give them the political right to vote and to be voted for; render it feasible for them to enter the arena of political strife, to become canvassers in elections and candidates for office, and what remains of family union will soon be dissolved. The wife may espouse one political party, and the husband another, and it may well happen that the husband and wife may be rival candidates for the same office, and one or the other doomed to the mortification of defeat. Will the husband like to see his wife enter the lists against him, and triumph over him? Will the wife, fired with political ambition for place or power, be pleased to see her own husband enter the lists against her, and succeed at her expense? Will political rivalry and the passions it never fails to engender increase the mutual affection of husband and wife for each other, and promote domestic union and peace, or will it not carry into the bosom of the family all the strife, discord, anger, and division of the political canvass? . . .

Woman was created to be a wife and a mother; that is her destiny. To that destiny all her instincts point, and for it nature has specially qualified her. Her proper sphere is home, and her proper function is the care of the household, to manage a family, to take care of children, and attend to their early training. For this she is endowed with patience, endurance, passive courage, quick sensibilities, a sympathetic nature, and great executive and administrative ability. She was born to be a queen in her own household, and to make home cheerful, bright, and happy.

We do not believe women, unless we acknowledge individual exceptions, are fit to have their own head. The most degraded of the savage tribes are those in which women rule, and descent is reckoned from the mother instead of the father. Revelation asserts, and universal experience proves that the man is the head of the woman,

---

*The following document consists of two articles by Orestes A. Brownson: "The Woman Question. Article I [from the *Catholic World*, May 1869]," in Henry F. Brownson, ed., *The Works of Orestes A. Brownson*, XVIII (Detroit, 1885), 388–89; and "The Woman Question. Article II [a review of Horace Bushnell, *Women's Suffrage: The Reform against Nature* (New York, 1869), from *Brownson's Quarterly Review* for October 1873]," in Henry F. Brownson, *op. cit.*, p. 403.

and that the woman is for the man, not the man for the woman; and his greatest error, as well as the primal curse of society is that he abdicates his headship, and allows himself to be governed, we might almost say, deprived of his reason, by woman. It was through the seductions of the woman, herself seduced by the serpent, that man fell, and brought sin and all our woe into the world. She has all the qualities that fit her to be a help-meet of man, to be the mother of his children, to be their nurse, their early instructress, their guardian, their life-long friend; to be his companion, his comforter, his consoler in sorrow, his friend in trouble, his ministering angel in sickness; but as an independent existence, free to follow her own fancies and vague longings, her own ambition and natural love of power, without masculine direction or control, she is out of her element, and a social anomaly, sometimes a hideous monster, which men seldom are, excepting through a woman's influence. This is no excuse for men, but it proves that women need a head, and the restraint of father, husband, or the priest of God.

Remarks of Senator George G. Vest in Congress (1887)*

Mr. VEST. . . . . If this Government, which is based on the intelligence of the people, shall ever be destroyed it will be by injudicious, immature, or corrupt suffrage. If the ship of state launched by our fathers shall ever be destroyed, it will be by striking the rock of universal, unprepared suffrage. . . .

The Senator who last spoke on this question refers to the successful experiment in regard to woman suffrage in the Territories of Wyoming and Washington. Mr. President, it is not upon the plains of the sparsely settled Territories of the West that woman suffrage can be tested. Suffrage in the rural districts and sparsely settled regions of this country must from the very nature of things remain pure when corrupt everywhere else. The danger of corrupt suffrage is in the cities, and those masses of population to which civilization tends everywhere in all history. Whilst the country has been pure and patriotic, cities have been the first cancers to appear upon the body-politic in all ages of the world.

Wyoming Territory! Washington Territory! Where are their large cities? Where are the localities in those Territories where the strain upon popular government must come? The Senator from New Hampshire [Henry W. Blair—*Ed.*], who is so conspicuous in this movement, appalled the country some months since by his ghastly array of illiteracy in the Southern States. . . . That Senator proposes now to double, and more than double, that illiteracy. He proposes now to give the negro women of the South this right of suffrage, utterly unprepared as they are for it.

In a convention some two years and a half ago in the city of Louisville an intelligent negro from the South said the negro men could not vote the Democratic

*The following remarks of Senator George G. Vest (Democrat, Missouri) may be found in the *Congressional Record*, 49th Congress, 2d Session, January 25, 1887, p. 986.

ticket because the women would not live with them if they did. The negro men go out in the hotels and upon the railroad cars. They go to the cities and by attrition they wear away the prejudice of race; but the women remain at home, and their emotional natures aggregate and compound the race-prejudice, and when suffrage is given them what must be the result? . . .

I pity the man who can consider any question affecting the influence of woman with the cold, dry logic of business. What man can, without aversion, turn from the blessed memory of that dear old grandmother, or the gentle words and caressing hand of that dear blessed mother gone to the unknown world, to face in its stead the idea of a female justice of the peace or township constable? For my part I want when I go to my home—when I turn from the arena where man contends with man for what we call the prizes of this paltry world—I want to go back, not to be received in the masculine embrace of some female ward politician, but to the earnest, loving look and touch of a true woman. I want to go back to the jurisdiction of the wife, the mother; and instead of a lecture upon finance or the tariff, or upon the construction of the Constitution, I want those blessed, loving details of domestic life and domestic love.

. . . I speak now respecting women as a sex. I believe that they are better than men, but I do not believe they are adapted to the political work of this world. I do not believe that the Great Intelligence ever intended them to invade the sphere of work given to men, tearing down and destroying all the best influences for which God has intended them.

The great evil in this country to-day is in emotional suffrage. The great danger to-day is in excitable suffrage. If the voters of this country could think always coolly, and if they could deliberate, if they could go by judgment and not by passion, our institutions would survive forever, eternal as the foundations of the continent itself; but massed together, subject to the excitements of mobs and of these terrible political contests that come upon us from year to year under the autonomy of our Government, what would be the result if suffrage were given to the women of the United States?

Women are essentially emotional. It is no disparagement to them they are so. It is no more insulting to say that women are emotional than to say that they are delicately constructed physically and unfitted to become soldiers or workmen under the sterner, harder pursuits of life.

What we want in this country is to avoid emotional suffrage, and what we need is to put more logic into public affairs and less feeling. There are spheres in which feeling should be paramount. There are kingdoms in which the heart should reign supreme. That kingdom belongs to woman. The realm of sentiment, the realm of love, the realm of the gentler and the holier and kindlier attributes that make the name of wife, mother, and sister next to that of God himself.

I would not, and I say it deliberately, degrade woman by giving her the right of suffrage. I mean the word in its full signification, because I believe that woman as she is to-day, the queen of the home and of hearts, is above the political collisions of this world, and should always be kept above them. . . .

It is said that the suffrage is to be given to enlarge the sphere of woman's influence. Mr. President, it would destroy her influence. It would take her down from that pedestal where she is to-day, influencing as a mother the minds of her offspring, influencing by her gentle and kindly caress the action of her husband toward the good and pure.

People v. Hall, 1854

Bias against Chinese and other colored "races" was endemic in Nineteenth Century California, but perhaps no single document so well demonstrates that bias as this majority opinion handed down by the Chief Justice of the California Supreme Court. Since Chinese miners lived in small, segregated groups, the practical effect of this decision was to declare "open season" on Chinese, since crimes against them were likely to be witnessed only by other Chinese.

The People, Respondent, v. George W. Hall, Appellant

The appellant, a free white citizen of this State, was convicted of murder upon the testimony of Chinese witnesses.

The point involved in this case, is the admissibility of such evidence.

The 394th section of the Act Concerning Civil Cases, provides that no Indian or Negro shall be allowed to testify as a witness in any action or proceeding in which a White person is a party.

The 14th section of the Act of April 16th, 1850, regulating Criminal Proceedings, provides that "No Black, or Mulatto person, or Indian, shall be allowed to give evidence in favor of, or against a white man."

The true point at which we are anxious to arrive, is the legal signification of the words, "Black, Mulatto, Indian and White person," and whether the Legislature adopted them as generic terms, or intended to limit their application to specific types of the human species.

Before considering this question, it is proper to remark the difference between the two sections of our Statute, already quoted, the latter being more broad and comprehensive in its exclusion, by use of the word "Black," instead of Negro.

Conceding, however, for the present, that the word "Black," as used in the 14th section, and "Negro," in 394th, are convertible terms, and that the former was intended to include the latter, let us proceed to inquire who are excluded from testifying as witnesses under the term "Indian."

When Columbus first landed upon the shores of this continent, in his attempt to discover a western passage to the Indies, he imagined that he had accomplished the object of his expedition, and that the Island of San Salvador was one of those Islands of the Chinese sea, lying near the extremity of India, which had been described by navigators.

Acting upon this hypothesis, and also perhaps from the similarity of features and physical conformation, he gave to the Islanders the name of Indians, which appellation was universally adopted, and extended to the aboriginals of the New World, as well as of Asia.

From that time, down to a very recent period, the American Indians and the Mongolian, or Asiatic, were regarded as the same type of human species. . . .

. . . That this was the common opinion in the early history of American legislation, cannot be disputed, and, therefore, all legislation upon the subject must have borne relation to that opinion. . . .

. . . In using the words, "No Black, or Mulatto person, or Indian shall be allowed to give evidence for or against a White person," the Legislature, if any intention can be ascribed to it, adopted the most comprehensive terms to embrace every known class or shade of color, as the apparent design was to protect the White person from the influence of all testimony other than that of persons of the same caste. The use of these terms must, by every sound rule of construction, exclude every one who is not of white blood. . . .

. . . We have carefully considered all the consequences resulting from a different rule of construction, and are satisfied that even in a doubtful case we would be impelled to this decision on grounds of public policy.

The same rule which would admit them to testify, would admit them to all the equal rights of citizenship, and we might soon see them at the polls, in the jury box, upon the bench, and in our legislative halls.

This is not a speculation which exists in the excited and overheated imagination of the patriot and statesman, but it is an actual and present danger.

The anomalous spectacle of a distinct people, living in our community, recognizing no laws of this State except through necessity, bringing with them their prejudices and national feuds, in which they indulge in open violation of law; whose mendacity is proverbial; a race of people whom nature has marked as inferior, and who are incapable of progress or intellectual development beyond a certain point, as their history has shown; differing in language, opinions, color, and physical conformation; between whom and ourselves nature has placed an impassable difference, is now presented, and for them is claimed, not only the right to swear away the life of a citizen, but the further privilege of participating with us in administering the affairs of our Government. . . .

. . . For these reasons, we are of opinion that the testimony was inadmissible. . . .

9

Dred Scott v. *Sanford,* 1857

The question is simply this: Can a negro, whose ancestors were imported into this country, and sold as slaves, become a member of the political community formed and brought into existence by the Constitution of the United States, and as such become entitled to all the rights, and privileges, and immunities, guarantied by that instrument to the citizen? One of which rights is the privilege of suing in a court of the United States in the cases specified in the Constitution.

It will be observed, that the plea applies to that class of persons only whose ancestors were negroes of the African race, and imported into this country, and sold and held as slaves. The only matter in issue before the court, therefore, is whether the descendants of such slaves, when they shall be emancipated, or who are born of parents who had become free before their birth, are citizens of a State, in the sense in which the word citizen is used in the Constitution of the United States. And this being the only matter in dispute on the pleadings, the court must be understood as speaking in his opinion of that class only, that is, of those persons who are the descendants of Africans who were imported into this country, and sold as slaves.

It becomes necessary, therefore, to determine who were citizens of the several States when the Constitution was adopted. And in order to do this, we must recur to the Governments and institutions of the thirteen colonies, when they separated from Great Britain and formed new sovereignties, and took their places in the family of independent nations. We must inquire who, at that time, were recognised as the people or citizens of a State, whose rights and liberties had been outraged by the English Government; and who declared their independence, and assumed the powers of Government to defend their rights by force of arms.

In the opinion of the court, the legislation and histories of the times, and the language used in the Declaration of Independence, show, that neither the class of persons who had been imported as slaves, nor their descendants, whether they had become free or not, were then acknowledged as a part of the people, nor intended to be included in the general words used in that memorable instrument.

It is difficult at this day to realize the state of public opinion in relation to that unfortunate race, which prevailed in the civilized and enlightened portions of the world at the time of the Declaration of Independence, and when the Constitution of the United States was formed and adopted. But the public history of every European nation displays it in a manner too plain to be mistaken.

They had for more than a century before been regarded as beings of an inferior order, and altogether unfit to associate with the white race, either in social or political relations; and so far inferior, that they had no rights which the white man was bound to respect; and that the negro might justly and lawfully be reduced to slavery for his benefit. He was bought and sold, and treated as an ordinary article of merchandise and traffic, whenever a profit could be made by it. This opinion was at that time fixed and universal in the civilized portion of the white race. It was regarded as an axiom in morals as well as in politics, which no one thought of disputing, or supposed to be open to dispute; and men in every grade and position in society daily and habitually acted upon it in their private pursuits, as well as in matters of public concern, without doubting for a moment the correctness of this opinion.

And in no nation was this opinion more firmly fixed or more uniformly acted upon than by the English Government and English people. They not only seized them on the coast of Africa, and sold them or held them in slavery for their own use, but they took them as ordinary articles of merchandise to every country where they could make a profit on them, and were far more extensively engaged in this commerce than any other nation in the world.

The opinion thus entertained and acted upon in England was naturally impressed upon the colonies they founded on this side of the Atlantic. And, accordingly, a negro of the African race was regarded by them as an article of property, and held, and bought and sold as such, in every one of the thirteen colonies which united in the Declaration of Independence, and afterwards formed the Constitution of the United States. The slaves were more or less numerous in the different colonies, as slave labor was found more or less profitable. But no one seems to have doubted the correctness of the prevailing opinion of the time.

The legislation of the different colonies furnishes positive and indisputable proof of this fact.

The language of the Declaration of Independence is equally conclusive:

It begins by declaring that, "when in the course of human events it becomes necessary for one people to dissolve the political bands which have connected them with another, and to assume among the powers of the earth the separate and equal station to which the laws of nature and nature's God entitle them, a decent respect for the opinions of mankind requires that they should declare the causes which impel them to the separation."

It then proceeds to say: "We hold these truths to be self-evident: that all men are created equal; that they are endowed by their Creator with certain unalienable rights; that among them is life, liberty, and the pursuit of happiness; that to secure these rights, Governments are instituted, deriving their just powers from the consent of the governed."

The general words above quoted would seem to embrace the whole human family, and if they were used in a similar instrument at this day would be so understood. But it is too clear for dispute, that the enslaved African race were not intended to be included, and formed no part of the people who framed and adopted this declaration; for if the language, as understood in that day, would embrace them, the conduct of the distinguished men who framed the Declaration of Independence would have been utterly and flagrantly inconsistent with the principles they asserted; and instead of the sympathy of mankind, to which they so confidently appealed, they would have deserved and received universal rebuke and reprobation.

Yet the men who framed this declaration were great men—high in literary acquirements—high in their sense of honor, and incapable of asserting principles inconsistent with those on which they were acting. They perfectly understood the meaning of the language they used, and how it would be understood by others; and they knew that it would not in any part of the civilized world be supposed to embrace the negro race, which, by common consent, had been excluded from civilized Governments and the family of nations, and doomed to slavery. They spoke and acted according to the then established doctrines and principles, and in the ordinary language of the day, and no one misunderstood them. The unhappy black race were separated from the white by indelible marks, and laws long before established, and were never thought of or spoken of except as property, and when the claims of the owner or the profit of the trader were supposed to need protection.

This state of public opinion had undergone no change when the Constitution was adopted, as is equally evident from its provisions and language.

The brief preamble sets forth by whom it was formed, for what purposes, and for whose benefit and protection. It declares that it is formed by the *people* of the United States; that is to say, by those who were members of the different political communities in the several States; and its great object is declared to be to secure the blessings of liberty to themselves and their posterity. It speaks in general terms of the *people* of the United States, and of *citizens* of the several States, when it is providing for the exercise of the powers granted or the privileges secured to the citizen. It does not define what description of persons are intended to be included under these terms, or who shall be regarded as a citizen and one of the people. It uses them as terms so well understood, that no further description or definition was necessary.

But there are two clauses in the Constitution which point directly and specifically to the negro race as a separate class of persons, and show clearly that they were not regarded as a portion of the people or citizens of the Government then formed.

One of these clauses reserves to each of the thirteen States the right to import slaves until the year 1808, if it thinks proper. And the importation which it thus sanctions was unquestionably of persons of the race of which we are speaking, as the traffic in slaves in the United States had always been confined to them. And by the other provision the States pledge themselves to each other to maintain the right of property of the master, by delivering up to him any slave who may have escaped from his service, and be found within their respective territories. By the first above-mentioned clause, therefore, the right to purchase and hold this property is directly sanctioned and authorized for twenty years by the people who framed the Constitution. And by the second, they pledge themselves to maintain and uphold the right of the master in the manner specified, as long as the Government they then formed should endure. And these two provisions show, conclusively, that neither the description of persons therein referred to, nor their descendants, were embraced in any of the other provisions of the Constitution; for certainly these two clauses were not intended to confer on them or their posterity the blessings of liberty, or any of the personal rights so carefully provided for the citizen.

Upon the whole, therefore, it is the judgment of this court, that it appears by the record before us that the plaintiff in error is not a citizen of Missouri, in the sense in which that word is used in the Constitution; and that the Circuit Court of the United States, for that reason, had no jurisdiction in the case, and could give no judgment in it. Its judgment for the defendant must, consequently, be reversed, and a mandate issued, directing the suit to be dismissed for want of jurisdiction. *

10

The Emancipation Proclamation

Abraham Lincoln

Emancipation Proclamation by the President of the United States of America: A Proclamation

January 1, 1863

Whereas, on the twenty-second day of September, in the year of our Lord one thousand eight hundred and sixty two, a proclamation was issued by the President of the United States, containing, among other things, the following, to wit:

"That on the first day of January, in the year of our Lord one thousand eight hundred and sixty-three, all persons held as slaves within any State or designated part of a State, the people whereof shall then be in rebellion against the United States, shall be then, thenceforward, and forever free; and the Executive Govern-

---

*Benjamin C. Howard, *Report of the Decision of the Supreme Court of the United States in the Case Dred Scott.* . . (Washington, 1857), 9, 13–14, 15–17, 60.

ment of the United States, including the military and naval authority thereof, will recognize and maintain the freedom of such persons, and will do no act or acts to repress such persons, or any of them, in any efforts they may make for their actual freedom.

"That the Executive will, on the first day of January aforesaid, by proclamation, designate the States and parts of States, if any, in which the people thereof, respectively, shall then be in rebellion against the United States; and the fact that any State, or the people thereof, shall on that day be, in good faith, represented in the Congress of the United States by members chosen thereto at elections wherein a majority of the qualified voters of such State shall have participated, shall, in the absence of strong countervailing testimony, be deemed conclusive evidence that such State, and the people thereof, are not then in rebellion against the United States."

Now, therefore I, Abraham Lincoln, President of the United States, by virtue of the power in me vested as Commander-in-Chief, of the Army and Navy of the United States in time of actual armed rebellion against authority and government of the United States, and as a fit and necessary war measure for suppressing said rebellion, do, on this first day of January, in the year of our Lord one thousand eight hundred and sixty-three, and in accordance with my purpose so to do publicly proclaimed for the full period of one hundred days, from the day first above mentioned, order and designate as the States and parts of States wherein the people thereof respectively, are this day in rebellion against the United States, the following, to wit:

Arkansas, Texas, Louisiana, (except the Parishes of St. Bernard, Plaquemines, Jefferson, St. Johns, St. Charles, St. James[,] Ascension, Assumption, Terrebonne, Lafourche, St. Mary, St. Martin, and Orleans, including the City of New-Orleans) Mississippi, Alabama, Florida, Georgia, South-Carolina, North-Carolina, and Virginia (except the forty-eight counties designated as West Virginia, and also the counties of Berkley, Accomac, Northampton, Elizabeth-City, York, Princess Ann, and Norfolk, including the cities of Norfolk & Portsmouth [)]; and which excepted parts are, for the present, left precisely as if this proclamation were not issued.

And by virtue of the power, and for the purpose aforesaid, I do order and declare that all persons held as slaves within said designated States, and parts of States, are, and henceforward shall be free; and that the Executive government of the United States, including the military and naval authorities thereof, will recognize and maintain the freedom of said persons.

And I hereby enjoin upon the people so declared to be free to abstain from all violence, unless in necessary self-defence; and I recommend to them that, in all cases when allowed, they labor faithfully for reasonable wages.

And I further declare and make known, that such persons of suitable condition, will be received into the armed service of the United States to garrison forts, positions, stations, and other places, and to man vessels of all sorts in said service.

And upon this act, sincerely believed to be an act of justice, warranted by the

Constitution, upon military necessity, I invoke the considerate judgment of mankind, and the gracious favor of Almighty God.

In witness whereof, I have hereunto set my hand and caused the seal of the United States to be affixed.

Done at the City of Washington, this first day of January, in the year of our Lord one thousand eight hundred and sixty-three, and of the Independence of the United States of America the eighty-seventh.

By the President:
Abraham Lincoln

William H. Steward,
Secretary of State*

11

United States Constitution:
Thirteenth (1865), Fourteenth (1868), and Fifteenth (1870) Amendments

Amendment XIII (Ratified December 6, 1865). *Section 1.* Neither slavery nor involuntary servitude, except as a punishment for crime whereof the party shall have been duly convicted, shall exist within the United States, or any place subject to their jurisdiction.

Section 2. Congress shall have power to enforce this article by appropriate legislation.

Amendment XIV (Ratified July 9, 1868). *Section 1.* All persons born or naturalized in the United States, and subject to the jurisdiction thereof, are citizens of the United States and of the state wherein they reside. No State shall make or enforce any law which shall abridge the privileges or immunities of citizens of the United States; nor shall any State deprive any person of life, liberty, or property, without due process of law; nor deny to any person within its jurisdiction the equal protection of the laws.

*Basler, *op. cit.*, VI, 28–30.

Section 2. Representatives shall be apportioned among the several states according to their respective numbers, counting the whole number of persons in each state, excluding Indians not taxed. But when the right to vote at any election for the choice of Electors for President and Vice-President of the United States, Representatives in Congress, the executive and judicial officers of a State, or the members of the Legislature thereof, is denied to any of the male inhabitants of such State, being twenty-one years of age, and, citizens of the United States, or in any way abridged, except for participation in rebellion, or other crime, the basis of representation therein shall be reduced in the proportion which the number of such male citizens shall bear to the whole number of male citizens twenty-one years of age in such State.

Section 3. No person shall be a Senator or Representative in Congress, or elector of President and Vice-President, or hold any office, civil or military, under the United States, or under any State, who, having previously taken an oath, as a member of Congress, or as an officer of the United States, or as an executive or judicial officer of any State, to support the Constitution of the United States, shall have engaged in insurrection or rebellion against the same, or given aid or comfort to the enemies thereof. But Congress may by a vote of two-thirds of each House, remove such disability.

Section 4. The validity of the public debt of the United States, authorized by law, including debts incurred for payment of pensions and bounties for services in suppressing insurrection or rebellion, shall not be questioned. But neither the United States nor any State shall assume or pay any debt or obligation incurred in aid of insurrection or rebellion against the United States, or any claim for the loss or emancipation of any slave; but all such debts, obligations, and claims, shall be held illegal and void.

Section 5. The Congress shall have power to enforce, by appropriate legislation, the provisions of this article.

Amendment XV (Ratified February 3, 1870). *Section 1.* The right of citizens of the United States to vote shall not be denied or abridged by the United States or by any State on account of race, color, or previous condition of servitude.

Section 2. The Congress shall have power to enforce this article by appropriate legislation.

12

The Black Codes

W. E. B. Du Bois

The whole proof of what the South proposed to do to the emancipated Negro, unless restrained by the nation, was shown in the Black Codes passed after Johnson's accession, but representing the logical result of attitudes of mind existing when Lincoln still lived. Some of these were passed and enforced. Some were passed and afterward repealed or modified when the reaction of the North was realized. In other cases, as for instance, in Louisiana, it is not clear just which laws were retained and which were repealed. In Alabama, the Governor induced the legislature not to enact some parts of the proposed code which they overwhelmingly favored.

The original codes favored by the Southern legislatures were an astonishing affront to emancipation and dealt with vagrancy, apprenticeship, labor contracts, migration, civil and legal rights. In all cases, there was plain and indisputable attempt on the part of the Southern states to make Negroes slaves in everything but name. They were given certain civil rights: the right to hold property, to sue and be sued. The family relations for the first time were legally recognized. Negroes were no longer real estate.

Yet, in the face of this, the Black Codes were deliberately designed to take advantage of every misfortune of the Negro. Negroes were liable to a slave trade under the guise of vagrancy and apprenticeship laws; to make the best labor contracts, Negroes must leave the old plantations and seek better terms; but if caught wandering in search of work, and thus unemployed and without a home, this was vagrancy, and the victim could be whipped and sold into slavery. In the turmoil of war, children were separated from parents, or parents unable to support them properly. These children could be sold into slavery, and "the former owner of said minors shall have the preference." Negroes could come into court as witnesses only in cases in which Negroes were involved. And even then, they must make their appeal to a jury and judge who would believe the word of any white man in preference to that of any Negro on pain of losing office and caste.

The Negro's access to the land was hindered and limited; his right to work was curtailed; his right of self-defense was taken away, when his right to bear arms was stopped; and his employment was virtually reduced to contract labor with penal servitude as a punishment for leaving his job. And in all cases, the judges of the Negro's guilt or innocence, rights and obligations were men who believed firmly, for the most part, that he had "no rights which a white man was bound to respect."

Making every allowance for the excitement and turmoil of war, and the mentality of a defeated people, the Black Codes were infamous pieces of legislation.

Let us examine these codes in detail.[1] They covered, naturally, a wide range of subjects. First, there was the question of allowing Negroes to come into the state. In South Carolina the constitution of 1865 permitted the Legislature to regulate immigration, and the consequent law declared "that no person of color shall migrate into and reside in this State, unless, within twenty days after his arrival within the same, he shall enter into a bond, with two freeholders as sureties . . . in a penalty of one thousand dollars, conditioned for his good behavior, and for his support."

Especially in the matter of work was the Negro narrowly restricted. In South Carolina, he must be especially licensed if he was to follow on his own account any employment, except that of farmer or servant. Those licensed must not only prove their fitness, but pay an annual tax ranging from $10–$100. Under no circumstances could they manufacture or sell liquor. Licenses for work were to be granted by a judge and were revokable on complaint. The penalty was a fine double the amount of the license, one-half of which went to the informer.

Mississippi provided that "every freedman, free Negro, and mulatto shall on the second Monday of January, one thousand eight hundred and sixty-six, and annually thereafter, have a lawful home or employment, and shall have written evidence thereof . . . from the Mayor . . . or from a member of the board of police . . . which licenses may be revoked for cause at any time by the authority granting the same."

Detailed regulation of labor was provided for in nearly all these states.

Louisiana passed an elaborate law in 1865, to "regulate labor contracts for agricultural pursuits." Later, it was denied that this legislation was actually enacted but the law was published at the time and the constitutional convention of 1868 certainly regarded this statute as law, for they formally repealed it. The law required all agricultural laborers to make labor contracts for the next year within the first ten days of January, the contracts to be in writing, to be with heads of families, to embrace the labor of all the members, and to be "binding on all minors thereof." Each laborer, after choosing his employer, "shall not be allowed to leave his place of employment, until the fulfillment of his contract, unless by consent of his employer, or on account of harsh treatment, or breach of contract on the part of the employer; and if they do so leave, without cause or permission, they shall forfeit all wages earned to the time of abandonment. . . .

"In case of sickness of the laborer, wages for the time lost shall be deducted, and where the sickness is feigned for purposes of idleness, . . . and also should refusal to work be continued beyond three days, the offender shall be reported to a justice of the peace, and shall be forced to labor on roads, levees, and other public works, without pay, until the offender consents to return to his labor. . . .

"When in health, the laborer shall work ten hours during the day in summer, and nine hours during the day in winter, unless otherwise stipulated in the labor contract; he shall obey all proper orders of his employer or his agent; take proper care of his work mules, horses, oxen, stock; also of all agricultural implements; and employers shall have the right to make a reasonable deduction from the laborer's wages for injuries done to animals or agricultural implements committed to his care, or for bad or negligent work. Bad work shall not be allowed. Failing to obey reasonable orders, neglect of duty and leaving home without permission, will be deemed disobedience. . . . For any disobedience a fine of one dollar shall be imposed on the offender. For all lost time from work hours, unless in case of sickness, the laborer shall be fined twenty-five cents per hour. For all absence from home without leave, the laborer will be fined at the rate of two dollars per day. Laborers will not be required to labor on the Sabbath except to take the necessary care of stock and other property on plantations and do the necessary cooking and household duties, unless by special contract. For all thefts of the laborers from the employer of agricultural products, hogs, sheep, poultry or any other property of the employer, or willful destruction of property or injury, the laborer shall pay the employer double the amount of the value of the property stolen, destroyed or injured, one half to be paid to the employer, and the other half to be placed in the general fund provided for in this section. No live stock shall be allowed to laborers without the permission of the employer. Laborers shall not receive visitors during work hours. All difficulties arising between the employers and laborers, under this section, shall be settled, and all fines be imposed, by the former; if not satisfactory to the laborers, an appeal may be had to the nearest justice of the peace and two freeholders, citizens, one of said citizens to be selected by the employer and the other by the laborer; and all fines imposed and collected under this section shall be deducted from the wages due, and shall be placed in a common fund, to be divided among the other laborers employed on the plantation at the time when their full wages fall due, except as provided for above."

Similar detailed regulations of work were in the South Carolina law. Elaborate provision was made for contracting colored "servants" to white "masters." Their masters were given the right to whip "moderately" servants under eighteen. Others were to be whipped on authority of judicial officers. These officers were given authority to return runaway servants to their masters. The servants, on the other hand, were given certain rights. Their wages and period of service must be specified in writing, and they were protected against "unreasonable" tasks, Sunday and night work, unauthorized attacks on their persons, and inadequate food.

Contracting Negroes were to be known as "servants" and contractors as "masters." Wages were to be fixed by the judge, unless stipulated. Negroes of ten years of age or more without a parent living in the district might make a valid contract for a year or less. Failure to make written contracts was a misdemeanor, punishable by a fine of $5 to $50; farm labor to be from sunrise to sunset, with intervals for meals; servants to rise at dawn, to be careful of master's property and answerable for property lost or injured. Lost time was to be deducted from wages. Food and clothes might be deducted. Servants were to be quiet and orderly and to go to bed at reasonable hours. No night work or outdoor work in bad weather was to be asked, except in cases of necessity, visitors not allowed without the master's consent. Servants leaving employment without good reason must forfeit wages. Masters might discharge servants for disobedience, drunkenness, disease, absence, etc.

Enticing away the services of a servant was punishable by a fine of $20 to $100. A master could command a servant to aid him in defense of his own person, family or property. House servants at all hours of the day and night, and at all days of the weeks, "must answer promptly all calls and execute all lawful orders. . . ."

Mississippi provided "that every civil officer shall, and every person may, arrest and carry back to his or her legal employer any freedman, free Negro, or mulatto who shall have quit the service of his or her employer before the expiration of his or her term of service without good cause; and said officer and person shall be entitled to receive for arresting and carrying back every deserting employee aforesaid the sum of five dollars, and ten cents per mile from the place of arrest to the place of delivery, and the same shall be paid by the employer and held as a set-off for so much against the wages of said deserting employee."

It was provided in some states, like South Carolina, that any white man, whether an officer or not, could arrest a Negro. "Upon view of a misdemeanor committed by a person of color, any person present may arrest the offender and take him before a magistrate, to be dealt with as the case may require. In case of a misdemeanor committed by a white person toward a person of color, any person may complain to a magistrate, who shall cause the offender to be arrested, and according to the nature of the case, to be brought before himself, or be taken for trial in the district court."

On the other hand, in Mississippi, it was dangerous for a Negro to try to bring a white person to court on any charge. "In every case where any white person has been arrested and brought to trial, by virtue of the provisions of the tenth section of the above recited act, in any court in this State, upon sufficient proof being made to the court or jury, upon the trial before said court, that any freedman, free Negro or mulatto has falsely and maliciously caused the arrest and trial of said white person or persons, the court shall render up a judgment against said freedman, free Negro or mulatto for all costs of the case, and impose a fine not to exceed fifty dollars, and imprisonment in the county jail not to exceed twenty days; and for a failure of said freedman, free Negro or mulatto to pay, or cause to be paid, all costs, fines and jail fees, the sheriff of the county is hereby authorized and required, after giving ten days' public notice, to proceed to hire out at public outcry, at the court-house of the county, said freedman, free Negro or mulatto, for the shortest time to raise the amount necessary to discharge said freedman, free Negro or mulatto from all costs, fines, and jail fees aforesaid."

Mississippi declared that: "Any freedman, free Negro, or mulatto, committing riots, routs, affrays, trespasses, malicious mischief and cruel treatment to animals, seditious speeches, insulting gestures, language or acts, or assaults on any person, disturbance of the peace, exercising the functions of a minister of the gospel without a license from some regularly organized church, vending spirituous or intoxicating liquors, or committing any other misdemeanor, the punishment of which is not specifically provided for by law, shall, upon conviction thereof, in the county court, be fined not less than ten dollars, and not more than one hundred dollars, and may be imprisoned, at the discretion of the court, not exceeding thirty days. . . ."

The most important and oppressive laws were those with regard to vagrancy and apprenticeship. Sometimes they especially applied to Negroes; in other cases, they were drawn in general terms but evidently designed to fit the Negro's condition and to be enforced particularly with regard to Negroes.

The Virginia Vagrant Act enacted that "any justice of the peace, upon the complaint of any one of certain officers therein named, may issue his warrant for the apprehension of any person alleged to be a vagrant and cause such person to be apprehended and brought before him; and that if upon due examination said justice of the peace shall find that such person is a vagrant within the definition of vagrancy contained in said statute, he shall issue his warrant, directing such person to be employed for a term not exceeding three months, and by any constable of the county wherein the proceedings are had, be hired out for the best wages which can be procured, his wages to be applied to the support of himself and his family. The said statute further provides, that in case any vagrant so hired shall, during his term of service, run away from his employer without sufficient cause, he shall be apprehended on the warrant of a justice of the peace and returned to the custody of his employer, who shall then have, free from any other hire, the services of such vagrant for one month in addition to the original term of hiring, and that the employer shall then have power, if authorized by a justice of the peace, to work such vagrant with ball and chain. The said statute specified the persons who shall be considered vagrants and liable to the penalties imposed by it. Among those declared to be vagrants are all persons who, not having the wherewith to support their families, live idly and without employment, and refuse to work for the usual and common wages given to other laborers in the like work in the place where they are."

In Florida, January 12, 1866: "It is provided that when any person of color shall enter into a contract as aforesaid, to serve as a laborer for a year, or any other specified term, on any farm or plantation in this State, if he shall refuse or neglect to perform the stipulations of his contract by willful disobedience of orders, wanton impudence or disrespect to his employer, or his authorized agent, failure or refusal to perform the work assigned to him, idleness, or abandonment of the premises or the employment of the party with whom the contract was made, he or she shall be liable, upon the complaint of his employer or his agent, made under oath before any justice of the peace of the county, to be arrested and tried before the criminal court of the county, and upon conviction shall be subject to all the pains and penalties prescribed for the punishment of vagrancy."

In Georgia, it was ruled that "All persons wandering or strolling about in idleness, who are able to work, and who have no property to support them; all persons leading an idle, immoral, or profligate life, who have no property to support them and are able to work and do not work; all persons able to work having no visible and known means of a fair, honest, and respectable livelihood; all persons having a fixed abode, who have no visible property to support them, and who live by stealing or by trading in, bartering for, or buying stolen property; and all professional gamblers living in idleness, shall be deemed and considered vagrants, and shall be indicated as such, and it shall be lawful for any person to arrest said vagrants and have them bound over for trial to the next term of the country court, and upon conviction, they shall be fined and imprisoned or sentenced to work on the public works, for not longer than a year, or shall, in the discretion of the court, be bound over for trial to the next term of the country court, and upon conviction, they shall be fined and imprisoned or sentenced to work on the public works, for not longer than a year, or shall, in the discretion of the court, be bound out to some person for a time not longer than one year, upon such valuable consideration as the court may prescribe."

Mississippi provided "That all freedmen, free Negroes, and mulattoes in this state over the age of eighteen years, found on the second Monday in January, 1866, or thereafter, with no lawful employment or business, or found unlawfully assembling themselves together, either in the day or night time, and all white persons so assembling with freedmen, free Negroes or mulattoes, or usually associating with freedmen, free Negroes or mulattoes on terms of equality, or living in adultery or fornication with a freedwoman, free Negro or mulatto, shall be deemed vagrants, and on conviction thereof shall be fined in the sum of not exceeding, in the case of a freedman, free Negro or mulatto, fifty dollars, and a white man two hundred dollars and imprisoned, at the discretion of the court, the free Negro not exceeding ten days, and the white men not exceeding six months."

Sec. 5 provides that "all fines and forfeitures collected under the provisions of this act shall be paid into the county treasury for general county purposes, and in case any freedman, free Negro or mulatto, shall fail for five days after the imposition of any fine or forfeiture upon him or her, for violation of any of the provisions of this act to pay the same, that it shall be, and is hereby made, the duty of the Sheriff of the proper county to hire out said freedman, free Negro or mulatto, to any person who will, for the shortest period of service, pay said fine or forfeiture and all costs; *Provided*, a preference shall be given to the employer, if there be one, in which case the employer shall be entitled to deduct and retain the amount so paid from the wages of such freedman, free Negro or mulatto, then due or to become due; and in case such freedman, free Negro or mulatto cannot be hired out, he or she may be dealt with as a pauper. . . ."

In Alabama, the "former owner" was to have preference in the apprenticing of a child. This was true in Kentucky and Mississippi.

Mississippi "provides that it shall be the duty of all sheriffs, justices of the peace, and other civil officers of the several counties in this state to report to the probate courts of their respective counties semi-annually, at the January and July terms of said courts, all freedmen, free Negroes and mulattoes, under the age of eighteen, within their respective counties, beats, or districts, who are orphans, or whose parent or parents have not the means, or who refuse to provide for and support said minors, and thereupon it shall be the duty of said probate court to order the clerk of said court to apprentice said minors to some competent and suitable person, on such terms as the court may direct, having a particular care to the interest of said minors; *Provided*, that the former owner of said minors shall have the preference when, in the opinion of the court, he or she shall be a suitable person for that purpose. . . ."

"Capital punishment was provided for colored persons guilty of willful homicide, assault upon a white woman, impersonating her husband for carnal purposes, raising an insurrection, stealing a horse, a mule, or baled cotton, and housebreaking. For crimes not demanding death Negroes might be confined at hard labor, whipped, or transported; 'but punishments more degrading than imprisonment shall not be imposed upon a white person for a crime not infamous.'"[2]

In most states Negroes were allowed to testify in courts but the testimony was usually confined to cases where colored persons were involved, although in some states, by consent of the parties, they could testify in cases where only white people were involved. . . .

Mississippi simply reenacted her slave code and made it operative so far as punishments were concerned. "That all the penal and criminal laws now in force in this State, defining offenses, and prescribing the mode of punishment for crimes and misdemeanors committed by slaves, free Negroes or mulattoes, be and the same are hereby reenacted, and declared to be in full force and effect, against freedmen, free Negroes, and mulattoes, except so far as the mode and manner of trial and punishment have been changed or altered by law."

North Carolina, on the other hand, abolished her slave code, making difference of punishment only in the case of Negroes convicted of rape. Georgia placed the fines and costs of a servant upon the master. "Where such cases shall go against the servant, the judgment for costs upon written notice to the master shall operate as a garnishment against him, and he shall retain a sufficient amount for the payment thereof, out of any wages due to said servant, or to become due during the period of service, and may be cited at any time by the collecting officer to make answer thereto."

The celebrated ordinance of Opelousas, Louisiana, shows the local ordinances regulating Negroes. "No Negro or freedman shall be allowed to come within the limits of the town of Opelousas without special permission from his employer, specifying the object of his visit and the time necessary for the accomplishment of the same.

"Every Negro freedman who shall be found on the streets of Opelousas after ten o'clock at night without a written pass or permit from his employer, shall be imprisoned and compelled to work five days on the public streets, or pay a fine of five dollars.

"No Negro or freedman shall be permitted to rent or keep a house within the limits of the town under any circumstances, and anyone thus offending shall be ejected, and compelled to find an employer or leave the town within twenty-four hours.

"No Negro or freedman shall reside within the limits of the town of Opelousas who is not in the regular service of some white person or former owner, who shall be held responsible for the conduct of said freedman.

"No Negro or freedman shall be permitted to preach, exhort, or otherwise declaim to congregations of colored people without a special permission from the Mayor or President of the Board of Police, under the penalty of a fine of ten dollars or twenty days' work on the public streets.

"No freedman who is not in the military service shall be allowed to carry firearms, or any kind of weapons within the limits of the town of Opelousas without the special permission of his employer, in writing, and approved by the Mayor or President of the Board.

"Any freedman not residing in Opelousas, who shall be found within its corporate limits after the hour of 3 o'clock, on Sunday, without a special permission from his employer or the Mayor, shall be arrested and imprisoned and made to work two days on the public streets, or pay two dollars in lieu of said work."[3]

Of Louisiana, Thomas Conway testified February 22, 1866: "Some of the leading officers of the state down there—men who do much to form and control the opinions of the masses—instead of doing as they promised, and quietly submitting to the authority of the government, engaged in issuing slave codes and in promulgating them to their subordinates, ordering them to carry them into execution, and this to the knowledge of state officials of a higher character, the governor and others. And the men who issued them were not punished except as the military authorities punished them. The governor inflicted no punishment on them while I was there, and I don't know that, up to this day, he has ever punished one of them. These codes were simply the old black code of the state, with the word 'slave' expunged, and 'Negro' substituted. The most odious features of slavery were preserved in them. . . ."[4]

NOTES

1. Quotations from McPherson, *History of United States During Reconstruction*, pp. 29–44.

2. Simkins and Woody, *South Carolina During Reconstruction*, pp. 49, 50.

3. Warmoth, *War, Politics and Reconstruction*, p. 274.

4. *Report on the Joint Committee on Reconstruction*, 1866, Part IV, pp. 78–79.

13

Bradwell v. *Illinois*, 1873

Mid-nineteenth century feminists, many of them diligent workers in the cause of abolition, looked to Congress after the Civil War for an express guarantee of equal rights for men and women. Viewed in historical perspective, their expectations appear unrealistic. A problem of far greater immediacy faced the nation. Moreover, the common law heritage, ranking the married woman in relationship to her husband as "something better than his dog, a little dearer than his horse,"[1] was just beginning to erode. Nonetheless, the text of the fourteenth amendment appalled the proponents of a sex equality guarantee. Their concern centered on the abortive second section of the amendment, which placed in the Constitution for the first time the word "male." Threefold use of the word "male," always in conjunction with the term "citizens," caused concern that the grand phrases of the first section of the fourteenth amendment would have, at best, qualified application to women.[2]

For more than a century after the adoption of the fourteenth amendment, the judiciary, with rare exceptions, demonstrated utmost deference to sex lines drawn by the legislature. . . .

The Court's initial examination of a woman's claim to full participation in society through entry into a profession traditionally reserved to men came in 1873 in Bradwell v. Illinois.[3] Myra Bradwell's application for a license to practice law had been denied by the Illinois Supreme Court solely because she was a female. The Supreme Court affirmed this judgment with only one dissent, recorded but not explained, by Chief Justice Chase. Justice Miller's opinion for the majority was placed on two grounds: (1) since petitioner was a citizen of Illinois, the privileges and immunities clause of article IV, section 2 of the Federal Constitution[4] was inapplicable to her claim; and (2) since admission to the bar of a state is not one of the privileges and immunities of United States citizenship, the fourteenth amendment did not secure the asserted right. Justice Bradley, speaking for himself and Justices Swayne and Field, chose to place his concurrence in the judgment on broader grounds. He wrote[5]:

> [T]he civil law, as well as nature herself, has always recognized a wide difference in the respective spheres and destinies of man and woman. Man is, or should be, woman's protector and defender. The natural and proper timidity and delicacy which belongs to the female sex evidently unfits it for many of the occupations of civil life. The constitution of the family organization, which is founded in the divine ordinance, as well as in the nature of things, indicates the domestic sphere as that which properly belongs to the domain and functions of womanhood. The harmony, not to say identity, of interests and views which belong, or should belong, to the family institution is repugnant to the idea of a woman adopting a distinct and independent career from that of her husband. So firmly fixed was this sentiment in the founders of the common law that it became a maxim of that system of jurisprudence that a woman had no legal existence separate from her husband, who was regarded as her head and representative in the social state and, notwithstanding some recent modifications of this civil status, many of the special rules of law flowing from and dependent upon this cardinal principle still exist in full force in most States. One of these is, that a married woman is incapable, without her husband's consent, of making contracts which shall be binding on her or him. This very incapacity was one circumstance which the Supreme Court of Illinois deemed important in rendering a married woman incompetent fully to perform the duties and trusts that belong to the office of an attorney and counsellor.
>
> It is true that many women are unmarried and not affected by any of the duties,

complications, and incapacities arising out of the married state, but these are exceptions to the general rule. The paramount destiny and mission of woman are to fulfil the noble and benign offices of wife and mother. This is the law of the Creator. And the rules of civil society must be adapted to the general constitution of things, and cannot be based upon exceptional cases.

The humane movements of modern society, which have for their object the multiplication of avenues for woman's advancement, and of occupations adapted to her condition and sex, have my heartiest concurrence. But I am not prepared to say that it is one of her fundamental rights and privileges to be admitted into every office and position, including those which require highly special qualifications and demanding special responsibilities. In the nature of things it is not every citizen of every age, sex, and condition that is qualified for every calling and position. It is the prerogative of the legislator to prescribe regulations founded on nature, reason, and experience for the due admission of qualified persons to professions and callings demanding special skill and confidence. This fairly belongs to the police power of the State; and, in my opinion, in view of the peculiar characteristics, destiny, and mission of woman, it is within the province of the legislature to ordain what offices, positions, and callings shall be filled and discharged by men, and shall receive the benefit of those energies and responsibilities, and that decision and firmness which are presumed to predominate in the sterner sex.

Although the method of communication between the Creator and the judge is never disclosed, "divine ordinance" has been a dominant theme in decisions justifying laws establishing sex-based classifications.[6] Well past the middle of the twentieth century laws delineating "a sharp line between the sexes"[7] were sanctioned by the judiciary on the basis of lofty inspiration as well as restrained constitutional interpretation. . . .

NOTES

1. Alfred Lord Tennyson, Locksley Hall (1842); see Johnston, Sex and Property: The Common Law Tradition, The Law School Curriculum, and Developments Toward Equality, 47 N.Y.U.L. Rev. 1033, 1044–1070 (1972); pp. 163–183 infra.

2. E. Flexner, Century of Struggle 142–55 (1959).

3. 83 U.S. (16 Wall.) 130, 21 L. Ed. 442 (1873).

4. Article IV, section 2 reads: "The Citizens of each State shall be entitled to all Privileges and Immunities of Citizens in the several States."

5. 83 U.S. (16 Wall.) at 141–42.

6. E.g., State v. Heitman, 105 Kan. 139, 146–47, 181 P. 630. 633–34 (1919); State v. Bearcub, 1 Or. App. 579, 580, 465 P. 2d 252, 253 (1970).

7. Goesaert v. Cleary, 335 U.S. 464, 466, 69 S. Ct. 198, 199, 93 L. Ed. 163, 165 (1948). *Goesaert* was disapproved in Craig v. Boren, 429 U.S. 190, 210 n. 23, 97 S. Ct. 451, 463, 50 L. Ed. 2d 397, 414 (1976).

14

Minor v. Happersett, 1875

"In this case the court held that although women were citizens, the right to vote was not a privilege or immunity of national citizenship before adoption of the 14th Amendment, nor did the amendment add suffrage to the privileges and immunities of national citizenship. Therefore, the national government could not require states to permit women to vote."*

15

California Constitution, 1876

In 1876, at the height of the anti-Chinese movement, California adopted a new constitution. Its anti-Chinese provisions, largely unenforceable, represent an accurate measure of public feeling.

Article XIX

Section 1. The Legislature shall prescribe all necessary regulations for the protection of the State, and the counties, cities, and towns thereof, from the burdens and evils arising from the presence of aliens, who are or may become vagrants, paupers, mendicants, criminals, or invalids afflicted with contagious or infectious

*From *Congressional Quarterly's Guide to the U.S. Supreme Court,* 1979, p. 631.

diseases, and from aliens otherwise dangerous or detrimental to the well-being or peace of the State, and to impose conditions upon which such persons may reside in the State, and to provide means and mode of their removal from the State upon failure or refusal to comply with such conditions; provided, that nothing contained in this section shall be construed to impair or limit the power of the Legislature to pass such police laws or other regulations as it may deem necessary.

Section 2. No corporation now existing or hereafter formed under the laws of this State, shall, after the adoption of this Constitution, employ, directly or indirectly, in any capacity, any Chinese or Mongolian. The Legislature shall pass such laws as may be necessary to enforce this provision.

Section 3. No Chinese shall be employed on any State, county, municipal, or other public work, except in punishment for crime.

Section 4. The presence of foreigners ineligible to become citizens of the United States is declared to be dangerous to the well-being of the State, and the Legislature shall discourage their immigration by all the means within its power. Asiatic coolieism is a form of human slavery, and is forever prohibited in this State; and all contracts for coolie labor shall be void. All companies or corporations, whether formed in this country or any foreign country, for the importation of such labor, shall be subject to such penalties as the Legislature may prescribe. The Legislature shall delegate all necessary power to the incorporated cities and towns of this State for the removal of Chinese without the limits of such cities and towns, or for their location within prescribed portions of those limits; and it shall also provide the necessary legislation to prohibit the introduction into this State of Chinese after the adoption of this Constitution. This section shall be enforced by appropriate legislation.

16

Elk v. *Wilkins,* November 3, 1884

John Elk, an Indian who had voluntarily separated himself from his tribe and taken up residence among the whites, was denied the right to vote in Omaha, Nebraska, on the ground that he was not a citizen. The Supreme Court considered the question of whether Elk had been made a citizen by the Fourteenth Amendment and decided against him.

. . . The plaintiff, in support of his action, relies on the first clause of the first section of the Fourteenth Article of Amendment of the Constitution of the United States, by which "all persons born or naturalized in the United States, and subject to the jurisdiction thereof, are citizens of the United States and of the State wherein they reside;" and on the Fifteenth Article of Amendment, which provides that "the right of citizens of the United States to vote shall not be denied or abridged by the United States or by any State on account of race, color, or previous condition of servitude." . . .

The petition, while it does not show of what Indian tribe the plaintiff was a member, yet, by the allegations that he "is an Indian, and was born within the United States," and that "he had severed his tribal relation to the Indian tribes," clearly implies that he was born a member of one of the Indian tribes within the limits of the United States, which still exists and is recognized as a tribe by the government of the United States. Though the plaintiff alleges that he "had fully and completely surrendered himself to the jurisdiction of the United States," he does not allege that the United States accepted his surrender, or that he has ever been naturalized, or taxed, or in any way recognized or treated as a citizen, by the State or by the United States. Nor is it contended by his counsel that there is any statute or treaty that makes him a citizen.

The question then is, whether an Indian, born a member of one of the Indian tribes within the United States, is, merely by reason of his birth within the United States, and of his afterwards voluntarily separating himself from his tribe and taking up his residence among white citizens, a citizen of the United States, within the meaning of the first section of the Fourteenth Amendment of the Constitution. . . .

Indians born within the territorial limits of the United States, members of, and owing immediate allegiance to, one of the Indian tribes (an alien, though dependent, power), although in a geographical sense born in the United States, are no more "born in the United States and subject to the jurisdiction thereof," within the meaning of the first section of the Fourteenth Amendment, than the children of subjects of any foreign government born within the domain of that government, or the children born within the United States, of ambassadors or other public ministers of foreign nations.

This view is confirmed by the second section of the Fourteenth Amendment, which provides that "representatives shall be apportioned among the several States according to their respective numbers, counting the whole number of persons in each State, excluding Indians not taxed." Slavery having been abolished, and the persons formerly held as slaves made citizens, this clause fixing the apportionment of representatives has abrogated so much of the corresponding clause of the original Constitution as counted only three-fifths of such persons. But Indians not taxed are still excluded from the count, for the reason that they are not citizens. Their absolute exclusion from the basis of representation, in which all other persons are now included, is wholly inconsistent with their being considered citizens. . . .

The plaintiff, not being a citizen of the United States under the Fourteenth

Amendment of the Constitution, has been deprived of no right secured by the Fifteenth Amendment, and cannot maintain this action.*

17

Plessy v. Ferguson, 1896

After the collapse of Reconstruction governments, southern whites began gradually to legalize the informal practices of segregation which obtained in the South. One such law was passed by the Louisiana legislature in 1890 and provided that "all railway companies carrying passengers . . . in this State shall provide separate but equal accommodations for the white and colored races."

Plessy vs. Ferguson tested the constitutionality of this recent trend in southern legislation. Plessy was a mulatto who, on June 7, 1892, bought a first-class ticket on the East Louisiana Railway for a trip from New Orleans to Covington, La., and sought to be seated in the "white" coach. Upon conviction of a violation of the 1890 statute, he appealed to the Supreme Court of Louisiana, which upheld his conviction, and finally to the U.S. Supreme Court, which pronounced the Louisiana law constitutional, on May 18, 1896. The defense of Plessy and attack on the Louisiana statute was in the hands of four men, the most famous of whom was Albion W. Tourgée. M. J. Cunningham, Attorney General of Louisiana, was assisted by two other lawyers in defending the statute. The majority opinion of the Court was delivered by Justice Henry B. Brown. John Marshall Harlan dissented and Justice David J. Brewer did not participate, making it a 7–1 decision.

In his dissent to this decision Harlan asserted that "Our Constitution is color-blind, and neither knows nor tolerates classes among citizens. In respect of civil rights, all citizens are equal before the law." He offered the prophecy that "the judgment rendered this day will, in time, prove to be quite as pernicious as the decision made by this tribunal in the Dred Scott *case."*

The constitutionality of this act is attacked upon the ground that it conflicts both with the Thirteenth Amendment of the Constitution, abolishing slavery, and the Fourteenth Amendment, which prohibits certain restrictive legislation on the part of the States.

1. That it does not conflict with the Thirteenth Amendment, which abolished

*112 *United States Reports: Cases Adjudged in the Supreme Court,* Banks & Brothers, New York.

slavery and involuntary servitude, except as a punishment for crime, is too clear for argument. Slavery implies involuntary servitude—a state of bondage: the ownership of mankind as a chattel, or at least the control of the labor and services of one man for the benefit of another, and the absence of a legal right to the disposal of his own person, property and services. . . .

A statute which implies merely a legal distinction between the white and colored races—a distinction which is founded in the color of the two races, and which must always exist so long as white men are distinguished from the other race by color—has no tendency to destroy the legal equality of the two races, or reestablish a state of involuntary servitude. Indeed, we do not understand that the Thirteenth Amendment is strenuously relied upon by the plaintiff in error in this connection.

2. By the Fourteenth Amendment, all persons born or naturalized in the United States, and subject to the jurisdiction thereof, are made citizens of the United States and of the State wherein they reside; and the States are forbidden from making or enforcing any law which shall abridge the privileges or immunities of citizens of the United States, or shall deprive any person of life, liberty or property without due process of law, or deny to any person within their jurisdiction the equal protection of the laws. . . .

The object of the amendment was undoubtedly to enforce the absolute equality of the two races before the law, but in the nature of things it could not have been intended to abolish distinctions based upon color, or to enforce social, as distinguished from political equality, or a commingling of the two races upon terms unsatisfactory to either. Laws permitting, and even requiring, their separation in places where they are liable to be brought into contact do not necessarily imply the inferiority of either race to the other, and have been generally, if not universally, recognized as within the competency of the state legislatures in the exercise of their police power. The most common instance of this is connected with the establishment of separate schools for white and colored children, which has been held to be a valid exercise of the legislative power even by courts of States where the political rights of the colored race have been longest and most earnestly enforced. . . .

While we think the enforced separation of the races, as applied to the internal commerce of the State, neither abridges the privileges or immunities of the colored man, deprives him of his property without due process of law, nor denies him the equal protection of the laws, within the meaning of the Fourteenth Amendment, we are not prepared to say that the conductor, in assigning passengers to the coaches according to their race, does not act at his peril, or that the provision of the second section of the act, that denies to the passenger compensation in damages for a refusal to receive him into the coach in which he properly belongs, is a valid exercise of the legislative power. Indeed, we understand it to be conceded by the State's attorney, that such part of the act as exempts from liability the railway company and its officers is unconstitutional. The power to assign to a particular coach obviously implies the power to determine to which race the passenger belongs, as well as the power to determine who, under the laws of the particular State, is to be deemed a white, and who a colored person. . . .

It is claimed by the plaintiff in error that, in any mixed community, the reputation of belonging to the dominant race, in this instance the white race, is *property*, in the same sense that a right of action, or of inheritance, is property. Conceding this to be so, for the purposes of this case, we are unable to see how this statute deprives him of, or in any way affects his right to, such property. If he be a white man and assigned to a colored coach, he may have his action for damages against the company for being deprived of his so called property. Upon the other hand, if he be a colored man and be so assigned, he has been deprived of no property, since he is not lawfully entitled to the reputation of being a white man.

In this connection, it is also suggested by the learned counsel for the plaintiff in error that the same argument that will justify the state legislature in requiring railways to provide separate accommodations for the two races will also authorize them to require separate cars to be provided for the people whose hair is of a certain color, or who are aliens, or who belong to certain nationalities, or to enact laws requiring colored people to walk upon one side of the street, and white people upon the other, or requiring white men's houses to be painted white, and colored men's black, or their vehicles or business signs to be of different colors, upon the theory that one side of the street is as good as the other, or that a house or vehicle of one color is as good as one of another color. The reply to all this is that every exercise of the police power must be reasonable, and extend only to such laws as are enacted in good faith for the promotion for the public good, and not for the annoyance or oppression of a particular class. . . .

We consider the underlying fallacy of the plaintiff's argument to consist in the assumption that the enforced separation of the two races stamps the colored race with a badge of inferiority. If this be so, it is not by reason of anything found in the act, but solely because the colored race chooses to put that construction upon it. The argument necessarily assumes that if, as has been more than once the case, and is not unlikely to be so again, the colored race should become the dominant power in the state legislature, and should enact a law in precisely similar terms, it would thereby relegate the white race to an inferior position. We imagine that the white race, at least, would not acquiesce in this assumption. The argument also assumes that social prejudices may be overcome by legislation, and that equal rights cannot be secured to the negro except by an enforced commingling of the two races. We cannot accept this proposition. If the two races are to meet upon terms of social equality, it must be the result of natural affinities, a mutual appreciation of each other's merits and a voluntary consent of individuals.*

Plessy vs. Ferguson, 163 U.S. 537 *United States Reports: Cases Adjudged in the Supreme Court* (New York, Banks & Brothers, 1896).

18

United States Constitution:
Nineteenth Amendment (1920)

Amendment XIX (ratified August 18, 1920). *Section 1.* The right of citizens of the United States to vote shall not be denied or abridged by the United States or by any State on account of sex.

Section 2. Congress shall have power to enforce this Article by appropriate legislation.

Korematsu v. United States, 1944

The present case involved perhaps the most alarming use of executive military authority in our nation's history. Following the bombing of Pearl Harbor in December, 1941, the anti-Japanese sentiment on the West Coast brought the residents of the area to a state of near hysteria; and in February, 1942, President Roosevelt issued an executive order authorizing the creation of military areas from which any or all persons might be excluded as the military authorities might decide. On March 2, the entire West Coast to a depth of about forty miles was designated by the commanding general as Military Area No. 1, and he thereupon proclaimed a curfew in that area for all persons of Japanese ancestry. Later he ordered the compulsory evacuation from the area of all persons of Japanese ancestry, and by the middle of the summer most of these people had been moved inland to "war relocation centers," the American equivalent of concentration camps. Congress subsequently made it a crime to violate these military orders. Of the 112,000 persons of Japanese ancestry involved, about 70,000 were native-born American citizens, none of whom had been specifically accused of disloyalty. Three cases were brought to the Supreme Court as challenging the right of the government to override in this manner the customary civil rights of these citizens. In Hirabayashi v. United States, 320 U.S. 81 (1943), the Court upheld the curfew regulations as a valid military measure to prevent espionage and sabotage. "Whatever views we may entertain regarding the loyalty to this country of the citizens of Japanese ancestry, we cannot reject as unfounded the judgment of the military authorities and of Congress that there were disloyal members of that population, whose number and strength could not be precisely and quickly ascertained. We cannot say that the war-making branches of the Government did not have ground for believing that in a critical hour such persons could not readily be isolated and separately dealt with, and constituted a menace to the national defense and safety. . . ." While emphasizing that distinctions based on ancestry were "by their very nature odious to a free people" the Court nonetheless felt "that in time of war residents having ethnic affiliations with an invading enemy may be a greater source of danger than those of a different ancestry."

While the Court, in the present case, held valid the discriminatory mass evacuation of all persons of Japanese descent, it also held in Ex parte Endo, 323 U.S. 283 (1944), that an American citizen of Japanese ancestry whose loyalty to this country had been established could not constitutionally be held in a War Relocation Center but must be unconditionally released. The government had allowed persons to leave the Relocation Centers under conditions and restrictions which aimed to guarantee that there should not be "a dangerously disorderly migration of unwanted people to unprepared communities." Permission to leave was granted only if the applicant had the assurance of a job and a place to live, and wanted to go to a place "approved" by the War Relocation Authority. The Court held that the sole purpose of the evacuation and detention program was to protect the war effort against sabotage and espionage. "A person who is concededly loyal presents no problem of espionage or sabotage. . . . He who is loyal is by definition not a spy or a saboteur." It therefore follows that the authority to detain a citizen of Japanese ancestry ends when his loyalty is established. To hold otherwise would be to justify his detention not on grounds of military necessity but purely on grounds of race.

Although no case reached the Court squarely challenging the right of the government to incarcerate citizens of Japanese ancestry pending a determination of their loyalty, the tenor of the opinions leaves little doubt that such action would have been sustained. The present case involved only the right of the military to evacuate such persons from the West Coast. Mr. Justice Murphy, one of three dissenters, attacked the qualifications of the military to make sociological judgments about the effects of ancestry, and pointed out that the time consumed in evacuating these persons (eleven months) was ample for making an orderly inquiry into their individual loyalty.

Mr. Justice Black delivered the opinion of the Court, saying in part:

The petitioner, an American citizen of Japanese descent, was convicted in a federal district court for remaining in San Leandro, California, a "Military Area," contrary to Civilian Exclusion Order No. 34 of the Commanding General of the Western Command, U.S. Army, which directed that after May 9, 1942, all persons of Japanese ancestry should be excluded from that area. No question was raised as to petitioner's loyalty to the United States. The Circuit Court of Appeals affirmed, and the importance of the constitutional question involved caused us to grant certiorari.

It should be noted, to begin with, that all legal restrictions which curtail the civil rights of a single racial group are immediately suspect. That is not to say that all such restrictions are unconstitutional. It is to say that courts must subject them to the most rigid scrutiny. Pressing public necessity may sometimes justify the existence of such restrictions; racial antagonism never can.

In the instant case prosecution of the petitioner was begun by information charging violation of an Act of Congress, of March 21, 1942, 56 Stat. 173, which provides that ". . . whoever shall enter, remain in, leave, or commit any act in any military area or military zone prescribed, under the authority of an Executive order of the President, by the Secretary of War, or by any military commander designated by the Secretary of War, contrary to the restrictions applicable to any such area or zone or contrary to the order of the Secretary of War or any such military commander, shall, if it appears that he knew or should have known of the existence and extent of the restrictions or order and that his act was in violation thereof, be guilty of a misdemeanor and upon conviction shall be liable to a fine of not to exceed $5,000 or to imprisonment for not more than one year, or both, for each offense."

Exclusion Order No. 34, which the petitioner knowingly and admittedly violated was one of a number of military orders and proclamations, all of which were substantially based upon Executive Order No. 9066, 7 Fed. Reg. 1407. That order, issued after we were at war with Japan, declared that "the successful prosecution of the war requires every possible protection against espionage and against sabotage to national-defense material, national-defense premises, and national-defense utilities. . . ."

One of the series of orders and proclamations, a curfew order, which like the exclusion order here was promulgated pursuant to Executive Order 9066, subjected all persons of Japanese ancestry in prescribed West Coast military areas to remain in their residences from 8 p.m. to 6 a.m. As is the case with the exclusion order here, that prior curfew order was designed as a "protection against espionage and against sabotage." In Kiyoshi Hirabayashi v. United States, 320 U.S. 81, we sustained a conviction obtained for violation of the curfew order. The Hirabayashi conviction and this one thus rest on the same 1942 Congressional Act and the same basic executive and military orders, all of which orders were aimed at the twin dangers of espionage and sabotage.

The 1942 Act was attacked in the Hirabayashi case as an unconstitutional delegation of power; it was contended that the curfew order and other orders on which it rested were beyond the war powers of the Congress, the military authorities and of the President, as Commander in Chief of the Army; and finally that to apply the curfew order against none but citizens of Japanese ancestry amounted to a constitutionally prohibited discrimination solely on account of race. To these questions, we gave the serious consideration which their importance justified. We upheld the curfew order as an exercise of the power of the government to take steps necessary to prevent espionage and sabotage in an area threatened by Japanese attack.

In the light of the principles we announced in the Hirabayashi case, we are unable to conclude that it was beyond the war power of Congress and the Executive to exclude those of Japanese ancestry from the West Coast war area at the time they did. True, exclusion from the area in which one's home is located is a far greater deprivation than constant confinement to the home from 8 p.m. to 6 a.m. Nothing short of apprehension by the proper military authorities of the gravest imminent danger to the public safety can constitutionally justify either. But exclusion from a threatened area, no less than curfew, has a definite and close relationship to the prevention of espionage and sabotage. The military authorities, charged with the primary responsibility of defending our shores, concluded that curfew provided inadequate protection and ordered exclusion. They did so, as pointed out in our Hirabayashi opinion, in accordance with Congressional authority to the military to say who should, and who should not, remain in the threatened areas.

In this case the petitioner challenges the assumptions upon which we rested our conclusions in the Hirabayashi case. He also urges that by May 1942, when Order No. 34 was promulgated, all danger of Japanese invasion of the West Coast had disappeared. After careful consideration of these contentions we are compelled to reject them.

Here, as in the Hirabayashi case, ". . . we cannot reject as unfounded the judgment of the military authorities and of Congress that there were disloyal members of that population, whose number and strength could not be precisely and quickly ascertained. We cannot say that the warmaking branches of the Government did not have ground for believing that in a critical hour such persons could not readily be isolated and separately dealt with, and constituted a menace to the national defense and safety, which demanded that prompt and adequate measures be taken to guard against it."

Like curfew, exclusion of those of Japanese origin was deemed necessary because of the presence of an unascertained number of disloyal members of the group, most of whom we have no doubt were loyal to this country. It was because we could not reject the finding of the military authorities that it was impossible to bring about an immediate segregation of the disloyal from the loyal that we sustained the validity of the curfew order as applying to the whole group. In the instant case, temporary exclusion of the entire group was rested by the military on the same ground. The judgment that exclusion of the whole group was for the same reason a military imperative answers the contention that the exclusion was in the nature of group punishment based on antagonism to those of Japanese origin. That there were members of the group who retained loyalties to Japan has been confirmed by investigations made subsequent to the exclusion. Approximately five thousand American citizens of Japanese ancestry refused to swear unqualified allegiance to the United States and to renounce allegiance to the Japanese Emperor, and several thousand evacuees requested repatriation to Japan.

We uphold the exclusion order as of the time it was made and when the petitioner violated it. . . . In doing so, we are not unmindful of the hardships imposed by it upon a large group of American citizens. . . . But hardships are part of war, and war is an aggregation of hardships. All citizens alike, both in and out of uniform, feel the impact of war in greater or lesser measure. Citizenship has its responsibilities as well as its privileges, and in time of war the burden is always heavier. Compulsory exclusion of large groups of citizens from their homes, except under circumstances of direst emergency and peril, is inconsistent with our basic governmental institution. But when under conditions of modern warfare our shores are threatened by hostile forces, the power to protect must be commensurate with the threatened danger. . . .

[The Court dealt at some length with a technical complication which arose in the case. On May 30, the date on which Korematsu was charged with remaining unlawfully in the prohibited area, there were two conflicting military orders outstanding, one forbidding him to remain in the area, the other forbidding him to leave but ordering him to report to an assembly center. Thus, he alleged, he was punished for doing what it was made a crime to fail to do. The Court held the orders not to be contradictory, since the requirement to report to the assembly center was merely a step in an orderly program of compulsory evacuation from the area.]

It is said that we are dealing here with the case of imprisonment of a citizen in a concentration camp solely because of his ancestry, without evidence or inquiry concerning his loyalty and good disposition towards the United States. Our task would be simple, our duty clear, were this a case involving the imprisonment of a loyal citizen in a concentration camp because of racial prejudice. Regardless of the true nature of the assembly and relocation centers—and we deem it unjustifiable to call them concentration camps with all the ugly connotations that term implies— we are dealing specifically with nothing but an exclusion order. To cast this case into outlines of racial prejudice, without reference to the real military dangers which were presented, merely confuses the issue. Korematsu was not excluded from the Military Area because of hostility to him or his race. He was excluded because we are at war with the Japanese Empire, because the properly constituted military authorities feared an invasion of our West Coast and felt constrained to take proper security measures, because they decided that the military urgency of the situation demanded that all citizens of Japanese ancestry be segregated from the West Coast temporarily, and finally, because Congress reposing its confidence in this time of war in our military leaders—as inevitably it must—determined that they should have the power to do just this. There was evidence of disloyalty on the part of some, the military authorities considered that the need for action was great, and time was short. We cannot—by availing ourselves of the calm perspective of hindsight—now say that at that time these actions were unjustified.

Affirmed.

Mr. Justice Frankfurter wrote a concurring opinion. Justices Roberts, Murphy, and Jackson each wrote a dissenting opinion.

20

Brown v. Board of Education of Topeka, 1954

Mr. Chief Justice Warren delivered the opinion of the Court.

These cases come to us from the States of Kansas, South Carolina, Virginia, and Delaware. They are premised on different facts and different local conditions, but a common legal question justifies their consideration together in this consolidated opinion.[1]

In each of the cases, minors of the Negro race, through their legal representatives, seek the aid of the courts in obtaining admission to the public schools of their community on a nonsegregated basis. In each instance, they had been denied admission to schools attended by white children under laws requiring or permitting segregation according to race. This segregation was alleged to deprive the plaintiffs of the equal protection of the laws under the Fourteenth Amendment. In each of the cases other than the Delaware case, a three-judge federal district court denied relief to the plaintiffs on the so-called "separate but equal" doctrine announced by this Court in Plessy v. Ferguson, 163 U.S. 537. Under that doctrine, equality of treatment is accorded when the races are provided substantially equal facilities, even though these facilities be separate. In the Delaware case, the Supreme Court of Delaware adhered to that doctrine, but ordered that the plaintiffs be admitted to the white schools because of their superiority to the Negro schools.

The plaintiffs contend that segregated public schools are not "equal" and cannot be made "equal," and that hence they are deprived of the equal protection of the laws. Because of the obvious importance of the question presented, the Court took jurisdiction.[2] Argument was heard in the 1952 Term, and reargument was heard this Term on certain questions propounded by the Court. . . .[3]

In approaching this problem, we cannot turn the clock back to 1868 when the Amendment was adopted, or even to 1896 when Plessy v. Ferguson was written. We must consider public education in the light of its full development and its present place in American life throughout the Nation. Only in this way can it be determined if segregation in public schools deprives these plaintiffs of the equal protection of the laws.

Today, education is perhaps the most important function of state and local governments. Compulsory school attendance laws and the great expenditures for education both demonstrate our recognition of the importance of education to our democratic society. It is required in the performance of our most basic public responsibilities, even service in the armed forces. It is the very foundation of good citizenship. Today it is a principal instrument in awakening the child to cultural values, in preparing him for later professional training, and in helping him to adjust normally to his environment. In these days, it is doubtful that any child may reasonably be expected to succeed in life if he is denied the opportunity of an education. Such an opportunity, where the state has undertaken to provide it, is a right which must be made available to all on equal terms.

We come then to the question presented: Does segregation of children in public schools solely on the basis of race, even though the physical facilities and other "tangible" factors may be equal, deprive the children of the minority group of equal educational opportunities? We believe that it does.

In Sweatt v. Painter, in finding that a segregated law school for Negroes could not provide them equal educational opportunities, this Court relied in large part on "those qualities which are incapable of objective measurement but which make for greatness in a law school." In McLaurin v. Oklahoma State Regents, the Court, in requiring that a Negro admitted to a white graduate school be treated like all other students, again resorted to intangible considerations: ". . . his ability to study, to engage in discussions and exchange views with other students, and in general, to learn his profession." Such considerations apply with added force to children in grade and high schools. To separate them from others of similar age and qualifications solely because of their race generates a feeling of inferiority as to their status in the community that may affect their hearts and minds in a way unlikely ever to be undone. The effect of this separation on their educational opportunities was well stated by a finding in the Kansas case by a court which nevertheless felt compelled to rule against the Negro plaintiffs:

> Segregation of white and colored children in public schools has a detrimental effect upon the colored children. The impact is greater when it has the sanction of the law; for the policy of separating the races is usually interpreted as denoting the inferiority of the negro group. A sense of inferiority affects the motivation of a child to learn. Segregation with the sanction of law, therefore, has a tendency to [retard] the educational and mental development of negro children and to deprive them of some of the benefits they receive in a racial[ly] integrated school system.[4]

Whatever may have been the extent of psychological knowledge at the time of Plessy v. Ferguson, this finding is amply supported by modern authority.[5] Any language in Plessy v. Ferguson contrary to this finding is rejected.

We conclude that in the field of public education the doctrine of "separate but equal" has no place. Separate educational facilities are inherently unequal. Therefore, we hold that the plaintiffs and others similarly situated for whom the actions have been brought are, by reason of the segregation complained of, deprived of the equal protection of the laws guaranteed by the Fourteenth Amendment. This disposition makes unnecessary any discussion whether such segregation also violates the Due Process Clause of the Fourteenth Amendment.

Because these are class actions, because of the wide applicability of this decision, and because of the great variety of local conditions, the formulation of decrees in these cases presents problems of considerable complexity. On reargument, the consideration of appropriate relief was necessarily subordinated to the primary question —the constitutionality of segregation in public education. We have now announced that such segregation is a denial of the equal protection of the laws. In order that we may have the full assistance of the parties in formulating decrees, the cases will be restored to the docket, and the parties are requested to present further argument on Questions 4 and 5 previously propounded by the Court for the reargument this Term.[6] The Attorney General of the United States is again invited to participate. The Attorneys General of the states requiring or permitting segregation in public education will also be permitted to appear as amici curiae upon request to do so by September 15, 1954, and submission of the briefs by October 1, 1954.

It is so ordered.

NOTES

1. In the Kansas case, Brown v. Board of Education, the plaintiffs are Negro children of elementary school age residing in Topeka. They brought this action in the United States District Court for the District of Kansas to enjoin enforcement of a Kansas statute which permits, but does not require, cities of more than 15,000 population to maintain separate school facilities for Negro and white students. Kan. Gen. Stat. §72-1724 (1949). Pursuant to that authority, the Topeka Board of Education elected to establish segregated elementary schools. Other public schools in the community, however, are operated on a nonsegregated basis. The three-judge District Court, convened under 28 U.S.C. §§2281 and 2284, found that segregation in public education has a detrimental effect upon Negro children, but denied relief on the ground that the Negro and white schools were substantially equal with respect to buildings, transportation, curricula, and educational qualifications of teachers. 98 F. Supp. 797. The case is here on direct appeal under 28 U.S.C. §1253. [The Topeka, Kansas case would be analogous to a Northern school case inasmuch as the school segregation that existed in Topeka was not mandated by state law, and some of the system was integrated. It would be eighteen years before the Court would accept another such case for review. Keyes v. School District No. 1, Denver, 445 F.2d 990 (10th Cir. 1971), *cert. granted*, 404 U.S. 1036 (1972)].

In the South Carolina case, Briggs v. Elliot, the plaintiffs are Negro children of both elementary and high school age residing in Clarendon County. They brought this action in the United States District Court for the Eastern District of South Carolina to enjoin enforcement of provisions in the state constitution and statutory code which require the segregation of Negroes and whites in public schools. S.C. Const., Art. XI, §7; S.C. Code §5377 (1942). The three-judge District Court, convened under 28 U.S.C. §§2281 and 2284, denied the requested relief. The court found that the Negro schools were inferior to the white schools and ordered the defendants to begin immediately to equalize the facilities. But the court sustained the validity of the contested provisions and denied the plaintiffs admission to the white schools during the equalization program. 98 F. Supp. 529. This Court vacated the

District Court's judgment and remanded the case for the purpose of obtaining the court's views on a report filed by the defendants concerning the progress made in the equalization program. 342 U.S. 350. On remand, the District Court found that substantial equality had been achieved except for buildings and that the defendants were proceeding to rectify this inequality as well. 103 F. Supp. 920. The case is again here on direct appeal under 28 U.S.C. §1253.

In the Virginia case, Davis v. County School Board, the plaintiffs are Negro children of high school age residing in Prince Edward County. They brought this action in the United States District Court for the Eastern District of Virginia to enjoin enforcement of provisions in the state constitution and statutory code which require the segregation of Negroes and whites in public schools. Va. Const., §140; Va. Code §22-221 (1950). The three-judge District Court, convened under 28 U.S.C. §2281 and 2284, denied the requested relief. The court found the Negro school inferior in physical plant, curricula, and transportation, and ordered the defendants forthwith to provide substantially equal curricula and transportation and to "proceed with all reasonable diligence and dispatch to remove" the inequality in physical plant. But, as in the South Carolina case, the court sustained the validity of the contested provisions and denied the plaintiffs admission to the white schools during the equalization program. 103 F. Supp. 337. The case is here on direct appeal under 28 U.S.C. §1253.

In the Delaware case, Gebhart v. Belton, the plaintiffs are Negro children of both elementary and high school age residing in New Castle County. They brought this action in the Delaware Court of Chancery to enjoin enforcement of provisions in the state constitution and statutory code which require the segregation of Negroes and whites in public schools. Del. Const., Art. X, §2; Del. Rev. Code §2631 (1935). The chancellor gave judgment for the plaintiffs and ordered their immediate admission to schools previously attended only by white children, on the ground that the Negro schools were inferior with respect to teacher training, pupil-teacher ratio, extracurricular activities, physical plant, and time and distance involved in travel. 87 A.2d 862. The Chancellor also found that segregation itself results in an inferior education for Negro children (see note 4, infra), but did not rest his decision on that ground. Id., at 865. The Chancellor's decree was affirmed by the Supreme Court of Delaware, which intimated, however, that the defendants might be able to obtain a modification of the decree after equalization of the Negro and white schools had been accomplished. 91 A.2d 137, 152. The defendants, contending only that the Delaware courts had erred in ordering the immediate admission of the Negro plaintiffs to the white schools, applied to this Court for certiorari. The writ was granted, 344 U.S. 891. The plaintiffs, who were successful below, did not submit a cross-petition.

2. 344 U.S. 1, 141, 891.

3. 345 U.S. 972. The Attorney General of the United States participated both Terms as amicus curiae.

4. A similar finding was made in the Delaware case: "I conclude from the testimony that in our Delaware Society, State-imposed segregation in education itself results in the Negro children, as a class, receiving educational opportunities which are substantially inferior to those available to white children otherwise similarly situated." 87 A.2d 862, 865.

5. K. B. Clark, Effect of Prejudice and Discrimination on Personality Development (Midcentury White House Conference on Children and Youth, 1950); Witmer and Kotinsky, Personality in the Making (1952), c. VI; Deutscher and Chein, The Psychological Effects of Enforced Segregation: A Survey of Social Science Opinion, 26 J. Psychol. 259 (1948); Chein, What are the Psychological Effects of Segregation Under Conditions of Equal Facilities?, 3 Int. J. Opinion and Attitude Res. 229 (1949); Brameld, Educational Costs, in Discrimination

and National Welfare (MacIver, ed., 1949), 44–48; Frazier, The Negro in the United States (1949), 674–681. And see generally Myrdal, An American Dilemma (1944).

6. "4. Assuming it is decided that segregation in public schools violates the Fourteenth Amendment

"(a) would a decree necessarily follow providing that, within the limits set by normal geographic school districting, Negro children should forthwith be admitted to schools of their choice, or

"(b) may this Court, in the exercise of its equity powers, permit an effective gradual adjustment to be brought about from existing segregated systems to a system not based on color distinctions?

"5. On the assumption on which questions 4(a) and (b) are based, and assuming further that this Court will exercise its equity powers to the end described in question 4(b),

"(a) should this Court formulate detailed decrees in these cases;

"(b) if so, what specific issues should the decrees reach;

"(c) should this Court appoint a special master to hear evidence with a view to recommending specific terms for such decrees;

"(d) should this Court remand to the courts of first instance with directions to frame decrees in these cases, and if so what general directions should the decrees of this Court include and what procedures should the courts of first instance follow in arriving at the specific terms of more detailed decrees?"

21

Roe v. Wade, 1973

This historic decision legalized a woman's right to terminate her pregnancy by abortion. The ruling was based upon the right of privacy founded on both the Fourteenth and Ninth Amendments to the Constitution. The court ruled that this right of privacy protected the individual from interference by the state in the decision to terminate a pregnancy by abortion during the early portion of the pregnancy. At the same time, it recognized the interest of the state in regulating decisions concerning the pregnancy during the latter period as the fetus developed the capacity to survive outside the woman's body.

22

The Equal Rights Amendment (Defeated)

Equality of rights under the law shall not be denied or abridged by the United States or any State on account of sex.

23

Bowers v. Hardwick, 1986

Justice WHITE delivered the opinion of the Court.

In August 1982, respondent Hardwick (hereafter respondent) was charged with violating the Georgia statute criminalizing sodomy by committing that act with another adult male in the bedroom of respondent's home. After a preliminary hearing, the District Attorney decided not to present the matter to the grand jury unless further evidence developed.

Respondent then brought suit in the Federal District Court, challenging the constitutionality of the statute insofar as it criminalized consensual sodomy. He asserted that he was a practicing homosexual, that the Georgia sodomy statute, as administered by the defendants, placed him in imminent danger of arrest, and that the statute for several reasons violates the Federal Constitution. . . .

[2] This case does not require a judgment on whether laws against sodomy between consenting adults in general, or between homosexuals in particular, are wise or desirable. It raises no question about the right or propriety of state legislative decisions to repeal their laws that criminalize homosexual sodomy, or of state-court

decisions invalidating those laws on state constitutional grounds. The issue presented is whether the Federal Constitution confers a fundamental right upon homosexuals to engage in sodomy and hence invalidates the laws of the many States that still make such conduct illegal and have done so for a very long time. The case also calls for some judgment about the limits of the Court's role in carrying out its constitutional mandate.

We first register our disagreement with the Court of Appeals and with respondent that the Court's prior cases have construed the Constitution to confer a right of privacy that extends to homosexual sodomy and for all intents and purposes have decided this case. . . .

Accepting the decisions in these cases . . . we think it evident that none of the rights announced in those cases bears any resemblance to the claimed constitutional right of homosexuals to engage in acts of sodomy that is asserted in this case. No connection between family, marriage, or procreation on the one hand and homosexual activity on the other has been demonstrated, either by the Court of Appeals or by respondent. Moreover, any claim that these cases nevertheless stand for the proposition that any kind of private sexual conduct between consenting adults is constitutionally insulated from state proscription is unsupportable. Indeed, the Court's opinion in *Carey* twice asserted that the privacy right, which the *Griswold* line of cases found to be one of the protections provided by the Due Process Clause, did not reach so far. . . .

Precedent aside, however, respondent would have us announce, as the Court of Appeals did, a fundamental right to engage in homosexual sodomy. This we are quite unwilling to do. It is true that despite the language of the Due Process Clauses of the Fifth and Fourteenth Amendments, which appears to focus only on the processes by which life, liberty, or property is taken, the cases are legion in which those Clauses have been interpreted to have substantive content, subsuming rights that to a great extent are immune from federal or state regulation or proscription. Among such cases are those recognizing rights that have little or no textual support in the constitutional language. *Meyer, Prince,* and *Pierce* fall in this category, as do the privacy cases from *Griswold* to *Carey.*

Striving to assure itself and the public that announcing rights not readily identifiable in the Constitution's text involves much more than the imposition of the Justices' own choice of values on the States and the Federal Government, the Court has sought to identify the nature of the rights qualifying for heightened judicial protection. In *Palko v. Connecticut.* . . (1937), it was said that this category includes those fundamental liberties that are "implicit in the concept of ordered liberty," such that "neither liberty nor justice would exist if [they] were sacrificed." A different description of fundamental liberties appeared in *Moore v. East Cleveland.* . . (1977) (opinion of POWELL, J.), where they are characterized as those liberties that are "deeply rooted in this Nation's history and tradition.". . .

It is obvious to us that neither of these formulations would extend a fundamental right to homosexuals to engage in acts of consensual sodomy. Proscriptions against that conduct have ancient roots. . . . Sodomy was a criminal offense at common law and was forbidden by the laws of the original thirteen States when they ratified the Bill of Rights. In 1868, when the 24 States and the District of Columbia continue to provide criminal penalties for sodomy performed in private and between consenting adults. . . . Against this background, to claim that a right to engage in such conduct is "deeply rooted in this Nation's history and tradition" or "implicit in the concept of ordered liberty" is, at best, facetious.

[3] Nor are we inclined to take a more expansive view of our authority to discover new fundamental rights imbedded in the Due Process Clause. The Court is most vulnerable and comes nearest to illegitimacy when it deals with judge-made constitutional law having little or no cognizable roots in the language or design of the Constitution. . . .

Respondent, however, asserts that the result should be different where the homosexual conduct occurs in the privacy of the home. He relies on *Stanley v. Georgia*, . . . (1969), where the Court held that the First Amendment prevents conviction for possessing and reading obscene material in the privacy of one's home: "If the First Amendment means anything, it means that a State has no business telling a man, sitting alone in his house, what books he may read or what films he may watch.". . .

Stanley did protect conduct that would not have been protected outside the home, and it partially prevented the enforcement of state obscenity laws; but the decision was firmly grounded in the First Amendment. The right pressed upon us here has no similar support in the text of the Constitution, and it does not qualify for recognition under the prevailing principles for construing the Fourteenth Amendment. Its limits are also difficult to discern. Plainly enough, otherwise illegal conduct is not always immunized whenever it occurs in the home. Victimless crimes, such as the possession and use of illegal drugs, do not escape the law where they are committed at home. *Stanley* itself recognized that its holding offered no protection for the possession in the home of drugs, firearms, or stolen goods. . . . And if respondent's submission is limited to the voluntary sexual conduct between consenting adults, it would be difficult, except by fiat, to limit the claimed right to homosexual conduct while leaving exposed to prosecution adultery, incest, and other sexual crimes even though they are committed in the home. We are unwilling to start down that road.

[4] Even if the conduct at issue here is not a fundamental right, respondent asserts that there must be a rational basis for the law and that there is none in this case other than the presumed belief of a majority of the electorate in Georgia that homosexual sodomy is immoral and unacceptable. This is said to be an inadequate rationale to support the law. The law, however, is constantly based on notions of morality, and if all laws representing essentially moral choices are to be invalidated under the Due Process Clause, the courts will be very busy indeed. Even respondent makes no such claim, but insists that majority sentiments about the morality of homosexuality should be declared inadequate. We do not agree, and are unpersuaded that the sodomy laws of some 25 States should be invalidated on this basis.

Accordingly, the judgment of the Court of Appeals is
Reversed.

24

Gay/Lesbian Rights:
Report from the Legal Front

Arthur S. Leonard

In the twenty-one years since the Stonewall uprising in New York City, legal battles have produced major changes in the status of gay men and lesbians. The repeal or reform of sodomy laws has removed the stigma of criminality from gay sexual practices in half the states, comprising over half the nation's population. Civil rights protections have been enacted in more than sixty-five municipalities, in seventeen counties, in Wisconsin and Massachusetts, and in the District of Columbia; new laws are on the horizon. Some courts have recognized that antigay government policies present problems under the Constitution. A few municipalities have embraced new definitions of family life that include lesbian and gay relationships.

But there's still a long way to go. The trend toward decriminalization of gay sex has been halted by AIDS, and court challenges to those laws have hit a major stumbling block in the Supreme Court's 1986 *Bowers v. Hardwick* decision, which upheld Georgia's sodomy law. As a result of the AIDS epidemic, the energy of the gay rights movement has been sidetracked into fighting for civil rights protections for persons infected with HIV and pressuring government to allocate more money for research, education and treatment and to cut red tape so that experimental drugs are made available. Meanwhile, the growing trend toward recognizing domestic partnerships is being vigorously challenged by right-wing "family protection" groups.

What follows is a brief survey of major developments in the law in three areas that are on the cutting edge of gay and lesbian rights: sodomy laws, antigay discrimination by the military and family rights for homosexual partners.

Sodomy Laws

Prohibitions of sodomy in English common law were adopted after the Revolution by the American states. In 1961 Illinois became the first state to repeal its sodomy law, and others followed suit over the next two decades. Some states retained penalties for sodomy by unmarried adults. (Such was the case in New York until 1980, when the law was invalidated by the State Supreme Court.) Others, such as

313

Texas, passed reforms that reduced penalties and penalized sodomy only between persons of the same sex. By the early 1970s it was clear that the drive for legislative repeal was losing steam, so the gay legal movement shifted its energies to the courts, hoping to capitalize on liberal trends in constitutional law from the Warren Court era, particularly the expansion of the right of privacy. In *Griswold v. Connecticut* and *Roe v. Wade* the Court had affirmed the right of individuals to determine important aspects of their sex lives, and in *Stanley v. Georgia* it overturned on privacy grounds a statute banning possession of pornography.

In 1985 the U.S. Court of Appeals for the Eleventh Circuit ruled in Michael Hardwick's case that Georgia's sodomy law could not stand, absent a compelling state interest that would justify invading the bedrooms of citizens and policing consensual behavior. The court's opinion, which was the first federal appellate court condemnation of a sodomy law, galvanized the gay rights movement. If the ruling withstood appeal, all state and federal sodomy laws might be struck down overnight. (Federal law forbids sodomy among members of the military and in federal parks and buildings.) But on June 30, 1986, the Supreme Court reversed the lower court's decision. Justice Byron White's opinion characterized as "facetious" the argument that gay people have a "fundamental right" to engage in consensual sex, upheld the State of Georgia's assertion that the law was needed to promote morality and disclaimed consideration of equal protection issues.

The shortest judicial route to sodomy-law reform was thus blocked, but opinion polls showing that a majority of Americans disagreed with the *Hardwick* decision gave hope for future change. Thousands of gays and lesbians, shocked out of their complacency, began providing financial support to the movement for the first time. New challenges to sodomy laws were filed in state courts in Texas, Michigan and Minnesota, building on the trend toward fighting for more expansive civil liberties protections under state constitutions, and grass-roots movements for legislative reform have sprung up in several states.

The Military

Discrimination against gays and lesbians in the armed forces is deeply entrenched. Discharges of military personnel solely because of their homosexuality has led to many lawsuits over the past twenty years. Because the military's exclusion policy is based on status rather than conduct, the most promising constitutional recourse is equal protection. The Fourteenth Amendment requires the states to guarantee to all people living under their jurisdiction "equal protection of the laws." The Supreme Court has held that the Fifth Amendment's due process clause imposes a simple obligation on the federal government. Even before *Hardwick*, a major conflict was brewing over whether discrimination against gays and lesbians violates this obligation.

The Supreme Court has generally recognized that government policies almost always make categorical distinctions that favor one group over another, and it has deferred legislative judgment, so long as it appears to have a rational basis. Certain classifications, however, naturally arouse suspicions that they are based on prejudice. The Courts treated as "suspect" those classifications, such as race, that have a history of discriminatory use and for which it is unlikely a nonprejudicial justification exists. If a classification is suspect the government must demonstrate a compelling interest for adopting it. The Court has also recognized that classifications occasionally relevant to a legitimate governmental purpose, such as gender, carry enough discriminatory baggage to require heightened scrutiny. The challenge for gay rights advocates has been to convince courts that classifications that disadvantage gays are suspect.

Unfortunately, for many judges the fact that the Supreme Court has yet to recognize sexual orientation as a suspect classification is sufficient reason to reject a legal challenge. Others, confusing status (sexual orientation) and conduct (sexual behavior), assert that government may discriminate against categories of people presumed to engage in the conduct of which it disapproves, even when there is no evidence that a given individual has actually engaged in such conduct. For them, the *Hardwick* decision settled the matter.

In 1988, however, a three-judge panel of the U.S. Court of Appeals for the Ninth Circuit held in *Watkins v. United States*, a suit challenging the military's policy of excluding lesbians and gays, that *Hardwick* was not relevant. The judges embraced the distinction between status and conduct and found that the military's policy was explicitly premised on sexual orientation rather than sexual behavior. Soldiers who claimed that their conduct was an aberration (of the "I had too much to drink" variety) would not be discharged, while those identified as homosexuals would be, even if they had remained celibate.

Since Perry Watkins's homosexual conduct was not the issue, the Ninth Circuit panel said that the relevant question was whether unequal treatment based on his status was suspect. The majority concluded it was, because of the history of antigay prejudice and the centrality of sexual orientation as a virtually immutable characteristic of identity. Thus the government must show that the exclusion served a compelling interest.

This placed the Defense Department in an indefensible position, since its policies are based on speculation rather than evidence. The department's arguments were similar to those advanced during World War II against desegregation of the armed forces—that morale would be adversely affected, recruitment would be undermined and military discipline impaired—but they have been disproved by men and women who challenged the policies. Perry Watkins's homosexuality was well known to his fellow soldiers, but it had caused none of the problems raised by military lawyers, and he had received the highest fitness ratings for his performance.

The military's other argument was that gays are susceptible to blackmail and thus are security risks. This contention lost its credibility at a 1985 Senate hearing, when neither the Defense Intelligence Agency nor the F.B.I. was able to offer any solid evidence that incidents of blackmail had ever occurred.

In equal protection cases the Supreme Court has held that nonsuspect classifications will be sustained if they stand the rational basis test and are related to a legitimate government purpose. Under this test, the Court would accept the military's justifications cited above, since the Court is willing to indulge the fantasies of governmental bodies. But under the heightened scrutiny standard for a suspect category, these rationales for antigay discrimination collapse like a house of cards. The Defense Department's internal studies of homosexuality and the military, leaked during the fall of 1989, provide no support for its policies, and a strong argument can be made that the military's justifications fall short of meeting even the more permissive rationality standard.

The government petitioned for reconsideration in *Watkins*. An expanded panel of judges ordered the Army to offer Watkins the chance to re-enlist. Without deciding the constitutional question, the panel said the Army could not exclude Watkins because it had allowed him to re-enlist several times over a period of thirteen years even though it knew he was gay.

After the Ninth Circuit's decision, the Court of Appeals for the Seventh Circuit ruled on a similar suit brought by Miriam Ben Shalom, a lesbian Army Reserve sergeant. Like Watkins, Ben Shalom had received superior ratings and had been promoted to an important command position based on her performance and the recommendation of her commanding officer. Her military record did not sway the court, however. Fastening on magazine and newspaper articles about gays in government and the participation of Chicago Mayor Richard M. Daley in a gay rights march, the Court asserted that homosexuals did not meet one of the tests for determining whether a classification is suspect: political powerlessness of the disadvantaged group. Gays could ask Congress to rescind the exclusion and so did not need the assistance of the courts.

This reasoning ignored the consistent failure of Congress to pass pro-gay legislation. Even an innocuous bill requiring the Justice Department to tally incidents of antigay violence was stalled for more than a year while lesbian and gay groups negotiated a mildly antigay amendment for which timid senators could vote in preference to a draconian one introduced by Jesse Helms. In reality, gays' political power exists largely at the local level, encompassing a few city councils, state legislatures and some elected officials.

Citing *Hardwick*, the Seventh Circuit also ruled that the Army could assume from Ben Shalom's sexual orientation that she would inevitably engage in behavior that the government might forbid. The same analysis was recently embraced by a different panel of Ninth Circuit judges in *High Tech Gays v. Defense Industrial Security Clearance Office*, a discrimination suit brought by gay employees of defense contractors. The judges held that the Defense Department did not violate equal protection by initiating special investigations of gays when they applied for security clearances.

The Supreme Court ducked two opportunities to rule on the equal protection issue during its current term, including Ben Shalom's appeal, but cases are pending in the lower courts, so the issue will arise again. Since the Court always shows extreme deference to the "professional" judgment of the Pentagon, it seems unlikely that it will overrule policies excluding gays from the services, even if it were to subject those policies to heightened scrutiny. Given this reluctance, why bring these cases at all? Because no agency is so blatantly homophobic as the Defense Department. Furthermore, voluntary service to one's country is the right of every citizen. Finally, on a more practical note, many young people who enlist have not yet come to terms with their sexuality and are unaware of the policy excluding homosexuals. Imagine the difficulty of young people finally confronting their sexuality and then having to deal with military homophobia and heterosexism.

Family Rights

The newest battlefront for the lesbian and gay rights movement is the family. The right-wing calumny that gays are "antifamily" has been frequently disproved, most spectacularly through the "lesbian baby boom" and the incredible strength of gay relationships in the face of AIDS. Cases involving formerly married gay parents who have been denied child custody and visitation rights, or gays who have been declared unfit to adopt or provide foster care, continue to be decided with results that vary from state to state, but the major news lies in court rulings on the issues raised by lesbian motherhood and the premature deaths of gay men in committed-couple relationships.

Few topics have drawn more eager audiences at gay conferences than discussions of parenting. Many gays who count among their friends people who have been married and have children ask why they cannot also have a parenting experience. More lesbian couples are deciding to have children, frequently by one obtaining sperm from a male relative of the other so the child will be related to both. Some lesbian couples seek sperm from a gay male friend, and in some cases gay men have sought lesbians to share parenting responsibilities.

Legal intervention most frequently comes at the point when a lesbian relationship breaks up and the birth mother tries to limit her former partner's contact with the child, or the birth mother dies and the surviving woman's right to keep the child is challenged. Courts in Florida and Vermont recently recognized the parental status of the nonbirth mother in the latter situation, holding that she had rights superior to grandparents and other genetic relatives. Both courts, focusing on the quality of the relationship, recognized a true family tie that should not be broken.

The AIDS epidemic has hastened legal recognition of gay families, as surviving partners have gone to court to assert their rights. In California a man gave up his job to care full time for his partner. A spouse or family member who does this is entitled to unemployment benefits, but the man's employer contested his claim. An appeals judge said the former employee's reason for quitting came within the spirit of the spousal entitlement and awarded benefits.

Hospitals sometimes allow spouses access to patients while excluding all other visitors, and spouses are routinely briefed by medical staff and consulted about treatment. But gay partners of hospital patients frequently found themselves barred because hospitals refused to recognize their relationships. Lobbying and threatened lawsuits have led many hospitals to change these policies.

Surviving partners of people with AIDS were threatened with eviction from rent-regulated apartments in New York City by landlords eager to gain rent increases upon vacancy. In *Braschi v. Stahl Associates* New York State's highest court ruled in 1989 that survivors should be treated as family members under a rent-control regulation barring such evictions. Three judges agreed on a functional definition of family based on emotional and economic commitment rather than technicalities such as a marriage license. A fourth judge concurred, arguing that it would be irrational to deny the surviving gay partner the benefit of the regulation.

Although *Braschi* appeared to be limited to the narrow issue of tenant succession, its symbolic impact was enormous because of the widespread news media attention it drew. In the year since the decision was announced it has been codified and extended by administrative and judicial action, it has inspired a New York City mayoral executive order and introduction of a domestic partnership bill in the New York State Legislature and it has even been cited by an appellate judge as justification for a new approach to the problem of child custody and visitation rights of lesbian partners.

Braschi came in the wake of increasing legislative recognition of lesbian and gay families. San Francisco's Board of Supervisors had unanimously passed a domestic partnership ordinance (later narrowly repealed in a referendum), and the Los Angeles City Council had resolved to accept the concept of domestic partnerships between unmarried persons as recommended by a Family Diversity Task Force convened by a Council member. West Hollywood, California; Madison, Wisconsin; and Seattle have passed domestic partnership ordinances, and the District of Columbia appointed a commission to study the issue. Extending legal recognition to alternative families is in the air, and gay families may benefit from the resulting restructuring of social and legal policies.

There are busy times ahead for the advocates of legal and political rights for lesbians and gays. Legislative initiatives continue in the areas of immigration policy, bias-motivated crime and public employment rights outside the military. The new prudery represented by the Helms amendment to last year's National Endowment for the Arts budget authorization has opened a major battlefront over homoeroticism in the arts. We have come a long way in the twenty-one years since Stonewall, but the road ahead continues to pose major challenges.

Suggestions for Further Reading

Acuna, Rudolpho: *Occupied America: A History of Chicanos*, Harper and Row, New York, 1987.

Aptheker, B.: *Woman's Legacy: Essays on Race, Sex, and Class in American History*, University of Massachusetts Press, Amherst, 1982.

Baxendall, R., L. Gordon and S. Reverby: *America's Working Women: A Documentary History—1600 to the Present*, Random House, New York, 1976.

Berry, M. F. and J. W. Blassingame: *Long Memory: The Black Experience in America*, Oxford University Press, New York, 1982.

Boyer, R. O. and H. Morais: *Labor's Untold Story*, United Electrical, Radio and Machine Workers of America, New York, 1972.

Cluster, D. (ed.): *They Should Have Served That Cup of Coffee*, South End Press, Boston, 1979.

Cott, Nancy F.: *Root of Bitterness: Documents of the Social History of American Women*, Northeastern Press, Boston, 1986.

Deitz, James L.: *Economic History of Puerto Rico: Institutional Change and Capitalist Development*, Princeton University Press, Princeton, New Jersey, 1986.

Duberman, Martin Baum, Martha Vicinus and George Chauncey, Jr.: *Hidden From History: Reclaiming the Gay and Lesbian Past*, New American Library, New York, 1989.

Flexner, E.: *Century of Struggle*, Harvard University Press, Cambridge, Massachusetts, 1976.

Gee, E. (ed.): *Counterpoint: Perspectives on Asian Americans*, Asian American Studies Center, University of California, Los Angeles, 1976.

Giddings, P.: *When and Where I Enter: The Impact of Black Women on Race and Sex in America*, Bantam Books, New York, 1976.

Jacobs, P., and S. Landau (eds.): *To Serve the Devil: vol.1, Natives and Slaves: vol.2, Colonials and Sojourners: A Documentary Analysis of America's Racial History and Why It Has Been Kept Hidden*, Vintage Books, New York, 1971.

Katz, Jonathan: *Gay American History: Lesbians and Gay Men in the U.S.: A Documentary History*, Avon Books, New York, 1984.

Mintz, Sidney: *Caribbean Transformations*, Johns Hopkins Press, Baltimore, Maryland, 1974.

Stampp, K. M.: *The Peculiar Institution: Slavery in the Ante-Bellum South*, Vintage, New York, 1956.

Takaki, Ronald: *From Different Shores: Perspectives on Race and Culture in America*, Oxford, New York, 1987.

United States Commission on Human Rights, Washington, D.C., 1981.

K. Wagenheim and O. J. Wagenheim (eds.): *The Puerto Ricans: A Documentary History*, Praeger, New York, 1973.

PART VI

Creating and Maintaining Hierarchy: Stereotypes, Ideology, Language, and Social Control

More than two thousand years ago, Plato wrote *The Republic*, one of the most important books about politics and the social order ever written. Plato believed that people were born with different capacities and that the key to the ideal society was for each person to occupy that place in society for which he or she was naturally suited. Once those best qualified to rule were in power, the most important thing would be to guard against social change because any change would be a change for the worse.

To this end, Plato outlined a set of myths that would be taught to people at an early age to ensure that they were disinclined to tamper with the structure of the Republic. They are to be told that some people are born with iron and brass in their souls, some with silver, and others with gold, and that these metals indicate each individual's proper place in society. Those born with gold are to rule, assisted by those with silver, over those with iron and brass. Thus, the assignment of social class in Plato's Republic is to be viewed as natural and unchangeable, not arbitrary and reversible.

Plato's motives for prohibiting social change were laudable. In his Republic, the rulers, being uninterested in either personal wealth or power, would rule reluctantly out of a sense of responsibility. Guided by principles of justice and the highest considerations of morality, they would simply maintain the society so that it functioned in the best interests of all its members. For the most part, people who have exercised political power in the real world have ignored Plato's advice about what suits a person to rule, but have embraced his suggestions about how to maintain power through the exercise of social control. Tanks in the streets and armed militia are not particularly good long-term devices for keeping a population in check. Although crude force can be effective in the short run, it serves as a constant reminder to oppressed people that they are not free and gives them a focus for their anger and an impetus for rebellion.

Plato was correct that the most effective way for rulers to maintain power is to persuade those they rule that the situation is natural, inevitable, and desirable. It is here that stereotypes, ideology, and language have their role to play. Each is a way of persuading people that differences in wealth, power, and opportunity are reflections of natural differences among people, not a result of the economic and political organization of the society. Thus, each is a way of persuading people that inequality is inevitable and beyond change, not arbitrary and alterable.

In our society, stereotypes, ideology, and language have played a critical role in perpetuating racism, sexism, and class privilege, even at those times when the law has been used as a vehicle to fight discrimination rather than maintain it. Furthermore, race, class, and gender biases perpetuated in these subtle and largely unconscious ways manage to deflect attention from those who profit from the current organization of society. Because of this, many ordinary working people have come to believe that the greatest obstacle to their advancement comes from the demands for equity made by either women, or Black women, or white women, or people of color, or white men, or white people, rather than a small and powerful group of wealthy white men who reap the benefits of racism, sexism, and class oppression.

Stereotypes are used to ascribe incorrectly certain characteristics to whole groups of people and then explain or excuse social problems in light of these characteristics. For example, high unemployment among African-American and Latino men in our society is often attributed to the "fact" that this group is "lazy" and "irresponsible" rather than to the combined effects of racism and the particular way we organize our economic life. The underrepresentation of women in positions of leadership is explained by the "fact" that they are "naturally" less aggressive than men; the large gap in wages between men and women is explained by "natural" differences in ability or by emphasizing woman's "natural" role as homemaker and man's as breadwinner and so on, rather than the needs of capitalism and male dominance.

In addition to creating and maintaining mistaken beliefs about the reason for unequal distribution of wealth, power, and opportunity, stereotypes can play an important role in reconciling individuals to discriminatory treatment. If women and people of color internalize prevailing stereotypes about their group as they are encouraged to do, they come to believe that they themselves are inadequate and unqualified, and thus they blame themselves for their failures, even when they are clearly the victims of discrimination. Stereotypes are not merely broad generalizations we impose on others; they are ways of seeing "women" or "Chicanos" or "workers" that we internalize and use to define and limit ourselves and our expectations.

Ideology, or a set of incorrect beliefs that rationalize the status quo, supports or buttresses the impact of stereotyping by further distorting our perceptions of ourselves and each other. For example, stories in the media as well as all forms of advertising create the impression that particular groups—say, women or African-Americans—have made enormous strides in all areas of society, implying that they are now the recipients of special treatment that give them an advantage over white men and other groups. Never mind that statistics paint a very different picture. The force of ideology distorts our perception of the world to the extent that even women earning a fraction of what men earn for comparable work may not recognize that they are victims of discrimination.

Moreover, negative stereotypes of women and African-Americans combine with ideology so that success by members of these groups is viewed with suspicion as undeserved. Consequently, an individual can have a distorted perception of how well certain groups are doing and then blame the supposed success of these groups for his or her own frustrations and failure. For example, some people view their inability to gain admission to college as the fault of a minority group that supposedly gets preferential treatment instead of as a result of inadequate funding for public higher education.

In this way, the power of ideology helps explain why people live in one of the wealthiest societies the world has ever known, but never question why a good education continues to be a privilege enjoyed by some rather than a right for all. The same holds true with respect to housing, medical care, food, clothing, and other basic necessities. Instead of our being encouraged to ask why so much suffering and deprivation exist in the midst of such wealth, the prevailing racist and sexist ideology and stereotyping encourages us to redefine social problems as individual pathology. A good illustration of this way of seeing the world came in the mid-1980s when the mayor of New York City toured publicly financed housing facilities, which were in abominable and subhuman living condition. The mayor's comment was that some people simply prefer to live this way.

Language encourages various individuals and groups to think of themselves in ways that undermine their sense of personhood and dignity. Referring to a fifty-year-old female office worker as a "girl" is part of the package that results in paying her an inferior wage, expecting her to make coffee and run errands for her boss on her lunch hour, and failing to treat her with appropriate respect. That many women claim to be flattered by being referred to as a "girl" or being called "honey" or "sweetheart" by men they hardly know only shows how successful language and ideology have been in getting women to internalize a self-image that perpetuates their own lack of power and dignity.

The selections in Part VI focus on the ways in which stereotypes, language, and ideology operate as forms of social control. They show the variety of ways in which the unconscious beliefs we hold about ourselves and others reinforce existing social roles and class positions and blunt social criticism. Many of the articles underscore the point made in Part II that stereotyping distorts the accuracy of our perceptions of others and dulls our critical abilities. In "Self-Fulfilling Stereotypes," Mark Snyder uses examples from current psychological research to show how important our expectations are in shaping our behavior and experience. As he points out, some of the most interesting studies being done in the field of education show that teachers' expectations are at least as important as "innate ability" in determining how well young children do in school. These expectations are often shaped unconsciously by the racist and sexist stereotypes that pervade our language.

The many ways in which our language smuggles in negative images of women and people of color are explored in the selections by Robert B. Moore and Haig Bosmajian. Language can provide valuable clues to unconscious attitudes in a society but some people have difficulty analyzing language because they dismiss it as trivial or because they have trouble believing that *what* we call something affects *how* we feel about it. These selections ask us to take language seriously. Taken together with Richard Mohr's discussion of gay stereotypes and Jean Kilbourne's account of images of women in advertising, these selections suggest that language, stereotyping, and ideology often result in the creation of "the other," a way of seeing members of certain groups that strips them of their humanity and makes it possible for us to treat them in ways that would otherwise horrify us. Carole Sheffield's article on hate-violence (Selection 9) describes and analyzes some of the consequences of these depictions.

While many people are inclined to think of stereotypes and biased language as crude and obvious, that is not always the case. As Herbert Gans' analysis of the term "underclass" makes clear, even technical jargon may carry with it implications about those being described which creates and/or perpetuates stereotypes. Like William Ryan, Gans is concerned with the way in which stereotypes and ideology can reinforce the status quo by directing our attention away from the economic and social arrangements that perpetuate unequal treatment and encouraging us to blame the victims of these institutions for their own misery. Ryan's article introduces us to the technique he calls "blaming the victim," which effectively allows people to recognize injustice without assuming responsibility for it or acknowledging the need to make basic changes in our social and economic institutions.

In Selection 8, William Chafe examines the impact of both race and gender stereotypes and ideology by drawing an analogy between sex and race. He argues persuasively that both racism and sexism function analogously as forms of social control. Although Chafe suggests he is comparing the experiences of white women with those of African-Americans, a careful reading of this essay suggests he is really comparing the experience of white women to those of white men. The reader might be interested to see whether Chafe's claim about racism and sexism and social control holds up equally well when we construct similar accounts of the experiences of African-American *women* as well as members of other racial/ethnic groups discussed in this book. Chafe begins by analyzing how stereotypes, ideology, and language function to distort our expectations, perceptions, and experience and then proceeds to ask whose interests are served by this distortion.

Often, people become overwhelmed and discouraged when they realize how much our unconscious images and beliefs affect our ways of seeing each other and the world and, as a result, fail to go on to analyze the consequences of ideology. Believing that people are naturally prejudiced and can't change is one more bit of ideology that prevents us from taking control of our lives. And ideology is dangerous because it prevents us from questioning prevailing social and economic arrangements and asking whether they serve the best interest of all the people. By dividing us from each other and confusing us as to who really profits from these arrangements, ideology and stereotypes imprison us in a false world. In the next and final part of this book, a number of thinkers will offer their suggestions about how to move beyond race, class, and gender divisions.

Self-Fulfilling Stereotypes

Mark Snyder

Gordon Allport, the Harvard psychologist who wrote a classic work on the nature of prejudice, told a story about a child who had come to believe that people who lived in Minneapolis were called monopolists. From his father, moreover, he had learned that monopolists were evil folk. It wasn't until many years later, when he discovered his confusion, that his dislike of residents of Minneapolis vanished.

Allport knew, of course, that it was not so easy to wipe out prejudice and erroneous stereotypes. Real prejudice, psychologists like Allport argued, was buried deep in human character, and only a restructuring of education could begin to root it out. Yet many people whom I meet while lecturing seem to believe that stereotypes are simply beliefs or attitudes that change easily with experience. Why do some people express the view that Italians are passionate, blacks are lazy, Jews materialistic, and lesbians mannish in their demeanor? In the popular view, it is because they have not learned enough about the diversity among these groups and have not had enough contact with members of the groups for their stereotypes to be challenged by reality. With more experience, it is presumed, most people of good will are likely to revise their stereotypes.

My research over the past decade convinces me that there is little justification for such optimism—and not only for the reasons given by Allport. While it is true that deep prejudice is often based on the needs of pathological character structure, stereotypes are obviously quite common even among fairly normal individuals. When people first meet others, they cannot help noticing certain highly visible and distinctive characteristics: sex, race, physical appearance, and the like. Despite people's best intentions, their initial impressions of others are shaped by their assumptions about such characteristics.

What is critical, however, is that these assumptions are not merely beliefs or attitudes that exist in a vacuum; they are reinforced by the behavior of both prejudiced people and the targets of their prejudice. In recent years, psychologists have collected considerable laboratory evidence about the processes that strengthen stereotypes and put them beyond the reach of reason and good will.

My own studies initially focused on first encounters between strangers. It did not take long to discover, for example, that people have very different ways of treating those whom they regard as physically attractive and those whom they consider physically unattractive, and that these differences tend to bring out precisely those kinds of behavior that fit with stereotypes about attractiveness.

In an experiment that I conducted with my colleagues Elizabeth Decker Tanke and Ellen Berscheid, pairs of college-age men and women met and became acquainted in telephone conversations. Before the conversations began, each man received a Polaroid snapshot, presumably taken just moments before, of the woman he would soon meet. The photograph, which had actually been prepared before the experiment began, showed either a physically attractive woman or a physically unattractive one. By randomly choosing which picture to use for each conversation, we insured that there was no consistent relationship between the attractiveness of the woman in the picture and the attractiveness of the woman in the conversation.

By questioning the men, we learned that even before the conversations began, stereotypes about physical attractiveness came into play. Men who looked forward to talking with physically attractive women said that they expected to meet decidedly sociable, poised, humorous, and socially adept people, while men who thought that they were about to get acquainted with unattractive women fashioned images of rather unsociable, awkward, serious, and socially inept creatures. Moreover, the men proved to have very different styles of getting acquainted with women whom they thought to be attractive and those whom they believed to be unattractive. Shown a photograph of an attractive woman, they behaved with warmth, friendliness, humor, and animation. However, when the woman in the picture was unattractive, the men were cold, uninteresting, and reserved.

These differences in the men's behavior elicited behavior in the women that was consistent with the men's stereotyped assumptions. Women who were believed (unbeknown to them) to be physically attractive behaved in a friendly, likeable, and sociable manner. In sharp contrast, women who were perceived as physically unattractive adopted a cool, aloof, and distant manner. So striking were the differences in the women's behavior that they could be discerned simply by listening to tape recordings of the woman's side of the conversations. Clearly, by acting upon their stereotyped beliefs about the women whom they would be meeting, the men had initiated a chain of events that produced *behavioral confirmation* for their beliefs.

Similarly, Susan Anderson and Sandra Bem have shown in an experiment at Stanford University that when the tables are turned—when it is women who have pictures of men they are to meet on the telephone—many women treat the men according to their presumed physical attractiveness, and by so doing encourage the men to confirm their stereotypes. Little wonder, then, that so many people remain convinced that good looks and appealing personalities go hand in hand.

Sex and Race

It is experiments such as these that point to a frequently unnoticed power of stereotypes: the power to influence social relationships in ways that create the illusion of reality. In one study, Berna Skrypnek and I arranged for pairs of previously unacquainted students to interact in a situation that permitted us to control the information that each one received about the apparent sex of the other. The two people were seated in separate rooms so that they could neither see nor hear each other. Using a system of signal lights that they operated with switches, they negotiated a division of labor, deciding which member of the pair would perform each of several tasks that differed in sex-role connotations. The tasks varied along the dimensions of masculinity and femininity: sharpen a hunting knife (masculine), polish a pair of shoes (neutral), iron a shirt (feminine).

One member of the team was led to believe that the other was, in one condition of the experiment, male; in the other, female. As we had predicted, the first member's belief about the sex of the partner influenced the outcome of the pair's negotiations. Women whose partners believed them to be men generally chose stereotypically masculine tasks; in contrast, women whose partners believed that they were women usually chose stereotypically feminine tasks. The experiment thus suggests that much sex-role behavior may be the product of other people's stereotyped and often erroneous beliefs.

In a related study at the University of Waterloo, Carl von Baeyer, Debbie Sherk, and Mark Zanna have shown how stereotypes about sex roles operate in job interviews. The researchers arranged to have men conduct simulated job interviews with women supposedly seeking positions as research assistants. The investigators informed half of the women that the men who would interview them held traditional views about the ideal woman, believing her to be very emotional, deferential to her husband, home-oriented, and passive. The rest of the women were told that their interviewer saw the ideal woman as independent, competitive, ambitious, and dominant. When the women arrived for their interviews, the researchers noticed that most of them had dressed to meet the stereotyped expectations of their prospective interviewers. Women who expected to see a traditional interviewer had chosen very feminine-looking makeup, clothes, and accessories. During the interviews (videotaped through a one-way mirror) these women behaved in traditionally feminine ways and gave traditionally feminine answers to questions such as "Do you have plans to include children and marriage with your career plans?"

Once more, then, we see the self-fulfilling nature of stereotypes. Many sex differences, it appears, may result from the images that people create in their attempts to act out accepted sex roles. The implication is that if stereotyped expectations about sex roles shift, behavior may change, too. In fact, statements by people who have undergone sex-change operations have highlighted the power of such expectations in easing adjustment to a new life. As the writer Jan Morris said in recounting the story of her transition from James to Jan: "The more I was treated as a woman, the more woman I became."

The power of stereotypes to cause people to confirm stereotyped expectations can also be seen in interracial relationships. In the first of two investigations done at Princeton University by Carl Word, Mark Zanna, and Joel Cooper, white undergraduates interviewed both white and black job applicants. The applicants were actually confederates of the experimenters, trained to behave consistently from interview to interview, no matter how the interviewers acted toward them.

To find out whether or not the white interviewers would behave differently toward white and black job applicants, the researchers secretly videotaped each interview and then studied the tapes. From these, it was apparent that there were substantial differences in the treatment accorded blacks and whites. For one thing, the interviewers' speech deteriorated when they talked to blacks, displaying more errors in grammar and pronunciation. For another, the interviewers spent less time with blacks than with whites and showed less "immediacy," as the researchers called it, in their manner. That is, they were less friendly, less outgoing, and more reserved with blacks.

In the second investigation, white confederates were trained to approximate the immediate or the nonimmediate interview styles that had been observed in the first investigation as they interviewed white job applicants. A panel of judges who evaluated the tapes agreed that applicants subjected to the nonimmediate styles performed less adequately and were more nervous than job applicants treated in the immediate style. Apparently, then, the blacks in the first study did not have a chance to display their qualifications to the best advantage. Considered together, the two investigations suggest that in interracial encounters, racial stereotypes may constrain behavior in ways to cause both blacks and whites to behave in accordance with those stereotypes.

Rewriting Biography

Having adopted stereotyped ways of thinking about another person, people tend to notice and remember the ways in which that person seems to fit the stereotype, while resisting evidence that contradicts the stereotype. In one investigation that I conducted with Seymour Uranowitz, student subjects read a biography of a fictitious woman named Betty K. We constructed the story of her life so that it would fit the stereotyped images of both lesbians and heterosexuals. Betty, we wrote, never had a steady boyfriend in high school, but did go out on dates. And although we gave her a steady boyfriend in college, we specified that he was more of a close friend than anything else. A week after we had distributed this biography, we gave our subjects some new information about Betty. We told some students that she was now living with another woman in a lesbian relationship; we told others that she was living with her husband.

To see what impact stereotypes about sexuality would have on how people remembered the facts of Betty's life, we asked each student to answer a series of questions about her life history. When we examined their answers, we found that the students had reconstructed the events of Betty's past in ways that supported their own stereotyped beliefs about her sexual orientation. Those who believed that Betty was a lesbian remembered that Betty had never had a steady boyfriend in high school, but tended to neglect the fact that she had gone out on many dates in college. Those who believed that Betty was now a heterosexual tended to remember that she had formed a steady relationship with a man in college, but tended to ignore the fact that this relationship was more of a friendship than a romance.

The students showed not only selective memories but also a striking facility for interpreting what they remembered in ways that added fresh support for their stereotypes. One student who accurately remembered that a supposedly lesbian Betty never had a steady boyfriend in high school confidently pointed to the fact as an early sign of her lack of romantic or sexual interest in men. A student who correctly remembered that a purportedly lesbian Betty often went out on dates in college was sure that these dates were signs of Betty's early attempts to mask her lesbian interests.

Clearly, the students had allowed their preconceptions about lesbians and heterosexuals to dictate the way in which they interpreted and reinterpreted the facts of Betty's life. As long as stereotypes make it easy to bring to mind evidence that supports them and difficult to bring to mind evidence that undermines them, people will cling to erroneous beliefs.

Stereotypes in the Classroom and Work Place

The power of one person's beliefs to make other people conform to them has been well demonstrated in real life. Back in the 1960s, as most people well remember, Harvard psychologist Robert Rosenthal and his colleague Lenore Jacobson entered elementary-school classrooms and identified one out of every five pupils in each room as a child who could be expected to show dramatic improvement in intellectual achievement during the school year. What the teachers did not know was that the children had been chosen on a random basis. Nevertheless, something happened in the relationships between teachers and their supposedly gifted pupils that led the children to make clear gains in test performance.

It can also do so on the job. Albert King, now a professor of management at Northern Illinois University, told a welding instructor in a vocational training center that five men in his training program had unusually high aptitude. Although these five had been chosen at random and knew nothing of their designation as high-aptitude workers, they showed substantial changes in performance. They were absent less often than were other workers, learned the basics of the welder's trade in about half the usual time, and scored a full 10 points higher than other trainees on a welding test. Their gains were noticed not only by the researcher and by the welding instructor, but also by other trainees, who singled out the five as their preferred co-workers.

Might not other expectations influence the relationships between supervisors and workers? For example, supervisors who believe that men are better suited to some jobs and women to others may treat their workers (wittingly or unwittingly) in ways that encourage them to perform their jobs in accordance with stereotypes about differences between men and women. These same stereotypes may determine who gets which job in the first place. Perhaps some personnel managers allow stereotypes to influence, subtly or not so subtly, the way in which they interview job candidates, making it likely that candidates who fit the stereotypes show up better than job-seekers who do not fit them.

Unfortunately, problems of this kind are compounded by the fact that members of stigmatized groups often subscribe to stereotypes about themselves. That is what Amerigo Farina and his colleagues at the University of Connecticut found when they measured the impact upon mental patients of believing that others knew their psychiatric history. In Farina's study, each mental patient cooperated with another person in a game requiring teamwork. Half of the patients believed that their partners knew they were patients, the other half believed that their partners thought they were nonpatients. In reality, the nonpatients never knew a thing about anyone's psychiatric history. Nevertheless, simply believing that others were aware of their history led the patients to feel less appreciated, to find the task more difficult, and to perform poorly. In addition, objective observers saw them as more tense, more anxious, and more poorly adjusted than patients who believed that their status was not known. Seemingly, the belief that others perceived them as stigmatized caused them to play the role of stigmatized patients.

Consequences for Society

Apparently, good will and education are not sufficient to subvert the power of stereotypes. If people treat others in such a way as to bring out behavior that supports stereotypes, they may never have an opportunity to discover which of their stereotypes are wrong.

I suspect that even if people were to develop doubts about the accuracy of their stereotypes, chances are they would proceed to test them by gathering precisely the evidence that would appear to confirm them.

The experiments I have described help to explain the persistence of stereotypes. But, as is so often the case, solving one puzzle only creates another. If by acting as if false stereotypes were true, people lead others, too, to act as if they were true, why do the stereotypes not come to *be* true? Why, for example, have researchers found so little evidence that attractive people are generally friendly, sociable, and outgoing and that unattractive people are generally shy and aloof?

I think that the explanation goes something like this: Very few among us have the kind of looks that virtually everyone considers either very attractive or very unattractive. Our looks make us rather attractive to some people but somewhat less attractive to other people. When we spend time with those who find us attractive, they will tend to bring out our more sociable sides, but when we are with those who find us less attractive, they will bring out our less sociable sides. Although our actual physical appearance does not change, we present ourselves quite differently to our admirers and to our detractors. For our admirers we become attractive people, and for our detractors we become unattractive. This mixed pattern of behavior will prevent the development of any consistent relationship between physical attractiveness and personality.

Now that I understand some of the powerful forces that work to perpetuate social stereotypes, I can see a new mission for my research. I hope, on the one hand, to find out how to help people see the flaws in their stereotypes. On the other hand, I would like to help the victims of false stereotypes find ways of liberating themselves from the constraints imposed on them by other members of society.

2

Racism in the English Language

Robert B. Moore

Language and Culture

An integral part of any culture is its language. Language not only develops in conjunction with a society's historical, economic and political evolution; it also reflects that society's attitudes and thinking. Language not only *expresses* ideas and concepts but actually *shapes* thought.[1] If one accepts that our dominant white culture is racist, then one would expect our language—an indispensable transmitter of culture—to be racist as well. Whites, as the dominant group, are not subjected to the same abusive characterization by our language that people of color receive. Aspects of racism in the English language that will be discussed in this essay include terminology, symbolism, politics, ethnocentrism, and context.

Before beginning our analysis of racism in language we would like to quote part of a TV film review which shows the connection between language and culture.[2]

> Depending on one's culture, one interacts with time in a very distinct fashion. One example which gives some cross-cultural insights into the concept of time is language. In Spanish, a watch is said to "walk." In English, the watch "runs." In German, the watch "functions." And in French, the watch "marches." In the Indian culture of the Southwest, people do not refer to time in this way. The value of the watch is displaced with the value of "what time it's getting to be." Viewing these five cultural perspectives of time, one can see some definite emphasis and values that each culture places on time. For example, a cultural perspective may provide a clue to why the negative stereotype of the slow and lazy Mexican who lives in the "Land of

Manana" exists in the Anglo value system, where time "flies," the watch "runs" and "time is money."

A Short Play on "Black" and "White" Words

Some may blackly (angrily) accuse me of trying to blacken (defame) the English language, to give it a black eye (a mark of shame) by writing such black words (hostile). They may denigrate (to cast aspersions; to darken) me by accusing me of being blackhearted (malevolent), of having a black outlook (pessimistic, dismal) on life, of being a blackguard (scoundrel)—which would certainly be a black mark (detrimental fact) against me. Some may black-brow (scowl at) me and hope that a black cat crosses in front of me because of this black deed. I may become a black sheep (one who causes shame or embarrassment because of deviation from the accepted standards), who will be blackballed (ostracized) by being placed on a blacklist (list of undesirables) in an attempt to blackmail (to force or coerce into a particular action) me to retract my words. But attempts to blackjack (to compel by threat) me will have a Chinaman's chance of success, for I am not a yellow-bellied Indian-giver of words, who will whitewash (cover up or gloss over vices or crimes) a black lie (harmful, inexcusable). I challenge the purity and innocence (white) of the English language. I don't see things in black and white (entirely bad or entirely good) terms, for I am a white man (marked by upright firmness) if there ever was one. However, it would be a black day when I would not "call a spade a spade," even though some will suggest a white man calling the English language racist is like the pot calling the kettle black. While many may be niggardly (grudging, scanty) in their support, others will be honest and decent—and to them I say, that's very white of you (honest, decent).

The preceding is of course a white lie (not intended to cause harm), meant only to illustrate some examples of racist terminology in the English language.

Obvious Bigotry

Perhaps the most obvious aspect of racism in language would be terms like "nigger," "spook," "chink," "spic," etc. While these may be facing increasing social disdain, they certainly are not dead. Large numbers of white Americans continue to utilize these terms. "Chink," "gook," and "slant-eyes" were in common usage among U.S. troops in Vietnam. An NBC nightly news broadcast, in February 1972, reported that the basketball team in Pekin, Illinois, was called the "Pekin Chinks" and noted that even though this had been protested by Chinese Americans, the term continued to be used because it was easy, and meant no harm. Spiro Agnew's widely reported "fat Jap" remark and the "little Jap" comment of lawyer John Wilson during the Watergate hearings, are surface indicators of a deep-rooted Archie Bunkerism.

Many white people continue to refer to Black people as "colored," as for instance in a July 30, 1975 *Boston Globe* article on a racist attack by whites on a group of Black people using a public beach in Boston. One white person was quoted as follows:

> We've always welcomed good colored people in South Boston but we will not tolerate radical blacks or Communists. . . . Good colored people are welcome in South Boston, black militants are not.

Many white people may still be unaware of the disdain many African Americans have for the term "colored," but it often appears that whether used intentionally or unintentionally, "colored" people are "good" and "know their place," while "Black" people are perceived as "uppity" and "threatening" to many whites. Similarly, the term "boy" to refer to African American men is now acknowledged to be a demeaning term, though still in common use. Other terms such as "the pot calling the kettle black" and "calling a spade a spade" have negative racial connotations but are still frequently used, as for example when President Ford was quoted in February 1976 saying that even though Daniel Moynihan had left the U.N., the U.S. would continue "calling a spade a spade."

Color Symbolism

The symbolism of white as positive and black as negative is pervasive in our culture, with the black/white words used in the beginning of this essay only one of many aspects. "Good guys" wear white hats and ride white horses, "bad guys" wear black hats and ride black horses. Angels are white, and devils are black. The definition of *black* includes "without any moral light or goodness, evil, wicked, indicating disgrace, sinful," while that of *white* includes "morally pure, spotless, innocent, free from evil intent."

A children's TV cartoon program, *Captain Scarlet*, is about an organization called Spectrum, whose purpose is to save the world from an evil extraterrestrial force called the Mysterons. Everyone in Spectrum has a color name—Captain Scarlet, Captain Blue, etc. The one Spectrum agent who has been mysteriously taken over by the Mysterons and works to advance their evil aims is Captain Black. The person who heads Spectrum, the good organization out to defend the world, is Colonel White.

Three of the dictionary definitions of white are "fairness of complexion, purity, innocence." These definitions affect the standards of beauty in our culture, in which whiteness represents the norm. "Blondes have more fun" and "Wouldn't you really rather be a blonde" are sexist in their attitudes toward women generally, but are racist white standards when applied to third world women. A 1971 *Mademoiselle* advertisement pictured a curly-headed, ivory-skinned woman over the caption, "When you go blonde go all the way," and asked: "Isn't this how, in the back of your mind, you always wanted to look? All wide-eyed and silky blonde down to there, and innocent?" Whatever the advertising people meant by this particular woman's innocence, one must remember that "innocent" is one of the definitions of the word white. This standard of beauty when preached to all women is racist. The statement "Isn't this how, in the back of your mind, you always wanted to look?" either ignores third world women or assumes they long to be white.

Time magazine in its coverage of the Wimbledon tennis competition between the black Australian Evonne Goolagong and the white American Chris Evert described Ms. Goolagong as "the dusky daughter of an Australian sheepshearer," while Ms. Evert was "a fair young girl from the middle-class groves of Florida." *Dusky* is a synonym of "black" and is defined as "having dark skin; of a dark color; gloomy; dark; swarthy." Its antonyms are "fair" and "blonde." *Fair* is defined in part as "free from blemish, imperfection, or anything that impairs the appearance, quality, or character; pleasing in appearance, attractive; clean; pretty; comely." By defining Evonne Goolagong as "dusky," *Time* technically defined her as the opposite of "pleasing in appearance; attractive; clean; pretty; comely."

The studies of Kenneth B. Clark, Mary Ellen Goodman, Judith Porter and others indicate that this persuasive "rightness of whiteness" in U.S. culture affects children before the age of four, providing white youngsters with a false sense of superiority and encouraging self-hatred among third world youngsters.

Ethnocentrism or from a White Perspective

Some words and phrases that are commonly used represent particular perspectives and frames of reference, and these often distort the understanding of the reader or listener. David R. Burgest[3] has written about the effect of using the terms "slave" or "master." He argues that the psychological impact of the statement referring to "the master raped his slave" is different from the impact of the same statement substituting the words: "the white captor raped an African woman held in captivity."

> Implicit in the English usage of the "master-slave" concept is ownership of the "slave" by the "master," therefore, the "master" is merely abusing his property (slave). In reality, the captives (slave) were African individuals with human worth, right and dignity and the term "slave" denounces that human quality thereby making the mass rape of African women by white captors more acceptable in the minds of people and setting a mental frame of reference for legitimizing the atrocities perpetuated against African people.

The term slave connotes a less than human quality and turns the captive person into a thing. For example, two McGraw-Hill Far Eastern Publishers textbooks (1970) stated, "At first it was the slaves who worked the cane and they got only food for it. Now men work cane and get money." Next time you write about slavery or read about it, try transposing all "slaves" into "African people held in captivity," "Black people forced to work for no pay" or "African people stolen from their families and societies." While it is more cumbersome, such phrasing conveys a different meaning.

Passive Tense

Another means by which language shapes our perspective has been noted by Thomas Greenfield,[4] who writes that the achievements of Black people—and Black people themselves—have been hidden in

> the linguistic ghetto of the passive voice, the subordinate clause, and the "understood" subject. The seemingly innocuous distinction (between active/passive voice) holds enormous implications for writers and speakers. When it is effectively applied, the rhetorical impact of the passive voice—the art of making the creator or instigator of action totally disappear from a reader's perception—can be devastating.

For instance, some history texts will discuss how European immigrants came to the United States seeking a better life and expanded opportunities, but will note that "slaves *were brought* to America." Not only does this omit the destruction of African societies and families, but it ignores the role of northern merchants and southern slaveholders in the profitable trade in human beings. Other books will state that "the continental railroad *was built*," conveniently omitting information about the Chinese laborers who built much of it or the oppression they suffered.

Another example. While touring Monticello, Greenfield noted that the tour guide

> made all the black people at Monticello disappear through her use of the passive voice. While speaking of the architectural achievements of Jefferson in the active voice, she unfailingly shifted to passive when speaking of the work performed by Negro slaves and skilled servants.

Noting a type of door that after 166 years continued to operate without need for repair, Greenfield remarks that the design aspect of the door was much simpler than the actual skill and work involved in building and installing it. Yet his guide stated: "Mr. Jefferson designed these doors . . ." while "the doors **were installed** in 1809." The workers who installed those doors were African people whom Jefferson held in bondage. The guide's use of the passive tense enabled her to dismiss the reality of Jefferson's slaveholding. It also meant that she did not have to make any mention of the skills of those people held in bondage.

Politics and Terminology

"Culturally deprived," "economically disadvantaged" and "underdeveloped" are other terms which mislead and distort our awareness of reality. The application of the term "culturally deprived" and third world children in this society reflects a value judgment. It assumes that the dominant whites are cultured and all others without culture. In fact, third world children generally are bicultural, and many are bilingual, having grown up in their own culture as well as absorbing the dominant culture. In many ways, they are equipped with skills and experiences which white youth have been deprived of, since most white youth develop in a monocultural, monolingual environment. Burgest[5] suggests that the term "culturally deprived" be replaced by "culturally dispossessed," and that the term "economically disadvantaged" be replaced by "economically exploited." Both these terms present a perspective and implication that provide an entirely different frame of reference as to the reality of the third world experience in U.S. society.

Similarly, many nations of the third world are described as "underdeveloped." These less wealthy nations are generally those that suffered under colonialism and neo-colonialism. The "developed" nations are those that exploited their resources and wealth. Therefore, rather than referring to these countries as "underdeveloped," a more appropriate and meaningful designation might be "over exploited." Again, transpose this term next time you read about "underdeveloped nations" and note the different meaning that results.

Terms such as "culturally deprived," "economically disadvantaged" and "underdeveloped" place the responsibility for their own conditions on those being so described. This is known as "Blaming the Victim."[6] It places responsibility for poverty on the victims of poverty. It removes the blame from those in power who benefit from, and continue to permit, poverty.

Still another example involves the use of "non-white," "minority" or "third world." While people of color are a minority in the U.S., they are part of the vast majority of the world's population, in which white people are a distinct minority. Thus, by utilizing the term minority to describe people of color in the U.S., we can lose sight of the global majority/minority reality—a fact of some importance in the increasing and interconnected struggles of people of color inside and outside the U.S.

To describe people of color as "non-white" is to use whiteness as the standard and norm against which to measure all others. Use of the term "third world" to describe all people of color overcomes the inherent bias of "minority" and "nonwhite." Moreover, it connects the struggles of third world people in the U.S. with the freedom struggles around the globe.

The term third world gained increasing usage after the 1955 Bandung Conference of "non-aligned" nations, which represented a third force outside of the two world superpowers. The "first world" represents the United States, Western Europe and their sphere of influence. The "second world" represents the Soviet Union and its sphere. The "third world" represents, for the most part, nations that were, or are, controlled by the "first world" or West. For the most part, these are nations of Africa, Asia and Latin America.

"Loaded" Words and Native Americans

Many words lead to a demeaning characterization of groups of people. For instance, Columbus, it is said, "discovered" America. The word *discover* is defined as "to gain sight or knowledge of something previously unseen or unknown; to discover may be to find some existent thing that was previously unknown." Thus, a continent inhabited by millions of human beings cannot be "discovered." For history books to continue this usage represents a Eurocentric (white European) perspective on world history and ignores the existence of, and the perspective of, Native Americans. "Discovery," as used in the Euro-American context, implies the right to take what one finds, ignoring the rights of those who already inhabit or own the "discovered" thing.

Eurocentrism is also apparent in the usage of "victory" and "massacre" to describe the battles between Native Americans and whites. *Victory* is defined in the dictionary as "a success or triumph over an enemy in battle or war; the decisive defeat of an opponent." *Conquest* denotes the "taking over of control by the victor, and the obedience of the conquered." *Massacre* is defined as "the unnecessary, indiscriminate killing of a number of human beings, as in barbarous warfare or persecution, or for revenge or plunder." *Defend* is described as "to ward off attack from; guard against assault or injury; to strive to keep safe by resisting attack."

Eurocentrism turns these definitions around to serve the purpose of distorting history and justifying Euro-American conquest of the Native American homelands. Euro-Americans are not described in history books as invading Native American lands, but rather as defending *their* homes against "Indian" attacks. Since European communities were constantly encroaching on land already occupied, then a more honest interpretation would state that it was the Native Americans who were "warding off," "guarding" and "defending" their homelands.

Native American victories are invariably defined as "massacres," while the indiscriminate killing, extermination and plunder of Native American nations by Euro-Americans is defined as "victory." Distortion of history by the choice of "loaded" words used to describe historical events is a common racist practice. Rather than portraying Native Americans as human beings in highly defined and complex societies, cultures and civilizations, history books use such adjectives as "savages," "beasts," "primitive," and "backward." Native people are referred to as "squaw," "brave," or "papoose" instead of "woman," "man," or "baby."

Another term that has questionable connotations is *tribe*. The Oxford English Dictionary defines this noun as "a race of people; now applied especially to a primary aggregate of people in a primitive or barbarous condition, under a headman or chief." Morton Fried,[7] discussing "The Myth of Tribe," states that the word "did not become a general term of reference to American Indian society until the nineteenth century. Previously, the words commonly used for Indian populations were 'nation' and 'people.'" Since "tribe" has assumed a connotation of primitiveness or backwardness, it is suggested that the use of "nation" or "people" replace the term whenever possible in referring to Native American peoples.

The term *tribe* invokes even more negative implications when used in reference to American peoples. As Evelyn Jones Rich[8] has noted, the term is "almost always used to refer to third world people and it implies a stage of development which is, in short, a put-down."

"Loaded" Words and Africans

Conflicts among diverse peoples within African nations are often referred to as "tribal warfare," while conflicts among the diverse peoples within European countries are never described in such terms. If the rivalries between the Ibo and the Hausa and Yoruba in Nigeria are described as "tribal," why not the rivalries between Serbs and Slavs in Yugoslavia, or Scots and English in Great Britain, Protestants and Catholics in Ireland, or the Basques and the Southern Spaniards in Spain? Conflicts among African peoples in a particular nation have religious, cultural, economic and/or political roots. If we can analyze the roots of conflicts among European peoples in terms other than "tribal warfare," certainly we can do the same with African peoples, including correct reference to the ethnic groups or nations involved. For example, the terms "Kaffirs," "Hottentot" or "Bushmen" are names imposed by white Europeans. The correct names are always those by which a people refer to themselves. (In these instances Xhosa, Khoi-Khoin and San are correct.[9])

The generalized application of "tribal" in reference to Africans—as well as the failure to acknowledge the religious, cultural and social diversity of African peoples—is a decidedly racist dynamic. It is part of the process whereby Euro-Americans justify, or avoid confronting, their oppression of third world peoples. Africa has been particularly insulted by this dynamic, as witness the pervasive "darkest Africa" image. This image, widespread in Western culture, evokes an Africa covered by jungles and inhibited by "uncivilized," "cannibalistic," "pagan," "savage" peoples. This "darkest Africa" image avoids the geographical reality. Less than 20 per cent of the African continent is wooded savanna, for example. The image also ignores the history of African cultures and civilizations. Ample evidence suggests this distortion of reality was developed as a convenient rationale for the European and American slave trade. The Western powers, rather than exploiting, were civilizing and christianizing "uncivilized" and "pagan savages" (so the rationalization went). This dynamic also served to justify Western colonialism. From Tarzan movies to racist children's books like *Doctor Dolittle* and *Charlie and the Chocolate Factory*, the image of "savage" Africa and the myth of "the white man's burden" has been perpetuated in Western culture.

A 1972 *Time* magazine editorial lamenting the demise of *Life* magazine, stated that the "lavishness" of *Life's* enterprises included "organizing safaris into darkest Africa." The same year, the *New York Times'* C. L. Sulzberger wrote that "Africa has a history as dark as the skins of many of its people." Terms such as "darkest Africa," "primitive," "tribe" ("tribal") or "jungle," in reference to Africa, perpetuate myths and are especially inexcusable in such large circulation publications.

Ethnocentrism is similarly reflected in the term "pagan" to describe traditional religions. A February 1973 *Time* magazine article on Uganda stated, "Moslems account for only 500,000 of Uganda's 10 million people. Of the remainder, 5,000,000 are Christians and the rest pagan." *Pagan* is defined as "Heathen, a follower of a polytheistic religion; one that has little or no religion and that is marked by a frank delight in and uninhibited seeking after sensual pleasures and material goods." *Heathen* is defined as "Unenlightened; an unconverted member of a people or nation that does not acknowledge the God of the Bible. A person whose culture or enlightenment is of an inferior grade, especially an irreligious person." Now, the people of Uganda, like almost all Africans, have serious religious beliefs and practices. As used by Westerners, "pagan" connotes something wild, primitive and inferior—another term to watch out for.

The variety of traditional structures that African people live in are their "houses," not "huts." A *hut* is "an often small and temporary dwelling of simple construction." And to describe Africans as "natives" (noun) is derogatory terminology—as in, "the natives are restless." The dictionary definition of *native* includes: "one of a people inhabiting a territorial area at the time of its discovery or becoming familiar to a foreigner; one belonging to a people having a less complex civilization." Therefore, use of "native," like use of "pagan" often implies a value judgment of white superiority.

Qualifying Adjectives

Words that would normally have positive connotations can have entirely different meanings when used in a racial context. For example, C. L. Sulzberger, the columnist of the *New York Times*, wrote in January 1975, about conversations he had with two people in Namibia. One was the white South African administrator of the country and the other a member of SWAPO, the Namibian liberation movement. The first is described as "Dirk Mudge, who as senior elected member of the administration is a kind of acting Prime Minister. . . ." But the second person is introduced as "Daniel Tijongarero, an intelligent Herero tribesman who is a member of SWAPO. . . ." What need was there for Sulzberger to state that Daniel Tijongarero is "intelligent"? Why not also state that Dirk Mudge was "intelligent"—or do we assume he wasn't?

A similar example from a 1968 *New York Times* article reporting on an address by Lyndon Johnson stated, "The President spoke to the well-dressed Negro officials and their wives." In what similar circumstances can one imagine a reporter finding it necessary to note that an audience of white government officials was "well-dressed?"

Still another word often used in a racist context is "qualified." In the 1960's white Americans often questioned whether Black people were "qualified" to hold public office, a question that was never raised (until too late) about white officials like Wallace, Maddox, Nixon, Agnew, Mitchell, et al. The question of qualifications has been raised even more frequently in recent years as white people question whether Black people are "qualified" to be hired for positions in industry and educational institutions. "We're looking for a qualified Black" has been heard again and again as institutions are confronted with affirmative action goals. Why stipulate that Blacks must be "qualified," when for others it is taken for granted that applicants must be "qualified."

Speaking English

Finally, the depiction in movies and children's books of third world people speaking English is often itself racist. Children's books about Puerto Ricans or Chicanos often connect poverty with a failure to speak English or to speak it well, thus blaming the victim and ignoring the racism which affects third world people regardless of their proficiency in English. Asian characters speak a stilted English ("Honorable so and so" or "Confucius say") or have a speech impediment ("roots or ruck," "very solly," "flied lice"). Native American characters speak another variation of stilted English ("Boy not hide. Indian take boy."), repeat certain Hollywood-Indian phrases ("Heap big" and "Many moons") or simply grunt out "Ugh" or "How." The repeated use of these language characterizations functions to make third world people seem less intelligent and less capable than the English-speaking white characters.

Wrap-Up

A *Saturday Review* editorial[10] on "The Environment of Language" stated that language

> . . . has as much to do with the philosophical and political conditioning of a society as geography or climate. . . . people in Western cultures do not realize the extent to which their racial attitudes have been conditioned since early childhood by the power of words to ennoble or condemn, augment or detract, glorify or demean. Negative language infects the subconscious of most Western people from the time they first learn to speak. Prejudice is not merely imparted or superimposed. It is metabolized in the bloodstream of society. What is needed is not so much a change in language as an awareness of the power of words to condition attitudes. If we can at least recognize the underpinnings of prejudice, we may be in a position to deal with the effects.

To recognize the racism in language is an important first step. Consciousness of the influence of language on our perceptions can help to negate much of that influence. But it is not enough to simply become aware of the affects of racism in conditioning attitudes. While we may not be able to change the language, we can definitely change our usage of the language. We can avoid using words that degrade people. We can make a conscious effort to use terminology that reflects a progressive perspective, as opposed to a distorting perspective. It is important for educators to provide students with opportunities to explore racism in language and to increase their awareness of it, as well as learning terminology that is positive and does not perpetuate negative human values.

NOTES

1. Simon Podair, "How Bigotry Builds Through Language," *Negro Digest*, March '67
2. Jose Armas, "Antonio and the Mayor: A Cultural Review of the Film," *The Journal of Ethnic Studies*, Fall,'75

3. David R. Burgest, "The Racist Use of the English Language," *Black Scholar*, Sept. '73

4. Thomas Greenfield, "Race and Passive Voice at Monticello," *Crisis*, April '75

5. David R. Burgest, "Racism in Everyday Speech and Social Work Jargon," *Social Work*, July '73

6. William Ryan, *Blaming the Victim*, Pantheon Books, '71

7. Morton Fried, "The Myth of Tribe," *National History*, April '75

8. Evelyn Jones Rich, "Mind Your Language," *Africa Report*, Sept./Oct. '74

9. Steve Wolf, "Catalogers in Revolt Against LC's Racist, Sexist Headings," *Bulletin of Interracial Books for Children*, Vol. 6, Nos. 3&4, '75

10. "The Environment of Language," *Saturday Review*, April 8,'67

Also see:

Roger Bastide, "Color, Racism and Christianity," *Daedalus*, Spring '67

Kenneth J. Gergen, "The Significance of Skin Color in Human Relations," *Daedalus*, Spring '67

Lloyd Yabura, "Towards a Language of Humanism," *Rhythm*, Summer '71

UNESCO, "Recommendations Concerning Terminology in Education on Race Questions," June '68

3

The Language of Sexism

Haig Bosmajian

While the language of racial and ethnic oppression is often blatant and relatively easy to identify, the language of sexism is more subtle and pervasive. Our everyday speech reflects the "superiority" of the male and the "inferiority" of the female, resulting in a master-subject relationship. The language of sexism relegates the woman to the status of children, servants, and idiots, to being the "second sex" and to virtual invisibility. The progress implied in the advertising slogan "You've come a long way, baby" notwithstanding, the language of sexism remains with us and exerts an influence on the male's attitudes towards and control over women and the women's attitudes toward themselves. More accurate than the above slogan is the feminist's response: "If I've come such a long way, how come you still call me baby?"

The need to eradicate the language of sexism to bring about equality of the sexes has been recognized by a variety of writers. Deborah Rosenfelt and Florence Howe have pointed out that "a number of reputable linguists believe that linguistic systems are partially determined by underlying metaphysical assumptions about the structure of reality. Linguists argue about the precise nature of the interaction between language, thought, and culture, but it seems clear that language as a form of social behavior does both reflect and help to perpetuate deeply held cultural attitudes. Among these attitudes—and this is an area that traditional linguists have hardly touched upon—are those concerning the relationships between men and women."[1] "By calling attention to sexist usage," continue Rosenfelt and Howe, "feminists hope to change not only the language—the surface behavior—but the underlying attitudes that determine and, in a constant interaction, are determined by the behavior."[2] . . .

Our sexist language, according to Aileen Hernandez, past president of the National Organization for Women, makes it abundantly clear that "in all areas that really count, we discount women." Sexist language manifests itself in various ways:

"'Mankind' is the generic term for all people or all males, but there is no similar dual meaning for 'womankind.' The masculine pronoun is used to refer to both men and women in general discussions.

"The Constitution of the United States is replete with sexist language—Senators and Representatives are 'he'; the President is obviously 'he' and even the fugitive from justice is 'he' in our Constitution. . . .

"But just in case we as women manage to escape the brainwashing that assigns us to 'our place' in the order of things, the language continues to get the message across.

"There is a 'housewife' but no 'househusband'; there's a 'housemother' but no 'housefather'; there's a 'kitchenmaid' but no 'kitchenman'; unmarried women cross the threshold from 'bachelor girl' to 'spinster' to 'old maid,' but unmarried men are 'bachelors' forever."[3]

Writing in *Women: A Journal of Liberation*, Emily Toth has observed that "generally, women lack their own words for professional positions: a woman must be a 'female judge,' 'female representative,' 'madam chairman,' or—a ghastly pun—a 'female mailman'."[4] She notes that "one textbook defines Standard English as that language spoken by 'educated professional people and their wives.'"[5] She might have added the *Webster's New World Dictionary of the American Language* definition of "honorarium": "a payment to a professional man for services on which no fee is set or legally obtainable."

Alma Graham tells us in an article titled "The Making of a Nonsexist Dictionary" that "at every level of achievement and activity—from primitive man to the man of the hour—woman is not taken into account. Consider the congressman. He is a man of the people. To prove that he's the best man for the job, he takes his case to the man in the street. He is a champion of the workingman. He speaks for the little man. He has not forgotten the forgotten man. And he firmly believes: one man, one vote. Consider the policeman or fireman, the postman or milkman, the clergyman or businessman."[6] So ingrained is the language of sexism that it is with great effort and some resistance that people will refer to a "jurywoman," "chairwoman," "churchwoman," or "journeywoman." Instead, the females all end up "countrymen," "middlemen," "selectmen," "jurymen" when these groups are referred to generally.

Not only does the woman end up a "man," she also finds herself labeled "he" or "him" or "his" when the pronoun is used as a neuter to designate anyone, female or male.

Lynne T. White, former president of Mills College, has commented on this problem of women coming out male through the use of masculine pronouns: "The grammar of English dictates that when a referent is either of indeterminate sex or both sexes, it shall be considered masculine. The penetration of this habit of language into the minds of little girls as they grow up to be women is more profound than most people, including most women, have recognized: it implies that personality is really a male attribute, and that women are human subspecies. . . . It would be a miracle if a girl-baby, learning to use the symbols of our tongue, could escape some wound to her self-respect; whereas a boy-baby's ego is bolstered by the pattern of our language."[7]

In her study dealing with the response of individuals to the pronoun "he" Virginia Kidd found that "the use of the male pronoun as the generic is not generally interpreted as representative of a neutral antecedent; that in fact the antecedent is considered male; that this interpretation of the antecedent as male is stronger in cases where the societal stereotypes of the male role coincides with the pronoun is often strong enough to be indicated in cases where other traits of the antecedent are admittedly unknown."[8] Kidd concludes that the results of her study "seem eminently clear: use of the masculine pronoun as the generic simply does not accomplish the purpose for which it is intended. The masculine pronoun does not suffice as a verbal indicator in situations where persons of either sex could be the antecedent."[9]

Rosenfelt and Howe report that "at a summer workshop a Feminist Press staff member used a simple device to illustrate the feelings of invisibility that the 'universal' *he* can arouse in women. She substituted the feminine pronoun: 'the teacher. . . she.' Finally a principal (male) could take it no longer. 'Why are you doing that, Marj?' he asked plaintively; 'why do you keep saying *she?*' With all eyes on her, Marj responded pleasantly, without embarrassment, 'why, I'm using the word generically.' Then there was laughter, an explosive release of tension. But the point had been made, and as the workshop went on, the participants were careful to use either he/she or the plural. Perhaps *he* was not so generic after all?"[10] . . .

There are many occasions when "women and men" would be more appropriate than "men and women." In fact, one might argue that since women are a majority in this nation we should henceforth always speak of "the women and men of this nation" instead of "the men and women of this nation." The firstness of the male has always appeared evident when male and female names are put side by side: Jack and Jill, Hansel and Gretel, Romeo and Juliet, Antony and Cleopatra, Dick and Jane, John and Marsha. As for the firstness of the female, there isn't much more than Snow White and the Seven Dwarfs.

In the church we have the "clergyman," the "altar boy," the Father, Son, and the

Holy Ghost. Males dominate in Christianity not only in language, but also in terms of the decision-making powers, a domination which can partly be attributed to the language of sexism. This male domination exists despite the fact that "every survey that measures sex differences in religiosity shows that females attend church more frequently than males, pray more often, hold firmer beliefs, cooperate more in church programs. This is true at all age levels from childhood to senior-citizen, and of both single and married women, of women gainfully employed and home-makers."[11] But what is a woman to do when in Scriptures she is told: "Wives, submit yourselves unto your own husbands, as unto the Lord"? This, in the same book, Ephesians, which tells children to obey their parents and tells servants to be obedient to their masters. Somehow, women, along with children and servants, end up subjects in the master-subject relationship.

The idea that women are to play a subservient role and not to be taken seriously has been perpetuated through the use of the word "lady." One might, at first glance, think that referring to a woman as a "lady" is something complimentary and desirable. Upon closer examination, however, "lady" turns out to be a verbal label connoting the non-seriousness of women.

Robin Lakoff has argued convincingly that "lady" is a euphemism. Of the euphemism generally she declares:

"When a word acquires a bad connotation by association with something people find unpleasant or embarrassing to think of, people will reach for substitutes for that word that do not have this uncomfortable effect—that is, euphemisms. What then happens is that, since feelings about the things or people referred to themselves are not altered by a change of name, the new name itself takes on the same old connotations, and a new euphemism must be found. It is no doubt possible to pick out those areas in which a society is feeling particular psychological strain or discomfort—areas where problems exist in a culture—by pinpointing those lexical items around which a great many euphemisms are clustered."[12] One has only to think of the numerous euphemisms we have for death, toilet, and certain dreaded diseases. Lakoff's point is that "unless we start feeling more respect for women, and at the same time less uncomfortable about them and their roles in society in relation to men, we cannot avoid *ladies* any more than we can avoid broads."[13]

In her discussion of the use of "lady" in job terminology, Lakoff writes: "For at least some speakers, the more demeaning the job, the more the person holding it (if female, of course) is likely to be described as a *lady*. Thus cleaning *lady* is at least as common as *cleaning woman*, *saleslady* as *saleswoman*. But one says, normally *woman doctor*. To say *lady doctor* is to be very condescending; it constitutes an insult. For men, there is no such dichotomy. *Garbage man* or *salesman* is the only possibility, never *garbage gentleman*."[14]

The non-seriousness of "lady" as contrasted to "woman" is exemplified further in the titles of organizations: "It seems that organizations of women who have a serious purpose (not merely that of spending time with one another) cannot use the word *lady* in their titles, but less serious ones may. Compare the *Ladies' Auxiliary* of a men's group, or the *Thursday Evening Ladies Browning and Garden Society* with *Ladies' Lib* or *Ladies Strike for Peace.*"[15]

One might try substituting "ladies" for "women" in the following: National Organization for Women; Harvard Medical and Dental School Committee on the Status of Women; Women's Studies Program; Radical Women; Black Women's Community Development Foundation. One seldom finds "lady" or "ladies" in titles of books which treat women seriously; substituting those terms for "woman" or "women" in the following titles clearly demonstrates that "lady" trivializes, denegrates: *The Natural Superiority of Women* by M. F. Ashley Montague; *Women and the Law* by Leo Kanowitz; *A Vindication of the Rights of Women* by Mary Wollstonecraft; *The Subjection of Women* by John S. Mill; *The Emancipation of Women* by V. I. Lenin; *The Ideas of the Woman Suffrage Movement* by Aileen Kraditor.

To those who say that the use of "lady" is simply a matter of being polite, Lakoff answers: "The concept of politeness thus invoked is the politeness used in dignifying or ennobling a concept that normally is not thought of as having dignity or nobility. It is this notion of politeness that explains why we have *cleaning lady*, but not normally *lady doctor*: a doctor does not need to be exalted by conventional expressions: she has dignity enough from her professional status. But a cleaning woman is in a very different situation, in which her occupational category requires ennobling. Then perhaps we can say that the very notion of womanhood, as opposed to manhood, requires ennobling since it lacks inherent dignity of its own; hence the word *woman* requires the existence of a euphemism like *lady*."[16] . . .

Linguistically, we live in a world of professional men and only men; unless the professional is identified as a "lady" or "woman" we assume the person to be a male. As Casey Miller and Kate Swift have observed: "When a woman or girl makes news, her sex is identified at the beginning of a story, if possible in the headline or its equivalent. The assumption, apparently, is that whatever event or action is being reported, a woman's involvement is less common and therefore more newsworthy than a man's. If the story is about achievement, the media have developed a special and extensive vocabulary to avoid the constant repetition of 'woman.' The results, 'Grandmother Wins Nobel Prize,' 'Blonde Hijacks Airliner,' 'Housewife to Run for Congress,' convey the kind of information that would be ludicrous in comparable headlines if the subjects were men."[17]

The nonseriousness and the triviality of women and their accomplishments have been further conveyed in that special language used to describe females in news features which report on their personal and sexual characteristics, a language seldom ever used in news features about men.

More often than not, the woman is identified in terms of her husband, while the story about a man usually makes no reference to his wife. For example, "in the recent discussion of possible Supreme Court nominees, one woman was mentioned prominently. In discussing her general qualifications for the office, and her background, *The New York Times* saw fit to remark on her 'bathing-beauty figure.' Note that is not only a judgment on a physical attribute totally removed from her qualifications for the Supreme Court, but that it is couched in terms of how a man would react to her figure, rather than being merely descriptive. So it is conceivable that a male prospective nominee might (but was not) have been described by the *Times* as 'well-preserved,' or 'athletic,' the reference in this case not invoking a judgment on the part of the opposite sex, and not as 'sexy'; but a woman appointee is described as though an entrant in a beauty contest: even an aspirant to a Supreme Court seat is judged in terms of her physical attractiveness to men."[18]

Commenting on this double standard treatment, one time Presidential press secretary Bill Moyers has said: "The obsolete treatment of women in the press has, I think contributed greatly to the anger many women feel. Why does the press identify Golda Meir as a grandmother but not Georges Pompidou as a grandfather? Why does the press talk of a female politician's hair coloring and dress style, but not the hair dye or tailor used by a Presidential candidate or Senator?"[19] . . .

The language of sexism not only portrays women as nonserious, as trivial, and as the "second sex," but it also contributes to her invisibility. In a world of "chairmen," "spokesmen," "statesmen," "repairmen," et cetera, the woman loses visibility. We know of the Neanderthal Man, the Java Man, and the Cro-Magnon Man, but never have we had a comparable pre-historic woman. The invisible woman remains linguistically invisible as long as "the assumption is that unless otherwise identified, people in general—including doctors and beggars—are men. It is a semantic mechanism that operates to keep women invisible: *man* and *mankind* represent everyone; *he* in generalized use refers to either sex; the 'land where our fathers died' is also the land of our mothers—although they go unsung."[20] . . .

The woman's efforts to achieve self-identity has been further complicated by the "street language" which labels her a sexual child object. She is openly called "babe," "toots," "chick," "doll," et cetera. All of these labels are associated with children, helplessness, and immaturity.

Dictionary definitions tell us a "babe" is "1. a baby; infant; hence, 2. a naive, gullible, or helpless person. 3.[slang], a girl or young woman, especially a pretty one." A "chick" is "1. a young chicken. 2. a young bird. 3. a child: term of endearment." A "tootsy" is "1. a child's or woman's small foot. 2. "toots"; and a "toots" is "[slang], darling, dear: affectionate or playful term of address." If a woman is not a "babe," "toots," or "chick," she can be a "doll." Doll: "1. a children's toy made to resemble a baby, child or grown person. 2. a pretty but rather stupid or silly girl or woman. 3. a pretty child. 4. [slang], any girl or young woman." And if the woman is not labeled any of these, she still can be a "girl." No matter how high in professional status or how old she may be, the woman can always be the "girl."

Three of the definitions of "girl" given by *Webster's New World Dictionary of the American Language* are: "1. a female child. 2. a young, unmarried woman. 3. a female servant." Lakoff has said of the use of the term "girl": "One seldom hears a man past the age of adolescence referred to as a boy, save in expressions like 'going out with boys,' which are meant to suggest an air of adolescent frivolity and irresponsibility. But women of all ages are 'girls'. . . . It may be that this use of *girl* is euphemistic in the sense in which *lady* is an euphemism: in stressing the idea of immaturity, it removes the sexual connotations lurking in women."

All of these terms identifying women with babies and children result in a portrayal of mature females as weak, silly, irresponsible and dependent. The women are infantalized through language.

The language of sexism, like the language of racism, leads to circularity in our thinking and behavior. Our sexist language does affect our attitudes and behavior which in turn affect our language. . . .

NOTES

1. Deborah Rosenfelt and Florence Howe, "Language and Sexism A Note," *MLA Newsletter*, (December 1973), p. 5.
2. *Ibid.*, p. 6.
3. Aileen Hernandez, "The Preening of America," *Star-News* (Pasadena, Calif.), 1971 New Year's edition.
4. Emily Toth, "How Can A Woman MAN the Barricades? Or—Linguistic Sexism Up Against the Wall, *Women: A Journal of Liberation*, 2 (1970), p. 57.
5. *Ibid.*
6. Alma Graham, "The Making of a Nonsexist Dictionary," ETC., 31 (March 1974), p. 63.
7. Cited in Kate Miller and Casey Smith, "De-Sexing the English Language," *Ms.*, (Spring 1972), p. 7.
8. Virginia Kidd, "A Study of the Images Produced Through the Use of the Male Pronoun As the Generic," *Movements: Contemporary Rhetoric and Communication*, 1 (Fall 1971), p. 27.
9. *Ibid.*, p. 28.
10. Rosenfelt and Howe, p. 5.
11. Joseph Fichter, "Holy Father Church," *Commonweal*, 92 (1970), p. 216.
12. Robin Lakoff, "Language and Woman's Place," *Language in Society*, II, p. 57.
13. *Ibid.*, pp. 58–59.
14. *Ibid.*, pp. 59–60.
15. *Ibid.*, p. 60.
16. *Ibid.*, p. 61.
17. Casey Miller and Kate Smith, "One Small Step for Genkind," *New York Times Magazine*, (April 16, 1972), p. 100.
18. Lakoff, p. 65.
19. Cited in Midge Kovacs, "Women: Correcting the Myths," *New York Times*, August 26, 1972, p. 25.
20. Miller and Smith, "One Small Step for Genkind," p. 36.

Beauty and the Beast of Advertising

Jean Kilbourne

"You're a Halston woman from the very beginning," the advertisement proclaims. The model stares provocatively at the viewer, her long blonde hair waving around her face, her bare chest partially covered by two curved bottles that give the illusion of breasts and a cleavage.

The average American is accustomed to blue-eyed blondes seductively touting a variety of products. In this case, however, the blonde is about five years old.

Advertising is an over $100 billion a year industry and affects all of us throughout our lives. We are each exposed to over 2,000 ads a day, constituting perhaps the most powerful educational force in society. The average adult will spend one and one-half years of his/her life watching television commercials. But the ads sell a great deal more than products. They sell values, images and concepts of success and worth, love and sexuality, popularity and normalcy. They tell us who we are and who we should be. Sometimes they sell addictions.

Advertising's foundation and economic lifeblood is the mass media, and the primary purpose of the mass media is to deliver an audience to advertisers, just as the primary purpose of television programs is to deliver an audience for commercials.

Adolescents are particularly vulnerable, however, because they are new and inexperienced consumers and are the prime targets of many advertisements. They are in the process of learning their values and roles and developing their self-concepts. Most teenagers are sensitive to peer pressure and find it difficult to resist or even question the dominant cultural messages perpetuated and reinforced by the media. Mass communication has made possible a kind of nationally distributed peer pressure that erodes private and individual values and standards.

But what does society, and especially teenagers, learn from the advertising messages that proliferate in the mass media? On the most obvious level they learn the stereotypes. Advertising creates a mythical, WASP-oriented world in which no one is ever ugly, overweight, poor, struggling or disabled either physically or mentally (unless you count the housewives who talk to little men in toilet bowls, animated germs in drains or muscle-bound giants clad in white clothing). And it is a world in which people talk only about products.

Housewives or Sex Objects

The aspect of advertising most in need of analysis and change is the portrayal of women. Scientific studies and the most casual viewing yield the same conclusion: Women are shown almost exclusively as housewives or sex objects.

The housewife, pathologically obsessed by cleanliness and lemon-fresh scents, debates cleaning products with herself and worries about her husband's "ring around the collar."

The sex object is a mannequin, a shell. Conventional beauty is her only attribute. She has no lines or wrinkles (which would indicate she had the bad taste and poor judgment to grow older), no scars or blemishes—indeed, she has no pores. She is thin, generally tall and long-legged, and, above all, she is young. All "beautiful" women in advertisements (including minority women), regardless of product or audience, conform to this norm. Women are constantly exhorted to emulate this ideal, to feel ashamed and guilty if they fail, and to feel that their desirability and lovability are contingent upon physical perfection.

Creating Artificiality

The image is artificial and can only be achieved artificially (even the "natural look" requires much preparation and expense). Beauty is something that comes from without; more than one million dollars is spent every hour on cosmetics. Desperate to conform to an ideal and impossible standard, many women go to great lengths to manipulate and change their faces and bodies. A woman is conditioned to view her face as a mask and her body as an object, as *things* separate from and more important than her real self, constantly in need of alteration, improvement, and disguise. She is made to feel dissatisfied with and ashamed of herself, whether she tries to achieve "the look" or not. Objectified constantly by others, she learns to objectify herself. (It is interesting to note that one in five college-age women have an eating disorder.)

"When *Glamour* magazine surveyed its readers in 1984, 75 percent felt too heavy and only 15 percent felt just right. Nearly half of those who were actually underweight reported feeling too fat and wanting to diet. Among a sample of college women, 40 percent felt overweight when only 12 percent actually were too heavy," according to Rita Freedman in her book *Beauty Bound*.

There is evidence that this preoccupation with weight begins at ever-earlier ages for women. According to a recent article in *New Age Journal*, "even grade-school girls are succumbing to stick-like-standards of beauty enforced by a relentless parade of wasp-waisted fashion models, movie stars and pop idols." A study by a University of California professor showed that nearly 80 percent of fourth-grade girls in the Bay Area are watching their weight.

A recent *Wall Street Journal* survey of students in four Chicago-area schools found that more than half the fourth-grade girls were dieting and three-quarters felt they were overweight. One student said, "We don't expect boys to be that handsome.

We take them as they are." Another added, "But boys expect girls to be perfect and beautiful. And skinny."

Dr. Steven Levenkron, author of *The Best Little Girl in the World*, the story of an anorexic, says his blood pressure soars every time he opens a magazine and finds an ad for women's fashions. "If I had my way," he said, "every one of them would have to carry a line saying, 'Caution: This model may be hazardous to your health.'"

Women are also dismembered in commercials, their bodies separated into parts in need of change or improvement. If a woman has "acceptable" breasts, then she must also be sure that her legs are worth watching, her hips slim, her feet sexy, and that her buttocks look nude under her clothes ("like I'm not wearin' nothin'"). This image is difficult and costly to achieve and impossible to maintain (unless you buy the product)—no one is flawless and everyone ages. Growing older is the great taboo. Women are encouraged to remain little girls ("because innocence is sexier than you think"), to be passive and dependent, never to mature. The contradictory message—"sensual, but not too far from innocence"—places women in a double bind; somehow we are supposed to be both sexy and virginal, experienced and naive, seductive and chaste. The disparagement of maturity is, of course, insulting and frustrating to adult women, and the implication that little girls are seductive is dangerous to real children.

Influencing Sexual Attitudes

Young people also learn a great deal about sexual attitudes from the media and from advertising in particular. Advertising's approach to sex is pornographic; it reduces people to objects and de-emphasizes human contact and individuality. This reduction of sexuality to a dirty joke and of people to objects is the real obscenity of the culture. Although the sexual sell, overt and subliminal, is at a fevered pitch in most commercials, there is at the same time a notable absence of sex as an important and profound human activity.

There have been some changes in the images of women. Indeed, a "new woman" has emerged in commercials in recent years. She is generally presented as superwoman, who manages to do all the work at home and on the job (with the help of a product, of course, not of her husband or children or friends), or as the liberated woman, who owes her independence and self-esteem to the products she uses. These new images do not represent any real progress but rather create a myth of progress, an illusion that reduces complex sociopolitical problems to mundane personal ones.

Advertising images do not cause these problems, but they contribute to them by creating a climate in which the marketing of women's bodies—the sexual sell and dismemberment, distorted body image ideal and children as sex objects—is seen as acceptable.

This is the real tragedy, that many women internalize these stereotypes and learn their "limitations," thus establishing a self-fulfilling prophecy. If one accepts these mythical and degrading images, to some extent one actualizes them. By remaining unaware of the profound seriousness of the ubiquitous influence, the redundant message and the subliminal impact of advertisements, we ignore one of the most powerful "educational" forces in the culture—one that greatly affects our self-images, our ability to relate to each other, and effectively destroys any awareness and action that might help to change that climate.

5

Anti-Gay Stereotypes

Richard D. Mohr

A recent Gallup poll found that only one in five Americans reports having a gay acquaintance.[1] This finding is extraordinary given the number of practicing homosexuals in America. Alfred Kinsey's 1948 study of the sex lives of 5000 white males shocked the nation: 37 percent had at least one homosexual experience to orgasm in their adult lives; an additional 13 percent had homosexual fantasies to orgasm; 4 percent were exclusively homosexual in their practices; another 5 percent had virtually no heterosexual experience, and nearly 20 percent had at least as many homosexual as heterosexual experiences.[2] With only slight variations, these figures held across all social categories: region, religion, political belief, class, income, occupation, and education.

Two out of five men one passes on the street have had orgasmic sex with men. Every second family in the country has a member who is essentially homosexual, and many more people regularly have homosexual experiences. Who are homosexuals? They are your friends, your minister, your teacher, your bankteller, your doctor, your mailcarrier, your secretary, your congressional representative, your sibling, parent, and spouse. They are everywhere, virtually all ordinary, virtually all unknown.

What follows? First, the country is profoundly ignorant of the actual experience of gay people. Second, social attitudes and practices that are harmful to gays have a much greater overall negative impact on society than is usually realized. Third, most gay people live in hiding—in the closet—making the "coming out" experience the central fixture of gay consciousness and invisibility the chief social characteristic of gays.

Society's ignorance of gay people is, however, not limited to individuals' lack of personal acquaintance with gays. Stigma against gay people is so strong that even discussions of homosexuality are taboo. This taboo is particularly strong in academe, where it is reinforced by the added fear of the teacher as molester. So even within the hearth of reason irrational forces have held virtually unchallenged and largely unchallengeable sway. The usual sort of clarifying research that might be done on a stigmatized minority has with gays only just begun—haltingly—in history, literature, sociology, and the sciences.

Yet ignorance about gays has not stopped people from having strong opinions about them. The void which ignorance leaves has been filled with stereotypes. Society holds chiefly two groups of antigay stereotypes; the two are an oddly contradictory lot. One set of stereotypes revolves around alleged mistakes in an individual's gender identity: lesbians are women that want to be, or at least look and act like, men—bulldykes, diesel dykes; while gay men are those who want to be, or at least look and act like, women—queens, fairies, limp-wrists, nellies. Gays are "queer," which, remember, means at root not merely weird but chiefly counterfeit—"he's as queer as a three dollar bill." These stereotypes of mismatched or fraudulent genders provide the materials through which gays and lesbians become the butts of ethnic-like jokes. These stereotypes and jokes, though derisive, basically view gays and lesbians as ridiculous.

Another set of stereotypes revolves around gays as a pervasive, sinister, conspiratorial, and corruptive threat. The core stereotype here is the gay person as child molester and, more generally, as sex-crazed maniac. These stereotypes carry with them fears of the very destruction of family and civilization itself. Now, that which is essentially ridiculous can hardly have such a staggering effect. Something must be afoot in this incoherent amalgam.

Sense can be made of this incoherence if the nature of stereotypes is clarified. Stereotypes are not *simply* false generalizations from a skewed sample of cases examined. Admittedly, false generalizing plays a part in most stereotypes a society holds. If, for instance, one takes as one's sample homosexuals who are in psychiatric hospitals or prisons, as was done in nearly all early investigations, not surprisingly one will probably find homosexuals to be of a crazed and criminal cast. Such false generalizations, though, simply confirm beliefs already held on independent grounds, ones that likely led the investigator to the prison and psychiatric ward to begin with. Evelyn Hooker, who in the mid-fifties carried out the first rigorous studies to use nonclinical gays, found that psychiatrists, when presented with results of standard psychological diagnostic tests—but with indications of sexual orientation omitted—were able to do no better than if they had guessed randomly in their attempts to distinguish gay files from nongay ones, even though the psychiatrists believed gays to be crazy and supposed themselves to be experts in detecting craziness.[3] These studies proved a profound embarrassment to the psychiatric establishment, the financial well-being of which was substantially enhanced by 'curing' allegedly insane gays. Eventually the studies contributed to the American Psychiatric Association's dropping homosexuality from its registry of mental illnesses in 1973.[4] Nevertheless, the stereotype of gays as sick continues apace in the mind of America.

False generalizations *help maintain* stereotypes; they do not *form* them. As the history of Hooker's discoveries shows, stereotypes have a life beyond facts. Their origin lies in a culture's ideology—the general system of beliefs by which it lives—and they are sustained across generations by diverse cultural transmissions, hardly any of which, including slang and jokes, even purport to have a scientific basis. Stereotypes, then, are not the products of bad science, but are social constructions that perform central functions in maintaining society's conception of itself.

On this understanding, it is easy to see that the antigay stereotypes surrounding gender identification are chiefly means of reinforcing still powerful gender roles in society. If, as this stereotype presumes (and condemns), one is free to choose one's social roles independently of gender, many guiding social divisions, both domestic and commercial, might be threatened. The socially gender-linked distinctions would blur between breadwinner and homemaker, protector and protected, boss and secretary, doctor and nurse, priest and nun, hero and whore, saint and siren, lord and helpmate, and God and his world. The accusations "fag" and "dyke" (which recent philology has indeed shown to be rooted in slang referring to gender-bending, especially cross-dressing)[5] exist in significant part to keep women in their place and to prevent men from breaking ranks and ceding away theirs.

The stereotypes of gays as child molesters, sex-crazed maniacs, and civilization destroyers function to displace (socially irresolvable) problems from their actual source to a foreign (and so, it is thought, manageable) one. Thus, the stereotype of child molester functions to give the family unit a false sheen of absolute innocence. It keeps the unit from being examined too closely for incest, child abuse, wife-battering, and the terrorism of constant threats. The stereotype teaches that the problems of the family are not internal to it, but external.

Because this stereotype has this central social function, it could not be dislodged even by empirical studies, paralleling Hooker's efforts, that showed heterosexuals to be child molesters to a far greater extent than the actual occurrence of heterosexuals in the general population.[6] But one need not even be aware of such debunking empirical studies in order to see the same cultural forces at work in the social belief that gays are molesters as in its belief that they are crazy. For one can see them now in society's and the media's treatment of current reports of violence, especially domestic violence. When a mother kills her child or a father rapes his daughter—regular Section B fare even in major urbane papers—this is never taken by reporters, columnists, or pundits as evidence that there is something wrong with heterosexuality or with traditional families. These issues are not even raised.

But when a homosexual child molestation is reported it is taken as confirming evidence of the way homosexuals are. One never hears of heterosexual murders, but one regularly reads of "homosexual" ones. Compare the social treatment of Richard Speck's sexually motivated mass murder in 1966 of Chicago nurses with that of John Wayne Gacy's serial murders of Chicago youths. Gacy was in the culture's mind taken as symbolic of gay men in general. To prevent the possibility that The Family was viewed as anything but an innocent victim in this affair, the mainstream press knowingly failed to mention that most of Gacy's adolescent victims were homeless hustlers, even though this was made obvious at his trial.[7] That knowledge would be too much for the six o'clock news and for cherished beliefs.

The stereotype of gays as sex-crazed maniacs functions socially to keep individuals' sexuality contained. For this stereotype makes it look as though the problem of how to address one's considerable sexual drives can and should be answered with repression, for it gives the impression that the cyclone of dangerous psychic forces is *out there* where the fags are, not within one's own breast. With the decline of the stereotype of the black man as raping pillaging marauder (found in such works as *Birth of a Nation, Gone with the Wind,* and *Soul on Ice*), the stereotype of gay men as sex-crazed maniacs has become more aggravated. The stereotype of the sex-crazed threat seems one that society desperately needs to have somewhere in its sexual cosmology.

For the repressed homosexual, this stereotype has an especially powerful allure—by hating it consciously, he subconsciously appears to save himself from himself, at least as long as the ruse does not exhaust the considerable psychic energies required to maintain it, or until, like ultraconservative Congressmen Robert E. Bauman (R-Md.) and Jon C. Hinson (R-Miss.), he is caught importuning hustlers or gentlemen in washrooms.[8] If, as Freud and some of his followers thought, everyone feels an urge for sex partners of both genders, then the fear of gays works to show us that we have not "met the enemy and he is us."[9]

By directly invoking sex acts, this second set of stereotypes is the more severe and serious of the two—one never hears child-molester jokes. These stereotypes are aimed chiefly against men, as in turn stereotypically the more sexed of the genders. They are particularly divisive for they create a very strong division between those conceived as "us" and those conceived as "them." This divide is not so strong in the case of the stereotype of gay men as effeminate. For women (and so the woman-like) after all do have their place. Nonstrident, nonuppity useful ones can even be part of "us," indeed, belong, like "our children," to "us." Thus, in many cultures with overweening gender-identified social roles (like prisons, truckstops, the armed forces, Latin America, and the Islamic world) only passive partners in male couplings are derided as homosexual.[10]

Because "the facts" largely do not matter when it comes to the generation and maintenance of stereotypes, the effects of scientific and academic research and of enlightenment generally will be, at best, slight and gradual in the changing fortunes of gays. If this account of stereotypes holds, society has been profoundly immoral. For its treatment of gays is a grand scale rationalization and moral sleight-of-hand. The problem is not that society's usual standards of evidence and procedure in coming to judgments of social policy have been misapplied to gays, rather when it comes to gays, the standards themselves have simply been ruled out of court and disregarded in favor of mechanisms that encourage unexamined fear and hatred.

Partly because lots of people suppose they do not know a gay person and partly through their willful ignorance of society's workings, people are largely unaware of the many ways in which gays are subject to discrimination in consequence of widespread fear and hatred. Contributing to this social ignorance of discrimination is the difficulty for gay people, as an invisible minority, even to complain of discrimination. For if one is gay, to register a complaint would suddenly target one as a stigmatized person, and so, in the absence of any protections against discrimination, would in turn invite additional discrimination.

Further, many people, especially those who are persistently downtrodden and so lack a firm sense of self to begin with, tend either to blame themselves for their troubles or to view their troubles as a matter of bad luck or as the result of an innocent mistake by others—as anything but an injustice indicating something wrong with society. Alfred Dreyfus went to his grave believing his imprisonment for treason and his degradation from the French military, in which he was the highest ranking Jewish officer, had all just been a sort of clerical error, merely requiring recomputation, rather than what it was—lightning striking a promontory from out of a storm of national bigotry.[11] The recognition of injustice requires doing something to rectify wrong; the recognition of systematic injustices requires doing something about the system, and most people, especially the already beleaguered, simply are not up to the former, let alone the latter.

For a number of reasons, then, discrimination against gays, like rape, goes seriously underreported. What do they experience? First, gays are subject to violence and harassment based simply on their perceived status rather than because of any actions they have performed. A recent extensive study by the National Gay and Lesbian Task Force found that over 90 percent of gays and lesbians had been victimized in some form on the basis of their sexual orientation.[12] Greater than one in five gay men and nearly one in ten lesbians had been punched, hit, or kicked; a quarter of all gays had had objects thrown at them; a third had been chased; a third had been sexually harassed and 14 percent had been spit on—all just for being perceived to be gay.

The most extreme form of antigay violence is queerbashing—where groups of young men target another man who they suppose is gay and beat and kick him unconscious and sometimes to death amid a torrent of taunts and slurs. Such seemingly random but in reality socially encouraged violence has the same social origin and function as lynchings of blacks—to keep a whole stigmatized group in line. As with lynchings of the recent past, the police and courts have routinely averted their eyes, giving their implicit approval to the practice.

Few such cases with gay victims reach the courts. Those that do are marked by inequitable procedures and results. Frequently judges will describe queerbashers as "just All-American Boys." In 1984, a District of Columbia judge handed suspended sentences to queerbashers whose victim had been stalked, beaten, stripped at knife point, slashed, kicked, threatened with castration, and pissed on, because the judge thought the bashers were good boys at heart—after all they went to a religious prep school.[13]

In the summer of 1984, three teenagers hurled a gay man to his death from a bridge in Bangor, Maine. Though the youths could have been tried as adults and normally would have been, given the extreme violence of their crime, they were tried rather as children and will be back on the streets again automatically when they turn twenty-one.[14]

Further, police and juries simply discount testimony from gays.[15] They typically construe assaults on and murders of gays as "justified" self-defense—the killer need only claim his act was a panicked response to a sexual overture.[16] Alternatively, when guilt seems patent, juries will accept highly implausible insanity or other "diminished capacity" defenses. In 1981 a former New York City Transit Authority policeman, later claiming he was just doing the work of God, machine-gunned down nine people, killing two, in two Greenwich Village gay bars. His jury found him innocent due to mental illness.[17] The best known example of a successful "diminished capacity" defense is Dan White's voluntary manslaughter conviction for the 1978 assassination of openly gay San Francisco city councilman Harvey Milk—Hostess Twinkies, his lawyer successfully argued, made him do it.[18]

These inequitable procedures and results collectively show that the life and liberty of gays, like those of blacks, simply count for less than the life and liberty of members of the dominant culture. . . .

NOTES

1. "Public Fears—And Sympathies," *Newsweek*, August 12, 1985, p. 23.

2. Alfred C. Kinsey, et al., *Sexual Behavior in the Human Male* (Philadelphia: Saunders, 1948), pp. 650–51. On the somewhat lower incidences of lesbianism, see Alfred C. Kinsey, et al., *Sexual Behavior in the Human Female* (Philadelphia: Saunders, 1953), pp. 472–75.

3. Evelyn Hooker, "The Adjustment of the Male Overt Homosexual," *Journal of Projective Techniques* (1957) 21:18–31, reprinted in Hendrik M. Ruitenbeck, ed., *The Problem of Homosexuality*, pp. 141–61, epigram quote from p. 149 (New York: Dutton, 1963).

4. See Ronald Bayer, *Homosexuality and American Psychiatry* (New York: Basic Books, 1981).

5. See Wayne Dynes, *Homolexis: A Historical and Cultural Lexicon of Homosexuality* (New York: Gay Academic Union, Gai Saber Monograph No. 4, 1985), s.v. dyke, faggot.

6. For studies showing that gay men are no more likely—indeed, are less likely—than heterosexuals to be child molesters and that the most widespread and persistent sexual abusers of children are the children's fathers, stepfathers or mother's boyfriends, see Vincent De Francis, *Protecting the Child Victim of Sex Crimes Committed by Adults* (Denver: The American Humane Association, 1969), pp. vii, 38, 69–70; A. Nicholas Groth, "Adult Sexual Orientation and Attraction to Underage Persons," *Archives of Sexual Behavior* (1978) 7:175–81; Mary J. Spencer, "Sexual Abuse of Boys," *Pediatrics* (July 1986) 78(1):133–38.

7. See Lawrence Mass, "Sanity in Chicago: The Trial of John Wayne Gacy and American Psychiatry," *Christopher Street* [New York] (June 1980) 4(7):26. See also Terry Sullivan, *Killer Clown* (New York: Grosset & Dunlap, 1983, pp. 219–25, 315–16; Tim Cahill, *Buried Dreams* (Toronto: Bantam Books, 1986), pp. 318, 352–53, 368–69.

8. For Robert Bauman's account of his undoing, see his autobiography, *The Gentleman from Maryland* (New York: Arbor House, 1986).

9. On Freud, see Timothy F. Murphy, "Freud Reconsidered: Bisexuality, Homosexuality, and Moral Judgment," *Journal of Homosexuality* (1984) 9(2–3):65–77.

10. On prisons, see Wayne Wooden and Jay Parker, *Men Behind Bars: Sexual Exploitation in Prison* (New York: Plenum, 1982). On the armed forces, see George Chauncey Jr.,

"Christian Brotherhood or Sexual Perversion? Homosexual Identities and the Construction of Sexual Boundaries in the World War One Era," *Journal of Social History* (1985) 19:189–211.

11. See Jean-Denis Bredin, *The Affair: The Case of Alfred Dreyfus*, trans. Jeffrey Mehlman (1983; New York: George Braziller, 1986), pp. 486–96.

12. National Gay and Lesbian Task Force, *Anti-Gay/Lesbian Victimization* (New York: National Gay and Lesbian Task Force, 1984). See also, "Anti-Gay Violence," Subcommitee on Criminal Justice, Committee on the Judiciary, House of Representatives, 99th Congress, 2nd Session, October 9, 1986, serial no. 132.

13. "Two St. John's Students Given Probation in Assault on Gay," *The Washington Post*, May 15, 1984, p. I.

The 1980 Mariel boatlift, which included thousands of gays escaping Cuban internment camps, inspired U.S. Federal District Judge A. Andrew Hauk in open court to comment of a Mexican illegal alien caught while visiting his resident alien daughter: "And he isn't even a fag like all these faggots we're letting in." *The Advocate* [Los Angeles], November 27, 1980, no. 306, p. 15. Cf. "Gay Refugees Tell of Torture, Oppression in Cuba," *The Advocate*, August 21, 1980, no. 299, pp. 15–16.

14. See *The New York Times*, September 17, 1984, p. D17 and October 6, 1984, p. 6.

15. John D'Emilio writes of the trial of seven police officers caught in a gay bar shakedown racket: "The defense lawyer cast aspersions on the credibility of the prosecution witnesses . . . and deplored a legal system in which 'the most notorious homosexual may testify against a policeman.' Persuaded by this line of argument, the jury acquitted all of the defendants." *Sexual Politics, Sexual Communities: The Making of a Homosexual Minority in the United States, 1940–1970* (Chicago: University of Chicago Press, 1983), p. 183.

16. See for discussion and examples, Pat Califia, "'Justifiable' Homicide?" *The Advocate*, May 12, 1983, no. 367, p. 12 and Robert G. Bagnall, et al., "Burdens on Gay Litigants and Bias in the Court System: Homosexual Panic, Child Custody, and Anonymous Parties," *Harvard Civil Rights-Civil Liberties Law Review* (1984) 19:498–515.

17. *The New York Times*, July 25, 1981, p. 27, and July 26, 1981, p. 25.

18. See Randy Shilts, *The Mayor of Castro Street: The Life and Times of Harvey Milk* (New York: St. Martin's, 1982), pp. 308–25.

6

Deconstructing the Underclass

Herbert Gans

A Matter of Definition?

Buzzwords for the undeserving poor are hardly new, for in the past the poor have been termed paupers, rabble, white trash, and the dangerous classes. Today, however, Americans do not use such harsh terms in their public discourse, whatever people may say to each other in private. Where possible, euphemisms are employed, and if they are from the academy, so much the better. A string of these became popular in the 1960s; the most famous is Oscar Lewis's anthropological concept *culture of poverty*, a term that became his generation's equivalent of underclass.

When Gunnar Myrdal invented or reinvented the term underclass in his 1962 book *Challenge to Affluence*, he used the word as a purely economic concept, to describe the chronically unemployed, underemployed, and underemployables being created by what we now call the post-industrial economy. He was thinking of people being driven to the margins, or entirely out, of the modern economy, here and elsewhere; but his intellectual and policy concern was with reforming that economy, not with changing or punishing the people who were its victims.

Some other academics, this author included, used the term with Myrdal's definition in the 1960s and 1970s. However, gradually the users shifted from Myrdal's concern with unemployment to poverty, so that by the late 1970s social scientists had begun to identify the underclass with acute or persistent poverty rather than joblessness. Around the same time a very different definition of the underclass also emerged that has become the most widely used, and is also the most dangerous.

That definition has two novel elements. The first is racial, for users of this definition see the underclass as being almost entirely black and Hispanic. Second, it adds a number of behavioral patterns to an economic definition—and almost always these patterns involve behavior thought to be undeserving by the definers.

Different definers concentrate on somewhat different behavior patterns, but most include antisocial or otherwise harmful behavior, such as crime. Many definers also focus on various patterns that are *deviant* or aberrant from what they consider middle class norms, but that in fact are not automatically or always harmful, such as common law marriage. Some definers even measure membership in the underclass by deviant answers to public opinion poll questions. . . .

In the past five years the term's diverse definitions have remained basically unchanged, although the defining attempt itself has occasioned a very lively, often angry, debate among scholars. Many researchers have accepted much or all of the now-dominant behavioral definition; some have argued for a purely economic one, like Myrdal's; and some—this author included—have felt that the term has taken on so many connotations of undeservingness and blameworthiness that it has become hopelessly polluted in meaning, ideological overtone and implications, and should be dropped—with the issues involved studied via other concepts. Basically the debate has involved positions usually associated with the Right and the Left, partisans of the former arguing that the underclass is the product of the unwillingness of the black poor to adhere to the American work ethic, among other cultural deficiencies, and the latter claiming that the underclass is a consequence of the development of the post-industrial economy, which no longer needs the unskilled poor.

The debate has swirled in part around William J. Wilson, the University of Chicago sociologist and author of *The Truly Disadvantaged* (1987), who is arguably the most prominent analyst of the underclass in the 1980s. He focuses entirely on the black underclass and insists that this underclass exists mainly because of large-scale and harmful changes in the labor market, and its resulting spatial concentration as well as the isolation of such areas from the more affluent parts of the black community. One of his early definitions also included a reference to aberrant behavior patterns, although his most recent one, offered in November 1989, centers around the notion of "weak attachment to the labor force," an idea that seems nearly to coincide with Myrdal's, especially since Wilson attributes that weakness to faults in the economy rather than in the jobless.

Wilson's work has inspired a lot of new research, not only about the underclass but about poverty in general, and has made poverty research funding, public and private, available again after a long drought. Meanwhile, various scholars have tried to resolve or reorient the political debate, but without much luck, for eventually the issue always boils down to whether the fault for being poor and the responsibility for change should be assigned more to poor people or more to the economy and the state. At the same time, journalistic use of the so-called behavioral definition of the underclass has increased—and so much so that there is a danger of researchers and policy analysts being carried along by the popularity of this definition of the term in the public discourse. . . .

The Power of Buzzwords and Labels

The behavioral definition of the underclass, which in essence proposes that some very poor people are somehow to be selected for separation from the rest of society and henceforth treated as especially undeserving, harbors many dangers—for their civil liberties and ours, for example, for democracy, and for the integration of society. But the rest of this essay will concentrate on what seem to me to be the major dangers for planners. The *first* danger of the term is its unusual power as a buzzword. It is a handy euphemism; while it seems inoffensively technical on the surface, it hides within it all the moral opprobrium Americans have long felt toward those poor people who have been judged to be undeserving. Even when it is being used by journalists, scholars, and others as a technical term, it carries with it this judgmental baggage. . . .

A *second* and related danger of the term is its use as a racial codeword that subtly hides anti-black and anti-Hispanic feelings. A codeword of this kind fits in with the tolerant public discourse of our time, but it also submerges and may further repress racial—and class—antagonisms that continue to exist, yet are sometimes not expressed until socio-political boiling points are reached. Racial and class codewords—and codewords of any kind—get in the way of planners, however, because the citizenry may read codewords even though planners are writing analytical concepts.

A *third* danger of the term is its flexible character. Given the freedom of definition available in a democracy, anyone can decide, or try to persuade others, that yet additional people should be included in the underclass. For example, it is conceivable that in a city, region, or country with a high unemployment rate, powerless competitors for jobs, such as illegal immigrants or even legal but recently arrived workers, might be added to the list of undeserving people. . . .

The *fourth* danger of the term, a particularly serious one, is that it is a synthesizing notion—or what William Kornblum has more aptly called a lumping one—that covers a number of different people. Like other synthesizing notions that have moved far beyond the researchers' journals, it has also become a stereotype. Stereotypes are lay generalizations that are necessary in a very diversified society, and are useful when they are more or less accurate. When they are not, however, or when they are also judgmental terms, they turn into *labels*, to be used by some people to judge, and usually to stigmatize, other people, often those with less power or prestige. . . .

Insofar as poor people keep up with the labels the rest of society sticks on them, they are aware of the latest one. We do not all know the "street-level" consequences of stigmatizing labels, but they cannot be good. One of the likely, and most dangerous, consequences of labels is that they can become self-fulfilling prophecies. People publicly described as members of the underclass may begin to feel that they *are* members of such a class and are therefore unworthy in a new way. At the least, they now have to fight against yet another threat to their self-respect, not to mention another reason for feeling that society would just as soon have them disappear.

More important perhaps, people included in the underclass are quickly treated accordingly in their relations with the private and public agencies in which, like the rest of us, they are embedded—from workplaces, welfare agencies, and schools to the police and the courts. We know from social research that teachers with negative images of their pupils do not expect them to succeed and thus make sure, often unconsciously, that they do not; likewise, boys from single parent families who are picked up by the police are often thought to be wild and therefore guilty because they are assumed to lack male parental control. We know also that areas associated with the underclass do not get the same level of services as more affluent areas. After all, these populations are not likely to protest. . . .

Social Policy Implications

The remaining dangers are more directly relevant for planners, other policy researchers, and policy makers. The most general one, and the *fifth* on my list, is the term's interference with antipoverty policy and other kinds of planning. This results in part from the fact that underclass is a quite distinctive synthesizing term that lumps together a variety of highly diverse people who need different kinds of help. Categorizing them all with one term, and a buzzword at that, can be disastrous, especially if the political climate should demand that planners formulate a single "underclass policy." Whether one thinks of the poorest of the poor as having problems or as making problems for others, or both, they cannot be planned for with a single policy. For example, educational policies to prevent young people from dropping out of school, especially the few good ones in poor areas, have nothing to do with housing policies for dealing with various kinds of homelessness and the lack of affordable dwellings. Such policies are in turn different from programs to reduce street crime, and from methods of discouraging the very poor from escaping into the addictions of drugs, alcohol, mental illness, or pentecostal religion—which has its own harmful side effects. To be sure, policies relevant to one problem may have positive overlaps for another, but no single policy works for all the problems of the different poverty-stricken populations. Experts who claim one policy can do it all, like education, are simply wrong.

This conclusion applies even to jobs and income grant policies. Although it is certain that all of the problems blamed on the people assigned to the underclass would be helped considerably by policies to reduce sharply persistent joblessness and poverty, *and generally before other programs are implemented*, these policies also have limits. While all poor people need economic help, such help will not alone solve other problems some of them have or make for others. Although the middle class does not mug, neither do *the* poor; only a small number of poor male youngsters and young adults do so. Other causal factors are also involved, and effective antipoverty planning has to be based on some understanding of these factors and how to overcome them. Lumping concepts like the underclass can only hurt this effort.

A related or *sixth* danger stems from the persuasive capacity of concepts or buzzwords. These terms may become so *reified* through their use that people think they represent actual groups or aggregates, and may also begin to believe that being in what is, after all, an imaginary group is a *cause* of the characteristics included in its definition. Sometimes journalists and even scholars—especially those of conservative bent—appear to think that becoming very poor and acting in antisocial or deviant ways is an *effect* of being in the underclass. When the underclass becomes a causal term, however, especially on a widespread basis, planners, as well as politicians and citizens, are in trouble; sooner or later, someone will argue that the only policy solution is to lock up everyone described as an underclass member.

Similar planning problems develop if and when the reification of a term leads to its being assigned *moral* causality. Using notions that blame victims may help the blamers to feel better by blowing off the steam of righteous indignation, but it does not eliminate the problems very poor people have or make. Indeed, those who argue that all people are entirely responsible for what they do sidestep the morally and otherwise crucial issue of determining how much responsibility should be assigned to people who lack resources, who are therefore under unusual stress, and who lack effective choices in many areas of life in which even moderate income people can choose relatively freely. . . .

The *seventh* danger of the term, and one also particularly salient for planners, stems from the way the underclass has been analyzed. As already noted, some researchers have tried to identify underclass neighborhoods. Planners must be especially sensitive to the dangers of the underclass neighborhood notion, because, once statistically defined "neighborhoods," or even sets of adjacent census tracts, are marked with the underclass label, the politicians who make the basic land use decisions in the community may propose a variety of harmful policies, such as moving all of a city's homeless into such areas, or declaring them ripe for urban renewal because of the undeservingness of the population. Recall that this is how much of the federal urban renewal of the 1950s and 1960s was justified. In addition, neighborhood policies generally rest on the assumption that people inside the boundaries of such areas are more homogeneous than they in fact are, and that they remain inside boundaries that are more often nothing but lines on a map. Since very poor people tend to suffer more from public policies than they benefit, and since they have fewer defenses than more affluent people against harmful policies, "neighborhood policies" may hurt more often than they will help.

A related danger—and my *eighth*—stems from William J. Wilson's "concentration and isolation" hypotheses. Wilson argues that the economic difficulties of the very poorest blacks are compounded by the fact that as the better-off blacks move out, the poorest are more and more concentrated, having only other very poor people, and the few institutions that minister to them, as neighbors. This concentration causes social isolation, among other things, Wilson suggests, because the very poor are now isolated from access to the people, job networks, role models, institutions, and other connections that might help them escape poverty.

Wilson's hypotheses, summarized all too briefly here, are now being accepted as dogma by many outside the research community. Fortunately, they are also being tested in a number of places, but until they are shown to be valid, planners should probably go slowly with designing action programs—especially programs to reduce concentration. In the minimal-vacancy housing markets in which virtually all poor people live, such a policy might mean having to find a new, and surely more costly, dwelling unit, or having to double up with relatives, or in some cases being driven into shelters or into the streets. Even if working- and middle-class areas were willing to accept relocatees from deconcentrated areas, a response that seems unlikely, the relocatees could not afford to live in such areas—although many would flourish if they had the money to do so. Meanwhile, the dysfunctions of dispersal may be as bad as those of overconcentration, not because the latter has any virtues, but because, until an effective jobs-and-income-grants program has gone into operation, requiring very poor people to move away from the neighborly support structures they *do* have may deprive them of their only resources.

While it may be risky to attempt deconcentration at this stage, it is worth trying to reduce isolation. One form of isolation, the so-called urban-suburban mismatch between jobless workers residing in cities and available suburban jobs, is already being attacked again, which is all to the good. Perhaps something has been learned from the failures of the 1960s to reduce the mismatch. We must bear in mind, however, that in some or perhaps many cases the physical mismatch is only a cover for class and racial discrimination, and the widespread unwillingness of white suburban employers—and white workers—to have black coworkers. . . .

The *ninth* danger is inherent in the concept of an underclass. While it assumes that the people assigned to the underclass are poor, the term itself sidesteps issues of poverty. It also permits analysts to ignore the dramatic recent increases in certain kinds of poverty, or persisting poverty, and hence the need for resuming effective antipoverty programs. For example, terms like underclass make it easier for conservative researchers to look at the homeless mainly as mentally ill or the victims of rent control, and frees them of any need to discuss the disappearance of jobs, SROs, and other low income housing.

Indeed, to the extent that the underclass notion is turned into a synonym for the undeserving poor, the political conditions for reinstituting effective antipoverty policy are removed. If the underclass is undeserving, then the government's responsibility is limited to beefing up the courts and other punitive agencies and institutions that try to isolate the underclass and protect the rest of society from it. Conversely, the moral imperative to help the poor through the provision of jobs and income grants is reduced. Describing the poor as undeserving has long been an effective if immoral short-term approach to tax reduction. . . .

NOTES

I am grateful to Michael Katz for his helpful comments on an earlier draft of this essay.

Kornblum, William. 1984. Lumping the Poor: What *Is* the Underclass. *Dissent*. September: 295–302.

Lewis, Oscar. 1969. The Culture of Poverty. In *On Understanding Poverty*, edited by Daniel P. Moynihan. New York: Basic.

Myrdal, Gunnar. 1962. *The Challenge to Affluence*. New York: Pantheon.

Wilson, William J. 1987. *The Truly Disadvantaged: The Inner City, the Underclass, and Public Policy*. Chicago: University of Chicago Press.

7

Blaming the Victim

William Ryan

Twenty years ago, Zero Mostel used to do a sketch in which he impersonated a Dixiecrat Senator conducting an investigation of the origins of World War II. At the climax of the sketch, the Senator boomed out, in an excruciating mixture of triumph and suspicion, "What was Pearl Harbor *doing* in the Pacific?" This is an extreme example of Blaming the Victim.

Twenty years ago, we could laugh at Zero Mostel's caricature. In recent years, however, the same process has been going on every day in the arena of social problems, public health, anti-poverty programs, and social welfare. A philosopher might analyze this process and prove that, technically, it is comic. But it is hardly ever funny.

Consider some victims. One is the miseducated child in the slum school. He is blamed for his own miseducation. He is said to contain within himself the causes of his inability to read and write well. The shorthand phrase is "cultural deprivation," which, to those in the know, conveys what they allege to be inside information: that the poor child carries a scanty pack of cultural baggage as he enters school. He doesn't know about books and magazines and newspapers, they say. (No books in the home; the mother fails to subscribe to *Reader's Digest*.) They say that if he talks at all—an unlikely event since slum parents don't talk to their children—he certainly doesn't talk correctly. (Lower-class dialect spoken here, or even—God forbid!—Southern Negro.) (*Ici on parle nigra.*) If you can manage to get him to sit in a chair, they say, he squirms and looks out the window. (Impulse-ridden, these kids, motoric rather than verbal.) In a word he is "disadvantaged" and "socially deprived," they say, and this, of course, accounts for his failure (*his* failure, they say) to learn much in school.

Note the similarity to the logic of Zero Mostel's Dixiecrat Senator. What is the culturally deprived child *doing* in the school? What is wrong with the victim? In pursuing this logic, no one remembers to ask questions about the collapsing buildings and torn textbooks, the frightened, insensitive teachers, the six additional desks in the room, the blustering, frightened principals, the relentless segregation, the callous administrator, the irrelevant curriculum, the bigoted or cowardly members of the school board, the insulting history book, the stingy taxpayers, the fairy-tale readers, or the self-serving faculty of the local teachers' college. We are encouraged to confine our attention to the child and to dwell on all his alleged defects. Cultural deprivation becomes an omnibus explanation for the educational disaster area known as the inner-city school. This is Blaming the Victim.

Pointing to the supposedly deviant Negro family as the "fundamental weakness of the Negro community" is another way to blame the victim. Like "cultural deprivation," "Negro family" has become a shorthand phrase with stereotyped connotations of matriarchy, fatherlessness, and pervasive illegitimacy. Growing up in the "crumbling" Negro family is supposed to account for most of the racial evils in America. Insiders have the word, of course, and know that this phrase is supposed to evoke images of growing up with a long-absent or never-present father (replaced from time to time perhaps by a series of transient lovers) and with bossy women ruling the roost, so that the children are irreparably damaged. This refers particularly to the poor, bewildered male children, whose psyches are fatally wounded and who are never, alas, to learn the trick of becoming upright, downright, forthright all-American boys. Is it any wonder the Negroes cannot achieve equality? From such families! And, again, by focusing our attention on the Negro family as the apparent *cause* of racial inequality, our eye is diverted. Racism, discrimination, segregation, and the powerlessness of the ghetto are subtly, but thoroughly, downgraded in importance.

The generic process of Blaming the Victim is applied to almost every American problem. The miserable health care of the poor is explained away on the grounds that the victim has poor motivation and lacks health information. The problems of slum housing are traced to the characteristics of tenants who are labeled as "Southern rural migrants" not yet "acculturated" to life in the big city. The "multiproblem" poor, it is claimed, suffer the psychological effects of impoverishment, the "culture of poverty," and the deviant value system of the lower classes; consequently, though unwittingly, they cause their own troubles. From such a viewpoint, the obvious fact that poverty is primarily an absence of money is easily overlooked or set aside.

The growing number of families receiving welfare are fallaciously linked together with the increased number of illegitimate children as twin results of promiscuity and sexual abandon among members of the lower orders. Every important social problem—crime, mental illness, civil disorder, unemployment—has been analyzed within the framework of the victim-blaming ideology. . . .

I have been listening to the victim-blamers and pondering their thought processes for a number of years. That process is often very subtle. Victim-blaming is cloaked in kindness and concern, and bears all the trappings and statistical furbelows of scientism; it is obscured by a perfumed haze of humanitarianism. In observing the process of Blaming the Victim, one tends to be confused and disoriented because those who practice this art display a deep concern for the victims that is quite genuine. In this way, the new ideology is very different from the open prejudice and reactionary tactics of the old days. Its adherents include sympathetic social scientists with social consciences in good working order, and liberal politicians with a genuine commitment to reform. They are very careful to dissociate themselves from vulgar Calvinism or crude racism; they indignantly condemn any notions of innate wickedness or genetic defect. "The Negro is *not born* inferior," they shout apoplectically. "Force of circumstance," they explain in reasonable tones, "has *made* him inferior." And they dismiss with self-righteous contempt any claims that the poor man in America is plainly unworthy or shiftless or enamored of idleness. No, they say, he is "caught in the cycle of poverty." He is trained to be poor by his culture and his family life, endowed by his environment (perhaps by his ignorant mother's outdated style of toilet training) with those unfortunately unpleasant characteristics that make him ineligible for a passport into the affluent society.

Blaming the Victim is, of course, quite different from old-fashioned conservative ideologies. The latter simply dismissed victims as inferior, genetically defective, or morally unfit; the emphasis is on the intrinsic, even hereditary, defect. The former shifts its emphasis to the environmental causation. The old-fashioned conservative could hold firmly to the belief that the oppressed and the victimized were born that way—"that way" being defective or inadequate in character or ability. The new ideology attributes defect and inadequacy to the malignant nature of poverty, injustice, slum life, and racial difficulties. The stigma that marks the victim and accounts for his victimization is an acquired stigma, a stigma of social, rather than genetic, origin. But the stigma, the defect, the fatal difference—though derived in the past from environmental forces—is still located *within* the victim, inside his skin. With such an elegant formulation, the humanitarian can have it both ways. He can, all at the same time, concentrate his charitable interest on the defects of the victim, condemn the vague social and environmental stresses that produced the defect (some time ago), and ignore the continuing effect of victimizing social forces (right now). It is a brilliant ideology for justifying a perverse form of social action designed to change, not society, as one might expect, but rather society's victim.

As a result, there is a terrifying sameness in the programs that arise from this kind of analysis. In education, we have programs of "compensatory education" to build up the skills and attitudes of the ghetto child, rather than structural changes in the schools. In race relations, we have social engineers who think up ways of "strengthening" the Negro family, rather than methods of eradicating racism. In health care, we develop new programs to provide health information (to correct the supposed ignorance of the poor) and to reach out and discover cases of untreated illness and disability (to compensate for their supposed unwillingness to seek treatment). Meanwhile, the gross inequities of our medical care delivery systems are left completely unchanged. As we might expect, the logical outcome of analyzing social problems in terms of the deficiencies of the victim is the development of programs aimed at correcting those deficiencies. The formula for action becomes extraordinarily simple: change the victim.

All of this happens so smoothly that it seems downright rational. First, identify a social problem. Second, study those affected by the problem and discover in what ways they are different from the rest of us as a consequence of deprivation and injustice. Third, define the differences as the cause of the social problem itself. Finally, of course, assign a government bureaucrat to invent a humanitarian action program to correct the differences.

Now no one in his right mind would quarrel with the assertion that social problems are present in abundance and are readily identifiable. God knows it is true that when hundreds of thousands of poor children drop out of school—or even graduate from school—they are barely literate. After spending some ten thousand hours in the company of professional educators, these children appear to have learned very little. The fact of failure in their education is undisputed. And the racial situation in America is usually acknowledged to be a number one item on the nation's agenda. Despite years of marches, commissions, judicial decisions, and endless legislative remedies, we are confronted with unchanging or even widening racial differences in achievement. In addition, despite our assertions that Americans get the best health care in the world, the poor stubbornly remain unhealthy. They lose more work because of illness, have more carious teeth, lose more babies as a result of both miscarriage and infant death, and die considerably younger than the well-to-do.

The problems are there, and there in great quantities. They make us uneasy. Added together, these disturbing signs reflect inequality and a puzzlingly high level of unalleviated distress in America totally inconsistent with our proclaimed ideals and our enormous wealth. This thread—this rope—of inconsistency stands out so visibly in the fabric of American life, that it is jarring to the eye. And this must be explained, to the satisfaction of our conscience as well as our patriotism. Blaming the Victim is an ideal, almost painless, evasion.

The second step in applying this explanation is to look sympathetically at those who "have" the problem in question, to separate them out and define them in some way as a special group, a group that is *different* from the population in general. This is a crucial and essential step in the process, for that difference is in itself hampering and maladaptive. The Different Ones are seen as less competent, less skilled, less knowing—in short, less human. The ancient Greeks deduced from a single characteristic, a difference in language, that the barbarians—that is, the "babblers" who spoke a strange tongue;—were wild, uncivilized, dangerous, rapacious, uneducated, lawless, and, indeed, scarcely more than animals. Automatically labeling strangers as savages, weird and inhuman creatures (thus explaining difference by exaggerating difference) not infrequently justifies mistreatment, enslavement, or even extermination of the Different Ones.

Blaming the Victim depends on a very similar process of identification (carried out, to be sure, in the most kindly, philanthropic, and intellectual manner) whereby the victim of social problems is identified as strange, different—in other words, as a barbarian, a savage. Discovering savages, then, is an essential component of, and prerequisite to, Blaming the Victim, and the art of Savage Discovery is a core skill that must be acquired by all aspiring Victim Blamers. They must learn how to demonstrate that the poor, the black, the ill, the jobless, the slum tenants, are different and strange. They must learn to conduct or interpret the research that shows how "these people" think in different forms, act in different patterns, cling to different values, seek different goals, and learn different truths. Which is to say that they are strangers, barbarians, savages. This is how the distressed and disinherited are redefined in order to make it possible for us to look at society's problems and to attribute their causation to the individuals affected. . . .

Blaming the Victim can take its place in a long series of American ideologies that have rationalized cruelty and injustice.

Slavery, for example, was justified—even praised—on the basis of a complex ideology that showed quite conclusively how useful slavery was to society and how uplifting it was for the slaves.[1] Eminent physicians could be relied upon to provide the biological justification for slavery since after all, they said, the slaves were a separate species—as, for example, cattle are a separate species. No one in his right mind would dream of freeing the cows and fighting to abolish the ownership of cattle. In the view of the average American of 1825, it was important to preserve slavery, not simply because it was in accord with his own group interests (he was not fully aware of that), but because reason and logic showed clearly to the reasonable and intelligent man that slavery was good. In order to persuade a good and moral man to *do* evil, then, it is not necessary first to persuade him to *become* evil. It is only necessary to teach him that he is doing good. No one, in the words of a legendary newspaperman, thinks of himself as a son of a bitch.

In late-nineteenth-century America there flowered another ideology of injustice that seemed rational and just to the decent, progressive person. But Richard Hofstadter's analysis of the phenomenon of Social Darwinism[2] shows clearly its functional role in the preservation of the *status quo*. One can scarcely imagine a better fit than the one between this ideology and the purposes and actions of the robber barons, who descended like piranha fish on the America of this era and picked its bones clean. Their extraordinarily unethical operations netted them not only hundreds of millions of dollars but also, perversely, the adoration of the nation. Behavior that would be, in any more rational land (including today's America), more than enough to have landed them all in jail, was praised as the very model of a captain of modern industry. And the philosophy that justified their thievery was such that John D. Rockefeller could actually stand up and preach it in church. Listen as he speaks in, of all places, Sunday school: "The growth of a large business is merely a survival of the fittest. . . . The American Beauty rose can be produced in the splendor and fragrance which bring cheer to its beholder only by sacrificing the early buds which grow up around it. This is not an evil tendency in business. It is merely the working-out of a law of nature and a law of God."[3]

This was the core of the gospel, adapted analogically from Darwin's writings on evolution. Herbert Spencer and, later, William Graham Sumner and other beginners in the social sciences considered Darwin's work to be directly applicable to social processes: ultimately as a guarantee that life was progressing toward perfection but, in the short run, as a justification for an absolutely uncontrolled laissez-faire economic system. The central concepts of "survival of the fittest," "natural selection," and "gradualism" were exalted in Rockefeller's preaching to the status of laws of God and Nature. Not only did this ideology justify the criminal rapacity of those who rose to the top of the industrial heap, defining them automatically as naturally superior (this was bad enough), but at the same time it also required that those at the bottom of the heap be labeled as patently *unfit*—a label based solely on their position in society. According to the law of natural selection, they should be, in Spencer's judgment, eliminated. "The whole effort of nature is to get rid of such, to clear the world of them and make room for better."

For a generation, Social Darwinism was the orthodox doctrine in the social sciences, such as they were at that time. Opponents of this ideology were shut out of respectable intellectual life. The philosophy that enabled John D. Rockefeller to justify himself self-righteously in front of a class of Sunday school children was not the product of an academic quack or a marginal crackpot philosopher. It came directly from the lectures and books of leading intellectual figures of the time, occupants of professorial chairs at Harvard and Yale. Such is the power of an ideology that so neatly fits the needs of the dominant interests of society.

If one is to think about ideologies in America in 1970, one must be prepared to consider the possibility that a body of ideas that might seem almost self-evident is, in fact, highly distorted and highly selective; one must allow that the inclusion of a specific formulation in every freshman sociology text does not guarantee that the particular formulation represents abstract Truth rather than group interest. It is important not to delude ourselves into thinking that ideological monstrosities were constructed by monsters. They were not; they are not. They are developed through a process that shows every sign of being valid scholarship, complete with tables of numbers, copious footnotes, and scientific terminology. Ideologies are quite often academically and socially respectable and in many instances hold positions of exclusive validity, so that disagreement is considered unrespectable or radical and risks being labeled as irresponsible, unenlightened, or trashy.

Blaming the Victim holds such a position. It is central in the mainstream of contemporary American social thought, and its ideas pervade our most crucial assumptions so thoroughly that they are hardly noticed. Moreover, the fruits of this ideology appear to be fraught with altruism and humanitarianism, so it is hard to believe that it has principally functioned to block social change.

A major pharmaceutical manufacturer, as an act of humanitarian concern, has distributed copies of a large poster warning, "LEAD PAINT CAN KILL!" The poster, featuring a photograph of the face of a charming little girl, goes on to explain that if children *eat* lead paint, it can poison them, they can develop serious symptoms, suffer permanent brain damage, even die. The health department of a major American city has put out a coloring book that provides the same information. While the poster urges parents to prevent their children from eating paint, the coloring book is more vivid. It labels as neglectful and thoughtless the mother who does not keep her infant under constant surveillance to keep it from eating paint chips.

Now, no one would argue against the idea that it is important to spread knowledge about the danger of eating paint in order that parents might act to forestall their children from doing so. But to campaign against lead paint *only* in these terms is destructive and misleading and, in a sense, an effective way to support and agree with slum landlords—who define the problem of lead poisoning in precisely these terms.

This is an example of applying an exceptionalistic solution to a universalistic problem. It is not accurate to say that lead poisoning results from the actions of individual neglectful mothers. Rather, lead poisoning is a social phenomenon supported by a number of social mechanisms, one of the most tragic by-products of the systematic toleration of slum housing. In New Haven, which has the highest reported rate of lead poisoning in the country, several small children have died and many others have incurred irreparable brain damage as a result of eating peeling paint. In several cases, when the landlord failed to make repairs, poisonings have occurred time and again through a succession of tenancies. And the major reason for the landlord's neglect of this problem was that the city agency responsible for enforcing the housing code did nothing to make him correct this dangerous condition.

The cause of the poisoning is the lead in the paint on the walls of the apartment in which the children live. The presence of the lead is illegal. To use lead paint in a residence is illegal; to permit lead paint to be exposed in a residence is illegal. It is not only illegal, it is potentially criminal since the housing code does provide for criminal penalties. The general problem of lead poisoning, then, is more accurately analyzed as the result of a systematic program of lawbreaking by one interest group in the community, with the toleration and encouragement of the public authority charged with enforcing that law. To ignore these continued and repeated law violations, to ignore the fact that the supposed law enforcer actually cooperates in lawbreaking, and then to load a burden of guilt on the mother of a dead or dangerously ill child is an egregious distortion of reality. And to do so *under the guise* of public-spirited and humanitarian service to the community is intolerable.

But this is how Blaming the Victim works. The righteous humanitarian concern displayed by the drug company, with its poster, and the health department, with its coloring book, is a genuine concern, and this is a typical feature of Blaming the Victim. Also typical is the swerving away from the central target that requires systematic change and, instead, focusing in on the individual affected. The ultimate effect is always to distract attention from the basic causes and to leave the primary social injustice untouched. And, most telling, the proposed remedy for the problem is, of course, to work on the victim himself. Prescriptions for cure, as written by the Savage Discovery set, are invariably conceived to revamp and revise the victim, never to change the surrounding circumstances. They want to change his attitudes, alter his values, fill up his cultural deficits, energize his apathetic soul, cure his character defects, train him and polish him and woo him from his savage ways.

Isn't all of this more subtle and sophisticated than such old-fashioned ideologies as Social Darwinism? Doesn't the change from brutal ideas about survival of the fit (and the expiration of the unfit) to kindly concern about characterological defects (brought about by stigmas of social origin) seem like a substantial step forward?

Hardly. It is only a substitution of terms. The old, reactionary exceptionalistic formulations are replaced by new progressive, humanitarian exceptionalistic formulations. In education, the outmoded and unacceptable concept of racial or class differences in basic inherited intellectual ability simply gives way to the new notion of cultural deprivation: there is very little functional difference between these two ideas. In taking a look at the phenomenon of poverty, the old concept of unfitness or idleness or laziness is replaced by the newfangled theory of the culture of poverty. In race relations, plain Negro inferiority—which was good enough for old-fashioned conservatives—is pushed aside by fancy conceits about the crumbling Negro family. With regard to illegitimacy, we are not so crass as to concern ourselves with immorality and vice, as in the old days; we settle benignly on the explanation of the "lower-class pattern of sexual behavior," which no one condemns as evil, but which is, in fact, simply a variation of the old explanatory idea. Mental illness is no longer defined as the result of hereditary taint or congenital character flaw; now we have new causal hypotheses regarding the ego-damaging emotional experiences that are supposed to be the inevitable consequence of the deplorable child-rearing practices of the poor.

In each case, of course, we are persuaded to ignore the obvious; the continued blatant discrimination against the Negro, the gross deprivation of contraceptive and adoption services to the poor, the heavy stresses endemic in the life of the poor. And almost all our make-believe liberal programs aimed at correcting our urban problems are off target; they are designed either to change the poor man or to cool him out.

We come finally to the question, Why? It is much easier to understand the process of Blaming the Victim as a way of thinking than it is to understand the motivation for it. Why do Victim Blamers, who are usually good people, blame the victim? The development and application of this ideology, and of all the mythologies associated with Savage Discovery, are readily exposed by careful analysis as hostile acts—one is almost tempted to say acts of war—directed against the disadvantaged, the distressed, the disinherited. It is class warfare in reverse. Yet those who are most fascinated and enchanted by this ideology tend to be progressive, humanitarian, and, in the best sense of the word, charitable persons. They would usually define themselves as moderates or liberals. Why do they pursue this dreadful war against the poor and the oppressed?

Put briefly, the answer can be formulated best in psychological terms—or, at least, I, as a psychologist, am more comfortable with such a formulation. The highly charged psychological problem confronting this hypothetical progressive, charitable person I am talking about is that of reconciling his own self-interest with the promptings of his humanitarian impulses. This psychological process of reconciliation is not worked out in a logical, rational, conscious way; it is a process that takes place far below the level of sharp consciousness, and the solution—Blaming the Victim—is arrived at subconsciously as a compromise that apparently satisfies both his self-interest and his charitable concerns. Let me elaborate.

First, the question of self-interest or, more accurately, class interest. The typical Victim Blamer is a middle-class person who is doing reasonably well in a material way; he has a good job, a good income, a good house, a good car. Basically, he likes the social system pretty much the way it is, at least in broad outline. He likes the two-party political system, though he may be highly skilled in finding a thousand minor flaws in its functioning. He heartily approves of the profit motive as the propelling engine of the economic system despite his awareness that there are abuses of that system, negative side effects, and substantial residual inequalities.

On the other hand, he is acutely aware of poverty, racial discrimination, exploitation, and deprivation, and, moreover, he wants to do something concrete to ameliorate the condition of the poor, the black, and the disadvantaged. This is not an extraneous concern; it is central to his value system to insist on the worth of the individual, the equality of men, and the importance of justice.

What is to be done, then? What intellectual position can he take, and what line of action can he follow that will satisfy both of these important motivations? He quickly and self-consciously rejects two obvious alternatives, which he defines as "extremes." He cannot side with an openly reactionary, repressive position that accepts continued oppression and exploitation as the price of a privileged position for his own class. This is incompatible with his own morality and his basic political principles. He finds the extreme conservative position repugnant.

He is, if anything, more allergic to radicals, however, than he is to reactionaries. He rejects the "extreme" solution of radical social change, and this makes sense since such radical social change threatens his own well-being. A more equitable distribution of income might mean that he would have less—a smaller or older house, with fewer yews or no rhododendrons in the yard, a less enjoyable job, or, at the least, a somewhat smaller salary. If black children and poor children were, in fact, reasonably educated and began to get high S.A.T. scores, they would be competing with *his* children for the scarce places in the entering classes of Harvard, Columbia, Bennington, and Antioch.

So our potential Victim Blamers are in a dilemma. In the words of an old Yiddish proverb, they are trying to dance at two weddings. They are old friends of both brides and fond of both kinds of dancing, and they want to accept both invitations. They cannot bring themselves to attack the system that has been so good to them, but they want so badly to be helpful to the victims of racism and economic injustice.

Their solution is a brilliant compromise. They turn their attention to the victim in his post-victimized state. They want to bind up wounds, inject penicillin, administer morphine, and evacuate the wounded for rehabilitation. They explain what's wrong with the victim in terms of social experiences *in the past*, experiences that have left wounds, defects, paralysis, and disability. And they take the cure of these wounds and the reduction of these disabilities as the first order of business. They want to make the victims less vulnerable, send them back into battle with better weapons, thicker armor, a higher level of morale.

In order to do so effectively, of course, they must analyze the victims carefully, dispassionately, objectively, scientifically, empathetically, mathematically, and hardheadedly, to see what made them so vulnerable in the first place.

What weapons, now, might they have lacked when they went into battle? Job skills? Education?

What armor was lacking that might have warded off their wounds? Better values? Habits of thrift and foresight?

And what might have ravaged their morale? Apathy? Ignorance? Deviant lower-class cultural patterns?

This is the solution of the dilemma, the solution of Blaming the Victim. And those who buy this solution with a sigh of relief are inevitably blinding themselves to the basic causes of the problems being addressed. They are, most crucially, rejecting the possibility of blaming, not the victims, but themselves. They are all unconsciously passing judgments on themselves and bringing in a unanimous verdict of Not Guilty.

If one comes to believe that the culture of poverty produces persons *fated* to be poor, who can find any fault with our corporation-dominated economy? And if the Negro family produces young men *incapable* of achieving equality, let's deal with that first before we go on to the task of changing the pervasive racism that informs and shapes and distorts our every social institution. And if unsatisfactory resolution of one's Oedipus complex accounts for all emotional distress and mental disorder, then by all means let us attend to that and postpone worrying about the pounding day-to-day stresses of life on the bottom rungs that drive so many to drink, dope, and madness.

That is the ideology of Blaming the Victim, the cunning Art of Savage Discovery. The tragic, frightening truth is that it is a mythology that is winning over the best people of our time, the very people who must resist this ideological temptation if we are to achieve nonviolent change in America.

NOTES

1. For a good review of this general ideology, see I. A. Newby, *Jim Crow's Defense* (Baton Rouge: Louisiana State University Press, 1965).

2. Richard Hofstadter, *Social Darwinism in American Thought* (revised ed.; Boston: Beacon Press, 1955).

3. William J. Ghent, *Our Benevolent Feudalism* (New York: The Macmillan Co., 1902), p. 29.

Sex and Race:
The Analogy of Social Control

William Chafe

. . . Analogies should not be limited to issues of substance alone, nor is their purpose to prove that two categories or objects are exactly identical. According to the dictionary, an analogy is "a relation of likeness . . . consisting in the resemblance not of the things themselves but of two or more attributes, circumstances or effects." Within this context, the purpose of an analogy is to illuminate a process or relationship which might be less discernible if only one or the other side of the comparison were viewed in isolation. What, then, if we look at sex and race as examples of how social control is exercised in America, with the primary emphasis on what the analogy tells us about the modes of control emanating from the dominant culture? Throughout the preceding discussion, the strongest parallels dealt with the use of stereotypes and ascribed attributes to define the respective position of women and blacks in the society. Thus what if the nature of the analogy is not in the *substance* of the material existence which women and blacks have experienced but in the *forms* by which others have kept them in "their place" and prevented them from challenging the status quo?

The virtues of such an approach are many. First, it provides greater flexibility in exploring how the experience of one group can inform the study of another. Second, it has the potential of developing insights into the larger processes by which the status quo is perpetuated from generation to generation. In this sense, it can teach us about the operation of society as a whole and the way in which variables like sex and race have been made central to the division of responsibilities and power within the society. If the forms of social control used with blacks and women resemble each other in "two or more attributes, circumstances, or effects," then it may be possible to learn something both about the two groups and how the status quo has been maintained over time. The best way to pursue this, in turn, is through looking closely at the process of social control as it has operated on one group, and then comparing it with the process and experience of the second group.

In his brilliant autobiographical novel *Black Boy*, Richard Wright describes what it was like to grow up black in the Jim Crow South. Using his family, the church, his classmates, his jobs, and his fantasies as stage-pieces for his story, Wright plays out the themes of hunger, fear, and determination which permeated his young life. Above all, he provides a searing account of how white Southerners successfully controlled the lives and aspirations of blacks. A series of concentric circles of social control operated in devastating fashion to limit young blacks to two life options— conformity to the white system, or exile.*

The outermost circle of control, of course, consisted of physical intimidation. When Richard asked his mother why black men did not fight white men, she responded, "The white men have guns and the black men don't." Physical force, and ultimately the threat of death, served as a constant reminder that whites held complete power over black lives. Richard saw that power manifested repeatedly. When his Uncle Hoskins dared to start his own saloon and act independently of the white power structure, he was lynched. The brother of one of Richard's schoolmates suffered a similar fate, allegedly for fooling with a white prostitute. When Richard worked for a clothing store, he frequently saw the white manager browbeat or physically attack black customers who had not paid their bills on time. When one woman came out of the store in a torn dress and bleeding, the manager said, "That's what we do to niggers when they don't pay their bills."[1]

The result was pervasive fear, anchored in the knowledge that whites could unleash vicious and irrational attacks without warning. Race consciousness could be traced, at least in part, to the tension which existed between anger at whites for attacking blacks without reason, and fear that wanton violence could strike again at any time, unannounced and unrestrained. "The things that influenced my conduct as a Negro," Richard wrote, "did not have to happen to me directly; I needed but to hear of them to feel their full effects in the deepest layers of my consciousness. Indeed the white brutality that I had not seen was a more effective control of my behavior than that which I knew . . . as long as it remained something terrible and yet remote, something whose horror and blood might descend upon me at any moment, I was compelled to give my entire imagination over to it, an act which blocked the springs of thought and feelings in me."[2]

The second circle of control rested in white domination of the economic status of black people. If a young black did not act the part of "happy nigger" convincingly, the employer would fire him. Repeatedly, Richard was threatened with the loss of work because he did not keep his anger and independence from being communicated to his white superiors. "Why don't you laugh and talk like the other niggers?" one employer asked. "Well, sir, there is nothing much to say or smile about," Richard said. "I don't like your looks nigger. Now git!" the boss ordered. Only a limited number of economic roles were open to blacks, and if they were not played

---

*Despite the problems created by using a novel for purposes of historical analysis, the interior perspective that is offered outweighs the limitations of "subjectiveness." Wright has been criticized for being overly harsh and elitist in his judgment of his black peers. His depiction of the conditions blacks had to cope with, on the other hand, corresponds well with the historical record. In the cases of both women and blacks, novels provide a vividness of detail and personal experience necessary to understand the larger processes at work in the society, but for the most part unavailable in conventional historical sources.

according to the rules, the job would be lost. A scarce supply of work, together with the demand that it be carried out in a deferential manner, provided a powerful guarantee that blacks would not get out of line.[3]

Significantly, the highest status jobs in the black community—teachers, ministers, civil servants—all depended ultimately upon acting in ways that pleased the white power structure.* One did not get the position at the post office or in the school system without being "safe"—the kind of person who would not make trouble. The fundamental precondition for success in the black community, therefore, was acting in ways that would not upset the status quo. When Richard tried to improve his own occupational chances and learn the optical trade, the white men who were supposed to teach him asked: "What are you trying to do, get smart, nigger?"[4]

The third circle of control consisted of the psychological power of whites to define and limit the reach of black aspirations. The sense people have of who they are and what they might become is tied intimately to the expectations communicated to them by others. The verbal cues, the discouragement or encouragement of authority figures, the picture of reality transmitted by friends or teachers—all of these help to shape how people think of themselves and their life chances. Stated in another way, human beings can envision careers as doctors and lawyers or a life of equality with others only to the extent that someone holds forth these ideals as viable possibilities.

Within this realm of social psychology, white Southerners exerted a pervasive and insidious control upon blacks. When Richard took his first job in a white household, he was given a bowl of molasses with mold on it for breakfast, even as his employers ate bacon and eggs. The woman he worked for asked what grade he was in, and when he replied the seventh, she asked, "Then why are you going to school?" When he further answered, "Well, I want to be a writer," she responded: "You'll never be a writer . . . who on earth put such ideas into your nigger head?" By her response, the woman attempted to undercut whatever sense of possibility Richard or other young blacks might have entertained for such a career. In effect, the woman had defined from a white perspective the outer boundaries of a black person's reality. As Richard noted, "She had assumed that she knew my place in life, what I felt, what I ought to be, and I resented it with all my heart. . . . perhaps I would never be a writer; but I did not want her to say so." In his own time Richard Wright was able to defy the limits set upon his life by white people. But for the overwhelming majority of his fellow blacks, the ability of whites to intimidate them psychologically diminished the chance that they would be able to aspire realistically to a life other than that assigned them within a white racist social structure.[5]

---

*There is an important distinction, of course, between jobs which were tied to white support and those with an indigenous base in the black community. Black doctors, morticians, and barbers, for example, looked to the black community itself for their financial survival; hence they could be relatively free of white domination. On the other hand, the number of such independent positions was small. Although many people would include ministers in such a category, the visibility of the ministerial role created pressure from blacks concerned with the stability and safety of their churches for ministers to avoid a radical protest position. That started to change during the civil rights movement.

The most devastating control of all, however, was that exercised by the black community itself out of self-defense. In the face of a world managed at every level by white power, it became an urgent necessity that black people train each other to adapt in order to survive. Thus the most profound and effective socialization toward accepting the racial status quo came from Richard's own family and peer group. It was Richard's mother who slapped him into silence "out of her own fear" when he asked why they had not fought back after Uncle Hoskins's lynching. To even ask the question posed a threat to safety. Similarly, it was Richard's Uncle Tom who insisted that Richard learn, almost by instinct, how to be accommodating. If Richard did not learn, the uncle said, he would never amount to anything and would end up on the gallows. Indeed, Richard would survive only if somebody broke his spirit and set the "proper" example.[6]

The instances of social control from within the black community abound in Wright's *Black Boy*. It was not only the white employer, but almost every black he knew, who opposed Richard's writing aspirations. "From no quarter," he recalled, "with the exception of the Negro newspaper editor, had there come a single encouraging word . . . I felt that I had committed a crime. Had I been aware of the full extent to which I was pushing against the current of my environment, I would have been frightened altogether out of my attempts at writing." The principal of his school urged vehemently that Richard give a graduation speech written by the principal rather than by Richard himself so that the proper tone of accommodation could be struck; the reward for going along was a possible teaching job. Griggs, Richard's best friend, was perhaps the most articulate in demanding that Richard control his instincts. "You're black and you don't act a damn bit like it." When Richard replied, "Oh Christ, I can't be a slave," Griggs responded with the ultimate lesson of reality: "But you've got to eat . . . when you are in front of white people, think before you act, think before you speak . . . you may think I'm an Uncle Tom, but I'm not. I hate these white people, hate them with all my heart. But I can't show it; if I did, they'd kill me." No matter where he went or whom he talked to in his own community, Richard found, not support for his protest, but the warning that he must behave externally in the manner white people expected. Whatever the hope of ultimate freedom, survival was the immediate necessity. One could not fight another day if one was not alive.[7]

Paradoxically, even the outlets for resistance within the system provided a means of reinforcing it. There were many ways of expressing unhappiness with one's lot, and all were essential to let off steam. The gang on the corner constantly verbalized resentment and anger against the white oppressor. Yet the very fact that the anger had to be limited to words and out of the earshot of whites meant that in practical terms it was ineffectual. Humor was another form of resistance. Richard and his friends joked that, if they ate enough black-eyed peas and buttermilk, they would defeat their white enemies in a race riot with "poison gas." But the end of the joke was an acknowledgment that the only way in reality to cope with the "mean" white folks was to leave.[8]

Indeed, the most practical form of resistance—petty theft—almost seemed a ploy by white people to perpetuate the system. Just as modern-day department store owners tolerate a certain degree of employee theft as a means of making the workers think they are getting away with something so they will not demand higher wages, so white employers of black people appear to have intentionally closed their eyes to a great deal of minor stealing. By giving blacks a small sense of triumph, white employers were able to tie them even more closely into the system, and prevent them from contemplating outright defiance. As Wright observed:[9]

> No Negroes in my environment had ever thought of organizing . . . and petitioning their white employers for higher wages . . . They knew that the whites would have retaliated with swift brutality. So, pretending to conform to the laws of the whites, grinning, bowing, they let their fingers stick to what they could touch. And the whites seemed to like it.
>
> But I, who stole nothing, who wanted to look them straight in the face, who wanted to talk and act like a man, inspired fear in them. The southern whites would rather have had Negroes who stole work for them than Negroes who knew, however dimly, the worth of their own humanity. Hence, whites placed a premium upon black deceit; they encouraged irresponsibility, and their rewards were bestowed upon us blacks in the degree that we could make them feel safe and superior.

From a white point of view, a minor exercise of indirect and devious power by blacks was a small price to pay for maintaining control over the entire system. Thus, whites held the power to define black people's options, even to the point of controlling their modes of resistance. *

The result of all this was a system that functioned smoothly, with barely a trace of overt protest or dissension. Everyone seemed outwardly content with their place. At a very early age, Wright observed, "the white boys and the black boys began to play our traditional racial roles as though we had been born to them, as though it was in our blood, as though we were guided by instinct." For most people, the impact of a pervasive system of social control was total: resignation, a lowering of aspirations, a recognition of the bleakness of the future and the hopelessness of trying to achieve major change. In Wright's images life was like a train on a track; once headed in a given direction, there was little possibility of changing one's course. [10]

Wright himself, of course, was the exception. "Somewhere in the dead of the southern night," he observed, "my life had switched onto the wrong track, and without my knowing it, the locomotive of my heart was rushing down a dangerously steep slope, heading for a collision, heedless of the warning red lights that

---

*It is important to remember that there existed a life in the black community less susceptible to white interference on a daily basis. Black churches, lodges, and family networks provided room for individual self-expression and supplied emotional reinforcement and sustenance. In this connection it is no accident that black institutions are strongest in the South where, until recently, the vast majority of blacks resided. On the other hand, the freedom which did exist came to a quick end wherever blacks attempted to enter activities, occupations, or areas of aspiration involving whites; or defined as white-controlled. Thus even the realm where freedom existed was partially a reflection of white control.

blinked all about me, the sirens and the bells and the screams that filled the air." Wright had chosen the road of exile, of acute self-consciousness and alienation. For most blacks of his era, though, the warning red lights, the sirens, the bells, and the screams produced at least outward conformity to the status quo. In the face of forms of social control which effectively circumscribed one's entire life, there seemed no other choice. [11]

Obviously, women have not experienced overtly and directly the same kind of consistent physical intimidation that served so effectively to deter the black people of Richard Wright's childhood from resisting their condition. On the other hand, it seems clear that the physical strength and alleged dominance of men have been an important instrument of controlling women's freedom of action. The traditional image of the male as "protector" owes a great deal to the notion that women cannot defend themselves and that men must therefore take charge of their lives physically. The same notion of male strength has historically been responsible for restricting jobs involving heavy labor to men. Nor is the fear with which women view the potential of being struck or raped by a male lover, husband, or attacker an insignificant reality in determining the extent to which women historically have accepted the dominance of the men in their lives. Richard Wright observed that "the things that influenced my conduct . . . did not have to happen to me directly; I needed but to hear of them to feel their full effects. . . ." Similarly, women who have grown up with the image of powerful and potentially violent men need not have experienced a direct attack to share a sense of fear and intimidation. "Strength," the psychologist Jerome Kagan has observed, "is a metaphor for power." Thus, despite the substantive difference in the way women and blacks have been treated, the form of social control represented by physical strength has operated similarly for both groups. [12]

An even stronger case can be made for the way in which economic controls have succeeded in keeping blacks and women in their place. In 1898 Charlotte Perkins Gilman argued in *Women and Economics* that the root of women's subjection was their economic dependency on men. As long as women were denied the opportunity to earn their own living, she argued, there could never be equality between the sexes. The fact that women had to please their mates, both sexually and through other services, to ensure their survival made honest communication and mutual respect impossible. The prospect of a "present" from a generous husband, or a new car or clothes, frequently served to smooth over conflict, while the implicit threat of withholding such favors could be used to discourage carrying conflict too far. [13]

In fact, the issue of women not controlling their own money has long been one of the most painful and humiliating indexes of inequality between the sexes, especially in the middle class. Since money symbolizes power, having to ask others for it signifies subservience and an inferior status. Carol Kennicott, the heroine of Sinclair Lewis's *Main Street*, recognized the problem. After begging prettily for her household expenses early in her marriage, she started to demand her own separate funds. "What was a magnificent spectacle of generosity to you," she told her husband, "was a humiliation to me. You *gave* me money—gave it to your mistress if she was complaisant." Beth Phail, a character in Marge Piercy's novel *Small Changes*, experienced the same conflict with her husband, who was immediately threatened by the idea of her economic autonomy. Indeed, few examples of psychological control seem more pointed than those represented in husbands' treating their wives as not mature enough to handle their own money.[14]

Even the women who held jobs reflected the pattern by which economic power was used to control women's freedom of action. Almost all women workers were concentrated in a few occupations delineated as "woman's" work. As secretaries, waitresses, cooks, and domestic workers, women on the job conformed to the "service" image of their sex. Significantly, the highest status jobs available—nurses and teachers—tended to reinforce a traditional image of women and the status quo between the sexes, just as the highest jobs available within the black community—teachers and civil servants—reinforced a pattern of accommodation with the existing white power structure. Any woman who chose a "man's job" automatically risked a loss of approval, if not total hostility. For most, the option simply did not exist.

Even those in the most prestigious positions illustrated how money could be used as an instrument of social control. If they were to succeed in raising funds, college administrators in black and women's schools frequently found that they had to shape their programs in conformity to social values that buttressed the status quo. Booker T. Washington represented the most outstanding example of this phenomenon. Repeatedly he was forced to appease white racist presumptions in order to get another donation for Tuskegee. As the funnel through which all white philanthropic aid to blacks was channeled, Washington had to ensure that no money would be spent in a way which might challenge the political values of his contributors, even though privately he fought those political values. But Washington was not alone. During the 1830's Mary Lyons, head of Mt. Holyoke Seminary, agreed not to attend trustee meetings lest she offend male sensibilities, and Mary Alice Baldwin, the very effective leader of the Women's College of Duke University, felt it necessary to pay homage to the conservative tradition of "the Southern lady" as the price for sustaining support of women's education at Duke.[15]

In all of these instances, economic controls functioned in parallel ways to limit the freedom of women and blacks. If a group is assigned a "place," there are few more effective ways of keeping it there than economic dependency. Not only must the group in question conform to the expectations of the dominant class in order to get money to live; those who would do otherwise are discouraged by the fact that no economic incentives exist to reward those who challenge the status quo. The absence of financial support for those who dare to deviate from prescribed norms has served well to perpetuate the status quo in the condition of both women and blacks. "I don't want to be a slave," Richard Wright observed. "But you have to eat," Griggs replied.

The strongest parallel, however, consists of the way in which blacks and women have been given the psychological message that they should be happy with their "place." In both instances, this form of control has effectively limited aspiration to non-conventional roles. Although Beth Phail of *Small Changes* wanted to go to college and law school, her family insisted that her highest aspiration should be marriage and homemaking. A woman should not expect a career. Similarly, when Carol Kennicott told her college boy friend, "I want to do something with my life," he responded eagerly: "What's better than making a comfy home and bringing up some cute kids . . . ?" The small town atmosphere of Gopher Prairie simply reinforced the pressure to conform. Carol was expected to be a charming hostess, a dutiful wife, and a good homemaker, but not a career woman. Thus, as Sinclair Lewis observed, she was a "woman with a working brain and no work." The messages Carol received from her surroundings were not designed to give her high self-esteem. Her husband called her "an extravagant little rabbit," and his poker partners, she noted simply expected her "to wait on them like a servant."[16]

Although Carol's personality was atypical, her social experience was not. When high school girls entertained the possibility of a career, they were encouraged to be nurses, not doctors. The qualities that received the most praise were those tradition- ally associated with being a "lady," not an assertive individual ready to face the world. Significantly, both women and blacks were the victims of two devices de- signed to discourage non-conformity. Those who sought to protest their status, for example, were subjected to ridicule and caricature. The black protestor was almost certain to be identified with subversive activity, just as the women's rights advocate was viewed as unsexed and a saboteur of the family. (Ordinary blacks and females were subject to a gentler form of humor, no less insidious, as in the characters of Amos 'n Andy's "King Fish" or Lucille Ball's "Lucy.") In addition, it was not uncommon for blacks to be set against blacks and women against women in a competition which served primarily the interests of the dominant group. According to Judith Bardwick and Elizabeth Douvan, girls are socialized to use oblique forms of aggression largely directed at other females, while men's aggression is overt. The stereotype of women doing devious battle over an attractive man is an ingrained part of our folk tradition. Nor is the "divide and conquer" strategy a stranger to the history of black people, as when white workers sowed seeds of suspicion between Richard Wright and another black worker in order to make them fight each other for the entertainment of whites.[17]

In both cases the psychological form of social control has operated in a similar fashion. The aspirations, horizons, and self-images of blacks and women have been defined by others in a limiting and constrictive way. More often that not, the result historically has been an acceptance of society's perception of one's role. The prospect of becoming an architect, an engineer, or a carpenter is not easy to sustain in an envi- ronment where the very idea is dismissed as foolish or unnatural. Instead of encourage- ment to aspire to new horizons of achievement, the message transmitted to blacks and women has been the importance of finding satisfaction with the status quo.

But in the case of women, as with blacks, the most effective instrument of continued control has been internal pressure from the group itself. From generation to generation, mothers teach daughters to please men, providing the instruction that prepares the new generation to assume the roles of mothers and housewives. Just as blacks teach each other how to cope with "whitey" and survive within the system, women school each other in how to win a man, how to appear charming, where to "play a role" in order to avoid alienating a potential husband. When Beth in *Small Changes* rebelled against her husband and fought the idea of tying herself down with a child, it was the other women in her family who urged her to submit and at least give the *appearance* of accepting the role expected of her.[18]

In fact, dissembling in order to conform to social preconceptions has been a frequent theme of women's socialization. As Mirra Komarovsky has demonstrated, college women in the 1940's were taught to hide their real ability in order to make their male friends feel superior. "My mother thinks that it is very nice to be smart in college," one of Komarovsky's students noted, "but only if it doesn't take too much effort. She always tells me not to be too intellectual on dates, to be clever in a light sort of way." It is not difficult to imagine one woman saying to another as Griggs said to Richard Wright, "When you are around white people [men] you have to act the part that they expect you to act." Even if deception was the goal, however, the underlying fact was that members of the "oppressed" group acted as accomplices in perpetuating the status quo.[19]

The most effective device for maintaining internal group discipline was to ostracize those who did not conform. Richard Wright found himself singled out for negative treatment because he refused to accept authority and to smile and shuffle before either his teachers or white people. Beth Phail was roundly condemned by her sisters and mother for not pleasing her husband, and above all for not agreeing to have a child. And Carol Kennicott received hostile glances when she violated her "place" by talking politics with men or seeking to assume a position of independent leadership in the community of Gopher Prairie. The disapproval of her female peers was the most effective weapon used to keep her in line, and, when it appeared that she finally was going to have a child, her women friends applauded the fact that in becoming a mother she would finally get over all her strange ideas and settle down. As Sinclair Lewis observed, "She felt that willy-nilly she was being initiated into the assembly of housekeepers; with the baby for hostage, she would never escape."[20]

The pressure of one's own group represented a double burden. In an environment where success was defined as marriage, and fulfillment as being a happy homemaker, it was hard enough to fight the tide in the first place. If one did, however, there was the additional problem of being seen as a threat to all the other members of the group who had conformed. The resistance of blacks toward Richard Wright and of women toward Carol Kennicott becomes more understandable in light of the fact that in both cases the individual protestors, through their refusal to play the game according to the rules, were also passing judgment on those who accepted the status quo. Thus, historically, women and blacks have kept each other in line not only as a means of group self-defense—protecting the new generation from harm and humiliation—but also as a means of maintaining self-respect by defending the course they themselves have chosen.

Indeed, for women as well as for blacks, even the vehicles for expressing resentment became reinforcements of the status quo. For both groups, the church provided a central emotional outlet—a place where solidarity with one's own kind could be found, and where some protest was possible. Women's church groups provided not only a means of seeking reform in the larger society but also for talking in confidence to other women about the frustrations of being a woman in a male-dominated society. What social humorists have called "hen-sessions" were in fact group therapy encounters where women had a chance to voice their gripes. Humor was frequently a vehicle for expressing a bittersweet response to one's situation, bemoaning, even as one laughed, the pain of being powerless. But as in the case with blacks, venting one's emotions about a life situation—although necessary for survival—was most often an instrument for coping with the situation, rather than for changing it.

Perhaps the most subversive and destructive consequence of a pervasive system of social control is how it permeates every action, so that even those who are seeking to take advantage of the "enemy" end up supporting the system. When Shorty, the elevator man in *Black Boy* known for his wit and hostility to whites, needed some money for lunch one day, he told a white man he would not move the elevator until he got a quarter. "I'm hungry, Mr. White Man. I'm dying for a quarter," Shorty said. The white man responded by asking what Shorty would do for a quarter. "You can kick me for a quarter," Shorty said, bending over. At the end of the elevator ride, Shorty had his quarter. "This monkey's got the peanuts," he said. Shorty was right. He had successfully used racial stereotypes and his own role as a buffoon to get himself some lunch money. But in the process, the entire system of racial imbalance had been strengthened.[21]

Similar patterns run through the history of women's relationships to men. The coquette role is only the most extreme example of a type of manipulative behavior by women that seems to confirm invidious stereotypes. In the classic case of a wife trying to persuade her husband to go along with a desired course of action, the woman may play up to a man's vanity and reinforce his stereotyped notions about being a tower of strength and in control. Similarly, a female employee wishing advancement may adopt a flirtatious attitude toward a male superior. By playing a semi-seductive role and implying a form of sexual payoff for services rendered, she may achieve her immediate goal. But in each of these cases, the price is to become more entrapped in a set of distorted and unequal sex role stereotypes. The fact that overt power is not available and that the ability to express oneself honestly and openly has been denied leads to the use of covert and manipulative power. Thus, a woman may play dumb or a black may act deferential—conforming in each case to a stereotype—as a means of getting his or her way. But the result is pathological power that simply perpetuates the disease. The irony is that, even in trying to outwit the system of social control, the system prevails.

Basic to the entire system, of course, has been the extent to which a clearly defined role was "woven into the texture of things." For blacks the crucial moment might come as soon as they developed an awareness of whites. In the case of women, it more likely took place at puberty when the need to begin pleasing potential husbands was emphasized. In either case, what Richard Wright said about the process of socialization could be said of both groups. "I marveled," he wrote[22]:

at how smoothly the black boys [women] acted out the role . . . mapped out for them. Most of them were not conscious of living a special, separate, stunted way of life. Yet I knew that in some period of their growing up—a period that they had no doubt forgotten—there had been developed in them a delicate, sensitive controlling mechanism that shut off their minds and emotions from all that the white race [society] had said was taboo. Although they lived in America where in theory there existed equality of opportunity, they knew unerringly what to aspire to and what not to aspire to.

The corollary for both women and blacks, at least metaphorically, has been that those unable or unwilling to accept the role prescribed for them have been forced into a form of physical or spiritual exile. Richard Wright understood that continued accommodation with the white Southern system of racial oppression would mean the destruction of his integrity and individuality. "Ought one to surrender to authority even if one believed that the authority was wrong?" Wright asked. "If the answer was yes, then I knew that I would always be wrong, because I could never do it. . . . How could one live in a world in which one's mind and perceptions meant nothing and authority and tradition meant everything?" The only alternative to psychological death was exile, and Wright pursued that course, initially in Chicago, later in Paris. In her own way Carol Kennicott attempted the same journey. "I've got to find out what my work is," she told her husband. "I've been ruled too long by fear of being called things. I'm going away to be quiet and think. I'm—I'm going. I have a right to my own life." And Beth Phail finally fled her home and family because it was the only way to grow up, to find out what "she wanted," to learn how to be a person in her own right in the world.[23]

Although in reality only a few blacks and women took the exact course adopted by Richard Wright, Carol Kennicott, and Beth Phail, all those who chose to resist the status quo shared to some extent in the metaphor of exile. Whether the person was a feminist like Charlotte Perkins Gilman, a pioneer career woman such as Elizabeth Blackwell, a runaway slave like Frederick Douglass, or a bold race leader like W. E. B. Du Bois, the act of challenging prevailing norms meant living on the edge of alienation and apart from the security of those who accepted the status quo. Until and unless protest generated its own community of support which could provide a substitute form of security and reinforcement, the act of deviance promised to be painful and solitary.

This condition, in turn, reflected an experience of marginality which many blacks and women shared. In sociological terms, the "marginal" personality is someone who moves in and out of different groups and is faced with the difficulty of adjusting behavior to the norms of the different groups. By definition, most blacks and most women have participated in that experience, especially as they have been required to accommodate the expectations of the dominant group of white males. The very fact of having to adopt different modes of behavior for different audiences introduces an element of complexity and potential conflict to the lives of those who are most caught up in a marginal existence. House slaves, for example, faced the inordinately difficult dilemma of being part of an oppressed group of slaves even as they lived in intimacy with and under the constant surveillance of the white master-class, thereby experiencing in its most extreme form the conflict of living in two worlds.[24]

Ordinarily, the tension implicit in such a situation is deflected, or as Richard Wright observed, "contained and controlled by reflex." Most house slaves seemed to learn how to live with the conflict by repressing their anger and uneasiness. Coping with the situation became a matter of instinct. But it is not surprising that many slave revolts were led by those house slaves who could not resolve the conflict by reflex, and instead were driven to alienation and protest. For the minority of people who misinterpreted the cues given them or learned too late how to cope, consciousness of the conflict made instinctive conformity impossible. As Richard Wright observed, "I could not make subservience an automatic part of my behavior. . . . while standing before a white man . . . I had to figure out how to say each word . . . I could not grin . . . I could not react as the world in which I lived expected me to." The pain of self-consciousness made the burden almost unbearable. As Maya Angelou has written, awareness of displacement "is the rust on the razor that threatens the throat." In an endless string of injuries, it was the final insult.[25]

Dissenting blacks and women have shared this experience of being "the outsider." Unable to accept the stereotyped behavior prescribed for their group, they have, in Vivian Gornick's words, "stood beyond the embrace of their fellows." With acute vision, Gornick writes, the outsider is able to "see deeply into the circle, penetrating to its very center, his vision a needle piercing the heart of life. Invariably, what he sees is intolerable." On the basis of such a vision, exile is the only alternative available. Yet, ironically, it too serves to reinforce the status quo by removing from the situation those most likely to fight it. Until the members willing to resist become great enough, the system of social control remains unaltered.[26]

It seems fair to conclude, therefore, that a significant resemblance has existed in the forms of social control used to keep women and blacks in their "place." Despite profound substantive differences between women and blacks, and white women and black women, all have been victims of a process, the end product of which has been to take away the power to define one's own aspirations, destiny, and sense of self. In each case a relationship of subservience to the dominant group has been perpetuated by physical, economic, psychological, and internal controls that have functioned in a remarkably similar way to discourage deviancy and place a premium on conformity. "It was brutal to be Negro and have no control over my life," Maya Angelou observes in her autobiography. "It was brutal to be young and already trained to sit quietly." From a feminist perspective, the same words describe the process of control experienced by most women.[27]

The core of this process has been the use of a visible, physical characteristic as the basis for assigning to each group a network of duties, responsibilities, and attributes. It is the physical foundation for discriminatory treatment which makes the process of social control on sex and race distinctive from that which has applied to other oppressed groups. Class, for example, comes closest to sex and race as a source of massive social inequity and injustice. Yet in an American context, class has been difficult to isolate as an organizing principle. Because class is not associated with a visible physical characteristic and many working class people persist in identifying with a middle-class life-style, class is not a category easy to identify in terms of physical or psychological control. (The very tendency to abjure class consciousness in favor of a social mobility ethic, of course, is its own form of psychological control.) Ethnicity too has frequently served as a basis for oppression, but the ease with which members of most ethnic minorities have been able to "pass" into the dominant culture has made the structure of social control in those cases both porous and complicated. Thus although in almost every instance invidious treatment has involved the use of some form of physical, economic, psychological, or internal controls, the combinations have been different and the exceptions frequent.

The analogy of sex and race is distinctive, therefore, precisely to the extent that it highlights in pure form the process of social control which has operated to maintain the existing structure of American society. While many have been victimized by the same types of control, only in the case of sex and race—where physical attributes are ineradicable—have these controls functioned systematically and clearly to define from birth the possibilities to which members of a group might aspire. Perhaps for that reason sex and race have been cornerstones of the social system, and the source of values and attitudes which have both reinforced the power of the dominant class and provided a weapon for dividing potential opposition.

Finally, the analogy provides a potential insight into the strategies and possibilities of social change. If women and blacks have been kept in their "place" by similar forms of social control, the prerequisites for liberation may consist of overcoming those forms of social control through a similar process. In the case of both women and blacks, the fundamental problem has been that others have controlled the power to define one's existence. Thus, to whatever extent women and blacks act or think in a given way solely because of the expectation of the dominant group rather than from their own choice, they remain captive to the prevailing system of social control. The prototypical American woman, writes Vivian Gornick, is perceived as "never taking, always being taken, never absorbed by her own desire, preoccupied only with whether or not she is desired." Within such a context, the "other" is always more important than the "self" in determining one's sense of individual identity. It is for this reason that efforts by blacks and women toward group solidarity, control over one's own institutions, and development of an autonomous and positive self-image may be crucial in breaking the bonds of external dominance.[28]

Yet such a change itself depends on development of a collective consciousness of oppression and a collective commitment to protest. As long as social and political conditions, or the reluctance of group members to participate, preclude the emergence of group action, the individual rebel has little chance of effecting change. Thus the issue of social control leads inevitably to the question of how the existing cycle is broken. What are the preconditions for the evolution of group protest? How do external influences stimulate, or forestall, the will to resist? And through what modes of organization and action does the struggle for autonomy proceed? For these questions too, the analogy of sex and race may provide a useful frame of reference.

Whatever the case, it seems more productive to focus on forms of control or processes of change than to dwell on the substantive question of whether blacks and women have suffered comparable physical and material injury. Clearly, they have not. On the other hand when two groups exist in a situation of inequality, it may be self-defeating to become embroiled in a quarrel over which is more unequal or the victim of greater oppression. The more salient question is how a condition of inequality for both is maintained and perpetuated—through what modes is it reinforced? By that criterion, continued exploration of the analogy of sex and race promises to bring added insight to the study of how American society operates.

NOTES

1. Richard Wright, *Black Boy* (New York, 1937), pp. 48, 52, 150, 157. Quotations used by permission of the publishers Harper and Row, New York.
2. Wright, pp. 65, 150–51.
3. Wright, p. 159.
4. Wright, p. 164.
5. Wright, pp. 127–29.
6. Wright, pp. 139–40.
7. Wright, pp. 147, 153–55, 160–61.
8. Wright, pp. 68–71, 200.
9. Wright, p. 175.
10. Wright, p. 72.
11. Wright, p. 148.
12. Wright, pp. 150–51; Brownmiller, *Against Our Will*; Jerome Kagan and H. A. Moss, *Birth to Maturity* (New York, 1962).
13. Degler, "Introduction," *Women and Economics*.
14. Lewis, *Main Street*, pp. 74, 167; Marge Piercy, *Small Changes* (Greenwich, Conn., 1972), p. 33.
15. Louis P. Harlan, *Booker T. Washington 1856–1901* (New York, 1972); Ralph Ellison, *Invisible Man* (New York, 1952); Flexner, *Century of Struggle*, p. 33; and Dara DeHaven, "On Educating Women—The Co-ordinate Ideal at Trinity and Duke University," Masters thesis, Duke University, 1974.
16. Piercy, *Small Changes*, pp. 19–20, 29, 40–41; Lewis, *Main Street*, pp. 14–15, 86, 283.
17. Bardwick and Douvan, "Ambivalence: The Socialization of Women"; Wright, *Black Boy*, pp. 207–13.
18. Piercy, *Small Changes*, pp. 31, 34, 316–17.
19. Piercy, pp. 30–31, 34, 39; Mirra Komarovsky, "Cultural Contradictions and Sex Roles," *American Journal of Sociology* 52 (November 1946).
20. Lewis, *Main Street*, p. 234.
21. Wright, *Black Boy*. p. 199.
22. Wright, p. 172.
23. Wright, p. 144; Lewis, *Main Street*, pp. 404–5; Piercy, *Small Changes*, p. 41.
24. See Everett Hughes, "Social Change and Status Protest: An Essay on the Marginal

Man," *Phylon* 10 (December 1949); and Robert K. Merton, *Social Theory and Social Structure* (New York, 1965), pp. 225–50.

25. Wright, *Black Boy*, p. 130; Maya Angelou, *I Know Why the Caged Bird Sings*, p. 3.
26. Vivian Gornick, "Woman as Outsider," in Moran and Gornick, pp. 126–44.
27. Angelou, p. 153.
28. Gornick, p. 140.

Hate-Violence

Carole Sheffield

Hate-violence is not a new phenomenon in the United States. Our history reveals a pattern of violence, brutality, and bigotry against those defined as "other." The campaign of genocide against native peoples is the prototype of American hate-violence. In the first three hundred years of American history, hate-violence was often institutionally organized and sanctioned. The government and its agents were the perpetrators. State violence was committed against Native Americans, captured and enslaved Africans, African-Americans, workers, and citizens who protested against domestic and foreign policies. Hate-violence, however, has also always been spontaneous and unorganized. Violence against women and gay and lesbian people has been documented since the earliest settlements and illuminates the central role of violence in American life. Women's diaries, newspaper accounts, and case records of social work agencies (which date as far back as 1870) chronicle the high incidence of rape, sexual abuse of children, and wife beating. Men were executed for sodomy as early as 1624. Lesbian women and gay men have, for three centuries, been subjected to many forms of institutional violence including forced psychiatric treatment, castration and clitoridectomy (the removal of the clitoris), felony imprisonment and fines, and dishonorable discharge from the military (Herek 1989, p. 949).

Organized hate groups have played key roles in maintaining an environment of fear for minority Americans. The most well-known organized hate group, the Ku Klux Klan, was organized in 1865 out of the resentment and hatred many white Southerners felt after the Civil War, and emancipated Africans were its principal targets. The KKK has been responsible for some of the most brutal violence in our history. It has used whips, dynamite, hanging, acid-burning, tar-and-feathering, torture, shooting, stabbing, clubbing, fire-branding, castration, and other forms of mutilation (Bullard 1988, p. 24). Between 1889 and 1941, 3,811 black people were lynched in the United States. In 1981, Klansmen in Mobile, Alabama, stopped nineteen-year old Michael Donald as he was walking home from visiting relatives, cut his throat and hanged him from a tree limb in a residential neighborhood, because, as one of them put it, "they wanted to kill a black person" (Bullard 1988, p. 25). While the menace of the KKK has fluctuated over the years, it has never vanished. During the Civil Rights Movement, a particularly "active" time for the Klan, and up to the present, the Klan has developed ties with a number of hate groups, including the White Citizens Councils (organized to defy U.S. Supreme Court-ordered desegregation), the Skinheads, and the Aryan Nation and its various subsidiaries. The Christian Identity Movement, which includes the Order, the Covenant, the Sword, the Arm of the Lord, seeks to unite religious people with the white supremacy movement (Ostling 1986, p. 74).

The Center for Democratic Renewal reports that gay people are now included with Jews and African-Americans as the "favorite target for hate groups" (Herek 1989, p. 952). For example, a hate group called "Crusade Against Corruption" published a pamphlet entitled "Praise God for AIDS," which claimed that "AIDS is a racial disease of jews and negroids that also exterminates sodomites." They called for the segregation of high risk AIDS groups "so as to protect innocent white people from AIDS" (Herek 1989, p. 952). Similarly, the National States Rights Party's newspaper *Thunderbolt*, in a front page headline "Bisexuals Infect white Women with AIDS," claimed that "most bisexuals are Negroes who often seek affairs with White females" (Herek 1989, p. 952). Here the linkage between race-hate, gay-hate, and misogyny is evident. It is important to note that racism, anti-Semitism, and hatred of gay and lesbian people are not caused by Klan and neo-Nazi organizations; these groups merely attract individuals whose prejudice and bigotry have already developed.

The Incidence of Hate-Violence

The latter part of the twentieth century has seen an alarming rise of individual acts of hate-violence. While organized hate groups do advocate and promulgate violence, much, if not most, hate-violence is not the work of people associated with organized hate groups. Singling out individuals for apparently random attack because of their sex, skin color, ethnicity, religion, presumed or known affectional identification is a pattern of both historical and contemporary significance. Recent examples include cross burnings on the front lawns of African-American families; an attack on African-Americans who moved into a predominately white neighborhood in Philadelphia; continued attacks by neighborhood youths on families of Cambodian refugees who had to flee Brooklyn; the shootings of African-American joggers; the beating to death of a Chinese-American because he was presumed to be Japanese; the harassment of Laotian fishermen in Texas; the brutal attack on two men in Manhattan by a group of knife-and bat-wielding teenage boys shouting "Homos!" and "Fags!"; the assault on three women in Portland, Maine, after their assailant yelled anti-lesbian epithets at them; the stalking of two lesbian women while camping in Pennsylvania, and the brutal murder of one of them; the gang rape with bottles, lighted matches, and other implements of a gay man who was repeatedly told, "this is what faggots deserve"; the stabbing to death of a heterosexual man in San Francisco because he was presumed to be gay; and the gang rapes of a female jogger in Central Park and a mentally handicapped teenager in Glen Ridge, N.J. Unfortunately, the list goes on and on.

While no national data on the incidence of racial, ethnic, anti-gay and lesbian, and sexual violence exists, there is a remarkable and generally unchallenged consensus that hate-violence is not only extensive but that it may well be increasing, both in incidence and in brutality (Hernandez 1990, p. 845–6; Finn and McNeil 1988, p. 2; Lutz 1987, p. 11; Wexler and Marx 1986, p. 205). The data which support this view come from a variety of sources, including twelve states who monitor hate crime statistics (in advance of the recent federal mandate to do so); hearings; reports from various municipalities; the FBI Uniform Crime Reports and the National Crime Surveys data on rape; statistics collected by a number of concerned interest groups; and the media. For example, the Anti-Defamation League of B'nai B'rith reports that anti-Semitic incidents, ranging from desecration to murder, reached their highest level in 1989 since the organization began collecting statistics eleven years ago (Toner 1990, p. A16). The National Gay and Lesbian Task Force (NGLTF) reports that the incidence of anti-gay violence and victimization reported to its Violence Project has risen steadily—an increase of 142 percent from 1985 to 1986 and an increase of 42 percent in 1987. In 1988, there were seventy "gay-motivated" or "gay-related" murders (Herek 1989, p. 950).

The Center for Democratic Renewal conducted a nation-wide study on racist violence and documented nearly 3,000 incidents of race hate-violence between 1980 and 1986 (Lutz 1987, p. 91). The study also revealed a notably high level of violence aimed at interracial couples (p. 13). The Puerto Rican Legal Defense and Education Fund reports a significant increase in hate crimes against Latinos (Hernandez 1990, p. 846). In 1988, thirty state attorneys general reported that violence against individuals based on race is increasing (Hernandez 1990, p. 846, note 2). Despite the high incidence revealed by these varied sources, most also agree that there is considerable underreporting of hate-violence. As with sexual violence, insensitivity and prejudice of officials, blaming the victim (especially true of women, gay men, and lesbian women, who are often accused of "flaunting" their sexuality), shame, fear of exposure, and fear that little or nothing will be done contribute to underreporting.

Finally, recent studies and reports suggest that the incidence of hate-violence on college campuses is quite high. During the 1986–1987 academic year, the National Institute Against Prejudice and Violence documented racist incidents on 130 college campuses (Farrell and Jones 1988, p. 214). However, most colleges and universities do not have adequate reporting procedures and this data is also seriously underrepresentative of the actual incidence of campus hate-violence.

The Roots of Hate-Violence

Hate-violence is neither accidental nor coincidental. It is the result of acquired beliefs, stereotypes, expectations, and images that we have of ourselves and others. These beliefs, etc. are called "ideologies." An ideology is a system of beliefs about how things are and how things should be. As such, an ideology is both descriptive and prescriptive. It helps us to process and evaluate information and events, to determine what is right or wrong, good or bad. It helps us locate and understand our place in a complex world.

Ideologies, commonly known as "isms," address questions of social, economic, political, religious, and even scientific relations. The "isms" that are of primary concern in understanding the roots of hate-violence are racism, sexism, classism, and heterosexism. Each of these "isms" is based on conceptualizations of superiority and inferiority. In racism, white people are defined as naturally superior to people of color; in sexism, men are defined as superior to women; in classism, richer people are considered superior to poorer people; and in heterosexism, heterosexual people are considered superior to homosexual or bisexual people. Within each "ism" is an elaborate network of beliefs and stereotypes that attempts to justify and maintain the dominance and privilege of the superior group. Dominance is maintained by an allocation of scarce resources (employment, education, housing, health care, status, acceptance, etc.), which favors the "superior" group. Indeed, members of those groups defined as superior are taught to expect greater advantages and rewards than those who are defined as inferior and therefore less deserving.

Dominance is translated by the ideology(ies) into specific interests and privileges, which while collectively defined (by race, sex, ethnicity, religion, sexual orientation) are manifested in individual expectations of resources and privileges. Harassing people of color who move into white middle-class neighborhoods and gay and lesbian people who demonstrate affection are examples of hate-violence based on what the perpetrators of such violence often feel is a betrayal of what they were taught to expect about how the world is and should be. Because ideologies establish a framework for determining who is most and least deserving of opportunities for success and fulfillment, economic conditions play a key role in organizing hate and bigotry. Economic hardship is blamed on "reverse discrimination," inflated welfare rolls, and unfair advantages "given" to racial minorities and women by "lowering standards" in the competition for fewer jobs and shrinking resources. This is known as "scapegoating"; a process of placing blame for society's problems on people who are defined as inferior. Another striking example of scapegoating is the dramatic rise in anti-gay and lesbian violence since the beginning of the AIDS epidemic. AIDS, however, is not the cause of such violence but rather the rationale used by bigots to justify their acts of hatred.

Dominance is also maintained through the threat of force and the use of actual violence against those defined as inferior. All systems of oppression employ violence and the threat of violence as an institutionalized mechanism for maintaining the interests and privileges of the "superior" group. Indeed, while there are differences in the manifestations of racism, sexism, heterosexism, and classism, the commonality that underlies these ideologies is force and its threat. No aspect of well-being is more fundamental than freedom from ideologically motivated and justified violence; that is, personal harm that is motivated by hatred and fear of one's ascribed characteristics (Sheffield 1987, p. 171). Richard Wright (1945), in his autobiography *Black Boy*, makes explicit the fear and control of racial terrorism:

> The things that influenced my conduct as a Negro did not have to happen to me directly. I needed but to hear of them to feel their full effects in the deepest layers of my consciousness. Indeed, the white brutality that I had not seen was a more effective control of my behavior than that which I knew. . . . as long as it remained something terrible and yet remote, something whose horror and blood might descend upon me at any moment, I was compelled to give up my entire imagination over to it, an act which blocked the springs of thought and feelings in me (p. 190).

Sexual Terrorism

Violence against women constitutes a system of sexual terrorism—a system by which males frighten and, by frightening, dominate and control females (Sheffield 1987, pp. 171–189; Sheffield 1989, pp. 3–19). Sexual terrorism is manifested through actual and implied violence; and all females, irrespective of race, class, physical or mental abilities, and sexual orientation, are potential victims—at any age, at any time, or in any place. Sexual terrorism employs a variety of means: rape, battery, incestuous abuse, sexual abuse of children, sexual harassment, pornography, prostitution and sexual slavery, and murder.

Pervasive sexual danger is a basic reality for American women. The level of violence against women is at an all-time high and many believe that it is increasing. Also, many acts of sexual violence are more severe and brutal than ever before. There is an apparent increase in gang rapes, serial rapes, sexual torture, and sexualized murder. Approximately 1,500 women are killed every year by husbands and lovers (Uniform Crime Reports 1987, p. 11). Nine out of every ten females who are murdered are murdered by men (Uniform Crime Reports 1989, p. 11). "In 1990, more women were raped than in any year in United States history," according to research conducted for the U.S. Senate Judiciary Committee (Majority Staff Report 1991, p. i). The FBI reports that in 1990 12 rapes were committed every hour, one every five minutes, close to 300 per day (Majority Staff Report 1991, p. 2). FBI data, however, does not reflect the actual incidence of rape due to the significant underreporting of this crime. Furthermore, the rape rate has increased four times faster than the overall crime rate during the last decade (Majority Staff Report 1991, p. 4). Every 18 seconds a woman is beaten. An estimated 3 million to 4 million women a year are battered, largely by their husbands or men they know (Rasky 1990, p. A19). Domestic violence is the single largest cause of injury to women in the U.S.; 22–35 percent of emergency room visits by women are for injuries caused by battering (Warshaw 1989, pp. 506–507). The March of Dimes (Brygger 1990, p. 1) reports that domestic violence is a major cause of birth defects in the U.S. Research indicates that there are nearly 38 million adults who have been sexually abused as children; 8 million who have been the victims of childhood incest (Crewdson 1988, p. 81).

Violence and its corollary, fear, function to terrorize females and to maintain the patriarchal definition of woman's subordinate place (Sheffield 1987, p. 171). How much do women worry about rape? According to Margaret T. Gordon and Stephanie Riger's (1989) study of female fear, about a third of women said they worry once a month about being raped—or more often; many said more than once a day. When they think about rape, they feel terrified and somewhat paralyzed. Another third of women indicated that the fear of rape is "part of the background," "one of those things that's always there." Another third said they never worried about rape but admitted taking precautions, "sometimes elaborate ones," to try to avoid being raped (pp. 21–22).

Women's attempts to avoid rape and other forms of sexual assault and intrusion take many forms. Women change/restrict their behavior, lifestyles, bodies, and appearances; they will pay higher costs for housing, purchase and maintain cars in order to avoid public transportation, refuse employment in certain areas or at certain times—all in attempts to avoid sexual assault. In a system of sexual terrorism where unpredictable, indiscriminate, and arbitrary violence is an essential component of social control, these self-protective acts serve as ways for women to feel some measure of control over their lives. Adaptive behaviors are used by all victims of oppression and are functional, although not without cost, for one's psychological, if not physical, survival.

Not only are women's lives controlled by the threat or reality of men's sexual violence, but the research shows that for many women it is the men they know— those with whom they live, work, spend leisure time—who are the most likely to victimize them. A study of acquaintance rape on 32 college campuses revealed that 1 in 4 women were victims of rape or attempted rape; that 84 percent of those raped knew their attacker; and that 57 percent of the rapes occurred while on dates (Warshaw 1988, p. 11). This reality, in large measure, sets sexual violence apart from other forms of hate-violence. Victims of race-hate or religious or ethnic intolerance have the most to fear from strangers. While gay and lesbian youth are often subject to abuse in the home, the perpetrators of anti-lesbian and gay violence are also mostly strangers.

Violence against women by acquaintances or by strangers is an assertion of the individual power of males as well as the power of men as a class. In this way, the beliefs and attitudes which support male interests and privileges are reinforced and perpetuated in women's and men's daily lives. Furthermore, we live in a culture that celebrates aggressive masculinity and denigrates female sexuality. Female sexuality is defined as insatiable, lustful, even desirous of male aggression. The pervasive patriarchal myth that "all women secretly want to be raped" provides the lens through which women and girls are blamed for their victimization. This belief that women/girls are responsible for assaults committed against them is a primary reason for the low conviction rate of rapists (Stanko 1985; LaFree 1989).

Moreover, the image of the male as warrior and the female as enemy is concretized in films, television, advertising, music, literature, and pornography. Every day and everywhere, in the most routine and mundane ways, women and female children are reminded visually and verbally that they are sexually objectified and are potential targets of violence. This commodification of women as sex is a multi-billion dollar industry and further distinguishes sex hate from other forms of hate-violence.

Sexuality does, however, play a role in other forms of hate-violence. Sexual arrangements are socially constructed and are political in nature. They are often organized, imposed, propagandized, and enforced by a dominant group in order to further its aims. For example, the racist construction of the sexuality of Africans during slavery defined African men as sexual savages and particularly as rapists. This view provided the justification for lynchings, castration, and other brutal punishments designed to terrorize and control African men and the slave community as a whole. Similarly, African women were defined as sexual savages, as depraved, immoral, loose; available and eager for sexual relations with any man. These constructions of the sexuality of enslaved Africans were translated into stereotypes that persist today and influence the way society processes sexual assaults committed by African-American men or against African-American women. That African-American women are treated poorly by the criminal justice system when they are victims of sexual assault is well documented (hooks 1981; LaFree 1989).

Constructions of sexuality play a key role in hate-violence directed against lesbian women and gay men. Homosexuality has been constructed as deviant, sinful, sick, and dangerous. Homosexuality is seen as a perversion of heterosexuality: that is, a deviation from the "norm" of the aggressive, masculine man having sex with the passive, feminine woman. Thus, gay men are often denigrated with language infused with misogyny—"you faggot bitch." Lesbian women are often raped by men claiming that "sex" with them could turn them into heterosexuals. As with sexual violence, victim-blaming is pervasive in how society evaluates violence against lesbian and gay people. Recently, two college students were beaten in Philadelphia by several assailants who called them "faggots" and "pretty boys." The police refused to take a report on the assault because, they said, the victims provoked the incident by "sitting like that" (Roskey 1988, p. 18).

Hate-Violence and Social Control

The assessment of the impact and harm of hate-violence is a complex one, and a critical one as it points to the uniqueness and insidiousness of such violence. Hate-violence is motivated by social and political factors and is bolstered by belief systems which (attempt to) legitimate such violence. The intent of hate-violence is to harm both the individual victim and the group to which the victim belongs. It reveals that the personal is political; that such violence is *not* a series of isolated incidents but rather the consequence of a political culture which allocates rights, privilege and prestige according to biological or social characteristics. This is what distinguishes all forms of hate-violence from the random acts of violence that occur daily in this society. Ann Pellegrini (1990) argues that "hate crimes are not random acts. They target a person because of who she or he is; because of what she or he is taken to represent. The only thing random about a hate crime is which woman, which Korean-American, which African-American, which family with AIDS, is raped, assaulted, beaten with bats, left for dead, burned out of their home" (p. E13).

Furthermore, the harm from swastikas and other graffiti, racial epithets, cross-burnings, broken windows and other property destruction extends far beyond the material damage. Names and words that assail a person's basic identity and dignity are profoundly injurious. Many studies of raped and/or battered women reveal that the name-calling that accompanied the violence was described by the victims as being as hurtful as the actual violence. The manifestation of sexual violence, race-hate, religious intolerance, and hatred of gay and lesbian people in the form of assault or murder goes beyond the injured person or taken life. Hate-violence is a demonstration of power over the victim and the class to which the victim belongs; therefore, hate-violence victimizes an entire class of people. It functions to intimidate every member of the target group. Its purpose is to limit the rights and privileges of individuals/groups and to maintain the superiority of one group—its beliefs, values, and privileges—through terrorism.

Conclusion

On April 23, 1990 President George Bush signed the "Federal Hate Crimes Statistics Act." The Act requires the Justice Department to conduct a five-year statistical study on crimes that "manifest evidence of prejudice based on race, religion, sexual orientation, or ethnicity, including crimes of murder; non-negligent manslaughter; forcible rape; aggravated assault; simple assault; intimidation; arson; and destruction, damage or vandalism of property" (Rosenthal 1990, p. A14).

This law, noteworthy in that it represents a far-ranging consensus about the need to address hate-violence in America, and historic in that it recognizes that violence against gay and lesbian people is a crime of hatred and bigotry, is seriously flawed by its omission of sexual violence. * Counting hate crimes against women would reveal that 52 percent of the population is in serious jeopardy (Pellegrini 1990, p. E13). The exclusion of sex-hate as a form of hate-violence is not only a profound denial of the most pervasive form of violence in the United States but an attempt to deny the reality of patriarchal/sexist oppression and its interaction with other structures of power and privilege such as race, class, and sexuality. It is an attempt to have it both

---

*The Act was supported by a coalition, "The Coalition on Hate Crimes," of sixty civil rights, religious, peace, gay and lesbian, and ethnic rights groups. It received the support of both liberal Democrats and conservative Republicans. Women's rights groups such as the National Organization for Women and the National Coalition Against Domestic Violence were deliberately excluded from "The Coalition on Hate Crimes" (de santis 1990, p. 1).

ways: that is, to rage against such hate-violence when the victims are males (and occasionally females) and yet protect male superiority over women. The denial of sexual violence as a hate crime is purposeful for the status quo, for it would be detrimental to the social order to define men's violence against women as a serious, hateful crime. The basic reality of sexual violence is that ordinary women are victimized every day by ordinary men. In denying this, the law sets the stage for viewing other forms of hate-violence as something committed by the "extremists," "irrational," "socially maladjusted"—and not as a function of our shared political and cultural myths. Therefore, the basic social order will remain essentially unchallenged.

NOTES

Brygger, Mary Pat. 1990. "Beginning of National Domestic Violence Awareness Month." Washington, D.C.: National Woman Abuse Prevention Project.

Bullard, Sara (ed.). 1988. *The Ku Klux Klan: A history of racism and violence* (3rd. ed.). Montgomery, Alabama: The Southern Poverty Law Center.

Crewdson, John. 1988. *By Silence Betrayed: Sexual Abuse of Children in America*. New York: Harper and Row, Publishers.

Conyers, J. 1986. *Hearings on anti-gay/lesbian violence*. Washington, D.C.: U.S. House of Representatives Committee on the Judiciary, Subcommittee on Criminal Violence.

de santis, marie. 1990. "Hate Crimes Bill Excludes Women." *off our backs* xx: p. 1.

Farrell, Walter C. Jr., and Cloyzelle K. Jones. 1988. "Recent Racial Incidents in Higher Education: A Preliminary Perspective." *The Urban Review* 20:211–226.

Finn, Peter and Taylor McNeil. 1988. "Bias Crime and the Criminal Justice Response: A Summary Report Prepared for the National Criminal Justice Association." Washington, D.C.: U.S. Department of Justice.

Gordon, Linda. 1988. *Heroes of Their Own Lives: The Politics and History of Family Violence*. New York: Penguin Books.

Gordon, Margaret T. and Stephanie Riger. 1989. *The Female Fear*. New York: The Free Press.

Herek, Gregory M. 1989. "Hate Crimes Against Lesbians and Gay Men: Issues for Research and Policy." *American Psychologist* 44: 948–955.

Hernandez, Tanya Kateri. 1990. "Bias Crimes: Unconscious Racism in the Prosecution of 'Racially Motivated Violence'." *The Yale Law Journal* 99:845–864.

hooks, bell. 1981. *Ain't I A Woman: black women and feminism*. Boston: South End Press.

LaFree, Gary D. 1989. *Rape and Criminal Justice: The Social Construction of Sexual Assault*. Belmont, California: Wadsworth, Inc.

Lutz, Chris (compiler). 1987. *They Don't All Wear Sheets: A Chronology of Racist and Far Right Violence—1980–1986*. Atlanta: Center for Democratic Renewal.

Majority Staff Report. 1991. "Violence Against Women: The Increase of Rape in America 1990." Washington, D.C.: U.S. Senate, Committee on the Judiciary.

National Gay and Lesbian Task Force. 1990. "Anti-Gay Violence, Victimization and Defamation in 1989." Washington, D.C.

Ostling, Richard N. 1986. "A Sinister Search for 'Identity'." *Time* (October 20): 74.

Rasky, Susan F. 1990. "Bill on Sex Crime Assessed in Senate." *New York Times* (June 21): Sec. A, 19.

Rosenthal, Andrew. 1990. "President Signs Law for Study of Hate Crimes." *New York Times* (April 24): Sec. A, 14.

Roskey, Michael L. 1988. *Ideology in Instances of Anti-Gay Violence.* University of California at Irvine, unpublished dissertation.

Sheffield, Carole J. 1987. "Sexual Terrorism and the Social Control of Women." Pp. 177–189 in *Analyzing Gender,* edited by B. Hess and M. Marx Ferree. Newbury Park, California: Sage.

_____ 1989. "Sexual Terrorism." Pp. 3–19 in *Women: A Feminist Perspective,* edited by Jo Freeman. Palo Alto, California: Sage.

Stanko, Elizabeth A. 1985. *Intimate Intrusions: Women's Experience of Male Violence.* Boston: Routledge and Kegan Paul.

Toner, Robin. 1990. "Senate, 92 to 4, Wants U.S. Data on Crimes that Spring From Hate." *New York Times* (February 9): Sec. A, 16.

Uniform Crime Reports. 1987. Washington, D.C.: U.S. Department of Justice.

_____ 1989. Washington, D.C.: U.S. Department of Justice.

Walker, Lenore E. 1984. *The Battered woman Syndrome.* New York: Springer.

Warshaw, Carole. 1989. "Limitations of the Medical Model in the Care of Battered Women." *Gender & Society* 3: 506–517.

Warshaw, Robin. 1988. *I Never Called It Rape.* New York: Harper and Row, Publishers.

Wexler, Chuck and Gary T. Marx. 1986, "When Law and Order Works: Boston's Innovative Approach to the Problem of Racial Violence." *Crime and Delinquency* 32: 205–223.

Wright, Richard. 1945. *Black Boy.* New York: Harper and Row, Publishers.

Suggestions for Further Reading

Bastow, Susan: *Gender Stereotypes: Traditions and Alternatives,* Second Edition, Brooks-Cole Publishing Company, Pacific Grove, California, 1986.

Harding, S. & M. B. Hintikka: *Discovering Reality: Feminist Perspectives on Epistemology, Metaphysics, Methodology, and Philosophy of Science,* D. Reidel Publishing Co., Boston, 1983.

Hartman, Paul and Charles Husband: *Racism and The Mass Media,* Rowman and Littlefield, Totowa, New Jersey, 1974.

Kramarae, C., M. Schultz, and W. M. O'Barr (eds.): *Language and Power,* Sage Press, Beverly Hills, California, 1984.

Marcuse, H: *One-Dimensional Man,* Beacon Press, Boston, 1964.

Michaels, Leonard, et. al. (eds.): *The State of the Language,* University of California Press, 1979.

Spender, D: *Man Made Language,* Second Edition, Routledge and Kegan Paul, Boston, 1985.

Vetterling-Braggin: *Sexist Language,* Littlefield, Adams, and Co., 1981.

PART VII

Revisioning the Future

Developing an adequate understanding of the nature and causes of race, class, and gender oppression is a critical first step toward moving beyond them. Solutions to problems are generated, at least in part, by the way we pose them. That is why so much of this book is devoted to defining and analyzing the nature of the problem. Only when we appreciate the complex, subtle factors that operate together to create a society in which wealth, privilege, and opportunity are unequally divided will we be able to formulate viable proposals for changing those conditions.

What, then, have the selections in this book told us about racism, sexism, and class divisions? First, there is no single cause. Eliminating these forms of oppression will involve changes at the personal, social, political, and economic levels. It will require that we learn to think differently about ourselves and others and see the world through new categories. We will have to learn to pay close attention to our language, our attitudes, and our behavior and ask what values and forms of relationships are being created and maintained both consciously and unconsciously by them. It will mandate that (1) we reevaluate virtually every institution in society and critically appraise the ways in which it intentionally or unintentionally perpetuates the forms of discrimination we have been studying and (2) that we act to change them. In short, we will have to scrutinize every aspect of our economic, political, and social life with a view to asking whose interests are served and whose are denied by organizing our world in this way.

In the first two selections in this part Audre Lorde and Gloria Anzaldúa suggest that we will need to begin by redefining and rethinking the idea of difference. While acknowledging that real differences of race, age, and sex exist, Lorde argues that it is not these differences that separate us as much as it is our refusal to acknowledge them and the role they play in shaping our relationships and our society. Denying or distorting those differences keeps us apart; embracing those differences can provide a new starting point for us from which to work together to reconstruct our world. Gloria Anzaldúa is concerned with the way women of color deal with differences among themselves, and argues that many women of color have learned to see each other through the categories of inferiority/superiority that white people have constructed. She urges women of color to reject these categories and stand "on the ground of our own ethnic being." The poem that follows by Cherríe Moraga illustrates what it might mean to rethink difference. Moraga writes of discovering differences that were previously hidden from her and of thus finding a new basis for human community.

Ruth Sidel turns our attention to social policy. She suggests that young women today have unrealistic expectations about the kind of life they are likely to lead as adults. Wrapped up in a version of the American Dream that promises you can have it all, young women today are unprepared for the difficult choices they will have to make in a world where class, race, and gender inequities shape people's lives. After offering a brief survey of these unrealistic expectations, Sidel goes on to suggest the kinds of social policies that are necessary if we are to create a more humane society. Among them are fundamental changes in the workplace, education, and health care, and the availability of sex education and abortion. Arguing that the American Dream cannot and never could work for the vast majority of people in this society, Sidel suggests that a humane society will be one organized around the public good, not private profit.

Suzanne Pharr is also concerned with the relationship between economic policy and social justice. She argues that in a society organized to create and maintain an extremely unequal distribution of wealth, economics is "the underlying, driving force that keeps all oppression in place." Beginning with an analysis of our economic system, Pharr goes on to examine the ways in which homophobia and heterosexism operate as weapons of sexism which threaten all women with violence and keep race, class, and gender subordination and domination in place. She concludes her discussion by asking us to imagine what the world might be like, for both women and men, without homophobia in it.

Like Pharr, bell hooks is concerned with understanding the way in which sex, race, and class function as interlocking, mutually supportive, systems of domination. Like Lorde and Anzaldúa she urges us to rethink difference. While acknowledging past failures of much feminist theory to adequately deal with issues of race, racism, and class, hooks maintains that a revisioned feminism can provide the most comprehensive perspective from which to challenge all forms of oppression and domination. This is true because sexism is the form of oppression we confront throughout our daily lives; "sexism directly shapes and determines relations of power in our private lives, in familiar social spaces, in that most intimate context— home—and in that most intimate sphere of relations—family." hooks envisions a process of education and consciousness raising where women from diverse back- grounds come together in small groups to talk about feminism and to learn from each other, but she calls upon men as well to commit themselves to overthrowing patriarchal domination.

This part, and this book, conclude with poems by Maya Angelou and Marge Piercy which celebrate survival, transformation, and the human spirit. They remind us of the strength oppressed people have called upon to help them survive under inhumane conditions, and they encourage us with their vision of an indomitable human spirit that will not merely survive but, as William Faulkner once wrote, will prevail.

Age, Race, Class, and Sex:
*Women Redefining Difference**

Audre Lorde

Much of Western European history conditions us to see human differences in simplistic opposition to each other: dominant/subordinate, good/bad, up/down, superior/inferior. In a society where the good is defined in terms of profit rather than in terms of human need, there must always be some group of people who, through systematized oppression, can be made to feel surplus, to occupy the place of the dehumanized inferior. Within this society, that group is made up of Black and Third World people, working-class people, older people, and women.

As a forty-nine-year-old Black lesbian feminist socialist mother of two, including one boy, and a member of an interracial couple, I usually find myself a part of some group defined as other, deviant, inferior, or just plain wrong. Traditionally, in american society, it is the members of oppressed, objectified groups who are expected to stretch out and bridge the gap between the actualities of our lives and the consciousness of our oppressor. For in order to survive, those of us for whom oppression is as american as apple pie have always had to be watchers, to become familiar with the language and manners of the oppressor, even sometimes adopting them for some illusion of protection. Whenever the need for some pretense of communication arises, those who profit from our oppression call upon us to share our knowledge with them. In other words, it is the responsibility of the oppressed to teach the oppressors their mistakes. I am responsible for educating teachers who dismiss my children's culture in school. Black and Third World people are expected to educate white people as to our humanity. Women are expected to educate men. Lesbians and gay men are expected to educate the heterosexual world. The oppressors maintain their position and evade responsibility for their own actions. There is a constant drain of energy which might be better used in redefining ourselves and devising realistic scenarios for altering the present and constructing the future.

Institutionalized rejection of difference is an absolute necessity in a profit economy which needs outsiders as surplus people. As members of such an economy, we

*Paper delivered at the Copeland Colloquium, Amherst College, April 1980.

401

have *all* been programmed to respond to the human differences between us with fear and loathing and to handle that difference in one of three ways: ignore it, and if that is not possible, copy it if we think it is dominant, or destroy it if we think it is subordinate. But we have no patterns for relating across our human differences as equals. As a result, those differences have been misnamed and misused in the service of separation and confusion.

Certainly there are very real differences between us of race, age, and sex. But it is not those differences between us that are separating us. It is rather our refusal to recognize those differences, and to examine the distortions which result from our misnaming them and their effects upon human behavior and expectation.

Racism, the belief in the inherent superiority of one race over all others and thereby the right to dominance. Sexism, the belief in the inherent superiority of one sex over the other and thereby the right to dominance. Ageism. Heterosexism. Elitism. Classism.

It is a lifetime pursuit for each one of us to extract these distortions from our living at the same time as we recognize, reclaim, and define those differences upon which they are imposed. For we have all been raised in a society where those distortions were endemic within our living. Too often, we pour the energy needed for recognizing and exploring difference into pretending those differences are insurmountable barriers, or that they do not exist at all. This results in a voluntary isolation, or false and treacherous connections. Either way, we do not develop tools for using human difference as a springboard for creative change within our lives. We speak not of human difference, but of human deviance.

Somewhere, on the edge of consciousness, there is what I call a *mythical norm*, which each one of us within our hearts knows "that is not me." In america, this norm is usually defined as white, thin, male, young, heterosexual, christian, and financially secure. It is with this mythical norm that the trappings of power reside within society. Those of us who stand outside that power often identify one way in which we are different, and we assume that to be the primary cause of all oppression, forgetting other distortions around difference, some of which we ourselves may be practicing. By and large within the women's movement today, white women focus upon their oppression as women and ignore differences of race, sexual preference, class, and age. There is a pretense to a homogeneity of experience covered by the word *sisterhood* that does not in fact exist.

Unacknowledged class differences rob women of each others' energy and creative insight. Recently a women's magazine collective made the decision for one issue to print only prose, saying poetry was a less "rigorous" or "serious" art form. Yet even the form our creativity takes is often a class issue. Of all the art forms, poetry is the most economical. It is the one which is the most secret, which requires the least physical labor, the least material, and the one which can be done between shifts, in the hospital pantry, on the subway, and on scraps of surplus paper. Over the last few years, writing a novel on tight finances, I came to appreciate the enormous differences in the material demands between poetry and prose. As we reclaim our literature, poetry has been the major voice of poor, working class, and Colored women. A room of one's own may be a necessity for writing prose, but so are reams of paper, a typewriter, and plenty of time. The actual requirements to produce the visual arts also help determine, along class lines, whose art is whose. In this day of inflated prices for material, who are our sculptors, our painters, our photographers? When we speak of broadly based women's culture, we need to be aware of the effect of class and economic differences on the supplies available for producing art.

As we move toward creating a society within which we can each flourish, ageism is another distortion of relationship which interferes with our vision. By ignoring the past, we are encouraged to repeat its mistakes. The "generation gap" is an important social tool for any repressive society. If the younger members of a community view the older members as contemptible or suspect or excess, they will never be able to join hands and examine the living memories of the community, nor ask the all important question, "Why?" This gives rise to a historical amnesia that keeps us working to invent the wheel every time we have to go to the store for bread.

We find ourselves having to repeat and relearn the same old lessons over and over that our mothers did because we do not pass on what we have learned, or because we are unable to listen. For instance, how many times has this all been said before? For another, who would have believed that once again our daughters are allowing their bodies to be hampered and purgatoried by girdles and high heels and hobble skirts?

Ignoring the differences of race between women and the implications of those differences presents the most serious threat to the mobilization of women's joint power.

As white women ignore their built-in privilege of whiteness and define *woman* in terms of their own experience alone, then women of Color become "other," the outsider whose experience and tradition is too "alien" to comprehend. An example of this is the signal absence of the experience of women of Color as a resource for women's studies courses. The literature of women of Color is seldom included in women's literature courses and almost never in other literature courses, nor in women's studies as a whole. All too often, the excuse given is that the literatures of women of Color can only be taught by Colored women, or that they are too difficult to understand, or that classes cannot "get into" them because they come out of experiences that are "too different." I have heard this argument presented by white women of otherwise quite clear intelligence, women who seem to have no trouble at all teaching and reviewing work that comes out of the vastly different experiences of Shakespeare, Molière, Dostoyefsky, and Aristophanes. Surely there must be some other explanation.

This is a very complex question, but I believe one of the reasons white women have such difficulty reading Black women's work is because of their reluctance to see Black women as women and different from themselves. To examine Black women's literature effectively requires that we be seen as whole people in our actual complexities—as individuals, as women, as human—rather than as one of those problematic but familiar stereotypes provided in this society in place of genuine images of Black women. And I believe this holds true for the literatures of other women of Color who are not Black.

The literatures of all women of Color recreate the textures of our lives, and many white women are heavily invested in ignoring the real differences. For as long as any difference between us means one of us must be inferior, then the recognition of any difference must be fraught with guilt. To allow women of Color to step out of stereotypes is too guilt provoking, for it threatens the complacency of those women who view oppression only in terms of sex.

Refusing to recognize difference makes it impossible to see the different problems and pitfalls facing us as women.

Thus, in a patriarchal power system where whiteskin privilege is a major prop, the entrapments used to neutralize Black women and white women are not the same. For example, it is easy for Black women to be used by the power structure against Black men, not because they are men, but because they are Black. Therefore, for Black women, it is necessary at all times to separate the needs of the oppressor from our own legitimate conflicts within our communities. This same problem does not exist for white women. Black women and men have shared racist oppression and still share it, although in different ways. Out of that shared oppression we have developed joint defenses and joint vulnerabilities to each other that are not duplicated in the white community, with the exception of the relationship between Jewish women and Jewish men.

On the other hand, white women face the pitfall of being seduced into joining the oppressor under the pretense of sharing power. This possibility does not exist in the same way for women of Color. The tokenism that is sometimes extended to us is not an invitation to join power; our racial "otherness" is a visible reality that makes that quite clear. For white women there is a wider range of pretended choices and rewards for identifying with patriarchal power and its tools.

Today, with the defeat of ERA, the tightening economy, and increased conservatism, it is easier once again for white women to believe the dangerous fantasy that if you are good enough, pretty enough, sweet enough, quiet enough, teach the children to behave, hate the right people, and marry the right men, then you will be allowed to co-exist with patriarchy in relative peace, at least until a man needs your job or the neighborhood rapist happens along. And true, unless one lives and loves in the trenches it is difficult to remember that the war against dehumanization is ceaseless.

But Black women and our children know the fabric of our lives is stitched with violence and with hatred, that there is no rest. We do not deal with it only on the picket lines, or in dark midnight alleys, or in the places where we dare to verbalize our resistance. For us, increasingly, violence weaves through the daily tissues of our living—in the supermarket, in the classroom, in the elevator, in the clinic and the schoolyard, from the plumber, the baker, the saleswoman, the bus driver, the bank teller, the waitress who does not serve us.

Some problems we share as women, some we do not. You fear your children will grow up to join the patriarchy and testify against you, we fear our children will be dragged from a car and shot down in the street, and you will turn your backs upon the reasons they are dying.

The threat of difference has been no less blinding to people of Color. Those of us who are Black must see that the reality of our lives and our struggle does not make us immune to the errors of ignoring and misnaming difference. Within Black communities where racism is a living reality, differences among us often seem dangerous and suspect. The need for unity is often misnamed as a need for homogeneity, and a Black feminist vision mistaken for betrayal of our common interests as a people. Because of the continuous battle against racial erasure that Black women and Black men share, some Black women still refuse to recognize that we are also oppressed as women, and that sexual hostility against Black women is practiced not only by the white racist society, but implemented within our Black communities as well. It is a disease striking the heart of Black nationhood, and silence will not make it disappear. Exacerbated by racism and the pressures of powerlessness, violence against Black women and children often becomes a standard within our communities, one by which manliness can be measured. But these woman-hating acts are rarely discussed as crimes against Black women.

As a group, women of Color are the lowest paid wage earners in america. We are the primary targets of abortion and sterilization abuse, here and abroad. In certain parts of Africa, small girls are still being sewed shut between their legs to keep them docile and for men's pleasure. This is known as female circumcision, and it is not a cultural affair as the late Jomo Kenyatta insisted, it is a crime against Black women.

Black women's literature is full of the pain of frequent assault, not only by a racist patriarchy, but also by Black men. Yet the necessity for and history of shared battle have made us, Black women, particularly vulnerable to the false accusation that anti-sexist is anti-Black. Meanwhile, womanhating as a recourse of the powerless is sapping strength from Black communities, and our very lives. Rape is on the increase, reported and unreported, and rape is not aggressive sexuality, it is sexualized aggression. As Kalamu ya Salaam, a Black male writer points out, "As long as male domination exists, rape will exist. Only women revolting and men made conscious of their responsibility to fight sexism can collectively stop rape."[1]

Differences between ourselves as Black women are also being misnamed and used to separate us from one another. As a Black lesbian feminist comfortable with the many different ingredients of my identity, and a woman committed to racial and sexual freedom from oppression, I find I am constantly being encouraged to pluck out some one aspect of myself and present this as the meaningful whole, eclipsing or denying the other parts of self. But this is a destructive and fragmenting way to live. My fullest concentration of energy is available to me only when I integrate all the parts of who I am, openly, allowing power from particular sources of my living to flow back and forth freely through all my different selves, without the restrictions of externally imposed definition. Only then can I bring myself and my energies as a whole to the service of those struggles which I embrace as part of my living.

A fear of lesbians, or of being accused of being a lesbian, has led many Black women into testifying against themselves. It has led some of us into destructive alliances, and others into despair and isolation. In the white women's communities, heterosexism is sometimes a result of identifying with the white patriarchy, a rejection of that interdependence between women-identified women which allows the self to be, rather than to be used in the service of men. Sometimes it reflects a diehard belief in the protective coloration of heterosexual relationships, sometimes a self-hate which all women have to fight against, taught us from birth.

Although elements of these attitudes exist for all women, there are particular resonances of heterosexism and homophobia among Black women. Despite the fact that woman-bonding has a long and honorable history in the African and African-american communities, and despite the knowledge and accomplishments of many strong and creative women-identified Black women in the political, social and cultural fields, heterosexual Black women often tend to ignore or discount the existence and work of Black lesbians. Part of this attitude has come from an understandable terror of Black male attack within the close confines of Black society, where the punishment for any female self-assertion is still to be accused of being a lesbian and therefore unworthy of the attention or support of the scarce Black male. But part of this need to misname and ignore Black lesbians comes from a very real fear that openly women-identified Black women who are no longer dependent upon men for their self-definition may well reorder our whole concept of social relationships.

Black women who once insisted that lesbianism was a white woman's problem now insist that Black lesbians are a threat to Black nationhood, are consorting with the enemy, are basically un-Black. These accusations, coming from the very women to whom we look for deep and real understanding, have served to keep many Black lesbians in hiding, caught between the racism of white women and the homophobia of their sisters. Often, their work has been ignored, trivialized, or misnamed, as with the work of Angelina Grimke, Alice Dunbar-Nelson, Lorraine Hansberry. Yet women-bonded women have always been some part of the power of Black communities, from our unmarried aunts to the amazons of Dahomey.

And it is certainly not Black lesbians who are assaulting women and raping children and grandmothers on the streets of our communities.

Across this country, as in Boston during the spring of 1979 following the unsolved murders of twelve Black women, Black lesbians are spearheading movements against violence against Black women.

What are the particular details within each of our lives that can be scrutinized and altered to help bring about change? How do we redefine difference for all women? It is not our differences which separate women, but our reluctance to recognize those differences and to deal effectively with the distortions which have resulted from the ignoring and misnaming of those differences.

As a tool of social control, women have been encouraged to recognize only one area of human difference as legitimate, those differences which exist between women and men. And we have learned to deal across those differences with the urgency of all oppressed subordinates. All of us have had to learn to live or work or coexist with men, from our fathers on. We have recognized and negotiated these differences, even when this recognition only continued the old dominant/ subordinate mode of human relationship, where the oppressed must recognize the masters' difference in order to survive.

But our future survival is predicated upon our ability to relate within equality. As women, we must root our internalized patterns of oppression within ourselves if we are to move beyond the most superficial aspects of social change. Now we must recognize differences among women who are our equals, neither inferior nor superior, and devise ways to use each others' difference to enrich our visions and our joint struggles.

The future of our earth may depend upon the ability of all women to identify and develop new definitions of power and new patterns of relating across difference. The old definitions have not served us, nor the earth that supports us. The old patterns, no matter how cleverly rearranged to imitate progress, still condemn us to cosmetically altered repetitions of the same old exchanges, the same old guilt, hatred, recrimination, lamentation, and suspicion.

For we have, built into all of us, old blueprints of expectation and response, old structures of oppression, and these must be altered at the same time as we alter the living conditions which are a result of those structures. For the master's tools will never dismantle the master's house.

As Paulo Freire shows so well in *The Pedagogy of the Oppressed*,[2] the true focus of revolutionary change is never merely the oppressive situations which we seek to escape, but that piece of the oppressor which is planted deep within each of us, and which knows only the oppressors' tactics, the oppressors' relationships.

Change means growth, and growth can be painful. But we sharpen self-definition by exposing the self in work and struggle together with those whom we define as different from ourselves, although sharing the same goals. For Black and white, old and young, lesbian and heterosexual women alike, this can mean new paths to our survival.

> We have chosen each other
> and the edge of each others battles
> the war is the same
> if we lose
> someday women's blood will congeal
> upon a dead planet
> if we win
> there is no telling
> we seek beyond history
> for a new and more possible meaning.[3]

NOTES

1. From "Rape: A Radical Analysis, An African-American Perspective" by Kalamu ya Salaam in *Black Books Bulletin*, vol. 6, no. 4 (1980).

2. Seabury Press, New York, 1970.

3. From "Outlines," unpublished poem.

2

En rapport, In Opposition:
Cobrando cuentas a las nuestras

Gloria Anzaldúa

Watch For Falling Rocks

The first time I drove from El Paso to San Diego, I saw a sign that read *Watch for Falling Rocks*. And though I watched and waited for rocks to roll down the steep cliff walls and attack my car and me, I never saw any falling rocks. Today, one of the things I'm most afraid of are the rocks we throw at each other. And the resultant guilt we carry like a corpse strapped to our backs for having thrown rocks. We colored women have memories like elephants. The slightest hurt is recorded deep within. We do not forget the injury done to us and we do not forget the injury we have done another. For unfortunately we do not have hides like elephants. Our vulnerability is measured by our capacity for openness, intimacy. And we all know that our own kind is driven through shame or self-hatred to poke at all our open wounds. And we know they know exactly where the hidden wounds are.

> I keep track of all distinctions. Between past and present. Pain and pleasure. Living and surviving. Resistance and capitulation. Will and circumstances. Between life and death. Yes. I am scrupulously accurate. I have become a keeper of accounts.
> —Irena Klepfisz[1]

One of the changes that I've seen since *This Bridge Called My Back* was published[2] is that we no longer allow white women to efface us or suppress us. Now we do it to each other. We have taken over the missionary's "let's civilize the savage role," fixating on the "wrongness" and moral or political inferiority of some of our sisters, insisting on a profound difference between oneself and the *Other*. We have been indoctrinated into adopting the old imperialist ways of conquering and dominating, adopting a way of confrontation based on differences while standing on the ground of ethnic superiority.

408

In the "dominant" phase of colonialism, European colonizers exercise direct control of the colonized, destroy the native legal and cultural systems, and negate non-European civilizations in order to ruthlessly exploit the resources of the subjugated with the excuse of attempting to "civilize" them. Before the end of this phase, the natives internalize Western culture. By the time we reach the "neocolonialist" phase, we've accepted the white colonizers' system of values, attitudes, morality, and modes of production.[3] It is not by chance that in the more rural towns of Texas Chicano neighborhoods are called *colonias* rather than *barrios*.

There have always been those of us who have "cooperated" with the colonizers. It's not that we have been "won" over by the dominant culture, but that it has exploited pre-existing power relations of subordination and subjugation within our native societies.[4] The great White ripoff and they are still cashing in. Like our exploiters who fixate on the inferiority of the natives, we fixate on the fucked-upness of our sisters. Like them we try to impose our version of "the ways things should be"; we try to impose one's self on the *Other* by making her the recipient of one's negative elements, usually the same elements that the Anglo projected on us. Like them, we project our self-hatred on her; we stereotype her; we make her generic.

Just How Ethnic Are You?

One of the reasons for this hostility among us is the forced cultural penetration, the rape of the colored by the white, with the colonizers depositing their perspective, their language, their values in our bodies. External oppression is paralleled with our internalization of that oppression. And our acting out from that oppression. They have us doing to those within our own ranks what they have done and continue to do to us—*Othering* people. That is, isolating them, pushing them out of the herd, ostracizing them. The internalization of negative images of ourselves, our self-hatred, poor self-esteem, makes our own people the *Other*. We shun the white-looking Indian, the "high yellow" Black woman, the Asian with the white lover, the Native woman who brings her white girl friend to the Pow Wow, the Chicana who doesn't speak Spanish, the academic, the uneducated. Her difference makes her a person we can't trust. *Para que sea "legal,"* she must pass the ethnic legitimacy test we have devised. And it is exactly our internalized whiteness that desperately wants boundary lines (this part of me is Mexican, this Indian) marked out and woe to any sister or any part of us that steps out of our assigned places, woe to anyone who doesn't measure up to our standards of ethnicity. *Si no cualifica,* if she fails to pass the test, *le aventamos mierda en la cara, le aventamos piedras, la aventamos.* We throw shit in her face, we throw rocks, we kick her out. *Como gallos de pelea nos atacamos unas a las otras—mexicanas de nacimiento contra* the born-again *mexicanas.* Like fighting cocks, razor blades strapped to our fingers, we slash out at each other. We have turned our anger against ourselves. And our anger is immense. *Es un acido que corroe.*

Internal Affairs *o las que niegan a su gente*

Tu traición yo la llevo aquá muy dentro,
la llevo dentro de mi alma
dentro de mi corazón.
Tu traición.
    —Cornelio Reyna[5]

I get so tired of constantly struggling with my sisters. The more we have in common, including love, the greater the heartache between us, the more we hurt each other. It's excruciatingly painful, this constant snarling at our own shadows. Anything can set the conflict in motion: the lover getting more recognition by the community, the friend getting a job with higher status, a break-up. As one of my friends said, "We can't fucking get along."

So we find ourselves *entreguerras*,[6] a kind of civil war among intimates, an in-class, in-race, in-house fighting, a war with strategies, tactics that are our coping mechanisms, that once were our survival skills and which we now use upon one another,[7] producing intimate terrorism—a modern form of *las guerras floridas*, the war of flowers that the Aztecs practiced in order to gain captives for the sacrifices. Only now we are each other's victims, we offer the *Other* to our politically correct altar.

El deniego. The hate we once cast at our oppressors we now fling at women of our own race. Reactionary—we have gone to the other extreme—denial of our own. We struggle for power, compete, vie for control. Like kin, we are there for each other, but like kin we come to blows. And the differences between us and this new *Other* are not racial but ideological, not metaphysical but psychological. *Nos negamos a si mismas y el deniego nos causa daño.*

Breaking Out of the Frame

I'm standing at the sea end of the truncated Berkeley pier. A boat had plowed into the black posts gouging out a few hundred feet of structure, cutting the pier in two. I stare at the sea, surging silver-plated, between me and the loped-off corrugated arm, the wind whipping my hair. I look down, my head and shoulders, a shadow on the sea. Yemaya pours strings of light over my dull jade, flickering body, bubbles pop out of my ears. I feel the tension easing and, for the first time in months, the litany of work yet to do, of deadlines, that sings incessantly in my head, blows away with the wind.
    Oh, Yemaya, I shall speak the words
        you lap against the pier.
But as I turn away I see in the distance a ship's fin fast approaching. I see fish heads lying listless in the sun, smell the stench of pollution in the waters.

From where I stand, *queridas carnalas*—in a feminist position—I see, through a critical lens with variable focus, that we must not drain our energy breaking down the male/white frame (the whole of Western culture) but turn to our own kind and change our terms of reference. As long as we see the world and our experiences through white eyes—in a dominant/subordinate way—we're trapped in the tar and pitch of the old manipulative and strive-for-power ways.

Even those of us who don't want to buy in get sucked into the vortex of the dominant culture's fixed oppositions, the duality of superiority and inferiority, of subject and object. Some of us, to get out of the internalized neocolonial phase, make for the fringes, the Borderlands. And though we have not broken out of the white frame, we at least see it for what it is. Questioning the values of the dominant culture which imposes fundamental difference on those of the "wrong" side of the good/bad dichotomy is the first step. Responding to the *Other* not as irrevocably different is the second step. By highlighting similarities, downplaying divergences, that is, by *rapprochement* between self and *Other* it is possible to build a syncretic relationship. At the basis of such a relationship lies an understanding of the effects of colonization and its resultant pathologies.

We have our work cut out for us. Nothing is more difficult than identifying emotionally with a cultural alterity, with the *Other*. *Alter*: to make different; to castrate. *Altercate*: to dispute angrily. *Alter ego*: another self or another aspect of oneself. *Alter idem*: another of the same kind. Nothing is harder than identifying with an interracial identity, with a mestizo identity. One has to leave the permanent boundaries of a fixed self, literally "leave" oneself and see oneself through the eyes of the *Other*. Cultural identity is "nothing more nor less than the mean between selfhood and otherness. . . ."[8] Nothing scares the Chicana more than a quasi Chicana; nothing disturbs a Mexican more than an acculturated Chicana; nothing agitates a Chicana more than a Latina who lumps her with the *norteamericanas*. It is easier to retreat to the safety of difference behind racial, cultural and class borders. Because our awareness of the *Other* as object often swamps our awareness of ourselves as subject, it is hard to maintain a fine balance between cultural ethnicity and the continuing survival of that culture, between traditional culture and an evolving hybrid culture. How much must remain the same, how much must change.

For most of us our ethnicity is still the issue. Ours continues to be a struggle of identity—not against a white background so much as against a colored background. *Ya no estamos afuera o atras del marco de la pintura*—we no longer stand outside nor behind the frame of the painting. We are both the foreground, the background and the figures predominating. Whites are not the central figure, they are not even in the frame, though the frame of reference is still white, male and heterosexual. But the white is still there, invisible, under our skin—we have subsumed the white.

El desengaño/Disillusionment

And yes I have some criticism, some self-criticism. And no I will not make everything nice. There is shit among us we need to sift through. Who knows, there may be some fertilizer in it. I've seen collaborative efforts between us end in verbal abuse, cruelty and trauma. I've seen collectives fall apart, dumping their ideals by the wayside and treating each other worse than they'd treat a rabid dog. My momma said, "Never tell other people our business, never divulge family secrets." Chicano dirt you do not air out in front of white folks, nor lesbian dirty laundry in front of heterosexuals. The cultural things stay with la Raza. Colored feminists must present a united front in front of whites and other groups. But the fact is we are not united. (I've come to suspect that unity is another Anglo invention like their one sole god and the myth of the monopole.[9]) We are not going to cut through *la mierda* by sweeping the dirt under the rug.

We have a responsibility to each other, certain commitments. The leap into self-affirmation goes hand in hand with being critical of self. Many of us walk around with reactionary, self-righteous attitudes. We preach certain political behaviors and theories and we do fine with writing about them. Though we want others to live their lives by them, we do not live them. When we are called on it, we go into a self-defensive mode and denial just like whites did when we started asking them to be accountable for their race and class biases.

Las opuestas/Those in Opposition

In us, intra- and cross-cultural hostilities surface in not so subtle put-downs. *Las no comprometidas, las que negan a sus gente. Fruncemos las caras y negamos toda responsabilidad.* Where some of us racially mixed people are stuck in now is denial and its damaging effects. Denial of the white aspects that we've been forced to acquire, denial of our sisters who for one reason or another cannot "pass" as 100% ethnic—as if such a thing exists. Racial purity, like language purity, is a fallacy. Denying the reality of who we are destroys the basis needed from which to talk honestly and deeply about the issues between us. We cannot make any real connections because we are not touching each other. So we sit facing each other and before the words escape our mouths the real issues are blanked in our consciousness, erased before they register because it hurts too much to talk about them, because it makes us vulnerable to the hurt the *carnala* may dish out, because we've been wounded too deeply and too often in the past. So we sit, a paper face before another paper face— two people who suddenly cease to be real. *La no compasiva con la complaciente, lo incomunicado atorado en sus gargantas.*

We, the new Inquisitors, swept along with the "swing to the right" of the growing religious and political intolerance, crusade against racial heretics, mow down with the sickle of righteous anger our dissenting sisters. The issue (in all aspects of life) has always been when to resist changes and when to be open to them. Right now, this rigidity will break us.

Recobrando/Recovering

Una luz fria y cenicienta bañada en la plata palida del amanecer entra a mi escritorio and I think about the critical stages we feminists of color are going through, chiefly that of learning to live with each other as *carnalas, parientes, amantes,* as kin, as friends, as lovers. Looking back on the road that we've walked on during the last decade, I see many emotional, psychological, spiritual, political gains—primarily developing an understanding and acceptance of the spirituality of our root ethnic cultures. This has given us the ground from which to see that our spiritual lives are not split from our daily acts. *En recobrando* our affinity with nature and her forces (deities), we have "recovered" our ancient identity, digging it out like dark clay, pressing it to our current identity, molding past and present, inner and outer. Our clay-streaked faces acquiring again images of our ethnic self and self-respect taken from us by the *colonizadores.* And if we've suffered losses, if often in the process we have momentarily "misplaced" our *carnala*hood, our sisterhood, there beside us always are the women, *las mujeres.* And that is enough to keep us going.

By grounding in the earth of our native spiritual identity, we can build up our personal and tribal identity. We can reach out for the clarity we need. Burning sage and sweetgrass by itself won't cut it, but it can be a basis from which we act.

And yes, we are elephants with long memories, but scrutinizing the past with binocular vision and training it on the juncture of past with present, and identifying the options on hand and mapping out future roads will ensure us survival.

So if we won't forget past grievances, let us forgive. Carrying the ghosts of past grievances *no vale la pena.* It is not worth the grief. It keeps us from ourselves and each other; it keeps us from new relationships. We need to cultivate other ways of coping. I'd like to think that the in-fighting that we presently find ourselves doing is only a stage in the continuum of our growth, an offshoot of the conflict that the process of biculturation spawns, a phase of the internal colonization process, one that will soon cease to hold sway over our lives. I'd like to see it as a skin we will shed as we are born into the 21st century.

And now in these times of the turning of the century, of harmonic conversion, of the end of *El Quinto Sol* (as the ancient Aztecs named our present age), it is time we began to get out of the state of opposition and into *rapprochment,* time to get our heads, words, ways out of white territory. It is time that we broke out of the invisible white frame and stood on the ground of our own ethnic being.

NOTES

1. Irena Klepfisz, *Keeper of Accounts* (Montpelier, VT: Sinister Wisdom, 1982), 85.

2. According to Chela Sandoval, the publication of *Bridge* marked the end of the second wave of the women's movement in its previous form. *U.S. Third World Feminist Criticism: The Theory and Method of Oppositional Consciousness,* a dissertation in process.

3. Abdul R. JanMohamed, "The Economy of Manichean Allegory: The Function of Racial Difference in Colonialist Literature," *"Race," Writing, and Difference,* ed. Henry Louis Gates, Jr. (Chicago: University of Chicago Press, 1985), 80–81.

4. JanMohamed, 81.

5. A Chicano from Texas who sings and plays *bajo-sexto* in his *música norteña/conjunto.* "*Tu Traición*" is from the album *15 Exitasos,* Reyna Records, 1981.

6. *Entreguerras, entremundos/Inner Wars Among the Worlds* is the title of a forthcoming book of narratives/novel.

7. Sarah Hoagland, "Lesbian Ethics: Intimacy & Self-Understanding," *Bay Area Women's News*, May/June 1987, vol. 1, no. 2, 7.

8. Nadine Gordimer is quoted in JanMohamed's essay, 88.

9. Physicists are searching for a single law of physics under which all other laws will fall.

3

Up Against the Wall

Cherríe Moraga

The cold in my chest comes
from having to decide

while the ice builds up on *this* side
of my new-york-apt.-bldg.-window
whose death
has been marked
upon the collective forehead
of this continent, this
shattering globe
the most indelibly.

Indelible. A catholic word
I learned
when I learned
that there were catholics and there
were not.
　　　　But somehow
we did not count the Jews
among the have-nots, only protestants
with their cold & bloodless god
with no candles/no incense/no bloody
sacrifice or spirits
lurking.

Protestantism. The white people's
religion.

. . .

First time I remember
seeing pictures of the Holocaust
was in the ninth grade and the moving pictures
were already there in my mind
somehow *before* they showed me
what I already understood
that these people were killed
for the spirit-blood
that runs through them.

They were like us in this.
Ethnic people with long last names
with vowels at the end or the wrong
type of consonants
combined   a colored kind of white people.

But let me tell you
first time I saw an actual
picture glossy photo of a lynching
I was already grown & active
& living & loving Jewish.
Black. White. Puerto
Rican.
      And the image blasted
my consciousness   split it
wide   I
had never thought   seen
heard   of such a thing
never imagined the look
of the man   the weight
dead
hanging
swinging
heavy
the fact   of the white people
cold
bloodless
looking on   It

had never occurred to me
I tell you   I
the nuns
failed to mention
this could happen, too
how *could* such a thing happen?

because somehow dark real dark
was not quite real
people killed
but some
thing not
taken to heart
in the same way it feels
to see white shaved/starved
burned/buried
the boned bodies stacked & bulldozed
into huge craters made by men
and machines
and at fifteen
before that movie screen
I kept running through my mind
and I'm only one
count one
it could be me
it could be me
I'm nothing
to this cruelty.

. . .

Somehow tonight,
is it the particular coldness
where I sleep with a cap
to keep it out
that causes me to toss
and turn the events of the last weeks
the last years of my life
around in my sleep?

Is it the same white coldness
that forces my back up
against the wall—*choose.*
Choose.

I cannot
choose nor forget
how simple
to fall back
upon rehearsed racial memory.

I work to remember
what I never dreamed possible
what my consciousness could never
contrive.

Whoever I am

I must believe
I am not
and will never be
the only
one
who suffers.

4

Toward a More Caring Society

Ruth Sidel

We have listened as young women have talked about their dreams: their dreams of work, of success, of affluence; their dreams of love, of child rearing, of intimacy; their dreams of affiliation and of independence. We have also heard their concerns: concerns about balancing work and family, about needing to be able to go it alone, about finding that close personal relationship so many seek. And we have heard their despair: the despair of those who cannot envision a future beyond tomorrow, of those whose lives have been shaped at a young age by personal circumstances and social and economic forces often beyond their control, of eighteen- and nineteen-year-olds who seem old before their time.

In listening to these young women it is clear that twenty-five years after the publication of *The Feminine Mystique*, much has changed and much has remained the same. Women are attending college and graduate school in greater numbers than ever before. In the area of work, women have made great strides: the vast increase in the number of women in the labor force; the once unimaginable increase in the number of women in high-status, high-income professions; the growing acceptance, both on the part of women and on the part of many men, that women are competent, committed workers who can get the job done and achieve a considerable amount of their identity through their work roles. In keeping with their greatly increased presence in the world of work, women are often pictured by the media, by the fashion industry, even by politicians as serious, significant members of the labor force.

In recent years women have also gained greater control over their bodies. Largely because of the feminist movement, women have far greater understanding of how their bodies work, more control over their own fertility, and far greater participation in the process of childbirth. As this is being written, some of that control is under siege, particularly the right to abortion; but there have been significant strides nonetheless.

And, perhaps most important, many women recognize that they must make their own way in the world, that they must develop their own identity rather than acquire that identity through a relationship with a man. Woman after woman detailed her plan for becoming a full-fledged person, able to survive on her own; and woman after woman recognized that she must be able to support herself and, if she has them, her children as well.

But in other areas over this quarter-century there has been very little change, and some aspects of women's lives have deteriorated dramatically. Women are still all too often depicted in advertising, in films, on television, and by the fashion industry as sex objects. Women are still encouraged to focus on their looks—their bodies, their clothes, their makeup, their image. How women are supposed to look may have changed; but the tyranny of physical attractiveness, compounded by the need to appear "fit" and youthful, is omnipresent. Even in an event such as the women's final of the 1988 U.S. Open tennis tournament, in which Steffi Graf was trying to win her fourth major tournament of the year, thereby winning the "Grand Slam"—a feat accomplished by only four other players in the history of tennis—the good looks of her opponent, Gabriela Sabatini, were mentioned numerous times by the male television announcers, who were otherwise scrupulously nonsexist. It is noteworthy that in the record-breaking four-hour-and-fifty-four-minute men's final, which pitted Mats Wilander against Ivan Lendl, there was no mention of Wilander's rugged good looks. It is not, after all, simply how well women play the game but how they look while playing that counts as well.

The area of sex is still extraordinarily problematic for young women today. Of all the mine fields women must navigate, sex is one of the most complex and treacherous. The pressures to have sex are enormous and the pressures not to plan for sex nearly as great. Many young women are caught in this incredible bind: some are caught by ignorance, others by the desire to be part of the group; some by fear, others by the need to be held or "loved." And many are caught by the notion that having sex is cool, sophisticated, a rite of passage somehow required in today's culture. But it is still widely seen as something you do inadvertently, almost as an afterthought, for if a fifteen-, sixteen-, or seventeen-year-old plans for sex, goes to the local family-planning clinic for contraception, acknowledges her intention, takes responsibility for her actions, truly takes control, she is often seen by her peers, her family, even her community as deviant, as a "bad girl." To acquiesce is permissible; to choose clearly and consciously to embark on a sexual relationship is somehow reprehensible. One is reminded of many magazine advertisements that picture women being "carried away" by feeling or literally carried away by men, vignettes that are clearly metaphors for sex. Are we really saying that being carried away is appropriately feminine while being in control of one's actions is not?

But it is not only the objectification of women that remains a fact of life but the marginalization of women as well, particularly in the workplace and in positions of power. Contrary to the expectations of the young women I interviewed, female workers still occupy the lowest rungs of most occupations, including the prestigious professions they have recently entered in such large numbers. Women may have entered the labor market in record numbers in recent years, but they are still working predominantly in the lowest-paying jobs within the lowest-paying occupations.

In addition, it has become clear over the past decade that poverty dominates and determines the lives of millions of women in the United States. Today two out of three poor adults are women. Teen mothers, female heads of families, divorced women, many working women, elderly women, the "new poor" as well as those who have grown up in poverty are all at substantial risk of spending a significant part of their lives at or below the poverty line. And, of course, if women are poor, their children are poor. One out of five children under the age of eighteen and one out of four under the age of six live in poverty today. One out of every two young black children is officially poor. Perhaps most disturbing, moreover, are the sharp increases over the past decade in the number of children in families with incomes below the poverty line, a group that has been termed "the poorest of the poor." The vast majority of these families are headed by women.

Within this context, within the reality of women's true economic situation, what is surprising in talking with young women from various parts of the country—black women, white women, and Hispanic women; affluent, middle-class, and poor women; women who are headed for Ivy League colleges as well as high school dropouts—is the narrowness of their image of success, the uniformity of their dreams. The affluent life as symbolized by the fancy car, the "house on a hill," the "Bloomingdale's wardrobe," "giving everything to my children," was described yearningly time and time again. As if programmed, the same words, the same dreams tumbled out of the mouths of young women from very different backgrounds and life experiences. Success was seen, overwhelmingly, in terms of what they would be able to purchase, what kind of "life-style" they would have. The ability to consume in an upper-middle-class manner was often the ultimate goal. . . .

Few spoke of becoming a reporter or a journalist, of teaching or entering the ministry. Rarely did anyone speak of caring for the sick or helping the poor; only occasionally did someone hope to make difference in the lives of others. Even those planning to become social workers or nurses (and there were very few) spoke mainly of their concern that these professions would pay enough to enable them to live the life-style they hoped for. Are these young women programmed or "brainwashed," or are they too reflecting the tone—and the economic reality—or their time?

Are young women focusing on material possessions in part because they are at least something to hold on to, symbols of identity and security in an era of fragmented family life, insecure, often transient work relationships, and a vanishing sense of community? In any case, young women are surely reflecting the omnipresent message of television. As Todd Gitlin has stated:

> With few exceptions, prime time gives us people preoccupied with personal ambition . . . Personal ambition and consumerism are the driving forces in their lives. The sumptuous and brightly lit settings of most series amount to advertisements for a consumption-centered version of the good life, and this doesn't even take into consideration the incessant commercials, which convey the idea that human aspirations for liberty, pleasure, accomplishment, and status can be fulfilled in the realm of consumption.

Given the reality of the job market for women, what will become of their dreams of affluence? Given the reality of the structure of work and the availability of child care, what will become of their image of mothering? Have these young women, in fact, been sold a false dream? Have young women become encouraged to raise their expectations, only to see those expectations unfulfilled because there has not been comparable change within society? Have the major institutions that influence public opinion—the media, advertising, the fashion industry, as well as the industries that produce consumer goods and parts of the educational establishment— fostered these rising expectations because it suits their purposes and, in some cases, their profits? Has the dream of equal opportunity for women and men, of at least partial redistribution of power both within the family and in the society at large, been coopted and commodified, turned into a sprint for consumer goods rather than a long march toward a more humane life for all of us?

Have we indeed over the last quarter-century persuaded women that they, too, are entitled to their fair share of the American Dream, in their own right, not merely as appendages to the primary players, without changing the rules of the game in ways that would permit them truly to compete and succeed? Have women, in short, been hoodwinked into believing that they can "have it all, do it all, be it all" while society itself changes minimally? And have we somehow communicated to them that they must make it on their own, recreating the myth of the rugged individualist seeking the American Dream—alone? . . .

Much has been written about the difficult choices women currently have: how to balance marriage and career; how to balance motherhood and career; the timing of conception; the problems of a demanding job versus the demands and joys of motherhood. But these books, articles, television programs, and occasionally films put forth a largely false message: that the majority of women in late-twentieth-century America indeed have these choices to make. The illusion is abroad in the land that a young woman can simply "choose" to postpone pregnancy and marriage, acquire the education of her choice (which should, of course, be in a field in which jobs are available and well paying), and then step into the job of her choice. At that point, if she wishes, the man of her dreams will miraculously appear (and will be single and interested in "commitment"!), and, despite years of contraception and possibly even an abortion or two, she will promptly conceive, have a healthy baby or two, and live happily ever after. But of course we know life is not like that—at least not for the vast majority of women.

Most women do not have these magnificent choices. The education of many women is circumscribed by economics, by inferior schooling, and by the expectations of their social group. The jobs they will take are dictated far more by the economy, by what jobs are "open" to women, and by their own economic need than by individual choice. And, as we know all too well, controlling and timing fertility can be an extremely difficult and delicate task. Not only do many women become pregnant when they are unprepared for motherhood, but many cannot seem to have a child when they have been planning and longing for one for years. Moreover, many women grow up hungry, homeless, and hopeless, part of the underside of a society that is increasingly coming to resemble a third-world nation with its very rich and privileged and its very poor and despairing.

This illusion of choice is a major impediment to the establishment of conditions that would enable women—and indeed all people—to have real choices. Young women recognize that they are likely to participate actively in both work and home, in "doing" and "caring," but they fail to recognize what they must have in order to do so: meaningful options and supports in their work lives; in childbearing, child rearing, and the structure of their families; in housing, health care, and child care; and, above all, in the values by which they live their lives. Does emphasis on fashion, consumerism, and the lives of the rich and famous create the illusion of choice while diverting attention from serious discussion of policies that would give women genuine options? It is significant that during the 1988 presidential campaign legislation to raise the minimum wage, to provide parental leave, and to improve and expand the child care system—measures that would have significantly increased the life options of women and of all family members—were defeated, the latter two by a Republican filibuster. Despite the much-touted gender gap, little real attention was paid to policies that relate primarily to the well-being of women and children during the national campaign, a time when these issues could have been thoroughly discussed and debated. Do politicians really believe that women are not watching and listening? Are women perhaps *not* watching and listening? Or have they given up on a society that does not seem interested in addressing their needs?

For women to have real choices, we must develop a society in which women and children and indeed families of all shapes and sizes are respected and valued. Despite the mythology of American individualism, it is clear that most women cannot truly go it alone. The young women I interviewed know that they must be prepared to be part of the labor force and still be available to care for others—for children, for older family members, for friends, for lovers—but these often mutually exclusive tasks will be possible only when we develop a society that supports doing and caring. Men must take on caring functions; the society must take some of the responsibility for caring and above all must be restructured to permit, even to encourage, doing and caring. Women simply cannot do it all and cannot do it alone.

To suggest that aspects of American society must be significantly altered may seem to some to be utopian or at best visionary. In a time of corporate takeovers, insider trading, and lavish levels of private consumption, calling for fundamental restructuring of social and economic priorities may seem fatuous or at best naive. I do not mean to suggest that such restructuring will be accomplished easily or in the near future, but while many of these changes may take years or even decades to accomplish, if we are to bring about significant change in the twenty-first century, discussion and debate must be ongoing and must involve all sectors of society. It must be stressed, moreover, that most of these proposals have been outlined before and will be explored again and again. It is my hope that this discussion will add to the debate and will thereby further the process of developing a more humane environment in which we can all live, work, and care for one another.

First, I believe that fundamental change must be made in the workplace. Traditionally male-dominated professions cannot continue to expect their workers to function as if there were a full-time wife and mother at home. Most male workers no longer live in that never-never land; female workers surely do not. Alternative paths to partnerships, professorships, and promotion must be developed that will neither leave women once again at the bottom of the career ladder without real power and equal rewards nor force them to choose between a demanding work life and a demanding personal life.

Nor should women have to choose a middle ground between work and mothering. One compromise has been described as "sequencing"—establishing a career, leaving it to bring up the children, and then resuming work in a way that does not conflict with domestic responsibilities. Isn't that what many of us did in the fifties? Most women, clearly, cannot afford to sequence. Try telling a stitcher in a garment factory to sequence—or a waitress or a clerical worker. In addition to the loss of income, status, and seniority, the problem with these upper-middle-class "solutions," which are often unsatisfactory even for those who can afford them, is that once again they give the illusion of choice. For the vast majority of American women, sequencing is not possible, or even desirable. What we must develop are options for the millions of women who must work and for the millions of women who *want* to work, not the illusion of options applicable only to that minority of women who are part of affluent two-parent families and are willing to sacrifice their careers, their earning power, and often the real pleasure they obtain from work because the larger society is unwilling to meet women and families even halfway.

Another compromise suggested recently is institutionalizing within corporations one track for "'career primary'" women, who can "be worked long hours, promoted, relocated and generally treated like a man," and another for "career and 'family'" women, who will accept "lower pay and little advancement in return for a flexible schedule that allows . . .[them] to accommodate to family needs." This proposal clearly would legitimize the second-class status of any parent, mother, or father who wished to spend a significant amount of time on family responsibilities. Once again, we would be insisting that individuals and families bend to norms that are defined by employers and that primarily serve the needs of employers.

We must reevaluate our system of economic rewards. Do we really want our entertainers, our stockbrokers, our corporate executives, and our divorce lawyers making millions while our nurses and day-care workers barely scrape by? Do we really want the rich to get richer while the poor get poorer and the middle class loses ground? Do we really want to tell our young women that they must play traditional male roles in order to earn a decent living and that caregiving no longer counts, is no longer worth doing? . . .

Market forces cannot be permitted to rule in all spheres of American life. If our society is to be a caring, humane place to live, to rear our children, and to grow old, we must recognize that some aspects of life—the education of our young people, health care, child care, the texture of community life, the quality of the environment—are more important than profit. We as a nation must determine our priorities and act accordingly. If teaching, the care of young children, providing nursing care, and other human services are essential to the quality of life in the United States, then we must recruit our young people into these fields and pay them what the job is really worth. Only then will we be giving them, particularly our young women, real choices. If we want nurses to care for our sick, we must indicate by decent wages and working conditions that the job is valued by society. We must give nurses and other health workers real authority, a meaningful voice in the health-care system, and then, and only then, will some of our best and brightest and most caring women and men choose to enter nursing. Whatever happened to careers in community organizing, urban planning, Legal Aid, and public-health nursing? Young women and men will be able to consider these options only if they are decently paid, have a future and some degree of security and respect.

In this fin de siècle period of U.S. history characterized (in the words of John Kenneth Galbraith) by "private affluence" and "public squalor," it may be difficult to see our way clear to putting significantly larger amounts of money into health care, community organizing, education, or even a meaningful effort to deter young people from drug abuse, but we must recognize that these issues are central to the well-being of families and thus central to the very fabric and structure of American society. While the 1980s have surely been characterized by absorption with personal advancement and well-being (particularly economic and physical well-being), there are many indications that Americans are also concerned about the well-being of the society as a whole. Poll after poll has demonstrated that people *are* concerned about issues such as education and homelessness and *are* willing to make sacrifices to enable the society to deal more effectively with these problems.

Furthermore, it is often said that there is no money to truly make this into a "kinder, gentler nation" but we must remember that the United States spends $300 billion annually on arms, the U.S. Congress has approved the Bush administration's savings and loan bailout proposal that will cost nearly $160 billion over the next ten years, and the United States has one of the lowest tax rates, particularly for the wealthy, in the industrialized world. I suggest that the money *is* there. The issue is how we choose to allocate it.

What should our priorities be? Among them, parents must have some time at home with their children. Why can't parents of young children work a shorter day or week and not risk losing their jobs? Why aren't parents at the time of the birth or adoption of a baby guaranteed some paid time together with that infant when virtually every other industrialized country has some statutory maternity or parental leave? The parental leave bill that was killed during the 100th Congress called for unpaid leave for the parents of a newborn or newly adopted child. It would have affected only 5 percent of all businesses and 40 percent of all workers (the firms affected would have been those with fifty or more employees). It was estimated by Senator John H. Chafee, Republican of Rhode Island, that the cost would have been $160 million per year, which averages out to one cent per day for each covered employee. The bill also would have provided unpaid leave for parents with seriously ill children. As Senator Christopher J. Dodd, Democrat of Connecticut, a sponsor of the legislation, stated:

> Today fewer than one in ten American families have the luxury of having the mother at home with the children while the father is at work.
>
> In this nation today there are 8.7 million women as the sole providers of their families. They are taking care of 16 million kids who have no father at home. And when that child becomes sick or that employee becomes sick, we ought not to say to that family struggling to make ends meet: "Choose. Choose your child or choose your job."

No, women cannot make it alone. They cannot work and parent and care for their elderly relatives as well without a caring society. They cannot work and care for others without sufficient income, parental leave, real flex time, and a work environment that recognizes and understands that a rewarding private life takes time and energy.

Furthermore, that work environment must make it possible for both fathers and mothers to care for others. It must become acceptable in the United States for fathers to take leave to care for a new baby, to stay home with sick children, to leave work in time to pick up a child from day care or after-school care; for sons to attend to the needs of aging parents. It must even become acceptable for fathers to attend a school play or a Halloween party during the work day. Changing male roles may take years of resocialization and structural change within the society, but we must attempt it nonetheless. Mothers can no longer play the solitary domestic role—not while participating in the work force as well. If women are to do and to care, men must also do and care.

Perhaps a vignette from the life of one family and one work site illustrates the need to humanize the workplace. On November 21, 1985, the U.S. Senate agreed not to cast any votes between seven and nine p.m. The following letter was the reason for this unusual action:

Dear Senator Dole:
I am having my second-grade play tonight. Please make sure there aren't any votes between 7 and 9 so my daddy can watch me. Please come with him if you can.
Love,
Corinne Quayle

What is particularly remarkable about this incident is that when the final version of the Parental and Medical Leave Act was being written by the Senate Labor and Human Resources Committee, Vice-President J. Danforth Quayle, then a senator, vehemently opposed it and, according to one observer, "offered an amendment in committee that would assure that an employer enjoys the right to fire an employee who takes as much as one day off to be with a seriously ill child." As Judy Mann, the *Washington Post* columnist who brought this incident to light, wrote: "Quayle lives by a set of special rules for the privileged and well-connected and doesn't hesitate to impose another set of rules and obligations, harsher and devoid of compassion, on those who were not to the manner born. Either he doesn't know anything about the reality of most workers' lives, or he doesn't care."

The United States must also finally decide where it stands on the care of preschool children. By 1995 two-thirds of all preschool children (approximately 15 million) and more than three-quarters of all school-age children (approximately 34.4 million) will have mothers in the work force. In addition, 3.7 million mothers receiving welfare with 3.1 million children under six and 2.9 million school-age children will with the passage of recent welfare legislation be required to enter the work force or to participate in education and job-training courses. Day care must be provided for those single-parent families for at least one year. Today only 23 percent of all children of working parents attend full or part-time centers, which vary enormously in quality; an additional 23 percent are cared for in family day care, most of which is unlicensed and unsupervised. As Edward Zigler, director of the Bush Center in Child Development and Social Policy at Yale and one of the founders of the Head Start program, has recently stated, "All over America today we have hundreds of thousands of children in child-care settings that are so bad that their development is being compromised. . . . We are cannibalizing our children. I know that sounds awful, but when you see 13 babies in cribs and one adult caretaker . . . you see children who are being destroyed right after birth."

How will 50 to 60 million children whose mothers will be in the work force be cared for during the 1990s? The New York-based Child Care Action Campaign, whose blue-ribbon board includes experts in child care from all over the country, has urged every level of society to become involved in solving this child-care crisis. It has urged the federal government to establish a national child-care office and a "new and separate funding stream" for child care, to expand Head Start, and to set federal regulations on minimum standards. It has urged state and local governments to establish school-age-child-care programs, expand resource and referral programs, and raise the professional status and working conditions of child-care workers. It has urged employers to adopt flexible work schedules, to support community efforts to expand day-care centers and family day care, to invest in on-site centers, to help parents to pay for regular day care and emergency day care, and to allow employees to use their sick leave to care for ill children. . . .

One of the central components of all of these recommendations is adequate training, recompense, employment security, and status for caregivers at every level. By demeaning the role of caregiver, society demeans all women and indeed, to one extent or another, exploits all caregivers. It also sets up the exploitation of one group of women by another. The ripples are endless: from the middle-or upper-middle-class career mother who is "stressed out" by trying to do it all to the single mother who really *is* doing it all to the day-care worker who is working in inadequate conditions earning inadequate pay to the child-care worker/domestic who is often shamefully exploited in the home, society's fundamental disregard for caregivers and for raising children diminishes us all. Ultimately, of course, it is the children who suffer, but women at all levels suffer as well. And the poor, the nonwhite, those with least choice suffer the most.

Any society that really wants to enable women to be in control of their lives must provide a comprehensive program of sex education and contraception. Perhaps one of the most startling aspects of my interviews with young women and with relevant professionals was the sense that many young women are buffeted about by conflicting attitudes toward sexuality and indeed find it exceedingly difficult to determine what they themselves think and want. By the time they figure it out, it is often too late. They are pregnant and faced with a real Hobson's choice: to abort, or to have a baby at a time in their life when they are ill-prepared—economically, physically, socially, or psychologically—to care for a child. We know what it can do to both the mother and the child when the pregnancy is unplanned and the mother is unable to care for the infant properly. We must do everything possible to make every child a planned child, to make every child a wanted child.

We must learn from the experience of other industrialized countries, whose rate of unintended and teenage pregnancy is so much lower than our own. We must institute sex education in our schools at all levels. The ignorance on the part of young women is astonishing and serves no useful purpose. Moreover, in this era of AIDS and other sexually transmitted diseases, such ignorance can literally be life-threatening. We must increase the accessibility of contraceptives, whether through school-based clinics or community-based health centers. We should consider staffing these centers with midwives or other health professionals whose primary task would be to relate to young people, understand their needs, and help them to understand their choices. The empowerment of young women and men in the area of sexuality should be the central goal—empowerment through knowledge, empowerment through emotional maturity, empowerment through access to the health-care system. And teenagers must be assured of confidentiality whenever they are dealing with contraception or abortion.

As Lisbeth Schorr so forcefully points out in her recent book *Within Our Reach: Breaking the Cycle of Disadvantage,* "The knowledge necessary to reduce the growing toll of damaged lives is now available." We know what to do; we know what works. A school-based program in Baltimore, Maryland, illustrates what can be done. Starting in January 1982, professionals at Johns Hopkins University and the Baltimore Health Department and School Board collaborated in bringing sex education, reproduction-related medical services, and counseling to students in the junior high school and senior high school closest to Johns Hopkins Hospital. Both schools had all-black student bodies. Many of the young people lived in nearby high-rise public housing, and in the junior high school 85 percent were poor enough to qualify for the free-lunch program.

A nurse midwife and a social worker were placed in one school; a nurse practitioner and a social worker were placed in the other. The same professionals were available every afternoon, with physician backup if necessary, to provide relevant medical services at a clinic across the street. The teams gave classroom presentations, counseled individuals and small groups, and made appointments for further consultation, education, and treatment at the clinic. Medical services, including physical exams and contraceptives, were provided during a single visit and at no cost. Every effort was made to ensure that the students would see the same professionals each time they came, "in the belief that consistency of relationships builds trust, helps youngsters to synthesize what they have learned, and makes it possible for them to share very private concerns."

The demonstration program continued until June 1984. During the two-and-a-half years of its existence, the proportion of sexually active high-school students who had babies went down 25 percent; the proportion of girls who became sexually active by age fourteen dropped 40 percent, and the median age at which girls became sexually active rose by seven months, from age fifteen and a half before the program was started to a little over age sixteen at the program's end. This experience is yet another piece of evidence that knowledge about reproduction and access to contraception and to caring people who can discuss a young person's options rationally, with concern and yet with objectivity, can and does lessen the critical problem of teenage pregnancy.

Michael Carrera and Patricia Dempsey, director and former program coordinator of the Teen Primary Pregnancy Prevention Program of the Children's Aid Society in New York City, claim that what is needed is a "holistic approach." "It is our belief," they state, "that the teen pregnancy problem is largely a symptomatic response to greater social ills and because of this, it must concurrently be attacked on several levels. For example, unintended pregnancies among poor, urban teens can be more effectively curtailed if we reduce the impact of the institutional racism that is systemic in our society; if we provide quality education for everyone; and if we create more employment opportunities for young people and adults. If we could accomplish this, we would probably impact, in a more meaningful way, on the lives of teens than can any school or agency sexuality program."

Continued access to abortion must be guaranteed. Efforts to overturn or limit women's right to abortion must be vigorously resisted. For many young women, abortion is the only barrier between them and a life of poverty and despair. Until we stop giving our young women mixed messages—that it is desirable and sometimes even de rigueur to have sex but not legitimate to protect against pregnancy— abortion remains the only resource. Saying that one is for adoption, not abortion, may sound reasonable and "pro life"; but once young women are pregnant and decide to have the baby, giving it up for adoption is a wrenching decision, particularly for those young women who see little opportunity to make another life for themselves. Indeed, among the women I interviewed those who were most despairing about their lives were often those who had babies at a young age and could see no way out of the trap in which they found themselves. I am not suggesting that any of these issues—particularly ones as personal and as controversial as sex education and abortion—are easy to resolve in our complex heterogeneous society, but we must somehow develop a public policy that will help our young people become mature before they are thrust into parenting roles. Other societies have developed such policies; we must learn from them and develop our own.

In addition to giving women greater choice over sex and childbearing, we must stop exploiting women as sex objects. As long as the message of jean manufacturers, cereal companies, automobile conglomerates, and perfume distributors is that women are for sale along with the product, that women are, in a very real sense, just another commodity to be bought, used, and traded in when the model wears out, both men and women will perceive women in this way. And until we enable young women to responsibly say either yes or no to sex, to understand their options and the risks involved, we are not permitting them to be in charge of their own destiny. But we cannot expect young women to take control of their own destiny unless they can see alternatives, pathways that will lead to a rewarding life.

It is ironic that young women, a group outside the cultural mainstream in at least two fundamental ways, age and gender, have internalized that most mainstream of ideologies, the American Dream. After examining the realities of women's lives today, it is clear that the American Dream, at least as conventionally conceived, cannot be the blueprint for the majority of women. The fundamental components of the American Dream—an almost devout reliance on individualism; the notion that American society, particularly at the end of the twentieth century and the beginning of the twenty-first, is fluid enough to permit substantial upward mobility; the belief that hard work will lead to economic rewards, even for women, a group that has always been at the margins of the labor force; and the determined optimism in the face of massive social and economic problems—will not serve women well.

We must recognize that even for most men the American Dream, with its belief in the power of the individual to shape his or her own destiny, was a myth. Men usually did not "make it" alone; they did not, as the image goes, tame the West, develop industrial America, and climb the economic ladder alone—and they certainly did not do it while being the primary caregiver for a couple of preschoolers. Most of those men who "made it" in America, whom we think of when we reaffirm our belief in the American Dream, had women beside them every step of the way—women to iron their shirts, press their pants, mend their socks, cook their meals, bring up their children, and soothe them at the end of a hard day. They did not do it alone. They *still* don't do it alone. How can women do it alone? Who is there to mend and press their clothes, cook their meals, bring up their children, and soothe them at the end of a hard day? How can women possibly make it alone when they earn 65 percent of what men earn, when housing is virtually unaffordable for millions of families, when child care is scarce and all too often second-rate or worse? And where did they get the notion that they *should* be able to make it alone? It may be progress that many young women now realize that they cannot depend on marriage and a man for their identity, their protection, their daily bread; but is it progress or is it illusion for them to believe that they can do the caring and the doing and do it all on their own in a society that has done very little to make women truly independent?

The American Dream cannot really work for any of the groups of women I interviewed. Yes, some women will accomplish their dreams and live productive, rewarding lives; but most of them will have to make substantial compromises, scale down their ambitions, not be quite the kind of parent they hoped they would be. How will the New American Dreamers make it in law, medicine, or oceanography when the rules were made for men with an elaborate support system? How will they get to the top of their fields when our image of authority is still someone who is six feet tall in a blue suit, striped shirt, and not-too-bold red tie? How will they afford the co-op, the BMW, and the trips to Europe when they must often choose between sequencing, the "Mommy" track, part-time work, or leaving their field entirely in order to parent? And how will they resolve their guilt about what they are likely to perceive as less-than-adequate parenting when they must work to remain competitive in their field, to contribute to the maintenance of the family, or to function as its sole support?

Nor does the ideology of the American Dream serve the Neo-traditionalists well. Many of them place their faith in a loving, lasting marriage and hope to spend much of their lives caring for others. But what happens if disaster strikes or the marriage fails? Will they be prepared to go it alone? Will they really be prepared and able to take care of themselves and their children—and possibly their aging parents—with relatively few societal supports? And what if they cannot be home at three o'clock for cookies and milk? How will they feel about themselves as mothers?

And finally, of course, the ideology of the American Dream fails the Outsiders most abysmally and most tragically. Those who are truly outside the system—the homeless and the hungry, the poor and the near-poor, who know that America as it enters the 1990s has largely forgotten them, the millions of nonwhites who feel permanently outside the culture, the young people who leave high school functionally illiterate, those who feel like a "circle within a square," those who try to forget their sadness and anger through alcohol or drugs or, tragically, through suicide—what can the American Dream mean to them? To many it means that their inability to find the path to success is their own fault; for imbedded in the ideology of the

American Dream, inherent in that "I think I can" mentality, is the presumption that if we do not succeed in this land of milk and honey, in this world of infinite opportunity, it must be our fault. If everyone is so rich on "Dallas," "Dynasty," and "L.A. Law," if even blacks have made it on "The Cosby Show" and its spin-offs, if single women like Kate and Allie and married couples like Hope and Michael and rural/suburban people like Bob Newhart and his support group and urban people like Sam Malone and his gang at "Cheers" all live comfortable and relatively happy, contented lives, what must be wrong with those who feel like Outsiders, either temporarily or permanently? If the biggest problems are solvable in twenty-two minutes, what hope can there be for those of us so beyond the pale that we cannot think of solutions at all?

We must have the courage and the wisdom as a society to recognize that we need a new vision of America for the twenty-first century, perhaps even a new American Dream. We need a vision that recognizes that we cannot survive without one another, that families must have supports in order to thrive, that women cannot make it alone any more than men ever have.

We must provide many more paths toward a gratifying, economically secure life. Traditional male occupations cannot be the only routes to the good life; traditional female work must be restructured so that it too can lead to power, prestige, and a life of plenty. And the traditional male work style must give way, for both women and men, to the recognition that work is merely one aspect of life and that private concerns, family life, leisure activities, and participation in community life help to define who we are and must be seen as important both to the individual and to the society.

We must find ways of opening up American society to those who feel outside the system, to those who feel hopeless and despairing. We must educate all of our young people, not simply the most privileged. We must provide them with adequate housing, health care, nutrition, safe communities in which to grow, and, above all, a meaningful role in society. So many of them feel extraneous because so many of them are treated as extraneous, except, possibly, in their roles as consumers. Moreover, providing decent lives for the millions of young people who are Outsiders will provide decent jobs for millions of other Americans and, even more, the sense that one is participating in a worthwhile way in the life of the nation. But, of course, we will not make the society accessible to those who now consider themselves Outsiders unless power and wealth are distributed far more equitably. It has been said before, it will be said again, but it cannot be said too often: there is a greater gap today between the rich and the poor than at any point since the Bureau of the Census began collecting these data in 1947. In 1987 the wealthiest 40 percent of American families received 67.8 percent of the national family income, the highest percentage ever recorded, while the poorest 40 percent received 15.4 percent, the lowest percentage (along with that of 1986) ever recorded. Until we address these fundamental inequities, we cannot hope to enable our young people to become fully participating members of society.

These changes will not come about all at once or even, perhaps, in the near future. Changing our priorities is exceedingly difficult without strong national leadership pointing the way, but until we have representatives in Washington who will promote the public good rather than private gain we must develop leadership at the local level and work toward a more humane society step by step. We can raise these issues in our own communities and places of work. We can select one concern, such as child care or parental leave or flexible work hours, and together with others place that issue on the agenda of our employer, our union, or our local legislator. We can work with major national organizations to place family policy concerns on the national agenda. We must recognize that these concerns transcend the traditional barriers of class, race, gender, and age and form common cause with those who share our priorities.

Above all, we must develop a vision that recognizes that caring is as important as doing, that caring indeed *is* doing, and that caregivers, both paid and unpaid, are the foundation of a humane society and must be treasured and honored. We need a vision of America that recognizes that we must reorganize our social institutions— our family life, our schools, our places of work, and our communities—to enable all people to care for one another, to enable all people to work and to participate in the public life of the nation. Our courageous, insightful, persevering, and often wise young women deserve no less. Our young men deserve no less. Future generations deserve no less.

5

Homophobia as a Weapon of Sexism

Suzanne Pharr

Patriarchy—an enforced belief in male dominance and control—is the ideology and sexism the system that holds it in place. The catechism goes like this: Who do gender roles serve? Men and the women who seek power from them. Who suffers from gender roles? Women most completely and men in part. How are gender roles maintained? By the weapons of sexism: economics, violence, homophobia.

Why then don't we ardently pursue ways to eliminate gender roles and therefore sexism? It is my profound belief that all people have a spark in them that yearns for freedom, and the history of the world's atrocities—from the Nazi concentration camps to white dominance in South Africa to the battering of women—is the story of attempts to snuff out that spark. When that spark doesn't move forward to full flame, it is because the weapons designed to control and destroy have wrought such intense damage over time that the spark has been all but extinguished.

Sexism, that system by which women are kept subordinate to men, is kept in place by three powerful weapons designed to cause or threaten women with pain and loss. . . .

We have to look at economics not only as the root cause of sexism but also as the underlying, driving force that keeps all the oppressions in place. In the United States, our economic system is shaped like a pyramid, with a few people at the top, primarily white males, being supported by large numbers of unpaid or low-paid workers at the bottom. When we look at this pyramid, we begin to understand the major connection between sexism and racism because those groups at the bottom of the pyramid are women and people of color. We then begin to understand why there is such a fervent effort to keep those oppressive systems (racism and sexism and all the ways they are manifested) in place to maintain the unpaid and low-paid labor.

Susan DeMarco and Jim Hightower, writing for *Mother Jones*, report that *Forbes* magazine indicated that "the 400 richest families in America last year had an average net worth of $550 million each. These and less than a million other families—roughly one percent of our population—are at the prosperous tip of our society. . . . In 1976, the wealthiest 1 percent of America's families owned 19.2 percent of the nation's total wealth. (This sum of wealth counts all of America's cash, real estate, stocks, bonds, factories, art, personal property, and anything else of financial value.) By 1983, those at this 1 percent tip of our economy owned 34.3 percent of our wealth. . . . *Today, the top 1 percent of Americans possesses more net wealth than the bottom 90 percent.*" (My italics.) (*May, 1988, pp. 32–33*)

In order for this top-heavy system of economic inequity to maintain itself, the 90 percent on the bottom must keep supplying cheap labor. A very complex, intricate system of institutionalized oppressions is necessary to maintain the status quo so that the vast majority will not demand its fair share of wealth and resources and bring the system down. Every institution—schools, banks, churches, government, courts, media, etc—as well as individuals must be enlisted in the campaign to maintain such a system of gross inequity.

What would happen if women gained the earning opportunities and power that men have? What would happen if these opportunities were distributed equitably, no matter what sex one was, no matter what race one was born into, and no matter where one lived? What if educational and training opportunities were equal? Would women spend most of our youth preparing for marriage? Would marriage be based on economic survival for women? What would happen to issues of power and control? Would women stay with our batterers? If a woman had economic independence in a society where women had equal opportunities, would she still be thought of as owned by her father or husband?

Economics is the great controller in both sexism and racism. If a person can't acquire food, shelter, and clothing and provide them for children, then that person can be forced to do many things in order to survive. The major tactic, worldwide, is to provide unrecompensed or inadequately recompensed labor for the benefit of those who control wealth. Hence, we see women performing unpaid labor in the home or filling low-paid jobs, and we see people of color in the lowest-paid jobs available.

The method is complex: limit educational and training opportunities for women and for people of color and then withhold adequate paying jobs with the excuse that people of color and women are incapable of filling them. Blame the economic victim and keep the victim's self-esteem low through invisibility and distortion within the media and education. Allow a few people of color and women to succeed among the profitmakers so that blaming those who don't "make it" can be intensified. Encourage those few who succeed in gaining power now to turn against those who remain behind rather than to use their resources to make change for all. Maintain the myth of scarcity—that there are not enough jobs, resources, etc., to go around—among the middleclass so that they will not unite with laborers, immigrants, and the unemployed. The method keeps in place a system of control and profit by a few and a constant source of cheap labor to maintain it.

If anyone steps out of line, take her/his job away. Let homelessness and hunger do their work. The economic weapon works. And we end up saying, "I would do this or that—be openly who I am, speak out against injustice, work for civil rights, join a labor union, go to a political march, etc.—if I didn't have this job. I can't afford to lose it." We stay in an abusive situation because we see no other way to survive. . . .

Violence against women is directly related to the condition of women in a society that refuses us equal pay, equal access to resources, and equal status with males. From this condition comes men's confirmation of their sense of ownership of women, power over women, and assumed right to control women for their own means. Men physically and emotionally abuse women because they *can*, because they live in a world that gives them permission. Male violence is fed by their sense of their *right* to dominate and control, and their sense of superiority over a group of people who, because of gender, they consider inferior to them.

It is not just the violence but the threat of violence that controls our lives. Because the burden of responsibility has been placed so often on the potential victim, as women we have curtailed our freedom in order to protect ourselves from violence. Because of the threat of rapists, we stay on alert, being careful not to walk in isolated places, being careful where we park our cars, adding incredible security measures to our homes—massive locks, lights, alarms, if we can afford them—and we avoid places where we will appear vulnerable or unprotected while the abuser walks with freedom. Fear, often now so commonplace that it is unacknowledged, shapes our lives, reducing our freedom. . . .

Part of the way sexism stays in place is the societal promise of survival, false and unfulfilled as it is, that women will not suffer violence if we attach ourselves to a man to protect us. A woman without a man is told she is vulnerable to external violence and, worse, that there is something wrong with her. When the male abuser calls a woman a lesbian, he is not so much labeling her a woman who loves women as he is warning her that by resisting him, she is choosing to be outside society's protection from male institutions and therefore from wide-ranging, unspecified, ever-present violence. When she seeks assistance from woman friends or a battered women's shelter, he recognizes the power in woman bonding and fears loss of her servitude and loyalty: the potential loss of his control. The concern is not affectional/sexual identity: the concern is disloyalty and the threat is violence.

The threat of violence against women who step out of line or who are disloyal is made all the more powerful by the fact that women do not have to do anything— they may be paragons of virtue and subservience—to receive violence against our lives: the violence still comes. It comes because of the woman-hating that exists throughout society. Chance plays a larger part than virtue in keeping women safe. Hence, with violence always a threat to us, women can never feel completely secure and confident. Our sense of safety is always fragile and tenuous.

Many women say that verbal violence causes more harm than physical violence because it damages self-esteem so deeply. Women have not wanted to hear battered women say that the verbal abuse was as hurtful as the physical abuse: to acknowledge that truth would be tantamount to acknowledging that *virtually every woman is a battered woman*. It is difficult to keep strong against accusations of being a bitch, stupid, inferior, etc., etc. It is especially difficult when these individual assaults are backed up by a society that shows women in textbooks, advertising, TV programs, movies, etc., as debased, silly, inferior, and sexually objectified, and a society that gives tacit approval to pornography. When we internalize these messages, we call the result "low self-esteem," a therapeutic individualized term. It seems to me we should use the more political expression: when we internalize these messages, we experience *internalized sexism*, and we experience it in common with all women living in a sexist world. The violence against us is supported by a society in which woman-hating is deeply imbedded.

In "Eyes on the Prize," a 1987 Public Television documentary about the Civil Rights Movement, an older white woman says about her youth in the South that it was difficult to be anything different from what was around her when there was no vision for another way to be. Our society presents images of women that say it is appropriate to commit violence against us. Violence is committed against women because we are seen as inferior in status and in worth. It has been the work of the women's movement to present a vision of another way to be.

Every time a woman gains the strength to resist and leave her abuser, we are given a model of the importance of stepping out of line, of moving toward freedom. And we all gain strength when she says to violence, "Never again!" Thousands of women in the last fifteen years have resisted their abusers to come to this country's 1100 battered women's shelters. There they have sat down with other women to share their stories, to discover that their stories again and again are the same, to develop an analysis that shows that violence is a statement about power and control, and to understand how sexism creates the climate for male violence. Those brave women are now a part of a movement that gives hope for another way to live in equality and peace.

Homophobia works effectively as a weapon of sexism because it is joined with a powerful arm, heterosexism. Heterosexism creates the climate for homophobia with its assumption that the world is and must be heterosexual and its display of power and privilege as the norm. Heterosexism is the systemic display of homophobia in the institutions of society. Heterosexism and homophobia work together to enforce compulsory heterosexuality and that bastion of patriarchal power, the nuclear family. The central focus of the rightwing attack against women's liberation is that women's equality, women's self-determination, women's control of our own bodies and lives will damage what they see as the crucial societal institution, the nuclear family. The attack has been led by fundamentalist ministers across the country. The two areas they have focused on most consistently are abortion and homosexuality, and their passion has led them to bomb women's clinics and to recommend deprogramming for homosexuals and establishing camps to quarantine people with AIDS. To resist marriage and/or heterosexuality is to risk severe punishment and loss.

It is not by chance that when children approach puberty and increased sexual awareness they begin to taunt each other by calling these names: "queer," "faggot," "pervert." It is at puberty that the full force of society's pressure to conform to heterosexuality and prepare for marriage is brought to bear. Children know what we have taught them, and we have given clear messages that those who deviate from standard expectations are to be made to get back in line. The best controlling tactic at puberty is to be treated as an outsider, to be ostracized at a time when it feels most vital to be accepted. Those who are different must be made to suffer loss. It is also at puberty that misogyny begins to be more apparent, and girls are pressured to conform to societal norms that do not permit them to realize their full potential. It is at this time that their academic achievements begin to decrease as they are coerced into compulsory heterosexuality and trained for dependency upon a man, that is, for economic survival.

There was a time when the two most condemning accusations against a woman meant to ostracize and disempower her were "whore" and "lesbian." The sexual revolution and changing attitudes about heterosexual behavior may have led to some lessening of the power of the word *whore*, though it still has strength as a threat to sexual property and prostitutes are stigmatized and abused. However, the word *lesbian* is still fully charged and carries with it the full threat of loss of power and privilege, the threat of being cut asunder, abandoned, and left outside society's protection.

To be a lesbian is to be *perceived* as someone who has stepped out of line, who has moved out of sexual/economic dependence on a male, who is woman-identified. A lesbian is perceived as someone who can live without a man, and who is therefore (however illogically) against men. A lesbian is perceived as being outside the acceptable, routinized order of things. She is seen as someone who has no societal institutions to protect her and who is not privileged to the protection of individual males. Many heterosexual women see her as someone who stands in contradiction to the sacrifices they have made to conform to compulsory heterosexuality. A lesbian is perceived as a threat to the nuclear family, to male dominance and control, to the very heart of sexism.

Gay men are perceived also as a threat to male dominance and control, and the homophobia expressed against them has the same roots in sexism as does homophobia against lesbians. Visible gay men are the objects of extreme hatred and fear by heterosexual men because their breaking ranks with male heterosexual solidarity is seen as a damaging rent in the very fabric of sexism. They are seen as betrayers, as traitors who must be punished and eliminated. In the beating and killing of gay men we see clear evidence of this hatred. When we see the fierce homophobia expressed toward gay men, we can begin to understand the ways sexism also affects males through imposing rigid, dehumanizing gender roles on them. The two circumstances in which it is legitimate for men to be openly physically affectionate with one another are in competitive sports and in the crisis of war. For many men, these two experiences are the highlights of their lives, and they think of them again and again with nostalgia. War and sports offer a cover of all-male safety and dominance to keep away the notion of affectionate openness being identified with homosexuality. When gay men break ranks with male roles through bonding and affection outside the arenas of war and sports, they are perceived as not being "real men," that is, as being identified with women, the weaker sex that must be dominated and that over the centuries has been the object of male hatred and abuse. Misogyny gets transferred to gay men with a vengeance and is increased by the fear that their sexual identity and behavior will bring down the entire system of male dominance and compulsory heterosexuality.

If lesbians are established as threats to the status quo, as outcasts who must be punished, homophobia can wield its power over all women through lesbian baiting. Lesbian baiting is an attempt to control women by labeling us as lesbians because our behavior is not acceptable, that is, when we are being independent, going our own way, living whole lives, fighting for our rights, demanding equal pay, saying no to violence, being self-assertive, bonding with and loving the company of women, assuming the right to our bodies, insisting upon our own authority, making changes that include us in society's decision-making; lesbian baiting occurs when women are called lesbians because we resist male dominance and control. And it has little or nothing to do with one's sexual identity.

To be named as lesbian threatens all women, not just lesbians, with great loss. And any woman who steps out of role risks being called a lesbian. To understand how this is a threat to all women, one must understand that any woman can be called a lesbian and there is no real way she can defend herself: there is no way to credential one's sexuality. ("The Children's Hour," a Lillian Hellman play, makes this point when a student asserts two teachers are lesbians and they have no way to disprove it.) She may be married or divorced, have children, dress in the most feminine manner, have sex with men, be celibate—but there are lesbians who do all those things. *Lesbians look like all women and all women look like lesbians.* There is no guaranteed method of identification, and as we all know, sexual identity can be kept hidden. (The same is true for men. There is no way to prove their sexual identity, though many go to extremes to prove heterosexuality.) Also, women are not necessarily born lesbian. Some seem to be, but others become lesbians later in life after having lived heterosexual lives. Lesbian baiting of heterosexual women would not work if there were a definitive way to identify lesbians (or heterosexuals).

We have yet to understand clearly how sexual identity develops. And this is disturbing to some people, especially those who are determined to discover how lesbian and gay identity is formed so that they will know where to start in eliminating it. (Isn't it odd that there is so little concern about discovering the causes of heterosexuality?) There are many theories: genetic makeup, hormones, socialization, environment, etc. But there is no conclusive evidence that indicates that heterosexuality comes from one process and homosexuality from another.

We do know, however, that sexual identity can be in flux, and we know that sexual identity means more than just the gender of people one is attracted to and has sex with. To be a lesbian has as many ramifications as for a woman to be heterosexual. It is more than sex, more than just the bedroom issue many would like to make it: it is a woman-centered life with all the social interconnections that entails. Some lesbians are in long-term relationships, some in short-term ones, some date, some are celibate, some are married to men, some remain as separate as possible from men, some have children by men, some by alternative insemination, some seem "feminine" by societal standards, some "masculine," some are doctors, lawyers and ministers, some laborers, housewives and writers: what all share in common is a sexual/affectional identity that focuses on women in its attractions and social relationships.

If lesbians are simply women with a particular sexual identity who look and act like all women, then the major difference in living out a lesbian sexual identity as opposed to a heterosexual identity is that as lesbians we live in a homophobic world that threatens and imposes damaging loss on us for being *who we are*, for choosing to live whole lives. Homophobic people often assert that homosexuals have the choice of not being homosexual; that is, we don't have to act out our sexual identity. In that case, I want to hear heterosexuals talk about their willingness not to act out their sexual identity, including not just sexual activity but heterosexual social interconnections and heterosexual privilege. It is a question of wholeness. It is very difficult for one to be denied the life of a sexual being, whether expressed in sex or in physical affection, and to feel complete, whole. For our loving relationships with humans feed the life of the spirit and enable us to overcome our basic isolation and to be interconnected with humankind.

If, then, any woman can be named a lesbian and be threatened with terrible losses, what is it she fears? Are these fears real? Being vulnerable to a homophobic world can lead to these losses:

- *Employment.* The loss of job leads us right back to the economic connection to sexism. This fear of job loss exists for almost every lesbian except perhaps those who are self-employed or in a business that does not require societal approval. Consider how many businesses or organizations you know that will hire and protect people who are openly gay or lesbian.
- *Family.* Their approval, acceptance, love.

- *Children*. Many lesbians and gay men have children, but very, very few gain custody in court challenges, even if the other parent is a known abuser. Other children may be kept away from us as though gays and lesbians are abusers. There are written and unwritten laws prohibiting lesbians and gays from being foster parents or from adopting children. There is an irrational fear that children in contact with lesbians and gays will become homosexual through influence or that they will be sexually abused. Despite our knowing that 95 percent of those who sexually abuse children are heterosexual men, there are no policies keeping heterosexual men from teaching or working with children, yet in almost every school system in America, visible gay men and lesbians are not hired through either written or unwritten law.
- *Heterosexual privilege and protection*. No institutions, other than those created by lesbians and gays—such as the Metropolitan Community Church, some counseling centers, political organizations such as the National Gay and Lesbian Task Force, the National Coalition of Black Lesbians and Gays, the Lambda Legal Defense and Education Fund, etc.,—affirm homosexuality and offer protection. Affirmation and protection cannot be gained from the criminal justice system, mainline churches, educational institutions, the government.
- *Safety*. There is nowhere to turn for safety from physical and verbal attacks because the norm presently in this country is that it is acceptable to be overtly homophobic. Gay men are beaten on the streets; lesbians are kidnapped and "deprogrammed." The National Gay and Lesbian Task Force, in an extended study, has documented violence against lesbians and gay men and noted the inadequate response of the criminal justice system. One of the major differences between homophobia/heterosexism and racism and sexism is that because of the Civil Rights Movement and the women's movement racism and sexism are expressed more covertly (though with great harm); because there has not been a major, visible lesbian and gay movement, it is permissible to be overtly homophobic in any institution or public forum. Churches spew forth homophobia in the same way they did racism prior to the Civil Rights Movement. Few laws are in place to protect lesbians and gay men, and the criminal justice system is wracked with homophobia.
- *Mental health*. An overtly homophobic world in which there is full permission to treat lesbians and gay men with cruelty makes it difficult for lesbians and gay men to maintain a strong sense of well-being and self-esteem. Many lesbians and gay men are beaten, raped, killed, subjected to aversion therapy, or put in mental institutions. The impact of such hatred and negativity can lead one to depression and, in some cases, to suicide. The toll on the gay and lesbian community is devastating.
- *Community*. There is rejection by those who live in homophobic fear, those who are afraid of association with lesbians and gay men. For many in the gay and lesbian community, there is a loss of public acceptance, a loss of allies, a loss of place and belonging.

- *Credibility.* This fear is large for many people: the fear that they will no longer be respected, listened to, honored, believed. They fear they will be social outcasts.

The list goes on and on. But any one of these essential components of a full life is large enough to make one deeply fear its loss. A black woman once said to me in a workshop, "When I fought for Civil Rights, I always had my family and community to fall back on even when they didn't fully understand or accept what I was doing. I don't know if I could have borne losing them. And you people don't have either with you. It takes my breath away."

What does a woman have to do to get called a lesbian? Almost anything, sometimes nothing at all, but certainly anything that threatens the status quo, anything that steps out of role, anything that asserts the rights of women, anything that doesn't indicate submission and subordination. Assertiveness, standing up for oneself, asking for more pay, better working conditions, training for and accepting a non-traditional (you mean a man's?) job, enjoying the company of women, being financially independent, being in control of one's life, depending first and foremost upon oneself, thinking that one can do whatever needs to be done, but above all, working for the rights and equality of women.

In the backlash to the gains of the women's liberation movement, there has been an increased effort to keep definitions man-centered. Therefore, to work on behalf of women must mean to work against men. To love women must mean that one hates men. A very effective attack has been made against the word *feminist* to make it a derogatory word. In current backlash usage, *feminist* equals *man-hater* which equals *lesbian.* This formula is created in the hope that women will be frightened away from their work on behalf of women. Consequently, we now have women who believe in the rights of women and work for those rights while from fear deny that they are feminists, or refuse to use the word because it is so "abrasive."

So what does one do in an effort to keep from being called a lesbian? She steps back into line, into the role that is demanded of her, tries to behave in such a way that doesn't threaten the status of men, and if she works for women's rights, she begins modifying that work. When women's organizations begin doing significant social change work, they inevitably are lesbian-baited; that is, funders or institutions or community members tell us that they can't work with us because of our "man-hating attitudes" or the presence of lesbians. We are called too strident, told we are making enemies, not doing good. . . .

In my view, homophobia has been one of the major causes of the failure of the women's liberation movement to make deep and lasting change. (The other major block has been racism.) We were fierce when we set out but when threatened with the loss of heterosexual privilege, we began putting on brakes. Our best-known nationally distributed women's magazine was reluctant to print articles about lesbians, began putting a man on the cover several times a year, and writing articles about women who succeeded in a man's world. We worried about our image, our being all right, our being "real women" despite our work. Instead of talking about the elimination of sexual gender roles, we stepped back and talked about "sex role stereotyping" as the issue. Change around the edges for middleclass white women began to be talked about as successes. We accepted tokenism and integration, forgetting that equality for all women, for all people—and not just equality of white middleclass women with white men—was the goal that we could never put behind us.

But despite backlash and retreats, change is growing from within. The women's liberation movement is beginning to gain strength again because there are women who are talking about liberation for all women. We are examining sexism, racism, homophobia, classism, anti-Semitism, ageism, ableism, and imperialism, and we see everything as connected. This change in point of view represents the third wave of the women's liberation movement, a new direction that does not get mass media coverage and recognition. It has been initiated by women of color and lesbians who were marginalized or rendered invisible by the white heterosexual leaders of earlier efforts. The first wave was the 19th and early 20th century campaign for the vote; the second, beginning in the 1960s, focused on the Equal Rights Amendment and abortion rights. Consisting of predominantly white middleclass women, both failed in recognizing issues of equality and empowerment for all women. The third wave of the movement, multi-racial and multi-issued, seeks the transformation of the world for us all. We know that we won't get there until everyone gets there; that we must move forward in a great strong line, hand in hand, not just a few at a time.

We know that the arguments about homophobia originating from mental health and Biblical/religious attitudes can be settled when we look at the sexism that permeates religious and psychiatric history. The women of the third wave of the women's liberation movement know that *without the existence of sexism, there would be no homophobia*.

Finally, we know that as long as the word lesbian can strike fear in any woman's heart, then work on behalf of women can be stopped; the only successful work against sexism must include work against homophobia.

6

Feminism:
A Transformational Politic

bell hooks

We live in a world in crisis—a world governed by politics of domination, one in which the belief in a notion of superior and inferior, and its concomitant ideology—that the superior should rule over the inferior—effects the lives of all people everywhere, whether poor or privileged, literate or illiterate. Systematic dehumanization, worldwide famine, ecological devastation, industrial contamination, and the possibility of nuclear destruction are realities which remind us daily that we are in crisis. Contemporary feminist thinkers often cite sexual politics as the origin of this crisis. They point to the insistence on difference as that factor which becomes the occasion for separation and domination and suggest that differentiation of status between females and males globally is an indication that patriarchal domination of the planet is the root of the problem. Such an assumption has fostered the notion that elimination of sexist oppression would necessarily lead to the eradication of all forms of domination. It is an argument that has led influential Western white women to feel that feminist movement should be *the* central political agenda for females globally. Ideologically, thinking in this direction enables Western women, especially privileged white women, to suggest that racism and class exploitation are merely the offspring of the parent system: patriarchy. Within feminist movement in the West, this has led to the assumption that resisting patriarchal domination is a more legitimate feminist action than resisting racism and other forms of domination. Such thinking prevails despite radical critiques made by black women and other women of color who question this proposition. To speculate that an oppositional division between men and women existed in early human communities is to impose on the past, on these non-white groups, a world view that fits all too neatly within contemporary feminist paradigms that name man as the enemy and woman as the victim.

Clearly, differentiation between strong and weak, powerful and powerless, has been a central defining aspect of gender globally, carrying with it the assumption that men should have greater authority than women, and should rule over them. As significant and important as this fact is, it should not obscure the reality that women can and do participate in politics of domination, as perpetrators as well as victims—

441

that we dominate, that we are dominated. If focus on patriarchal domination masks this reality or becomes the means by which women deflect attention from the real conditions and circumstances of our lives, then women cooperate in suppressing and promoting false consciousness, inhibiting our capacity to assume responsibility for transforming ourselves and society.

Thinking speculatively about early human social arrangement, about women and men struggling to survive in small communities, it is likely that the parent-child relationship with its very real imposed survival structure of dependency, of strong and weak, of powerful and powerless, was a site for the construction of a paradigm of domination. While this circumstance of dependency is not necessarily one that leads to domination, it lends itself to the enactment of a social drama wherein domination could easily occur as a means of exercising and maintaining control. This speculation does not place women outside the practice of domination, in the exclusive role of victim. It centrally names women as agents of domination, as potential theoreticians, and creators of a paradigm for social relationships wherein those groups of individuals designated as "strong" exercise power both benevolently and coercively over those designated as "weak."

Emphasizing paradigms of domination that call attention to woman's capacity to dominate is one way to deconstruct and challenge the simplistic notion that man is the enemy, woman the victim; the notion that men have always been the oppressors. Such thinking enables us to examine our role as women in the perpetuation and maintenance of systems of domination. To understand domination, we must understand that our capacity as women and men to be either dominated or dominating is a point of connection, of commonality. Even though I speak from the particular experience of living as a black woman in the United States, a white-supremacist, capitalist, patriarchal society, where small numbers of white men (and honorary "white men") constitute ruling groups, I understand that in many places in the world oppressed and oppressor share the same color. I understand that right here in this room, oppressed and oppressor share the same gender. Right now as I speak, a man who is himself victimized, wounded, hurt by racism and class exploitation is actively dominating a woman in his life—that even as I speak, women who are ourselves exploited, victimized, are dominating children. It is necessary for us to remember, as we think critically about domination, that we all have the capacity to act in ways that oppress, dominate, wound (whether or not that power is institutionalized). It is necessary to remember that it is first the potential oppressor within that we must resist—the potential victim within that we must rescue—otherwise we cannot hope for an end to domination, for liberation.

This knowledge seems especially important at this historical moment when black women and other women of color have worked to create awareness of the ways in which racism empowers white women to act as exploiters and oppressors. Increasingly this fact is considered a reason we should not support feminist struggle even though sexism and sexist oppression is a real issue in our lives as black women (see, for example, Vivian Gordon's *Black Women, Feminism, Black Liberation: Which Way?*). It becomes necessary for us to speak continually about the convictions that inform our continued advocacy of feminist struggle. By calling attention to inter-locking systems of domination—sex, race, and class—black women and many other groups of women acknowledge the diversity and complexity of female experience, of our relationship to power and domination. The intent is not to dissuade people of color from becoming engaged in feminist movement. Feminist struggle to end patriarchal domination should be of primary importance to women and men glo-bally not because it is the foundation of all other oppressive structures but because it is that form of domination we are most likely to encounter in an ongoing way in everyday life.

Unlike other forms of domination, sexism directly shapes and determines rela-tions of power in our private lives, in familiar social spaces, in that most intimate context—home—and in that most intimate sphere of relations—family. Usually, it is within the family that we witness coercive domination and learn to accept it, whether it be domination of parent over child, or male over female. Even though family relations may be, and most often are, informed by acceptance of a politic of domination, they are simultaneously relations of care and connection. It is this convergence of two contradictory impulses—the urge to promote growth and the urge to inhibit growth—that provides a practical setting for feminist critique, resis-tance, and transformation.

Growing up in a black, working-class, father-dominated household, I exper-ienced coercive adult male authority as more immediately threatening, as more likely to cause immediate pain than racist oppression or class exploitation. It was equally clear that experiencing exploitation and oppression in the home made one feel all the more powerless when encountering dominating forces outside the home. This is true for many people. If we are unable to resist and end domination in relations where there is care, it seems totally unimaginable that we can resist and end it in other institutionalized relations of power. If we cannot convince the mothers and/or fathers who care not to humiliate and degrade us, how can we imagine convincing or resisting an employer, a lover, a stranger who systematically humiliates and degrades?

Feminist effort to end patriarchal domination should be of primary concern precisely because it insists on the eradication of exploitation and oppression in the family context and in all other intimate relationships. It is that political movement which most radically addresses the person—the personal—citing the need for trans-formation of self, of relationships, so that we might be better able to act in a revolutionary manner, challenging and resisting domination, transforming the world outside the self. Strategically, feminist movement should be a central compo-nent of all other liberation struggles because it challenges each of us to alter our person, our personal engagement (either as victims or perpetrators or both) in a system of domination.

Feminism, as liberation struggle, must exist apart from and as a part of the larger struggle to eradicate domination in all its forms. We must understand that patriar-chal domination shares an ideological foundation with racism and other forms of group oppression, that there is no hope that it can be eradicated while these systems remain intact. This knowledge should consistently inform the direction of feminist theory and practice. Unfortunately, racism and class elitism among women has frequently led to the suppression and distortion of this connection so that it is now necessary for feminist thinkers to critique and revise much feminist theory and the direction of feminist movement. This effort at revision is perhaps most evident in the current widespread acknowledgement that sexism, racism, and class exploitation constitute interlocking systems of domination—that sex, race, and class, and not sex alone, determine the nature of any female's identity, status, and circumstance, the degree to which she will or will not be dominated, the extent to which she will have the power to dominate.

While acknowledgement of the complex nature of woman's status (which has been mòst impressed upon everyone's consciousness by radical women of color) is a significant corrective, it is only a starting point. It provides a frame of reference which must serve as the basis for thoroughly altering and revising feminist theory and practice. It challenges and calls us to re-think popular assumptions about the nature of feminism that have had the deepest impact on a large majority of women, on mass consciousness. It radically calls into question the notion of a fundamentally common female experience which has been seen as the prerequisite for our coming together, for political unity. Recognition of the inter-connectedness of sex, race, and class highlights the diversity of experience, compelling redefinition of the terms for unity. If women do not share "common oppression," what then can serve as a basis for our coming together?

Unlike many feminist comrades, I believe women and men must share a common understanding—a basic knowledge of what feminism is—if it is ever to be a powerful mass-based political movement. In *Feminist Theory: from margin to center*, I suggest that defining feminism broadly as "a movement to end sexism and sexist oppression" would enable us to have a common political goal. We would then have a basis on which to build solidarity. Multiple and contradictory definitions of feminism create confusion and undermine the effort to construct feminist movement so that it addresses everyone. Sharing a common goal does not imply that women and men will not have radically divergent perspectives on how that goal might be reached. Because each individual starts the process of engagement in feminist struggle at a unique level of awareness, very real differences in experience, perspective, and knowledge make developing varied strategies for participation and transformation a necessary agenda.

Feminist thinkers engaged in radically revisioning central tenets of feminist thought must continually emphasize the importance of sex, race and class as factors which *together* determine the social construction of femaleness, as it has been so deeply ingrained in the consciousness of many women active in feminist movement that gender is the sole factor determining destiny. However, the work of education for critical consciousness (usually called consciousness-raising) cannot end there. Much feminist consciousness-raising has in the past focussed on identifying the particular ways men oppress and exploit women. Using the paradigm of sex, race, and class means that the focus does not begin with men and what they do to women, but rather with women working to identify both individually and collectively the specific character of our social identity.

Imagine a group of women from diverse backgrounds coming together to talk about feminism. First they concentrate on working out their status in terms of sex, race, and class using this as the standpoint from which they begin discussing patriarchy or their particular relations with individual men. Within the old frame of reference, a discussion might consist solely of talk about their experiences as victims in relationship to male oppressors. Two women—one poor, the other quite wealthy—might describe the process by which they have suffered physical abuse by male partners and find certain commonalities which might serve as a basis for bonding. Yet if these same two women engaged in a discussion of class, not only would the social construction and expression of femaleness differ, so too would their ideas about how to confront and change their circumstances. Broadening the discussion to include an analysis of race and class would expose many additional differences even as commonalities emerged.

Clearly the process of bonding would be more complex, yet this broader discussion might enable the sharing of perspectives and strategies for change that would enrich rather than diminish our understanding of gender. While feminists have increasingly given "lip service" to the idea of diversity, we have not developed strategies of communication and inclusion that allow for the successful enactment of this feminist vision.

Small groups are no longer the central place for feminist consciousness-raising. Much feminist education for critical consciousness takes place in Women's Studies classes or at conferences which focus on gender. Books are a primary source of education which means that already masses of people who do not read have no access. The separation of grassroots ways of sharing feminist thinking across kitchen tables from the spheres where much of that thinking is generated, the academy, undermines feminist movement. It would further feminist movement if new feminist thinking could be once again shared in small group contexts, integrating critical analysis with discussion of personal experience. It would be useful to promote anew the small group setting as an arena for education for critical consciousness, so that women and men might come together in neighborhoods and communities to discuss feminist concerns.

Small groups remain an important place for education for critical consciousness for several reasons. An especially important aspect of the small group setting is the emphasis on communicating feminist thinking, feminist theory, in a manner that can be easily understood. In small groups, individuals do not need to be equally literate or literate at all because the information is primarily shared through conversation, in dialogue which is necessarily a liberatory expression. (Literacy should be a goal for feminists even as we ensure that it not become a requirement for participation in feminist education.) Reforming small groups would subvert the appropriation of feminist thinking by a select group of academic women and men, usually white, usually from privileged class backgrounds.

Small groups of people coming together to engage in feminist discussion, in dialectical struggle make a space where the "personal is political" as a starting point for education for critical consciousness can be extended to include politicization of the self that focusses on creating understanding of the ways sex, race, and class together determine our individual lot and our collective experience. It would further feminist movement if many well known feminist thinkers would participate in small groups, critically re-examining ways their works might be changed by incorporating broader perspectives. All efforts at self-transformation challenge us to engage in ongoing, critical self-examination and reflection about feminist practice, about how we live in the world. This individual commitment, when coupled with engagement in collective discussion, provides a space for critical feedback which strengthens our efforts to change and make ourselves new. It is in this commitment to feminist principles in our words and deeds that the hope of feminist revolution lies.

Working collectively to confront difference, to expand our awareness of sex, race, and class as interlocking systems of domination, of the ways we reinforce and perpetuate these structures, is the context in which we learn the true meaning of solidarity. It is this work that must be the foundation of feminist movement. Without it, we cannot effectively resist patriarchal domination; without it, we remain estranged and alienated from one another. Fear of painful confrontation often leads women and men active in feminist movement to avoid rigorous critical encounter, yet if we cannot engage dialectically in a committed, rigorous, humanizing manner, we cannot hope to change the world. True politicization—coming to critical consciousness—is a difficult, "trying" process, one that demands that we give up set ways of thinking and being, that we shift our paradigms, that we open ourselves to the unknown, the unfamiliar. Undergoing this process, we learn what it means to struggle and in this effort we experience the dignity and integrity of being that comes with revolutionary change. If we do not change our consciousness, we cannot change our actions or demand change from others.

Our renewed commitment to a rigorous process of education for critical consciousness will determine the shape and direction of future feminist movement. Until new perspectives are created, we cannot be living symbols of the power of feminist thinking. Given the privileged lot of many leading feminist thinkers, both in terms of status, class, and race, it is harder these days to convince women of the primacy of this process of politicization. More and more, we seem to form select interest groups composed of individuals who share similar perspectives. This limits our capacity to engage in critical discussion. It is difficult to involve women in new processes of feminist politicization because so many of us think that identifying men as the enemy, resisting male domination, gaining equal access to power and privilege is the end of feminist movement. Not only is it not the end, it is not even the place we want revitalized feminist movement to begin. We want to begin as women seriously addressing ourselves, not solely in relation to men, but in relation to an entire structure of domination of which patriarchy is one part. While the struggle to eradicate sexism and sexist oppression is and should be the primary thrust of feminist movement, to prepare ourselves politically for this effort we must first learn how to be in solidarity, how to struggle with one another.

Only when we confront the realities of sex, race, and class, the ways they divide us, make us different, stand us in opposition, and work to reconcile and resolve these issues will we be able to participate in the making of feminist revolution, in the transformation of the world. Feminism, as Charlotte Bunch emphasizes again and again in *Passionate Politics*, is a transformational politics, a struggle against domination wherein the effort is to change ourselves as well as structures. Speaking about the struggle to confront difference, Bunch asserts:

> A crucial point of the process is understanding that reality does not look the same from different people's perspective. It is not surprising that one way feminists have come to understand about differences has been through the love of a person from another culture or race. It takes persistence and motivation—which love often engenders—to get beyond one's ethnocentric assumptions and really learn about other perspectives. In this process and while seeking to eliminate oppression, we also discover new possibilities and insights that come from the experience and survival of other peoples.

Embedded in the commitment to feminist revolution is the challenge to love. Love can be and is an important source of empowerment when we struggle to confront issues of sex, race, and class. Working together to identify and face our differences— to face the ways we dominate and are dominated—to change our actions, we need a mediating force that can sustain us so that we are not broken in this process, so that we do not despair.

Not enough feminist work has focussed on documenting and sharing ways individuals confront differences constructively and successfully. Women and men need to know what is on the other side of the pain experienced in politicization. We need detailed accounts of the ways our lives are fuller and richer as we change and grow politically, as we learn to live each moment as committed feminists, as comrades working to end domination. In reconceptualizing and reformulating strategies for future feminist movement, we need to concentrate on the politicization of love, not just in the context of talking about victimization in intimate relationships, but in a critical discussion where love can be understood as a powerful force that challenges and resists domination. As we work to be loving, to create a culture that celebrates life, that makes love possible, we move against dehumanization, against domination. In *Pedagogy of the Oppressed*, Paulo Freire evokes this power of love, declaring:

> I am more and more convinced that true revolutionaries must perceive the revolution, because of its creative and liberating nature, as an act of love. For me, the revolution, which is not possible without a theory of revolution—and therefore science—is not irreconcilable with love . . . The distortion imposed on the word "love" by the capitalist world cannot prevent the revolution from being essentially loving in character, nor can it prevent the revolutionaries from affirming their love of life.

That aspect of feminist revolution that calls women to love womanness, that calls men to resist dehumanizing concepts of masculinity, is an essential part of our struggle. It is the process by which we move from seeing ourselves as objects to acting as subjects. When women and men understand that working to eradicate patriarchal domination is a struggle rooted in the longing to make a world where everyone can live fully and freely, then we know our work to be a gesture of love. Let us draw upon that love to heighten our awareness, deepen our compassion, intensify our courage, and strengthen our commitment.

7

Still I Rise

Maya Angelou

You may write me down in history
With your bitter, twisted lies,
You may trod me in the very dirt
But still, like dust, I'll rise.

Does my sassiness upset you?
Why are you beset with gloom?
'Cause I walk like I've got oil wells
Pumping in my living room.

Just like moons and like suns,
With the certainty of tides,
Just like hopes springing high,
Still I'll rise.

Did you want to see me broken?
Bowed head and lowered eyes?
Shoulders falling down like teardrops,
Weakened by my soulful cries.

Does my haughtiness offend you?
Don't you take it awful hard
'Cause I laugh like I've got gold mines
Diggin' in my own back yard.

You may shoot me with your words,
You may cut me with your eyes,
You may kill me with your hatefulness,
But still, like air, I'll rise.

Does my sexiness upset you?
Does it come as a surprise
That I dance like I've got diamonds
At the meeting of my thighs?

Out of the huts of history's shame
I rise
Up from a past that's rooted in pain
I rise
I'm a black ocean, leaping and wide,
Welling and swelling I bear in the tide.

Leaving behind nights of terror and fear
I rise
Into a daybreak that's wondrously clear
I rise
Bringing the gifts that my ancestors gave,
I am the dream and the hope of the slave.
I rise
I rise
I rise.

The woman in the ordinary*

Marge Piercy

The woman in the ordinary pudgy downcast girl
is crouching with eyes and muscles clenched.
Round and pebble smooth she effaces herself

*From *Circles on the Water* by Marge Piercy.

under ripples of conversation and debate.
The woman in the block of ivory soap
has massive thighs that neigh,
great breasts that blare and strong arms that trumpet.
The woman of the golden fleece
laughs uproariously from the belly
inside the girl who imitates
a Christmas card virgin with glued hands,
who fishes for herself in other's eyes,
who stoops and creeps to make herself smaller.
In her bottled up is a woman peppery as curry,
a yam of a woman of butter and brass,
compounded of acid and sweet like a pineapple,
like a handgrenade set to explode,
like goldenrod ready to bloom.

Suggestions for Further Reading

Bowser, B. P. and R. G. Hunt: *Impacts of Racism on White Americans*, Sage Publications, Beverly Hills, California, 1981.

deLone, Richard H.: *Small Futures*, Harcourt Brace Jovanovich, Inc., 1979.

Eisenstein, Z. R.: *Feminism and Sexual Equality*, Monthly Review Press, New York, 1984.

Lynch, James: *Prejudice Reduction in the Schools*, Nichols Publishing Company, New York, 1987.

Marable, M.: *Black American Politics from the Washington Marches to Jesse Jackson*, Schocken, New York, 1985.

Pogrebin, L. C.: *Growing Up Free*, Bantam Books, New York, 1981.

Shalom, S.: *Socialist Visions*, South End Press, Boston, 1980.

The Women's Economic Agenda Working Group of the Institute for Policy Studies: *Toward Economic Justice for Women: A National Agenda for Change*, Institute for Policy Studies, Washington, DC, 1985.

"Aqui No Se Habla Español," by Shirley Perez West. "Did Tavern Single Out Three Women?" *Eugene Register,* December 6, 1990. Reprinted by permission.

"S.I. Man Stabbed Dead on Beach," by James C. McKinley, Jr. Copyright © 1990 by *The New York Times.* Reprinted by permission.

"Rewards and Opportunities: The Politics and Economics of Class in the U.S.," by Gregory Mantsios, Queens College, The City University of New York. Reprinted by permission of the author.

"Three Realities: Minority Life in America." Permission granted by The Business Higher Education Forum, c/o American Council on Education, One Dupont Circle, Suite 800, Washington, D.C. 20036.

"Middle Class Blacks Try to Grip a Ladder While Lending a Hand," by Isabel Wilkerson. Copyright © 1990 by The New York Times Company. Reprinted by permission.

"The Poverty Industry," by Theresa Funiciello. *Ms.* Magazine, November/December 1990. Reprinted by permission of *Ms.* Magazine.

"The Wage Gap: Myths and Facts" from The National Committee on Pay Equity, Washington, D.C. Reprinted by permission.

"Being Poor Isn't Enough," by Tim Wise, from *Dollars and Sense,* October 1990, p. 5.

"And the Rich Got Richer. . . ," *Dollars and Sense,* October, 1990, p. 5.

Reprinted by permission of Macmillan Publishing Company, from "Racial And Economic Minorities: An Overview," by Beth Hess, Elizabeth W. Markson, and Peter J. Stein. Copyright © 1985 by Macmillan Publishing Company.

"Sun Chief: Autobiography of a Hopi Indian," edited by Leo W. Simmons (Yale University Press, 1942). Reprinted by permission, Yale University Press.

"A Farewell to Manzanar" from *Farewell to Manzanar* by Jeanne Wakatsuki Houston and James D. Houston. Copyright © 1973 by James D. Houston. Reprinted by permission of Houghton Mifflin Co.

Francisco Jimenez, "The Circuit," *The Arizona Quarterly* (Autumn, 1973) by permission of the author.

"The Puerto Rican Community in the South Bronx," by Clara E. Rodriguez. From "Racial and Ethnic Minorities: An Overview," in *Sociology,* 3rd edition, by Beth Hess, Elizabeth W. Markson, and Peter J. Stein. Copyright © 1991 by Macmillan Publishing Company. Reprinted with the permission of Macmillan Publishing Company.

"'Nopalitos': The Making of Fiction," by Helena Maria Viramontes. From *Breaking Boundaries: Latina Writing and Critical Readings,* Asuncion Horno-Delgado, Eliana Ortega, Nina M. Scott, and Nancy Saporta Sternbach, eds. (Amherst, U Mass Press, 1989). Copyright © 1989 by The University of Massachusetts Press.

"Suicide Note." Reprinted from *Shedding Silence* by Janice Mirikitani, with permission from Celestial Arts, Berkeley, CA.

"The Gap between Striving and Achieving: The Case of Asian American Women," by Deborah Woo. From *Making Waves* by Asian Women United of California. Copyright © 1989 by Asian Women United of California. Reprinted by permission of Beacon Press.

"Black Hispanics: The Ties That Bind," by Vivian Brady, from Centro.

"Blacks and Hispanics: A Fragile Alliance," by Jacqueline Conciatore and Roberto Rodriguez. Reprinted from *Black Issues in Higher Education,* October 11, 1990. Reprinted by permission of the authors.

"Legal Alien," by Pat Mora. Permission granted by Arte Publico Press, University of Houston, MD Anderson Library, Room 2, Houston, Texas, 77204-2090.

"Her Rites of Passage," by Lynda Marin, from *Making Faces, Making Soul, Haciendo Caras.* Reprinted by permission of Aunt Lute Foundation.

"is not so gd to be born a girl," by Ntozake Shange, from *Black Scholar,* Vol. 10, May–June, 1979. Reprinted by permission of the author.

"The Tyranny of Slenderness," by Kim Chernin. From *The Obsession* by Kim Chernin. Copyright © 1981 by Kim Chernin. Reprinted by permission of HarperCollins.

"Bloody and Bowed," by Anna Quindlen. Copyright © 1990 by The New York Times Company. Reprinted by permission.

"He Defies You Still: The Memoirs of a Sissy," by Tommi Avicolli, in Radical Teacher, #24, pp. 4–5 and in *Men Freeing Men,* edited by Francis Baumli, Atlantis Press. Copyright © 1985 by Tommi Avicolli. Reprinted by permission of the author.

"Silent Scream," by Carole R. Simmons. Reprinted with permission of Carole R. Simmons, copyright © 1987.

"Being Black is Dangerous to Your Health," by Denise Foley. Reprinted by permission of *Prevention* Magazine. Copyright © 1991, Rodale Press, Inc. All rights reserved.

"The Case of Sharon Kowalski and Karen Thompson: Ableism, Heterosexism, and Sexism," by Joan L. Griscom. Reprinted by permission of the author.

"Poem for the Young White Man Who Asked Me How I, an Intelligent, Well-read Person Could Believe in the War between Races," by Lorna Dee Cervantes. Reprinted from *Emplunada*, by Lorna Dee Cervantes, by permission of the University of Pittsburgh Press. © 1981 by Lorna Dee Cervantes.

"Listening," by Sey Chassler, from *Ms.* Magazine, August, 1984. Reprinted by permission of Sey Chassler.

"Indian Tribes: A Continuing Quest for Survival." Reprinted by permission of U.S. Commission on Human Rights.

"Race and the American Legal Process," by A. Leon Higginbotham, Jr. From *In the Matter of Color: Race and the American Legal Process: The Colonial Period*, New York: Oxford University Press, 1978.

"Declarations of Sentiments and Resolutions, Seneca Falls Convention, 1848," excerpts from *Up from the Pedestal*, by Aileen S. Kraditor. Reprinted by permission of Times Books, a division of Random House, Inc.

"The Antisuffragists: Selected Papers, 1852–1887," excerpts from *Up from the Pedestal*, by Aileen S. Kraditor. Reprinted by permission of Times Books, a division of Random House, Inc.

People v. Hall, 1854, from *American Racism: Exploration of the Nature of Prejudice*, by Roger Daniels and Harry H. L. Kitano, Prentice Hall, 1970.

"The Black Codes" from *Black Reconstruction* by W. E. B. Du Bois (Harcourt Brace Jovanovich, Inc., 1935). Reprinted by permission of David G. Du Bois.

Bradwell v. Illinois, 1873, from *Cases and Materials on Sex-Based Discrimination*, 2nd Edition by Herma Hill Kay with permission of the West Publishing Company.

Bowers v. Hardwick, 1986. Reprinted with permission from 106 S. Court 2841. Copyright © 1989 by West Publishing.

"Gay/Lesbian Rights: Report from the Legal Front," by Arthur S. Leonard, *The Nation* Magazine/ The Nation Co. © 1990.

"Self-Fulfilling Stereotypes," by Mark Snyder, *Psychology Today*, July 1982, pp. 60–68. Reprinted with permission from *Psychology Today* Magazine. Copyright © 1982 American Psychological Association.

"Racism in the English Language," reprinted, by permission, from *Racism in the English Language* by Robert B. Moore, Council on Interracial Books for Children, 1976. Write the Council at 1841 Broadway, New York, N.Y. 10023 for a free catalog of antiracist, antisexist materials.

"The Language of Sexism," by Haig Bosmajian from *The Language of Oppression*, Public Affairs Press, 1974.

"Beauty and the Beast of Advertising," by Jean Kilbourne. Reprinted with permission from the Winter, 1990 issue of *Media & Values* Magazine: *Redesigning Women*, published by the Center for Media and Values, Los Angeles, California.

"Anti-Gay Stereotypes," by Richard D. Mohr. From *Gays/Justice: A Study of Ethics, Society and Law.* New York: Columbia University Press, pp. 21–27.

"Deconstructing the Underclass," by Herbert J. Gans, APA Journal 271: Summer 1990.

"Blaming the Victim," by William Ryan. From *Blaming the Victim*, copyright © 1971 by William Ryan. Reprinted by permission of Pantheon Books, a division of Random House.

"Sex and Race: The Analogy of Social Control," by William Chafe. From *Women and Equality: Changing Patterns in American Culture* by William C. Chafe. Copyright © 1977 by Oxford University Press, Inc. Reprinted by permission.

"Hate-Violence," by Carole Sheffield. Copyright © by Carole Sheffield. Reprinted by permission of the author, William Paterson College, Wayne, N.J. 07470.

"Age, Race, Class, and Sex: Women Redefining Difference," by Audre Lord. From *Sister Outsider*, copyright © 1984 by Audre Lord, The Crossing Press, Freedom, CA.

"En Rapport, In Opposition: Cobrando Cuentas a las Nuestras," by Gloria Anzaldúa. From *Making Faces, Making Soul/Haciendo Caras*, by Gloria Anzaldúa, © 1990. Reprinted by permission of Aunt Lute Books.

"Up Against the Wall," by Cherríe Moraga. From *Loving the War Years* (Boston: South End Press, 1983). Reprinted by permission.

"Toward a More Caring Society," by Ruth Sidel. From *On Her Own* by Ruth Sidel. Copyright © 1990 by Ruth Sidel. Used by permission of Viking Penguin.

"Revisioning the Future," by Suzanne Pharr. Reprinted from *Homophobia: A Weapon of Sexism* by Suzanne Pharr.

"Feminism: A Transformational Politic," by bell hooks. Reprinted from *Talking Back: Thinking Feminist, Thinking Black* by bell hooks, with permission from the publisher, South End Press.

"Still I Rise," by Maya Angelou. From *And Still I Rise*, Maya Angelou, New York, N.Y., Random House, 1978.

"The woman in the ordinary," by Marge Piercy. From *Circles on the Water* by Marge Piercy, copyright © 1982 by Marge Piercy. Reprinted by permission of Alfred A. Knopf, Inc.